Preparation for the *NEW* GED

HIGH SCHOOL EQUIVALENCY EXAMINATION

Preparation for the New GED

HIGH SCHOOL EQUIVALENCY EXAMINATION

by Seymour Barasch, M.A.
Ronald Kappraff, Ed. D.
Robert Ganz, M.A., M.B.A.
Barbara Hull, M.L.S.

ARCO
New York

Eleventh Edition

ARCO

Simon & Schuster, Inc.
Gulf+Western Building
One Gulf+Western Plaza
New York, NY 10023

DISTRIBUTED BY PRENTICE HALL TRADE

Manufactured in the United States of America

2 3 4 5 6 7 8 9 10

LIBRARY OF CONGRESS
Library of Congress Cataloging-in-Publication Data

Barasch, Seymour.

Preparation for the new GED high school equivalency examination / by Seymour Barasch . . . [et al.].
p. cm.
Rev. ed. of: GED. 10th ed. c1986.
"An Arco book."
Includes index.
ISBN 0-13-698789-3 (pbk.)

1. General educational development tests—Study guides. 2. High school equivalency examinations—Study guides. I. Barasch, Seymour. GED. II. Title. III. Title: GED high school equivalency examination.
LB3060.33.G45B36 1988
373.12′64—dc19 87-24602
CIP

Table of Contents

PART V. READING SKILLS REVIEW

PART VI. MATH REVIEW FOR GED CANDIDATES

PART VII. TWO COMPLETE SAMPLE TESTS

FOREWORD

Congratulations on making the decision to get your high school diploma by preparing to take the GED high school equivalency diploma test. The high school diploma is an important document to have. With a diploma you can take advantage of education and training opportunities beyond the high school level and increase your earning potential by as much as fifty percent.

Since 1971, the GED Testing Program has enabled over six million adults to obtain high school credentials. By following the advice in this book, you, too, can earn a high school equivalency diploma and increase your chances of success in your work and in your life.

Preparation for the New GED is an attempt to help you, the GED candidate, gain a clear idea of what to expect and how to prepare for the GED examination. It will give you a fair and reasonable explanation of testing procedures, scoring information, and useful test-taking hints. It will not give you any questions or answers from an actual examination. But the Diagnostic Test, the two full-length Practice Tests, and the practice questions for each subject area, will give you an understanding of the kinds of questions you may expect. You will find that this book is a useful guide for taking and passing the GED exam with the least possible heartache and headache.

This book has been revised to more effectively cover all of the originally required material as well as the new sections in the GED exam. Seymour Barasch, the principal author of the original version of this text, interviewed many GED diploma winners to get their valuable experience on the exam. For the past two years we have been in constant touch with the American Council on Education, reading their up-to-date changes to the new GED format, telephoning them for clarifications, attending meetings, and preparing the most effective GED book possible. Discussions with GED classes and teachers have also helped us to prepare this powerful, easy-to-use preparation book.

The authors of this revision are master teachers who have had many years of teaching experience at the secondary school level and are all very active in their own professional organizations. Their dedication to meaningful education is reflected in the high quality of this book and in its usefulness to you in getting your High School Equivalency Diploma.

INTRODUCTION

WHAT IS THE GED?

The General Educational Development (GED) Tests are a series of examinations which are designed to determine whether the person taking them has the literacy and computational skills equivalent to those of the upper two-thirds of the students currently graduating from high schools in the United States. The tests are sponsored by the American Council on Education, a nonprofit educational organization located in Washington, D.C. The tests were designed and developed by the Educational Testing Service of Princeton, New Jersey, the same agency that produces the Scholastic Aptitude Tests taken by prospective college students.

Since 1942, many millions of adults have earned their high school credentials by passing the GED tests. Approximately 800,000 adults take the GED test each year and over 500,000 of them are awarded high school equivalency diplomas. Although passing rates vary widely from state to state, about seventy percent of all test-takers pass the five-part exam. All fifty states, the District of Columbia, six United States territories and possessions, and ten Canadian provinces use GED results as the basis for issuing high school equivalency diplomas. All tests are administered under the supervision of state or (in Canada) provincial offices at designated GED testing centers (there are about 2900 such centers) and the standards for a passing grade are set by each state or province. In addition, federal and state correctional and health institutions and the military services also administer the tests to persons under their purview.

What do the tests measure? According to the American Council on Education, the tests measure "broad concepts and general knowledge, not how well they [candidates] remember details, precise definitions or historical facts. Thus, the tests do not penalize candidates who lack recent academic or classroom experience or who have acquired their education informally."

There have been many versions and forms of the test. The latest version of the GED Test is being introduced on a state-by-state basis throughout 1988.

HOW HAS THE GED CHANGED?

This book was written to prepare you to successfully pass the newly revised GED exam. The new items appearing in this exam include the following:

1. A two-part Writing Skills Test consisting of
   a. Conventions of English—a test of your ability to recognize and correct errors in written English

b. Essay Writing—a test that requires you to write a composition of about 200 words giving an opinion or explaining an issue

2. Interpreting Literature and the Arts—a test of your ability to read and interpret passages taken from popular literature, classical literature or commentary (writings *about* literature and the arts)

In addition to these new sections, other changes in the revised GED exam include the following:

1. In the Social Studies and Science Tests—more questions that test your ability to think, rather than simply to memorize facts. These questions seek to find out whether you can
   a. comprehend new information
   b. apply what you have learned
   c. analyze a new idea by breaking it into parts
   d. evaluate items and make judgments about them
2. In the Mathematics Test—questions that test a more complete set of skills including
   a. solving number problems
   b. solving graph problems
   c. deciding whether a problem can be solved with the information given
   d, using many different arithmetic operations to solve a problem

WHAT SUBJECTS ARE TESTED IN THE GED BATTERY?

The English-language GED battery consists of five individual tests. Test 1, Writing Skills, contains two subsections: Conventions in English, consisting of 55 questions which ask you to identify errors in sentence structure, usage, capitalization, punctuation, and spelling/possessives/contractions; and an essay writing exercise to determine how well you write.

Test 2, Social Studies, contains 64 questions drawn from history, economics, geography, political science, and behavioral sciences. The questions are designed to test your understanding of the basic principles in each area by asking you to interpret reading passages, cartoons, graphs, and charts. You should be able to draw conclusions and identify cause-and-effect relationships based on the material presented. Although some factual knowledge is necessary to answer certain questions, most questions require only a wide general knowledge. The student who habitually reads a newspaper or one of the major weekly newsmagazines should not have too much difficulty with this segment.

Test 3, Science, is probably the most difficult of the five segments. The 66 questions are drawn from the areas of biology, earth science, chemistry, and physics. Some of the questions require specific knowledge but most test for an understanding of basic scientific principles and ideas. Answering the questions requires a combination of excellent reading skills, specific knowledge, and the ability to interpret scientific data.

Test 4, Interpreting Literature and the Arts, contains 45 questions based on excerpts from classical and popular literature and commentaries about literature and the arts. The passages may be drawn from newspapers, magazines, novels, short stories, poetry, and drama. The literary readings generally emphasize the work of current authors rather than that of famous writers from the distant past.

Test 5, Mathematics, is the part of the exam most universally feared by candidates. It really shouldn't be. Most of the 56 questions can be solved using the basic arithmetic operations of addition, subtraction, multiplication, and division. There is a substantial number of algebra, measurement, and geometry questions on the test, as well as some number theory, statistics, and probability. Most questions are presented as word problems. Many questions involve a real-life situation or ask you to interpret information presented in graphs, charts, tables, or diagrams. You are not allowed to bring a calculator to the test but will be given a sheet of important formulas to help you solve some of the problems on the exam. All scrap paper will be collected with your test.

PREPARING TO TAKE THE TEST

There are two kinds of tests. The most widespread is called a *power* test, and it measures what you know, not how fast you can produce an answer. In a power test, you are generally given a liberal amount of time to complete a specific number of tasks or to answer a specific number of questions. The second kind of test is called a *time* test. In a time test, you are competing with the other candidates to see who can give the greatest number of correct answers within a very limited amount of time. The Scholastic Aptitude Test is an example of a rigidly enforced time test, because it is essentially a competition among prospective college entrants to determine who will achieve the highest marks and be rewarded with admission to desired colleges.

The GED battery of tests is a blend of a power test and a time test, with greater emphasis on what you know than on how fast you can work out the correct answers. In the GED, you are in competition only with yourself. Of course, you should aim at getting the highest scores you can, but remember that you are not competing with anyone else.

Although the GED is not precisely a time test, there are time limits. Therefore, it is important that you learn to pace yourself. The allowed time for each test is always announced or written on the blackboard by the exam proctor so that you can tell how much time you have. If possible, bring a watch to the exam so that you can keep track of your progress.

In most of the tests, the easiest questions come first, and you should be able to dispose of them quickly. The later questions are apt to be more complex and difficult and therefore greater effort—and time—will be needed to solve them. Always answer the questions you are sure of first, then go back and spend additional time on the ones that you find more difficult.

FORMAT OF THE NEW GED TEST BATTERY

Subject	Number of Questions	Time Allowed
Test 1. Writing Skills		
Part I. Conventions of Written English Sentence Structure (25%) Usage (25%) Capitalization (10%) Punctuation (20%) Spelling/Possessives/ Contractions (20%)	55	75 minutes
Part II. Essay	1	45 minutes
Test 2. Social Studies History (25%) Economics (20%) Geography (15%) Political Science (20%) Behavioral Science (20%)	64	85 minutes
Test 3. Science Life Science (50%) Biology Physical Science (50%) Physics Chemistry Earth Science	66	95 minutes
Test 4. Interpreting Literature and the Arts Popular Literature (50%) Classical Literature (25%) Commentary (25%)	45	65 minutes
Test 5. Mathematics Measurement (30%) Algebra (30%) Geometry (20%) Numeration (10%) Statistics 10%)	56	90 minutes

Each of the questions on the GED includes five possible answers, and only one of the five is correct. If you're sure of the correct answer, don't waste time working through the other possibilities. Go on to the next question.

Pay attention to words like "but," "not," "however," "always," "only," and "never." They are often key indicators that signal major ideas. Be wary of absolutes like "greatest" or "least" or "lowest" because they may indicate the need for a negative (no) response.

The new GED exam contains a total of 286 multiple-choice questions and 1 essay to be answered in 7 hours and 35 minutes. The chart on page 4 indicates the makeup of a typical GED Test Battery.

NATURE OF THE QUESTIONS

TEST 1. WRITING SKILLS

The Writing Skills Test consists of two basic parts: Conventions of Written English Test and The Essay Test.

A. Conventions of Written English—Items in the Conventions of Written English Test are based on paragraphs of about 10–12 sentences in length. Some of the sentences are correct. Others contain a single error. The errors will be of the following types:

- Sentence structure
- Usage
- Capitalization
- Punctuation
- Spelling, possessives, or contractions

1. Sentence Structure—Sentence Structure is represented by approximately 15 of the 55 questions in this test. These questions test your ability to recognize such errors as sentence fragments, run-on sentences, comma splices, improper coordination, improper subordination, and lack of clarity.
2. Usage—Usage is also represented by about 15 questions per test. These questions cover errors in subject-verb agreement, verb tense, and pronoun reference.
3. Capitalization—Capitalization is tested in approximately 5 questions per test. The questions concern the rules of capitalization as they relate to proper nouns and adjectives, titles, dates, places, and seasons.
4. Punctuation—Errors in punctuation form the basis of approximately 10 questions on each test. Many of these questions test for correct use of the comma (in series, between independent clauses, after introductory elements or introductory dependent clauses, and with appositives).

5. Spelling/Possessives/Contractions—Approximately 10 questions per test are concerned with frequently misspelled words and proper use of troublesome possessives, contractions, and homonyms (words that sound alike but have different meanings).

There are three types of questions used to measure Writing Skills. They are the following:

1. Sentence Correction (50% or approximately 5 out of every 10 sentences)
2. Sentence Revision (35% or about 3 out of every 10 sentences)
3. Construction Shift (15% or about 2 out of every 10 sentences)

B. The Essay—You will have 45 minutes to write an essay on a single topic. In your essay you will be required to present an opinion or an explanation regarding a situation about which adults would be expected to have some general knowledge. The essay will be graded on a six-point scale. Two judges will evaluate each essay for its overall effectiveness. A score of "6" will be given to a paper which is effectively written, well organized, and contains few writing errors; a score of "1" will be given to an essay which has not answered the question, is poorly organized, and is full of grammatical errors.

TEST 2. SOCIAL STUDIES

Subject matter for Social Studies Test items is drawn from topics in history, geography, economics, political sciences, and the behavioral sciences such as psychology, sociology and anthropology.

Questions may often combine more than one subject area. For example, a question about legislation to limit acid rain might combine the concepts of political science, economics, and geography. When considering an answer, you should think of it as relating to an individual, or to a member of a social group such as a family, local community, a nation, or to the global community.

Social Studies questions will not be solely based on memory but will challenge you to make use of everyday decision-making skills. Often they will include a short reading passage or a picture such as a map, a cartoon, or a graph. Problems will measure your ability to understand the questions, to apply them to other situations, to analyze specific parts of them, and to evaluate their accuracy.

TEST 3. SCIENCE

The subject matter for science items is drawn from life sciences (biology), earth science, physics, and chemistry. Major themes include change, conservation of mass and energy, interactions, relationships, and time and space. Questions often combine topics rather than sticking to a single subject area.

Questions on the Science Test are equally divided between life science (biology) and physical science (earth science, chemistry, and physics). Most questions require thinking rather than memory skills, with an emphasis on common, everyday decision-making skills. The types of questions and the frequency with which they appear in the test are as follows:

1. Did you understand the idea presented? (20%)
2. Can you apply something you just learned to an altogether different use? (30%)
3. How does something work? Can you analyze the steps? (30%)
4. Can you judge whether a statement is correct? (20%)

TEST 4. INTERPRETING LITERATURE AND THE ARTS

This is the first time this test will be given in the GED exam. Reading material is chosen from three areas:

1. Popular Literature (50%)—good examples of contemporary fiction, non-fiction, and poetry that will probably be read for many years to come
2. Classical Literature (25%)—writings from the past: 19th and 20th century
3. Commentary (25%)—reviews of the arts such as TV programs, films, books, etc.

Approximately six questions will be asked after each reading passage. These questions will test just how well you have understood the passages, can apply the knowledge to other situations, and are able to analyze the elements of style and structure in the reading passages.

TEST 5. MATHEMATICS

The mathematics section consists of problem solving in the following areas:

1. Measurement—perimeter, area, volume, rate of motion, rate of interest, time, and money
2. Algebra—translating word problems, setting up equations, solving equations, inequalities, quadratic equations, linear functions, factoring, and algebraic fractions
3. Geometry—parallel and perpendicular lines, triangle theory, slope, Pythagorean theorem, congruent, similar, isosceles, and right triangles

4. Number Relationships—sequences with fractions and decimals, comparing data, exponents, and scientific notation
5. Data Analysis—calculating mean, median, ratio, and simple probability, interpreting graphs and tables

Thinking skills are stressed. To limit the amount of memorizing required, a page of mathematical formulas is provided for reference.

HOW TO TAKE THE GED TEST

It is not unusual to dislike the concept of tests. Most adults fear tests because they evoke bad memories from childhood when tests given by teachers were always a chore and often a punishment. Therefore, it is important to understand that tests are essentially ways of measuring what you have learned and are not punishments. If you are afraid of tests, the best way to combat that fear is take them as frequently as possible. In this case, familiarity breeds a healthy contempt and can reduce anxiety. Practice tests, such as the ones in this book, give you a chance to simulate in private what you will confront when you actually take the GED battery.

When you are satisfied that you are prepared to take the GED, consider the following test-taking tips:

1. Read every question carefully before attempting to answer it. If you don't understand what is required, ask the proctor for help.
2. Answer the easiest questions first. If you have absolutely no idea about how to answer a particular question, go on to the next one and come back to it later.
3. Try to avoid careless errors, which may occur when you misunderstand what is requested. Do not do more than is required and do not assume that the test is trying to trick you. It probably isn't.
4. Leave no questions unanswered. Since you are not penalized for an incorrect answer on the GED, answer every question. Even when you do not have the vaguest notion about the correct answer, you have a twenty percent chance of being right. By eliminating obviously silly answers, you raise your chances of choosing the right answer.
5. Bring chewing gum or hard candy with you to the test. Believe it or not, quietly chewing gum or sucking on hard candy tends to relieve nervousness, according to several prominent psychologists. You won't be allowed to smoke in the test room.
6. Make sure you hand in all your papers and that they all include your name and/or your identifying number and other requested information. Your answers cannot be marked unless your properly identified answer sheet is given to the proctor at the end of the test.
7. Be careful. Make certain that you fill in the blank spaces exactly as you had intended. For example, did you answer question 5 by marking the box reserved for question 6? Did you choose a "correct" answer when the "wrong" answer was requested? Did you answer every question?

WHAT IS A PASSING SCORE?

GED scores are reported as standard scores ranging from 20 to 80 for each test. The raw score (or number of questions answered correctly) is converted to a standard score so that all tests and all forms of the GED battery may be evaluated similarly.

To be successful in passing the GED in most states, a candidate must get a total minimum standard score of 225 on the five tests, with no score of less than 35 on any single test. In general, that means that a candidate who answers just over half of the questions in each test correctly will get a passing score.

The table on page 10 indicates the minimum passing scores currently in effect in each state, territory and province. When the minimum standard score is given at 35 *and* 45, this means no test score less than 35 and an average no lower than 45 for the entire battery for a total standard score of 225. When the minimum standard score is given as 35 *or* 45, this means no test score less than 35 or if one or more scores are less than 35 an average of 45 for the entire battery.

To be certain of earning a GED certificate or diploma, candidates should aim to score substantially above the minimum score on as many tests as possible. However, those who fall short of passing a single test or several tests can retake only those sections on which they failed to attain a minimum passing score. Information on retaking the GED test battery is available from the Education Department of each state.

MINIMUM PASSING SCORES

State	Minimum Scores
Alabama	35 and 45
Alaska	35 and 45
Arizona	35 and 45
Arkansas	35 and 45
California	40 and 45
Colorado	35 and 45
Connecticut	35 and 45
Delaware	40 and 45
District of Columbia	35 and 45
Florida	40 and 45
Georgia	35 and 45
Hawaii	35 and 45
Idaho	35 and 45
Illinois	35 and 45
Indiana	35 and 45
Iowa	35 and 45
Kansas	35 and 45
Kentucky	35 and 45
Louisiana	40 and 45
Maine	35 and 45
Maryland	40 and 45
Massachusetts	35 and 45
Michigan	35 and 45
Minnesota	35 and 45
Mississippi	40 or 45
Missouri	35 and 45
Montana	35 and 45
Nebraska	40 or 45
Nevada	35 and 45
New Hampshire	35 and 45
New Jersey	40 and 45
New Mexico	40 or 45
New York	40 and 45
North Carolina	35 and 45
North Dakota	40 or 50
Ohio	35 and 45
Oklahoma	40 and 45
Oregon	40 each text
Pennsylvania	35 and 45
Rhode Island	35 and 45
South Carolina	45 average
South Dakota	40 and 45
Tennessee	35 and 45
Texas	40 or 45
Utah	40 and 45
Vermont	35 and 45
Virginia	35 and 45
Washington	35 and 45
West Virginia	40 and 45
Wisconsin	35 and 45
Wyoming	35 and 45

Canadian Province or Territory	Minimum Scores
Alberta	45 each test
British Columbia	45 each test
Manitoba	45 each test
New Brunswick	35 and 45 (French) 45 each test (Eng.)
Newfoundland	40 and 45
Northwest Territories	40 and 45
Nova Scotia	45 each test
Prince Edward Island	45 each test
Saskatchewan	45 each test
Yukon Territory	45 each test

U.S. Territory or Other	
American Samoa	40 each test
Canal Zone	40 and 45
Guam	35 and 45
Kwajalein Island	35 and 45
Marshall Islands	40 and 45
Puerto Rico	35 and 45
Virgin Islands	35 and 45

TIPS FOR THE TEACHER

More often than not, GED teachers get little or no orientation on the nature of the actual tests their students must eventually face. It would be enlightening, of course, if GED teachers were able to see or to take the actual examination in order to know specifically the kinds of questions their students must face. Unfortunately, current GED regulations do not allow this. If you, as a teacher, were to take the test, you would be violating the policies of the GED Testing Service and the laws of the state where you teach.

There is an alternative. The half-length *Official Practice Tests* (Forms AA and BB) and the accompanying *Teacher's Manual* are available for a nominal fee from Cambridge Publishing Company, 888 Seventh Avenue, New York, NY 10106, or in Canada from Allyn and Bacon, 791 St. Clair Ave. West, Toronto, Canada M6C 1B8. These materials were developed by the American Council on Education to provide teachers with complete information about the tests without breaching the security of the actual test.

You may buy the practice tests and the manual or, better still, have your school administrator obtain them in bulk. Let your students work on the practice tests in order to develop a familiarity with the tests. The results will also be an indication of whether they are ready to take the full-length tests.

Another source of information is *The GED Testing Program, Policies & Centers,* which is also published by the GED Testing Service. It breaks down the policies and requirements for issuance of GED diplomas on a state-by-state basis (there are no absolute or uniform requirements nationwide) and gives the methods and costs of applying to take the tests in each state. This source also lists the locations of test centers where the GED exam battery is given, plus the name of the chief examiner at each location.

HOW TO USE THIS BOOK

This book will familiarize you with the GED test and testing conditions. Candidates who know what to expect have a far better chance of succeeding on the GED than those who face the test "cold." It is frightening to take any test without preparation or advance knowledge—and fear can prevent even the most experienced test-takers from doing their best.

The Practice Tests in this book are as much like the actual GED test as possible. They cover each of the five subject areas using the same kinds of questions, the same directions, and the same time limits as the actual test. Taking these Practice Tests will show you what you know (and do not know) about the GED test so that you can direct your study to the areas that are most important for you.

Start by taking the Diagnostic Exam following the step-by-step procedure below:

1. Read all directions carefully and follow them exactly.
2. Stick to the time limits given for each test.
3. Enter your answers on the tear-out answer sheet provided for the test.
4. When you have completed the entire exam, compare your answers with the correct answers given at the end of the test battery.
5. Count the total number of correct answers for each of the five tests and enter this number in the box provided on your answer sheet.
6. Add the five subtotals to obtain your total score for the test battery.
7. Use the Error Analysis Chart following the Diagnostic Exam to see where you are strong and where you are weak. This chart breaks down each test in the Diagnostic GED test battery into content areas. In the column headed "Questions," circle the number of every question you answered incorrectly. Count the number of circles in each content area and write the total number missed in the column headed "Number Incorrect." A large number of incorrect responses in a particular area indicates the need for further study in that area.
8. Start your review by consulting the Explanatory Answers to all questions you missed.
9. Turn next to the Skills Reviews provided in Parts 2, 3, 4, 5, and 6 of this book. Pay particular attention to the areas in which your Error Analysis showed you to be weak.
10. Take the two Complete Practice Tests at the end of this book, following the procedure outlined in steps 1 through 8.

Part I

A Diagnostic Test

DIRECTIONS FOR TAKING THE DIAGNOSTIC TEST

There are five tests in the Diagnostic Exam: Test 1—Writing Skills, Test 2—Social Studies, Test 3—Science, Test 4—Interpreting Literature and the Arts, and Test 5—Mathematics. Each test has a different time limit and a different set of directions.

Plan to take an entire test at one time. Follow the directions given at the start of each test.

Tear out the answer sheet on page 17 and use it to mark your answers to all questions.

As you complete each test, check your answers with the Answer Key on page 103. On your answer sheet, mark an X through each incorrect answer. Then turn to the Error Analysis chart on page 106 and circle the number of each question you answered incorrectly.

The Error Analysis shows you the subject area of each test question. Once you have circled all your incorrect answers, count the number of circles in each subject area and write that number in the column marked "Number Wrong."

Use your Error Analysis to determine which content areas you need to study most in order to raise your GED score. Parts II through VI of this book provide skills reviews and practice questions for each GED subject area. Read the review and answer the practice questions to help strengthen the areas where you are weak.

At the end of this book are two more Sample GED Exams. Take these exams just as you took the Diagnostic Exam. They will provide valuable practice for the GED exam, and they will help you to decide whether you are ready for the "real thing."

Answer Sheet GED Sample Test

Correct answers for this test appear on page 89.

TEST 1: WRITING SKILLS - PART 1 Number correct ☐

1 ① ② ③ ④ ⑤	15 ① ② ③ ④ ⑤	29 ① ② ③ ④ ⑤	43 ① ② ③ ④ ⑤
2 ① ② ③ ④ ⑤	16 ① ② ③ ④ ⑤	30 ① ② ③ ④ ⑤	44 ① ② ③ ④ ⑤
3 ① ② ③ ④ ⑤	17 ① ② ③ ④ ⑤	31 ① ② ③ ④ ⑤	45 ① ② ③ ④ ⑤
4 ① ② ③ ④ ⑤	18 ① ② ③ ④ ⑤	32 ① ② ③ ④ ⑤	46 ① ② ③ ④ ⑤
5 ① ② ③ ④ ⑤	19 ① ② ③ ④ ⑤	33 ① ② ③ ④ ⑤	47 ① ② ③ ④ ⑤
6 ① ② ③ ④ ⑤	20 ① ② ③ ④ ⑤	34 ① ② ③ ④ ⑤	48 ① ② ③ ④ ⑤
7 ① ② ③ ④ ⑤	21 ① ② ③ ④ ⑤	35 ① ② ③ ④ ⑤	49 ① ② ③ ④ ⑤
8 ① ② ③ ④ ⑤	22 ① ② ③ ④ ⑤	36 ① ② ③ ④ ⑤	50 ① ② ③ ④ ⑤
9 ① ② ③ ④ ⑤	23 ① ② ③ ④ ⑤	37 ① ② ③ ④ ⑤	51 ① ② ③ ④ ⑤
10 ① ② ③ ④ ⑤	24 ① ② ③ ④ ⑤	38 ① ② ③ ④ ⑤	52 ① ② ③ ④ ⑤
11 ① ② ③ ④ ⑤	25 ① ② ③ ④ ⑤	39 ① ② ③ ④ ⑤	53 ① ② ③ ④ ⑤
12 ① ② ③ ④ ⑤	26 ① ② ③ ④ ⑤	40 ① ② ③ ④ ⑤	54 ① ② ③ ④ ⑤
13 ① ② ③ ④ ⑤	27 ① ② ③ ④ ⑤	41 ① ② ③ ④ ⑤	55 ① ② ③ ④ ⑤
14 ① ② ③ ④ ⑤	28 ① ② ③ ④ ⑤	42 ① ② ③ ④ ⑤	**GO ON TO WRITING SKILLS-PART II**

TEST 2: SOCIAL STUDIES Number correct ☐

1 ① ② ③ ④ ⑤	18 ① ② ③ ④ ⑤	35 ① ② ③ ④ ⑤	52 ① ② ③ ④ ⑤
2 ① ② ③ ④ ⑤	19 ① ② ③ ④ ⑤	36 ① ② ③ ④ ⑤	53 ① ② ③ ④ ⑤
3 ① ② ③ ④ ⑤	20 ① ② ③ ④ ⑤	37 ① ② ③ ④ ⑤	54 ① ② ③ ④ ⑤
4 ① ② ③ ④ ⑤	21 ① ② ③ ④ ⑤	38 ① ② ③ ④ ⑤	55 ① ② ③ ④ ⑤
5 ① ② ③ ④ ⑤	22 ① ② ③ ④ ⑤	39 ① ② ③ ④ ⑤	56 ① ② ③ ④ ⑤
6 ① ② ③ ④ ⑤	23 ① ② ③ ④ ⑤	40 ① ② ③ ④ ⑤	57 ① ② ③ ④ ⑤
7 ① ② ③ ④ ⑤	24 ① ② ③ ④ ⑤	41 ① ② ③ ④ ⑤	58 ① ② ③ ④ ⑤
8 ① ② ③ ④ ⑤	25 ① ② ③ ④ ⑤	42 ① ② ③ ④ ⑤	59 ① ② ③ ④ ⑤
9 ① ② ③ ④ ⑤	26 ① ② ③ ④ ⑤	43 ① ② ③ ④ ⑤	60 ① ② ③ ④ ⑤
10 ① ② ③ ④ ⑤	27 ① ② ③ ④ ⑤	44 ① ② ③ ④ ⑤	61 ① ② ③ ④ ⑤
11 ① ② ③ ④ ⑤	28 ① ② ③ ④ ⑤	45 ① ② ③ ④ ⑤	62 ① ② ③ ④ ⑤
12 ① ② ③ ④ ⑤	29 ① ② ③ ④ ⑤	46 ① ② ③ ④ ⑤	63 ① ② ③ ④ ⑤
13 ① ② ③ ④ ⑤	30 ① ② ③ ④ ⑤	47 ① ② ③ ④ ⑤	64 ① ② ③ ④ ⑤
14 ① ② ③ ④ ⑤	31 ① ② ③ ④ ⑤	48 ① ② ③ ④ ⑤	**STOP**
15 ① ② ③ ④ ⑤	32 ① ② ③ ④ ⑤	49 ① ② ③ ④ ⑤	
16 ① ② ③ ④ ⑤	33 ① ② ③ ④ ⑤	50 ① ② ③ ④ ⑤	
17 ① ② ③ ④ ⑤	34 ① ② ③ ④ ⑤	51 ① ② ③ ④ ⑤	

TEST 3: SCIENCE Number correct ☐

1 ① ② ③ ④ ⑤	6 ① ② ③ ④ ⑤	11 ① ② ③ ④ ⑤	16 ① ② ③ ④ ⑤
2 ① ② ③ ④ ⑤	7 ① ② ③ ④ ⑤	12 ① ② ③ ④ ⑤	17 ① ② ③ ④ ⑤
3 ① ② ③ ④ ⑤	8 ① ② ③ ④ ⑤	13 ① ② ③ ④ ⑤	18 ① ② ③ ④ ⑤
4 ① ② ③ ④ ⑤	9 ① ② ③ ④ ⑤	14 ① ② ③ ④ ⑤	19 ① ② ③ ④ ⑤
5 ① ② ③ ④ ⑤	10 ① ② ③ ④ ⑤	15 ① ② ③ ④ ⑤	20 ① ② ③ ④ ⑤

TEST 3: SCIENCE (Con't)

21 ① ② ③ ④ ⑤
22 ① ② ③ ④ ⑤
23 ① ② ③ ④ ⑤
24 ① ② ③ ④ ⑤
25 ① ② ③ ④ ⑤
26 ① ② ③ ④ ⑤
27 ① ② ③ ④ ⑤
28 ① ② ③ ④ ⑤
29 ① ② ③ ④ ⑤
30 ① ② ③ ④ ⑤
31 ① ② ③ ④ ⑤
32 ① ② ③ ④ ⑤
33 ① ② ③ ④ ⑤
34 ① ② ③ ④ ⑤
35 ① ② ③ ④ ⑤
36 ① ② ③ ④ ⑤
37 ① ② ③ ④ ⑤
38 ① ② ③ ④ ⑤
39 ① ② ③ ④ ⑤
40 ① ② ③ ④ ⑤
41 ① ② ③ ④ ⑤
42 ① ② ③ ④ ⑤
43 ① ② ③ ④ ⑤
44 ① ② ③ ④ ⑤
45 ① ② ③ ④ ⑤
46 ① ② ③ ④ ⑤
47 ① ② ③ ④ ⑤
48 ① ② ③ ④ ⑤
49 ① ② ③ ④ ⑤
50 ① ② ③ ④ ⑤
51 ① ② ③ ④ ⑤
52 ① ② ③ ④ ⑤
53 ① ② ③ ④ ⑤
54 ① ② ③ ④ ⑤
55 ① ② ③ ④ ⑤
56 ① ② ③ ④ ⑤
57 ① ② ③ ④ ⑤
58 ① ② ③ ④ ⑤
59 ① ② ③ ④ ⑤
60 ① ② ③ ④ ⑤
61 ① ② ③ ④ ⑤
62 ① ② ③ ④ ⑤
63 ① ② ③ ④ ⑤
64 ① ② ③ ④ ⑤
65 ① ② ③ ④ ⑤
66 ① ② ③ ④ ⑤

STOP

TEST 4: INTERPRETING LITERATURE AND THE ARTS

Number correct ☐

1 ① ② ③ ④ ⑤
2 ① ② ③ ④ ⑤
3 ① ② ③ ④ ⑤
4 ① ② ③ ④ ⑤
5 ① ② ③ ④ ⑤
6 ① ② ③ ④ ⑤
7 ① ② ③ ④ ⑤
8 ① ② ③ ④ ⑤
9 ① ② ③ ④ ⑤
10 ① ② ③ ④ ⑤
11 ① ② ③ ④ ⑤
12 ① ② ③ ④ ⑤
13 ① ② ③ ④ ⑤
14 ① ② ③ ④ ⑤
15 ① ② ③ ④ ⑤
16 ① ② ③ ④ ⑤
17 ① ② ③ ④ ⑤
18 ① ② ③ ④ ⑤
19 ① ② ③ ④ ⑤
20 ① ② ③ ④ ⑤
21 ① ② ③ ④ ⑤
22 ① ② ③ ④ ⑤
23 ① ② ③ ④ ⑤
24 ① ② ③ ④ ⑤
25 ① ② ③ ④ ⑤
26 ① ② ③ ④ ⑤
27 ① ② ③ ④ ⑤
28 ① ② ③ ④ ⑤
29 ① ② ③ ④ ⑤
30 ① ② ③ ④ ⑤
31 ① ② ③ ④ ⑤
32 ① ② ③ ④ ⑤
33 ① ② ③ ④ ⑤
34 ① ② ③ ④ ⑤
35 ① ② ③ ④ ⑤
36 ① ② ③ ④ ⑤
37 ① ② ③ ④ ⑤
38 ① ② ③ ④ ⑤
39 ① ② ③ ④ ⑤
40 ① ② ③ ④ ⑤
41 ① ② ③ ④ ⑤
42 ① ② ③ ④ ⑤
43 ① ② ③ ④ ⑤
44 ① ② ③ ④ ⑤
45 ① ② ③ ④ ⑤

STOP

TEST 5: MATHEMATICS

Number correct ☐

1 ① ② ③ ④ ⑤
2 ① ② ③ ④ ⑤
3 ① ② ③ ④ ⑤
4 ① ② ③ ④ ⑤
5 ① ② ③ ④ ⑤
6 ① ② ③ ④ ⑤
7 ① ② ③ ④ ⑤
8 ① ② ③ ④ ⑤
9 ① ② ③ ④ ⑤
10 ① ② ③ ④ ⑤
11 ① ② ③ ④ ⑤
12 ① ② ③ ④ ⑤
13 ① ② ③ ④ ⑤
14 ① ② ③ ④ ⑤
15 ① ② ③ ④ ⑤
16 ① ② ③ ④ ⑤
17 ① ② ③ ④ ⑤
18 ① ② ③ ④ ⑤
19 ① ② ③ ④ ⑤
20 ① ② ③ ④ ⑤
21 ① ② ③ ④ ⑤
22 ① ② ③ ④ ⑤
23 ① ② ③ ④ ⑤
24 ① ② ③ ④ ⑤
25 ① ② ③ ④ ⑤
26 ① ② ③ ④ ⑤
27 ① ② ③ ④ ⑤
28 ① ② ③ ④ ⑤
29 ① ② ③ ④ ⑤
30 ① ② ③ ④ ⑤
31 ① ② ③ ④ ⑤
32 ① ② ③ ④ ⑤
33 ① ② ③ ④ ⑤
34 ① ② ③ ④ ⑤
35 ① ② ③ ④ ⑤
36 ① ② ③ ④ ⑤
37 ① ② ③ ④ ⑤
38 ① ② ③ ④ ⑤
39 ① ② ③ ④ ⑤
40 ① ② ③ ④ ⑤
41 ① ② ③ ④ ⑤
42 ① ② ③ ④ ⑤
43 ① ② ③ ④ ⑤
44 ① ② ③ ④ ⑤
45 ① ② ③ ④ ⑤
46 ① ② ③ ④ ⑤
47 ① ② ③ ④ ⑤
48 ① ② ③ ④ ⑤
49 ① ② ③ ④ ⑤
50 ① ② ③ ④ ⑤
51 ① ② ③ ④ ⑤
52 ① ② ③ ④ ⑤
53 ① ② ③ ④ ⑤
54 ① ② ③ ④ ⑤
55 ① ② ③ ④ ⑤
56 ① ② ③ ④ ⑤

STOP

TEST 1. WRITING SKILLS

This test has two parts. Part I measures your ability to recognize errors in written material. Part II tests your ability to write a short essay.

PART I. RECOGNIZING AND CORRECTING ERRORS

Time: 75 Minutes—55 Questions

Directions:
This test consists of several paragraphs in which each sentence is numbered. Some of the sentences within each paragraph contain errors in sentence structure, usage, or mechanics. Other sentences are correct as written. Following each paragraph are questions based upon it. Read the paragraph first, then answer the questions about it. For each item, choose the answer that would result in the most effective writing of the sentence. The best answer must be consistent with the meaning and tone of the paragraph. Record your answers in the Writing Skills section of the answer sheet.

FOR EXAMPLE:

Often their are two equally effective ways to solve a problem.

What correction should be made to this sentence?

(1) replace their with there
(2) change are to is
(3) change two to too
(4) insert a comma after equally
(5) no change is necessary

● ② ③ ④ ⑤

In this example, the word *their,* which means "belonging to them," is incorrectly substituted for the word *there.* To indicate this correction, mark answer space 1 on your answer sheet.

Items 1 to 8 are based on the following paragraph:

(1) People who smoke have a ten times greatest chance of getting cancer than people who don't smoke. (2) Overall, smoking causes 30 percent of all cancer deaths. (3) The risk of getting lung cancer from cigarettes increased with the number you smoke, how long you have been smoking, and how deeply you inhale. (4) Smoking also has been linked to cancers of the larynx, esophagus, pancreas, bladder, kidney, and mouth. (5) Although stopping is better, switching to low-tar, low-nicotine cigarettes may reduce somewhat your risk of developing lung cancer if you do not inhaled more deeply, take more puffs, or smoke more cigarettes than you did before you switched. (6) However, switching to low-tar, low-nicotine cigarettes will not reduce your risks of developing other cancers and diseases, such as heart disease. (7) Animal studies also have confirmed that basic by-products (tar) producing by smoking marijuana can cause cancers. (8) Once you quit smoking, your risks began to decrease at once. (9) The only way to elimenate your cancer risks due to smoking is not to smoke at all.

1. Sentence 1: **People who smoke have a ten times greatest chance of getting cancer than people who don't smoke.**

   What correction should be made to this sentence?

   (1) change who smoke to who smoked
   (2) change have to had
   (3) change greatest to greater
   (4) change don't smoke to don't smoking
   (5) no correction is necessary

2. Sentence 3: **The risk of getting lung cancer from cigarettes increased with the number you smoke, how long you have been smoking, and how deeply you inhale.**

   What correction should be made to this sentence?

   (1) change risk to risks
   (2) change the spelling of cigarettes to cigaretes
   (3) change increased to increases
   (4) change smoke to smoked
   (5) change inhale to inhaled

3. Sentence 4: **Smoking also has been linked to cancers of the larnyx, esophagus, pancreas, bladder, kidney, and mouth.**

   Which of the following is the best way to write the underlined portion of this sentence? If you think the original is the best way to write the sentence, choose option (1).

   (1) cancers of the larynx, esophagus, pancreas, bladder, kidney, and mouth.
   (2) Cancers of the larynx, esophagus, pancreas, bladder, kidney, and mouth.
   (3) cancers: of the larynx, esophagus, pancreas, bladder, kidney, and mouth.
   (4) Cancers of the Larynx, Esophagus, Pancreas, Bladder, Kidney, and Mouth.
   (5) cancers: of the Larynx, Esophagus, Pancreas, Bladder, Kidney, and Mouth.

4. Sentence 5: **Although stopping is better, switching to low-tar, low-nicotine cigarettes may reduce somewhat your risk of developing lung cancer if you do not inhaled more deeply, take more puffs, or smoke more cigarettes than you did before you switched.**

   What correction should be made to this sentence?

   (1) delete the comma after better
   (2) insert a colon after cigarettes
   (3) insert a comma after cancer
   (4) change inhaled to inhale
   (5) change take to took

5. Sentence 6: **However, switching to low-tar, low-nicotine cigarettes will not reduce your risks of developing other cancers and diseases, such as heart disease.**

If you rewrote sentence 6 beginning with
Even though you switch to low-tar, low-nicotine cigarettes,
the next words should be

(1) a cigarette
(2) you will not reduce
(3) your reduction of risks
(4) reducing risks
(5) having reduced your risks

6. Sentence 7: **Animal studies also have confirmed that basic by-products (tar) producing by smoking marijuana can cause cancers.**

   What correction should be made to this sentence?

   (1) delete the word also
   (2) change confirmed to confirm
   (3) change the spelling of basic to bassic
   (4) delete the parentheses around tar
   (5) change producing to produced

7. Sentence 8: **Once you quit smoking, your risks began to decrease at once.**

   Which of the following is the best way to write the underlined portion of this sentence? If you think the original is the best way to write the sentence, choose option (1).

   (1) your risks began to decrease
   (2) your risk began to decrease
   (3) your risks beginning to decrease
   (4) your risks to begin decreasing
   (5) your risks begin to decrease

8. Sentence 9: **The only way to elimenate your cancer risks due to smoking is not to smoke at all.**

   What correction should be made to this sentence?

   (1) change the spelling of elimenate to eliminate
   (2) change the spelling of way to weigh
   (3) change due to do
   (4) change to smoke to to be smoking
   (5) no correction is necessary

GO ON TO THE NEXT PAGE

Items 9 to 17 are based on the following paragraph.

(1) Most carriers begin work early in the morning, in some cases as early as 4 a.m. if they have routes in the business district. (2) Carriers spend most of their time outdoors, and deliver mail in all kinds of whether. (3) Even those who drive often must walk when making deliveries, they must lift heavy sacks of parcel post when loading their vehicles. (4) A carrier's schedule has its advantages: Carriers who begin work early in the morning are through by early afternoon, and they spend most of the day on his own, relatively free from direct supervision. (5) Working conditions of clerks vary to accomodate work arrangements and the type of laborsaving machinery availible. (6) In small post offices, clerks may use a handtruck to move heavy mail sacks from one part of the building to another and sort mail by hand. (7) In large post offices and mail processing centers, chutes and conveyers move the mail, and much of the sorting is done with machines. (8) When not operating a letter sorting machine, clerks usually are on their feet, reaching for sacks and trays of mail and placing packages and bundles into sacks and trays. (9) Distribution clerks may become board with the routine of sorting mail unless they try to improve their speed and accuracy. (10) Many work at night or on weekends because most large post offices process mail around the clock, and the largest volume of mail is sorting during the evening and night shifts. (11) Window clerks, on the other hand, have a greater variety of duties, frequent contact with the public, and a generally less strenuous job, although they are held responsible for the assigned stamp stock and postal fund.

9. Sentence 1: **Most carriers begin work early in the morning, in some cases as early as 4 a.m. if they have routes in the business district.**

   What correction should be made to this sentence?

   (1) change begin to began
   (2) insert a comma after cases
   (3) change the spelling of routes to roots
   (4) change the spelling of business to bussiness
   (5) no correction is necessary

10. Sentence 2: **Carriers spend most of their time outdoors, and deliver mail in all kinds of whether.**

    What correction should be made to this sentence?

    (1) change the spelling of Carriers to Carrier's
    (2) change spend to spent
    (3) change their to there
    (4) insert a comma after mail
    (5) change whether to weather

11. Sentence 3: **Even those who drive often must walk when making deliveries, they must lift heavy sacks of parcel post when loading their vehicles.**

    Which of the following is the best way to write the underlined portion of this sentence? If you think the original is the best way to write this sentence, choose option (1).

    (1) deliveries, they
    (2) deliveries. They
    (3) deliveries; and they
    (4) deliveries they
    (5) deliveries: they

12. Sentence 4: **A carrier's schedule has its advantages: Carriers who begin work early in the morning are through by early afternoon, and they spend most of the day on his own, relatively free from direct supervision.**

    Which of the following is the best way to write the underlined portion of this sentence? If you think the original is the best way to write the sentence, choose option (1).

    (1) on his own
    (2) his own way
    (3) on their own
    (4) by their own
    (5) on one's own

13. Sentence 5: **Working conditions of clerks vary to accomodate work arrangements and the type of laborsaving machinery availible.**

What correction should be made to this sentence?

(1) change spelling of conditions to condetions
(2) change vary to very
(3) change the spelling of accomodate to accomadate
(4) change the spelling of arrangements to arrangments
(5) change the spelling of availible to available

14. Sentence 6: **In small post offices, clerks may use a handtruck to move heavy mail sacks from one part of the building to another and sort mail by hand.**

If you rewrote sentence 6 beginning with Moving heavy mail sacks, the next word should be

(1) small
(2) clerks
(3) may
(4) part
(5) building

15. Sentence 9: **Distribution clerks may become board with the routine of sorting mail unless they try to improve their speed and accuracy.**

What correction should be made to this sentence?

(1) change clerks to clerk
(2) change become to became
(3) change board to bored
(4) insert a comma after mail
(5) insert a comma after unless

16. Sentence 10: **Many work at night or on weekends because most large post offices process mail around the clock, and the largest volume of mail is sorting during the evening and night shifts.**

What correction should be made to this sentence?

(1) insert a period after weekends
(2) change the spelling of process to proccess
(3) insert a comma between mail and around
(4) change sorting to sorted
(5) no correction is necessary

17. Sentence 11: **Window clerks, on the other hand, have a greater variety of duties, frequent contact with the public, and a generally less strenuous job, although they are held responsible for the assigned stamp stock and postal fund.**

What correction should be made to this sentence?

(1) change spelling of variety to variaty
(2) change spelling of strenuous to strenous
(3) change although to all though
(4) change spelling of responsible to responsable
(5) no correction is necessary

GO ON TO THE NEXT PAGE

Items 18 to 27 are based on the following paragraph:

(1) Residents of Montana laughingly refer to the small, windblown settlement of Ekalaka in the eastern badlands as "Skeleton flats," but as curious as it may sound, the name is appropriate. (2) So many fossils have been dug up in this otherwise unremarkable town that it has become a paradise for paleontologists, because scientists who use fossils to study prehistoric life forms. (3) In fact, dinosaur bones are plentiful in this area, ranchers have been known to use them as doorstops! (4) Ekalaka's fame began to grow more than 50 years ago when Walter H Peck, whose hobby was geology, found the bones of a Stegosaurus, a huge, plant-eating dinosaur. (5) The entire population soon took up Peck's pastime, and alot of people began digging for dinosaur bones. (6) Led by the local science teacher, new finds were sought and they rarely returned empty-handed. (7) It would seem there is no end to the fossil riches and they are Ekalaka. (8) Among the most valuable finds are the remains of a Brontosaurus, an 80-foot-long monster that probably weighed 40 tons. (9) The skeleton of a Triceratops was also found. (10) The head of this prehistoric giant alone weighed more than 1000 pounds. (11) Careful searching also yields small fossilized fishes, complete with stony scales, and the remains of a huge sea reptile.

18. Sentence 1: **Residents of Montana laughingly refer to the small, windblown settlement of Ekalaka in the eastern badlands as "Skeleton flats," but as curious as it may sound, the name is appropriate.**

    Which of the following is the best way to write the underlined portion of this sentence? If you think the original is the best way to write the sentence, choose option (1).

    (1) as "Skeleton flats,"
    (2) as Skeleton flats,
    (3) as Skeleton flats;
    (4) as "Skeleton Flats,"
    (5) as "skeleton flats,"

19. Sentence 2: **So many fossils have been dug up in this otherwise unremarkable town that it has become a paradise for paleontologists, because scientists who use fossils to study prehistoric life forms.**

    Which of the following is the best way to write the underlined portion of this sentence? If you think the original is the best way to write the sentence, choose option (1).

    (1) paleontologists, because scientists
    (2) paleontologists, scientists
    (3) paleontologists. Because scientists
    (4) paleontologists. Scientists
    (5) paleontologists scientists

20. Sentence 3: **In fact, dinosaur bones are plentiful in this area, ranchers have been known to use them as doorstops!**

    Which of the following is the best way to write the underlined portion of this sentence? If you think the original is the best way to write the sentence, choose option (1).

    (1) area, ranchers have
    (2) area, even though ranchers
    (3) area despite ranchers
    (4) area ranchers have
    (5) area. Ranchers have

21. Sentence 4: **Ekalaka's fame began to grow more than 50 years ago when Walter H Peck, whose hobby was geology, found the bones of a Stegosaurus, a huge, plant-eating dinosaur.**

    What correction should be made to this sentence?

    (1) change Ekalaka's to Ekalakas
    (2) add a period after Walter H
    (3) change the comma after Peck to a semicolon
    (4) change spelling of geology to Geology
    (5) change the spelling of Stegosaurus to stegosaurus

22. Sentence 5: **The entire population soon took up Peck's pastime, and alot of people began digging for dinosaur bones.**

What correction should be made to this sentence?

(1) change the spelling of population to popullation
(2) change the spelling of pastime to pasttime
(3) change the spelling of and to And
(4) change the spelling of alot to a lot
(5) no correction is necessary

23. Sentence 6: **Led by the local science teacher, new finds were sought and they rarely returned empty-handed.**

Which of the following is the best way to write the underlined portion of this sentence? If you think the original is the best way to write the sentence, choose option (1).

(1) new finds were sought
(2) people sought new finds
(3) seeking new finds
(4) bones were all around
(5) that looked for fossils

24. Sentence 7: **It would seem there is no end to the fossil riches and they are Ekalaka.**

Which of the following is the best way to write the underlined portion of this sentence? If you think the original is the best way to write the sentence, choose option (1).

(1) and they are Ekalaka.
(2) that Ekalaka passed.
(3) and contain Ekalaka.
(4) to be found in Ekalaka.
(5) and Ekalaka's.

25. Sentence 8: **Among the most valuable finds are the remains of a Brontosaurus, an 80-foot-long monster that probably weighed 40 tons.**

What correction should be made to this sentence?

(1) change Among to Between
(2) change the spelling of valuable to valubale
(3) change are to were
(4) insert a comma after monster
(5) change the spelling of weighed to waved

26. Sentences 9 and 10: (9) **The skeleton of a Triceratops was also found.** (10) **The head of this prehistoric giant alone weighed more than 1000 pounds.**

The most effective combination of sentences 9 and 10 would include which of the following groups of words?

(1) The skeleton being prehistoric
(2) A Triceratops weighed more
(3) The head of a Triceratops
(4) the head was found
(5) The giant weighed

27. Sentence 11: **Careful searching also yields small fossilized fishes, complete with stony scales, and the remains of a huge sea reptile.**

What correction should be made to this sentence?

(1) change careful to carefully
(2) insert a comma after searching
(3) change yields to yielded
(4) change complete to completing
(5) no correction is necessary

GO ON TO THE NEXT PAGE

Items 28 to 37 are based on the following paragraph:

(1) Certain groups of jobseekers face special difficulties in obtaining suitable employment. (2) All too often, veterans, youth, handicapped persons, minorities, and women experiences difficulty in the labor market. (3) The reasons for job market disadvantage vary, for sure. (4) People may have trouble setting career goals and looked for work for reasons as different as a limited command of English, a prison record, or lack of self-confidence. (5) Some people are held back by their background—by growing up in a setting that provided only a few role models and little exposure to the wide range of opportunities in the world of work. (6) A growing number of communities had career counseling, training, and placement services for people with special needs. (7) Programs sponsored by many organizations, including churches and synagogues, nonprofit organizations, social service agencies, the state public employment service, and vocational rehabilitation agencies. (8) Some of the most successful programs provide, the extensive support that disadvantaged job seekers require. (9) They begin by helping clients resolve personal, family, or other fundamentel problems that prevent them from finding or keeping a suitable job. (10) Some agencies that serve special groups provide a variety of supportive services designed to help people find and kept jobs.

28. Sentence 1: **Certain groups of jobseekers face special difficulties in obtaining suitable employment.**

What correction should be made to this sentence?

(1) change certain to certian
(2) insert an apostrophe after jobseekers
(3) change special to spesial
(4) insert a comma after difficulties
(5) no correction is necessary

29. Sentence 2: **All too often, veterans, youth, handicapped persons, minorities, and women experiences difficulty in the labor market.**

Which of the following is the best way to write the underlined portion of this sentence? If you think the original is the best way to write the sentence, choose option (1).

(1) women experiences difficulty
(2) woman experiences difficulty
(3) men and women experiences difficulty
(4) women experience difficulty
(5) women experiencing difficulty

30. Sentence 3: **The reasons for job market disadvantage vary, for sure.**

Which of the following is the best way to write the underlined portion of this sentence? If you think the original is the best way to write the sentence, choose option (1).

(1) for sure
(2) of course
(3) although
(4) because
(5) all too soon

31. Sentence 4: **People may have trouble setting career goals and looked for work for reasons as different as a limited command of English, a prison record, or lack of self-confidence.**

Which of the following is the best way to write the underlined portion of this sentence? If you think that the original is the best way to write the sentence, choose option (1).

(1) goals and looked for work
(2) goals. And looked for work
(3) goals. They looked for work
(4) goals and looking for work
(5) goals and he looks for work

32. Sentence 5: **Some people are held back by their background—by growing up in a setting that provided only a few role models and little exposure to the wide range of opportunities in the world of work.**

If you rewrote sentence 5 beginning with
Settings that provide
the next words should be

(1) few role models
(2) background of people
(3) wide ranges
(4) work opportunities
(5) exposure to work

33. Sentence 6: **A growing number of communities had career counseling, training, and placement services for people with special needs.**

Which of the following is the best way to write the underlined portion of this sentence? If you think the original is the best way to write the sentence, choose option (1).

(1) communities had career
(2) communities have career
(3) community had career
(4) community are career
(5) communities are career

34. Sentence 7: **Programs sponsored by many organizations, including churches and synagogues, nonprofit organizations, social service agencies, the state public employment service, and vocational rehabilitation agencies.**

What correction should be made to this sentence?

(1) insert are after programs
(2) change the comma after synagogue to a colon
(3) remove the comma after organizations
(4) change the period after rehabilitation agencies to a semicolon
(5) no correction is necessary

35. Sentence 8: **Some of the most successful programs provide, the extensive support that disadvantaged jobseekers require.**

Which of the following is the best way to write the underlined portion of this sentence? If you think the original is the best way to write the sentence, choose option (1).

(1) provide, the extensive
(2) provide. The extensive
(3) provide and the extensive
(4) provide: the extensive
(5) provide the extensive

36. Sentence 9: **They begin by helping clients resolve personal, family, or other fundamentel problems that prevent them from finding or keeping a suitable job.**

What correction should be made to this sentence?

(1) change They to There
(2) insert a comma after helping
(3) change the spelling of fundamentel to fundamental
(4) change prevent to prevention
(5) change keeping to keep

37. Sentence 10: **Some agencies that serve special groups provide a variety of supportive services designed to help people find and kept jobs.**

What correction should be made to this sentence?

(1) change serve to served
(2) change provide to provided
(3) insert a semicolon after services
(4) change kept to keep
(5) no correction is necessary

GO ON TO THE NEXT PAGE

Items 38 to 47 are based on the following paragraph.

(1) Sophia Loren once confessed to an interviewer that she had always loved pasta and eating it "by the ton." (2) Most women would eat tons, too, if they could end up with a figure like Sophia's, but they don't and won't because they think pasta's fattening. (3) Well, relax, ladies. (4) Nutritionists said a pasta is not as bad as you might think. (5) Two ounces of dry pasta—which is an average dinner portion —contain about 210 calories. (6) Just like a baked potato, its not the pasta that's fattening, but the stuff one slathers over it that makes the calorie count jump. (7) Pasta to hold its own in the nutrition department, too. (8) No one knows who invented pasta, but it is mentioned in Chinese writings from about 5,000 B.C. (9) Marco Polo uses to get the credit for introducing pasta to Italy, but that legend was laid to rest when scholars unearthed an Italian cookbook with pasta recipes published around 1290—at least five years before Marco returned from his wanderings through Asia. (10) Now experts believe that Indians, Arabs, or Mongols introduced pasta to Italy; as early as the 11th century, though some think the Etruscans were using it in pre-Roman days. (11) Though theirs no historical documentation, it's not too hard to imagine how pasta was invented. (12) Somewhere, someone must have carelessly or experimentally dropped a blob of paste made from flour and water into a pot of boiling water and, after tasting it, decided the acident was worth repeating.

38. Sentence 1: **Sophia Loren once confessed to an interviewer that she had always loved pasta and eating it "by the ton."**

Which of the following is the best way to write the underlined portion of this sentence? If you think the original is the best way to write the sentence, choose option (1).

(1) pasta and eating
(2) pasta and ate
(3) pasta by eat
(4) pasta or eat
(5) pasta by ate

39. Sentence 2: **Most women would eat tons, too, if they could end up with a figure like Sophia's, but they don't and won't because they think pasta's fattening.**

If sentence 2 were to be rewritten in more formal language, it would include which of the following group of words?

(1) they don't and won't
(2) would eat tons, too
(3) they refuse to
(4) pasta's fattening
(5) great figure

40. Sentence 4: **Nutritionists said a pasta is not as bad as you might think.**

Which of the following is the best way to write the underlined portion of this sentence? If you think the original is the best way to write the sentence, choose option (1).

(1) Nutritionists said a pasta
(2) Nutritionists say that pasta
(3) Nutritionists, say that pasta
(4) Nutritionists, said that pasta
(5) Nutritionists to say that pasta

41. Sentence 5: **Two ounces of dry pasta—which is an average dinner portion—contain about 210 calories.**

What correction should be made to this sentence?

(1) change two to 2
(2) change ounces to ounzes
(3) change which to witch
(4) change dinner to diner
(5) no correction is necessary

42. Sentence 6: **Just like a baked potato, its not the pasta that's fattening, but the stuff one slathers over it that makes the calorie count jump.**

Which of the following is the best way to write the underlined portion of this sentence? If you think the original is the best way to write the sentence, choose option (1).

(1) its not the pasta that's fattening
(2) it not the pasta that's fattening
(3) it's not the pasta that fattening

(4) it's not the pasta thats fattening
(5) it's not the pasta that's fattening

43. Sentence 7: **Pasta to hold its own in the nutrition department, too.**

Which of the following is the best way to write the underlined portion of this sentence? If you think the original is the best way to write the sentence, choose option (1).

(1) Pasta to hold
(2) Pasta holding
(3) Pasta in order to hold
(4) Pasta can hold
(5) Pasta would be held

44. Sentence 9: **Marco Polo uses to get the credit for introducing pasta to Italy, but that legend was laid to rest when scholars unearthed an Italian cookbook with pasta recipes published around 1290—at least five years before Marco returned from his wanderings through Asia.**

Which of the following is the best way to write the underlined portion of this sentence? If you think the original is the best way to write the sentence, choose option (1).

(1) Marco Polo uses
(2) Marco Polo to use
(3) Marco Polo using
(4) Marco Polo use
(5) Marco Polo used

45. Sentence 10: **Now experts believe that Indians, Arabs, or Mongols introduced pasta to Italy; as early as the 11th century, though some think the Etruscans were using it in pre-Roman days.**

What correction should be made to this sentence?

(1) insert a colon after that
(2) change Indians to indians
(3) remove the semicolon after Italy
(4) change the comma to a colon after century
(5) change Etruscans to etruscans

46. Sentence 11: **Though theirs no historical documentation, it's not too hard to imagine how pasta was invented.**

What correction should be made to this sentence?

(1) replace Though with Although
(2) replace theirs with there's
(3) change it's to its
(4) change was to is
(5) no correction is necessary

47. Sentence 12: **Somewhere, someone must have carelessly or experimentally dropped a blob of paste made from flour and water into a pot of boiling water and, after tasting it, decided the acident was worth repeating.**

What correction should be made to this sentence?

(1) change carelessly to carelesly
(2) change experimentally to experimenttally
(3) change acident to accident
(4) change repeating to repeting
(5) no correction is necessary

GO ON TO THE NEXT PAGE

Items 48 to 55 are based on the following paragraph:

(1) Osteoarthritis, a degenerative joint disease, occur most often in men and women over 50. (2) It is believed to be related from the wear and tear of the hardest working joints of the body and to other uncertain and unknown factors. (3) The cartilage that protects the ends of the bones in the joints is worn away due to weakness of the supporting structures, such as the tendons, ligaments, and muscles. (4) The bones then great against each other with accompanying pain and a decrease in mobility. (5) In the beginning only one joint may be affected, but as time goes on different joints can begin to hurt, usually one at a time. (6) Some people with osteoarthritis don't even know they have them even though X-rays show joint damage. (7) For those who do have trouble, the major symptoms are pain in and around joints and noticeable loss of ability to move joints easily. (8) In advanced cases joints taken on an outwardly knobby look.

48. Sentence 1: **Osteoarthritis, a degenerative joint disease, occur most often in men and women over 50.**

    What correction should be made to this sentence?

    (1) delete the comma after osteoarthritis
    (2) change disease to diseases
    (3) change occur to occurs
    (4) change the spelling of often to offen
    (5) no change is necessary

49. Sentence 2: **It is believed to be related from the wear and tear of the hardest working joints of the body and to other uncertain and unknown factors.**

    What correction should be made to this sentence?

    (1) change the spelling of believed to beleived
    (2) change from to to
    (3) insert a comma after body
    (4) change the spelling of uncertain to uncertian
    (5) no correction is necessary

50. Sentence 3: **The cartilage that protects the ends of the bones in the joints is worn away due to weakness of the supporting structures, such as the tendons, ligaments and muscles.**

    If you rewrote sentence 3 beginning with Bone ends protected by cartilage in the joints the next word should be

    (1) joined
    (2) is
    (3) was
    (4) weakness
    (5) are

51. Sentence 4: **The bones then great against each other with accompanying pain and a decrease in mobility.**

    What correction should be made to this sentence?

    (1) change then to than
    (2) change great to grate
    (3) change the spelling of accompanying to acompanying
    (4) insert a colon after the word pain
    (5) no correction is necessary

52. Sentence 5: **In the beginning only one joint may be affected, but as time goes on different joints can begin to hurt, usually one at a time.**

    What correction should be made to this sentence?

    (1) change the spelling of beginning to begining
    (2) change affected to effected
    (3) change spelling of different to differant
    (4) delete the comma after hurt
    (5) no correction is necessary

53. Sentence 6: **Some people with osteoarthritis don't even know they have them even though X-rays show joint damage.**

    What correction should be made to this sentence?

(1) change don't to didn't
(2) change know to knew
(3) change them to it
(4) change though to through
(5) change show to showed

54. Sentence 7: **For those who do have trouble, the major symptoms are pain in and around joints and noticeable loss of ability to move joints easily.**

What correction should be made to this sentence?

(1) delete the comma after trouble
(2) change are to is
(3) change the spelling of noticeable to noticable
(4) change move to moving
(5) no correction is necessary

55. Sentence 8: **In advanced cases, joints taken on an outwardly knobby look.**

Which of the following is the best way to write the underlined portion of this sentence? If you think that the original way is the best way to write the sentence, choose option (1).

(1) joints taken on an outwardly
(2) joint taken on an outwardly
(3) joints have taken on an outwardly
(4) joint took on an outwardly
(5) joints taked on an outwardly

END OF WRITING SKILLS TEST PART I

PART II. ESSAY TEST

Time: 45 Minutes— 1 Essay

Directions:

This part of the GED is designed to find out how well you write. You will be given one question which asks you to explain something or to present an opinion on an issue. In constructing your answer for this part of the exam, you should take the following steps:

1. Before you begin to write your answer, read all of the material accompanying the question.
2. Carefully plan what you will say before you begin to write.
3. Use the blank pages in the test booklet (or scratch paper provided for you) to make notes to plan your essay.
4. Write your answer on the separate answer sheet.
5. Carefully read over what you have written and make any changes that will improve your work.
6. Check your paragraphing, sentence structure, spelling, punctuation, capitalization, and usage, and correct any errors.

You will have 45 minutes to write a response to the question you are given. Write clearly with a ballpoint pen so the evaluators can read what you have written. Any notes you make on the blank pages or scratch paper will not be included in your evaluation.

Your essay will be scored by at least two trained readers who will evaluate the paper according to its overall impact. They will be concerned with how clearly you made your main points, how thoroughly your ideas are supported, and how effective and correct your writing is throughout the entire composition. You will receive no credit for writing on a topic other than the one assigned.

SAMPLE TOPIC

Some people think exercise and diet are good for you. Others believe they can be carried to extremes with fad diets and too much exercise. What do you think? Write a composition of 200 words in which you give your opinion on this issue. Be specific, and use examples to support your view.

Use this page for notes.

END OF WRITING SKILLS TEST PART II

TEST 2. SOCIAL STUDIES

Time: 85 Minutes—64 Questions

Directions:

The Social Studies Test consists of multiple-choice questions intended to measure your knowledge of general concepts in history, economics, geography, and political and behavioral science. The questions are based on reading passages, maps, graphs, charts, and cartoons. For each question, first study the information given and then answer the questions about it. You may refer to the readings or graphs as often as necessary in order to answer the questions. Record your answers in the Social Studies section of your answer sheet.

FOR EXAMPLE:

Which medium most regularly presents opinions and interpretations of the news?

(1) national television news programs
(2) local television news programs
(3) newspaper editorial pages
(4) teletype news agency reports
(5) radio news broadcasts

The correct answer is "newspaper editorial pages." Therefore, you should mark answer space 3 on your answer sheet.

Items 1 to 4 refer to the following selection.

Modern cartography was born in royal France during the latter part of the seventeenth century when King Louis XIV offered a handsome prize for anyone who could devise a method for accurately determining longitude. For two thousand years, sailors had been trying to find an exact way to locate different places on earth. The circumference of the earth had been calculated by the Greek Eratosthenes four hundred years before the birth of Christ, but as late as 1650, it was still difficult to exactly locate any single position on a map, and particularly difficult to determine longitude on land or sea. Longitude is used to determine the distance of a place east or west of a point of reference. By the end of the seventeenth century, two instruments had been invented which would provide greater accuracy in calculating longitude. The two new instruments were the telescope and the accurate clock. One final instrument remained to be devised. It was perfected by John Harrison in the latter part of the eighteenth century. It was called a chronometer.

1. Which of the following was the main benefit of the birth of modern cartography?

(1) more accurate clocks
(2) the determination of the exact location of the North Pole
(3) newer and better maps
(4) the introduction of excellent telescopes
(5) the invention of the chronometer

2. Which of the following statements can be inferred from this paragraph?

(1) John Harrison was a Frenchman.
(2) The French government was interested in accurate maps.
(3) The clock was invented in the seventeenth century.
(4) Because maps were inaccurate, people rarely travelled on land or sea.
(5) The telescope and the accurate clock were invented around 1780.

3. Which of the following was adopted as a direct result of modern cartography?

(1) radar as a time measurement
(2) plutonium temperature recording devices
(3) pollution control devices
(4) armaments by France
(5) universally accepted time zones

4. Which of the following statements is best supported by the information presented in this paragraph?

(1) Sailors and members of King Louis XIV's court were the only ones concerned with accurately determining longitude.
(2) King Louis XIV frequently offered large prizes for new discoveries, but this was the largest yet.
(3) Relatively little was discovered during King Louis XIV's reign.
(4) Everyone in the society was aware of these new instruments and the general public began to travel a great deal.
(5) King Louis XIV had an interest in worldwide exploration.

GO ON TO THE NEXT PAGE

Items 5 to 8 refer to the above cartoon:

5. Which of the following groups or situations does the restaurant in the cartoon represent?

(1) the fast food industry
(2) worldwide poverty and hunger
(3) the oil crisis
(4) the American people
(5) workers and employees

6. Which of the following is a hypothesis suggested by this cartoon?

(1) Americans eat out a great deal, especially at inexpensive fast food restaurants.
(2) Americans are unwilling to accept newcomers easily. As a result, immigrants tend to live in isolated groups.
(3) Americans have become much more open to dietary innovations.
(4) Americans have a tendency to eat too much convenience and snack food.
(5) A wide variety of nationalities make up American culture.

7. What would someone who disagrees with the cartoonist's view call this restaurant?

(1) "The Stew Pot"
(2) "The Salad Bowl"
(3) "Goulash to Go"
(4) "The Soup Bowl"
(5) "Sauce Supreme"

8. Which of the following statements is best supported by evidence presented in this cartoon?

(1) There is a wide variety of foods offered at fast food restaurants.
(2) The United States is made up of immigrants from many nations.
(3) The cost of food keeps rising.
(4) American food is imported from Europe.
(5) A balanced diet is very important to good health.

Items 9 to 12 refer to the following passage:

The years immediately prior to World War I were years of great labor unrest in the United States, growing labor bitterness, and high unemployment. Hourly wages for skilled workers were as low as fifteen cents. It was then that the Ford Motor Company, in the closing days of 1913, announced that it would pay a guaranteed five dollars a day to every one of its workers—two to three times what was then the standard wage. Henry Ford learned from a partner that his company's wage bill would almost triple overnight and that only a radical and highly visible action could have a useful result. Before Ford changed the whole labor economy of the United States with that one announcement, labor turnover at Ford Motor Company had been so high that, in 1912, 60,000 men had to be hired to retain 10,000 workers. With the new wage, turnover almost disappeared. The resulting savings were so great that despite sharply rising costs, Ford produced and sold its Model T at a lower price and higher profit than ever before—and achieved market domination. At the same time, Ford's action transformed American industrial society, establishing the American industrial society, establishing the American working man as fundamentally middle class.

adapted from *Management* by Peter Drucker, Harper and Row: New York 1974

9. What was the purpose of the guaranteed five-dollar-a-day wage, according to the passage?

    (1) to increase production
    (2) to reduce employee turnover
    (3) to raise the employee's standard of living
    (4) to attract the best workers
    (5) not specifically given in this paragraph

10. What was the result of this change in pay patterns?

    (1) increased car production
    (2) reduced employee turnover
    (3) improved worker morale
    (4) all of the above
    (5) none of the above

11. What does the author mean when he states that Ford's five-dollar-a-day wage transformed American industrial society?

    (1) It changed pay patterns in industry.
    (2) It made the labor movement a radical activity.
    (3) It caused the organization of General Motors.
    (4) It caused the workers to organize.
    (5) It resulted in a better car.

12. Which of the following is suggested by this paragraph?

    (1) Ford was the first to offer his workers job security, effectively transforming industrial society.
    (2) The American working man became part of the middle class because of an increased salary.
    (3) Henry Ford was following the lead of European industrialists.
    (4) The labor unrest was caused by high unemployment.
    (5) The pay increase was solely Ford's idea.

<u>Items 13 to 15</u> refer to the following statement.

Nations sent early explorers for three reasons: gold, glory, and God. Later explorers were sent out for raw materials, trading posts, and places to colonize.

13. According to this statement, which of the following could be considered an early explorer or exploration?

    (1) The Dutch East India Company trading with the Indians for fur
    (2) Sieur de la Salle setting up trading posts
    (3) James Oglethorpe settling in Savannah, Georgia
    (4) Francisco Coronado searching for the Seven Cities of Cibola in Arizona and New Mexico
    (5) The Dutch settling Albany, New York, which they called Fort Orange

14. According to this statement, which of the following could be considered a later explorer or exploration?

    (1) Cortes stealing the Incas' treasures from the Yucatan
    (2) Sir Francis Drake returning to England with a cargo of Spanish silver
    (3) Lewis and Clark's mapping of the territory West of the Mississippi acquired in the Louisiana Purchase
    (4) Ponce de Leon searching for the Fountain of Youth
    (5) none of the above

15. According to this passage, which of the following motivated early explorers?

    (1) hopes of fame and fortune
    (2) a desire for better living conditions
    (3) a need for religious freedom
    (4) a belief that the monarchy was always right
    (5) a search for spices to preserve meats

Items 16 to 21 refer to the stock market report below.

52-Week High	52-Week Low	Stock	Div	Yld %	PE Ratio	Sales 100s	High	Low	Last	Chg.
21⅜	8⅝	CenSoya	.84	5.3	7	x107	16	15½	16	+ ¼
27⅞	21¼	CenTel	2.00	8.8	7	59	22⅞	22⅝	22⅝	− ⅜
52⅛	19½	CentrDat	1.00	3.5	10	131	29¼	28⅛	28⅞	+ ¾
9¾	6¾	CntryTel	.66	8.0	5	37	8⅜	8¼	8¼	− ⅛
17⅛	11⅜	Crt-teed	.90	6.4	64	26	14¼	13⅞	14⅛	+ ⅛
29⅜	11¾	CessAir	.40	1.8	15	398	23½	22⅜	22⅝	− ½
28⅞	19⅝	Chmpin	1.48	5.7	8	2674	26¼	25⅞	26⅛	− ⅛
28½	19¼	Chml pf	1.20	4.7	. . .	10	25½	25½	25½	−1
53½	50	Chml	4.60	8.8	. . .	32	52⅝	52	52¼	− ⅛
12⅛	7¾	ChampSp	.80	8.5	8	446	9⅜	9	9⅜	− ⅛
44¼	15¾	ChartCo	1.00	5.1	2	457	19⅞	19½	19¾	+ ¼
37½	10⅝	ChartCo wt		. . .	. . .	95	13	12⅝	12¾	− ¼
22⅜	11¼	ChartCo pf	1.65	12.5	. . .	80	13¼	13	13¼	+ ⅛
11⅞	8¾	ChasFd	80e	6.7	. . .	37	11⅞	11⅝	11⅞	+ ⅛
47	33¼	ChasM	2.80	6.8	4	710	41⅞	41⅛	41⅜	− ⅞
47	40¾	ChasM pf	5.25	12.3	. . .	13	42¾	42	42¾	+ ¾
10¾	7	Chelsea	.60	6.2	6	28	9¾	9½	9¾	− ⅛
44⅞	33¼	ChmNY	3.48	8.5	4	139	41⅜	41	41⅛	− ⅛
21⅞	16⅝	ChNY pr	1.87	9.6	. . .	28	19¾	19⅜	19½	− ¼
26⅞	16½	ChesVa	.96	3.8	8	39	25¾	25¾	25½	+ ⅜
31¾	19⅛	ChesPn	1.28	4.5	9	1786	28⅞	28⅛	28⅜	− ⅛
44⅛	25	Chessie	2.56	5.8	6	258u	44⅜	43¾	44	. . .
31½	10¼	ChiMlw		. . .	42	455	31¼	29⅛	31¼	+1⅝
44½	15¾	ChiMlw pf		. . .	. . .	77u	47¼	45¾	47¼	+3
25⅞	16⅞	ChiPneT	2.00	9.1	7	43	22	21⅜	22	+ ¼
6⅞	3⅛	ChkFull	.20e	3.3	7	62	6¼	6	6⅛	. . .
29¼	13¾	ChrisCff	.52t	2.1	6	61	24¾	24⅜	24⅜	− ¼
13⅜	6	Christn	.40e	3.4	11	2	11⅝	11⅝	11⅜	− ⅛
26⅛	14⅝	Chroma	1.10	5.1	7	16	22	21⅜	21⅝	− ⅜
100½	62⅛	Chroma pf	5.00	5.9	. . .	6	85½	84½	84½	−4¼
11⅝	5½	Chrysler		. . .	. . .	979	8⅝	8½	8½	− ¼
6	2	Chrys wt		. . .	. . .	49	4⅜	4¼	4¼	− ¼
14⅞	6⅛	Chyrs pf		. . .	. . .	132	8⅞	8½	8⅝	− ⅛
29¾	18⅜	ChurCh	.72	2.8	9	x373	26¼	25⅞	26	+ ⅜
29⅝	23	CinBell	2.52	8.7	7	5	29	29	29	. . .
19⅛	14¾	CinGe	2.04	12.5	7	118	16⅜	16	16⅜	+ ¼
46	33	CinG pf	4.75	12.4	. . .	z40	38¼	38¼	38¼	+ ¼

16. Which stock showed the greatest change in price from the day before?

    (1) Chml pf
    (2) ChiMlw
    (3) ChiMlw pf
    (4) Chroma pf
    (5) CinBell

17. Which stock is selling closest to its highest selling price for the entire year?

    (1) CentrDat
    (2) Chml pf
    (3) Chas Fd
    (4) Chessie
    (5) Chroma

18. If John wanted to buy 100 shares of ChesVa, about how much would he spend?

    (1) $ 25.50
    (2) $ 255.00
    (3) $ 2550.00
    (4) $25500.00
    (5) cannot be determined from the information given

19. How much would one share of CenTel cost at its lowest price that day?

    (1) $22.50
    (2) $22.60
    (3) $22.63
    (4) $22.70
    (5) $22.75

20. Which stock pays the highest dividend?

    (1) ChasM pf
    (2) ChkFull
    (3) Chmpin
    (4) CenSoya
    (5) cannot be determined by the data given

21. Which stock has experienced the greatest stability in the last year?

    (1) Chml pf
    (2) Chas Fd
    (3) CntryTel
    (4) Chelsea
    (5) ChkFull

GO ON TO THE NEXT PAGE

Items 22 to 27 refer to the following information:

Throughout American history, people have been selected for positions within the government and in private companies in several ways. Some of these ways are still used today; others have fallen into disfavor. Listed below are five methods that have been used for candidate evaluation and promotion.

1. **The "spoils system"**—candidates are selected for positions based on their membership in a political party and/or for supporting their candidate's election bid
2. **The merit system**—an impartial body tests and evaluates job applicants
3. **The "Old Boy" network**—people are placed in high-status jobs because they are members of the upper-middle and upper class
4. **Nepotism**—positions are awarded based on a candidate's relationship to a person within the company
5. **Networking**—people look for positions through social contacts

Each of the following statements describes an aspect of the application review process. Choose the system in which the process would most likely occur. The categories may be used more than once in the set of items but no one question has more than one best answer.

22. Brian Parker's mother is the assistant vice president of the Amalgamated Tool Company. Rather than being given the expected entry-level position in the stock room, Brian starts work as a floor manager. Which of the following systems was used to evaluate Brian's qualifications?

    (1) the spoils system
    (2) the merit system
    (3) the "Old Boy" network
    (4) nepotism
    (5) networking

23. In 1883 Congress passed the Pendleton Act, setting up the Civil Service Commission. This impartial body was to test and rate applicants for federal jobs. Which system did this Act establish?

    (1) the spoils system
    (2) the merit system
    (3) the "Old Boy" network
    (4) nepotism
    (5) networking

24. Somerset St. Pierre's father is the president of a major oil company. His mother is active in many charitable organizations. In addition, his parents are friends with many socially important people. Somerset, like his father and grandfather, attended the exclusive and expensive preparatory high school, Wooded Hills. When Somerset was graduated from an Ivy League college, his father's friend told him about an excellent position in an investment banking firm. Under which system did Somerset receive his job?

    (1) the spoils system
    (2) the merit system
    (3) the "Old Boy" network
    (4) nepotism
    (5) networking

25. In 1939 Congress passed the Hatch Act, providing that federal employees may not be asked for political contributions and may not actively participate in political affairs. The Act was passed to lessen the influence of

    (1) the spoils system
    (2) the merit system
    (3) the "Old Boy" network
    (4) nepotism
    (5) networking

26. Meredith Jones met Nancy Grant at a party. They had lunch twice, and through Nancy, Meredith became acquainted with a handful of people in real estate, a field she has tried hard to break into. She invited several of these people to a barbecue, and carefully kept in touch with them all. Several months later, one of them offered Meredith a job in a newly opened real estate office. Under which system did Meredith get her job offer?

    (1) the spoils system
    (2) the merit system
    (3) the "Old Boy" network
    (4) nepotism
    (5) networking

27. Christopher McGivern was a loyal volunteer for Senator Halloway's campaign. After the senator won re-election, Christopher was given a very well-paying position on the senator's staff. Which system was the senator using to justify giving Christopher a job?

    (1) the spoils system
    (2) the merit system
    (3) the "Old Boy" network
    (4) nepotism
    (5) networking

GO ON TO THE NEXT PAGE

Items 28 to 31 refer to the following selection.

The human body is well suited for the ingestion of alcohol and for its rapid utilization. As with other substances, alcohol is absorbed into the intestine, but it is also absorbed by the stomach, by the lungs when inhaled, and by the rectum when administered as an enema. Once in the bloodstream, it is the liver's job to oxidize the alcohol. Even the sturdiest liver can handle only about one ounce of alcohol per hour. Excess alcohol remains in the bloodstream and is partially exhaled through the lungs, providing law authorities with a method of measuring the quantity of alcohol ingested. Alcohol in the brain can cause the lifting of inhibition. Fortunately, the brain is not organically altered by moderate amounts of alcohol that can affect behavior. Prolonged, heavy use of alcohol can have harmful effects on both liver and brain cells.

28. Which of the following statements about alcohol is best supported by evidence presented in the article?

(1) It can be drunk easily in great quantities.
(2) It can be handled quickly and efficiently by the liver.
(3) It is absorbed into the bloodstream from many parts of the body.
(4) It is controlled without much trouble by the brain.
(5) It can damage the liver and brain when consumed in excess.

29. What does the author mean by "organically altered"?

(1) effectively neutralized
(2) quickly sterilized
(3) physically changed
(4) psychologically damaged
(5) efficiently vaporized

30. How can a state police breath-test analyzer detect if a driver has been drinking in excess?

(1) Excess alcohol in the blood can leave through exhalation.
(2) The driver's statements will be incoherent.
(3) The radar will show excessive speed.
(4) Excess alcohol in the brain lifts inhibitions.
(5) The driver will be unable to walk a straight line.

31. The author of the paragraph is providing

(1) scientific writing
(2) orthodox analysis
(3) reader education
(4) generalized discussion
(5) theoretical abstractions

Women play an important role in the labor market

Women as a proportion of . . .

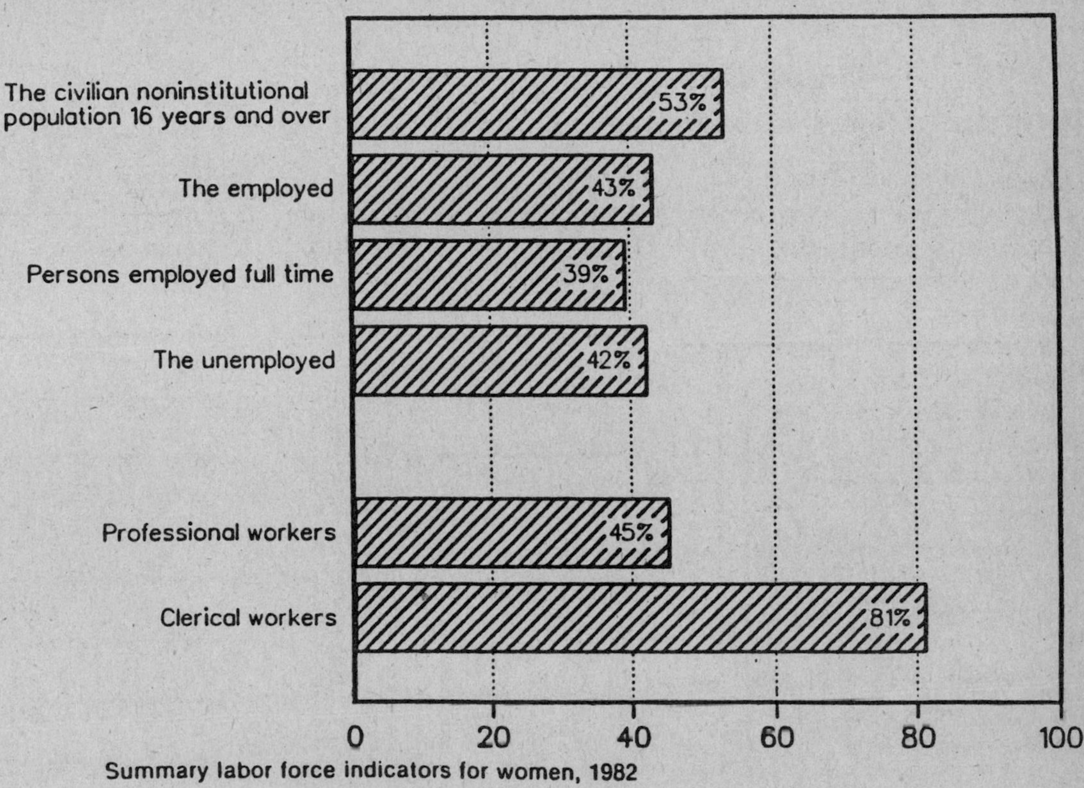

Summary labor force indicators for women, 1982

Items 32 and 33 refer to the above graph.

32. According to the graph above, which of the following statements may be supported as accurate?

    I. 45% of employed women are professional workers.
    II. 43% of women are unemployed.
    III. Women are not a minority.
    IV. Four out of five clerical workers are women.

    (1) I, II, and III only
    (2) I, II, and IV only
    (3) I and II only
    (4) II and IV only
    (5) III and IV only

33. Which of the following statements is supported by the information depicted in the graph above?

    (1) Women are a minority group.
    (2) Women will never achieve economic equality with men.
    (3) The U.S. economy would be seriously damaged if women were not available to the labor force
    (4) A high proportion of women will continue to be unemployed
    (5) Fewer women are likely to be trained as professional workers.

GO ON TO THE NEXT PAGE

Item 34 refers to the following graphs.

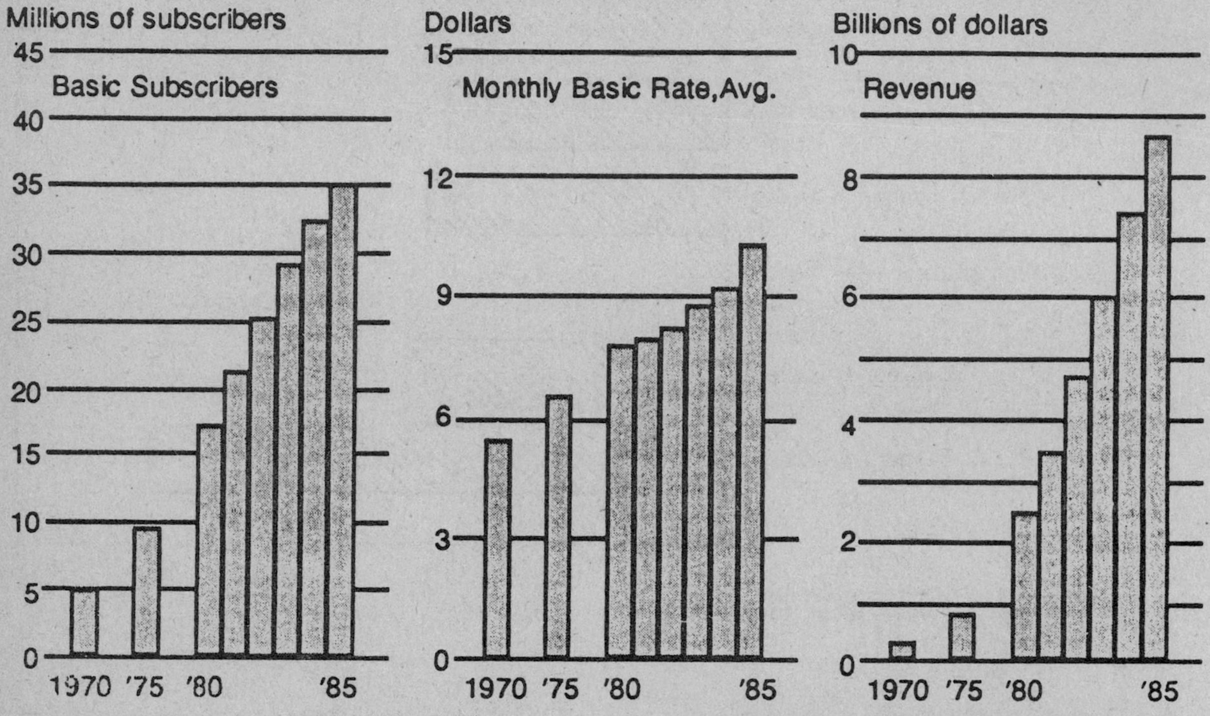

34. Based on the graphs shown above, which of the following statements could you most strongly support?

    (1) The number of cable television subscribers will continue to grow.
    (2) The average monthly fee is unlikely to increase much through the 1990's.
    (3) The cable television industry has enjoyed huge growth in total revenue and number of subscribers between 1975 and 1985.
    (4) Cable television has become a less profitable business than network television.
    (5) Revenue from cable is likely to drop after 1990.

Items 35 to 38 refer to the information below.

In the time of George Washington perhaps one in fifteen Americans was entitled to vote. Since then, many of the various restrictions that prevented certain people from voting have been eliminated by a combination of constitutional amendment, congressional action, and court decision. Restrictions on the right to vote have varied over time, and have included these requirements as well as others:

Property ownership——all thirteen colonies considered men without property unable to make proper decisions about government.

Condition of servitude—although three-fifths of the slave population was counted for purposes of representation in the House of Representatives, slaves were not entitled to vote.

Poll tax——————produced revenue for the states but effectively barred poor people from exercising the franchise.

Sex discrimination——women were allowed to vote in 1869, but only in Wyoming. Popular opinion viewed women as uninterested, incapable, or likely to obey their husbands.

Indirect elections———the Founding Fathers felt full democracy would lead to rash and unhealthy decisions about government.

Identify the voting restriction that was removed by each of the following constitutional amendments:

35. In 1964 the Twentieth Amendment effectively outlawed this limitation on the right to vote.

(1) property ownership
(2) condition of servitude
(3) poll tax
(4) sex discrimination
(5) indirect elections

36. The national debate on this limitation finally ended in 1920 with the passage of the Nineteenth Amendment.

(1) property ownership
(2) condition of servitude
(3) poll tax
(4) sex discrimination
(5) indirect elections

37. The passage of the Fourteenth and Fifteenth Amendments removed this limitation to the right to vote.

(1) property ownership
(2) condition of servitude
(3) poll tax
(4) sex discrimination
(5) indirect elections

38. After the Seventeenth Amendment was ratified in 1913, senators were no longer elected by each state legislature.

(1) property ownership
(2) condition of servitude
(3) poll tax
(4) sex discrimination
(5) indirect elections

GO ON TO THE NEXT PAGE

Item: 39 is based on the map shown above.

39. The center of population is defined as that point at which an imaginary flat, weightless, and rigid map of the U.S. would balance if weights of identical value were placed on it so that each weight represented the location of one person on the date of the census. What is the best conclusion that can be drawn by studying the map above?

(1) Ohio, Indiana, and Illinois were not part of the original thirteen colonies.
(2) Cities on the Mississippi River had a greater opportunity for growth.
(3) People moved from more sparsely populated areas to more crowded ones.
(4) The American population has experienced the greatest growth in the western portion of the country.
(5) The American population has experienced the greatest growth in the eastern half of the country.

Items 40 to 43 refer to the following selection.

Since the middle of 1980, most major household appliances have been carrying yellow-and-black Energy Guide labels. These federally designated labels tell the shopper the estimated cost of operating the appliance displayed and help him or her decide which one to buy. The labels are on new models of refrigerator-freezers, freezers, dishwashers, clothes washers, room air conditioners, furnaces, and water heaters. Television sets, home heating equipment (excluding furnaces), kitchen ranges and ovens, clothes dryers, humidifiers, and dehumidifiers are not labeled because the Federal Trade Commission has determined that there is little difference in energy consumption among the various makes and models. The cost of running each designated item is based upon the cost of energy from the local utility. Electricity is measured in cents per kilowatt-hour. Each label gives the average yearly cost of running the appliance.

40. Based on the paragraph above, what is the purpose of Energy Guide labels?

    (1) to help the consumer understand the cost of operation
    (2) to help the consumer make a logical purchase
    (3) to help the consumer conserve energy
    (4) all of the above
    (5) none of the above

41. Which appliances must carry Energy Guide labels?

    (1) freezers, television sets, clothes washers, clothes dryers
    (2) room air conditioners, television sets, furnaces, and water heaters
    (3) refrigerator-freezers, clothes washers, furnaces, and water heaters
    (4) freezers, dehumidifiers, clothes washers, and furnaces
    (5) freezers, television sets, dehumidifiers, clothes washers

42. According to the passage, which of the following units is used to measure the basic cost of energy?

    (1) British Thermal Units
    (2) wattage
    (3) energy efficiency ratings
    (4) kilowatt-hours
    (5) amperes

43. Which of the following statements about Energy Guide labels is best supported by evidence given in the selection?

    (1) They represent an effort to restrict imports.
    (2) They will reduce the high cost of appliance repairs.
    (3) They will eventually be present on all appliances.
    (4) They may help conserve finite energy resources.
    (5) They will help reduce the national debt.

Item 44

The Federal Bureau of Investigation reports that the following occurred in 1979:

A serious crime every 2.6 seconds
A theft every 4.8 seconds
A burglary every 10 seconds
A violent crime every 27 seconds
A car or truck theft every 29 seconds

An assault every 51 seconds
A robbery every 68 seconds
A forcible rape every 7 minutes
A murder every 24 minutes

44. From the data above, it would be very easy to classify the United States as a "violent" society. The data seem to indicate that

    (1) crime in America is on the increase
    (2) crime is basically an urban problem
    (3) violent crime is getting worse
    (4) the statistics given are debatable and probably unreliable
    (5) none of the above

GO ON TO THE NEXT PAGE

Item 45 refers to the following graph:

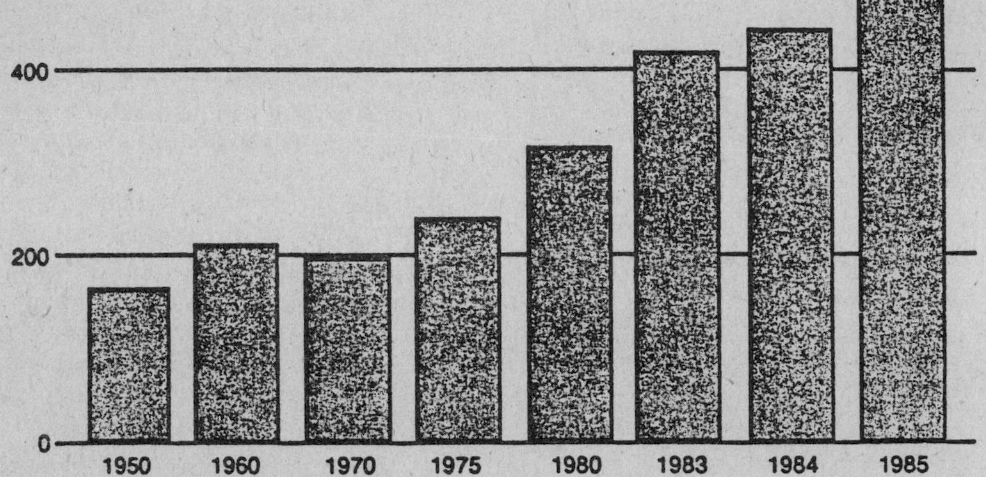

45. Assuming that the expenditure for prison construction generally followed the number of prisoners, choose the line graph that would most nearly describe the outlay for construction of prisons and rehabilitation centers.

(1)

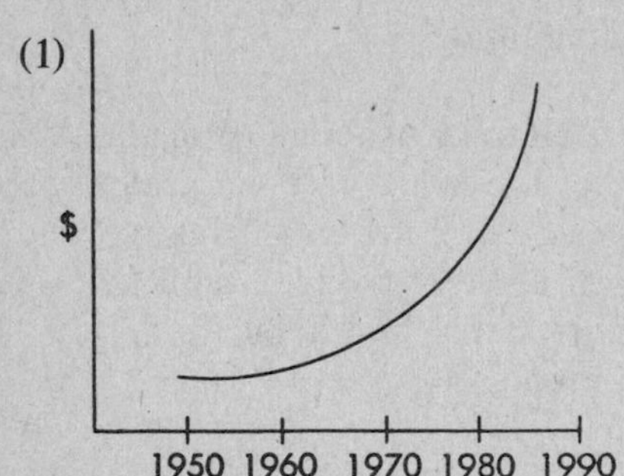

(2)

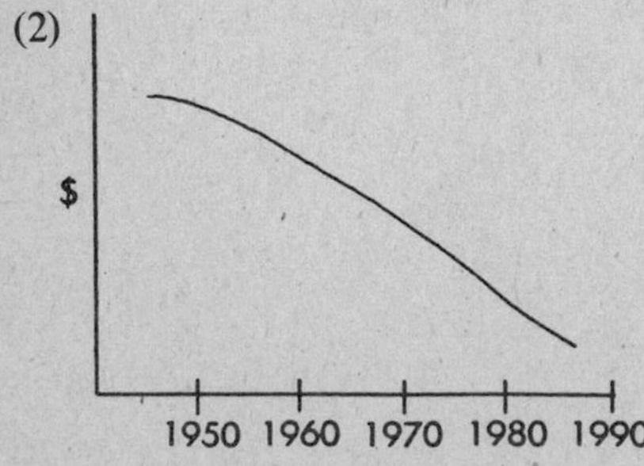

(3)

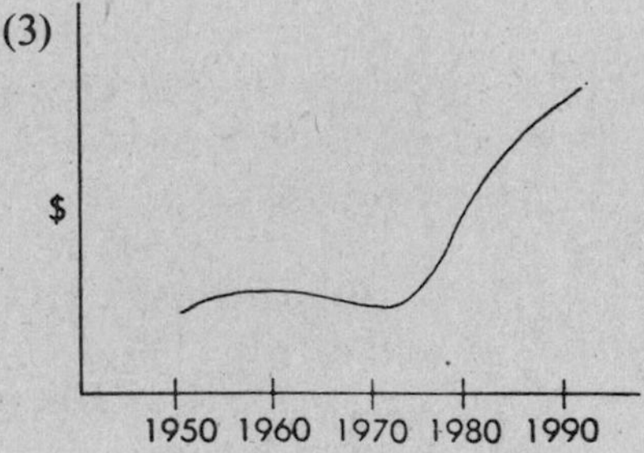

(4)

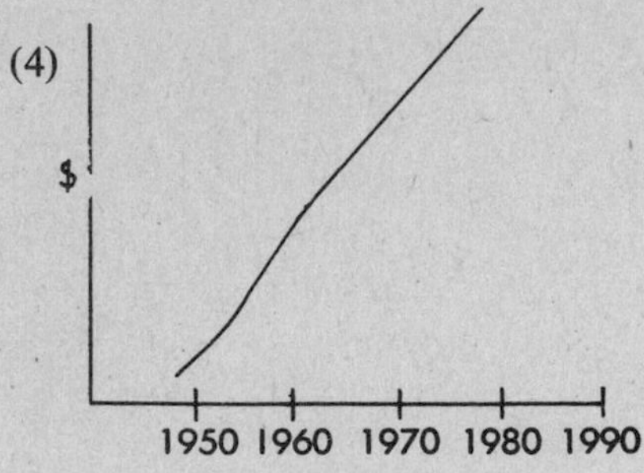

(5)

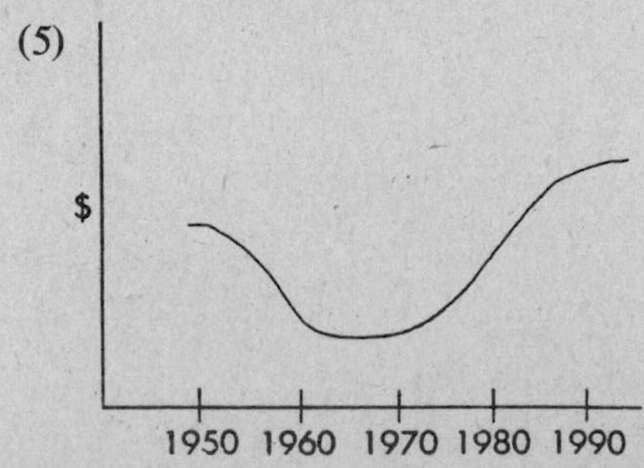

46. In 1947, President Truman announced that "it must be the policy of the United States to support free peoples who are resisting attempted subjugation by named minorities or by outside pressures." This statement became known as the Truman Doctrine.

Based on the information given in the above paragraph, which of the following is one *effect* of the Truman Doctrine?

(1) Greece, in economic chaos as a result of Axis occupation there in World War II, came under attack from Communist guerrillas.
(2) Tito split from Russia.
(3) With American military aid, Greece put down Communist guerrilla attacks.
(4) Turkey was under pressure from Russia for concessions in the Dardanelles, the straits connecting the Black Sea and the Mediterranean.
(5) Russian troops suppressed the Hungarian freedom fighters, successfully smashing the revolution.

47. In 1947, Secretary of State George C. Marshall offered economic aid to all European nations (including Russia and her satellites) to enable them to recover from the destruction of World War II. He said, "Our policy is not directed against any country or doctrine but against hunger, desperation, and chaos."

Based on the information given in the above paragraph, which of the following is one *cause* of the Marshall Plan?

(1) World War II had crippled the economies of European nations, victor and vanquished alike.
(2) Mutually profitable trade was reestablished between the United States and Europe.
(3) The danger of Communism in Western Europe was lessened.
(4) Western European countries moved toward economic unity.
(5) Russia condemned the Marshall Plan as a scheme of American capitalists to gain economic and political control over Europe.

GO ON TO THE NEXT PAGE

Item 48 refers to the following graphs.

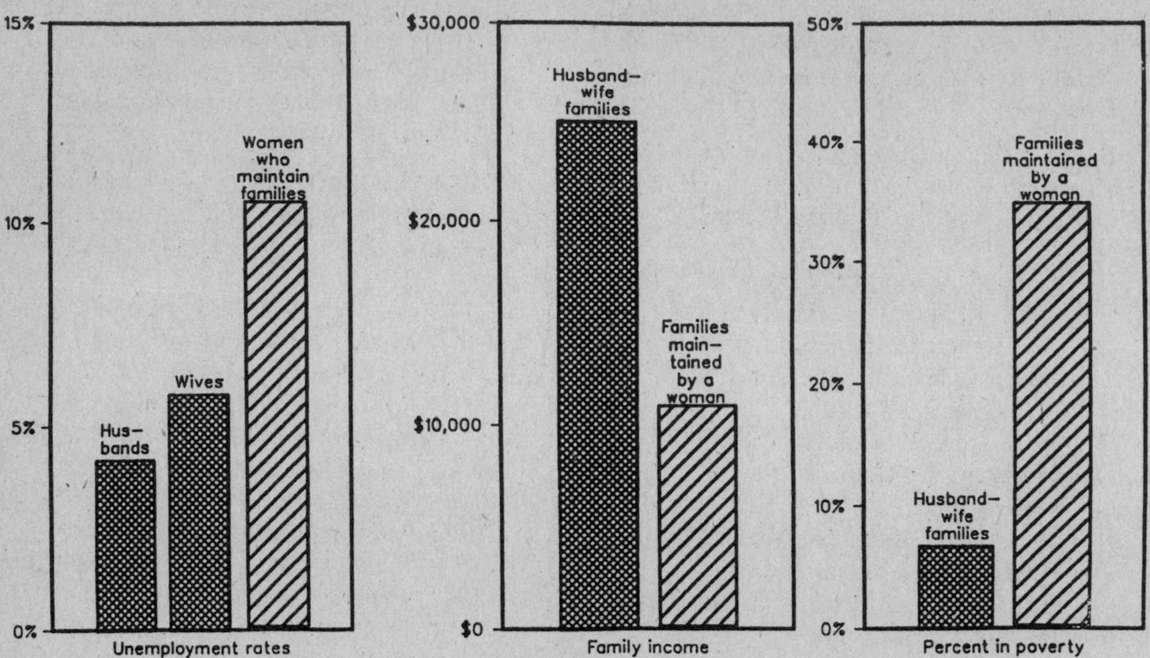

Unemployment, income, and poverty status of families by type of family, 1981

48. Which of the following conclusions is supported by the data shown in the three graphs above?

(1) Households headed by women are more likely to face serious economic problems.
(2) Women without children have lower unemployment rates.
(3) Men earn more than women.
(4) Family income increases when wives enter the workforce.
(5) 40% of all families live in poverty.

49. Most of the major newspapers in the United States are associated with a specific city and print general news about both the nation and the city in which the newspaper is published. Which of the following newspapers is not associated, in content, with a particular city?

(1) *The New York Times*
(2) *The Washington Post*
(3) *The Boston Globe*
(4) *The St. Louis Post-Dispatch*
(5) *The Wall Street Journal*

Items 50 to 52 refer to the following paragraph and chart.

The following chart shows how the United States government supported scientific research and development (R&D) over an eleven-year period and how that money was distributed among the various states. The bars indicate differences during three time periods.

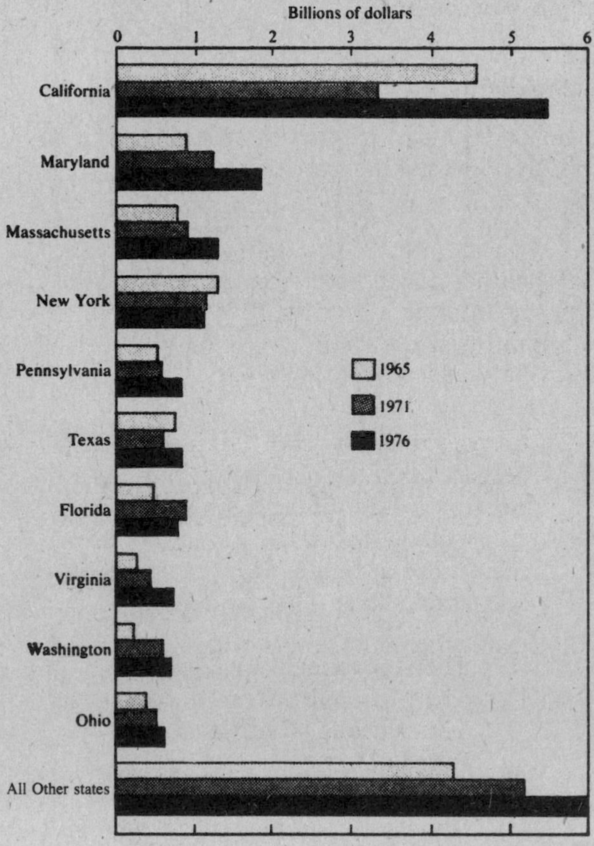

Source: National Science Foundation

50. Based on this chart, what happened to money for scientific research and development over the time period shown?

    (1) It increased dramatically.
    (2) It decreased dramatically.
    (3) It probably just kept up with inflation.
    (4) It enabled dramatic scientific breakthroughs.
    (5) It helped the Defense Department increase its effectiveness.

51. Which combination of states had the largest share of funds in 1971?

    (1) California, Pennsylvania, and Texas
    (2) Maryland, Massachusetts, and New York
    (3) California, Florida, and Texas
    (4) Pennsylvania, Texas, and Florida
    (5) New York, Pennsylvania, and Virginia

52. Which state had the largest percentage decline in funds over the time period of the chart?

    (1) Florida
    (2) New York
    (3) California
    (4) Texas
    (5) Virginia

GO ON TO THE NEXT PAGE

Items 53 to 59 refer to the information below.

As part of its regulatory and educational activities, the federal government has established agencies that issue a wide variety of consumer information publications. These publications are available free or for a small cost. Listed below are six such agencies and the topics of the consumer material they publish.

1. **The Department of Agriculture**——discusses food, clothing, housing
2. **National Bureau of Standards**——translates technical research findings by the government into terms that will be useful to consumers
3. **National Highway Safety Bureau**—provides information on safety aspects of automobile performance
4. **Federal Trade Commission**———alerts consumers to common types of fraudulent claims and deceptive practices
5. **Cooperative Extension Service**——administered by state universities; issues bulletins on homemaking, gardening, and farming

Each of the following statements describes a topic that would be of concern to one of the agencies listed above. Choose the agency that would be most likely to publish material on this topic. The categories may be used more than once in the set of items but no question has more than one best answer.

53. Provides information about acceleration and passing times and distances on tire reserve loads (the capacity of tires to bear additional weight) and on stopping distances.

(1) The Department of Agriculture
(2) The National Bureau of Standards
(3) The National Highway Safety Bureau
(4) The Federal Trade Commission
(5) Cooperative Extension Service

54. Advises that ads recruiting prospects to breed chinchillas for profit "present a glowing picture of large sums of money easily made through the breeding of chinchillas at home. Most such ads have one serious flaw. They are false."

(1) The Department of Agriculture
(2) The National Bureau of Standards
(3) The National Highway Safety Bureau
(4) The Federal Trade Commission
(5) Cooperative Extension Service

55. Advises that a certain vegetable glue "paste" is suitable for use only with paper and has "poor moisture resistance and low strength."

    (1) The Department of Agriculture
    (2) The National Bureau of Standards
    (3) The National Highway Safety Bureau
    (4) The Federal Trade Commission
    (5) Cooperative Extension Service

56. Provides information on consumer problems with lawn grubs and spider mites.

    (1) The Department of Agriculture
    (2) The National Bureau of Standards
    (3) The National Highway Safety Bureau
    (4) The Federal Trade Commission
    (5) Cooperative Extension Service

57. Provides information on the movement of food from the farm to the market and offers tips about its preparation. Also provides a handy way to figure nutritional value.

    (1) The Department of Agriculture
    (2) The National Bureau of Standards
    (3) The National Highway Safety Bureau
    (4) The Federal Trade Commission
    (5) Cooperative Extension Service

58. Its recent publications include

    Food Hints for Teenage Athletes (Ohio State University)

    Be a Smarter Shopper (Cornell University, New York)

    Refinishing Furniture (University of Illinois)

    (1) The Department of Agriculture
    (2) The National Bureau of Standards
    (3) The National Highway Safety Bureau
    (4) The Federal Trade Commission
    (5) Cooperative Extension Service

59. Agency to contact to obtain information about health care providers. They published a booklet entitled *How to Avoid Quackery.*

    (1) The Department of Agriculture
    (2) The National Bureau of Standards
    (3) The National Highway Safety Bureau
    (4) The Federal Trade Commission
    (5) Cooperative Extension Service

GO ON TO THE NEXT PAGE

Items 60 to 64 are based on the following selection:

The central belief of Hinduism is that there is one Universal Spirit, or Eternal Essence, without beginning or end, called Brahman. Brahman (World-Soul) is the three-in-one God: Brahma, The Creator; Vishnu, The Preserver; and Shiva, The Destroyer.

Hindus believe that this trinity embodies the processes of life and death, and that Brahman is continually creating, evolving, and destroying the world. At the end of a cycle, called a "day of Brahma," Shiva destroys the old world, Brahma creates a new one, and Vishnu appears on earth in different human forms, or incarnations, to preserve the world and to guide and enlighten man.

Hinduism is the only religion that believes in a caste system. The Brahmans originally were at the top of the caste system, for they were the ones who spoke to the gods for the people. Next came the Kshatriyas, or warriors. Below the warriors were the Vaisyas (herdsmen, farmers, and skilled craftsmen). The Sudras made up the lowest caste. Outside these four orders were the outcastes or "untouchables." The untouchables performed unpleasant tasks that upper caste members didn't care to do.

Hinduism links the caste system with the theory of reincarnation. Hindus believe that the soul wanders from body to body and is continuously reborn. In each reincarnation a man must accept and perform the duties of the caste into which he is born. Thus, each soul through good and virtuous living can rise to the next higher caste in its next rebirth.

60. According to this passage, what would a farmer who led a virtuous life be reincarnated as?

(1) an Untouchable
(2) a Sudra
(3) a Brahman
(4) a Kshatriya
(5) an animal or person of his choice

61. Based on the information in the passage, what will occur after a "day of Brahma" has ended?

(1) The Kshatriyas destroy the old cycle.
(2) Shiva preserves the world.
(3) Brahma creates a new cycle.
(4) The lowest caste does the hardest work.
(5) The Vaisyas enlighten the people.

62. According to this selection, when does reincarnation take place?

(1) at the moment an old cycle ends and a new one begins
(2) when the soul is continually reborn
(3) when Brahma, the Creator, so decides
(4) when Vishnu appears on earth in different forms
(5) when a man accepts the duties of his caste

63. According to this passage, which of the following might an Untouchable do?

(1) rise up in revolt
(2) raise sheep
(3) fight in religious holy wars
(4) speak to the gods for the people
(5) work as a streetsweeper

64. Based on the information in this article, what does Hinduism offer that best explains its appeal?

(1) the hope of rebirth in a better social position
(2) a way to rid oneself of guilt
(3) the chance to be an untouchable
(4) a chance to be reborn as Vishnu
(5) the belief that love cuts across social caste

END OF SOCIAL STUDIES TEST

TEST 3. SCIENCE

Time: 95 Minutes—66 Questions

Directions:

The Science Test consists of multiple-choice questions intended to measure general concepts in biology, earth science, physics, and chemistry. Some of the questions are based on short readings. Others are based on graphs, charts, tables, or diagrams. For each question, study the information given and then answer the question or questions based upon it. Refer to the information as often as necessary in answering the questions. Record your answer in the Science section of your answer sheet.

FOR EXAMPLE:

A physical change may alter the state of matter, but does not change its chemical composition. Which of the following is NOT a physical change?

(1) boiling water
(2) dissolving salt in water
(3) shaving wood
(4) rusting metal
(5) breaking glass

When metal rusts a new substance is formed. This is a chemical, not a physical, change. Therefore, answer space 4 should be marked on your answer sheet.

Items 1 to 4 refer to the following article.

For breakfast aboard Spacelab the Blue Shift enjoys orange drink, peaches, scrambled eggs, sausages, cocoa, and sweet rolls. The food as well as the food preparation facilities could easily be the envy of many earthbound chefs, homemakers, and diners. Crew members can select from a menu almost as varied and certainly as tasty and nutritious as in most homes or restaurants. One crew member can prepare meals for his shift in about five minutes. Members of the Blue and Red Shifts may eat breakfast and dinner together on some missions if schedules permit.

In a galley to the left of the bunks are an oven, hot and cold water dispensers, and a pantry stocked with seventy-four kinds of food and twenty different beverages. There are drinking cups and eating utensils.

There is no refrigerator and none is needed. To save weight and space, most onboard foods are dehydrated by a freeze-drying process developed especially for space use. Ample water for reconstituting these foods is provided by the fuel cells, which deliver clean water as a by-product of their electricity-generating chemical processes.

Some foods are stored in conventional sealed, heat-sterilized cans or plastic pouches. A few foods, such as cookies and nuts, are in ready-to-eat form. Meals provide for an average of 2,700 calories daily.

1. According to the passage, which of the following choices best describes the difference between the food eaten on earth and the food eaten in space?

   (1) Food eaten in space is more fattening.
   (2) Food eaten in space can be prepared more quickly.
   (3) Food eaten on earth is saltier.
   (4) People on earth eat food higher in carbohydrates.
   (5) Astronauts are better cooks than earthbound people.

2. Which of the following best defines the word "reconstituting"?

   (1) bring back to original form
   (2) recooking to change the shape
   (3) refining into a purer substance
   (4) scrambling up the contents
   (5) chopping into smaller pieces

3. What can be inferred from the fact that the astronauts consume 2,700 calories daily?

   (1) Astronauts are large-framed people who tend to overeat.
   (2) People need additional calories in space.
   (3) Astronauts eat less than people on earth.
   (4) Space flight makes people hungry.
   (5) 2,700 calories represent the recommended daily allowance.

4. Based on the information given, which of the following statements is (are) statements of fact, rather than opinion?

   A. Food served in space has been dehydrated to save space.

   B. Food served on earth has a better appearance than food served in space.

   C. It takes just a few minutes to prepare a meal in space.

   D. Food just tastes better in space!

   (1) A only
   (2) A and B
   (3) A and C
   (4) C only
   (5) A, B, and D

Items 5 to 8 are based on the chart on the next page.

5. According to the chart, when is the greatest amount of oxygen consumed during each stage?

   (1) between 10° and 20°
   (2) between 20° and 30°
   (3) between 30° and 40°
   (4) between 40° and 50°
   (5) between 50° and 55°

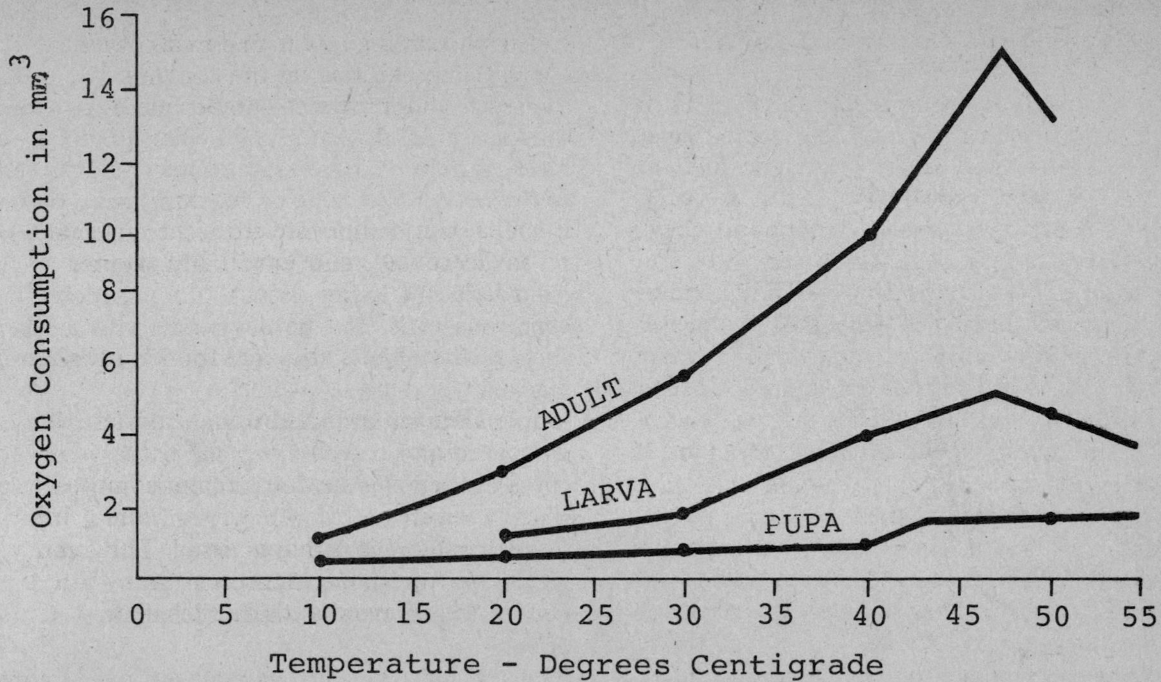

Relation of Oxygen Consumption of Fruitflies to Temperature During the Larval, Pupal, and Adult Stages

6. According to the chart, what was the highest stage of oxygen production in the adult?

   (1) 2 to 6 mm^3
   (2) 4 to 6 mm^3
   (3) 6 to 8 mm^3
   (4) 8 to 10 mm^3
   (5) 10 to 14 mm^3

7. Which of the following can be inferred from the information on the chart?

   (1) Fruitflies can reach maturity without oxygen.
   (2) Adult fruitflies need more oxygen than pupa.
   (3) Larva do well in temperatures between 5° and 15°.
   (4) The oxygen consumption of pupa greatly increases as they grow.
   (5) Larva grow faster than pupa.

8. We can infer that this information can be used for which of the following reasons?

   (1) to increase growth in seasonal plants
   (2) to inhibit growth in roaches
   (3) to increase lab production of fruitflies
   (4) to test new instruments
   (5) to test new hormone therapies

GO ON TO THE NEXT PAGE

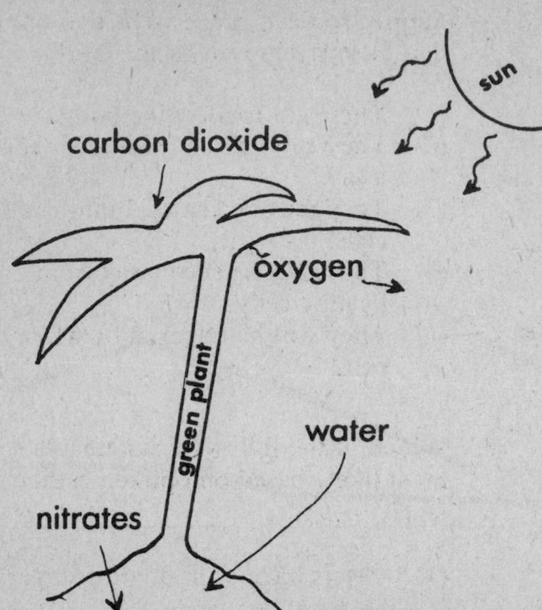

Green plants carry out photosynthesis.

9. As illust. ..ed in the diagram above, when green plants carry out photosynthesis, they take carbon dioxide and water and in the presence of sunlight, change the raw materials into sugar and oxygen. Which of the following is the chemical formula for photosynthesis?

    (1) $C_6H_{12}O_6 + C_6H_{12}O_6 \rightarrow C_{12}H_{22}O_{11} + H_2O$
    (2) $6CO_2 + 12H_2O \rightarrow C_6H_{12}O_6 + 6H_2O + 6O_2$
    (3) $NaOH + HCl \rightarrow NaCl + H_2O$
    (4) $C_6H_{12}0_6 \rightarrow 2C_2H_5OH + 2CO_2 + H_2O$
    (5) $2H_2O \rightarrow 2H_2 + O_2$

Items 10 to 14 are based on the following article.

The laser has been around only a couple of decades, but it does so many things so well that it's already pretty integrated into almost everyone's daily living. One important use is in surgery. A laser beam has some properties that, for certain kinds of surgery, make it eminently substitutable for a scalpel or other conventional surgery tools.

Laser surgery has been going on for only about fifteen years. Lasers used for surgery do their work by destroying tissue, or cells, in a process called photocoagulation necrosis. The heat or energy from the laser is absorbed by the cell's moisture, which thus is turned into vapor and dissipated. Solids that remain when all moisture has been removed are ash and may be disposed of by suction, sponging or brushing away. Often tissue is not completely turned to ash, but is no longer living, and eventually sloughs away from adjacent living tissue. Tumors, including cancerous cells, can be destroyed with a laser such as the CO_2 if they can be identified and reached.

To make a cut or incision, a narrow laser beam is focused and played along the path where the cut is desired. Tissue destruction is limited to a specific width and depth with minimal injury to adjacent or underlying tissue. The beam is played into the same incision as many times as needed to achieve the desired length and depth of cut.

Lasers have certain advantages over more conventional surgical methods, principally these:

- There is little or no touch or pressure contact on the tissues involved. This is important in certain kinds of operations, such as some types of brain surgery, when harm can result from applying pressure or movement against areas adjacent to where the surgery is being performed.
- Laser surgery's employment of heat and the minimal contact with tissue make for sterile conditions that are highly desirable for reducing the risks of infection.
- Laser surgery can be carried out in highly localized sites in the body, and the precision of lasers makes them valuable for microsurgery. When surgery is done under a magnifying lens it's easier to see and thus work on tiny, intricate or delicate parts of various systems in the body. There are laser setups or rigs for freehand, micro-, and electromechanically assisted surgery.
- With certain lasers, a surgeon can work in the nose, ears, mouth, throat, vagina, and other close areas. In conventional surgery, extra cutting may be required to open up such areas enough to use a scalpel or other conventional surgical instrument.
- Because lasers operate by vaporization of and destruction of tissues, healing is usually prompt and there is a minimum of scarring and swelling, its advocates claim.

10. According to the passage, which of the following choices best defines a laser?

(1) a beam of light rays
(2) a metal cutting tool
(3) a diamond-tipped drill
(4) a tool that has yet to be invented
(5) a tool that will someday replace doctors

11. As used in this passage, the word "vaporization" is best defined in which of the following choices?

(1) exploding a cancer cell
(2) removing moisture from a cell
(3) melting ice to form water
(4) sponging away dead cells
(5) slicing cancer cells into small sections

12. Which of the following is NOT an advantage of laser surgery, according to the passage?

(1) reduces scarring and swelling
(2) reduces amount of cutting necessary
(3) reduces risk of infection
(4) reduces risk of cancer
(5) reduces risk of harm to adjacent tissues

13. According to this passage, what may happen to dead cancer cells that are not completely removed by the laser?

(1) They will reinfect the body.
(2) They can still be brushed or sponged away.
(3) They may be changed into healthy cells.
(4) They may be shed away from healthy cells.
(5) They will be attacked by white blood cells.

14. Which of the following statements is most likely based on opinion rather than fact?

(1) Lasers have been used in surgery for about fifteen years.
(2) Lasers destroy healthy as well as infected tissue.
(3) Laser surgery lessens pressure to adjacent areas.
(4) Laser surgery usually heals promptly.
(5) Lasers are the best tools to use in surgery.

GO ON TO THE NEXT PAGE

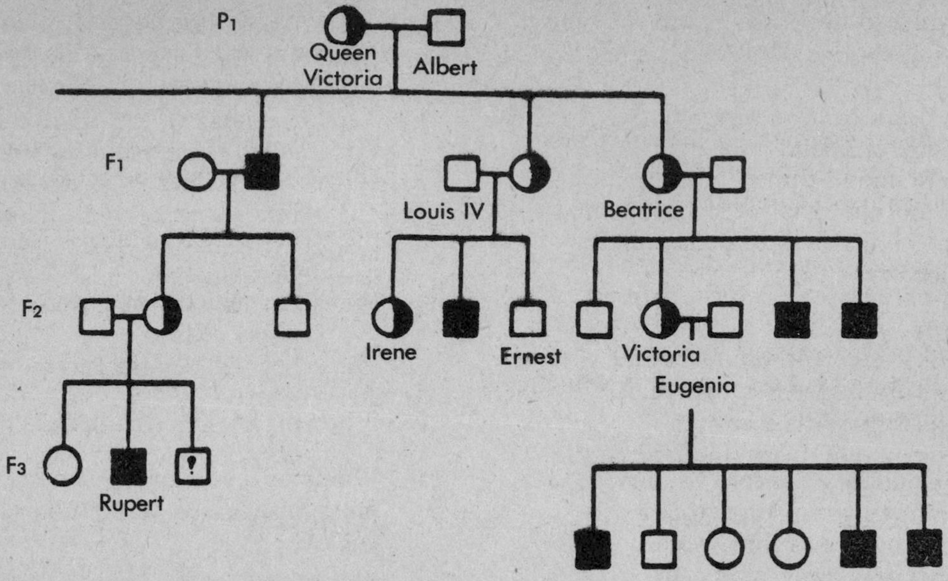

○ female normal

□ male normal

■ male hemophiliac

◐ female carrier

Items 15 to 19 are based on the above chart.

The accompanying pedigree chart shows only a part of Queen Victoria's descendants. The family tree indicates no history of hemophilia (a disease in which the blood fails to clot properly) for either parent prior to the P1 generation.

15. Which assumption about the P1 generation is true?

(1) Albert did not carry the gene for hemophilia.
(2) Queen Victoria had two X chromosomes, each with a gene for hemophilia.
(3) Neither Albert nor Victoria had a gene for hemophilia.
(4) Albert was probably a carrier of the gene for hemophilia.
(5) Albert has hemophilia.

16. Which is the best reason for assuming Louis IV had no gene for hemophilia?

(1) His son, Ernest, did not have hemophilia.
(2) He produced no children with the disease.
(3) His daughter, Irene, did not have hemophilia.
(4) Only females carry the gene for hemophilia.
(5) Louis IV did not exhibit any symptoms of the disease.

17. If Beatrice had married a hemophiliac, what is the probability that her daughters would have been afflicted with the disease?

(1) 0%
(2) 25%
(3) 50%
(4) 75%
(5) 100%

18. Theoretically, what is the probability that Victoria Eugenia's sons could have been afflicted with hemophilia?

(1) 0%
(2) 25%
(3) 33%

(4) 50%
(5) 75%

19. From the information on the chart, what is the most reasonable explanation that Rupert exhibits hemophilia?

    (1) A mutation occurred on the Y-chromosome which he received from his father.
    (2) His mother suffered from the disease and transmitted it to him.
    (3) His father was a carrier.
    (4) His maternal grandfather had the disease.
    (5) His father had the disease.

20. Precipitation refers to the forms of condensation that fall to earth. Which of the following is NOT a form of precipitation?

    (1) dust
    (2) rain
    (3) sleet
    (4) hail
    (5) snow

Items 21 to 24 are based on the following selection.

An immense cloud of glassy powder, spewed from a volcano somewhere in the western United States some ten million years ago, drifted downwind over the Great Plains and finally settled to earth in what is now northeastern Nebraska. The prodigious ashfall blanketed hundreds of square miles. Herds of rhinoceroses, three-toed horses, camels, and tiny saber-toothed deer, confused and choking, perished in the blizzard of abrasive dust.

On a far vaster scale, the disaster was a prehistoric prototype of recent ashfalls from the eruptions of Mount St. Helens in the Cascade Range of Washington.

Along a streambed in northern Antelope County, Nebraska, I have discovered dramatic evidence of the ancient catastrophe. Excavating the ashy filling of the prehistoric water hole, my crew and I from the University of Nebraska State Museum have dug up the skeletons of several hundred victims of the dusty cataclysm. The skeletons, some intertwined and piled on top of one another, have lain buried, mostly in undisturbed death poses, for millions of years since the animals were overwhelmed.

Michael R. Voorhies, "Ancient Ashfall Creates a Pompeii of Prehistoric Animals," *National Geographic*, Vol. 159, No. 1, January, 1984.

21. As it is used in the passage, which of the following choices best defines the word "cataclysm"?

    (1) chasm
    (2) soot
    (3) storm
    (4) disaster
    (5) flood

22. Which of the following overwhelmed the animals?

    (1) hot lava
    (2) volcanic dust
    (3) earthquakes
    (4) loud sounds
    (5) a violent storm

23. Which animals died in the prehistoric ashfall?

    (1) saber-toothed tigers
    (2) dinosaurs
    (3) rhinoceroses
    (4) tiny horses
    (5) huge elephants

24. From the information in the passage, what can we infer to be the author's occupation?

    (1) miner
    (2) writer
    (3) television commentator
    (4) cowboy
    (5) archeologist

GO ON TO THE NEXT PAGE

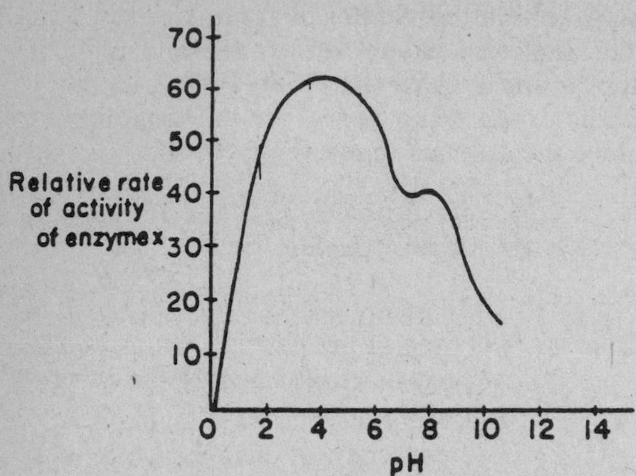

Questions 25–28 refer to the graph above.

25. Which of the following conclusions is supported by the graph?

    (1) pH has no effect on enzyme action.
    (2) The relative rate of enzyme x is constant.
    (3) The rate of enzyme action varies with the pH.
    (4) Plants grow best in strong sunlight.
    (5) Enzyme x increases in volume as the pH increases.

26. According to the graph, between which pH values does the rate of activity of enzyme increase most?

    (1) 0 and 2
    (2) 2 and 4
    (3) 4 and 6
    (4) 6 and 8
    (5) 8 and 10

27. Which of the following processes could be the subject of this graph?

    (1) digestion
    (2) evaporation
    (3) photosynthesis
    (4) sleep
    (5) respiration

28. Based on the information on the graph and the fact that 7 represents neutrality, numbers less than 7 represent acidity, and numbers greater than 7 represent alkalinity on the pH scale, which of the following would be true?

    (1) Water with a reading of 7 would be salty.
    (2) Adding acidic lemon juice to a solution will decrease its pH.
    (3) All enzymes increase their activity in an acidic environment.
    (4) pH remains constant, no matter what is added.
    (5) Some enzymes react to differences in pH.

29. A scientist did the following experiment: He covered two petri dishes with the same type of bacteria. Then he put a drop of penicillin on one dish and a drop of chemical "X" on the other. Several hours later he saw the results as shown in the diagram below. What can you infer from looking at the diagram?

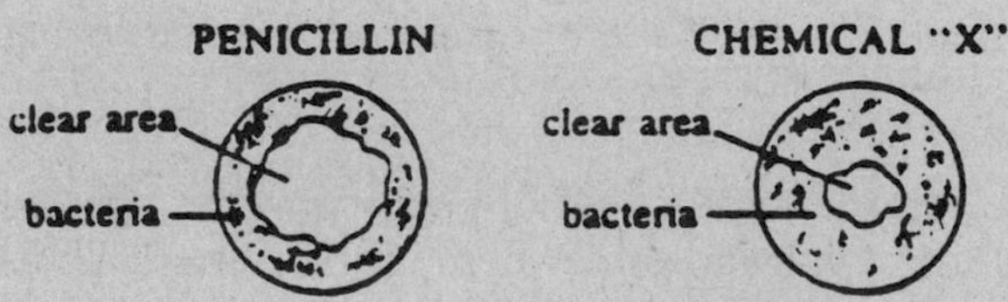

    (1) Chemical "X" could not kill any bacteria.
    (2) Chemical "X" is a stronger antibiotic than penicillin.
    (3) Chemical "X" is penicillin because penicillin kills germs.
    (4) Nothing can be determined by looking at the diagram.
    (5) Chemical "X" is a weaker antibiotic than penicillin.

Items 30 to 36 are based upon the following selection.

Biofeedback is a treatment technique in which people are trained to improve their health by using signals from their own bodies. Physical therapists use biofeedback to help stroke victims regain movement in paralyzed muscles. Psychologists use it to help tense and anxious clients learn to relax. Specialists in many different fields use biofeedback to help their patients cope with pain.

Chances are you have used biofeedback yourself. You've used it if you have ever taken your temperature or stepped on a scale. The thermometer tells you whether you're running a fever, the scale whether you've gained weight. Both devices "feed back" information about your body's condition. Armed with this information, you can take steps to improve the condition. When you're running a fever, you go to bed and drink plenty of fluids. When you've gained weight, you resolve to eat less and sometimes you do.

Clinicians rely on complicated biofeedback machines in somewhat the same way that you rely on your scale or thermometer. Their machines can detect a person's internal bodily functions with far greater sensitivity and precision than a person can alone. This information may be valuable. Both patients and therapists use it to gauge and direct the progress of treatment.

For patients, the biofeedback machine acts as a kind of sixth sense which allows them to "see" or "hear" activity inside their bodies. One commonly used type of machine, for example, picks up electrical signals in the muscles. It translates these signals into a form that patients can detect: It triggers a flashing light bulb, perhaps, or activates a beeper every time muscles grow more tense. If patients want to relax tense muscles, they try to slow down the flashing or beeping.

Like a pitcher learning to throw a ball across homeplate, the biofeedback trainee, in an attempt to improve a skill, monitors performance. When a pitch is off the mark, the ballplayer adjusts the delivery so that he performs better the next time he tries. When the light flashes or the beeper beeps too often, the biofeedback trainee makes internal adjustments which alter the signals. The biofeedback therapist acts as a coach, standing at the sidelines setting goals and limits on what to expect and giving hints on how to improve performance.

30. Which of the following is NOT an example of the use of biofeedback?

    (1) measuring electrical impulses
    (2) stepping on a scale
    (3) jumping rope
    (4) taking your temperature
    (5) monitoring performance

31. Which of the following statements represents a conclusion made by the author of this article?

    (1) All patients have a biofeedback "sixth sense."
    (2) Many of us have used forms of biofeedback without realizing it.
    (3) Biofeedback will enable each of us to become excellent ballplayers.
    (4) Biofeedback affects only motor skills.
    (5) Muscle tension can be reduced by the use of a beeper.

32. In which of the following situations might biofeedback prove helpful?

    (1) relieving the pain of childbirth
    (2) curing an upper respiratory infection
    (3) curing a case of poison ivy
    (4) straightening a crooked spine
    (5) preventing hair loss

33. A newspaper article on biofeedback contained the following statements:

    A. Biofeedback is the greatest invention since the wheel.
    B. Nothing cures a backache like biofeedback.
    C. In selected cases, biofeedback has helped alleviate pain.
    D. In no time flat, biofeedback will help you deal with today's anxieties.

    Which of the above statements is (are) most likely based on fact rather than opinion?

    (1) only A
    (2) only B
    (3) A and D
    (4) C and D
    (5) only C

34. Which of the following people will most likely derive the greatest success from biofeedback?

(1) those unaware of how biofeedback works
(2) those unconcerned with how biofeedback works
(3) those hostile to biofeedback
(4) those who cooperate actively with the process
(5) those undecided about the process

35. Which of the following factors must be assumed if biofeedback is to succeed?

(1) Internal organs work independently.
(2) Biofeedback can only succeed with trained assistants.
(3) People can actively affect the working of their internal organs.
(4) External events do not affect the biofeedback process.
(5) Biofeedback can only be used with machines.

•36. From the information in the article, you can infer that which of the following treatments is best suited for curing a broken leg?

(1) over-the-counter medications
(2) biofeedback
(3) surgery
(4) psychological counseling
(5) warm compresses alternated with cold packs

Item 37 is based on the following information.

Instincts are involuntary actions that are inborn. Some scientists believe that human beings possess no instincts. Everything they do has to be learned. You are observing examples of instincts when you watch a spider spinning a web, a bird building a nest, or a beaver building a dam. Humans learn habits. A habit is an action that is repeated so often that it can be done without a second thought. Typing without looking at the keys or biting one's nails are examples of habits.

37. Which of the following is properly matched?

(1) habit—an ant builds a colony
(2) instinct—a baby cries
(3) habit—a prairie dog digs a tunnel
(4) instinct—a man jumps when a car beeps its horn
(5) habit—a driver stops at a red light

Items 38 to 42 are based on the following graph.

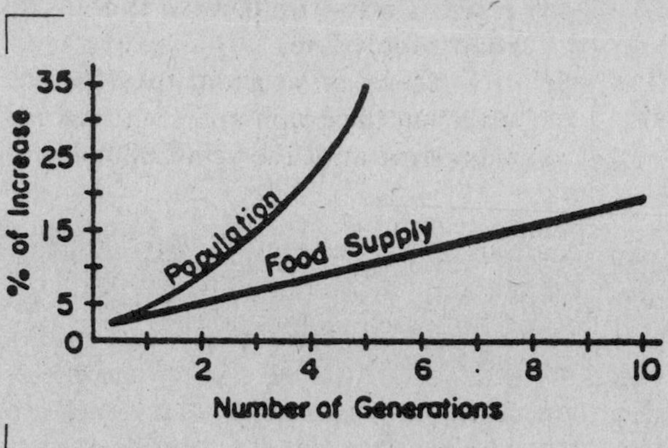

Darwin got some of his ideas for the Theory of Natural Selection from Malthus' *An Essay on the Principle of Population*. Malthus' ideas are represented on the graph above.

38. According to the information on the graph, what was Malthus' theory?

(1) Population increases arithmetically; food increases geometrically.
(2) There will always be sufficient food for the population.
(3) Eventually, food production will outstrip population increases.
(4) Population increases faster than food supply.
(5) The fittest will survive.

39. Specifically, Malthus' ideas most directly lent support to which of Darwin's ideas?

(1) variation
(2) overproduction
(3) adaptation
(4) inheritance of variations
(5) survival of the fittest

40. If the food supply trend line continues as indicated on the graph, what will probably eventually happen to the population curve?

(1) It will reach a peak and then drop downward until it again meets the food supply trend line.
(2) It will level off at about the 45% point on the graph and continue indefinitely at this level.
(3) The slope of the curve will decrease.
(4) It will always run parallel to the food supply line.
(5) It will level off at about the 75% point on the graph and continue at this point until the year 2000.

41. A group of nations are trying to change the outcome of Malthus' theory. Which of the following factors do they have to take into consideration to do so?

A. war
B. famine
C. improved agriculture
D. medical advances

(1) A only
(2) A and B
(3) A and C
(4) A and D
(5) A, B, C, and D

42. Which of the following will feel most likely the effect of Malthus' theory first?

A. China
B. America
C. Africa
D. Canada

(1) A and B
(2) A and C
(3) C alone
(4) A and D
(5) A, B, and C

43. Sublimation is the process of changing a substance from a solid to a gas. Since most substances first become a liquid, sublimation is an unusual event. Which of the following elements could sublime when heated?

(1) Br_2 (liquid)
(2) I_2 (solid)
(3) H_2 (gas)
(4) F_2 (gas)
(5) Cl_2 (gas)

Items 44 and 45 relate to the following information.

When an object moves at a constant speed, the distance it travels is equal to the rate it travels, times the total time it travels:

R(rate) × T(time) = D(distance)

44. The average speed of a runner in a 400-meter race is 8.0 meters per second. How long, in seconds, did it take this runner to complete the race?

(1) 80
(2) 50
(3) 40
(4) 32
(5) 10

45. Sharon finished the 20-mile race in 2.5 hours. What was her rate of speed in miles per hour?

(1) 1
(2) 5
(3) 8
(4) 10
(5) 15

GO ON TO THE NEXT PAGE

PERIODIC TABLE OF THE ELEMENTS

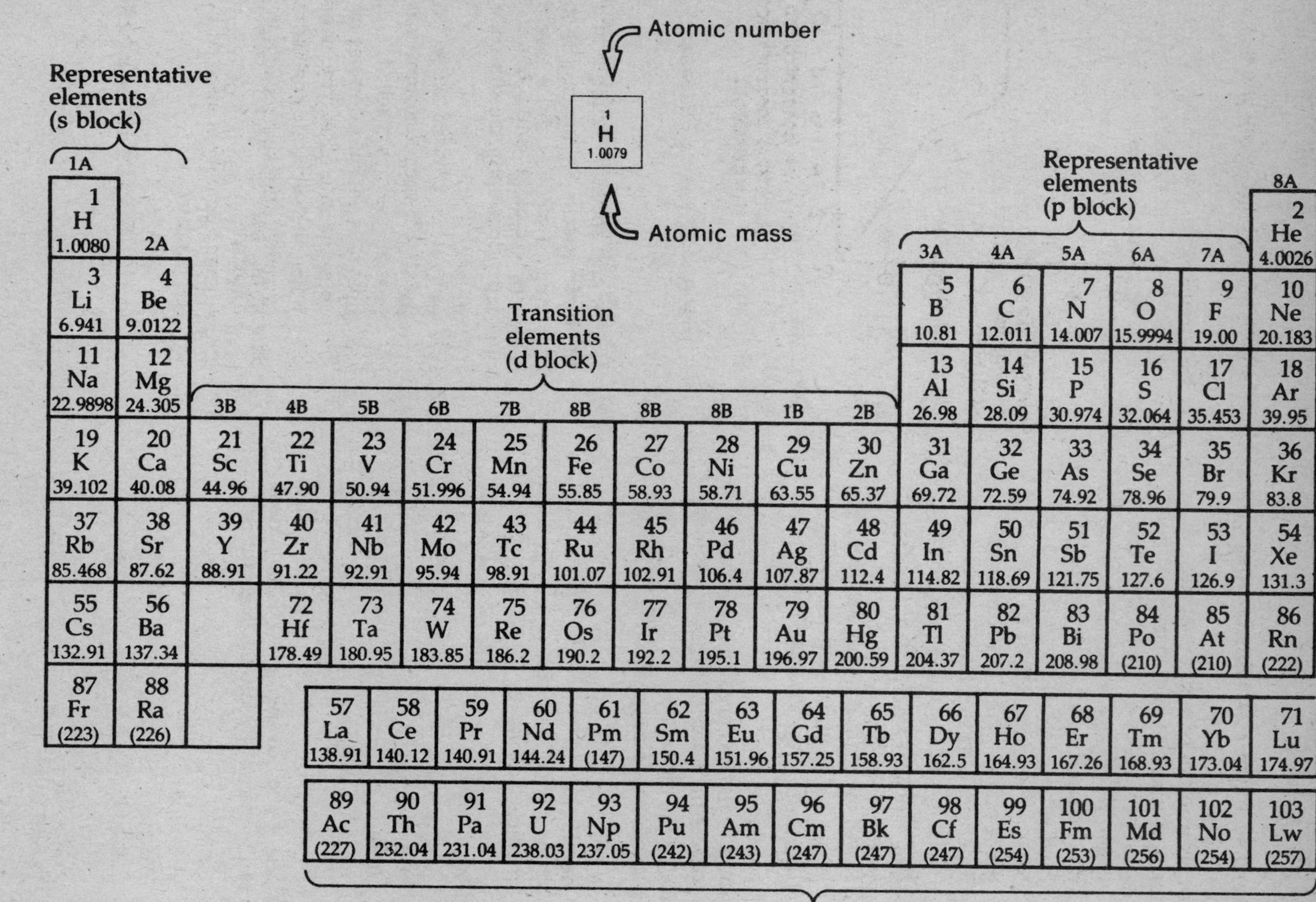

1A	2A	3B	4B	5B	6B	7B	8B	8B	8B	1B	2B	3A	4A	5A	6A	7A	8A
1 H 1.0080																	2 He 4.0026
3 Li 6.941	4 Be 9.0122											5 B 10.81	6 C 12.011	7 N 14.007	8 O 15.9994	9 F 19.00	10 Ne 20.183
11 Na 22.9898	12 Mg 24.305											13 Al 26.98	14 Si 28.09	15 P 30.974	16 S 32.064	17 Cl 35.453	18 Ar 39.95
19 K 39.102	20 Ca 40.08	21 Sc 44.96	22 Ti 47.90	23 V 50.94	24 Cr 51.996	25 Mn 54.94	26 Fe 55.85	27 Co 58.93	28 Ni 58.71	29 Cu 63.55	30 Zn 65.37	31 Ga 69.72	32 Ge 72.59	33 As 74.92	34 Se 78.96	35 Br 79.9	36 Kr 83.8
37 Rb 85.468	38 Sr 87.62	39 Y 88.91	40 Zr 91.22	41 Nb 92.91	42 Mo 95.94	43 Tc 98.91	44 Ru 101.07	45 Rh 102.91	46 Pd 106.4	47 Ag 107.87	48 Cd 112.4	49 In 114.82	50 Sn 118.69	51 Sb 121.75	52 Te 127.6	53 I 126.9	54 Xe 131.3
55 Cs 132.91	56 Ba 137.34		72 Hf 178.49	73 Ta 180.95	74 W 183.85	75 Re 186.2	76 Os 190.2	77 Ir 192.2	78 Pt 195.1	79 Au 196.97	80 Hg 200.59	81 Tl 204.37	82 Pb 207.2	83 Bi 208.98	84 Po (210)	85 At (210)	86 Rn (222)
87 Fr (223)	88 Ra (226)																

57 La 138.91	58 Ce 140.12	59 Pr 140.91	60 Nd 144.24	61 Pm (147)	62 Sm 150.4	63 Eu 151.96	64 Gd 157.25	65 Tb 158.93	66 Dy 162.5	67 Ho 164.93	68 Er 167.26	69 Tm 168.93	70 Yb 173.04	71 Lu 174.97
89 Ac (227)	90 Th 232.04	91 Pa 231.04	92 U 238.03	93 Np 237.05	94 Pu (242)	95 Am (243)	96 Cm (247)	97 Bk (247)	98 Cf (247)	99 Es (254)	100 Fm (253)	101 Md (256)	102 No (254)	103 Lw (257)

Items 46 and 47 refer to the table on page 68.

46. There was no potassium left in the chemical storeroom. Which atom is most similar in properties to potassium (K)?

    (1) P
    (2) Al
    (3) Na
    (4) Ca
    (5) Mg

47. The elements in the periodic table are arranged according to their

    (1) atomic numbers
    (2) atomic masses
    (3) conductivity
    (4) mass number
    (5) oxidation states

Item 48 refers to the following graph.

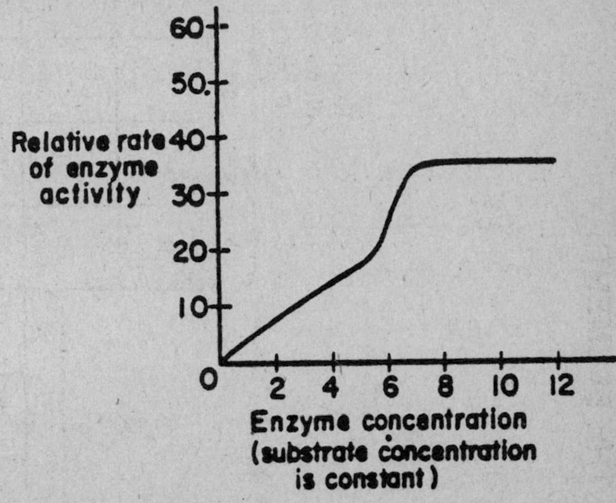

48. What is indicated by the information on this graph?

    (1) The rate of enzyme action is directly dependent upon the substrate concentration.
    (2) The rate of enzyme action becomes stabilized when a certain enzyme concentration is reached.
    (3) Enzyme concentration has no effect upon the rate of enzyme action.
    (4) When the substrate concentration is increased, the enzyme action is decreased.
    (5) Enzyme activity is affected by temperature.

GO ON TO THE NEXT PAGE

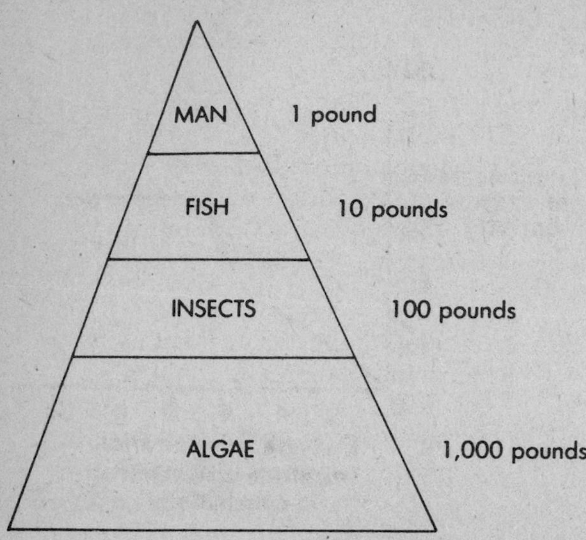

Items 49 to 51 are based on the food pyramid above.

The diagram above represents a food pyramid. It shows how many pounds of food are needed to sustain the animal above it.

49. According to this food pyramid, how many pounds of fish would it take to sustain a 100-pound man?

 (1) 10
 (2) 100
 (3) 1000
 (4) more than 1000
 (5) more than 10,000

50. From the information provided by this pyramid, how do insects get their energy?

 (1) They swim in the water.
 (2) They are eaten by fish.
 (3) They are eaten by algae.
 (4) They eat algae.
 (5) They feed on human blood.

51. Which of the following would result if the fish were removed from this pyramid?

 (1) The number of insects would increase.
 (2) The number of insects would decrease.
 (3) The amount of algae would increase.
 (4) The number of men would increase.
 (5) The insects would starve.

Items 52 to 58 refer to the following article.

The sun is at its strongest and most harmful during the hours from 10 a.m. to 2 p.m. Anyone wishing to minimize the effects of the sun or to avoid heat stroke would do well to confine his or her sunning to other than midday hours.

Ultraviolet radiation is worse at these hours, and it's that type of radiation from the sun that causes sunburns, tans the skin and leaves permanent damage. Excessive ultraviolet radiation will cause hardening and thickening of the epidermis (outer skin) of those who tan readily, and blotching or freckling of the skin of those who don't. Over the long run, the sun's rays will leave the skin tough, leathery, pebbly, and dry, with surface wrinkles much like those of old shoes.

Skins of individuals are affected differently by the sun. It depends on the amount of the naturally occurring skin pigment, melanin, that an individual's system produces. Persons with darker skins produce larger amounts of melanin. They also tan quicker and with less trouble than those with fair skin. Tanning is especially difficult for those Celtic and other blue-eyed and green-eyed peoples of northern European origins.

Ultraviolet radiation from the sun or other sources is the leading cause of skin cancer in people. According to estimates by the National Cancer Institute, each year more than 300,000 cases of basal cell and squamous cell cancer occur in the United States.

The third type of skin cancer—melanoma—is much more deadly than the others. It's not as clear that ultraviolet rays cause melanoma as it is that they cause basal cell and squamous cell cancer, although it's strongly suspected that they do.

52. According to the article, which of the following causes the most damage to the skin?

    (1) ultraviolet rays
    (2) flares
    (3) early morning sun
    (4) melanin
    (5) alpha waves

53. According to the article, people who wish to have youthful looking skin should do which of the following?

    (1) get a tan
    (2) wear heavy makeup
    (3) thicken their epidermis
    (4) avoid the sun
    (5) wear dark glasses

54. Which of the following is the most deadly form of skin cancer?

    (1) basal cell carcinoma
    (2) squamous cell carcinoma
    (3) leukemia
    (4) epidermis cell carcinoma
    (5) melanoma

55. We can infer from the article that which of the following groups of people is most susceptible to skin cancer?

    (1) dark-eyed, dark-haired people
    (2) those who freckle and sunburn easily
    (3) people with dark skin and lighter hair
    (4) those who frequent tanning salons
    (5) people from warm climates

56. From the information presented in the article, what can we infer dermatologists believe?

    (1) Sunbathing in moderation is harmless.
    (2) Sunbathing is harmless if a tanning lotion is used.
    (3) Sunbathing is foolhardy.
    (4) Tanning parlors present no risk.
    (5) It is only harmful to sunbathe between 10 a.m. and 2 p.m.

57. According to the article, what happens when skin is exposed to sunlight?

    (1) Light-skinned people produce the greatest amounts of melanin.
    (2) Those who tan easily will suffer no damage from the sun.
    (3) Skin cells are likely to produce melanomas.
    (4) The likelihood of developing skin cancer increases.
    (5) People with darker skins produce enough melanin to sunbathe any time.

58. We can infer that people continue to get suntans for which of the following reasons?

    (1) There has been no publicity concerning the danger of the tanning.
    (2) Most doctors endorse suntanning.
    (3) Articles such as this one exaggerate the dangers of the sun.
    (4) Few people have skin that is affected by the sun.
    (5) Few people feel they are at risk of getting skin cancer.

GO ON TO THE NEXT PAGE

SELECTED RADIOISOTOPES		
Nuclide	*Half-Life*	*Particle Emission*
^{14}C	5730 y	β^-
^{60}Co	5.3 y	β^-
^{147}Cs	30.23 y	β^-
^{220}Fr	27.5 s	α
^{3}H	12.26 y	β^-
^{131}I	8.07 d	β^-
^{10}K	1.28×10^9 y	β^+
^{42}K	12.4 h	β^-
^{32}P	14.3 d	β^-
^{226}Ra	1600 y	α
^{90}Sr	28.1 y	β^-
^{238}U	7.1×10^4 y	α
^{238}U	4.51×10^9 y	α
y = years; d = days; h = hours; s = seconds		

Items 59 to 62 refer to the chart above.

Half-life is the period of time required for the disintegration of one half of the atoms in a sample of some specific radioactive substance.

59. Suppose you have 100 grams of each of the following radioisotopes. Which will have the most atoms remaining after 1 year?

(1) ^{32}P
(2) ^{226}Ra
(3) ^{90}Sr
(4) ^{235}U
(5) ^{238}U

60. How many grams of ^{220}Fr will remain if you hold 100 grams for 110 seconds?

(1) 62.50
(2) 50.00
(3) 12.50
(4) 6.25
(5) 1.00

61. According to the table, what portion of the original quantity of ^{60}Co will remain at the end of 10.6 years?

(1) $\frac{1}{2}$
(2) $\frac{1}{4}$
(3) $\frac{1}{8}$
(4) $\frac{1}{16}$
(5) $\frac{1}{32}$

62. Based on the table, which of the following radioisotopes will disintegrate most rapidly?

(1) ^{60}Co
(2) ^{42}K
(3) ^{3}H
(4) ^{131}I
(5) ^{32}P

Items 63 to 66 are based on the following selection.

GALE WARNING: When winds of 38–55 miles per hour (33–48 knots) are expected, a gale warning is added to the advisory message.

STORM WARNING: When winds of 55–74 miles per hour (48–64 knots) are expected, a storm warning is added to the advisory message.

When gale or storm warnings are part of a tropical cyclone advisory, they may change to a hurricane warning if the storm continues along the coast.

HURRICANE WATCH: If the hurricane continues its advance and threatens coastal and inland regions, a hurricane watch is added to the advisory, covering a specified area and duration. A hurricane watch means that hurricane conditions are a real possibility; it does not mean they are imminent. When a hurricane watch is issued, everyone in the area covered by the watch should listen for further advisories and be prepared to act quickly if hurricane warnings are issued.

HURRICANE WARNING: When hurricane conditions are expected within 24 hours, a hurricane warning is added to the advisory. Hurricane warnings identify coastal areas where winds of at least 74 miles per hour are expected to occur. A warning may also describe coastal areas where dangerously high water or exceptionally high waves are forecast, even though winds may be less than hurricane force.

When the hurricane warning is issued, all precautions should be taken immediately. Hurricane warnings are seldom issued more than 24 hours in advance. If the hurricane's path is unusual or erratic, the warnings may be issued only a few hours before the beginning of hurricane conditions.

63. At which of the following wind speeds are gale warnings issued?

(1) 20 mph
(2) 30 mph
(3) 40 mph
(4) 60 mph
(5) 80 mph

64. "Citizens, store your food and water. Board up your windows and move to your storm cellars."

Which of the following would this message be issued for?

(1) weather report
(2) gale warning
(3) storm warning
(4) hurricane watch
(5) hurricane warning

65. According to the passage, hurricanes are especially dangerous in which of the following areas?

(1) major cities
(2) prairies
(3) near high buildings
(4) coastal areas
(5) the ocean

66. We can infer from the passage that hurricanes are dangerous for which of the following reasons?

(1) flood
(2) electrical shocks
(3) power loss
(4) food spoilage
(5) disruption of services

END OF SCIENCE TEST

TEST 4. INTERPRETING LITERATURE AND THE ARTS

Time: 65 Minutes—45 Questions

Directions:

This test consists of multiple-choice questions based on a variety of excerpts from popular and classical literature and articles about literature or the arts. Each selection is followed by a number of questions. Read each selection and then answer the questions based upon it. You may refer to the reading as often as necessary to answer the questions. Record your answers in the Interpreting Literature and the Arts section of your answer sheet.

FOR EXAMPLE:

He died at eventide . . . I saw his breath beat quicker and quicker, pause, and then his little soul leapt like a star that travels in the night and left a world of darkness in its train. The day changed not . . . Only in the chamber of death writhed the world's most piteous thing—a childless mother.

The reader can infer that death has come to

(1) an old man
(2) a favorite dog
(3) a child
(4) a mother
(5) a soldier

The correct answer is "a child"; therefore, you should blacken answer space 3 on your answer sheet.

Items 1 to 3 are based on the following article.

WHAT DID H. L. MENCKEN THINK OF AMERICAN CULTURE?

Virginia is the best of the South to-day, and Georgia is perhaps the worst. The one is simply senile; the other is crass, gross, vulgar and obnoxious. Between lies a vast plain of mediocrity, stupidity, lethargy, almost of dead silence. In the North, of course, there is also grossness, crassness, vulgarity. The North, in its way, is also stupid and obnoxious. But nowhere in the North is there such complete sterility, so depressing a lack of all civilized aspiration. One would find it difficult to unearth a second-rate city between the Ohio and the Pacific that isn't struggling to establish an orchestra, or setting up a little theater, or going in for an art gallery, or making some other effort to get into touch with civilization. These efforts often fail, and sometimes they succeed rather absurdly, but under them there is at least an impulse that deserves respect, and there is the impulse to seek beauty and experiment with ideas, and so to give the life of every day a certain dignity and purpose. You will find no such impulse in the South. There are no committees down there cadging subscriptions for orchestras; if a string quartet is ever heard there, the news of it has never come out; an opera troupe, when it roves the land, is a nine days' wonder. The little theater movement has swept the whole country, enormously augmenting the public interest in sound plays, giving new dramatists their chance, forcing reforms upon the commercial theater. Everywhere else the wave rolls high—but along the line of the Potomac it breaks upon a rock-bound shore. There is no little theater beyond. There is no gallery of pictures. No artist ever gives exhibitions. No one talks of such things. No one seems to be interested in such things.

1. When it was first printed in 1917 this article produced a ferocious reaction in the South. What does the author ask the reader to believe?

   (1) Art galleries were flourishing in California.
   (2) There was no culture in America.
   (3) Artists are not restricted in the United States.
   (4) The "little theater" movement was flourishing in the United States.
   (5) Southern culture was dried up or nonexistent.

2. The writing is characterized by its

   (1) subtle wit
   (2) vague references
   (3) calm rationality
   (4) infuriating directness
   (5) scholarly approach

3. If Mr. Mencken was thinking of setting up a traveling theater company, in the South, he would probably choose to establish it in the state of

   (1) Georgia
   (2) Alabama
   (3) Florida
   (4) Virginia
   (5) Mississippi

Items 4 to 9 are based on the following article.

HOW DID FREDERICK DOUGLASS GET AN EDUCATION?

From this time I was most narrowly watched. If I was in a separate room any considerable length of time, I was sure to be suspected of having a book, and was at once called to give an account of myself. All this, however, was too late. The first step had been taken. Mistress, in teaching me the alphabet, had given me the inch, and no precaution could prevent me from taking the ell.

The plan which I adopted, and the one by which I was most successful, was that of making friends of all the little white boys whom I met in the street. As many of these as I could, I converted into teachers. With their kindly aid, obtained at different times and in different places, I finally succeeded in learning to read. When I was sent on errands, I always took my book with me, and by doing one part of my errand quickly, I found time to get a lesson before my return. I used also to carry bread with me, enough of which was always in the house, and to which I was always welcome; for I was much better off in this regard than many of the poor white children in our neighborhood. This bread I used to bestow upon the hungry little urchins, who, in return, would give me the more valuable bread of knowledge.

I am strongly tempted to give the names of two or three of those little boys, as a testimonial of the gratitude and affection I bear them; but prudence forbids;—not that it would injure me, but it might embarrass them; for it is almost an unpardonable offense to teach slaves to read in this Christian country. It is enough to say of the dear little fellows that they lived on Philpot Street, very near Durgin and Bailey's ship-yard. I used to talk this matter of slavery over with them. I would sometimes say to them, I wished I could be as free as they would be when they got to be men. "You will be free as soon as you are twenty-one, but I am a slave for life! Have not I as good a right to be free as you have?" These words seemed to trouble them; they would express for me the liveliest sympathy, and console with the hope that something would occur by which I might be free.

from *Narrative of the Life of Frederick Douglass*

4. Based on information in this selection, when was Frederick Douglass' *Narrative* written?

   (1) during the Middle Ages
   (2) during the Renaissance
   (3) before the Civil War
   (4) between 1880 and 1900
   (5) after 1900

5. According to the information in the passage, how did Douglass learn to read?

   (1) by his own efforts
   (2) from his mistress
   (3) with the help of young white boys
   (4) by using his time in a clever way
   (5) by going to school

6. Which of the following would be the most suitable title for this selection?

   (1) The Yearning for Freedom
   (2) The Burning for Success
   (3) As the World Turns
   (4) How I Learned to Read
   (5) A Lover is Spurned

7. Why does Douglass withhold the names of his young white friends?

   (1) They asked him not to give their names.
   (2) They might be embarrassed.
   (3) He never learned their names.
   (4) He had forgotten their names.
   (5) He feared injury to himself.

8. Douglass states that ". . . in teaching me the alphabet (she) had given me an inch, and no precaution could prevent me from taking the ell." This can be interpreted as which of the following?

   (1) The use of knowledge is a criminal conspiracy.
   (2) Once started, learning is self-generating.
   (3) A slave could not be stopped from reading.
   (4) The alphabet is a powerful tool.
   (5) Douglass' need to know was a powerful motivator.

9. Judging from the selection, which of the following choices would best describe Douglass' character?
   (1) brave but unforgiving
   (2) courageous and determined
   (3) cowardly and bitter
   (4) a seeker after knowledge
   (5) lazy and selfish

Items 10 to 13 are based on the following selection.

WHAT CAN BE FOUND ON MOUNT KILIMANJARO?

Kilimanjaro is a snow-covered mountain 19,710 feet high, and is said to be the highest mountain in Africa. Its western summit is called by the Masai "Ngaje Ngaj," the House of God. Close to the western summit there is the dried and frozen carcass of a leopard. No one has explained what the leopard was seeking at that altitude.

from Ernest Hemingway, "The Snows of Kilimanjaro," in *The Short Stories of Ernest Hemingway.* Copyright © 1936 by Ernest Hemingway; Copyright renewed. Reprinted with the permission of Charles Scribner's Sons.

10. From the information in the paragraph, what does the carcass of the dead leopard seem to indicate?

    (1) We may all be searching for things we don't understand.
    (2) Animals may have souls.
    (3) Africa is a strange and exotic place.
    (4) Snow and ice are important preservatives.
    (5) The Masai are religious people.

11. According to the paragraph, what can we infer the Masai are?

    (1) a British-controlled African tribe
    (2) an African people
    (3) a chain of African mountains
    (4) a peculiar language phenomenon
    (5) leopard hunters

12. Which of the following choices best describes the style of this paragraph?

    (1) tough, spare and direct
    (2) flowering and poetic
    (3) obscure and mystical
    (4) wordy and indirect
    (5) somber and dark

13. What does the carcass of the leopard near the summit of Kilimanjaro probably indicate?

    (1) Hunters had driven it there.
    (2) It was a religious object placed there by Masai.
    (3) Conservationists must do more to protect animals.
    (4) There once was a watering hole at that spot.
    (5) Cannot be determined from the paragraph.

Items 14 to 17 are based on the following selection.

WHAT DID PRESIDENT LINCOLN MEAN WHEN HE GAVE THIS SPEECH?

. . . It is for us the living, rather, to be dedicated here to the unfinished work which they who fought here have thus far so nobly advanced. It is rather for us to be here dedicated to the great task remaining before us—that from these honored dead we take increased devotion to that cause for which they gave the last full measure of devotion—that we here highly resolve that these dead shall not have died in vain—that this nation, under God, shall have a new birth of freedom, and that government of the people, by the people, for the people shall not perish from the earth.

14. What was Abraham Lincoln memorializing when he made this famous speech in 1863?

    (1) soldiers who died in battle
    (2) slaves who had demonstrated for freedom
    (3) Pennsylvania Quakers who valued personal liberty
    (4) people who had supported the war effort
    (5) members of the government

15. What was Lincoln doing when he spoke of "government of the people, by the people, for the people"?

    (1) using a literary device to better make his point
    (2) trying to embarrass the Confederates
    (3) appealing to the baser instincts of the audience

(4) trying to restore faith in his administration
(5) abdicating his authority

16. Where was this speech most likely delivered?

(1) in a private home
(2) before members of Congress
(3) on the radio
(4) in a cemetery
(5) in a church

17. Which of the following words most closely defines the tone of this passage?

(1) calm
(2) earnest
(3) inflammatory
(4) bewildered
(5) impassioned

Items 18 to 22 are based on the following selection.

WHAT IS THIS MOTHER TELLING HER SON?

MOTHER TO SON

Well, son, I'll tell you.
Life for me ain't been no crystal stair.
It's had tacks in it,
And splinters,
And boards torn up,
And places with no carpet on the floor
Bare
But all the time
I'se been a-climbin' on,
And reachin' landin's.
And turnin' corners,
And sometimes goin' in the dark
Where there ain't been no light.
So, boy, don't you turn back.
Don't you set down on the steps
'Cause you finds it kinder hard.
Don't you fall now—
For I'se still goin', honey,
I'se still climbin'
And life for me ain't been no crystal stair.

Langston Hughes

18. What does the "crystal stair" symbolize in this poem?

(1) a life filled with hardships and problems
(2) a life filled with comforts and riches
(3) the front entrance to their house
(4) the love between the mother and the son
(5) the entranceway to heaven

19. What was the mother's advice to her son?

(1) marry a rich girl
(2) buy a lottery ticket
(3) try to overcome your problems
(4) accept life the way it is
(5) carry a hatred of the people who won't give you a break

20. In lines 3 to 6, the mother speaks of "tacks," "boards torn up" and "places with no carpet." To what do these terms refer?

(1) goals to be attained
(2) problems in life
(3) poverty of spirit
(4) lies and deception
(5) hesitation

21. Which of the following words most closely describes the tone of this poem?

(1) despairing
(2) mysterious
(3) determined
(4) uncertainty
(5) idealistic

22. If confronted with a ten-page research assignment, what would the son in this poem most likely do?

(1) work on it until it was finished
(2) complain to the teacher
(3) ask his parents to do the research
(4) procrastinate
(5) daydream and not do the work

GO ON TO THE NEXT PAGE

Items 23 to 28 refer to the following story.

WHAT WAS THE COST OF STAYING WITH THE HERD?

For every boss there were at least ten "just common hands." Some hired for money and some for fun; some to be going somewhere and some to leave somewhere; some for experience and some to escape experience. Whoever and whatever they were, irrespective of color, age, or position, a good hand stayed with the herd. That was his test.

Staying with the herd denoted a certain amount of endurance. Above that, it denoted pluck, loyalty, trustworthiness, honor. The range had no higher compliment to pay horse or man than to call him a "stayer."

On the first day of March, 1892, an outfit of **LFD** cowboys began trailing a herd of three-year-old steers northeast from their range down in New Mexico to Amarillo in the Panhandle of Texas. The third evening out, the northern rim of the sky had a blue-black tinge; before the second guard came in, a cold norther was blowing hard; by daylight, the sky was spattering snow. No break in the rolling plains offered protection. It is against the nature of cattle to travel against a blizzard, but, urged on by the never-turn-back men, the **LFD** steers kept their northward course.

Among the men on guard the first half of the night was a youthful Negro named George, the only Negro cowboy in the outfit. He was not warmly clad. A cowboy on guard with him named Mack McAvoy saw how cold George was and heard his spasms of coughing.

"George," he said, "we can hold the cattle without you. Go to the wagon and turn your horse loose and cover up."

George's teeth were chattering as he answered, "I can stand it if the rest of you all can."

The two men remained halted a little while near each other, the cattle being temporarily quiet. To quote McAvoy, "Presently I saw George lean over his saddle horn, coughing and sounding as if he were losing his breath. Then he went to the ground. He had simply frozen to death sitting on his horse."

The next day the **LFD** men placed George's body in the chuck wagon and drove to the top of the highest rise of land overlooking the Palo Duro. They dug a hole deep enough so that coyotes would not dig the body out. Then they rolled the cowboy in his blankets so that dirt would not get into his face and covered him up. They left him there on the lone prairie with only a stub of hackberry for a headboard.

There was no inscription on this grave marker. Yet in the imagination of those who know, there is a marker there, granite in durability, graved with these words:

HE STAYED WITH THE HERD.

23. According to the selection, what happened when George died?

    (1) The coyotes began to howl.
    (2) He fell off his horse.
    (3) The cattle refused to go on.
    (4) Winter had just ended.
    (5) The men from Palo Duro mourned.

24. Which of the following statements can be inferred from evidence presented in this selection?

    (1) Widespread cattle losses occurred in 1892.
    (2) Mack had been a medical intern.
    (3) Experience was essential to be a "hand."
    (4) The cattle were about to break loose.
    (5) George was a novice.

25. According to the information in the selection, which of the following best describes the grave marker?

    (1) It was knocked down by dirt and wind.
    (2) It was carved by Mack McAvoy.
    (3) It was made in Palo Duro.
    (4) It existed in the cowboys' minds.
    (5) It was made of granite.

26. Which of the following words best describes the tone of this selection?

    (1) respectful
    (2) bemused
    (3) contemplative
    (4) hostile
    (5) fearful

27. Why did McAvoy suggest George go back to the wagon?

    (1) McAvoy disliked George.
    (2) The cattle were quiet that night.
    (3) George was not a good cowboy.
    (4) George was not dressed for the cold.
    (5) George's horse needed rest.

28. According to the definition given in the selection, what did George do to meet the test of the stayer?

    (1) kept the cattle going through the blizzard
    (2) froze to death
    (3) refused to leave the herd
    (4) talked back to McAvoy
    (5) was buried on the range

GO ON TO THE NEXT PAGE

Items 29 to 32 refer to the following story.

WHY WAS THE BEGGAR BLIND?

The beggar was coming down the avenue as Mr. Parson emerged from his hotel.

He was a blind beggar, carrying the traditional battered cane. He was a shaggy, thick-necked fellow; his coat was greasy about the lapels and pockets, his hand splayed over the cane's crook in a futile sort of clinging.

Mr. Parsons noted the clack-clack approach of the slightless man and felt a sudden sort of pity for all blind creatures. And, thought Mr. Parsons, he was very glad to be alive. A few years ago he had been little more than a skilled laborer; now he was successful, respected, admired. Insurance . . . And he had done it alone, unaided, struggling beneath handicaps.

"Listen, guv'nor.[1] Just a minute of your time. I ain't no beggar, guv'nor. I got a handy little article here"—he fumbled until he could press a small object in Mr. Parson's hand—"that I sell. One buck. Best cigarette lighter ever made."

Mr. Parson stood there, somewhat annoyed and embarrassed. He was a handsome figure in his immaculate gray suit and gray hat and Malacca stick.[2] Of course the man with the cigarette lighters could not see him . . . "But I don't smoke," he said.

"Listen, I bet you know plenty people who smoke. And, mister, you wouldn't mind helping a poor guy out?"

Mr. Parson sighed and felt in his pocket. He brought out the two half dollars and pressed them into the man's hands. He hesitated, not wanting to be boorish and inquisitive, even with a blind peddler. "Have you lost your sight entirely?"

"Fourteen years, guv'nor." Then he added with an insane sort of pride: "Westbury, sir. I was one of 'em."

"Westbury," repeated Mr. Parsons. "Ah, yes. The chemical explosion . . . The papers haven't mentioned it for years."

"You want to know how I lost my eyes?" cried the man. "Well, here it is!" His words fell with the bitter and studied drama of a story often told, and told for money. "I was there in C shop, last of all the folks rushing out. Out in the air there was a chance, even with the buildings exploding right and left. And just as I was about there, crawling along between those big vats, a guy behind me grabs my legs. He says, 'Let me past, you—!' Maybe he was nuts. I dunno. I try to forgive him in my heart, guv'nor. But he was bigger than me. He hauls me back and climbs right over me. And he gets out, and I lie there with all that poison gas pouring down on all sides of me, and flame and stuff . . ." He swallowed—a studied sob—and stood dumbly expectant. "That's the story, guv'nor."

"Not quite," said Mr. Parsons.

The blind peddler shivered crazily. "Not quite, what do you mean, you—?"

"The story is true;" Mr. Parson said, "except that it is the other way around."

"Other way around?" he croaked unamiably. "Say, guv'nor—"

"I was in C shop," said Mr. Parsons. "It was the other way. You were the fellow who hauled back on me and climbed over me. You were bigger than I was, Markwardt."

The blind man stood for a long time, swallowing hoarsely. He gulped: "Parsons. By God. I thought you—." And then he screamed fiendishly: "Yes. Maybe so. Maybe so. But I'm blind! You got away, but I'm blind'.

"Well," said Mr. Parsons, "don't make such a row about it, Markwardt, . . . So am I."

Adapted from "A Man Who Had No Eyes" by Mackinlay Kantor

[1]guv'nor—a slang term of address used to a stranger or one's superior or employer.
[2]Malacca stick—a light walking stick made from rattan.

29. What can be inferred about the narrator of the story from the information given?

(1) He worked with Markwardt and Parsons.
(2) He is blind.
(3) He is a young boy.
(4) He has befriended Parsons.
(5) He has eyesight.

30. The title of this story is "A Man Who Had No Eyes." What does this title refer to?

(1) the people who lost their eyesight in the Westbury explosion
(2) Markwardt's inability to admit the truth
(3) the supervisor at C shop
(4) a person in Parson's hotel who develops chemicals
(5) both Parson's and Markwardt's blindness

31. The reader can infer that Markwardt has repeated his story many times when the author says,

(1) "His words fell with the bitter and studied drama of a story often told, and told for money"
(2) "The blind man stood for a long time, swallowing hoarsely."
(3) "He brought out the two half dollars and pressed them into the man's hands."
(4) "The blind peddler shivered crazily."
(5) "Westbury, sir. I was one of 'em."

32. How does the author establish a contrast between Parson and Markwardt?

(1) different disabilities
(2) levels of diction
(3) their marriages
(4) opposing political views
(5) their destinations

GO ON TO THE NEXT PAGE

Items 33 to 36 refer to the following poem.

WHERE IS THE HIGHWAYMAN HEADED?

THE HIGHWAYMAN

The wind was a torrent of darkness among the gusty trees,
The moon was a ghostly galleon tossed upon cloudy seas,
The road was a ribbon of moonlight over the purple moor,
And the highwayman came riding—
Riding—riding—
The highwayman came riding, up to the old inn-door.

He'd a French cocked-hat on his forehead, a bunch of lace at his chin,
A coat of the claret velvet, and breeches of brown doeskin;
They fitted with never a wrinkle: his boots were up to the thigh!
And he rode with a jewelled twinkle,
His pistol butts a-twinkle,
His rapier hilt a-twinkle, under the jewelled sky.

Over the cobbles he clattered and clashed in the dark innyard,
And he tapped with his whip on the shutters, but all was locked and barred;
He whistled a tune to the window, and who should be waiting there
But the landlord's black-eyed daughter,
Bess, the landlord's daughter,
Plaiting a dark red love-knot into her long black hair.

And dark in the dark old inn-yard a stable-wicket creaked
Where Tim, the ostler, listened; his face was white and peaked;
His eyes were hollows of madness, his hair like mouldy hay,
But he loved the landlord's daughter,
The landlord's red-lipped daughter;
Dumb as a dog he listened, and he heard the robber say—

"One kiss, my bonny sweetheart, I'm after a prize tonight,
But I shall be back with the yellow gold before the morning light;
Yet, if they press me sharply, and harry me through the day,
Then look for me by moonlight,
Watch for me by moonlight,
I'll come to thee by moonlight, though hell should bar the way."

by Alfred Noyes

33. The first ten lines are an example of which of the following?

    (1) personification
    (2) a haiku
    (3) a sonnet
    (4) an extended metaphor
    (5) a stanza

34. How does the highwayman appear to be dressed?

    (1) to conceal his identity
    (2) in dull, dark clothing
    (3) in loose-fitting clothes
    (4) as a resplendent gentleman
    (5) without frills

35. Another term for a highwayman would be a

    (1) toll collector
    (2) robber
    (3) model for men's clothing
    (4) bridegroom
    (5) stable hand

36. It may be inferred from the poem that the highwayman was in danger because

    (1) Bess did not like him
    (2) his horse was lame and he would be thrown
    (3) Tim was jealous of him
    (4) he owed the landlord back rent
    (5) he was as "Dumb as a dog"

GO ON TO THE NEXT PAGE

Items 37 to 40 refer to the following selection.

WHAT MAKES A LADY?

HIGGINS You let her alone, mother. Let her speak for herself. You will jolly soon see whether she has an idea that I havnt put into her head or a word that I havnt put into her mouth. I tell you I have created this thing out of the squashed cabbage leaves of Covent Garden.

LIZA Will you drop me altogether now that the experiment is over, Colonel Pickering?

PICKERING Oh dont. You mustnt think of it as an experiment. It shocks me, somehow.

LIZA Oh, I'm only a squashed cabbage leaf . . .

PICKERING [*Impulsively.*] No.

LIZA [*Continuing quietly.*] . . . but I owe so much to you that I should be very unhappy if you forgot me.

PICKERING It's very kind of you to say so, Miss Doolittle.

LIZA But it was from you that I learnt really nice manners; and that is what makes one a lady, isn't it? You see it was so very difficult for me with the example of Professor Higgins always before me. I was brought up to be just like him, unable to control myself, and using bad language on the slightest provocation.

HIGGINS Well!!

PICKERING Oh, thats only his way, you know. He doesnt mean it.

LIZA [*Continuing.*] It was just like learning to dance in the fashionable way: there was nothing more than that in it. But do you know what began my real education?

PICKERING What?

LIZA [*Stopping her work for a moment.*] Your calling me Miss Doolittle that day when I first came to Wimpole Street. That was the beginning of self-respect for me. [*She resumes her stitching.*] And there were a hundred little things you never noticed, because they came naturally to you. Things about standing up and taking off your hat and opening doors . . .

PICKERING Oh, that was nothing.

LIZA Yes: things that showed you thought and felt about me as if I were something better than a scullerymaid. You never took off your boots in the dining room when I was there.

PICKERING You mustn't mind that. Higgins takes off his boots all over the place.

LIZA I know. I am not blaming him. It is his way, isn't it? But it made such a difference to me that you didn't do it. I shall always be a flower girl to Professor Higgins, because he always treats me as a flower girl, and always will; but I know I can be a lady to you, because you always treat me as a lady, and always will.

PICKERING Well, this is really very nice of you, Miss Doolittle.

LIZA I should like you to call me Eliza, now, if you would.

PICKERING Thank you. Eliza, of course.

LIZA And I should like Professor Higgins to call me Miss Doolittle.

HIGGINS I'll see you damned first.

MRS HIGGINS Henry! Henry!

PICKERING [*Laughing.*] Why don't you slang back at him? Don't stand it. It would do him a lot of good.

LIZA I can't. I could have done it once; but now I can't go back to it. You told me, you know, that when a child is brought to a foreign country, it picks up the language in a few weeks, and forgets its own. Well, I am a child in your country. I have forgotten my own language, and can speak nothing but yours. That's the real breakoff with the corner of Tottenham Court Road. Leaving Wimpole Street finishes it.

PICKERING [*Much alarmed.*] Oh! but you're coming back to Wimpole Street, aren't you? Youll forgive Higgins?

HIGGINS [*Rising.*] Forgive! Will she, by George! Let her go. Let her find out how she can get on without us. She will relapse into the gutter in three weeks without me at her elbow.

37. By asking that Higgins call her "Miss Doolittle," what does Eliza indicate?

(1) that Higgins has just arrived
(2) the many injustices she felt from being a flower girl
(3) her admiration for Higgins
(4) her willingness to continue her education
(5) her displeasure that Higgins treats her like a maid

38. What do the "squashed cabbage leaves" in lines 5-6 refer to?

(1) Eliza's rustic ways
(2) an experiment involving Mrs. Higgins' flowers
(3) an invitation to a flower festival
(4) the rotting vegetables of Covent Garden
(5) Colonel Pickering's country estate

39. What does Higgins mean in his last speech when he says, "She will relapse into the gutter"?

(1) He admires Eliza for her spunk.
(2) Eliza will lose all grace and manners.
(3) Eliza will become ill.
(4) Eliza's drinking problem will become more pronounced.
(5) Eliza will live in a shanty hut with the other street urchins.

40. If Eliza were alive today, which of the following would she most likely endorse?

(1) free higher education for everyone
(2) giving everyone a patch of land to garden
(3) selling flowers at tourist attractions
(4) taking off your boots in the dining room
(5) referring to people only by their last names

GO ON TO THE NEXT PAGE

Items 41 to 45 refer to the following passage.

WHY IS THIS CHOREOGRAPHER BEING HONORED?

Fifty-three years ago, Anna Sokolow choreographed her first hit. She didn't open on Broadway, and she hadn't set the dances for a Hollywood smash. For Sokolow, as for a host of other artists laboring during that near-forgotten era, success in the 1930s wasn't measured by society's applause—it was measured in political clout. Her first "hit" was a dance for an anti-war congress convened in New York. She was twenty-three years old.

Today, Sokolow's success can be reckoned in much the same terms. In a career spanning five tumultuous decades, she has consistently created dances of uncompromising conviction. Sometimes in the limelight, most often just outside it, Sokolow the choreographer and teacher—she stopped performing in the mid-1950s—has fostered development of modern dance around the world. Although she has choreographed for Broadway, opera, and television, and has staged dances for such well-known troupes as Joffrey Ballet, Netherlands Dance Theatre, and Alvin Ailey's American Dance Theater, Sokolow's most enduring effort hasn't won her many curtain calls. Quietly, she has demonstrated the necessity for the modern artist to renew herself—to reject past rules, even her own, in the search for her own voice. Such renewal is the most "modern" of modern dance's legacies. At seventy-six, Sokolow still modestly pursues the truth.

When she was twenty-four, Sokolow toured the Soviet Union as a guest artist. Starting in 1939, she worked regularly in Mexico, establishing the country's first modern dance company. Her first trip to Israel, in 1953, aroused a deep feeling for her Jewish heritage, for it initiated over thirty years of teaching and choreographing for a variety of groups in that land.

Sokolow has said (*Dance Magazine,* July 1965) that her 1953 dance *Lyric Suite* marked a turning point in her development as a choreographer. "It was then that I began to find a language of movement for myself," she noted. A dance mounted by many companies, *Lyric Suite* has often served as introduction to the mature Sokolow's recurring themes of loneliness and alienation, here somewhat tempered. In *Rooms* (1955), perhaps her most famous dance, Sokolow caught postwar urban anxiety in a particularly chilling—and accurate—way. She continued to make overtly political works as well.

In acknowledgment of Sokolow's achievements, the National Foundation for Jewish Culture will honor her at a gala benefit performance September 20 at the Joyce Theater in New York. Featuring Ze'eva Cohen, Pearl Lang, Sophie Maslow, Meredith Monk, Ohad Naharin, and members of the Players' Project, among others, the evening also opens the foundation's international conference, Jews and Judaism in Dance: Reflections and Celebrations. This conference celebration, which promises to reveal the rich heritage of so many Jewish artists—particularly in contemporary American dance—is appropriately inaugurated with an ovation for Anna Sokolow.

Gary Parks, ''Anna Sokolow: Choreographer Without Compromise,'' *Dance Magazine,* September 1986.

41. Why does the reviewer consider Anna Sokolow to be in the forefront of modern dance?

    (1) Her dances have political themes.
    (2) She stresses compromise.
    (3) Alvin Ailey and Joffrey Ballet have used her dances.
    (4) She combines her heritage with classical technique.
    (5) She rejects even her own rules to create new work.

42. What is the most prevalent theme in Sokolow's dances?

    (1) political struggle
    (2) alienation
    (3) ethnic pride
    (4) war
    (5) parental respect

43. Which of the following statements about Anna Sokolow can be inferred from the passage?

    (1) She intends to produce at least ten more dances.
    (2) She was once a Nazi prisoner of war.
    (3) She has had fierce disagreements with Harvard's performing arts department.
    (4) She is concerned with Russian artists scorned by their government.
    (5) She demanded more recognition than she received.

44. Based on the passage, which of the following statements best describes Anna Sokolow's life?

    (1) She was forced to stop dancing because of her political views.
    (2) She has had little effect on modern dance.
    (3) Her most important work has been widely acclaimed by popular audiences.
    (4) She has continued to follow her inner voice.
    (5) In her later years, she ceased her political activities.

45. At the base of Anna Sokolow's work is her belief that the purpose of dance is to

    (1) entertain
    (2) pursue the truth
    (3) generate income
    (4) attract supporters
    (5) stage "hits"

END OF LITERATURE AND THE ARTS TEST

TEST 5. MATHEMATICS

Time: 90 Minutes—56 Questions

Directions:

The Mathematics Test consists of multiple-choice questions covering the areas of arithmetic, algebra, and geometry. The problems emphasize the practical aspects of mathematics necessary to the solution of everyday problems. A page of formulas is provided for reference in solving the problems presented. However, you will have to determine which formula (if any) is needed to solve a particular problem. Read each problem carefully and then work out the solution on your own before looking at the answer choices. Work quickly, but carefully, answering as many questions as you can. If a problem is too difficult for you, skip it and come back to it after you have completed all of the problems you know how to solve. Record your answers in the Mathematics section of your answer sheet.

FOR EXAMPLE:

Jill's drug store bill totals $8.68. How much change should she get if she pays with a $10.00 bill?

(1) $2.32
(2) $1.42
(3) $1.32
(4) $1.28
(5) $1.22

The correct answer is "$1.32." Therefore, you should mark answer space 3 on your answer sheet.

FORMULAS

Description	Formula
AREA (A) of a:	
square	$A=s^2$; where s=side
rectangle	$A=lw$; where l=length, w=width
parallelogram	$A=bh$; where b=base, h=height
triangle	$A=\frac{1}{2}bh$; where b=base, h=height
circle	$A=\pi r^2$; where $\pi=3.14$, r=radius
PERIMETER (P) of a:	
square	$P=4s$; where s=side
rectangle	$P=2l+2w$; where l=length, w=width
triangle	$P=a+b+c$; where a, b, and c are the sides
circumference (C) of a circle	$C=\pi d$; where $\pi=3.14$, d=diameter
VOLUME (V) of a:	
cube	$V=s^3$; where s=side
rectangular container	$V=lwh$; where l=length, w=width, h=height
cylinder	$V=\pi r^2 h$; where $\pi=3.14$, r=radius, h=height
Pythagorean relationship	$c^2=a^2+b^2$; where c=hypotenuse, a and b are legs of a right triangle
distance (d) between two points in a plane	$d=\sqrt{(x_2-x_1)^2+(y_2-y_1)^2}$; where (x_1, y_1) and (x_2, y_2) are two points in a plane
slope of a line (m)	$m=\frac{y_2-y_1}{x_2-x_1}$; where (x_1, y_1) and (x_2, y_2) are two points in a plane
mean	mean$=\frac{x_1+x_2+\cdots+x_n}{n}$; where the x's are the values for which a mean is desired, and n=number of values in the series
median	median=the point in an ordered set of numbers at which half of the numbers are above and half of the numbers are below this value
simple interest (i)	$i=prt$; where p=principal, r=rate, t=time
distance (d) as function of rate and time	$d=rt$; where r=rate, t=time
total cost (c)	$c=nr$; where n=number of units, r=cost per unit

1. A drill, .375 inches in diameter, is needed for a job. If the hardware store sells drills only in fractions of an inch, which one should be purchased?

   (1) $\frac{5}{8}$
   (2) $\frac{4}{5}$
   (3) $\frac{3}{4}$
   (4) $\frac{2}{3}$
   (5) $\frac{3}{8}$

2. A nonstop flight from Atlanta to London leaves Hart Field in Atlanta at 8:30 p.m. Eastern Standard Time and arrives in London at 8:15 a.m. Greenwich Mean Time. There is a 5-hour difference in the time between Atlanta and London. Therefore the amount of time spent in flight was

   (1) 3 hours and 30 minutes
   (2) 6 hours and 45 minutes
   (3) 11 hours and 45 minutes
   (4) 13 hours and 30 minutes
   (5) 16 hours and 45 minutes

3. Mrs. Smith plans to have a table pad made to fit her new round table. The price of table pads varies according to the area of the pad. If Mrs. Smith's table has a radius of 2 feet, in which of the following size ranges will she find the price for the pad she needs?

   (1) More than 2 square feet but less than 4 square feet
   (2) More than 4 square feet but less than 6 square feet
   (3) More than 6 square feet but less than 8 square feet
   (4) More than 8 square feet but less than 10 square feet
   (5) More than 12 square feet but less than 14 square feet

4. In which of the following equations is 4 the value of x?

   (1) $x^2 + x = 12$
   (2) $4x - 1 = 7$
   (3) $2x - 3 = 5$
   (4) $5x = 25$
   (5) $3x/2 + 5 = 17$

Items 5 and 6 refer to the following information.

Finishing time for the last three runners in the mini-marathon is as follows:

Runner	Hours	Minutes
#1	2	10
#2	2	13
#3	1	55

5. What was the average finishing time for these three runners?

   (1) 1 hour 55 minutes
   (2) 2 hours
   (3) 2 hours 6 minutes
   (4) 2 hours 10 minutes
   (5) 2 hours 13 minutes

6. How many minutes would runner #2 have had to take off his time in order to win the race?

   (1) 4
   (2) 6
   (3) 7
   (4) 13
   (5) Insufficient data is given to solve the problem.

7. A part-time worker at a fast food restaurant is paid $3.65 per hour. If he works 4 hours on Monday, 3 hours on Tuesday, 5 hours on Wednesday, 4 hours on Thursday, and 4 hours on Saturday his income could be expressed algebraically as x =

   (1) (4 + 3 + 5 + 4 + 6) + 3.65
   (2) (3.65) (4 × 3 × 5 × 4 × 6)
   (3) (3.65) (24)
   (4) (4 + 3 + 5 + 4 + 4) (3.65)
   (5) y

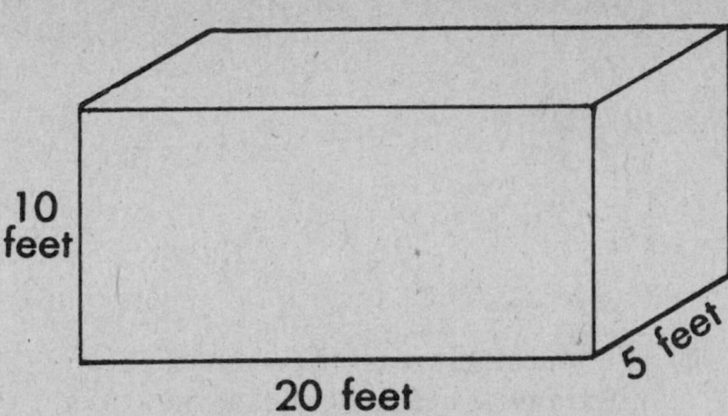

Items 8 and 9 are based on the above diagram.

8. Alice and Arthur want to paint the outside of the rectangular storage shed shown above. If each gallon of paint will cover 200 square feet, how many gallons of paint are needed to cover all the outside surfaces of the shed?

   (1) 1
   (2) 2
   (3) 3
   (4) 6
   (5) Insufficient data is given to solve the problem.

9. When they finished painting the shed, Alice and Arthur decided to use it to store 1-cubic-foot crates. How many such crates can be stored in the shed?

   (1) 10
   (2) 100
   (3) 750
   (4) 1000
   (5) Insufficient data is given to solve the problem.

10. The sum of 2 coins of value x and 3 coins of value y is 50 cents. If the value of y is 10 cents, which of the following equations can be used to solve for the value of x?

    (1) $x + y = 5$
    (2) $x + 3y = 50$
    (3) $2x = 50 - 3y$
    (4) $x = 50 - y$
    (5) $2x + y = 10$

Items 11 and 12 refer to the following information.

Mrs. Jones paid $180 a share for stock and bought 100 shares. The stock paid a quarterly dividend of $4.50 a share.

11. What rate of return did Mrs. Jones make on her stock in one year?

    (1) 7.5%
    (2) 9%
    (3) 10%
    (4) 14.5%
    (5) 16.5%

12. How much money did Mrs. Jones spend in order to purchase her stock?

    (1) $1800
    (2) $4500
    (3) $9000
    (4) $18,000
    (5) $18,450

13. The area of a square stamp is .64 inches. What is the length of one of its sides in inches?

    (1) .0008
    (2) .008
    (3) .08
    (4) .4
    (5) .8

14. Assume that the length of a meter is equal to 39 inches. If a yard is equal to 36 inches, which of the following choices best expresses the weight in grams of 2.17 yards of silk material?

(1) 2.17
(2) 2.30
(3) 2.36
(4) 2.43
(5) Insufficient data is given to solve the problem.

15. If 2 pints of milk cost $.80, how much money can you save by buying a gallon container at a cost of $3.00?

(1) $.10
(2) $.20
(3) $.30
(4) $.40
(5) $.50

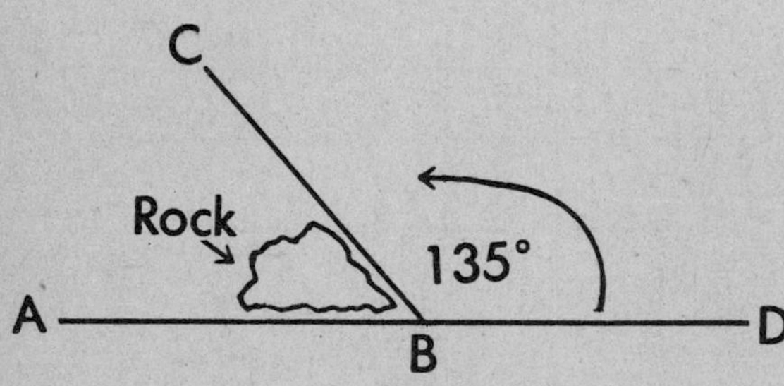

16. A gate, (BC), can swing open only 135 degrees because of a rock which is wedged behind it. Without the rock, the gate could swing all the way back against the fence, (AD), to form a straight angle. Find the number of degrees which the gate is prevented from opening (Angle ABC in the diagram above).

(1) 45
(2) 55
(3) 60
(4) 135
(5) 225

17. If you set out on a 250-mile drive at 10 a.m. and arrive at your destination at 2:10 p.m. on the same day, what was the average speed of your car in miles per hour for the entire drive?

(1) 45
(2) 50
(3) 55
(4) 60
(5) 75

18. If a machine operator produces 312 license plates each hour that he works and he works from 8:00 a.m. to 4:00 p.m. with one hour off for lunch and two 15-minute coffee breaks, how many license plates does he produce each day?

(1) 2028
(2) 2082
(3) 2184
(4) 2496
(5) 2802

19. If $x - 12 = y$ and $x = 3y$, then $y =$

(1) 2
(2) 4
(3) 6
(4) 8
(5) 10

20. Find the value of $3x^2 - 4x + 3$ if x is equal to 5.

(1) 2
(2) 38
(3) 54
(4) 58
(5) 98

21. In the diagram, a domino cube is drawn next to a domino box. At most, how many dominos can fit into the box (ignore the thickness of the box)?

(1) 20
(2) 25
(3) 36
(4) 48
(5) 60

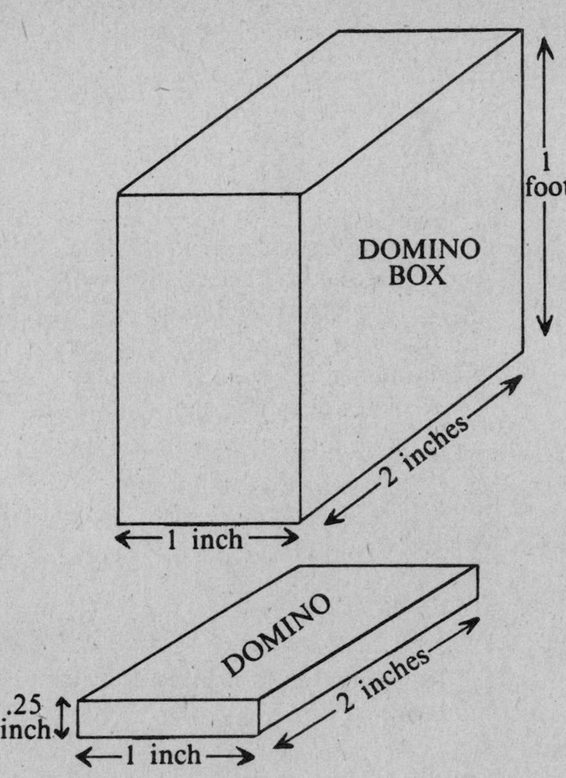

Items 22 and 23 refer to the following information.

A family has a monthly income of $3600. Their monthly expenditures are as shown in the graph below.

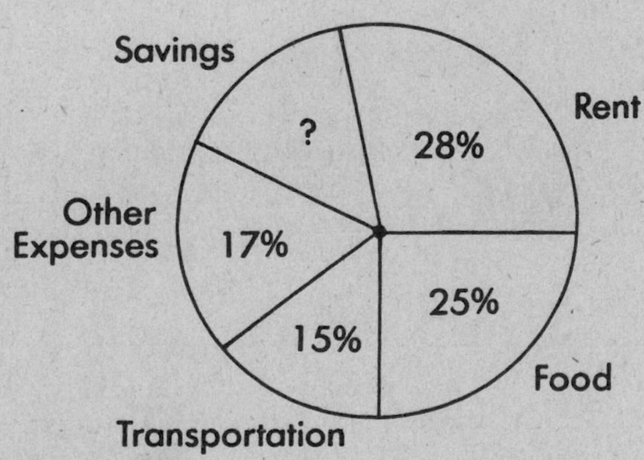

22. How much money does the family save in a year?

    (1) $6000
    (2) $6320
    (3) $6480
    (4) $6900
    (5) $7400

23. What is the cost of rent each month?

    (1) $612
    (2) $750
    (3) $1000
    (4) $1008
    (5) $1200

Item 24

The chart below shows the sexes of the children in the families living on our street.

FAMILY:	1	2	3	4	5
# BOYS: # GIRLS:	2 3	0 0	1 2	2 1	5 4

24. Compare the number of girls to boys.

    (1) $\frac{1}{2}$ more girls
    (2) 1 more girl
    (3) $\frac{1}{2}$ fewer girls
    (4) 1 fewer girl
    (5) They are the same

25. The circumference of the wheel on Tim's tricycle is $\frac{1}{4}$ the circumference of the wheel on his father's car. If the circumference of his father's wheel is 16 π, what is the radius of Tim's wheel?

    (1) 1
    (2) 2
    (3) 4
    (4) 16
    (5) 64

26. Solve the equation:

$$x/(-3) + 1 = 12$$

x will equal

(1) −39
(2) −36
(3) −33
(4) 11
(5) 12

27. A triangle is a musical instrument which can be made by bending a steel rod into the shape of a triangle. Each of the angles of the triangle used in the school orchestra measures 60°. One side of the triangle is 12 inches. How many inches of metal rod are needed for each instrument?

(1) 12
(2) 18
(3) 24
(4) 30
(5) 36

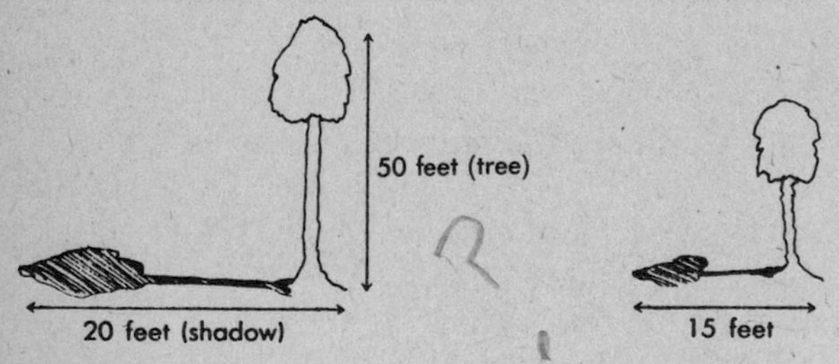

28. Two trees are 10 feet apart. The taller tree, which measures 50 feet in height, casts a shadow of 20 feet, while the shorter tree casts a shadow of 15 feet. If the sun is shining on each tree from the same angle, how tall is the shorter tree?

(1) 25 feet
(2) 30 feet
(3) 32.5 feet
(4) 35 feet
(5) 37.5 feet

29. Aunt Millie wants to boil water for tea. If the temperature of the water leaving the tap is 10°C how long would it take for the water to boil? (Answer in seconds.)

(1) 10
(2) 90
(3) 100
(4) 212
(5) Insufficient data is given to solve the problem.

30. During a sale, an item's selling price was reduced by 50 cents. If 50 items were sold on the first day of the sale, and X items were sold on the second day, then how many dollars did the store lose by not selling at the original price?

(1) 50
(2) 40
(3) 30
(4) 20
(5) Insufficient data is given to solve the problem.

31. Simplify the equation:

$$3x + 3y + x + 4y - 4x = 5$$

(1) $6x = 5$
(2) $7x + 7y = 5$
(3) $-x + 7y = 5$
(4) $7x - y = 5$
(5) $7y = 5$

Item 32 is based on the figures below and on the next page.

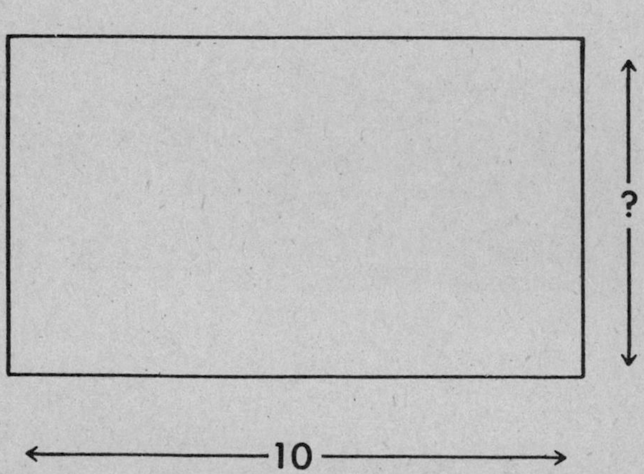

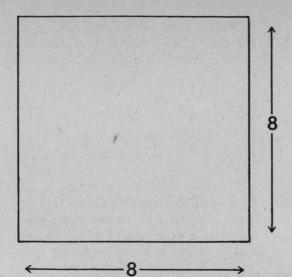

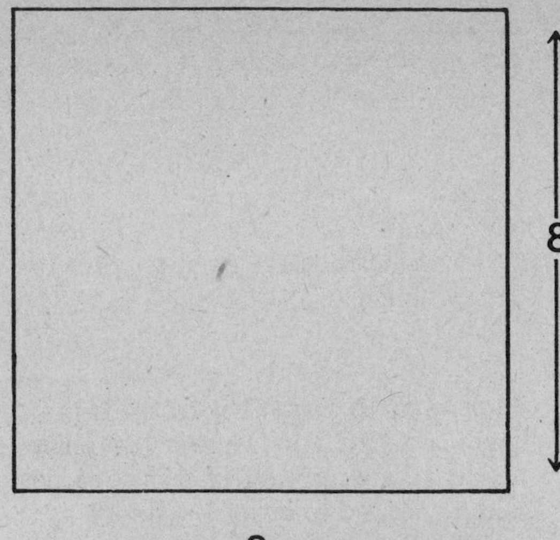

32. In the preceeding figures, what must the height of the rectangle be in order for its area to be equal to the area of the square?

    (1) 6.4
    (2) $\sqrt{8.1}$
    (3) $\sqrt{80}$
    (4) 11
    (5) Insufficient data is given to solve the problem.

33. Five soldiers are planning to rough it in field maneuvers for eight days. They must pack enough food to see them through the maneuvers, plus a spare ration of one day's food. If each soldier is allowed 36 ounces of food per day, approximately how much food is assigned to the group for the trip?

    (1) 18 lbs.
    (2) 100 lbs.
    (3) 162 lbs.
    (4) 180 lbs.
    (5) 324 lbs.

34. In $1\frac{1}{2}$ hours, the minute hand of a clock rotates through an angle equivalent to

    (1) 180°
    (2) 270°
    (3) 360°
    (4) 540°
    (5) 720°

Items 35 to 37 relate to the following information.

Jim and Jack were curious about the number of red cars they saw each day. One Saturday, they decided to keep track of the red cars that passed their house each hour. They recorded their findings in the table below.

Hour	1	2	3	4	5
Number of Red Cars	5	4	8	0	8

35. What was the mode?

    (1) 0
    (2) 4
    (3) 5
    (4) 8
    (5) 25

36. What was the average number of red cars that they saw?

    (1) 1
    (2) 2
    (3) 3
    (4) 4
    (5) 5

37. How many red cars would have to pass the house in the sixth hour to make the mean equivalent to 7?

    (1) 5
    (2) 7
    (3) 9
    (4) 15
    (5) 17

38. Simplify the equation:

$$5x + 5y + 5z = 5$$

    (1) $x + y + z = 1$
    (2) $21x = 5$
    (3) $5x + 11y + 5z = 1$
    (4) $11x + 5y + 5z = 5$
    (5) $21z = 1$

Items 39 and 40 refer to the following information.

The price of an airplane flight between Seattle and New York has risen as follows:

November 1985	$210.00
February 1986	245.00
June 1986	350.00
November 1986	390.00
February 1987	410.00

39. What is the percentage of change in the cost of a trip from Seattle to New York between February 1986 and February 1987?

(1) 40%
(2) 60%
(3) 67%
(4) 78%
(5) 87%

40. Natalie Bova and her husband decided to fly from Seattle to New York City to visit her parents. Natalie made the trip on October 30, 1986. Her husband followed her on November 2nd. What was the total cost of the two trips?

(1) $595
(2) $645
(3) $700
(4) $740
(5) $780

41. Sam wants to have a cushion made for his favorite lounge chair. The information he has is shown in the diagram below. Find the number of degrees in angle DAB if line ABC is a straight line and angle DBC equals 128°.

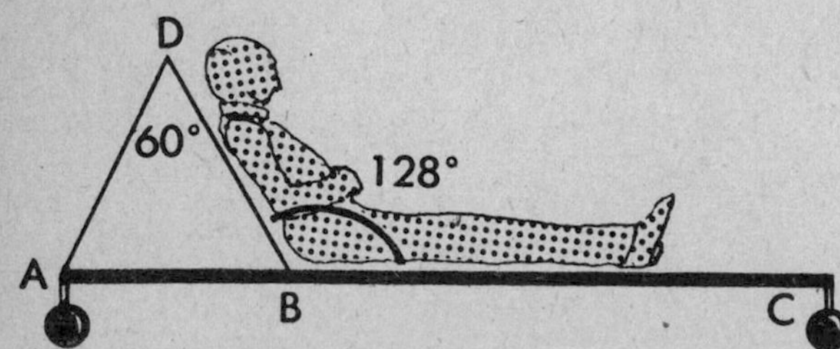

(1) 60°
(2) 64°
(3) 68°
(4) 72°
(5) Insufficient data given to solve the problem.

42. Sara wants to carpet her room. If the room is a square measuring 120 inches to a side, how many square feet of carpet will be needed to cover the floor?

(1) 144,000
(2) 1400
(3) 144
(4) 120
(5) 100

43. Taking inventory of the stock in the notions department, a clerk finds that she has only 3 partial spools of blue ribbon left. The first spool has $10\frac{2}{3}$ yards of ribbon, the second spool has $5\frac{3}{4}$ yards, and the third spool has $2\frac{1}{6}$ yards. How many yards of blue ribbon are available for sale?

(1) $18\frac{2}{3}$
(2) $18\frac{7}{12}$
(3) $18\frac{5}{6}$
(4) $19\frac{1}{2}$
(5) $19\frac{3}{4}$

44. A hole whose circumference was 2π feet long was cut in the ice with a saw. John wanted to do ice-fishing in a hole which had a circumference five times larger. What would be the radius of the larger hole in feet?

(1) 1
(2) 2
(3) 3
(4) 4
(5) 5

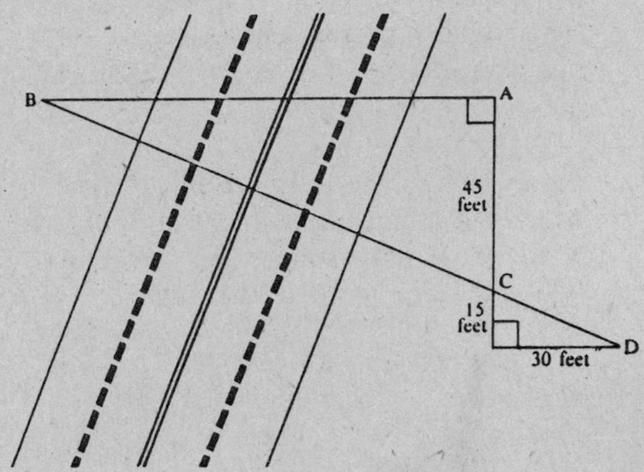

Items 45 and 46 are based on the diagram above.

45. A surveyor made the measurements shown above. What is the straight line distance from A to B across the highway?

    (1) 45
    (2) 60
    (3) 75
    (4) 90
    (5) 120

46. Find the length C to D.

    (1) $\sqrt{45}$
    (2) 45
    (3) 450
    (4) $\sqrt{1125}$
    (5) 1125

47. A machine is able to produce 3,500 parts an hour. However, the machine can only be run at 80% of its maximum speed if it is to be run efficiently without producing many unusable parts. How many usable parts can this machine produce in a 40-hour week?

    (1) 11,200
    (2) 14,000
    (3) 28,000
    (4) 112,000
    (5) 140,000

48. Under certain conditions sound travels at about 1100 feet per second. If 88 feet per second is approximately equal to 60 miles per hour, the speed of sound, under the above conditions, is closest to which speed in miles per hour.

    (1) 480 miles per hour
    (2) 750 miles per hour
    (3) 3280 miles per hour
    (4) 6600 miles per hour
    (5) 8800 miles per hour

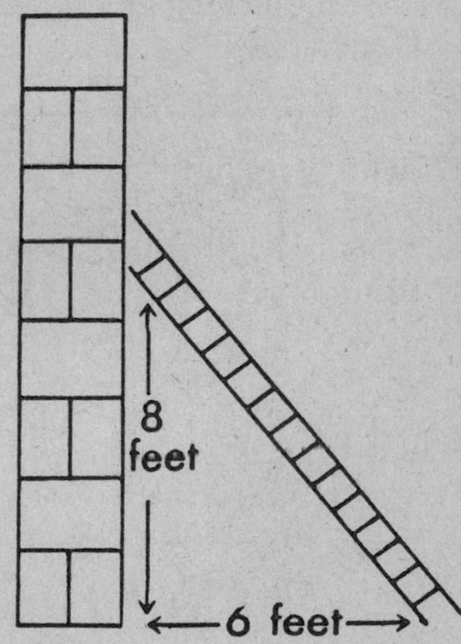

49. A ladder set 6 feet from the base of a wall reaches a point 8 feet high on the wall. How long is the ladder (in feet)?

    (1) 7
    (2) 10
    (3) 14
    (4) 15
    (5) 20

50. At the end of the day, in the toy department of a store, 14 dolls were bought and 3 were returned, netting a total sale of $44. How many dollars did each doll cost the customer?

(1) 4
(2) 14
(3) 44
(4) 44/7
(5) 44/17

51. A metal box is to be covered with paper. How many square inches of paper are needed in order to cover all sides of the box, if

width is W

length is L

height is H

(1) W + L + H
(2) W × L × H
(3) 2 × WLH
(4) 2W + 2L + 2H
(5) 2WL + 2 WH + 2 LH

52. If the box in problem 51 had dimensions 6 inches × 6 inches × 1 inch, and was filled with water, how many cubic inches of water would it hold?

(1) 100
(2) 96
(3) 50
(4) 36
(5) 24

Items 53 to 56 are based on the chart below.

The Consumer Dollar

53. The chart entitled The Consumer Dollar shows how much the value of the U.S. dollar has decreased since 1967.
    In what year did the 1967 dollar decrease to approximately half of its original value?

    (1) 1967
    (2) 1974
    (3) 1977
    (4) 1978
    (5) 1979

54. Michael purchased a radio for $100 in 1979. Its value in 1967 dollars would be

    (1) 10
    (2) 45
    (3) 80
    (4) 100
    (5) 140

55. Predict the most likely value of the dollar in 1980, compared to the 1967 dollar.

    (1) 20
    (2) 40
    (3) 45
    (4) 100
    (5) 140

56. What was the approximate average decrease in the value of the dollar between 1967 and 1979?

    (1) 1
    (2) 2
    (3) 3
    (4) 4
    (5) 5

END OF MATHEMATICS TEST

Answer Key for GED Diagnostic Test

After completing the Diagnostic Test, check your answers against the key answers that follow. Enter the total number of correct answers for each test in the box provided on your answer sheet. Then turn to the Error Analysis chart to see what your strengths and weaknesses are.

TEST 1. WRITING SKILLS—PART I

1. (3)
2. (3)
3. (1)
4. (4)
5. (2)
6. (5)
7. (5)
8. (1)
9. (5)
10. (5)
11. (2)
12. (3)
13. (5)
14. (2)
15. (3)
16. (4)
17. (5)
18. (4)
19. (2)
20. (5)
21. (2)
22. (4)
23. (2)
24. (4)
25. (3)
26. (3)
27. (3)
28. (5)
29. (4)
30. (2)
31. (4)
32. (1)
33. (2)
34. (1)
35. (5)
36. (3)
37. (4)
38. (2)
39. (3)
40. (2)
41. (5)
42. (5)
43. (4)
44. (5)
45. (3)
46. (2)
47. (3)
48. (3)
49. (2)
50. (5)
51. (2)
52. (5)
53. (3)
54. (5)
55. (3)

TEST 2. SOCIAL STUDIES

1. (3)
2. (2)
3. (5)
4. (5)
5. (4)
6. (5)
7. (2)
8. (2)
9. (5)
10. (4)
11. (1)
12. (2)
13. (4)
14. (3)
15. (1)
16. (4)
17. (3)
18. (3)
19. (3)
20. (1)
21. (3)
22. (4)
23. (2)
24. (3)
25. (1)
26. (5)
27. (1)
28. (5)
29. (3)
30. (1)
31. (3)
32. (5)
33. (3)
34. (3)
35. (3)
36. (4)
37. (2)
38. (5)
39. (4)
40. (4)
41. (3)
42. (4)
43. (4)
44. (5)
45. (3)
46. (3)
47. (1)
48. (1)
49. (5)
50. (3)
51. (3)
52. (2)
53. (3)
54. (4)
55. (2)
56. (5)
57. (1)
58. (5)
59. (4)
60. (4)
61. (3)
62. (2)
63. (5)
64. (1)

TEST 3. SCIENCE

1. (2)
2. (1)
3. (5)
4. (3)
5. (4)
6. (5)
7. (2)
8. (3)
9. (2)
10. (1)
11. (2)
12. (4)
13. (4)
14. (5)
15. (1)
16. (5)
17. (3)
18. (4)
19. (4)
20. (1)
21. (4)
22. (2)
23. (3)
24. (5)
25. (3)
26. (1)
27. (1)
28. (5)
29. (5)
30. (3)
31. (2)
32. (1)
33. (5)
34. (4)
35. (3)
36. (3)
37. (5)
38. (4)
39. (2)
40. (3)
41. (5)
42. (2)
43. (2)
44. (2)
45. (3)
46. (3)
47. (1)
48. (2)
49. (3)
50. (4)
51. (1)
52. (1)
53. (4)
54. (5)
55. (2)
56. (3)
57. (4)
58. (5)
59. (5)
60. (4)
61. (2)
62. (2)
63. (3)
64. (5)
65. (4)
66. (1)

TEST 4. INTERPRETING LITERATURE AND THE ARTS

1. (5)
2. (4)
3. (4)
4. (3)
5. (3)
6. (4)
7. (2)
8. (5)
9. (2)
10. (1)
11. (2)
12. (1)
13. (5)
14. (1)
15. (1)
16. (4)
17. (5)
18. (1)
19. (3)
20. (2)
21. (3)
22. (1)
23. (2)
24. (5)
25. (4)
26. (1)
27. (4)
28. (3)
29. (5)
30. (2)
31. (1)
32. (2)
33. (5)
34. (4)
35. (2)
36. (3)
37. (5)
38. (1)
39. (2)
40. (1)
41. (5)
42. (2)
43. (4)
44. (4)
45. (2)

TEST 5. MATHEMATICS

1. (5)
2. (2)
3. (5)
4. (3)
5. (3)
6. (5)
7. (4)
8. (3)
9. (4)
10. (3)
11. (3)
12. (4)
13. (5)
14. (5)
15. (2)
16. (1)
17. (4)
18. (1)
19. (3)
20. (4)
21. (4)
22. (3)
23. (4)
24. (5)
25. (2)
26. (3)
27. (5)
28. (5)
29. (5)
30. (5)
31. (5)
32. (1)
33. (2)
34. (4)
35. (4)
36. (5)
37. (5)
38. (1)
39. (3)
40. (4)
41. (3)
42. (5)
43. (2)
44. (5)
45. (4)
46. (4)
47. (4)
48. (2)
49. (2)
50. (1)
51. (5)
52. (4)
53. (4)
54. (2)
55. (2)
56. (4)

ERROR ANALYSIS FOR GED DIAGNOSTIC TEST

Circle the number of each question you answered incorrectly. Count the number of circles in each content area and write the total number missed in the column headed "Number Incorrect." A large number of incorrect responses in a particular area indicates the need for further study in that area.

Subject Area	Questions	No. Incorrect
TEST 1. WRITING SKILLS	55	
Sentence Structure	4, 5, 6, 11, 14, 16, 20, 24, 26, 30, 31, 32, 34, 37, 38, 39, 40, 43, 45, 49, 55	
Usage	1, 2, 7, 12, 19, 23, 25, 27, 29, 33, 41, 44, 48, 50, 53, 54	
Capitalization	3, 18	
Punctuation	21, 28, 35	
Spelling/Possessives/ Contractions	8, 9, 10, 13, 15, 17, 22, 36, 42, 46, 47, 51, 52	
TEST 2. SOCIAL STUDIES	64	
History	4, 5, 6, 7, 8, 13, 14, 15, 23, 25, 32, 39, 46, 47, 49, 50, 51, 57	
Economics	9, 10, 11, 12, 16, 17, 18, 19, 20, 21, 32, 33, 34, 40, 41, 42, 43, 47, 48, 50, 51, 52, 53, 54, 55, 56, 57, 59	
Geography	1, 2, 3, 39, 43, 60, 61, 62, 63, 64	
Political Science	23, 25, 27, 28, 29, 30, 31, 34, 35, 36, 37, 38, 44, 45, 47, 50, 51, 52, 53, 54, 55, 56, 57, 58, 59	
Behavioral Science	5, 6, 7, 8, 22, 24, 26, 32, 33, 44, 45, 48, 60, 61, 62, 63, 64	
TEST 3. SCIENCE	66	
Biology	5, 6, 7, 8, 9, 12, 13, 14, 15, 16, 17, 18, 19, 25, 26, 27, 28, 29, 30, 31, 32, 33, 34, 35, 36, 48	
Chemistry	43, 46, 47, 59, 60, 61, 62	
Earth Science	1, 2, 3, 4, 20, 21, 22, 23, 24, 38, 39, 40, 41, 42, 44, 50, 51, 64, 65, 66	
Physics	10, 11, 44, 45, 52, 53, 54, 55, 56, 57, 58	
TEST 4. INTERPRETING LITERATURE AND THE ARTS	45	
Popular Literature	1, 2, 3, 4, 5, 6, 7, 8, 9, 18, 19, 20, 21, 22, 23, 24, 25, 26, 27, 28, 29, 30, 31, 32	
Classical Literature	10, 11, 12, 13, 14, 15, 16, 17, 33, 34, 35, 36, 37, 38, 39, 40	
Commentary	41, 42, 43, 44, 45	
TEST 5. MATHEMATICS	56	
Measurement	2, 11, 12, 17, 18, 22, 23, 28, 29, 33, 34, 39, 40, 47, 48	
Algebra	4, 6, 7, 15, 19, 20, 25, 26, 30, 31, 38, 45, 46, 50	
Geometry	3, 8, 9, 14, 16, 27, 32, 41, 42, 49, 51, 52	
Numeration	1, 10, 21, 43, 44	
Statistics	5, 24, 35, 36, 37, 53, 54, 55, 56	

Explanatory Answers For GED Diagnostic Test

TEST 1. WRITING SKILLS—PART I

1. **(3)** Change *greatest* to *greater.* Use the *comparative* form (ends in -er) when comparing *two* things; use the *superlative* form (ends in -est) when comparing *three or more things*. Here, you are comparing two things—people who smoke to people who don't smoke, and so use the word "greater."

2. **(3)** To keep the tenses consistent within the paragraph, change the past tense *increased* to the present tense *increases.*

3. **(1)** *Cancers of the larynx, esophagus, pancreas, bladder, kidney, and mouth.* No correction is necessary since commas have been used properly and there is no need of capitalization.

4. **(4)** Change *inhaled* to *inhale* to make the verbs *inhale, take,* and *smoke* parallel. When you make the sentence elements parallel you make the sentence clearer.

5. **(2)** *You will not reduce.* The rewritten sentence reads: Even though you switch to low-tar, low-nicotine cigarettes, you will not reduce your risks of developing other cancers and diseases, such as heart disease. When used for a revision, choice (1) will not make sense. Choices (2), (3), and (5) will create awkard and wordy sentences, and choice (4) will create an incomplete sentence.

6. **(5)** Change *producing* to *produced* to ensure the correct meaning. The tar is not producing the smoking; the smoking is producing the tar.

7. **(5)** *Your risks begin to decrease.* Begin is required for the sense of the sentence and the tense of the paragraph.

8. **(1)** Change the spelling of *elimenate* to *eliminate. Way* and *weigh* and *due* and *do* are homonyms, words that sound alike but are spelled differently and have different meanings.

9. **(5)** No correction is necessary.

10. **(5)** Change *whether* to *weather.* Don't confuse "whether" (referring to alternate choices) with *weather,* atmospheric conditions such as rain or snow, the meaning required by the paragraph.

11. **(2)** *deliveries. They.* The original sentence is a comma splice.

12. **(3)** *On their own.* The sentence refers to carriers (plural) therefore it requires the plural *their.*

13. **(5)** Change the spelling of *availible* to *available.*

14. **(2)** Moving heavy mail sacks, *clerks* may use a hand truck. . . . A subject telling who did the moving must follow the phrase.

15. **(3)** Change *board* to *bored. Board* refers to a plank or a piece of wood. *Bored* refers to a feeling or state of mind.

16. **(4)** Change *sorting* to *sorted.* People do the sorting of the mail; it does not sort itself.

17. **(5)** No correction is necessary.

18. **(4)** *As "Skeleton Flats."* The name of a town is capitalized. In addition, the name of the town is put in quotes to indicate it is a nickname, to stress the point that the residents "laughingly" refer to it in a specific way.

19. **(2)** *paleontologists, scientists.* The second portion of the sentence explains the meaning of the word paleontologist, and is properly set off by commas.

20. **(5)** *area. Ranchers have.* The original sentence contains a comma splice.

21. **(2)** add a period after *Walter H.* Initials in a person's name are followed by a period.

22. **(4)** Change the spelling of *alot* to *a lot. A lot* is properly written as two words, not one.

23. **(2)** *people sought new finds.* Sentence is unclear in the original; in corrected version "they" refers to the people seeking bones.

24. **(4)** *To be found in Ekalaka.* This is the only response which provides coordination of sentence structure.

25. **(3)** Change *are* to *were.* Since the remains were already found (an act that occurred in the past), use the past tense "were" rather than the present tense "are."

26. **(3)** *The head of a Triceratops.* Logical and clearer sentences result when unnecessary words are eliminated, as is done in choice (3).

27, **(3)** Change *yields* to *yielded.* The sense of the paragraph requires a verb in the past tense.

28. **(5)** No correction is necessary.

29. **(4)** *Women experience difficulty.* In keeping with the paragraph, the verb should be in the present tense. To agree with the subject, the verb must be plural.

30. **(2)** *Of course.* This is the only grammatically correct and sensible choice.

31. **(4)** *Goals and looking for work.* For parallel structure in sentence, balance *setting* career goals with *looking* for work.

32. **(1)** Settings that provide *few role models* . . . is necessary for proper sentence structure and coordination.

33. **(2)** *Communities have career.* The paragraph is written in the present tense; this sentence should also be present tense to maintain the sense of the paragraph.

34. **(1)** Insert *are* after *programs.* Without *are* this is merely a sentence fragment.

35. **(5)** *Provide the extensive.* A comma is not required here; this would not logically break into two clauses or two sentences.

36. **(3)** Change the spelling of *fundamentel* to *fundamental.*

37. **(4)** Change *kept* to *keep.* Necessary for clarity and to maintain parallel structure (*find* and *keep*).

38. **(2)** *Pasta and ate.* Parallel construction: *loved* pasta and *ate* it.

39. **(3)** *They refuse to.* This is the only choice that does not contain any slang, contractions, or colloquialisms which are generally found in informal writing or everyday speech.

40. **(2)** *Nutritionists say that pasta.* The sentence (and paragraph) require the verb in the present tense.

41. **(5)** No correction is necessary.

42. **(5)** *It's not the pasta that's fattening.* It's means "it is." *Its* is a possessive form showing ownership (not a contraction, indicating a letter or letters have been omitted).

43. **(4)** *Pasta can hold.* As originally stated, sentence 7 is a sentence fragment.

44. **(5)** *Marco Polo used.* Usage requires a verb in the past tense.

45. **(3)** *remove the semicolon after Italy.* Splitting the sentence after Italy destroys the logical sense of the sentence.

46. **(2)** Replace *theirs* with *there's*. The sentence requires a noun and a verb, *there is,* which appears in the form of a contraction. The original sentence contains a homonym *theirs*.

47. **(3)** Change *acident* to *accident.*

48. **(3)** Change *occur* to *occurs.* The sentence is about one disease and requires a singular verb.

49. **(2)** Change *from* to *to.* The verb *relate* is commonly used with *to.*

50. **(5)** Bone ends protected by cartilage in the joints *are* . . . The plural subject "bone ends" requires the plural verb "are."

51. **(2)** Change *great* to *grate.* To irritate or rub against is the meaning required here: the verb to *grate,* not the homonym *great.*

52. **(5)** No correction is necessary.

53. **(3)** Change *them* to *it.* Osteoarthritis is a single ailment even though it ends in an 's'.

54. **(5)** No correction is necessary.

55. **(3)** *Joints have taken on an outwardly.* As originally written, this is a sentence fragment. To correct this, add the helping verb "have."

WRITING SKILLS—PART II

SAMPLE ESSAY RESPONSE

The evidence is in: Eating carefully and exercising moderately can improve your health and may even help you live longer. But overdoing anything is dangerous, and eating too little and exercising too much can hurt you. Moderate exercise and watching what you eat can help you feel better.

Exercise like walking or swimming is good for you. These sports work your muscles, and you are not likely to get hurt. Exercise lowers blood pressure and helps your heart work more efficiently. This may even help you live longer. Watching what you eat can also improve the way you feel. Fresh fruits and vegetables, whole grains, fish, and chicken are better for you than fatty or sugary foods. It is also important to keep your weight down, but not too low. The doctor can tell you what you should weigh. Unfortunately, some people carry the idea of diet and exercise too far.

Carrying diet and exercise to extremes can have tragic results Some people think they are too fat and so they diet and exercise too much. If they get too thin or gain and lose weight too quickly or too often, their hearts can fail. Other people let diet and exercise run their lives. They spend too much time worrying about what they eat and how much they work out. This is not healthy either. Some people even put babies on diets. This can be very dangerous, for babies need extra weight to grow correctly.

Eating a variety of healthful foods and keeping slim is good for you. Carefully planned out exercise helps you stay younger and healthier longer. But fitness freaks may cause themselves serious harm—even death. Remember: avoid extremes in diet and exercise.

TEST 2. SOCIAL STUDIES

1. **(3)** Cartography is the science of making maps. Being able to accurately determine longitude results in newer and better maps.

2. **(2)** Offering a "handsome"—meaning large—prize for better maps suggests the French government's interest in accuracy.

3. **(5)** The only direct consequence of improved maps was the ability of nations to agree on clearly defined time zones, since it was now possible to locate a single position on a map and determine longitude.

4. **(5)** King Louis XIV offered the prize because he was especially interested in expanding exploration.

5. **(4)** The restaurant represents the American population with its many different kinds of people.

6. **(5)** The cartoon suggests America is made up of a number of different nationalities, as indicated by foods representative of each culture.

7. **(2)** "The Melting Pot" suggests the different cultures that have formed America have "melted" together, obscuring individual cultural differences. Only "The Salad Bowl" disagrees with this view, suggesting that the cultures have been "tossed" together but have not blended.

8. **(2)** The different foods indicate the United States has been settled by people from many other countries.

9. **(5)** Although the passage details the effect of the five-dollar-a-day wage, it does not actually present Ford's reason for implementing such a policy. Causes and effects need to be clearly distinguished.

10. **(4)** The effects are clearly given in the paragraph.

11. **(1)** It changed pay patterns, but it did not directly cause answer choices (2), (3), or (5).

12. **(2)** The wage increase resulted in the working man's inclusion in the middle class. (1) is not proven by the passage; (3) European industrialists are never mentioned; and (4) confuses cause and effect.

13. **(4)** Francisco Coronado was looking for gold in the American southwest. The Seven Cities of Cibola were reported by Indians to be rich in gold, a precious metal sought by explorers.

14. **(3)** Mapping land already acquired implies Lewis and Clark were seeking raw materials and places to colonize. (1) and (2) sought treasure; (4) sought fame.

15. **(1)** "glory" is fame and fortune.

16. **(4)** Chroma pf went down $4\frac{1}{4}$ a share from its closing price the day before, the largest jump.

17. **(3)** Chas Fd closed at $11\frac{7}{8}$ which is the same as its 52-week highest selling price.

18. **(3)** 100 shares times $25.50 a share equals $2550. Even though you don't know if the stock was at its daily high or low, the other choices are too far off.

19. **(3)** CenTel's low for the day was 22 dollars plus $\frac{5}{8}$ of a dollar or about 63 cents.

20. **(1)** ChasM pf pays $5.25, the highest amount here.

21. **(3)** Cntry Tel had a high of 9 $\frac{3}{4}$ and a low of 6 $\frac{3}{4}$, a difference of 3 points. All others had a greater fluctuation.

22. **(4)** The preferential treatment shown to Brian because of his mother's position in the company is an example of nepotism.

23. **(2)** The Pendleton Act established the merit system.

24. **(3)** Awarding a job to a candidate because of social standing is an example of the "Old Boy" network in action.

25. **(1)** The Hatch Act greatly decreased the effects of the spoils system.

26. **(5)** Meredith made good use of networking when she cultivated the acquaintance of people in the field in which she wished to be employed.

27. **(1)** Christopher got his job as a result of the spoils system.

28. **(5)** Support for the fifth choice is found in the last sentence.

29. **(3)** "Altered" means "changed."

30. **(1)** When the liver has not yet oxidized all the alcohol, the unoxidized portion shows up as fumes being exhaled by the lungs. The breath analyzer can detect the presence of such fumes.

31. **(3)** The author is presenting some basic information to educate the reader rather than writing a scientific paragraph.

32. **(5)** III and IV only. Women are not a minority if they comprise 53% of the population under scrutiny. If 81% of all clerical workers are women, it is accurate to say that four out of five clerical workers are women. I and II are inaccurate because the graph depicts something different. It shows that 45% of all professional workers are women (*not* that 45% of employed women are professional workers) and that 43% of all the unemployed are women (not that 43% of women are unemployed). Neither I nor II is defensible since the total number of categories of women depicted would have to add up to 100%.

33. **(3)** The U.S. economy would be seriously damaged if women were not available to the labor force If women comprise nearly half of all employed workers (43%), nearly half of the professional workers (45%) and an overwhelming percentage of the clerical workers (81%), who could possibly replace them if they all left the job market at once? (1) is inaccurate as compared to the chart, while (2), (4), and (5) are unsupported since the chart offers no comparisons with men or future or past activity in the labor force.

34. **(3)** During the time period shown in the chart, cable television has experienced a huge increase in the number of basic subscribers, and the total amount of revenue. The average monthly basic rate has risen from less than six dollars to more than ten. The statement "The cable television industry has enjoyed huge growth in total revenue and number of subscribers between 1975 and 1985" can be supported. There is also some support for (1) and (2) since the trend shown for fifteen years is likely to continue; however, the support offered for choice (3) is stronger. The graphs offer no comparisons with network television nor any indication that revenue is likely to drop (4) and (5).

35. **(3)** The poll tax was outlawed in federal elections by the Twentieth Amendment, and Supreme Court decisions outlawed it in state and local elections.

36. **(4)** The Nineteenth Amendment entitled women to vote.

37. **(2)** The Fourteenth Amendment (ratified 1868) defined slaves as citizens and the Fifteenth (1870) gave them the right to vote.

38. **(5)** When the Seventeenth Amendment was ratified it provided for the direct election of senators, but left the Electoral College in place.

39. **(4)** If the "center" of the U.S. has shifted to the west, it is because the western portion of the country has added more "weight"; that is, population. (1) is irrelevant; (2) is not supportable since the center of population has jumped west of the Mississippi. (3) may be accurate with respect to certain periods of American history, but all the major cities are no longer concentrated on the eastern seaboard. (5) is inaccurate, since if this were true, the center would shift to the east.

40. **(4)** Each of the first three items is a purpose of the Energy Guide label.

41. **(3)** A careful reading of the paragraph will show that clothes dryers, dishwashers, and television sets are not labeled.

42. **(4)** Electricity is measured in kilowatt-hours.

43. **(4)** The Energy Guide labels were designed to help consumers conserve energy.

44. **(5)** You cannot make a comparison without data from previous years.

45. **(3)** The number of prisoners has increased quite sharply from 1975 on. The comparison between 1980 and 1985 suggests that the number of prisoners will continue to increase, and since the allocation of public monies for major problems usually suffers a considerable time lag, it is likely that there will be considerable public expenditures for prisons through the 1990's.

46. **(3)** is the only *effect* of the Truman Doctrine. Choices (1) and (4) are *causes,* not effects. (2) and (5) do not directly address the question.

47. **(1)** is the only cause; all the rest are effects.

48. **(1)** All three charts support the fact that female heads of households suffer economically: they have higher unemployment rates; their total income is lower; and a larger percentage are likely to fall below the definition of the poverty line. (2) is not addressed since we have no direct comparison for women with and without children; (3) is incorrect since we do not know who works in husband-wife families; (4) and (5) are not supported by the information supplied.

49. **(5)** *The Wall Street Journal* covers national and international events which affect all aspects of economic life. All the other newspapers have the name of a city in their title.

50. **(3)** By observation we can see that there was probably less than a fifty percent increase in available funds over the eleven years. The only possible option among all the answer choices is (3).

51. **(3)** The 1971 bar shows us that Florida and Texas combined had more funding than Pennsylvania and Texas combined. Add California and you have the largest combination.

52. **(2)** Only New York showed a consistent decline over the eleven-year period.

53. **(3)** National Highway Safety Bureau

54. **(4)** Federal Trade Commission

55. **(2)** National Bureau of Standards

56. **(5)** Cooperative Extension Service

57. **(1)** Department of Agriculture

58. **(5)** Cooperative Extension Service. Note that the booklets were published by university presses.

59. **(4)** Federal Trade Commission

60. **(4)** Farmers and herdsmen are Vaisyas. Kshatriya is the next higher caste.

61. **(3)** After the old "day" is over, Brahma creates a new cycle.

62. **(2)** As stated in paragraph 4, reincarnation takes place when the soul is continually reborn.

63. **(5)** The untouchables perform the tasks no one else wants to do.

64. **(1)** Hinduism offers a strong belief in reincarnation.

TEST 3. SCIENCE

1. **(2)** The passage states that it takes about five minutes to prepare a meal in space. It takes more time to prepare a meal in a conventional kitchen with conventional foods.

2. **(1)** The foods are "reconstituted" with the "ample water" provided by the fuel cells.

3. **(5)** Since the astronauts are given 2,700 calories daily and we are not told that they are in any way different from earthbound people, the only choice we can infer is that these calories represent a recommended daily allowance.

4. **(3)** Both A and C are facts; B and D are opinions, open to discussion and question.

5. **(4)** Between 40° and 50° the oxygen consumption of the three stages was at its highest.

6. **(5)** The highest stage of oxygen production in the adult was 10 to 14 mm^3, indicated by the sharp upturn in the line.

7. **(2)** Adult fruitflies need more oxygen than pupa, as indicated by the sharply rising line.

8. **(3)** Of the choices, the only one that the information applies to is (3). The experiment would be useful to increase lab production of fruitflies.

9. **(2)** During photosynthesis, carbon dioxide and water are changed to sugar and oxygen as indicated by formula (2). (1) is the formula of dehydration synthesis. (3) is the formula for combining sodium hydroxide and hydrochloric acid to form salt and water. (4) is fermentation, changing sugar to alcohol. (5) is electrolysis.

10. **(1)** In the first paragraph the laser is called a "beam." From this we can infer a laser is a "beam of light rays."

11. **(2)** Paragraph 2 explains how lasers destroy cells by removing water from them.

12. **(4)** Laser surgery can be used to destroy cancerous cells, but it does not reduce the risk of cancer. All of the other choices are specifically mentioned as advantages of laser surgery.

13. **(4)** The second paragraph states that dead cells that are not completely removed by the laser are sloughed off (cast off, discarded) from adjacent living tissue.

14. **(5)** The article does not state that lasers are the best tools, only that they are useful in certain situations. We have no way of knowing if other articles agree with this one. Choice (5), therefore, is opinion, not fact.

15. **(1)** According to the key, Albert was a normal male. Although hemophilia is a recessive trait, it is also sex-linked, according to the chart. A male would therefore need only one gene for hemophilia for the trait to appear. Since Albert was normal, it is evident that he had no gene for the disease.

16. **(5)** A male who has one gene for hemophilia has the disease. Since the chart shows that Louis IV was a normal male, we know he did not have any symptoms of the disease and was not a carrier of the gene for the disease.

17. **(3)** Beatrice was a carrier. Her marriage to a hemophiliac could be analyzed as follows:
    Key: XX—normal female; X*X*—female hemophiliac; XY— normal male; *X*Y—male hemophiliac.

Possible results: X*X* *X*Y
Female—50% X*X*-carrier
50% *XX*-hemophiliac
Male—50% *X*Y-hemophiliac
50% XY-normal

18. **(4)** Victoria Eugenia was a carrier. Her husband was normal. The results are as follows:
Female—50% X*X* carrier
50% XX normal
Male—50% *X*Y hemophiliac
50% XY normal

19. **(4)** Rupert's maternal grandfather was shown to have hemophilia (*X*Y). He transmitted the trait to his daughter, who was a carrier (X*X*). When this female married a normal male (XY), she transmitted the condition to her son, Rupert (*X*Y).

20. **(1)** Dust does not fit the definition; it is not condensation that falls to earth.

21. **(4)** The description of the death and destruction that followed the volcanic eruption indicates that "cataclysm" means disaster.

22. **(2)** Paragraph 1 states that the animals were killed by "the blizzard of abrasive dust."

23. **(3)** Of the choices given, only rhinoceroses are listed as victims of the dust storm, as stated in the first paragraph.

24. **(5)** The author states that he works for the University of Nebraska State Museum digging up skeletons. From this we can infer he is an archeologist.

25. **(3)** The graph shows the relative activity of enzyme x at various pH levels.

26. **(1)** At pH 4, relative rate of activity peaks at 60. However, the greatest increase in rate of activity is between pH 0 and 2 when activity increases from 0 to almost 50.

27. **(1)** Enzymes are used in digestion.

28. **(5)** Based on the graph and additional information, only choice (5) can be inferred. The graph indicates only that enzyme x reacts to pH differences; therefore it can be said that *some* enzymes react to differences in pH.

29. **(5)** The smaller clear area shows there are more bacteria growing. Thus, chemical X is a weaker antibiotic than penicillin.

30. **(3)** Jumping rope is not mentioned in the article as affecting biofeedback.

31. **(2)** The author generalizes that people use biofeedback without being aware of it. He cites taking your temperature or stepping on a scale as examples.

32. **(1)** As stated at the end of the first paragraph, biofeedback is used to help patients cope with pain.

33. **(5)** The first paragraph of the article states that biofeedback has been used to help some patients deal with pain. The other statements are based on opinion, not fact.

34. **(4)** From that material in the article, it can be inferred that those who actively cooperate in the process of biofeedback will achieve the greatest success.

35. **(3)** Biofeedback is built on the idea that people can affect the way their internal organs work. It can be inferred from the examples given that biofeedback can be used without machines or trained assistants.

36. **(3)** Surgery is the only treatment of the choices given that will "cure" a broken leg. Biofeedback might alleviate the pain, but it cannot cure the injury.

37. **(5)** A driver stopping at a red light is an example of a habit. All the other choices are incorrectly matched.

38. **(4)** According to the graph, Malthus stated that living things multiply in geometric ratio, while the food supply only increases in arithmetic ratio. In other words, population increases faster than food supply.

39. **(2)** According to the graph, the population is increasing faster than the food supply. Darwin stated that species tend to overproduce; that is, to produce more individuals than are needed for the species to survive.

40. **(3)** Since the slope of the population curve is increasing more than that of the food curve, starvation will probably occur, reducing the rate of population increase, and the slope of the curve, choice 3.

41. **(5)** All the choices listed have to be taken into consideration if the theory is to be affected.

42. **(2)** China and Africa have the greatest population density and least arable land, efficient agriculture, and transportation. They are already feeling the affects of the theory; China is trying to curb population and Africa has experienced severe famines.

43. **(2)** The only substance which can go from solid to gas is iodine. It is the only one in the solid phase.

44. **(2)** From the equation, $R \times T = D$, the question asks for the time ("how long") to complete the race. Thus the time must be found.
   Dividing both sides of the equation by R(rate) we get: $R \times T/R = D/R$ or, $T = D/R$. Substituting, we get $T = 400/8 = 50$ seconds.

45. **(3)** Substituting into the formula: $D = R \times T$, or solving for rate, $R = D/T$, we get $R = 20(\text{miles})/2.5(\text{hours}) = 8$ miles/hour.

46. **(3)** Atoms in the same groups (columns in the periodic table) behave similarly. K and Na are both in group 1.

47. **(1)** The first atom, hydrogen, has an atomic number 1 with 1 proton. Each larger atom gains 1 more proton as its atomic number increases.

48. **(2)** The relative rate of enzyme activity rises as the enzyme concentration increases until the concentration is about 7. At that point, the relative rate of enzyme activity levels off at about 35, and remains the same.

49. **(3)** The ratio is 1 to 10. A 100-pound man would need 1,000 pounds of fish.

50. **(4)** The insects get their energy by eating the organisms directly below them in the pyramid. That means the insects eat algae.

51. **(1)** The number of insects would increase because without the fish there would be nothing to kill them.

52. **(1)** The second paragraph states that ultraviolet rays are the type of radiation from the sun that leaves permanent damage.

53. **(4)** Sun damages the skin, according to the article.

54. **(5)** The last paragraph of the article states that melanoma is the most dangerous type of skin cancer.

55. **(2)** Those who freckle and sunburn easily are at the most risk from the sun.

56. **(3)** Any sunbathing, no matter when it is done, is dangerous, the article suggests.

57. **(4)** Exposure to the sun increases a person's chances of getting skin cancer.

58. **(5)** We can infer that few people believe they will be the ones to get skin cancer.

59. **(5)** ^{238}U has the longest half-life and therefore decays the slowest.

60. **(4)** Since the half-life for Fr is 27.5 seconds, then 110/27.5 = 4 half-lifes, therefore:

    1) 100 grams →50 grams
    2) 50 grams →25 grams
    3) 25 grams →12.5 grams
    4) 12.5 grams →6.25 grams

    (Note that each half-life causes $\frac{1}{2}$ of the sample to be used up.)

61. **(2)** The table shows that Co has a half-life of 5.3 years. At the end of 5.3 years $\frac{1}{2}$ of the original quantity of Co will remain. At the end of 10.6 years $\frac{1}{2}$ of $\frac{1}{2}$ or $\frac{1}{4}$ of the original quantity of Co will remain. If you started with 100 grams of Co, at the end of 5.3 years you would have 50 grams of Co. In another 5.3 years you would have 25 grams of Co. 25/100 = $\frac{1}{4}$.

62. **(2)** ^{42}K has a half-life of 12.4 hours. This is the shortest half-life of the choices offered and, therefore, ^{42}K decays most rapidly.

63. **(3)** Winds of 38–55 miles per hour are expected during a gale warning.

64. **(5)** Hurricane warnings require an immediate response to precautions, since such precautions are often issued with less than 24 hours' notice.

65. **(4)** According to the passage, coastal areas are especially dangerous during a hurricane, because of the danger of flood and high waves.

66. **(1)** Even though all the choices can be the result of a hurricane, the passage suggests that the most dangerous effect is flooding.

TEST 4. INTERPRETING LITERATURE AND THE ARTS

1. **(5)** Mencken characterizes the state of culture in the South as one of "almost dead silence" (line 5), of "complete sterility" (line 9), and lacking "all civilized aspirations" (line 10).

2. **(4)** The writing is like a billyclub. It hits the reader directly and hard. It is certainly not subtle, vague, or scholarly.

3. **(4)** All of the choices are southern states. However, in line 1, Mr. Mencken stated that Virginia was "the best."

4. **(3)** Douglass uses the present tense and indicates that slavery still exists. Slavery was declared void in the United States just after the Civil War.

5. **(3)** He made the boys into teachers, and they taught him to read.

6. **(4)** These paragraphs are about learning to read.

7. **(2)** Douglass states the reason in the first sentence of the third paragraph.

8. **(5)** The final clause refers to Douglass' own will.

9. **(2)** The whole tone of the passage indicates a strong and indomitable spirit, neither negative nor bitter.

10. **(1)** There are three clues that indicate the author here was explaining that we may all be looking for things we do not understand. These clues are: the inclusion of the word "God," indicating a search for meaning; setting the action on top of the highest mountain in Africa, to be closer to God perhaps; and the mystery of the dead leopard.

11. **(2)** Since the Masai are naming the western summit, they have to be a people, choice (1) or (2). Since the language they speak is clearly not English, we can eliminate (1). Therefore, the Masai must be an African people.

12. **(1)** There is no flowery and poetic wordy language here, just a direct statement of what the author is describing. Therefore, the best answer is (1).

13. **(5)** Since "no one has explained what the leopard was seeking," the answer remains a mystery, choice (5).

14. **(1)** Lincoln is speaking of those who died in battle, the soldiers.

15. **(1)** He was using a literary device to reinforce his point, that the soldiers' deaths will result in the birth of "a new freedom." The literary device was the repeated use of the word "people," for "democracy" literally means "rule of the people."

16. **(4)** The reference to the dead tells us this was delivered in a cemetery.

17. **(5)** The tone is impassioned, full of power and conviction. The ringing phrases "this nation under God" and "a new birth of freedom" tell us this.

18. **(1)** The mother said that her life ". . . ain't been no crystal stair." This meant that she had a difficult life.

19. **(3)** The mother's advice was to keep on going and overcome your problems.

20. **(2)** These are all potential problems in a staircase. They are used symbolically here, to represent problems in life.

21. **(3)** The mother says, "don't turn back," "don't you fall," and "I'se still climbin'," which sets an example of determination for the son.

22. **(1)** (See the answer to the preceding question.) A determined person would work at a project until it was completed.

23. **(2)** The author states, "then he went to the ground." Choice (2) explains this.

24. **(5)** George was an inexperienced cowboy, "He was not warmly clad." Experienced cowboys know to wear warm clothes in March in case a blizzard develops.

25. **(4)** The author says, "Yet in the imagination of those who know, there is a marker there. . . ." The grave marker existed only in their imagination.

26. **(1)** The tone is best described as "respectful" because the reader respects George for staying with the herd, the greatest test of a cowboy.

27. **(4)** As stated in the story, "McAvoy saw how cold George was" and suggested that he go back to the wagon to cover up.

28. **(3)** He stayed with the herd.

29. **(5)** The narrator sees all characters in the story. He describes the clothing of the two main characters. Don't confuse the narrator with Parsons, a character in the story.

30. **(2)** Markwardt has lied to himself and to others about the accident in C shop and thereby has handicapped himself from improving his situation.

31. **(1)** From this statement, the reader can infer that Markwardt told the C shop story often to obtain a few dollars from sympathetic listeners.

32. **(2)** The characters speak differently. Parsons uses the sentence structure and vocabulary associated with the upper middle class, while Markwardt uses the slang expressions typical of the lower class.

33. **(5)** The first ten lines form an organized unit which is set apart from the following lines. This is an example of a stanza.

34. **(4)** In stanza two, the highwayman is described as wearing lace, a red velvet coat, doeskin pants, and high boots. This is resplendent attire.

35. **(2)** The last line of the fourth stanza refers to the highwayman as a "robber."

36. **(3)** The fourth stanza reveals that Tim also loved the landlord's daughter and states that his eyes "were hollows of madness . . ."

37. **(5)** Liza is indicating her displeasure at the way Professor Higgins treats her. She insists on the formality of Miss Dolittle to put distance between them.

38. **(1)** Higgins refers to creating this thing out of "squashed cabbage leaves." This is a reference to Liza's background as a poor flower girl.

39. **(2)** The gutter is often associated with a fall from income, grace, or manners. Higgins believes the Liza will regress to her former ill-mannered ways without his help and guidance.

40. **(1)** Eliza has climbed the social ladder only through Higgins' help. She would welcome free higher education to give more people a chance to move up in the world.

41. **(5)** Anna Sokolow is considered to be at the forefront of modern dance because "She has demonstrated the necessity for the modern artist to renew herself—to reject past rules, even her own. . . ." (See lines *27–28.*)

42. **(2)** Sokolow's recurring themes are loneliness and alienation. (See line *47.*)

43. **(4)** Anna Sokolow has a "deep feeling for her Jewish heritage" and has made political works. She also toured the Soviet Union.

44. **(4)** She has continued "to find the language of movement" for herself (fourth paragraph), expressing her political views in modern terms.

45. **(2)** The last sentence of the second paragraph tells us that even at seventy-six, Anna Sokolow "still modestly pursues the truth."

TEST 5. MATHEMATICS

1. **(5)** Method I: .375 = $\frac{375}{1000}$. Then simplify this to $\frac{3}{8}$. Method II: .375 is smaller than .500 or $\frac{1}{2}$. Answer choices 1–4 are all greater than $\frac{1}{2}$. Choice 5 is the only possible answer.

2. **(2)** Add the time difference (5 hours) to the starting time:

   8:30 p.m. EST + 5 hours = 1:30 a.m. GMT
   1:30 a.m. to 8:15 a.m. = 6 hours 45 minutes

3. **(5)** Find the formula for area of a circle on the formula page. Using $A = \pi r^2$, solve for A:

   $A = 3.14 \times (2)^2$
   $A = 3.14 \times 4$
   A = More than 12 square feet

4. **(3)** Substitute 4 for x in each equation until you find one that is true:

(1) $(4)^2 + 4 = 16 + 4 \neq 12$
(2) $4\,(4) - 1 = 16 - 1 \neq 7$
(3) $2(4) - 3 = 8 - 3 = 5$ (This is the correct answer.)

5. **(3)** Change all times to minutes, then use the mean formula from the formula page:

2 hr 10 min = 120 + 10 = 130 min
2 hr 13 min = 120 + 13 = 133 min
1 hr 55 min = 60 + 55 = 115 min

$$\frac{130 + 133 + 115}{3} = \frac{378}{3} = 126$$

Divide by 60 to reconvert to hours:
$126 \div 60 = 2$ hr 6 min

An alternative and sometimes easier method to find an average:

2 hours is an approximation of the average, found by guessing.

value	*differences from 2 hours*
2 hr 10 min	+10
2 hr 13 min	+13
1 hr 55 min	−5

Find the sum of the differences, 18, and divide by number of values. $18 \div 3 = 6$, so add 6 to your guess; 2 hr + 6 min = *2 hr 6 min,* the average. This method avoids having to find the sum and dividing into all the values.

6. **(5)** To find out how much faster Runner #2 must run, we need to know the time of the winner. Without this, there is insufficient information to solve the problem.

7. **(4)** Organize your work carefully.

Hourly wage × Hours Worked = Total Income
($3.65) (4 + 3 + 5 + 4 + 4) = Total Income
The actual numerical solution is not asked for; just the equation you would use to solve the problem, which is choice 4.

8. **(3)** Draw the shed and write in the dimensions of each outside wall.

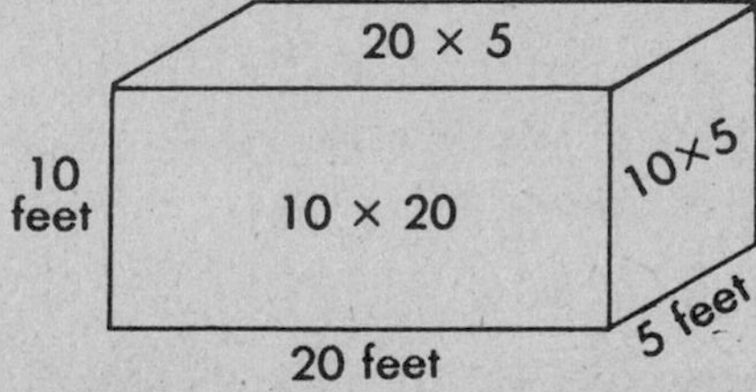

Using the formula for the area of a rectangle, find the area of each outside surface. Remember that the shed has 5 outside surfaces:

2 sides of 10×20
2 sides of 10×5
1 roof of 20×5

$$\text{Total area} = 2\,(10 \times 20) + 2\,(10 \times 5) + (20 \times 5)$$
$$= 400 + 100 + 100 = 600 \text{ square feet}$$

At 200 square feet per gallon, they need $\frac{600}{200} = 3$ gallons of paint.

9. **(4)** Use the formula for volume of a rectangular container: Volume(v) = $1 \times w \times h$, or $V = 20 \times 10 \times 5 = 1000$.

10. **(3)** Write the equation for the information given:

2 coins of value $x = 2x$
3 coins of value $y = 3y$
$2x + 3y = 50$ cents
Therefore $2x = 50 - 3y$

11. **(3)** Mrs. Jones received $4.50 × 4 = $18.00 each year for each share, since $4.50 was paid quarterly. (Quarterly means 4 times a year.) $18.00 represents $\frac{18}{180}$ or 10% of her investment.

12. **(4)** $180/share × 100 shares = $18,000.

13. **(5)** Know the squares of the numbers from 1–10. Here, 8 squared is 64. Reversing this, the square root of 64 is 8. And the square root of .64 is .8.

14. **(5)** The information given is all in measures of length (meters, inches, yards). The problem then asks for an answer in terms of weight (grams). There is not enough information given to solve the problem.

15. **(2)** If 2 pints of milk cost $.80, then 1 pint will cost $.40.

1 gallon = 4 quarts = 8 pints
.40 × 8 = $3.20
The saving is $3.20 − 3.00 = $0.20

16. **(1)** Angle ABC and Angle DBC (135°) are supplementary angles. That means the sum of these two angles is 180°.

Angle ABC + $135^\circ = 180^\circ$
Angle ABC = $180^\circ - 135^\circ = 45^\circ$

17. **(4)** 10 a.m. to 2:10 p.m. = 4 hr 10 min. Speed is measured in miles/hour. Use the given information to find this fraction:

    250 miles/4 hr 10 min

    4 hr 10 min = $4\frac{10}{60} = 4\frac{1}{6}$ hr

    $250/(4\frac{1}{6}) = 250 \div \frac{25}{6} = 250 \times \frac{6}{25} = 60$ mph

18. **(1)** First find the total number of hours the operator worked: From 8 a.m. to 4 p.m. = 8 hours. Subtract 1 hour for lunch plus two 15-minute breaks for a total of 1 hr + $\frac{1}{2}$ hr = $1\frac{1}{2}$ hr. Therefore the operator worked $8 - 1\frac{1}{2}$ or $6\frac{1}{2}$ hours. At a rate of 312 plates/hour, he produced $312 \times 6\frac{1}{2}$ or 2028 plates.

19. **(3)** Substitute x = 3y into the first equation:

    $x - 12 = y$
    $3y - 12 = y$

    Bring the y terms to the left and the numerical term to the right:

    $2y = 12$

    Divide both sides by 2:

    $y = 6$

20. **(4)** Substitute 5 for x in the quadratic equation:

    $3(5^2) - 4(5) + 3 =$
    $3(25) - 20 + 3 =$
    $75 - 20 + 3 = 58$

21. **(4)** Both length and width are the same for the dominos and the box. Can you see how the dominos will stack inside the box? Determine how many .25 inch-high dominos can fit into 1 foot:

    1 foot = 12 inches

    $12 \div .25 = 48$

22. **(3)** First calculate the amount spent on known items:

    28+25+15+17=85%. Subtract this figure from 100% to find out how much was saved: 100 − 85 = 15%. Multiply by total income, \$3600: .15 × 3600 = \$540 in 1 month, and 12 × 540 = \$6480 in 1 year.

23. **(4)** Since 28% is spent on rent, the cost of rent each month is .28 × \$3600 = \$1008.

24. **(5)** Find the mean number of boys and the mean number of girls using the formula for the mean from the formula page:

mean (boys) = (2+0+1+2+5)/5=10/5=2
mean (girls) = (3+0+2+1+4)/5=10/5=2

The average number of boys and girls is the same.

25. **(2)** From the formula page, the circumference of Dad's car wheel is $C = \pi d = \pi \times 16$. If Tim's tricycle wheel is $\frac{1}{4}$ of this, Tim's wheel is $\frac{1}{4}$ of 16π or 4π. Since $2 \times r = d$, we can write about Tim's bike: $C = \pi \times (2 \times r) = 4\pi$. Dividing both sides by 2 and then by π.

$$\frac{\not{2} \times \pi \times r}{\not{2}} = \frac{\overset{2}{\not{4}} \times \pi}{\not{2}}$$

$$\pi \times r = 2 \times \pi$$

$$r = 2$$

26. **(3)** x/(−3) + 1 = 12
Subtract 1 from each side: x/(−3) = 11
Multiply each side by −3: x = −33

27. **(5)** The triangle is an equilateral triangle since all angles are equal. Therefore, all sides are equal to 12 inches, and the perimeter is the sum of the sides: 12 + 12 + 12 = 36 inches.

28. **(5)** These trees and their shadows form similar triangles. Their corresponding sides and angles are proportional, so:

Big Tree Parts are proportional to the Small Tree Parts.

$$\frac{\text{height of big tree}}{\text{length of shadow}} = \frac{\text{height of small tree}}{\text{length of shadow}}$$

$$\frac{50}{20} = \frac{h}{15}$$

$$20h = 750$$

$$h = 37.5$$

Solving the proportion, we find that h = 37.5 feet.

29. **(5)** The time needed to boil water depends on several factors, namely, initial temperature, total amount of water, and the amount of heat supplied. Insufficient data is given, so the problem cannot be solved.

30. **(5)** If the number of items sold were 50 (on first day) and x (on the second day), the equation set-up is, $.50 \times (50 + x) = 25 + .50x$. But since x is unknown, no numerical value can be determined; insufficient data is given, choice (5).

31. **(5)** Add like terms of the left. Remember to add signed numbers correctly.

$$3x + 3y + x + 4y - 4x = 5$$
$$3x + x - 4x + 3y + 4y = 5$$
$$7y = 5$$

32. **(1)** According to the formula page, the formula for area of a square is $A = s^2$, where A = area and s = side. The side here is 8. The area of a rectangle, according to the formula, is A = lw, where A = area, l = length, and w = width. We know the length, 10, but not the width. If the areas of the two figures are the same, set them up as an equation
s^2 (square) = lw (rectangle)
$$8^2 = 10w$$
$$64 = 10w$$
$$64/10 = w$$
$$6.4 = w$$

33. **(2)** Each soldier needs 9 days' food rations (including the extra day). 36 ounces/day × 9 days is 324 ounces for each soldier. The group is 5 soldiers, therefore 324 ounces/soldier × 5 soldiers = 1620 ounces for the group. But the choices require pounds since there are 16 ounces/pound, 1620/16 = 100 lbs (approximately).

34. **(4)** In 1 hour the clocks rotates one revolution or 360°. One more half hour adds $\frac{1}{2}$ of a revolution or $\frac{360°}{2} = 180°$. Adding the two results, we get 360° + 180° = 540°.

35. **(4)** The mode is the highest frequency observation. Here it is 8 cars, which appeared twice, in hour 3 and hour 5.

36. **(5)** Using the mean formula from the formula page we find,

mean = sum of observations/# hours
mean = 5 + 4 + 8 + 0 + 8/5
mean = 25/5 = 5 red cars/hour

37. **(5)** Use the mean formula. However, the number in the 6th hour is unknown. Let R = number seen in 6th hour.

Mean = (sum of observations in 5 hours) + R/6 = 7

From question 36, we know that the sum of observations in 5 hours = 25

Therefore, 25 + R/6 = 7
Multiply both sides of equation by 6: 25 + R = 42
Subtract 25 from each side of equation: R = 17

38. **(1)** Divide both sides of the equation by 5:

$$\frac{5x + 5y + 5z}{5} = \frac{5}{5}$$

$$x + y + z = 1$$

39. **(3)** The percentage of change is equal to the difference divided by the Feb. 1986 figure, or

$$(410\text{-}245)/245 \times 100 =$$
$$165/245 \times 100 = 67\%.$$

40. **(4)** Oct. 30: $350 (see June 1986)
Nov. 2: $390 (see Nov. 1986)

Total $740

(Notice that the appropriate rates sometimes are not listed in a printed month, but in an overlapping month.)

41. **(3)** The sum of the angles of a triangle = 180°. Therefore, if two angles of a triangle are known, you can find the third angle:

DBA = 180° − 128° = 52°
ADB + DBA = 60° + 52° = 112°
DBA = 180° − 112° = 68°

42. **(5)** From the formula page we know that the area of a square = b^2. Therefore, the area of the room = 120 × 120 = 144,000 square inches. However, the problem asks for square feet.

144 square inches = 1 square foot
144,000/144 = 100 square feet

If you convert 120 inches to 10 feet at the start (120/12 = 10),

A = 10 × 10 = 100 square feet

43. **(2)** Change all fractions to fractions having the same denominator. Add the whole numbers, add the fractions, and combine the two sums:

$$10\tfrac{2}{3} = 10\tfrac{8}{12}$$
$$5\tfrac{3}{4} = 5\tfrac{9}{12}$$
$$2\tfrac{1}{6} = 2\tfrac{2}{12}$$

$$17\tfrac{19}{12} = 17 + 1\tfrac{7}{12} = 18\tfrac{7}{12}$$

44. **(5)** The smaller circumference is $\pi d = 2\pi$ ft.

The larger circumference is $5 \times 2\pi = 10\pi = \pi d$

Dividing both sides by π, $d = 10$; radius $= 10/2 = 5$.

45. **(4)** 90. Both triangles are similar, and their lengths are in proportion.

$$\frac{15 \text{ (smaller triangle)}}{45 \text{ (smaller triangle)}} = \frac{30 \text{ (larger triangle)}}{X \text{ (larger triangle)}}$$

Solve:

$$15X = 30 \times 45$$
$$15X = 1350$$
$$X = 90$$

46. **(4)** $\sqrt{1125}$. The triangle containing C and D is a right triangle. Using the pythagorean relationship, $c^2 = a^2 + b^2$, where c in the formula is the length CD. Substituting,

$C^2 = 15^2 + 30^2$, or
$C^2 = 225 + 900$,
$C^2 = 1125$, and taking the square root,
$C = \sqrt{1125}$

47. **(4)** At 80% of maximum speed the machine produces $3500 \times .8 = 2800$ parts per hour. In 40 hours it will produce $2800 \times 40 = 112{,}000$ parts

48. **(2)** A ratio can be made: $88/60 = 100/s$ (where s is the speed of sound in miles per hour).

Solve for s:

$$88s = 60 \times 100$$
$$88s = 66{,}000$$
$$s = 66{,}000/88 = 750 \text{ miles per hour}$$

49. **(2)** The figure formed by the wall, the ladder, and the ground is a right triangle. Use the Pythagorean theorem to find the length of the longer side (which is the ladder):

$$c^2 = a^2 + b^2$$
$$c^2 = 6^2 + 8^2$$
$$c^2 = 36 + 64 = 100$$
$$c = \sqrt{100} = 10$$

A quicker way to do this problem is to remember that there are two special right triangles with the ratios 3-4-5 and 5-12-13. Doubling the sides of the 3-4-5 right triangle results in a 6-8-10 triangle. Therefore, the ladder must be 10 feet long.

50. **(1)** Solve the equation using the following steps:

Add like terms on the left:

$$14S - 3S = 44$$
$$11S = 44$$

Divide both sides of the equation by the coefficient of S, or 11:

$$S = 44/11$$
$$S = \$4$$

51. **(5)** There are 6 sides to any rectangular container. If the length is L, the width is W and the height is H, then the total area is 2 (W × L) + 2 (L × H) + 2 (W × H) or 2WL + 2LH + 2WH.

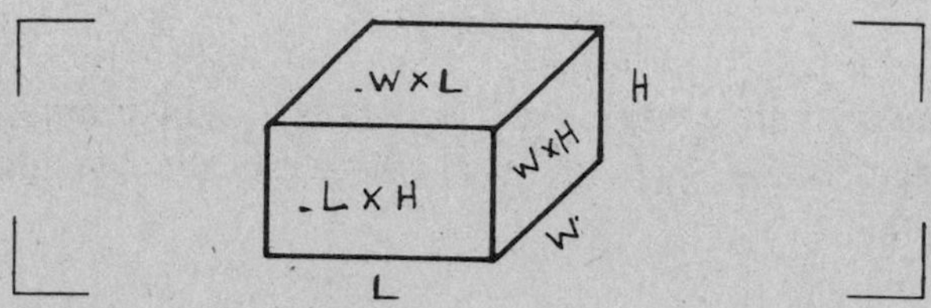

52. **(4)** The volume of the container is found by using the formula for volume of a rectangular container on the formula page:

$$V = 1 \times w \times h$$
$$= 6 \times 6 \times 1$$
$$= 36 \text{ cubic inches}$$

53. **(4)** The value of the dollar decreased from 100% of value (or $1.00) in 1967 to 50% of value (or 50 cents) in 1978. This can be found by locating the 50% mark on the right-hand scale and then finding the bar that reaches this mark. Reading from the scale at the bottom of the graph, you can see that the correct bar is the one for 1978.

54. **(2)** The value of $100 (1967) has decreased each year. $100 is worth only $45 in 1979.

55. **(2)** Extend the trend of the graph shown. The steps go downward and each height is approximately $4 or $5. The nearest choice is (2), $40 since $45 – $5 is $40.

56. **(4)** The average can be found by dividing the total decrease by the number of steps. (100 – 45)/12 = 4.2 which is closest to 4.

Part II

Writing Skills Review

SPELLING

GED writing questions test your knowledge of common spelling rules and your ability to spell frequently used, but often misspelled, words. You can raise your spelling score by learning the nine rules that follow and by working your way systematically through the list of commonly misspelled words.

Rule 1

If a one-syllable word ends with a short vowel and one consonant,

- DOUBLE THE FINAL CONSONANT before adding a suffix that begins with a vowel.
- DO NOT DOUBLE THE FINAL CONSONANT before adding a suffix that begins with a consonant, *or* if the word has two vowels before the consonant or ends in two consonants.

DOUBLE THE FINAL CONSONANT

-er	-er, -est	-y	-en	-ing	-ed
blotter	biggest	baggy	bidden	budding	rubbed
chopper	dimmer	blurry	bitten	quitting	scarred
clipper	fattest	funny	fatten	clipping	skipped
fitter	flatter	furry	flatten	dropping	stabbed
hopper	gladdest	muddy	gladden	fanning	stepped
plotter	grimmer	sloppy	hidden	fretting	stopped
quitter	hottest	starry	madden	grinning	tanned
shipper	madder	stubby	sadden	gripping	nodded
shopper	reddest	sunny	trodden	hopping	plotted

DO NOT DOUBLE THE FINAL CONSONANT

-ing, -ed, -er	-ly	-ness	-ful	-y
acting	badly	baseness	boastful	dirty
burned	dimly	bigness	baleful	dusky
cooker	gladly	coldness	doleful	fishy
climber	madly	dimness	fitful	frosty
coasting	manly	fatness	fretful	leafy
farmer	nearly	grimness	masterful	misty
feared	sadly	sadness	sinful	rainy
feasting	thinly	redness		soapy
quoted	trimly	wetness		weedy

Rule 2

If a word of more than one syllable ends with a short vowel and one consonant,

- DOUBLE THE FINAL CONSONANT before adding a suffix that begins with a vowel IF the accent is on the last syllable.
- DO NOT DOUBLE THE FINAL CONSONANT if the accent is not on the last syllable, or the suffix begins with a consonant.

DOUBLE THE FINAL CONSONANT

-ing, -ed	**-ence, -ent**	**-ance**	**-at**
befitting	abhorrence	acquittance	acquittal
befogged	concurrent	admittance	transmittal
committing	excellence	remittance	noncommittal
compelled	intermittent	transmittance	
controlling	occurrence		
disbarred	recurrent		
impelling			
incurred			
omitting	**-er**	**-en**	**-able**
permitted			
propelling	beginner	forbidden	controllable
regretted	propeller	forgotten	forgettable
submitting	transmitter		regrettable

DO NOT DOUBLE THE FINAL CONSONANT

ENDING IN *2* CONSONANTS	*2* VOWELS BEFORE THE FINAL CONSONANT	ACCENT NOT ON THE FINAL SYLLABLE	SUFFIX BEGINS WITH A CONSONANT
-ing, -ed	**-ing, -ed**	**-ing, -ed**	**-ment**
consenting	concealing	benefiting	allotment
converted	contained	blossomed	annulment
demanding	detaining	differed	commitment
diverted	disdained	gathered	deferment
requesting	refraining	limiting	equipment
subsisted	remounted	profited	interment
supplanting	restraining	quarreling	preferment
supported	retained	soliciting	
transcending	revealing	summoned	

Rule 3

If a word ends with a silent e,

- DROP THE E before adding a suffix that begins with a vowel.
- DO NOT DROP THE E before a suffix that begins with a consonant.

DROP THE SILENT E

-ing, -ed	-able	-ation	-ive
achieving	believable	admiration	abusive
balanced	debatable	continuation	appreciative
believing	desirable	declaration	creative
capsized	endurable	derivation	decorative
relieved	excitable	duplication	expensive
revolving	imaginable	exhalation	exclusive
telephoned	measurable	inclination	illustrative
trembling	observable	inhalation	intensive
trembled	pleasurable	quotation	repulsive

DO NOT DROP THE SILENT E

-ful	-ment	-ly	-ness
careful	achievement	accurately	completeness
disgraceful	amusement	affectionately	cuteness
distasteful	announcement	bravely	fineness
fateful	engagement	extremely	genuineness
hopeful	enlargement	genuinely	lameness
prideful	enslavement	immediately	lateness
tasteful	entanglement	intensely	likeness
vengeful	management	intimately	ripeness
wasteful	replacement	sincerely	wideness

EXCEPTIONS

acknowledgment	changeable	judgment	peaceable
acreage	chargeable	manageable	pronounceable
advantageous	duly	noticeable	replaceable
argument	dyeing	outrageous	serviceable
awful	exchanging		

Rule 4

To make a word plural,

- ADD -ES to words ending in s, x, z, ch, or sh.
- ADD -S to all other words.

ADD -S		ADD -ES	
advantages	croutons	annexes	fizzes
angles	distances	birches	hoaxes
beacons	effects	brushes	marshes
briquets	rings	caresses	witnesses
candles		coaches	

Rule 5

If a word ends with a y that has a vowel sound,

- CHANGE THE Y TO I before adding any suffix except one that begins with the letter i.
- DO NOT CHANGE THE Y if it is preceded by another vowel, or if the suffix begins with i.

CHANGE THE Y TO I

-er, -est, -ly, -ness	-ous	-ance, -ant	-able, -ful
craftier	ceremonious	alliance	beautiful
daintiest	harmonious	appliance	fanciful
healthier	industrious	compliant	justifiable
heavily	injurious	defiant	merciful
moldiness	luxurious	pliant	pitiable
moodiest	melodious	reliance	pliable
murkiness	mysterious		
steadily	studious		
sleepiness	victorious		

DO NOT CHANGE THE Y	EXCEPTIONS	
-ing	-ly, -ness	-ous
allying	dryly	beauteous
applying	dryness	bounteous
complying	shyly	duteous
defying	shyness	miscellaneous
fortifying	slyly	piteous
justifying	slyness	plenteous
pitying	spryly	
multiplying	wryly	
supplying		

Rule 6

Put i before e,
Except after c,
Or when sounded like a,
As in neighbor or weigh.

I BEFORE E	EXCEPT AFTER C	OR SOUNDS LIKE A	EXCEPTIONS
achieve	conceit	deign	ancient
believe	conceive	eight	conscience
fiend	ceiling	freight	deficient
fierce	deceit	inveigh	efficient
grief	deceive	neighbor	foreign
relieve	perceive	reign	glacier
reprieve	receipt	skein	heifer
retrieve	receive	vein	leisure
sieve		weigh	proficient
			weird

Rule 7

The suffix *-ful* never has two l's. When -ful is added to a word, the spelling of the base word does not change.

EXAMPLES

careful	disdainful	distasteful
forceful	grateful	hopeful
masterful	powerful	sorrowful

Rule 8

When the suffix *-ly* is added to a word, the spelling of the base word does not change.

EXAMPLES

coyly | quickly | frankly | swiftly | forcefully

EXCEPTIONS

When -ly is added to a word ending with -le, the e is replaced by a y.

forcibly
indelibly
despicably
probably
illegibly
suitably

When the base word ends with a y following a consonant, the y is changed to i before -ly.

busily
luckily
daintily
merrily
heavily
sleepily

Rule 9

When a syllable ends in a long vowel sound, that sound is made by the vowel alone: OPEN SYLLABLE.

A long vowel sound occurring in a one-syllable word, or in a syllable that ends with a consonant, is usually spelled by a vowel team: CLOSED SYLLABLE.

OPEN SYLLABLE	CLOSED SYLLABLE
recent	sublime
premium	infantile
sequence	crayon
stationary	attainment
fatality	cavalcade
abrasion	genteel
motivate	intercede
custodian	sincere
component	ridicule
proprietor	vestibule
microbe	clapboard
cyclone	disclose
cucumber	telescope
humane	growth

320 FREQUENTLY MISSPELLED WORDS

A poor speller can, in almost every case, become an excellent speller with perseverance and practice. The first step in spelling improvement is to find out which words are troublesome for you. The list that follows contains some of the most frequently misspelled words. Ask a friend to dictate this list to you. Write each word as it is read to you, then compare what you have written with the printed list. Place an X next to each word that you spelled incorrectly (and next to each word that you spelled correctly but were not sure of). For every word you misspelled:

1. LOOK at the word carefully.
2. PRONOUNCE each syllable clearly.
3. PICTURE the word in your mind.
4. WRITE the word correctly at least three times.

Test yourself again—and again—until you have mastered this entire list.

A

a lot
ability
absence
absent
across
abundance
accept
acceptable
accident
accidental
accommodate
accompanied
accomplish
accumulation
accurately
accuse
accustomed
ache
achieve
achievement
acknowledge
acknowledgment
acquaintance
acquainted
acquire
across
address
addressed
adequate
advantageous
advantage
advertise
advertisement

advice
advisable
advise
advisor
aerial
affect
affectionate
again
against
aggravate
aggressive
agree
aisle
all right
almost
already
although
altogether
always
amateur
American
among
amount
analysis
analyze
ancestor
angel
angle
annual
another
answer
antarctic
anticipate

antiseptic
anxious
apologize
apparatus
apparent
apparently
appear
appearance
appetite
application
apply
appreciate
appreciation
approach
appropriate
approval
approve
approximate
arctic
argue
arguing
argument
arouse

arrange
arrangement
article
artificial
ascend
asparagus
assistance
assistant
associate
association
attempt
attendance
attention
audience
August
author
automobile
autumn
auxiliary
available
avenue
awful
awkward

B

bachelor
balance
balloon
bankruptcy
bargain
barren
basic
basically
beautiful

because
become
before
beggar
beginning
begun
being
believe
benefit

benefited
between
bewilder
bicycle
board
bored
borrow
bottle
bottom
boundary
brake
breadth
breath
breathe
brilliant
building
bulletin
bureau
burial
buried
bury
bushes
business

C

cabinet
cafeteria
caffeine
calculator
calendar
campaign
capital
capitol
captain
career
careful
careless
carriage
carrying
category
ceiling
cemetery
cereal
certain
changeable
characteristic
charity
chief
chimney
choose
chose
cigarette
circumstance
congratulate
citizen
clothes
clothing
coarse
coffee
collect
college
column
comedy
comfortable
commitment
committed
committee
communicate
company
comparative
compel
competent
competition
competitor
compliment
conceal
conceit
conceivable
conceive
concentration
conception
condition
conference
confident
conquer
conscience
conscientious
conscious
consequence
consequently
considerable
consistency
consistent
consul
continual
continuous
controlled
controversy
convenience
convenient
conversation
corporal
corroborate
council
councilor
counsel
counselor
courage
courageous
course
courteous
courtesy
criticism
criticize
crucial
crystal
curiosity
curtain
customer
cylinder

D

daily
dairy
daughter
daybreak
dearth
death
deceit
deceive
December
deception
decide
decision
decisive
deed
definite
delicious
demur
dependent
deposit
derelict
descend
descent
descendant
describe
description
desert
desirable
despair
desperate
dessert
destruction
determine
develop
development
device
diary
dictator
dictatorship
died
difference
different
difficulty
dilapidated
dilemma
dinner
direction
disappear
disappoint
disappointment
disapproval
disapprove
disastrous
discipline
discover
discriminate
disease
dismal
dissatisfied
dissection
dissipate
distance
distinction
division
doctor
dollar
doubt
dozen
dying

E

earnest
easy
ecstasy
ecstatic
education
effect
efficiency
efficient
eight
either
eligibility
eligible
eliminate
embarrass

embarrassment
emergency
eminent
emphasis
emphasize
enclosure
encouraging
endeavor
engineer
English
enormous
enough
entrance
envelope
environment
equipment
equipped
especially
essential
evening
evident
exaggerate
exaggeration
examine
exceed
excellent
except
exceptional
exercise
exhausted
exhaustion
exhibition
exhilaration
existence
exorbitant
expense
experience
experiment
explain
explanation
extraordinary
extension
extreme

F

facility
factory
familiar
fascinate
fascinating
fatigue
February
fiend
fierce
financial
financier
flourish
forcibly
forehead
foreign
foreword
forfeit
formal
former
fortunate
forward
fourteen
fourth
frequent
freight
Friday
friend
frightening
fundamental
furniture
further

G

gallon
garden
gardener
gaseous
general
genius
geography
ghost
glacier
glandular
gnash
government
governor
grain
grammar
grandeur
grateful
great
grievance
grievous
grocery
guarantee
guard
guess
guidance

H

half
hallelujah
hammer
handkerchief
happiness
harassed
healthy
heard
heathen
heavily
heavy
height
heretic
heroes
heroine
hideous
himself
hoarse
holiday
hopeless
horrify
hospital
humorous
hundredth
hurried
hurrying
hygiene
hymn
hypocrisy

I

ignorance
imaginary
imbecile
imitation
immediately
immigrant
incidental
increase
incumbent
independence
independent
indispensable
inevitable
influence
influential
initiate
innocence
inoculate
inquiry
insistent
instantaneous
instead
instinct
integrity
intellectual
intelligence
intercede
interest
interfere
interference
interpreted
interruption
introduce
invitation
irrelevant
irresistible
irritable
island
its
it's
itself

J

January
jealous
jeopardy
jewelry
journal
judgment
judicial
justice
justification

K

kernel
kiln
kilometer
kilowatt
kindergarten
kitchen

knee
knew
knock
knot
know
knowledge

L

labor
laboratory
lacquer
laid
language
later
latter
laugh
legible
leisure
length
lesson
library
license
lieutenant
light

lightening
lightning
likelihood
likely
literal
literature
livelihood
loaf
loneliness
loose
lose
losing
lovable
loyal
loyalty

M

magazine
maintenance
maneuver
marriage
married
marry
match
material
materialize
mathematics
measure
medicine
memoir
million
miniature
minimum
miracle

miscellaneous
mischief
mischievous
misspell
misspelled
mistake
momentous
monkey
monotonous
moral
morale
mortgage
mountain
mournful
muscle
mysterious
mystery

N

narrative
naturally
necessary
needle

negligence
negligible
neighbor
neither

newspaper
newsstand
nickel

niece
ninth
noticeable

O

o'clock
oasis
obedient
obligatory
obsolescence
obstacle
occasion
occasional
occur
occurred
occurrence
ocean
offer
official
often
omission
omit

omitted
once
operate
opinion
opportune
opportunity
optimist
ordinance
origin
original
ornamental
oscillate
ought
ounce
outrageous
overcoat

P

paid
pamphlet
panicky
parallel
parallelism
particular
partner
pastime
patience
peace
peaceable
pear
peculiar
pencil
people
perceive
perception
perfect
perform
performance
perhaps
period
permanence
permanent
perpendicular
perseverance
persevere
persistent

persuade
personality
personal
personnel
persuade
persuasion
pertain
physician
picture
piece
plain
playwright
pleasant
please
pleasure
pocket
poison
policeman
political
population
portrayal
positive
possess
possession
possessive
possible
post office
potatoes

practical
prairie
precede
preceding
precise
predictable
prefer
preference
perferential
preferred
prejudice
preparation
prepare
prescription
presence
president
prevalent
primitive
principal
principle

privilege
probably
procedure
proceed
produce
professional
professor
profitable
prominent
promise
pronounce
pronunciation
propaganda
propellor
prophecy
prophet
prospect
psychology
pursue
pursuit

Q

quality
quantity
quarreling
quart
quarter

quiet
quintuple
quite
quotient

R

raise
realistic
realize
reason
rebellion
recede
receipt
receive
recipe
recognize
recommend
recuperate
reference
referred
rehearsal
reign
relevant
relieve
religious
remedy
renovate

repeat
repetition
repetitious
representative
requirements
resemblance
reservoir
resistance
resources
respectability
responsibility
restaurant
rhythm
rhythmical
ridiculous
right
role
roll
roommate
routine

S

sandwich
Saturday
scarcely
scene
scenery
schedule
science
scientific
scissors
season
secretary
seize
seizure
seminar
sense
separate
service
several
severely
shepherd
sheriff
shining
shoulder
shriek
siege
sight
signal
significance
significant
similar
similarity
sincerely
site
soldier
solemn
sophomore
soul

source
souvenir
special
specified
specimen
speech
stationary
stationery
statue
statute
stockings
stomach
straight
strength
strenuous
stretch
striking
studying
substantial
succeed
successful
sudden
sufficient
superintendent
suppress
surely
surgical
surprise
suspense
sweat
sweet
syllable
symmetrical
sympathy
sympathetic
synonym

T

technical
telegram
telephone
temperament
temperature
tenant
tendency
tenement
therefore
thorough
through
title

together
tomorrow
tongue
toward
tragedy
transferred
transient
treasury
tremendous
tries
truculent
truly

Tuesday
twelfth
twelve
typical
tyranny

U

umbrella
undoubtedly
unique
United States
university
unnecessary
unusual
usage
useful
usual

V

vacuum
valley
valuable
variety
vegetable
veil
vein
vengeance
versatile
vicinity
vicious
view
village
villain
visitor
voice
volume

W

waist
weak
wear
weather
Wednesday
week
weigh
weight
weird
wield
whether
which
while
whole
wholesome
wholly
whose
wretched
wouldn't
written

X-Y-Z

yacht
yield
zombie

PUNCTUATION AND CAPITALIZATION

Without punctuation, writing would be merely a jumble of words, difficult if not impossible to understand and open to all sorts of misinterpretation. Punctuation and capitalization are like signs along an unfamiliar road. They indicate when to stop, when to go, and when to slow down for a detour or a curve. You can master the mechanics of punctuation and capitalization by learning the simple rules that follow.

PUNCTUATION RULES

USE AN APOSTROPHE (')

1. *To indicate possession*
   Bob's hat; Burns' poems; Jones's houses
   Note: Use *apostrophe only* (without the s) for certain words that end in s:
   a. When *s* or *z* sound comes before the final *s*
      Moses' journey
      Cassius' plan
   b. after a plural noun
      girls' shoes
      horses' reins

   Where to place the apostrophe
   a. The apostrophe means *belonging to everything to the* left *of the apostrophe.*
   EXAMPLE:
   These (ladie's, ladies') blouses are on sale.
   ladie's means *belonging to ladie* (no such word)
   ladies' means *belonging to ladies* (this is correct)
   EXAMPLE:
   These (childrens', children's) coats are a good buy.
   childrens' means *belonging to childrens* (no such word)
   children's means *belonging to children* (this is correct)
   b. When two or more names comprise one firm, possession is indicated in the last name.
   EXAMPLES:
   Lansdale, Jackson and Roosevelt's law firm.
   Sacks and Company's sale.
   c. In a compound noun, separated by hyphens, the apostrophe belongs in the last syllable.
   EXAMPLE:
   father-in-law's
   Note: The *plurals* of compound nouns are formed by adding the s (no apostrophe, of course) to the *first* syllable: I have three *brothers-in-law.*

2. *For plurals of letters and figures*
   three d's; five 6's

3. *To show that a letter has been left out*
   let's (for let us)
   Note A: ours, yours, his, hers, its, theirs, and whose—all are possessive but have no apostrophe.
   Note B: The apostrophe is omitted occasionally in titles: Teachers College, Actors Equity Association.

USE A COLON (:)

1. *After such expressions as "the following," "as follows," and their equivalents*
   The sciences studied in high schools are as follows: biology, chemistry, and physics.

2. *After the salutation in a business letter*
   Gentlemen:
   Dear Mr. Jones:
   Note: A comma (see below) is used after the salutation in a friendly letter:
   Dear Ted,
   The semicolon is *never* used in a salutation.

3. *Between the figures for hours and minutes when expressing time*
   We set the alarm for 6:15, but we did not get up until 9:30.

USE A COMMA (,)

1. *To set off the name of the person being addressed*
   Mr. Adams, has the report come in yet?
   Are you sure, Betty, that this is the street?

2. *To set off appositives*—words that follow a noun or pronoun and mean the same as the noun or pronoun.
   Mr. Burke, our lawyer, gave us some good advice.

3. *To set off parenthetical expressions*—words that interrupt the flow of the sentence, such as *however, though, for instance, by the way.* If you would pause before and after saying such expressions, then they should be set off by commas.
   We could not, however, get him to agree.
   This book, I believe, is the best of its kind.

4. *After the closing of a letter*
   Sincerely,
   Truly yours,

5. *In dates and addresses*
   November 11, 1918
   Cleveland, Ohio

6. *Between the items in a series*
   We had soup, salad, ice cream, and milk for lunch.
   Note: You may omit the comma before the "and" in a series.

7. *After a phrase or clause at the beginning of a sentence (if the phrase or clause is long)*
   As I ran from the house on my way to work, my mother called me back to hand me my umbrella.

8. *To separate clauses in a long sentence*
   We travelled miles out of our way to visit Aunt Mary, but she was not at home when we arrived.

9. *To separate two words or figures that might otherwise be misunderstood.*
   Two weeks before, Jim had applied for a part-time job.
   On January 10, 23 workers were absent.

10. *Before a direct quotation*
    Mr. Arnold blurted out, "This is a fine mess!"

11. *To set off nonessential phrases and clauses—phrases or clauses that do not restrict the meaning of the thought which is modified*
    Air travel, *which may or may not be safe,* is an essential part of our way of life. (Nonessential clause—needs commas)
    Travel *which is on the ground* is safer than air travel. (Essential clause—no commas)

12. *To set off adjectives that follow the nouns they modify*
    The dog, frightened and hungry, ran home.

13. *To set off contrasting expressions that start with* not *or* though
    The girls, not the boys, started the fight.
    That car, though too expensive for me, is a very good buy.

14. *To set off introductory expressions such as* yes, no, well, why
    No, I don't like asparagus.
    Well, have you decided which one to buy?

USE A DASH (—)

1. *To break up a thought*
   There are five—remember I said five—good reasons to refuse their demands.

2. *Instead of parentheses*
   A beautiful horse—Black Beauty is its name—is the hero of the book.

USE AN EXCLAMATION MARK (!)

1. *After an expression of strong feeling*
   Ouch! I hurt my thumb.

USE A HYPHEN (-)

1. *To divide a word*
   mother-in-law
   Note: When written out, numbers from twenty-one through ninety-nine are hyphenated.

USE PARENTHESES ( )

1. *To set off that part of the sentence that is not absolutely necessary to the completeness of the sentence*
   I was about to remark (this may be repetition) that we must arrive there early.

2. *To enclose figures, letters, signs and dates in a sentence*
   Shakespeare (1564-1616) was a great dramatist.

The four forms of discourse are a) narration b) description c) exposition d) argument.

USE A PERIOD (.)

1. *After a complete thought unit*
   The section manager will return shortly.
2. *After an abbreviation*
   Los Angeles, Calif.
   Dr. James E. Brown

USE A QUESTION MARK (?)

1. *After a request for information*
   When do you leave for lunch?

USE QUOTATION MARKS (" ")

1. *To enclose what a person says directly*
   "No one could tell," she said, "that it would occur."
   He exclaimed, "This is the end!"
2. *To enclose the title of a short story, essay, short poem, song, or article (but not a book or play)*
   The song, "Tradition," is from *Fiddler on the Roof.*

USE A SEMICOLON (;)

1. *To avoid confusion with numbers*
   Add the following: $1.25; $7.50; and $12.89.
2. *Before explanatory words or abbreviations —namely, e.g.,* etc.
   We are able to supply you with two different types of paper; namely, lined and unlined.
   Note: The semicolon goes before the expression "namely." A comma follows the expression.
3. *To separate short statements of contrast*
   War is destructive; peace is constructive.

CAPITALIZATION RULES

1. *Capitalize the first word of a sentence.*
   With cooperation, a depression can be avoided.
2. *Capitalize all proper names.*
   America, General Motors, Abraham Lincoln, First Congregational Church
3. *Capitalize days of the week, months of the year and holidays.*
   The check was mailed on *Thursday,* the day before *Christmas.*
   Note: The seasons are not capitalized.
   In Florida, *winter* is mild.
4. *Capitalize the first word and all nouns in the salutation of a letter.*
   Dear Mr. Jones:
   (*but*—My *dear* Mr. Jones:)
5. *Capitalize the first word of the complimentary close of a letter.*
   Truly yours,
   (*but*—Very *truly* yours,)
6. *Capitalize the first and all other important words in a title.*
   The Art of *Salesmanship*
7. *Capitalize a word used as part of a proper name.*
   William *Street* (*but*—That *street* is narrow.)
   Morningside *Terrace* (*but*—We have a *terrace* apartment.)
8. *Capitalize titles, when they refer to a particular official or family member.*
   The report was read by *Secretary* Marshall.
   (*but*—Miss Shaw, our *secretary,* is ill.)
   Let's visit *Uncle* Harry.
   (*but*—I have three *uncles.*)
9. *Capitalize points of a compass, when they refer to particular regions of a country.*
   We're going *South* next week. (*but*—New York is *south* of *Albany.*)
   Note: Write: the Far West, the Pacific Coast, the Middle East, etc.
10. *Capitalize the first word of a direct quotation.*
    It was Alexander Pope who wrote, "*A* little learning is a dangerous thing."
    Note: When a direct quotation sentence is broken, the *first* word of the *second half* of the sentence is not capitalized.
    "Don't phone," Lilly told me, "*because* it will be too late."

THE ESSENTIALS OF ENGLISH GRAMMAR

PARTS OF SPEECH

A **noun** is the name of a person, place, thing, or idea:

teacher city desk democracy

Pronouns substitute for nouns:

he they ours those

An **adjective** describes a noun:

warm quick tall blue

A **verb** expresses action or state of being:

yell interpret feel are

An **adverb** modifies a verb, an adjective, or another adverb:

fast slowly friendly well

Conjunctions join words, sentences, and phrases:

and but or

A **preposition** shows position in time or space:

in during after behind

NOUNS

There are different kinds of nouns.

Common nouns are general:

house girl street city

Proper nouns are specific:

White House Jane Main Street New York

Collective nouns name groups:

team crowd organization Congress

Nouns have *cases:*

Nominative—the subject, noun of address, or predicate noun
Objective—the direct object, indirect object, or object of the preposition
Possessive—the form that shows possession

PRONOUNS

Antecedent of the pronoun—the noun to which a pronoun refers. A pronoun must agree with its antecedent in gender, person, and number.

There are several kinds of pronouns. (Pronouns also have cases.)

Demonstrative pronoun: this, that, these, those
Indefinite pronoun: all, any, nobody
Interrogative pronoun: who, which, what
Personal pronoun:

		Nominative Case	Objective Case	Possessive Case
Singular	1st person	I	me	mine
	2nd person	you	you	yours
	3rd person	he, she, it	him, her, it	his, hers
Plural	1st person	we	us	ours
	2nd person	you	you	yours
	3rd person	they	them	theirs

ADJECTIVES

Adjectives answer the questions "Which one?", "What kind?", and "How many?"

There are three uses of adjectives:

A **noun modifier** is usually placed directly before the noun it describes: He is a *tall* man.
A **predicate adjective** follows an inactive verb and modifies the subject:

He is *happy*. I feel *terrible*.

An **article** or **noun marker** are other names for these adjectives: the, a, an

ADVERBS

Adverbs answer the questions "Why?", "How?", "Where?", "When?", and "To what degree?"

Adverbs should not be used to modify nouns.

GRAMMAR RULES FOR GED CANDIDATES

1. The subject of a verb is in the nominative case even if the verb is understood and not expressed.

   Example: They are as old as *we*. (As we are.)

2. The word *who* is in the nominative case. *Whom* is in the objective case.

   Examples: The trapeze artist who ran away with the clown broke the lion tamer's heart.
   (*Who* is the subject of the verb *ran*.)
   The trapeze artist whom he loved ran away with the circus clown.
   (*Whom* is the object of the verb *loved*.)

3. The word *whoever* is in the nominative case. *Whomever* is in the objective case.

   Examples: Whoever comes to the door is welcome to join the party.
   (*Whoever* is the subject of the verb *comes*.)
   Invite whomever you wish to accompany you.
   (*Whomever* is the object of the verb *invite*.)

4. Nouns or pronouns connected by a form of the verb *to be* should always be in the nominative case.

   Example: It is I. (Not me!)

5. The object of a preposition or of a transitive verb should use a pronoun in the objective case.

   Examples: It would be impossible for you and *me* to do that job alone.
   (Use *me*, not *I*, because it is an object of the preposition *for*.)
   The attendant gave Tom and *me* keys to the locker.
   (Use *me*, not *I*, because it is an object of the verb *gave*.)

6. Do not use the possessive case when referring to an inanimate object.

   Example: He had difficulty with the management of the store.
   (Not—He had difficulty with the *store's* management.)

7. A pronoun agrees with its antecedent in person, number, gender, and case.

   Example: Since you were absent on Tuesday, you will have to ask Mary or Beth for her notes on the lecture.
   (Use *her*, not their, because two singular antecedents joined by *or* take a singular pronoun.)

8. A noun or pronoun modifying a gerund should be in the possessive case.

   Example: Is there any criticism of Arthur's going?
   (*Going* is a gerund. Therefore, it must be modified by *Arthur's*, not by Arthur.)

9. *Each, every, everyone, everybody, anybody, either, neither, no one, nobody,* and similar words are singular and require the use of singular verbs and pronouns.

   Examples: Each of the men in this class hopes to earn his high school diploma.
   (Use the singular verb form *hopes* and the singular pronoun *his* to agree with the singular subject *each*.)
   Neither of the women has completed her assignment.
   (Use the singular verb form *has completed* and the singular pronoun *her* to agree with the singular subject *neither*.)

10. When modifying the words *kind* and *sort*, the words *this* and *that* always remain in the singular.

    Examples: This kind of apple makes the best pie.
    That sort of behavior will result in severe punishment.

11. The word *don't* is never used with third person singular pronouns or nouns.

Example: She doesn't like classical music. It doesn't matter to me. (Not—*She don't* or *It don't*.)

12. A verb agrees in number with its subject. A verb should not be made to agree with a noun that is part of a phrase following the subject.

Examples: Mount Snow, one of my favorite ski areas, is in Vermont. (The singular subject *Mount Snow* takes the singular verb *is*.)
The mountains of Colorado, like those of Switzerland, offer excellent skiing. (The plural subject *mountains* takes the plural verb *offer*.)

13. The number of the verb is not affected by the addition to the subject of words introduced by *with, together with, no less than, as well as,* etc.

Example: The captain, together with the rest of the team, was delighted by the victory celebration. (The addition of the phrase *together with the rest of the team* does not change the fact that the subject of this sentence is the singular noun *captain* which requires the singular verb form *was delighted*.)

14. Singular subjects joined by the words *nor* and *or* take a singular verb.

Examples: Neither Adam nor Alex is able to come.
Either Eric or Mark has the key.

15. A subject consisting of two or more nouns joined by the word *and* takes a plural verb.

Example: Paul and Sue were the last to arrive.

16. A verb should agree in number with the subject, not with the predicate noun or pronoun.

Examples: Poor study habits are the leading cause of unsatisfactory achievement in school. (The plural subject *habits* takes the plural verb *are*.)
The leading cause of unsatisfactory achievement in school is poor study habits. (The singular subject *cause* takes the singular verb *is*.)

17. In sentences beginning with *there is* and *there are,* the verb should agree in number with the noun that follows it.

Examples: There isn't an unbroken bone in her body. (The singular subject *bone* takes the singular verb *is*.)
There are many choices to be made. (The plural subject *choices* takes the plural verb *are*.)

18. An adjective should not be used to modify a verb.

Example: He spoke slowly and carefully. (Not—He spoke *slow* and *careful*.)

19. Statements equally true in the past and in the present are usually expressed in the present tense.

Example: He said that Venus is a planet. (Not—He said that Venus *was* a planet.)

20. The word *were* is used to express a condition contrary to fact or a wish.

Example: I wish I were a movie star. (Not—I wish I *was* a movie star.)

CORRECT ENGLISH USAGE

The ability to choose and use the right word is an important part of the GED Writing Skills Test. The list that follows presents some of the most commonly misused words in the English language. Study it well and you will be rewarded with higher test scores.

accede—means *to agree with.*
concede—means *to yield,* but not necessarily in agreement.
exceed—means *to be more than.*
We shall *accede* to your request for more evidence.
To avoid delay, we shall *concede* that more evidence is necessary.
Federal expenditures now *exceed* federal income.

access—means *availability.*
excess—means *too much.*
The lawyer was given *access* to the grand jury records.
The expenditures this month are far in *excess* of income.

accept—means *to take when offered.*
except—means *excluding.* (preposition)
except—means *to leave out.* (verb)
The draft board will *accept* all seniors as volunteers before graduation.
All eighteen-year-olds *except* seniors will be called.
The draft board will *except* all seniors until after graduation.

adapt—means *to adjust to change.*
adopt—means *to take as one's own.*
adept—means *skillful.*
Children can *adapt* to changing conditions very easily.
The war orphan was *adopted* by the general and his wife.
Proper instruction makes children *adept* in various games.
NOTE: adapt *to,* adopt *by,* adept *in* or *at.*

adapted to—implies *original or natural suitability.*
The gills of the fish are *adapted to* underwater breathing.
adapted for—implies *created suitability.*
Atomic energy is constantly being *adapted for* new uses.
adapted from—implies *changes to be made suitable.*
Many of Richard Wagner's opera librettos were *adapted from* old Norse sagas.

addition—means *the act or process of adding.*
edition—means *a printing of a publication.*
In *addition* to a dictionary, he always used a thesaurus.
The first *edition* of Shakespeare's plays appeared in 1623.

advantage—means *a superior position.*
benefit—means *a favor conferred* or *earned* (as a profit).
He had an *advantage* in experience over his opponent.
The rules were changed for his *benefit.*
NOTE: to *take* advantage *of,* to *have* an advantage *over.*

adverse—(pronounced AD-verse) means *unfavorable.*
averse—(pronounced a-VERSE) means *disliking.*
He took the *adverse* decision in poor taste.
Many students are *averse* to criticism by their classmates.

advise—means *to give advice. Advise* is losing favor as a synonym for *notify.*
Acceptable: The teacher will *advise* the student in habits of study.
Unacceptable: We are *advising* you of a delivery under separate cover. (SAY: *notifying*)

affect—means *to influence.* (verb)
effect—means *an influence.* (noun)
effect—means *to bring about.* (verb)
Your education must *affect* your future.
The *effect* of the last war is still being felt.

A diploma *effected* a tremendous change in his attitude.

NOTE: *Affect* also has a meaning of *pretend.* She had an *affected* manner.

after—is unnecessary with the *past* participle.

SAY: *After* checking the timetable, I left for the station.

DON'T SAY: *After having checked* (omit *after*) the timetable, I left for the station.

ain't—is an *unacceptable* contraction for *am not, are not,* or *is not.*

aisle—is *a passageway* between seats.
isle—is *a small island.* (Both words rhyme with *pile.*)

all ready—means *everybody* or *everything ready.*
already—means *previously.*

They were *all ready* to write when the teacher arrived.

They had *already* begun writing when the teacher arrived.

alright—is *unacceptable.*
all right—is *acceptable.*

all together—means *everybody* or *everything together.*
altogether—means *completely.*

The boys and girls sang *all together.*

This was *altogether* strange for a person of his type.

all ways—means *in every possible way.*
always—means *at all times.*

He was in *all ways* acceptable to the voters.

His reputation had *always* been spotless.

allude—means *to make a reference to.*
elude—means *to escape from.*

Only incidentally does Coleridge *allude* to Shakespeare's puns.

It is almost impossible for one to *elude* tax collectors.

allusion—means *a reference.*
illusion—means *a deception of the eye or mind.*

The student made *allusions* to his teacher's habits.

Illusions of the mind, unlike those of the eye, cannot be corrected with glasses.

alongside of—means *side by side with.*

Bill stood *alongside of* Henry.

alongside—means *parallel to the side.*

Park the car *alongside* the curb.

alot—is *unacceptable.* It should always be written as two words: *a lot.*

among—is used with *more than two persons or things.*

NOTE: *Amongst* should be avoided.

between—is used with *two persons or things.*

The inheritance was equally divided *among* the four children.

The business, however, was divided *between* the oldest and the youngest one.

amount—applies to quantities *that cannot be counted one by one.*
number—applies to quantities *that can be counted one by one.*

A large *amount* of grain was delivered to the storehouse.

A large *number* of bags of grain was delivered.

annual—means *yearly.*
biannual—means *twice a year.* (*Semiannual* means the same.)
biennial—means *once in two years* or *every two years.*

anywheres—is *unacceptable.*
anywhere—is *acceptable.*

SAY we can't find it *anywhere.*

ALSO SAY *nowhere* (NOT nowheres), *somewhere* (NOT somewheres)

aren't I—is colloquial. Its use is to be discouraged.

SAY: *Am I not* entitled to an explanation? (preferred to *Aren't I . . .*)

as—(used as a conjunction) is followed by a verb.
like—(used as a preposition) is NOT followed by a verb.

Do *as* I do, not *as* I say.

Try not to behave *like* a child.

Unacceptable: He acts *like* I do.

as far as—expresses *distance.*
so far as—indicates *a limitation.*

We hiked *as far as* the next guest house.

So far as we know, the barn was adequate for a night's stay.

as good as—should be used *for comparisons only.*

This motel is *as good as* the next one.

NOTE: *As good as* does NOT mean *practically.*

Unacceptable: They *as good as* promised us a place in the hall.

Acceptable: They *practically* promised us a place in the hall.

as if—is correctly used in the expression, "He talked *as if* his jaw hurt him."

Unacceptable: "He talked *like* his jaw hurt him."

ascared—no such word. It is *unacceptable* for *scared.*

The child was *scared* of ghosts. (NOT *ascared.*)

ascent—is *the act of rising.*

assent—means *approval.*

The *ascent* to the top of the mountain was perilous.

Congress gave its *assent* to the President's emergency directive.

assay—means *to try* or *experiment.* (verb)

essay—means *an intellectual effort.* (noun)

We shall *assay* the ascent of the mountain tomorrow.

The candidate's views were expressed in a well-written *essay.*

attend to—means *to take care of.*

tend to—means *to be inclined to.*

One of the clerks will *attend to* mail in my absence.

Lazy people *tend* to gain weight.

back—should NOT be used with such words as *refer* and *return* since the prefix *re* means *back.*

Unacceptable: Refer *back* to the text, if you have difficulty recalling the facts.

backward / **backwards** } Both are *acceptable* and may be used interchangeably as an adverb.

We tried to run *backward.* (or *backwards*)

Backward as an adjective means *slow in learning.* (DON'T say *backwards* in this case)

A *backward* pupil should be given every encouragement.

berth—is *a resting place.*

birth—means *the beginning of life.*

The new liner was given a wide *berth* in the harbor.

He was a fortunate man from *birth.*

beside—means *close to.*

besides—refers *to something that has been added.*

He lived *beside* the stream.

He found wild flowers and weeds *besides.*

better—means *recovering.*

well—means *completely recovered.*

He is *better* now than he was a week ago.

In a few more weeks, he will be *well.*

both—means *two considered together.*

each—means *one of two or more.*

Both of the applicants qualified for the position.

Each applicant was given a generous reference.

NOTE: Avoid using such expressions as the following:

Both girls had a new typewriter. (Use *each girl* instead.)

Both girls tried to outdo the other. (Use *each girl* instead.)

They are *both* alike (Omit *both*).

breath—means *an intake of air.*

breathe—means *to draw air in and give it out.*

breadth—means *width.*

Before you dive in, take a very deep *breath.*

It is difficult to *breathe* under water.

In a square, the *breadth* should be equal to the length.

bring—means *to carry toward the person who is speaking.*

take—means *to carry away from the speaker.*

Bring the books here.

Take your raincoat with you when you go out.

broke—is the past tense of *break.*

broke—is *unacceptable* for *without money.*

He *broke* his arm.

"Go for broke" is a slang expression widely used in gambling circles.

bunch—refers to *things.*

group—refers to *persons* or *things.*

This looks like a delicious *bunch* of bananas.

What a well-behaved *group* of children!

NOTE: The colloquial use of bunch applied to *persons* is to be discouraged.

A *bunch* of the boys were whooping it up. (*Number* is preferable.)

certainly—(and *surely*) is an *adverb*.
sure—is an *adjective*.
He was *certainly* learning fast.
Unacceptable: He *sure* was learning fast.

cite—means *to quote*.
sight—means *seeing*.
site—means *a place for a building*.
He was fond of *citing* from the Scriptures.
The *sight* of the wreck was appalling.
The Board of Education is seeking a *site* for the new school.

coarse—means *vulgar* or *harsh*.
course—means a *path* or a *study*.
He was shunned because of his *coarse* behavior.
The ship took its usual *course*.
Which *course* in English are you taking?

come to be—should NOT be replaced with the expression *become to be*, since *become* means *come to be*.
True freedom will *come to be* when all tyrants have been overthrown.

comic—means *intentionally funny*.
comical—means *unintentionally funny*.
A clown is a *comic* figure.
The peculiar hat she wore gave her a *comical* appearance.

conscience—means *sense of right*.
conscientious—means *faithful*.
conscious—means *aware of one's self*.
Man's *conscience* prevents him from becoming completely selfish.
We all depend on him because he is *conscientious*.
The injured man was completely *conscious*.

considerable—is properly used *only as an adjective*, NOT as a noun.

cease—means *to end*.
seize—means *to take hold of*.
Will you please *cease* making those sounds?
Seize him by the collar as he comes around the corner.

cent—means *a coin*.
scent—means *an odor*.
sent—is the past tense of *send*.
The one-*cent* postal card is a thing of the past.
The *scent* of roses is pleasing.
We were *sent* to the rear of the balcony.

calendar—is a *system of time*.
calender—is *a smoothing and glazing machine*.
colander—is *a kind of sieve*.
In this part of the world, most people prefer the twelve-month *calendar*.
In ceramic work, the potting wheel and the *calender* are indispensable.
Garden-picked vegetables should be washed in a *colander* before cooking.

can—means *physically able*.
may—implies *permission*.
I *can* lift this chair over my head.
You *may* leave after you finish your work.

cannot help—must be followed by an *ing* form.
We cannot help *feeling* (NOT *feel*) distressed about this.
NOTE: *cannot help but* is *unacceptable*.

can't hardly—is a *double negative*. It is *unacceptable*.
SAY: The child *can hardly* walk in those shoes.

capital—is *the city*.
capitol—is *the building*.
Paris is the *capital* of France.
The Capitol in Washington is occupied by the Congress. (The Washington *Capitol* is capitalized.)
NOTE: *Capital* also means wealth.

compare to—means *to liken to something which has a different form*.
compare with—means *to compare persons or things with each other when they are of the same kind*.
contrast with—means *to show the difference between two things*.
A minister is sometimes *compared to* a shepherd.
Shakespeare's plays are often *compared with* those of Marlowe.
The writer *contrasted* the sensitivity of the dancer *with* the grossness of the pugilist.

complement—means *a completing part*.
compliment—is *an expression of admiration*.
His wit was a *complement* to her beauty.
He *complimented* her attractive hairstyle.

consul—means *a government representative*.
council—means *an assembly that meets for deliberation*.

counsel—means *advice.*
Americans abroad should keep in touch with their *consuls.*
The City *Council* enacts local laws and regulations.
The defendant heeded the *counsel* of his friends.

convenient to—should be followed by a *person.*
convenient for—should be followed by a *purpose.*
Will these plans be *convenient to* you?
You must agree that they are *convenient for* the occasion.

copy—is *an imitation of an original work.* (not necessarily an exact imitation)
facsimile—is *an exact imitation of an original work.*
The counterfeiters made a crude *copy* of the hundred-dollar bill.
The official government engraver, however, prepared a *facsimile* of the bill.

could of—is *unacceptable.* (*Should of* is also *unacceptable.*)
could have—is *acceptable.* (*Should have* is acceptable.)
Acceptable: You *could have* done better with more care.
Unacceptable: I *could of* won.
ALSO AVOID: *must of, would of.*

decent—means *suitable.*
descent—means *going down.*
dissent—means *disagreement.*
The *decent* thing to do is to admit your fault.
The *descent* into the cave was treacherous.
Two of the nine justices filed a *dissenting* opinion.

deduction—means *reasoning from the general (laws or principles) to the particular (facts).*
induction—means *reasoning from the particular (facts) to the general (laws or principles).*
All men are mortal. Since John is a man, he is mortal. (*deduction*)
There are 10,000 oranges in this truckload. I have examined 100 from various parts of the load and find them all of the same quality. I conclude that the 10,000 oranges are of this quality. (*induction*)

delusion—means *a wrong idea* that will probably influence action.
illusion—means *a wrong idea* that will probably *not* influence action.
People were under the *delusion* that the earth was flat.
It is just an *illusion* that the earth is flat.

desert—(pronounced DEZZ-ert) means *an arid area.*
desert—(pronounced di-ZERT) means *to abandon*; also *a reward or punishment.*
dessert—(pronounced di-ZERT) means *the final course of a meal.*
The Sahara is the world's most famous *desert.*
A husband must not *desert* his wife.
Execution was a just *desert* for his crime.
We had plum pudding for *dessert.*

different from—is *acceptable.*
different than—is *unacceptable.*
Acceptable: Jack is *different from* his brother.
Unacceptable: Florida climate is *different than* New York climate.

doubt that—is *acceptable.*
doubt whether—is *unacceptable.*
Acceptable: I *doubt that* you will pass this term.
Unacceptable: We *doubt whether* you will succeed.

dual—means *relating to two.*
duel—means *a contest between two persons.*
Dr. Jekyl had a *dual* personality.
Alexander Hamilton was fatally injured in a *duel* with Aaron Burr.

due to—is *unacceptable* at the beginning of a sentence. Use *because of, on account of,* or some similar expression instead.
Unacceptable: Due to the rain, the game was postponed.
Acceptable: Because of the rain, the game was postponed.
Acceptable: The postponement was *due to* the rain.

each other—refers to *two persons.*
one another—refers to *more than two persons.*
The two girls have known *each other* for many years.
Several of the girls have known *one another* for many years.

either . . . or—is used when referring to choices.
neither . . . nor—is the *negative form.*
Either you *or* I will win the election.
Neither Bill *nor* Henry is expected to have a chance.

eliminate—means *to get rid of.*
illuminate—means *to supply with light.*
Let us try to *eliminate* the unnecessary steps.
Several lamps were needed to *illuminate* the corridor.

emerge—means *to rise out of.*
immerge—means *to sink into* (also **immerse**).
The swimmer *emerged* from the pool.
The laundress *immerged* the dress in the tub of water.

emigrate—means *to leave one's country for another.*
immigrate—means *to enter another country.*
Many Norwegians *emigrated* from their homeland to America in the mid-1860's.
Today government restrictions make it more difficult for foreigners to *immigrate* to this country.

everyone—is written as one word when it is a *pronoun.*
every one—(two words) is used when each individual is stressed.
Everyone present voted for the proposal.
Every one of the voters accepted the proposal.
NOTE: *Everybody* is written as one word.

everywheres—is *unacceptable.*
everywhere—is *acceptable.*
We searched *everywhere* for the missing book.
NOTE: *Everyplace* (one word) is likewise *unacceptable.*

feel bad—means *to feel ill.*
feel badly—means *to have a poor sense of touch.*
I *feel bad* about the accident I saw.
The numbness in his limbs caused him to *feel badly.*

feel good—means *to be happy.*
feel well—means *to be in good health.*
I *feel* very *good* about my recent promotion.
Spring weather always made him *feel well.*

flout—means *to insult.*
flaunt—means *to make a display of.*
He *flouted* the authority of the principal.
Hester Prynne *flaunted* her scarlet "A."

formally—means *in a formal way.*
formerly—means *at an earlier time.*
The letter of reference was *formally* written.
He was *formerly* a delegate to the convention.

former—means *the first of two.*
latter—means *the second of two.*
The *former* half of the book was in prose.
The *latter* half of the book was in poetry.

forth—means *forward.*
fourth—*comes after third.*
They went *forth* like warriors of old.
The *Fourth* of July is our Independence Day.
NOTE: spelling of *forty* (40) and *fourteen* (14).

get—is a verb that strictly means *to obtain.*
Please *get* my bag.
There are many slang forms of GET that should be avoided:
AVOID: Do you *get* me? (SAY: Do you *understand* me?)
AVOID: You can't *get* away with it. (SAY: You won't *avoid* punishment if you do it.)
AVOID: *Get* wise to yourself. (SAY: *Use* common sense.)
AVOID: We didnt *get* to go. (SAY: We didn't *manage* to go.)

got—means *obtained.*
He *got* the tickets yesterday.
AVOID: You've *got* to do it. (SAY: You *have* to do it.)
AVOID: We *have got* no sympathy for them. (SAY: We *have* no sympathy for them.)
AVOID: They have *got* a great deal of property. (SAY: They *have* a great deal of property.)

hanged—is used in reference to a *person.*
hung—is used in reference to a *thing.*
The prisoner was *hanged* at dawn.
The picture was *hung* above the fireplace.

however—means *nevertheless.*
how ever—means *in what possible way.*
We are certain, *however,* that you will like this class.

We are certain that, *how ever* you decide to study, you will succeed.

if—introduces a *condition.*
whether—introduces a *choice.*
I shall go to Europe *if* I win the prize.
He asked me *whether* I intended to go to Europe. (not *if*)

if it was—implies that *something might have been true in the past.*
if it were—implies *doubt,* or indicates *something that is contrary to fact.*
If your book was there last night, it is there now.
If it were summer now, we would all go swimming.

in—usually refers to *a state of being.* (no motion)
into—is used for *motion from one place to another.*
The records are *in* that drawer.
I put the records *into* that drawer.
NOTE: "We were walking in the room" is correct even though there is motion. The motion is *not* from one place to another.

irregardless—is *unacceptable.*
regardless—is *acceptable.*
Unacceptable: Irregardless of the weather, I am going to the game.
Acceptable: Regardless of his ability, he is not likely to win.

its—means *belonging to it.*
it's—means *it is.*
The house lost *its* roof.
It's an exposed house, now.

kind of / **sort of** } are *unacceptable* for *rather.*
SAY: We are *rather* disappointed in you.

last—refers to *the final member in a series.*
latest—refers to *the most recent in time.*
latter—refers to *the second of two.*
This is the *last* bulletin. There won't be any other bulletins.
This is the *latest* bulletin. There will be other bulletins.
Of the two most recent bulletins, the *latter* is more encouraging.

lay—means *to place.*
lie—means *to recline.*

Note the forms of each verb:

TENSE	LIE (RECLINE)
Present	The child *is lying* down.
Past	The child *lay* down.
Pres. Perf.	The child *has lain* down.
TENSE	LAY (PLACE)
Present	He *is laying* the book on the desk.
Past	He *laid* the book on the desk.
Pres. Perf.	He *has laid* the book on the desk.

lightening—is the present participle of *to lighten.*
lightning—means *the flashes of light accompanied by thunder.*
Leaving the extra food behind resulted in *lightening* the pack.
Summer thunderstorms produce startling *lightning* bolts.

many—refers to *a number.*
much—refers to *a quantity in bulk.*
How *many* inches of rain fell last night?
I don't know; but I would say *much* rain fell last night.

may—is used in the *present tense.*
might—is used in the *past tense.*
We are hoping that he *may* come today.
He *might* have done it if you had encouraged him.

it's I—is always *acceptable.*
it's me—is *acceptable* only in colloquial speech or writing.

It's him / This is her / It was them — always *unacceptable*

It's he / This is she / It was they — always *acceptable*

noplace—as a solid word, is *unacceptable* for *no place* or *nowhere.*
Acceptable: You now have *nowhere* to go.

number—is singular *when the total is intended.*
The *number* (of pages in the book) is 500.
number—is plural *when the individual units are referred to.*

A *number of pages* (in the book) were printed in italic type.

of any—(and *of anyone*) is *unacceptable* for *of all*.
SAY: His was the highest mark *of all*. (NOT *of any* or *of anyone*)

off of—is *unacceptable*.
SAY: He took the book *off* the table.

out loud—is *unacceptable* for *aloud*.
SAY: He read *aloud* to his family every evening.

outdoor—(and *out-of-door*) is an adjective.
outdoors—is an adverb.
We spent most of the summer at an *outdoor* music camp.
Most of the time we played string quartets *outdoors*.
NOTE: *Out-of-doors* is *acceptable* in either case.

people—comprise *a united* or *collective group of individuals*.
persons—are *individuals that are separate and unrelated*.
Only five *persons* remained in the theater after the first act.
The *people* of New York City have enthusiastically accepted "Shakespeare-in-the-Park" productions.

persecute—means *to make life miserable for someone*. (Persecution is illegal.)
prosecute—means *to conduct a criminal investigation*. (Prosecution is legal.)
Some racial groups insist upon *persecuting* other groups.
The District Attorney is *prosecuting* the racketeers.

precede—means *to come before*.
proceed—means *to go ahead*. (*Procedure* is the noun.)
supersede—means *to replace*.
What were the circumstances that *preceded* the attack?
We can then *proceed* with our plan for resisting a second attack.
It is then possible that Plan B will *supersede* Plan A.

principal—means *chief* or *main* (as an adjective); *a leader* (as a noun).

principle—means *a fundamental truth* or *belief*.
His *principal* supporters came from among the peasants.
The *principal* of the school asked for cooperation from the staff.
Humility was the guiding *principle* of Buddha's life.
NOTE: *Principal* may also mean *a sum placed at interest*.
Part of his monthly payment was applied as interest on the *principal*.

sit—means *take a seat*. (intransitive verb)
set—means *place*. (transitive verb)
Note the forms of each verb:

TENSE	SIT (TAKE A SEAT)
Present	He *sits* on a chair.
Past	He *sat* on the chair.
Pres. Perf.	He *has sat* on the chair.
TENSE	SET (PLACE)
Present	He *sets* the lamp on the table.
Past	He *set* the lamp on the table.
Pres. Perf.	He *has set* the lamp on the table.

some time—means *a portion of time*.
sometime—means *at an indefinite time in the future*.
sometimes—means *occasionally*.
I'll need *some time* to make a decision.
Let us meet *sometime* after twelve noon.
Sometimes it is better to hesitate before signing a contract.

somewheres—is *unacceptable*.
somewhere—is *acceptable*.

stationary—means *standing still*.
stationery—means *writing materials*.
In ancient times people thought the earth was *stationary*.
We bought writing paper at the *stationery* store.

stayed—means *remained*.
stood—means *remained upright* or *erect*.
The army *stayed* in the trenches for five days.

The soldiers *stood* at attention for one hour.

sure—for *surely* is *unacceptable.*
SAY: You *surely* (NOT *sure*) are not going to write that!

take in—is *unacceptable* in the sense of *deceive* or *attend.*
SAY: We were *deceived* (NOT *taken in*) by his oily manner.
We should like to *attend* (NOT *take in*) a few plays during our vacation.

their—means *belonging to them.*
there—means *in that place.*
they're—means *they are.*
We took *their* books home with us.
You will find your books over *there* on the desk.
They're going to the ballpark with us.

theirselves—is *unacceptable* for *themselves.*
SAY: Most children of school age are able to care for *themselves* in many ways.

these kind—is *unacceptable.*
this kind—is *acceptable.*
I am fond of *this kind* of apples.
NOTE: *These kinds* would be also *acceptable.*

through—meaning *finished* or *completed* is *unacceptable.*
SAY: We'll finish (NOT *be through with*) the work by five o'clock.

try to—is *acceptable.*
try and—is *unacceptable.*
Try to come (NOT *try and* come).
NOTE: *plan on going* is *unacceptable; plan to go* is *acceptable.*

two—is the *numeral* 2.
to—means *in the direction of.*
too—means *more than* or *also.*
There are *two* sides to every story.
Three *twos* (or 2's) equal six.
We shall go *to* school.
We shall go, *too.*
The weather is *too* hot for school.

was / **were** } If something is contrary to fact (not a fact), use *were* in every instance.
I wish I *were* in Bermuda.
Unacceptable: If he *was* sensible, he wouldn't act like that.
(SAY: If he *were* . . .)

ways—is *unacceptable* for *way.*
SAY: We climbed a little way (NOT *ways*) up the hill.

went and took—(*went and stole,* etc.) is *unacceptable.*
SAY: They *stole* (NOT *went and stole*) our tools.

when—(and *where*) should NOT be used to introduce a definition of a noun.
SAY: A tornado *is a* twisting, high wind on land (NOT *is when a twisting, high wind is on land*).
A pool *is a place for swimming* (NOT *is where people swim*).

whereabouts—is *unacceptable* for *where.*
SAY: *Where* (NOT *whereabouts*) do you live?
NOTE: *Whereabouts* as a noun meaning a place is *acceptable.*
Do you know his *whereabouts?*

whether—should NOT be preceded by *of* or *as to.*
SAY: The President will consider the question *whether* (NOT *of whether*) it is better to ask for or demand higher taxes now.
He inquired *whether* (NOT *as to whether*) we were going or not.

which—is used *incorrectly* in the following expressions:
He asked me to stay, *which I did.* (CORRECT: He asked me to stay and I did.)
It has been a severe winter, *which* is unfortunate. (CORRECT: Unfortunately, it has been a severe winter.)
You did not write; besides *which* you have not telephoned. (CORRECT: Omit *which*)

while—is *unacceptable* for *and* or *though.*
SAY: The library is situated on the south side; (OMIT *while*) the laboratory is on the north side.
Though (NOT *while*) I disagree with you, I shall not interfere with your right to express your opinion.
Though (NOT *while*) I am in my office every day, you do not attempt to see me.

who / **whom** } The following is a method (without going into grammar rules) for determining when to use WHO or WHOM.
"Tell me (*who, whom*) you think should rep-

resent our company?"

STEP ONE: Change the who—whom part of the sentence to its natural order.

"You think (*who, whom*) should represent our company?"

STEP TWO: Substitute HE for WHO, HIM for WHOM.

"You think (*he, him*) should represent our company?"

You would say *he* in this case.

THEREFORE: "Tell me WHO you think should represent our company?" is correct.

who is
who am } Note these constructions.

It is I who *am* the most experienced.
It is he who *is* . . .
It is he or I who *am* . . .
It is I or he who *is* . . .
It is he and I who *are* . . .

whose—means *of whom.*
who's—means *who is.*

Whose is this notebook?
Who's in the next office?

THE GED WRITING SKILLS TEST

The multiple-choice questions in the Writing Skills Test measure your ability to recognize and correct errors in three areas:

Sentence Structure (35%)

Usage (35%)

Mechanics (30%)

Here are some examples of the kinds of errors you will be expected to recognize:

SENTENCE STRUCTURE ERRORS

1. Sentence fragments
   Susan bringing her books to the library.
   Mr. Smith having taken his daughter home.
2. Run-on sentences
   Jimmy watched the World Cup race his team lost.
   Marie enjoyed the movie her sister came.
3. Improper coordination
   Jeannie flies often and lives in Nashville.
4. Improper subordination
   We will continue to depend on local sales taxes even whenever the income tax is passed.
5. Lack of clarity due to misplaced modifiers or lack of parallelism
   Riding in the car, the light turned red.
   Betty likes skiing and to play tennis.

USAGE ERRORS

1. Lack of agreement between subject and verb
   Sam and Fred is here.
   Ron, like his two brothers, are short and muscular.

2. Incorrect verb tense
   When the teacher walks in, I sat down. (sequence of tenses)
   Tomorrow, Sandy went to work. (word clue to tense in the sentence)
   Bernie done the job. (verb form)

3. Incorrect pronouns
   Jimmy is a man which I love. (wrong relative pronoun)
   If one wants to earn money, you must get a job. (pronoun shift)
   He tried to plead his case to his children and his friends, but they wouldn't listen. (vague reference)
   The carpenter followed the plumber into his shop. (ambiguous reference)
   Russia was offered help, but they curtly rejected the assistance. (lack of agreement with antecedent)

MECHANICS ERRORS

1. Capitalization
   They planned to cook a chinese dinner. (proper adjectives)
   She booked a tour to italy. (proper nouns)
   Susan works for mayor Haley. (titles)
   Her birthday falls on memorial day. (dates)
   She lives at 893 Stone avenue. (addresses)
   He quit his job last Summer. (seasons)

2. Punctuation
   I need soda cups and paper plates. (comma between items in a series)
   Don wanted to stop for a drink but Janet wanted to finish shopping. (comma after introductory elements)
   When Marta arrived at her brother's house she could not believe the appearance of the basement. (comma after introductory dependent clauses)
   He looked, and decided to run. (overuse of commas)
   He dislikes sports for example and never watches baseball or football. (comma with appositives)

3. Spelling/Possessives/Contractions

   The weather is very changible. (commonly misspelled words)
   Her mothers old recipe made a delicious soup. (possessives)
   Your the tallest man on the team. (troublesome contractions)

Multiple choice WRITING SKILLS questions are always presented within a paragraph that averages ten to twelve sentences. When corrected, each paragraph becomes an example of good writing. Most questions do contain an error that must be identified and corrected. Some questions contain no error at all. At least a few contain errors in clarity or logic, the sort of mistakes that often hamper employees and students in everyday writing on the job or in school.

Writing skills questions may be asked in one of three ways:

SENTENCE CORRECTION QUESTIONS (50% OF THE TEST)

This type of question may test your knowledge in any area of sentence structure, usage, or mechanics. The question is always written with the following cue: WHAT CORRECTION SHOULD BE MADE TO THIS SENTENCE? Since no portion of the sentence is underlined, it is up to you to look at the entire sentence for any possible error in any of the three skills areas. Here's an example:

> When tickets went on sale for the rock concert, young people from miles around lining up at the box office.
> What correction should be made to this sentence?
>
> (1) change went to go
> (2) remove the comma after concert
> (3) change the spelling of people to people
> (4) change lining to lined
> (5) no correction is necessary

Answer: (4) As it stands, this is a sentence fragment, not a complete sentence. To make it complete you must change *lining* to *lined*, thus giving the sentence the verb it lacks.

SENTENCE REVISION QUESTIONS (35% OF THE TEST)

This type of question may test your skills in sentence structure, usage, and punctuation. It will always consist of a sentence with some portion underlined. The underlined portion may or may not contain an error, but you are being asked to look at that part of the sentence, and no other, in order to answer the question. A sentence revision question is always written with the cue: *Which of the following is the best way to write the underlined portion of this sentence? If you think the original is the best way to write the sentence, choose option (1).* Option 1 will *always* be a restatement of the sentence as it appears in the paragraph and in the separate question. Here is a sample question:

> Education is a life-long process, at every age we learn from family, friends and associates.
> Which of the following is the best way to write the underlined portion of this sentence? If you think the original is the best way to write the sentence, choose option (1).
> (1) process, at
> (2) process at
> (3) process. At
> (4) process: at
> (5) process of

Answer: (3) This sentence is an example of a comma splice (two complete sentences joined by a comma). To correct the error, separate the two sentences by changing process, at to process. At.

CONSTRUCTION SHIFT QUESTIONS
(15% OF THE TEST)

This type of question will test your skills in sentence structure, usage, and punctuation. Construction shift questions ask you to rewrite a sentence according to directions given to you. Your new sentence must be clearly and correctly stated, and it must have the same meaning as the original sentence. Here is an example of a construction shift question:

It is more rewarding to make friends than it is to be antisocial. If you rewrote this sentence beginning with *Making friends*, the next word should be
(1) than
(2) it
(3) is
(4) rewarding
(5) to

Answer: (3) The rewritten sentence will be: Making friends is more rewarding than being antisocial. Therefore, the word that follows *making friends* is *is*.

PRACTICE WITH GED-TYPE WRITING SKILLS QUESTIONS

The questions that follow are similar to the questions you will find in Part 1 of the Writing Skills Test. Writing Skills questions are based on paragraphs of ten to twelve sentences. Each sentence is numbered so that you can find it easily as you answer the questions about it. In each paragraph, some sentences are correct and others contain errors. The questions test your ability to recognize errors in a sentence and to choose the best way to correct them. Correct answers and explanations for these questions are given at the end of this chapter.

Directions:

Directions: This test consists of several paragraphs in which each sentence is numbered. Some of the sentences within each paragraph contain errors in sentence structure, usage, or mechanics. Other sentences are correct as written. Following each paragraph are questions based upon it. Read the paragraph first, then answer the questions about it. For each item, choose the answer that would result in the most effective writing of the sentence. The best answer must be consistent with the meaning and tone of the paragraph.

Items 1 to 12 refer to the following paragraph.

(1) Mutual help was been practiced since families first existed. (2) As social beings, all of us need to be accepted, cared for, and emotionally supported, we also find it satisfying to care for and support those around us. (3) Within the most natural "mutual help networks"—families and friends—we establish the one-to-one contact so important to our happiness and well-being. (4) This informal support is such a basic part of our social character that we are apt to take them for granted, but it clearly influences our ability to handle distressing events in our lives. (5) Many of our daily conversations are actually mutual counciling sessions, whereby we exchange the reassurance and advice that help us deal with routine stresses. (6) In fact researching scientists have found that there is a strong link between the strength of our social support systems and our health. (7) Many studies show that such support helps prevent ill health and promote recovery when an illness or accident does occur. (8) The personal support we receive from family and friends, besides, is only one part of the support network that helps sustain us through life. (9) As we develop social and intellectual, we tend to associate with others who have similar interests and beliefs. (10) In groups such as religious congregations, civic and fraternal organizations, and social clubs, members benefit from a shared identity and a sense of common purpose. (11) Some informal groups used to be aimed primarily at social enjoyment. (12) Other consumer-oriented groups come together to bring about social change: through combined efforts, the group can often promote or accomplish what the individual, acting alone, cannot.

1. Sentence 1: **Mutual help was been practiced since families first existed.**

   Which of the following is the best way to write the underlined portion of this sentence? If you think the original is the best way to write the sentence, choose option (1).

   (1) help was been practiced
   (2) help is been practiced
   (3) help is being practiced
   (4) help is practicing
   (5) help has been practiced

2. Sentence 2: **As social beings, all of us need to be accepted, cared for, and emotionally supported, we also find it satisfying to care for and support those around us.**

   Which of the following is the best way to write the underlined portion of the sentence? If you think the original is the best way to write the sentence, choose option (1).

   (1) supported, we also
   (2) supported we also
   (3) supported: we also
   (4) supported; We also
   (5) supported. We also

3. Sentence 3: **Within the most natural "mutual help networks"—families and friends—we establish the one-to-one contact so important to our happiness and well-being.**

   What correction should be made to this sentence?

   (1) remove the quotation marks around "mutual help network"
   (2) capitalize mutual help network
   (3) remove the dash after friends
   (4) insert a comma after contact
   (5) no correction is necessary

4. Sentence 4: **This informal support is such a basic part of our social character that we are apt to take them for granted, but it clearly influences our ability to handle distressing events in our lives.**

   What correction should be made to this sentence?

   (1) change is to was
   (2) change is to will be
   (3) change we are apt to they are apt
   (4) change to take them to to take it
   (5) no correction is necessary

5. Sentence 5: **Many of our daily conversations are actually mutual counciling sessions, whereby we exchange the reassurance and advice that help us deal with routine stresses.**

What correction should be made to this sentence?

(1) change the spelling of daily to dailey
(2) change are actually to were actually
(3) change the spelling of counciling to counseling
(4) change whereby to wherever
(5) no correction is necessary

6. Sentence 6: **In fact researching scientists have found that there is a strong link between the strength of our social support systems and our health.**

Which of the following is the best way to write the underlined portion of this sentence? If you think the original is the best way to write the sentence, choose option (1).

(1) fact researching scientists have found
(2) fact research scientists have found
(3) fact researched scientists have found
(4) researching scientists had found
(5) fact scientists have found research

7. Sentence 7: **Many studies show that such support helps prevent ill health and promote recovery when an illness or accident does occur.**

If you rewrote sentence 7 beginning with Ill health often can be prevented, the next words should be

(1) by many studies
(2) and recovery promoted
(3) that such support
(4) when an accident
(5) if an illness

8. Sentence 8: **The personal support we receive from family and friends, besides, is only one part of the support network that helps sustain us through life.**

Which of the following is the best way to write the underlined portion of this sentence? If you think the original is the best way to write the sentence, choose option (1).

(1) friends, besides, is
(2) friends, unless, is
(3) friends, either, is
(4) friends, neither, is
(5) friends, however, is

9. Sentence 9: **As we develop social and intellectual, we tend to associate with others who have similar interests and beliefs.**

Which of the following is the best way to write the underlined portion of this sentence? If you think the original is the best way to write the sentence, choose option (1).

(1) develop social and intellectual
(2) developed socially and intellectually
(3) developing social and intellectually
(4) develop socially and intellectually
(5) have developed social and intellectual

10. Sentence 10: **In groups such as religious congregations, civic and fraternal organizations, and social clubs, members benefit from a shared identity and a sense of common purpose.**

If you rewrote sentence 10 beginning with The benefit of a sense of common purpose and a shared identity, the next words should be

(1) is often obtained
(2) in groups
(3) in social clubs and civic groups
(4) group members
(5) in religious congregations

11. Sentence 11: **Some informal groups used to be aimed primarily at social enjoyment.**

Which of the following is the best way to write the underlined portion of this sentence? If you think the original is the best way to write the sentence, choose option (1).

(1) groups used to be aimed
(2) groups are aimed
(3) groups have been aimed
(4) groups were being aimed
(5) groups aimed

GO ON TO THE NEXT PAGE

12. Sentence 12: **Other consumer-oriented groups come together to bring about social change: through combined efforts, the group can often promote or accomplish what the individual, acting alone, cannot.**

    Which of the following is the best way to write the underlined portion of this sentence? If you think the original is the best way to write the sentence, choose option (1).

    (1) social change: through
    (2) social change through
    (3) social change, through
    (4) social change. Through
    (5) social change; Through

Items 13 to 22 refer to the following passage:

(1) Quality measurment is a comparatively modern development. (2) Man has been measured sizes and distances—more or less accurately—since the dawn of recorded history. (3) In ancient egypt, the length of the Pharaoh's foot was an official measurement. (4) But quality measurement did not appear until a few hundred years ago.

(5) Consumers in thirteenth-century England probably got the benifit of the first real quality standards when the king decreed "assizes" for bread. (6) These assizes were enforced by local officials to make sure that bakers gave full quality and wait to their loaves.

(7) Under the assize, "simnel loaves" had to be made from the finest white bread flower. (8) "Treet bread" was brown bread, fairly cloze to simnel loaf in quality. (9) There was also a "wastrel loaf," far inferior to the first two kinds. (10) "Horse bread" was made from beans, and seems to sell primarily to unwary travelers at the local inns. (11) The prices of the loaves were fixed, and the required weight of each kind was varied according to the price of the grain. (12) The standards weren't too exact, and local officials served as "graders" when there was a dispute.

13. Sentence 1: **Quality measurment is a comparatively modern development.**

    What correction should be made to this sentence?

    (1) capitalize measurment
    (2) change the spelling of measurment to measurement
    (3) change comparatively to comparative
    (4) change is to was
    (5) no correction is necessary

14. Sentence 2: **Man has been measured sizes and distances—more or less accurately—since the dawn of recorded history.**

    What correction should be made to this sentence?

    (1) change has to was
    (2) change measured to measuring
    (3) change sizes and distances to in size and distance
    (4) change accurately to accurate
    (5) no correction is necessary

15. Sentence 3: **In ancient egypt, the length of the Pharaoh's foot was an official measurement.**

    What correction should be made to this sentence?

    (1) change egypt to Egypt
    (2) change Pharaoh to pharaoh
    (3) change foot to feet
    (4) change the spelling of measurement to measurment
    (5) no correction is necessary

16. Sentence 4: **But quality measurement did not appear until a few hundred years ago.**

    If you rewrote sentence 4 beginning with Only a few hundred years ago the next words should be

    (1) but quality
    (2) measuring began
    (3) quality measurement
    (4) appearing
    (5) even quality

17. Sentence 5: **Consumers in thirteenth-century England probably got the benifit of the first real quality standards when the king decreed "assizes" for bread.**

    What correction should be made to this sentence?

    (1) change the spelling of thirteenth to Thirteenth
    (2) change the spelling of England to england
    (3) change the spelling of benifit to benefit
    (4) change the real to really
    (5) change decreed to degreed

18. Sentence 6: **These assizes were enforced by local officials to make sure that bakers gave full quality and wait in their loaves.**

    What correction should be made to this sentence?

    (1) change enforced to inforced
    (2) change make to made
    (3) change bakers to bakers'
    (4) change wait to weight
    (5) no correction is necessary

19. Sentence 7: **Under the assize, "simnel loaves" had to be made from the finest white bread flower.**

    What correction should be made to this sentence?

    (1) delete the comma after assize
    (2) change the spelling of loaves to loafs
    (3) change had to be made to had been made
    (4) change bread to bred
    (5) change flower to flour

20. Sentence 8: **"Treet bread" was brown bread, fairly cloze to simnel loaf in quality.**

    What correction should be made to this sentence?

    (1) remove the quotation marks around "Treet bread"
    (2) change was to were
    (3) change bread to bred
    (4) change cloze to close
    (5) add a comma after loaf

21. Sentence 10: **"Horse bread" was made from beans, and seems to sell primarily to unwary travelers at the local inns.**

    Which of the following is the best way to write the underlined portion of this sentence: If you think the original is the best way to write the sentence, choose option (1).

    (1) seems to sell
    (2) seems to be selling
    (3) was selling
    (4) seems to have been sold
    (5) seems selling

22. Sentence 12: **The standards weren't too exact, and local officials served as "graders" when there was a dispute.**

    Which of the following is the best way to write the underlined portion of this sentence? If you think the original is the best way, choose option (1).

    (1) weren't too exact, and
    (2) weren't to exact, and
    (3) weren't too exact; and
    (4) werent too exact, and
    (5) weren't too exacting, and

GO ON TO THE NEXT PAGE

Items 23 to 32 refer to the following paragraph.

(1) Legal Aid and Legal Services offices help people who cannot afford to hire private lawyers, and who meet financial eligibility requirements. (2) There are more than 1,000 of these offices around the country, staffed by lawyers, paralegals, and law students. (3) All offer free legal services by those who qualify. (4) In some cities, both Legal Aid or Legal Services offices are federally funded. (5) Legal Aid offices may also be financing state, local, or private funding, or by local Bar Associations. (6) The Legal Services Corporation in Washington, D. C., is funded by the Federal Government, and it, in turn, awards grants to local Legal Services programs around the country. (7) Also, many law schools throughout the nation conduct law clinics, where students assisted other lawyers as part of their training. (8) These offices generally offering legal assistance with problems such as landlord-tenant, credit, utilities, family issues, social security, welfare, unemployment, and worker's compensation. (9) Each legal aid office has its own board of directors that determines the prior office and the kinds of cases handled. (10) Whenever, the Legal Aid office serving your area may not handle all of the types of cases mentioned above. (11) However, these offices should be able to refer you to other local, state, or national organizations that can provide advice or help.

23. Sentence 1: **Legal Aid and Legal Services offices help people who cannot afford to hire private lawyers, and who meet financial eligibility requirements.**

If you rewrote sentence 1 beginning with People of limited financial resources the next words should be

(1) can find legal help
(2) cannot afford
(3) who help people
(4) help Legal Aid
(5) who hire private

24. Sentence 2: **There are more than 1,000 of these offices around the country, staffed by lawyers, paralegals, and law students.**

What correction should be made to this sentence?

(1) change There are to There're
(2) change these to this
(3) change the spelling of staffed to stafed
(4) capitalize lawyers
(5) no correction is necessary

25. Sentence 3: **All offer free legal services by those who qualify.**

Which of the following is the best way to write the underlined portion of this sentence? If you think the original is the best way to write the sentence, choose option (1).

(1) services by those
(2) services from those
(3) services unless those
(4) services to those
(5) services wherever those

26. Sentence 4: **In some cities, both Legal Aid or Legal Services offices are federally funded.**

What correction should be made to this sentence?

(1) remove comma after cities
(2) change Legal Aid to legal aid
(3) change or to and
(4) change are to were
(5) no correction is necessary

27. Sentence 5: **Legal Aid offices may also be financing state, local, or private funding, or by local Bar Associations.**

Which of the following is the best way to write the underlined portion of this sentence? If you think the original is the best way to write the sentence, choose option (1).

(1) also be financing
(2) also have financed
(3) finance
(4) be financed
(5) also be financed by

28. Sentence 7: **Also, many law schools throughout the nation conduct law clinics,**

where students assisted other lawyers as part of their training.

Which of the following is the best way to write the underlined portion of this sentence? If you think the original is the best way to write the sentence, choose option (1).

(1) students assisted other
(2) students assist other
(3) student assists other
(4) students have assisted
(5) students will be assisting

29. Sentence 8: **These offices generally offering legal assistance with problems such as landlord-tenant, credit, utilities, family issues, social security, welfare, unemployment, and worker's compensation.**

What correction should be made to this sentence?

(1) change These offices to This office
(2) change offering to offer
(3) insert a colon after such as
(4) change worker's to workers'
(5) no correction is necessary

30. Sentence 9: **Each legal aid office has its own board of directors that determines the prior office and the kinds of cases handled.**

What correction should be made to this sentence?

(1) change legal aid to Legal Aid
(2) change determines to which has determined
(3) change prior to priorities of the
(4) change office to offices
(5) no correction is necessary

31. Sentence 10: **Whenever, the Legal Aid office serving your area may not handle all of the types of cases mentioned above.**

Which of the following is the best way to write the underlined portion of this sentence? If you think the original is the best way to write the sentence, choose option (1).

(1) Whenever, the Legal
(2) In case the Legal
(3) Therefore, the Legal
(4) Unless, the Legal
(5) Basically the Legal

32. Sentence 11: **However, these offices should be able to refer you to other local, state, or national organizations that can provide advice or help.**

What correction should be made to this sentence?

(1) delete However,
(2) Change offices to officers
(3) change the spelling of refer to reffer
(4) change advice to advise
(5) no correction is necessary

GO ON TO THE NEXT PAGE

Items 33 to 42 refer to the following paragraph.

(1) Physical fitness activities begin with plays early in life, starting with arm and leg movements in infancy. (2) As children grow, they need the guidence of parents, teachers, coaches, recreation directors, and physicians in selecting individual and team play activities for physical and emotional development. (3) Unless helping to build physical fitness and a sense of physical power, play is a child's outlet for expressing joy, frustration, anger, and pride. (4) Group play and sports encourage growth in emotional stability and maturity and offer that good feeling of "belonging." (5) The ability to win or lose gracefully and to take pride in the success of others are added values learned through these activities who also provide lessons in honesty, cooperation, teamwork, tolerance, and consideration for others. (6) Parents and teachers know that when students are in good health, they get better grades in school, gaining in self-esteem and self-confidence. (7) It's one more reason for schools to provide physical fitness programs for all students—kindergarden through high school and college. (8) Schools and parents need to take an active interest and, where possible, works together in creating physical education programs in which all students, whatever their capabilities or special needs, can take part. (9) Physical fitness training programs help students understand relationships of exercise, diet, rest, and relaxation to all aspects of health. (10) Well-planned physical education programs helping children establish lifetime patterns of wholesome and rewarding physical activities.

33. Sentence 1: **Physical fitness activities begin with plays early in life, starting with arm and leg movements in infancy.**

What correction should be made to this sentence?

(1) change activities to activity
(2) change begin to begun
(3) change plays to play
(4) change arm and leg to arms and legs
(5) no correction is necessary

34. Sentence 2: **As children grow, they need the guidence of parents, teachers, coaches, recreation directors, and physicians in selecting individual and team play activities for physical and emotional development.**

What correction should be made to this sentence?

(1) change grow to growing
(2) change the spelling of guidence to guidance
(3) change selecting to selected
(4) change the spelling of development to developement
(5) no correction is necessary

35. Sentence 3: **Unless helping to build physical fitness and a sense of physical power, play is a child's outlet for expressing joy, frustration, anger, and pride.**

Which of the following is the best way to write the underlined portion of this sentence? If you think the original is the best way to write the sentence, choose option (1).

(1) Unless helping to build
(2) Besides helping to build
(3) Wherever helping to build
(4) Helping to build
(5) However helping to build

36. Sentence 4: **Group play and sports encourage growth in emotional stability and maturity and offer that good feeling of "belonging."**

If you rewrote sentence 4 beginning with Emotional stability and maturity the next words would be

(1) encourage growth
(2) offer "belonging"
(3) and sports
(4) feel that
(5) are encouraged

37. Sentence 5: **The ability to win or lose gracefully and to take pride in the success of others are added values learned through these activities who also provide lessons in honesty, cooperation, teamwork, tolerance, and consideration for others.**

Which of the following is the best way to write the underlined portion of this sentence? If you think the original is the best way to write the sentence, choose option (1).

(1) who also provide
(2) whom also provide
(3) who provided
(4) which also provide
(5) that provides

38. Sentence 6: **Parents and teachers know that when students are in good health, they get better grades in school, gaining in self-esteem and self-confidence.**

What correction should be made to this sentence?

(1) capitalize teachers
(2) change are to were
(3) delete the comma after health
(4) change get better to getting better
(5) no correction is necessary

39. Sentence 7: **It's one more reason for schools to provide physical fitness programs for all students—kindergarden through high school and college.**

What correction should be made to this sentence?

(1) change It's to Its
(2) change schools to school's
(3) change the spelling of kindergarden to kindergarten
(4) change through to threw
(5) change the spelling of college to colledge

40. Sentence 8: **Schools and parents need to take an active interest and, where possible, works together in creating physical education programs in which all students, whatever their capabilities or special needs, can take part.**

What correction should be made to this sentence?

(1) change need to needing
(2) change works to work
(3) change creating to created
(4) change whatever to whoever
(5) no correction is necessary

41. Sentence 9: **Physical fitness training programs help students understand relationships of exercise, diet, rest, and relaxation to all aspects of health.**

What correction should be made to this sentence?

(1) remove programs
(2) change help to helping
(3) change understand to understanding
(4) add a colon after relationships
(5) no correction is necessary

42. Sentence 10: **Well-planned physical education programs helping children establish lifetime patterns of wholesome and rewarding physical activities.**

Which of the following is the best way to write the underlined portion of this sentence? If you think the original is the best way to write the sentence, choose option (1).

(1) helping children establish
(2) can help children establish
(3) helping children establishing
(4) helping children to establish
(5) help children's establishing

GO ON TO THE NEXT PAGE

Items 43 to 52 refer to the following paragraph.

(1) Like the United States today, Athens had courts where a wrong might be righted. (2) Since any citizen might accuse another of a crime, the Athenian courts of law was very busy. (3) In fact, unless a citizen was unusually peaceful or very unimportant, they would be sure to appear in the courts at least once every few years.

(4) At a trial, both the accuser or the person accused were allowed a certain time to speak. (5) The length of time marked by a water clock. (6) Free men testified under oath as they do today, but the oath of a slave was counted as worthless.

(7) Judging a trial, a jury was chosen from the members of the assembly who had reached 30 years of age. (8) The Athenian juries were very large, often consisting of 201, 401, 501, 1,001 or more men, depending upon the importance of the case being tried. (9) The juryman swore by the gods to listen carefully to both sides of the question and to given his honest opinion of the case. (10) Each juryman gave his decision by depositing a white or black stone in a box. (11) To keep citizens from being too careless in accusing each other, there was a rule that if the person accused did not recieve a certain number of negative votes, the accuser was condemned instead.

43. Sentence 1: **Like the United States today, Athens had courts where a wrong might be righted.**

Which of the following is the best way to write the underlined portion of this sentence? If you think the original is the best way to write the sentence, choose option (1).

(1) wrong might be righted
(2) wrong should be righted
(3) wrong might have been righted
(4) wrong was righted
(5) wrong could have been righted

44. Sentence 2: **Since any citizen might accuse another of a crime, the Athenian courts of law was very busy.**

What correction should be made to this sentence?

(1) change the spelling of citizen to citisen
(2) change the spelling of accuse to acuse
(3) change the spelling of Athenian to athenian
(4) change was to were
(5) no correction is necessary

45. Sentence 3: **In fact, unless a citizen was unusually peaceful or very unimportant, they would be sure to appear in the courts at least once every few years.**

What correction should be made to this sentence?

(1) delete the comma after fact
(2) change was to were
(3) change the spelling of peaceful to peacefull
(4) change they to he
(5) insert a comma after courts

46. Sentence 4: **At a trial, both the accuser or the person accused were allowed a certain time to speak.**

What correction should be made to this sentence?

(1) delete the comma after trial
(2) change both to each
(3) change or to and
(4) change were to was
(5) no correction is necessary

47. Sentence 5: **The length of time marked by a water clock.**

Which of the following is the best way to write the underlined portion of this sentence? If you think the original is the best way to write the sentence, choose option (1).

(1) marked by
(2) marking by
(3) is marked by
(4) was marked by
(5) to be marked by

48. Sentence 6: **Free men testified under oath as they do today, but the oath of a slave was counted as worthless.**

Which of the following is the best way to write the underlined portion of this sentence? If you think the original is the best way to write the sentence, choose option (1).

(1) do today, but the
(2) did today, but the
(3) did today. But the
(4) do today and the
(5) do today; but the

49. Sentence 7: **Judging a trial, a jury was chosen from the members of the assembly who had reached 30 years of age.**

What correction should be made to this sentence?

(1) change Judging to To judge
(2) change was to were
(3) change from to among
(4) change spelling of assembly to asembly
(5) change who to whom

50. Sentence 8: **The Athenian juries were very large, often consisting of 201, 401, 501, 1,001 or more men, depending upon the importance of the case being tried.**

If you rewrote sentence 8 beginning with Depending upon the importance, the next words should be

(1) of the Athenian juries
(2) 201, 401, 501, 1,001
(3) being tried
(4) juries were very
(5) of the case

51. Sentence 9: **The juryman swore by the gods to listen carefully to both sides of the question and to given his honest opinion of the case.**

What correction should be made to this sentence?

(1) change swore to swear
(2) insert a comma after gods
(3) change carefully to careful
(4) change both to each
(5) change given to give

52. Sentence 11: **To keep citizens from being too careless in accusing each other, there was a rule that if the person accused did not recieve a certain number of negative votes, the accuser was condemned instead.**

What correction should be made to this sentence?

(1) change the too to to
(2) change there to their
(3) change the spelling of recieve to receive
(4) change the spelling of negative to negetive
(5) no correction is necessary

ANSWER KEY FOR WRITING SKILLS PRACTICE QUESTIONS

1. (5)	12. (4)	23. (1)	33. (3)	43. (1)
2. (5)	13. (2)	24. (5)	34. (2)	44. (4)
3. (5)	14. (2)	25. (4)	35. (2)	45. (4)
4. (4)	15. (1)	26. (3)	36. (5)	46. (3)
5. (3)	16. (3)	27. (5)	37. (4)	47. (4)
6. (2)	17. (3)	28. (2)	38. (5)	48. (1)
7. (2)	18. (4)	29. (2)	39. (3)	49. (1)
8. (5)	19. (5)	30. (3)	40. (2)	50. (5)
9. (4)	20. (4)	31. (3)	41. (5)	51. (5)
10. (1)	21. (4)	32. (5)	42. (2)	52. (3)
11. (2)	22. (1)			

EXPLANATIONS FOR WRITING SKILLS PRACTICE QUESTIONS

1. **(5)** *help has been practiced.* The correct verb form for an action begun in the past and still going on is *has been practiced.*

2. **(5)** *supported. We also.* The original sentence contains a comma splice.

3. **(5)** No correction is necessary.

4. **(4)** Change *to take them* to *to take it.* The pronoun refers to *support,* which is singular. Therefore, *it* is correct.

5. **(3)** change the spelling of *counciling* to *counseling.*

6. **(2)** *fact research scientists have found.* An adjective is needed to modify *scientists. Research* is an adjective; *researching* is a verb form.

7. **(2)** *and recovery promoted.* Ill health can often be prevented and recovery promoted by such support. This arrangement preserves the meaning of the sentence and the parallel structure as well.

8. **(5)** *friends, however, is.* Besides means "in addition to." There are no cues for neither (nor) and either (or). Unless does not make sense. *However,* meaning "nevertheless," is the only sensible choice.

9. **(4)** *develop socially and intellectually.* Social and intellectual are adjectives which normally modify a noun; develop requires the adverbs socially and intellectually.

10. **(1)** *are often obtained.* The benefit of a sense of common purpose and a shared identity are often obtained from groups such as religious congregations, civic and fraternal organizations, and social clubs. This is the only logical sequence among the choices.

11. **(2)** *groups are aimed.* Tense reflects the entire paragraph.

12. **(4)** *social change. Through.* A period is necessary to correct the original comma splice.

13. **(2)** Change the spelling of *measurment* to *measurement.*

14. **(2)** Change *measured* to *measuring.* Has been measuring shows an action that started in the past and continues in the present.

15. **(1)** Change *egypt* to *Egypt.* Names of countries are capitalized as proper nouns.

16. **(3)** *quality measurement.* Only a few hundred years ago quality measurement began to appear. Only logical choice for a coherent sentence.

17. **(3)** Change the spelling of *benifit* to *benefit.*

18. **(4)** Change *wait* to *weight.* Wait and weight are homonyms; weight refers to heaviness or lightness, not the length of time the baker has been standing around while his loaves bake.

19. **(5)** Change *flower* to *flour.* Flowers bloom on a tree, plant, or bush; flour is the baker's raw material for bread.

20. **(4)** Change the spelling of *cloze* to *close.*

21. **(4)** *Seems to have been sold.* Examine the tense of the other verbs in the paragraph. Everything took place a long time ago.

22. **(1)** *Weren't too exact and.* No correction is necessary.

23. **(1)** *can find legal help.* People of limited financial resources can find legal help at Legal Aid and Legal Services offices. This is the only choice that allows you to form a sentence that means the same as the original sentence.

24. **(5)** No correction is necessary.

25. **(4)** *services to those.* People who qualify (above) are the ones who receive the services, not offer them.

26. **(3)** change *or* to *and.* Both is a cue for the use of and rather than or.

27. **(5)** *also be financed by.* Any other choice destroys the meaning of the sentence.

28. **(2)** *students assist other.* Tense should reflect the rest of the paragraph.

29. **(2)** Change *offering* to *offer.* This change makes a sentence fragment a sentence.

30. **(3)** Change *prior* to *priorities of the.* Prior means earlier; without a noun the sentence is senseless.

31. **(3)** *Therefore, the Legal.* Therefore is used in the sense of drawing a conclusion from the previous sentence.

32. **(5)** No correction is necessary.

33. **(3)** Change *plays* to *play.* The word play is needed for sense; it refers to the things children do for fun. Plays refers to dramatic performances.

34. **(2)** Change the spelling of *guidence* to *guidance.*

35. **(2)** *Besides helping to build.* The author is building a case for physical fitness. Sentence three adds more supporting details, and the use of besides (meaning in addition to) supports the author's purpose in writing the paragraph.

36. **(5)** *are encouraged.* Emotional stability and maturity are encouraged by group play and sports. This is the only logical answer that preserves the general meaning of the sentence.

37. **(4)** *which also provide.* The pronoun needed refers to activities (a thing, not a person). *Who* refers only to people; *which* refers to things.

38. **(5)** No correction is necessary.

39. **(3)** Change the spelling of *kindergarden* to *kindergarten.*

40. **(2)** Change *works* to *work.* The plural subject (schools and parents) requires a plural verb (work).

41. **(5)** No correction is necessary.

42. **(2)** *can help children establish.* As written, this is a sentence fragment; choice 2 most closely harmonizes with the tone and voice of the paragraph.

43. **(1)** *wrong might be righted.* No correction is necessary.

44. **(4)** change *was* to *were.* The verb must agree in number with the subject; *courts were* is correct.

45. **(4)** change *they* to *he.* The pronoun refers to *a citizen;* therefore, a singular, not a plural, pronoun is required.

46. **(3)** change *or* to *and.* The cue is the word *both,* which should be followed by *and.*

47. **(4)** *was marked by.* The addition of the verb *was* makes the original sentence fragment into a complete sentence.

48. **(1)** *do today, but the.* No correction is necessary.

49. **(1)** change *Judging* to *To judge.* The infinitive form is needed.

50. **(5)** *of the case.* Depending upon the importance *of the case* being tried, Athenian juries could consist of 201, 401, 501, 1,001 or more men.

51. **(5)** change *given* to *give.* To keep the ideas parallel, the sentence needs two similar structures: He swore *to listen* and *to give.*

52. **(3)** change the spelling of *recieve* to *receive.* Remember the rule for "i before e, except after c . . ."

ERROR ANALYSIS FOR WRITING SKILLS PRACTICE QUESTIONS

BY CONTENT:		**No. Incorrect**
SENTENCE STRUCTURE:	1, 4, 6, 11, 20, 24, 26, 31, 32, 34, 37, 38, 43, 55	
USAGE:	2, 5, 7, 9, 12, 14, 16, 17, 23, 25, 27, 29, 30, 33, 39, 40, 44, 48, 49, 50, 53	
MECHANICS:	3, 8, 10, 13, 15, 18, 19, 21, 22, 28, 35, 36, 41, 42, 45, 46, 47, 51, 52, 54	
BY TYPE OF QUESTION:		
SENTENCE CORRECTION:	1, 2, 4, 6, 8, 9, 10, 13, 15, 16, 17, 21, 22, 25, 27, 28, 34, 36, 37, 41, 45, 46, 47, 48, 49, 51, 52, 53, 54	
SENTENCE REVISION:	3, 7, 11, 12, 18, 19, 20, 23, 24, 29, 30, 31, 33, 35, 38, 40, 42, 43, 44, 55	
CONSTRUCTION SHIFT:	5, 14, 26, 32, 39, 50	

THE GED ESSAY TEST

The new GED Test now includes an essay segment. The essay test consists of a single topic on which you are expected to write a well-organized, well-stated response in the forty-five minutes allowed. GED essay questions fall into two types: Exposition and Persuasion.

WHAT IS EXPOSITION?

Exposition means writing designed to convey information. Expository writing is *informative* writing. It explains or gives directions. Most of the practical writing you will do in the years to come—papers and examinations, job applications, business reports, insurance claims, your last will and testament—are examples of expository writing. That is why it is a part of this test, because it is so important to your life.

WHAT IS PERSUASION?

Persuasion is the ability to use language to move an audience to action or belief. There are three main ways to persuade someone:

1. Appeal to his emotion
2. Appeal to his sense of reason
3. Appeal to his ethics—his sense of right and wrong

Argumentation is the form of persuasion that appeals to reason. While an argument may be more concerned with following a line of reasoning than making someone act, it must nonetheless convince its audience that what you have to say is worthwhile.

Whichever type of question you get, expository or persuasive, you will have to logically state your case, answering the question fully with specific details and examples.

HOW IS THE GED ESSAY SCORED?

GED essays are read and scored by two trained readers. They read the paper as a whole, evaluating its overall effectiveness. Thus, your paper can have a few errors and still get a very good grade; they are looking more for logic and a complete, well-supported answer to the question.

The score used by GED readers ranges from a one (low) to a six (high). The two readers' scores are then added, resulting in a range of scores from 2 to 12. This total essay score is added to your score on the multiple-choice section of the Writing Skills Test to form a total score on a scale of 20 to 80.

WHAT EACH GRADE ON THE SCALE OF 1 TO 6 MEANS

1. These papers lack a clear plan of action and organization. There is also great weakness in skills such as grammar, usage, punctuation, spelling, correct sentences and paragraphs, and capitalization. Not only has the writer of a 1 paper not proven his point, but he has not proven any point at all.
2. These papers have very weak details and examples. The ideas are not fully developed or proven. The level of reasoning is unsophisticated and displays a lack of understanding of the thesis. There are a lot of generalizations that are not backed up with specific details. There may be conflicting purposes rather than one clear plan of action. There are also a great many errors in usage and skills, as in the 1 papers.
3. These papers are not well organized and simply list details rather than developing supporting examples. While the purpose may be correctly *stated* (unlike the 1 and 2 papers, which do not make a point at all), the purpose is still not well supported with details and examples. There is also weakness with skills, as in the 1 and 2 papers.
4. These papers show a clear plan and method of organization, although the supporting detail could be stronger. There are errors in usage and skills, but they are not intrusive enough to destroy the plan of action or the point being made.
5. These papers show a very clear organization and enough support for each point being made so that the reader is convinced of the logic of the writer's argument. The writer also shows a maturity of thought as well as writing, and may present ideas that show a level of sophistication beyond the topic, although always clearly *related to the topic.* There may be some minor writing errors, but they do not interrupt the flow of ideas and proofs.
6. These papers have a very clear "voice" or point of view. The topic is not only well proven, but there is a flair or style in word and example choice that clearly demonstrates the writer's ideas and maturity. The supporting details are especially effective because they are specific and very clearly prove the point under discussion. There may be an error or two, but the writer clearly shows an understanding of the rules of English grammar and usage.

A SAMPLE ESSAY QUESTION:

Let's look at a sample GED Essay Question and the various ways in which different examinees answered. Look carefully at each written response so you may determine how the various scores (range 1–6) were assigned.

> EXAMPLE:
> There has been a great deal of attention paid recently to the problem of drinking and driving. The laws on DWI have become much stiffer. Discuss the advantages and disadvantages of stiffer penalties for driving while intoxicated. Be specific.

SAMPLE ESSAY A

Personally, I think the drinking law should be raised, one reason is there would be less people getting in accidents, many accidents are caused by drunk drivers. The people usually involved in DWI's are all young kids who are under pressure try to act cool and instead injure someone's life. Many kids drinking are not responsible enough and take other people's lives in there hands this is ruining many peoples lives and also society is getting worse. The problem would almost be solved if the laws was raised, putting drinking in the hands of youngsters is like giving a baby coffee, there not of right mind to make a decision whether to take it or not. I think that many teens are to young and therefore I think that the laws should be raised if it were lowered it would only be more problems. The lawmakers are making a right move in order to make society better if they keep doing things to prevent teens to drink this country will have a better chance at surviving problems. I'm glad that the law was raised so that my life wasn't taken in the hands of one irresponsible teenager. That's why I think drunk driving laws should be raised.

Evaluation: This essay is poorly organized and fails to prove the point. There are far too many serious writing errors, especially in sentence construction. Some examples of poor sentences include:

> Personally, I think the drinking law should be raised, one reason is there would be less people getting into accidents, many accidents are caused by drunk drivers.

This is called a *run-on,* which means there are several complete sentences tacked together without proper punctuation. The first sentence ends after the word "raised"; the second, after the word "accidents." After each of these words there should be periods or words that serve as *conjunctions,* such as "and," "or," or "for." In addition to the technical writing problems, the groups of words that are linked do not make the author's point.

Another example of a weak sentence would be:

> Many kids drinking are not responsible enough and take other people's lives in there hands this is ruining many peoples lives and also society is getting worse.

This is also a *run-on,* and should properly end after the word "hands." The ideas do not prove the point and show a lack of logic.

Because of errors such as these, this paper would receive a grade in the *1 to 2 range* as a very weak essay. Let's see what can be done to improve it. The author's ideas are:

Advantages of stiffer penalties	Disadvantages of stiffer penalties
fewer accidents	

The author blames most of the DWI problems on teenagers who cause most of the accidents by their irresponsible attitudes. As we can see, there are not enough *advantages* and *disadvantages* here to make the point. Further, the author's logic is weak. It *may* be correct that the DWI situation is mainly the result of irresponsible teenagers, but nowhere does the author provide facts to back this assertion up. Let's look at another response to the same question.

Here's another possible answer:

SAMPLE ESSAY B

I think the drinking age should be raised because most of the accidents caused today are by young teenage kids who are drunk while they are driving. They nearly kill people because they are drunk. I think the age should be raised to 25 years old because by then many people would have thier heads together and they would know whether they should drive or not at that time.

However, many teenage kids or older would not listen to the law and they would drink anyway. I think the cops should check people more to see if they are drunk and if they should get a ticket of a certain amount, depending on how drunk they are or how much damage they have done. People should listen and obey the law (if it ever came about) and less people would probably be killed in automobile accidents involving people who are drinking.

Evaluation: Let's see the advantages and disadvantages here.

Advantages to stiffer DWI penalties	Disadvantages to stiffer DWI penalties
would prevent teenagers from DWI	teenagers would not listen
fewer accidents	

Again we can see that there are not enough advantages and disadvantages here to completely make the point. Teenagers are again blamed, and once again there is no proof to back up the author's belief that teenagers are the cause of most of the accidents involving drugs and/or alcohol. While the point about tickets is a good one, it does not have a place in this essay, which is concerned with the advantages and disadvantages of stiffer penalties for DWI. Remember that you will not get credit for answers that do not pertain to the question. The skills are rather good here, and so this paper would be in the *2–3 range,* providing a partial answer to the question.

SAMPLE ESSAY C

> Read this essay and see what "grade" you would assign it. How well does it answer the question? Is there enough specific detail to make the point? Are the skills strong? Is there evidence of an individual "style" or "voice" that makes the paper even more persuasive?

Drinking and driving laws need to be stiffer. When a person drinks and drives he or she is not only taking their own lives, but other innocent lives with them. The government should put very strict laws on those who drink and drive because maybe they will have a second thought about stepping into a car while intoxicated.

There are no advantages to drinking and driving. It is a very foolish thing. The disadvantages are that you will be punished if you violate the law, but that is no one else's fault but your own, for you brought it on yourself.

The advantage to stiffer penalties is that maybe people will stay away from alcohol, if they are driving alone. From my own opinion, I think there are no disadvantages to stiffer penalties.

When a person gets behind the wheel of a car, while intoxicated, they are not aware of many things that are going on around them. This causes them to do things that cause accidents, and many times, take people's lives. Drinking and driving is a very serious and foolish thing to do. Intoxicated drivers deserve a harsh penalty so they won't do it again.

Evaluation: You can see that this paper is much better structured than the previous ones. First of all, the paragraphs use the words "advantages" and "disadvantages" and clearly address themselves to the question. Let's take it apart.

Advantages to stiffer DWI laws	Disadvantages to stiffer DWI laws
will prevent deaths ("second thought")	you will be punished
people will stay away from alcohol	

There are clear divisions and a clear reasoning going on here. While there could be far more specific examples, the paper demonstrates control of the subject and a clear understanding of the question. There is also some style, in phrases such as "There are no advantages to drinking and driving," and "It is a very foolish thing." This paper would *rate a 4* on the scale. With more specific examples, it could very easily be a 5 or 6.

Let's look at one more essay:

SAMPLE ESSAY D

While all concerned agree that something has to be done about the problem of driving while intoxicated, there are both advantages and disadvantages to increasing the penalties. The advantages include the obvious saving of lives and property, while the disadvantages include providing incentive for those inclined to break laws to continue to show they can do so. There is little doubt, however, that the advantages vastly outweigh the disadvantages.

The main advantage of tightening the punishment for driving while under the influence of alcohol or drugs would be the protection of lives. There are so many innocent people killed every year by intoxicated drivers that citizens have been moved to take matters in their own hands. Candy Lightner, the mother of a sixteen-year-old daughter killed by a drunken driver, formed an organization called M.A.D.D. (Mothers Against Drunken Drivers) to educate people about the dangers of driving while under the influence. The Scandinavian countries, where alcoholism and driving has long been a problem, have greatly increased penalties for those convicted of driving drunk, and they found that the death rate has dropped significantly. They have mandatory jail sentences and publish the names of offenders. If even one life was saved through stiffer legislation, it would be worth it.

The disadvantages could include the portion of society that feels duty bound to break rules and might take increased DWI penalties as a sign that they should try to "beat the system." This could actually raise the number of serious accidents. There is also the problem of how to enact the laws. A recent proposal, involving hosts who can be held responsible for allowing drunken guests to leave their parties, has been greeted with a great deal of disapproval. Despite this, many bars are already limiting their "Happy Hours," especially in Connecticut.

Regardless of those who object to a tightening of DWI laws, it seems clear that something has to be done to decrease the number of deaths related to drivers on the roads when they clearly should not be. A series of stiffer laws seems to be the best way to accomplish the saving of lives. It's worked in other countries, and it can work here too.

Evaluation: The topic sentence clearly states the question and the points to be covered. The points include:

Advantages	Disadvantages
saving of lives and property	providing incentive for people to break the law

And the paragraph concludes with the author's point: The advantages far outweigh the disadvantages.

The second paragraph clearly states that the protection of lives is the main advantage of stiffer DWI laws. There are *two* specific examples to back this up:

Candy Lightner, founder of MADD

Result of tigher laws in Scandinavian countries

These are excellent examples because they *specifically* prove the point under discussion.

The third paragraph also has a clear specific example, involving the recent "host law," holding those who let drunken drivers leave their homes responsible for the results. It also discusses the recent change in Connecticut "happy hour" rules. Both these examples serve to make the point.

The conclusion has a sentence that sums up each major point and clearly states the writer's conviction that stiffer DWI laws would help all of us in preventing unnecessary deaths.

This would be a 6 paper, because it uses clear specific examples and good organization to make the point. It has a clear voice or tone—the author is obviously very concerned about this issue. The word choice is appropriate and the grammar and usage correct.

PLANNING YOUR ESSAY

GETTING STARTED

The first thing you must always do when answering an essay question is look at the question and see what it asks you to do. Ask yourself these questions:

What must I prove?

How many things am I being asked to do?

How many paragraphs will I need for this?

Look at this sample question:

> FOR EXAMPLE:
>
> A generation ago, young people took it for granted that they would marry and soon after become parents. Today's young couples seem to be putting off parenthood well into their marriages, and a significant number are not having children at all. Discuss the advantages and disadvantages of having children. Be specific.

Go back to the three questions and answer each one:

What must I prove?
You are asked to discuss the advantages and disadvantages of having children. Remember, you will receive no credit if you do not answer what is asked of you.

How many things am I being asked to do?
You are asked to discuss two things: *advantages* and *disadvantages.* You may have as many advantages and disadvantages as you like, but you must represent both sides.

How many paragraphs will I need for this?
You will need four paragraphs, to be broken down as follows:

1. Introduction
2. One side—either advantages or disadvantages
3. The other side—either advantages or disadvantages
4. Conclusion

Now, rephrase the question so you are sure you've understood what is asked of you. This can be one of the most important steps in any paper you write, for you must answer the question and if you rush in without fully understanding what the question is asking, you may lose all credit.

Rephrasing:____

____

____

Rephrasing:____

____

____

There are few things as frightening as staring at a blank sheet of paper, knowing that you only have a few minutes in which to write an essay. Where do you start? This can be really upsetting in a pressured exam, for you do not have the time to stop and think for awhile, and you are not allowed to talk to people and get their help. There is no time to revise and rewrite the paper; the first draft will have to stand as the final draft.

How do you begin? Is it best to just take a deep breath and plunge right in? Or are you better off planning for a few moments, even though it seems like everyone around you is already writing?

It Is Always Better to Plan Before You Write

It is ALWAYS worth the time to set up a plan of action, even though it looks as if you might be left behind, since everyone else just seems to start writing. A plan always makes a better finished project, especially in a timed exam, when you will not have the luxury of a revision. The ideas will flow with greater logic and clarity if you have a plan. There are several different ways to plan—select the one that is best for you.

ONE WAY TO PLAN: THE EGO METHOD

One of the best ways to set up an essay involves the following steps.

1. *Write down all the possible ideas you can think of on the topic.* Do not stop and consider your ideas, and try not to even lift your pen off the paper. Just write as many things as you can think of as fast as you can. This should take no more than *one* or *two* minutes. For example, look back to our question:

> FOR EXAMPLE:
>
> A generation ago, young people took it for granted that they would marry and soon after become parents. Today's young couples seem to be putting off parenthood well into their marriages, and a significant number are not having children at all. Discuss the advantages and disadvantages of having children. Be specific.

Allowing one to two minutes, you might write something like this:

money	time	career	jobs	love
housing	travel	friendships	responsibilities	continuation
families	fear	divorce	stepchildren	unity
money	material things	schooling	job advancement	purpose

2. *Eliminate* all the things you have doubles of, would rather not write about because you're not too well-versed in them, or are too general and vague. So you would cross off:

~~money~~	time	~~career~~	jobs	love
housing	~~travel~~	friendships	responsibilities	continuation
families	~~fear~~	divorce	stepchildren	~~unity~~
money	material things	schooling	job advancement	purpose

You have written "money" twice, so one gets crossed off; "career" and "jobs" are the same; "fear" is too general; and so forth. This should take another minute. Now you have a list of possible things to discuss, and are no longer staring at a blank sheet of paper.

This whole process should take 1 to 3 minutes—no more!

3. Now *group* the items into possible paragraphs. Look back at the question to arrange the groups.

Advantages of having children	Disadvantages of having children
love	schooling
families	jobs

or

friendships	responsibilities
love	money

4. Last *organize* the groups into possible ways to answer the question: Each Roman numeral (I, II, III, IV, etc.) stands for a paragraph. Each capital letter (A, B, C, etc.) stands for a subheading.

I. Introduction—There are advantages and disadvantages of having children

II. Advantages of having children
  A. Friendships
  B. Love

III. Disadvantages of having children
  A. Money
  B. Responsibilities

IV. Conclusion—pick a side

or

I. Introduction—There are advantages and disadvantages to having children

II. Advantages of having children
    A. Love
    B. Families

III. Disadvantages of having children
    A. Schooling
    B. Jobs

IV. Conclusion—pick a side

This is called the EGO method:

E	Eliminate	(as you crossed off items that you did not need)
G	Group	(as you grouped the items into possible paragraphs)
O	Organize	(as you organized the items into a possible answer)

Remember, this entire process is designed to be done very quickly. From start to finish, it should only take a few moments. Do not spend more than 5 minutes organizing your answer or you may not have time to complete the essay.

The advantages of this method, or any planning, are that you have organized and arranged your thoughts into a unified whole. Your answer will make a great deal more sense and you won't find that you complete a paragraph and then exclaim, "Oh! I forgot the point about . . ." and have to insert arrows and various messy signs.

Outlines Are Important

Outlining is one of the most valuable things you can do to ensure a good grade on the essay. It helps you plan and make sure you are really proving your point with good, specific details.

There are many ways to do outlines, depending on the amount of time you have and the amount of detail you need. For our purposes here, we will follow a very specific outline, printed below. Do not worry about spelling and punctuation; just concentrate on getting down the most important points in a very brief amount of time. Focus on DETAIL to make sure you have made your point.

Follow this plan:

I. Topic paragraph
    A. Topic sentence (rephrase question)
    B. Sentence that introduces second paragraph
    C. Sentence that introduces third paragraph
    D. Sentence that leads into the second paragraph. This is optional.

II. The first point you have to make. It may be advantages, disadvantages, or just your first topic under discussion.
    A. Topic sentence
    B. Your first point (or advantage, etc.)
        1. Detail about the point
        2. Detail about the point

C. Your second point
 1. Detail
 2. Detail
D. Optional summary of the points made in the paragraph

III. Your second point (which may be disadvantages, etc.)
 A. Topic sentence
 B. Your first point
  1. Detail
  2. Detail
 C. Your second point
  1. Detail
  2. Detail
 D. Optional conclusion

IV. Conclusion to the essay
 A. Topic sentence—rephrases the question
 B. Sentence that summarizes the second paragraph
 C. Sentence that summarizes the third paragraph
 D. Overall conclusion that makes your point

A SECOND WAY TO PLAN: THE QAD METHOD

There are many other ways to plan your essay. One that many find helpful is called

Q Question
A Answer
D Detail

and goes like this:

Question: Some believe that college is a waste of time and money, while others feel it is a valuable tool for happiness and success. Explain the advantages and disadvantages of going to college. Be specific.

Answer:

Advantages	Disadvantages
become better educated	expensive
meet people	lose time on career
form new interests	a lot of what you learn not useful in career
gain appreciation of culture	difficult to do

Details: There are two ways to do this.
You can ask yourself the following questions, when they apply:

What happens?	Where?
When?	Why?
How?	Who?

or

List specific details you can use in the essay.

Advantages

I became better educated when I took Math 101 and Chemistry. Even though I can't use either one of these courses in my job, I really feel it is important to understand how these fields work. I enjoyed learning about radical numbers and quadratic equations, and found the way molecules work fascinating. I think I'm more well-rounded for having studied these areas.

I met a lot of interesting people in college, people I would never have encountered in my home town. I remember especially someone from Hawaii and a few people from England and France, who told me all about their lives and culture. I still write to the Hawaiian and I stayed with my British friend last summer.

I became interested in gems and physical education in college, two fields I ignored in high school. The course in Jewelry Arts showed me all sorts of things I had never seen before—how to solder and hammer metal—and Physical Education got me involved in tennis and golf.

Disadvantages

My college charges $150.00 for one credit of study, and you need 125 credits to graduate. Counting room and board and fees, that's more than my parents paid for their first two homes combined!

I want to begin a career in landscaping and I can't afford to lose two or four years in a liberal arts college. I know there's a need for landscaping in my neighborhood and if I get started fast, I could have a thriving business.

I resent having to take Math and Science, which will be of no use to me in my planned career as a sales representative. Why should I spend all that time and money on something I'll never use?

WRITING YOUR ESSAY

TOPIC SENTENCES ARE A MUST

In a way, writing a good topic sentence is like aiming a gun: If the topic sentence is aimed correctly, the whole paragraph will hit its mark, and prove your point.

- *Every paragraph must have a topic sentence.* This includes the first, second, third, and last.
- The topic sentence expresses the main idea—the topic—of the paragraph.
- The topic sentence must join together all the ideas expressed in the paragraph.
- The topic sentence must be *limited* enough to be developed within a single paragraph but *broad* enough to have all the ideas that you need in that paragraph. The more specific your topic sentence, the more detailed and descriptive your paragraph will be.

Limiting a Topic Sentence

Remember: A topic sentence has an idea that can be fully proven in one paragraph. For example, the sentence "You can learn a lot about human nature just by observing people" is so broad that it cannot be proven in one single paragraph. But if we write

> FOR EXAMPLE:
>
> "You can learn a lot about human nature by watching people at a bus station"

or

> FOR EXAMPLE:
>
> "You can learn a lot about human nature by watching people at the beach"

we have a topic that we can prove in one paragraph.

Expressing a Clear Controlling Idea

Another way to look at topic sentences is through the *controlling idea.* This a *key word* or a *group of words* that expresses the basic idea of the sentence. When the controlling idea is clear, the entire sentence will be specific and clear.

Directions:

Circle the controlling idea in the following sentences.

Example: An encyclopedia is a handy book for students.
"Handy" is the *controlling idea,* and in the paragraph that follows, you will explain *how* the encyclopedia is handy.

1. Obtaining a driver's license is a difficult experience.
2. I have had several unusual experiences on dates.
3. Traveling by train has several advantages over traveling by car.
4. There are three steps in barbecuing hot dogs.
5. Good English is clear, appropriate, and vivid.

Answers:

1. difficult experience
2. unusual experiences
3. several advantages
4. three steps
5. clear, appropriate, vivid

USING SPECIFIC WORDS

To prove your point and make your writing interesting, you have to use specific words and phrases.

Directions:
Select the most specific word from the list below in each example to make the most precise sentence.

Example: His face was ____ with fright.
colorless scarlet chalky pale

The answer is "chalky," for "colorless" and "pale" are too vague. "Scarlet" is also incorrect, for your face does not become scarlet (red) when you are afraid. "Chalky" is the best word, for in addition to color—a pale, dry white—it implies a *texture*—dry and lifeless. It is the most descriptive word and the one that will make this sentence most effective.

1. He wore a ____ shirt.
   scarlet colored red bright-colored
2. The playground was a sea of mud after the ____.
   cloudburst precipitation rain moisture
3. The sun is high and hot; the air is sultry; it is ____ time.
   siesta sleep nap rest

Answers:

1. "Scarlet" is the most specific here, as it describes a bright red. Then would come:
   red
   bright-colored
   colored
2. "Cloudburst" describes a specific kind of precipitation, a sudden, sharp downpour. In order of specific nature:
   rain
   precipitation (can also be snow, sleet, hail)
   moisture
3. "Siesta" describes a nap that is taken when it is very warm during the middle of the day and is thus the most precise. Then would come:
   nap a short sleep
   sleep a type of rest
   rest any sitting down and relaxing

PROOFREADING CAN RAISE YOUR SCORE

There is a great tendency to stand up the very minute you have finished writing and rush out of the room, relieved that it is all over. While we all have this feeling, *you must allow time for proofreading.* You can save yourself a great many unnecessary errors if you proofread your essay.

After you finish writing, leave a few minutes to check over what you said. Make sure of the following:

- Did you answer the question?
- Did you provide good, *specific* detail to support your ideas?
- Did you organize your answer in the best possible way to make your point clearly?
- Did you check over what you said for errors in spelling, grammar, punctuation, words misused, and so forth?

This is time very well spent. You must check over what you said, but *be sure to read what is there, not what you think is there.* Do not read too quickly, and go back over passages that seem unclear to you. Some find it helpful to put another piece of paper over the lines to help you focus on only one line at a time. In any event, make sure you check what you have said, even if all others are getting up around you. You'll be the winner if you do.

BEFORE YOU GO ON TO THE SAMPLE TOPICS, REVIEW THESE TIPS FOR WRITING BETTER ESSAYS:

1. Sit in a quiet room all alone, without a television or radio. Make the room conditions as close to exam conditions as possible.
2. Allow yourself forty-five minutes.
3. ORGANIZE before you write. We suggest the EGO method. This means you will
   —Write down all the ideas you can think of about the question
   —Eliminate all doubles or vague ideas
   —Group the ideas into a form that will answer the question
   —Organize an outline and begin to write
   This whole process should only take a few moments.
4. After you finish writing, be sure to *proofread.* This is well worth the few moments it will take you. Check to make sure that you have provided specific examples, that you have proved what was asked of you, that you have corrected all spelling, grammar, punctuation, capitalization errors.
5. Try to turn in the best possible essay every time you write. Make each practice session count.
6. Try to get someone to read your essays over and offer advice. They will be able to help you clear up any confusion in your thinking and make sure that you have proved your point.

SAMPLE ESSAY TOPICS FOR PRACTICE:

Directions:
Each of the following essay topics is very much like what you will encounter on the GED. Answer them as though you were actually taking the exam.

1. Recent antismoking laws have touched off a great deal of controversy, as antismokers feel their health is being endangered by smokers, and smokers feel they are being denied their rights by antismoking legislation. State your opinion concerning the antismoking laws and back it up with specific examples.
2. "When all guns are outlawed, only outlaws will have guns" a bumper sticker reads. Discuss the advantages and disadvantages of gun control.
3. Many states are passing laws so students cannot graduate without passing a series of competency exams. Is this good or bad? State your opinion and support with details.
4. Women have made noteworthy strides in changing the way they live and, by extension, the shape of the American family. Do you feel the so-called "Women's Liberation" movement is a good or bad thing? Support with specific examples.
5. Some feel there should be a freeze on all spending for nuclear weapons. Others believe that we will be left behind if we do not increase allocations for nuclear technology. Take a side on this issue and support your opinion with specific details.
6. Discuss the advantages and disadvantages of the social security system. Support your opinion with specific details.
7. "Buy American," orders a roadside billboard. Discuss the advantages and disadvantages of buying goods manufactured in the United States in preference to foreign products.
8. Discuss the advantages and disadvantages of the new legalization regulations for undocumented aliens. Support your opinions with specific details.
9. "Seat belts save lives" according to the television commercials. It has been shown that a greater number of Americans are surviving serious automobile accidents. Some people feel that passive restraint systems, such as air bags, could increase the survival rate even more, especially if they were required in every automobile sold in the U.S. State your opinion concerning passive restraints and back it up with specific details.
10. Many gasoline stations in the country are dropping the sale of leaded gasoline. Irate automobile drivers have criticized the fuel companies and feel that they are being forced to "trade in" their old reliable jalopies for more complicated and expensive new models. Share your opinion on this situation and be sure to back it up with specific examples.

Part III

Social Studies Review

ALL ABOUT THE SOCIAL STUDIES TEST

The GED Social Studies Test covers the following subject areas:

History (25%)

Economics (20%)

Political Science (20%)

Geography/Area Studies (15%)

Behavioral Sciences (20%)

Many of the questions concern knowledge or skills taken from more than one subject area. For example, a single question may actually draw upon your knowledge of economic, geographic, political, and historical concepts in the process of asking you to make a decision or to solve a problem. Some of the questions concern global issues such as how American history influences world affairs or how world affairs have altered the course of American history.

WHAT ARE THE QUESTIONS LIKE ON THE SOCIAL STUDIES TEST?

All questions in the GED Social Studies Test will be multiple-choice questions, with five possible answers. You will be required to pick the best possible answer of the five. Each test contains 64 questions. Most of these questions (about two-thirds) are based on written (printed) information. This information may be taken from any number of places: a speech, an editorial, a magazine article, a diary, a historic document, etc. The remaining questions are based on some sort of illustration: a table, a pie chart, an editorial cartoon, a map, a bar graph, etc.

Most questions will be arranged in sets. A typical set might begin with an excerpt from a magazine article followed by five or six questions. Another set could begin with a table of business activity followed by four or five questions. The remaining questions in the test will be single questions based on a very short reading or a single illustration.

GED Social Studies questions test your knowledge of important principles, concepts, events, and relationships. You will be asked to demonstrate a variety of reasoning skills in answering these questions:

1. Understanding the meaning of both written and illustrated questions. (comprehension)

Can you restate information that was written or pictured in the original question?
Can you summarize, that is, restate briefly, the important idea(s) of a reading passage, or picture?
Can you determine the implications of a particular piece of information or event, that is, can you draw an inference?

2. Taking the information or ideas in a question and applying it to a specific situation given in the question(s). (Application)

   Can you apply a principle to a new situation, not necessarily one you may have studied in a class?

3. Breaking down information into smaller parts/Looking at the relationships between the various parts of (larger) complete ideas. (Analysis)

   Can you tell the difference between a fact and an opinion or a hypothesis?
   Can you pick out the unstated assumptions in a question or a table or a reading passage?
   Can you separate a conclusion from the various supporting statements that help you reach that conclusion?
   Can you pick out cause and effect relationships?

4. Making judgments about the validity or accuracy of information or methods used to gather information or research data. (Evaluation)

   Can you look at information presented in a question and decide whether it really supports a hypothesis, conclusion, or generalization?
   Do you understand that certain values have often entered into the development of particular beliefs, policies, or instances of decision-making?
   Are you able to look critically at the accuracy of facts which are offered as "proof"?
   Can you find logical mistakes in arguments?

If you've decided at this point that the reasoning skills needed for the GED are rather overwhelming, remember this: You need to answer just about half of the questions correctly to pass the GED Social Studies Test.

WHAT TOPICS ARE COVERED ON THE SOCIAL STUDIES TEST?

The following outline of areas from which social studies questions may be drawn is reprinted by permission of the GED Testing Service of the American Council on Education.

Social Studies questions may be drawn from any of the following areas:

I. United States History
   A. A New World and a new nation
      1. Beginnings in Europe: background for discovery
      2. Colonization in North America

3. Struggle for control by Spanish, English, and French
4. Thirteen English colonies
5. American colonial development: economic, social, cultural development

B. Growth and change
1. The Revolutionary War; a national government
2. Expansion and creation of economic and geographic regions
3. National issues: slavery, secession, states' rights

C. Civil War and Reconstruction

D. Rise of industrial America
1. Western frontier: settlement and way of life
2. Industrial Revolution
3. Labor and immigration
4. Growth of cities
5. Social and cultural trends
6. Problems of industrialization
7. Reforms: suffrage for women, welfare, education

E. Crisis and reform
1. Beginnings of reform: farmers and workers, political machines, rise of labor, NAACP
2. Protests and politics
3. Progressive era

F. United States becomes a world power
1. Expansion and imperialism: Spanish-American War
2. World War I; isolationism
3. The Twenties: prosperity, the Stock Market Crash, the Depression
4. The New Deal
5. World War II; United Nations
6. The Fifties: Cold War, Korean War
7. The Sixties and Seventies: The New Frontier, The Great Society, Vietnam, Watergate, arms race, civil rights movement
8. The Eighties: economic problems, involvement in the Mideast and Central America

G. Facing challenges of the modern world
1. Power and responsibility in a nuclear age
2. Working for peace
3. Postindustrial economy, high technology and communications, shifts in the work force
4. Global interdependence: information explosion, space exploration

II. Geography

A. Basic principles, concepts, and tools of geography
1. The earth and its people: population distribution, migration
2. Maps and globes
3. Latitude and longitude
4. Climate and its importance to human society
5. Natural resources
6. Land, water, air of the earth
7. Regions of the earth

B. Major cultural regions: the United States and Canada, Latin America, Northwestern Europe, Mediterranean countries and the Middle East, the USSR and Eastern Europe, the Far East, Africa south of the Sahara, the Pacific

1. Climate
2. Topography
3. Natural resources
4. Economic development
5. Cultural influences
6. Standard of living

C. Using the world's resources: toward a better world
1. World trade
2. Preserving the world's environment
3. Resources and developing nations
4. Urban and rural life

III. Economics

A. The meaning of economics

B. Comparison of modern (mixed) economic systems: capitalism, communism, socialism

C. Businesses in a free enterprise system
1. How business is organized
2. Economic markets
3. Supply and demand
4. How prices are determined
5. Competition and monopoly

D. Production
1. Role of production
2. Deciding what and how to produce and distribute
3. Production of goods and services, mass production, craftsmanship

E. Consumers
1. Role of the consumer in the economy
2. Money management: investment, insurance, savings
3. Advertising
4. Consumer budgeting: credit and contracts

F. Financial institutions
1. Money and monetary policy
2. Banking and interest
3. Financial institutions other than banks

G. Government's role in the economy (national, state, local)
1. Taxes and other sources of revenue
2. Government expenditures, services, national debt, balancing the budget
3. Consumer protection and education
4. Business regulation

H. How the overall economy behaves
1. Measuring the economy: GNP, Consumer Price Index, wages
2. How the economy grows: new industries, development, expanding markets
3. Problems of growth: economic classes, materialism, resource depletion, chemical waste
4. Economic fluctuations, business cycles
5. Inflation and deflation, recession
6. Policies for stabilization of the economy: fiscal and monetary
7. Formulating modern economic policy, a complex task

I. Labor and the economy
1. Labor market: union and non-union labor

2. Distribution of income: profit and wages, economic classes
3. Collective bargaining, strikes, and picketing
4. Productivity
5. Unemployment: causes, how to reduce it

J. Foreign trade
1. Imports and exports
2. Balance of trade
3. Multinational corporations
4. Foreign competition

IV. Political Science

A. Nature of political systems
1. Government and society: importance and the basic role of government
2. Types of modern governments
3. Meaning of democracy

B. The American political system
1. Declaration of Independence and the United States Constitution
2. American federalism: national, state, and local governments

C. American political process
1. Political party system
2. Right to vote and voter behavior
3. Nominations and elections
4. Public opinion and pressure groups
5. Active citizenship

D. National executive branch
1. Office and powers of the president
2. Office and powers of the vice president
3. The cabinet
4. The Civil Service
5. Executive agencies

E. National legislative branch
1. Legislative powers
2. House of Representatives
3. Senate
4. The making of the law

F. National judicial branch
1. United States system of justice: importance of law and the legal system
2. Federal court system
3. Role of the Supreme Court
4. Civil liberties and civil rights
5. Equal justice for all

G. State governments
1. Nature of state governments
2. State executive, legislative, and judicial branches
3. Financing state government

H. Local governments
1. Importance/function
2. Governing the communities: cities, towns, counties
3. Financing local governments

I. Government and general welfare
1. Federal revenues and expenditures

2. Money and banking policies
3. Government and business: capitalism/socialism
4. Labor and Social Security
5. Agriculture and conservation
6. Federal agencies

J. The United States in today's world
1. American foreign policy
2. United States and international organizations
3. Population explosion, technological revolutions, meeting social responsibilities: health, education, welfare, crime, and other problems

V. Behavioral Sciences

A. From the psychologist's point of view
1. What psychology is
2. Primary needs for survival and well-being
3. Understanding human behavior: measures of personality and intellect
4. Heredity and environment
5. Principles of learning
6. Beliefs, feelings, attitudes: male/female roles

B. From the sociologist's point of view
1. What sociology is
2. Groups: family, schools, peer groups, behavior in small groups, other social institutions
3. Social stratification: social class, occupational scale, ethnic background, norms and values

C. From the anthropologist's point of view
1. What anthropology is
2. Culture: social relationships, religious expression, problems of society, when cultures meet, race and prejudice
3. The search for identity

AMERICAN HISTORY

Directions:
For each question, circle the number of the response that best answers the question or completes the statement. Correct and explanatory answers are provided at the end of the chapter.

Items 1 and 2 refer to the graph below.

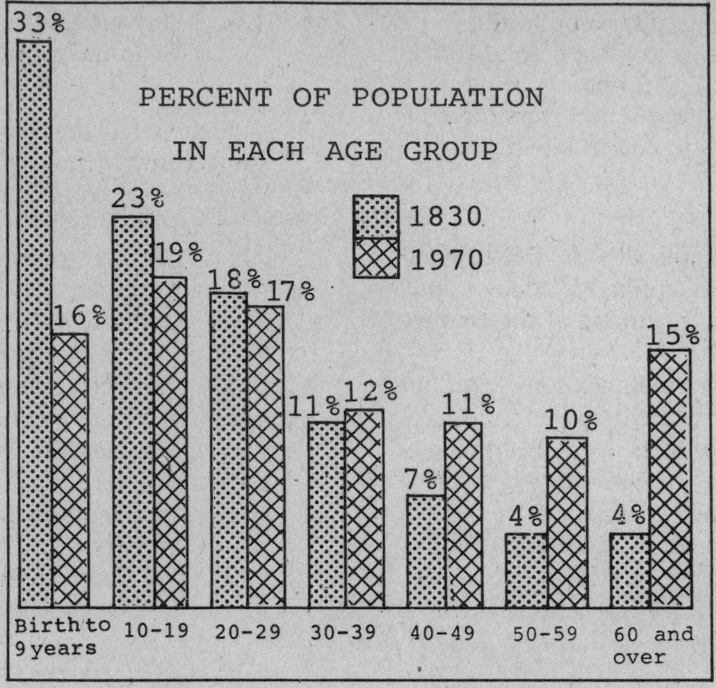

U.S. Population by Age Group 1830 and 1970

1. From 1830 to 1970, the smallest change in the percent of population occurred within which age group?

   (1) birth to 9 years
   (2) 10–19
   (3) 20–29
   (4) 40–49
   (5) 50–59

2. The information in the graph would be useful to officials of the federal government who are planning programs concerning

   (1) defense
   (2) mass transit
   (3) Social Security System
   (4) public works projects
   (5) nuclear power plants

3. The basic reason for the support of public education in the United States has been to provide

   (1) skilled workers for industry
   (2) trained persons for the professions
   (3) educated leaders for government service
   (4) knowledgeable social studies teachers
   (5) informed citizens for a democratic society

4. United States immigration policy has been characterized by

   (1) a preference for Asian peoples
   (2) continued willingness to welcome the oppressed of other nations
   (3) a preference for unskilled laborers
   (4) unrestricted immigration for all religious groups
   (5) periods of openness and periods of restriction

5. Which statement concerning immigration to the United States would be most difficult to prove?

   (1) The peak of immigration occurred between 1890 and 1910.
   (2) Many recent immigrants to the United States came from Asia and South America.
   (3) Immigrants have made many

contributions to the cultural development of the United States.
(4) Many immigrants came to the United States to escape undesirable conditions in Europe.
(5) The prejudice of employers forced immigrants to accept low-paying jobs.

6. Which best explains why divorce rates in the United States are higher today than they were at the beginning of the century?

(1) Marriage is no longer considered an important element in society.
(2) Divorce statistics at the beginning of the century were not accurate.
(3) Divorce rates generally increase during periods of economic instability.
(4) Social and legal restrictions concerning divorce have been reduced.
(5) Many modern religious leaders are now in favor of divorce.

7. Which statement is most accurate concerning various utopian communities in the 19th century?

(1) They were subsidized by the federal government.
(2) They were based on a belief that people could be improved by a better social environment.
(3) They were populated mainly by the upper classes.
(4) They were organized primarily to secure material wealth for their members.
(5) They were supported by a majority of the established churches.

GO ON TO THE NEXT PAGE

Items 8 and 9 refer to the map below.

State Population—Percent Change. 1980 to 1985

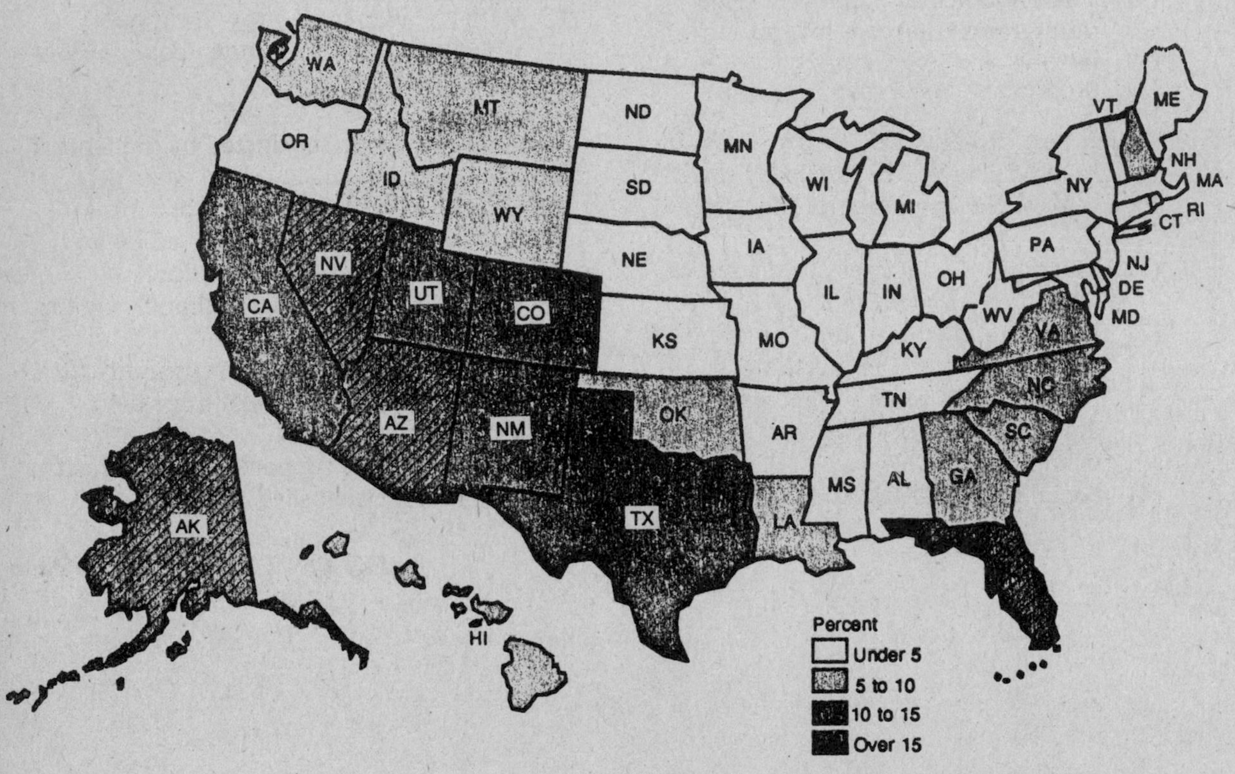

8. Which areas of the United States show the greatest changes in population between 1980 and 1985?

   (1) The Southeast and the Northwest
   (2) The North Central states and the Northwest
   (3) The North Central states and the South Atlantic region
   (4) The West and the Northeast
   (5) The Southwest and the Far West

9. Based on the map above, an employee looking for a new job might list which of the following states as a possible location for employment?

   (1) Arizona and Oklahoma
   (2) California and Alaska
   (3) Kentucky and Michigan
   (4) Louisiana and New Hampshire
   (5) Virginia and Wyoming

10. From 1840 to 1900, each new group of immigrants to the United States contributed to the upward social mobility of the previous groups by

    (1) creating a climate for social reform
    (2) stimulating interest in free public education
    (3) reinforcing the ethnic heritage of earlier immigrants
    (4) returning to their countries of origin
    (5) filling the unskilled and semiskilled jobs

11. In the United States, upward social mobility has been encouraged by the institution of

    (1) local zoning regulations
    (2) social welfare
    (3) public education
    (4) revenue sharing
    (5) progressive taxation

Items 12 and 13 refer to the information below.

"In the new code of law of which I suppose it will be necessary for you to make, I desire you would remember the ladies and be more generous and favorable to them than your ancestors. Do not put such unlimited power into the hands of husbands. Remember, all men would be tyrants if they could. If particular care and attention is not paid to the ladies, we are determined to foment a rebellion, and will not hold ourselves bound by any laws in which we have no voice or representation."

12. The writer of these lines might be described today as a

    (1) socialist
    (2) revolutionary
    (3) feminist
    (4) patriot
    (5) civil rights advocate

13. The writer's argument and choice of words reflect the language and political vocabulary of a specific time period in United States history. This period is most likely

    (1) early colonial period
    (2) Revolutionary War
    (3) War of 1812
    (4) annexation of Texas
    (5) 1850's

Items 14 to 16 are based on the following cartoon.

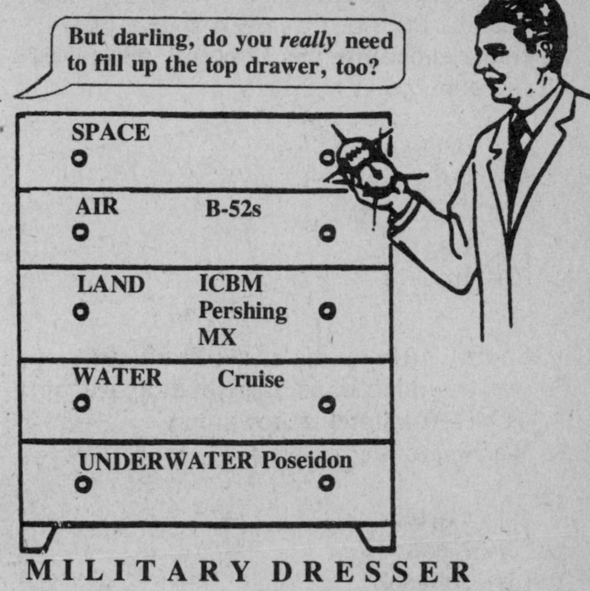

14. The best title for this cartoon is

    (1) Planning the Bedroom Furniture
    (2) Cooperative Planning
    (3) Arms Storage
    (4) Danger Under the Sea
    (5) Science Fiction Thriller

15. The cartoonist implies that

    (1) the submarine is the most important weapon
    (2) we have enough weapons already
    (3) the U.S. and U.S.S.R. should negotiate
    (4) we need more weapons below the earth
    (5) the military budget is too low

16. Nuclear weapons exist everywhere *but*

    (1) in space
    (2) in the air
    (3) on land
    (4) on the water
    (5) under the water

GO ON TO THE NEXT PAGE

17. In 1979 Russia invaded this Asian country and installed a Soviet-controlled government. Within two years _____ had become the world's largest source of refugees because nearly twenty percent of the population had fled.

    (1) Afghanistan
    (2) Lebanon
    (3) Cambodia
    (4) Iran
    (5) Iraq

18. Shortly after taking office, President _____ was wounded in an assassination attempt as he left a hotel in downtown Washington.

    (1) Carter
    (2) Kennedy
    (3) Johnson
    (4) Reagan
    (5) Ford

19. The Middle East has long been a volatile area of the world which has engaged American, French, and other Western interests. On October 23, 1983, terrorists set off explosives in _____, killing 299 members of the French and American peacekeeping forces.

    (1) Damascus, Syria
    (2) Tehran, Iran
    (3) Athens, Greece
    (4) Beirut, Lebanon
    (5) Jerusalem, Israel

20. In 1984, Congress passed a bill to create a new federal holiday. This new holiday commemorates the birthday of

    (1) John F. Kennedy
    (2) Abraham Lincoln
    (3) Martin Luther King, Jr.
    (4) Robert F. Kennedy
    (5) George Washington

Items 21 to 24 are based on the information below.

The attitudes and values of a democratic society are expressed in a variety of ways throughout history. The views of some members of a society often tend to express the underlying doubts, animosities, or culturally accepted reasons for pursuing war, even when this pursuit conflicts with the values of a democratic society. Each of the following quotations represents the time period of a particular conflict in which the United States was engaged. Choose the conflict each statement is most closely related to.

21. "Sic semper tyrannis! The South is avenged!"

    (1) Civil War
    (2) Spanish-American War
    (3) World War I
    (4) World War II
    (5) Vietnamese Conflict

22. "The tree of liberty must be refreshed from time to time with the blood of patriots and tyrants. It is its natural manure."

    (1) French and Indian War
    (2) American Revolution
    (3) War of 1812
    (4) Civil War
    (5) Spanish-American War

23. "A splendid little war"

    (1) Civil War
    (2) Spanish-American War
    (3) World War I
    (4) Korean Conflict
    (5) Vietnamese Conflict

24. "Wrong and morally wrong in its conduct and consequences, it was nevertheless not evil, in intent or origin. What propelled us into this war was a corruption of the generous, idealistic, liberal impulse."

    (1) American Revolution
    (2) Spanish-American War
    (3) World War II
    (4) Korean Conflict
    (5) Vietnamese Conflict

Items 25 and 26 are based on the following information.

In the 1880's large industrial monopolies controlled many industries. For example: the steel, oil, and meat-packing industries were each controlled by one major company. The result was that the consumer had to pay artificially high prices for these goods. Eventually laws were enacted to protect the consumers.

25. The writers who described the evils of the monopolies were called

    (1) communists
    (2) libertarians
    (3) progressives
    (4) labor leaders
    (5) muckrakers

26. One of the laws that was enacted to curb monopolies was the

    (1) Stamp Act
    (2) Sherman Anti-Trust Act
    (3) National Recovery Act
    (4) Great Society
    (5) Marshall Plan

Items 27 and 28 refer to the information below.

The selection below is a portion of a letter written by George Washington in 1790 during his first term as President of the United States:

The Citizens of the United States of America have a right to applaud themselves for having given to mankind examples of an enlarged and liberal policy; a policy worthy of imitation. All possess alike liberty of conscience and immunities of citizenship. It is now no more that toleration is spoken of, as if it was by the indulgence of one class of people, that another enjoyed the exercise of their inherent natural rights. For happily the Government of the United States, which gives to bigotry no sanction, to persecution no assistance, requires only that they who live under its protection, should demean themselves as good citizens, in giving it on all occasions their effectual support.

27. Ironically, at this time, the only persons who were allowed to vote were

    (1) native born men and women
    (2) veterans of the Revolutionary War
    (3) white male property owners
    (4) signers of the Declaration of Independence
    (5) Blacks and Orientals

28. It was another 130 years before women were given the vote. The women who lobbied and won passage of the Nineteenth Amendment to the Constitution were known as

    (1) Feminists
    (2) Suffragettes
    (3) Liberationists
    (4) Know-Nothings
    (5) Locofocos

29. During the westward movement of the nineteenth century, the Indians of the Plains were finally subdued. Which factor contributed most to their eventual confinement on the reservations?

    (1) the construction of the railroads
    (2) cattle drives along the route of the Chisholm Trail
    (3) U.S. cavalry warfare against Indians
    (4) the invention of the Conestoga wagon
    (5) the destruction of the buffalo

30. In the 1870's in the Middle West, a strong political movement was established to help farmers who were overcharged by the railroads. This movement was called

    (1) The Ku Klux Klan
    (2) The National Socialist Party
    (3) The Congress of Industrial Organization
    (4) The Grange
    (5) The Democratic Party

END OF AMERICAN HISTORY TEST

ANSWER KEY FOR AMERICAN HISTORY QUESTIONS

1. (3)	9. (2)	17. (1)	25. (5)
2. (3)	10. (5)	18. (4)	26. (2)
3. (5)	11. (3)	19. (4)	27. (3)
4. (5)	12. (3)	20. (3)	28. (2)
5. (5)	13. (2)	21. (1)	29. (5)
6. (4)	14. (3)	22. (2)	30. (4)
7. (2)	15. (2)	23. (2)	
8. (5)	16. (1)	24. (5)	

EXPLANATIONS FOR AMERICAN HISTORY QUESTIONS

1. **(3)** The 20–29 category shows a mere 1% change.

2. **(3)** The greatest change in population took place in the over-60 category. These people would receive important benefits from Social Security.

3. **(5)** Education has been viewed as an effective method for producing citizens who are capable of making intelligent decisions in a democratic way.

4. **(5)** United States immigration policy has varied drastically over the years, swinging from periods of unrestricted immigration to periods of severe restrictions on immigration.

5. **(5)** While all of the statements might be correct, prejudice is difficult to prove by looking at statistics.

6. **(4)** The divorce rate has increased because the social and legal restrictions against divorce have been reduced. What might have been headline news forty years ago receives only lip service today.

7. **(2)** Utopian communities of the nineteenth century were developed with the belief that given a better social environment, people would develop into better citizens.

8. **(5)** The darker the shading on a given state, the greater the change in population. A group of dark shaded states clustered together could be

identified as a region of great population change. Florida, part of the southeastern seaboard, the Southwest and most of the Northwest conform to this description. Choice (5) is the only one with two items drawn from this list of regions.

9. **(2)** States with the highest population growth are often the states with the greatest number of new jobs created by a demand for housing and other services. California and Alaska show the darkest shading of any pair of states listed in the choices.

10. **(5)** Generally, each new immigrant group filled the unskilled or semiskilled jobs. In the meantime, the previous groups moved upwards to better jobs and/or property ownership.

11. **(3)** It has been widely acknowledged that many American children have surpassed their parents due to the provision of free public education in the United States.

12. **(3)** In this 1777 letter to John Adams, her husband, Abigail Adams clearly pleads the case of women at the time of the Revolutionary War.

13. **(2)** Abigail Adams' style and word choice echo those of her husband and other leaders of the American colonies who deliberated and/or propagandized the cause of the Declaration of Independence.

14. **(3)** The cartoon depicts arms storage.

15. **(2)** The implication of the cartoon is that we have enough weapons already.

16. **(1)** The "Military Dresser" shows weapons everywhere except in space.

17. **(1)** In 1981 Afghanistan topped all other countries in the number of residents fleeing their homeland.

18. **(4)** President Reagan was wounded by John Hinckley in March, 1980, but recovered from the gun wound.

19. **(4)** American Marines and French troops, part of the international peacekeeping force in Beirut, Lebanon, were killed by truck bomb attacks on Sunday morning, October 23, 1983.

20. **(3)** Beginning in 1985, the third Monday in January became a federal holiday honoring the memory of Martin Luther King, Jr.

21. **(1)** Spoken after Booth assassinated Lincoln at Ford's Theater on April 14, 1865, these words typified the lingering animosity of the Reconstruction period to follow.

22. **(2)** Jefferson wrote these words in 1787 during the Revolutionary War.

23. **(2)** These words were spoken by John Hay, Secretary of State, in 1898. The Spanish-American was the "littlest" of American wars, and highly manipulated by interests other than those of the territories directly involved.

24. **(5)** Alexander Bickel wrote these words in *The Morality of Consent,* after the conclusion of the Vietnamese Conflict.

25. **(5)** The "muckrakers" were authors who wrote about the abuses of the people by big business.

26. **(2)** The Sherman Anti-Trust Act of 1890 was the first Federal act which sought to declare monopolies and attempts to restrain trade illegal.

27. **(3)** Early in the life of the Republic, only white male property owners were allowed to vote.

28. **(2)** The women who advocated and worked for their own right to vote were known as Suffragettes.

29. **(5)** The final destruction of the buffalo by hunters and builders eliminated the major food supply of the Indians who became dependent on the favor of the federal government and confined to the reservations.

30. **(4)** The Grange movement was started by farmers who wanted to end the high rates that they were charged by the railroads to transport their crops to market.

Economics

Directions:

For each question, circle the number of the response that best answers the question or completes the statement. Correct and explanatory answers are provided at the end of the chapter.

YEAR	WHEAT PRODUCTION (thousands of bushels)	PRICE OF WHEAT (cents per bushel)
1875	2,450	51.9
1880	2,706	49.0
1885	3,058	42.2

1. The data in the chart above could best be used to illustrate which economic concept?

   (1) recession
   (2) inflation
   (3) interdependence
   (4) free enterprise
   (5) supply and demand

2. "When prices of conventional fuels rise sufficiently to match the cost of solar energy, then solar energy will be able to supply more than 10% of our needs."

   In order to bring about greater use of solar energy, the author of this statement is relying primarily upon

   (1) the market system to cause consumers to switch to solar energy
   (2) government policy to encourage solar energy at the expense of other fuels
   (3) technological breakthroughs to reduce the cost of solar energy
   (4) changes in the attitude of big business toward solar energy
   (5) increase in availability of solar energy

3. Which statement concerning business enterprise in the United States is an opinion?

   (1) The corporation is an important form of business organization.
   (2) Some companies control all phases of production from the acquisition of raw materials to the final sale of the product.
   (3) Monopolies tend to eliminate the need for price competition.
   (4) Large-scale producers in an industry offer better personal services than do small-scale producers.
   (5) Mergers of many smaller companies have created a number of giant corporations.

4. The statement, "Today, the dollar is worth about forty-five cents," describes

   (1) inflation
   (2) prices
   (3) supply and demand
   (4) taxation
   (5) deflation

5. A short period of somewhat decreased business activity is known as a

   (1) boom
   (2) depression
   (3) recession
   (4) crash
   (5) demand

6. The theory that government should *not* interfere in economic affairs is known as

   (1) laissez-faire
   (2) populism
   (3) supply-side economics
   (4) socialism
   (5) capitalism

7. Under this system, the government owns nearly all the means of production and directs all important economic activities. It determines wages and prices and decides what to produce and in how great a quantity. The system is called

   (1) capitalism
   (2) fascism
   (3) communism

(4) anarchy
(5) none of the above

8. According to the theory of supply and demand, as the price of an article decreases

   (1) the quantity demanded will usually fall
   (2) the quantity demanded will fall and then rise
   (3) the quantity demanded will not change
   (4) the quantity demanded will usually rise
   (5) the quantity demanded will always fall

9. The money supply of the United States is regulated by the

   (1) United States Department of the Treasury
   (2) Treasurer of the United States
   (3) U.S. Bureau of Engraving and Printing
   (4) Federal Reserve System
   (5) Central Bank

10. In order to achieve agreement between employers and employees, labor and management use the process of

    (1) wildcat strike
    (2) arbitration
    (3) collective bargaining
    (4) boycott
    (5) blacklist

11. In order to compute the income taxes you owe the federal government this year, your employer is required to give you a _____ that lists your earnings and withholding for the past year.

    (1) 1040A form
    (2) W2 form
    (3) Social Security form
    (4) exemption statement
    (5) W4 form

12. Americans pay many different types of taxes to federal, state, and local governments. Choose the best example of a tax that we do NOT pay in the United States.

    (1) payroll taxes
    (2) excise taxes
    (3) value-added taxes
    (4) sales taxes
    (5) income taxes

13. The major purpose of our tax system is to provide funds for the operation of the government. But taxes are also levied in order to

    (1) develop or protect certain industries
    (2) redistribute income
    (3) influence personal spending
    (4) educate the young
    (5) all of the above

14. A tax on perfume is an example of a(n)

    (1) income tax
    (2) excise tax
    (3) property tax
    (4) estate tax
    (5) stock transfer tax

15. Susan Johnson earned $15,000 last year. Sam Milner earned $63,000 last year. Each person was required to pay a special tax of $350. Which of the following terms best describes this tax?

    (1) proportional
    (2) regressive
    (3) inexpensive
    (4) progressive
    (5) unearned

16. Payments to a worker, his dependents, and/or survivors in the event of retirement, disability or death are generally covered by the system of insurance known as

    (1) unemployment compensation
    (2) Social Security
    (3) workman's compensation
    (4) pension fund
    (5) profit sharing

17. Most Americans seek to reduce the financial losses caused by sickness, accident, fire, theft or old age through the use of a cooperative risk-sharing plan called

(1) workman's compensation
(2) Medicare
(3) pension funds
(4) trusts
(5) insurance

Items 18 to 20 refer to the following graph.

U.S. BALANCE OF INTERNATIONAL PAYMENTS

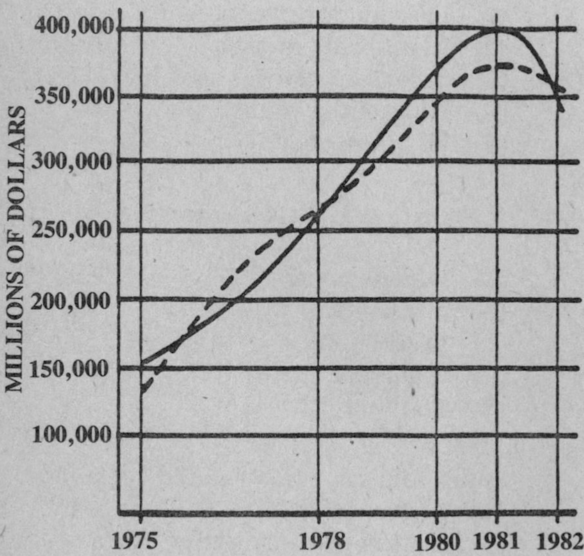

Exports of goods and services: ———
Imports of goods and services: – – – –

18. According to the graph, the value of goods and services exported by the United States exceeded the value of goods and services imported during the year

(1) 1976
(2) 1977
(3) 1980
(4) 1982
(5) Graph does not reveal this information.

19. The value of goods and services imported by the United States exceeded the value of goods and services exported during the year

(1) 1975
(2) 1979
(3) 1980
(4) 1981
(5) 1982

20. By how many millions of dollars did exports exceed imports in 1980? (Answer in millions of dollars).

(1) 4,000
(2) 10,000
(3) 40,000
(4) 60,000
(5) 100,000

Items 21 to 23 refer to the following article.

Advertising of nonprescription medicine has become a frequent source of confusion and wasteful expense. Sometimes it can even damage health. Among heavily advertised patent medicines are those that claim to have rejuvenating powers and are sold to elderly people. One leading gerontologist has pointed out that most such medicines generally contain vitamins and alcohol; and that the alcohol is cheaper at the liquor store and most people do not need extra vitamins.

Television is especially convincing in the sale of drugs and medicine because it can show pseudoscientific demonstrations, featuring actors who look and speak authoritatively—as if they were actually doctors, dentists, or scientists.

One of the most worrisome areas of medical promotions features the products which are sold to arthritis sufferers. Deceitful advertising victimizes five million arthritis sufferers at a cost of hundreds of millions of dollars each year. "Glorified aspirins" such as Arthrycin have been the biggest problem among misrepresented drugs, while vibrating machines are the most frequently oversold and useless mechanical devices. The "glorified aspirins" typically cost five to six dollars for 100 tablets, compared to ordinary aspirin which costs less than one-fifth of that amount.

21. According to the selection above, the most frequent victims of patent medicines are

(1) elderly people
(2) young children
(3) arthritis sufferers
(4) people with headaches
(5) people with dental problems

22. The concept of "rejuvenation" includes the idea of

(1) having a facelift
(2) relief from pain
(3) feeling young again
(4) getting rid of crutches
(5) getting drunk

23. Television as a sales medium is particularly effective because it

(1) conveys the appearance of authenticity
(2) is usually in color
(3) is often watched by old people and children
(4) costs nothing
(5) can be repeated incessantly

GO ON TO THE NEXT PAGE

Mortgage Table
30-Year Mortgage (Principal and Interest per month)

Mortgage Amount	Interest Rate 9%	10%	11%	12%	13%
$10,000	$ 81	$ 88	$ 95	$103	$111
$20,000	$161	$176	$190	$206	$221
$30,000	$242	$264	$286	$309	$330
$40,000	$322	$351	$381	$411	$442
$50,000	$402	$439	$476	$515	$553

Items 24 to 28 refer to the table above.

24. If Mr. and Mrs. Gray take a $40,000 mortgage at 11%, what will their mortgage payments be each month?

(1) $206
(2) $286
(3) $322
(4) $351
(5) $381

25. Which of the following statements is NOT supported by the information in the mortgage table?

(1) People will make higher mortgage payments as the interest rates increase.
(2) Mortgage payments will increase as the amount of money borrowed increases.
(3) It will cost more to borrow $10,000 at 13% than at 12%.
(4) It is more expensive to borrow $40,000 at 12% than $50,000 at 10%.
(5) It is cheaper to borrow $30,000 at 10% than at 12%.

26. What will a borrower pay in one year to borrow $50,000 at 9%?

(1) $402
(2) $4,824
(3) $5,530
(4) $50,000
(5) cannot be determined

27. Using the information from the table, what would you have to pay each month for a $25,000 mortgage at 11%?

(1) $176
(2) $190
(3) $238
(4) $286
(5) cannot be determined

28. What was the total interest paid during the term of a $10,000 mortgage at 12%?

(1) $10,000
(2) $27,080
(3) $37,080
(4) $40,000
(5) cannot be determined

29. The consumer price index, an economic measure published by the United States government, may rise in response to certain domestic or foreign events. Which of the following headlines would be LEAST likely to cause an increase in the consumer price index?

(1) "Bumper Harvest Expected in California"
(2) "Thousands of Chickens Slaughtered in Southeastern Drought"
(3) "Frost Hits Orange Groves in Coldest Florida Winter"
(4) "U.S. Imposes Tariffs on Imported Autos"
(5) "U.S. Embargo on Asian Microchips"

30. "Technology has developed to the point where most work which had been done by people having less than a high school education can now be done more cheaply by machines."

    This statement best supports which of the following conclusions?

    (1) The cost of providing a high school education to every citizen is very high.
    (2) A high school education is now required to operate the simplest machinery.
    (3) The need for white-collar workers will decrease in the future.
    (4) The need for blue-collar workers will increase in the future.
    (5) Dropouts will have greater difficulty finding employment.

ANSWER KEY FOR ECONOMICS QUESTIONS

1. (5)	9. (4)	17. (5)	24. (5)
2. (1)	10. (3)	18. (3)	25. (4)
3. (4)	11. (2)	19. (5)	26. (2)
4. (1)	12. (3)	20. (2)	27. (3)
5. (3)	13. (5)	21. (1)	28. (2)
6. (1)	14. (2)	22. (3)	29. (1)
7. (3)	15. (2)	23. (1)	30. (5)
8. (4)	16. (2)		

EXPLANATIONS FOR ECONOMICS QUESTIONS

1. **(5)** The data show that as the supply of wheat increased, the price decreased. This is an illustration of the concept of supply and demand.

2. **(1)** According to the author's point of view, solar energy will be used once its cost matches that of conventional fuels. If something is cheaper, and just as good or better, the consumer will buy it. This is an example of the market system at work.

3. **(4)** There is no way to prove this statement with facts. Each of the other statements could be supported by statistics.

4. **(1)** During inflation, money rapidly loses its buying power.

5. **(3)** A recession is less drastic than a depression or crash.

6. **(1)** Laissez-faire is the doctrine that holds that an economic system functions best when there is no government interference.

7. **(3)** Communism is the system described. (Contrast socialism and capitalism.)

8. **(4)** As the price decreases, demand will usually increase.

9. **(4)** The Federal Reserve System regulates the money supply. The Bureau of Engraving and Printing prints the money, but money is released at the discretion of the Federal Reserve.

10. **(3)** Collective bargaining is a procedure whereby an employer agrees to discuss working conditions with employee representatives. Boycott, strike, and arbitration usually reflect an impasse.

11. **(2)** The W2 form specifies earnings and withholding.

12. **(3)** Value-added taxes are taxes based on the increase in price or value at each level of production of a product. They are not levied in the United States.

13. **(5)** Choices (1), (2), (3) and (4) are all reasons for tax levies.

14. **(2)** Excise taxes are taxes on luxury items.

15. **(2)** Regressive taxes are those levied without regard to the income of the taxpayer.

16. **(2)** Social Security covers all these.

17. **(5)** Insurance serves as a means of guaranteeing individuals against losses of all kinds.

18. **(3)** To find a year in which exports exceeded imports, find a section of the graph where the solid line appears over the dotted line. This happens in 1979, 1980, and 1981.

19. **(5)** Imports exceed exports when the dotted line is over the solid line: 1976, 1977, 1978, 1982.

20. **(2)** Exports in 1980 = $360,000 million. Imports for 1980 = $350,000 million. The difference is 10,000 million.

21. **(1)** The third sentence states that the most heavily advertised patent medicines are those that claim to have rejuvenating powers; they are sold to the elderly. Another large group mentioned is arthritis sufferers, but many of these, too, are elderly.

22. **(3)** The root word means "young" as in "juvenile."

23. **(1)** Although all the answers are relatively correct, the best answer is (1) since the major idea of authenticity is stressed in the paragraphs.

24. **(5)** The table shows that $40,000 borrowed at 11% costs $381 per month.

25. **(4)** $40,000 borrowed at 12% costs $411 a month; $50,000 borrowed at 10% costs $439 a month. The $40,000 loan is cheaper, therefore choice (4) is false.

26. **(2)** A $50,000 loan at 9% costs $402 per month. $402 per month times 12 payments = $4,824 a year.

27. **(3)** The table does not give the payments for a $25,000 loan. You can estimate what these payments would be by using the figures given for a $20,000 loan and a $30,000 loan. A loan of $25,000 falls halfway between $20,000 and $30,000. Therefore, find the average:

$$\frac{\$190 + \$286}{2} = \$238$$

28. **(2)** This is a difficult question. $10,000 borrowed for 30 years at 12% costs $103 per month. Therefore $103 × 360 payments (12 months times 30 years) equals $37,080 principal and interest. Subtract the principal of $10,000 from $37,080 and $27,080 is interest.

29. **(1)** Each of the choices except choice (1) would have a negative effect on the economy of the U.S. Choice (1) would cause prices to go down since, by supply and demand, the supply is increasing, bringing the demand and the price down.

30. **(5)** The idea expressed is that education is necessary for employment since machines will do the unskilled work.

Political Science

Directions:

For each question, circle the number of the response that best answers the question or completes the statement. Correct and explanatory answers are provided at the end of the chapter.

1. Which factor appears to be most important to the success of a democratic form of government?

   (1) high industrial output
   (2) rich mineral resources
   (3) low interest rates
   (4) high literacy rate
   (5) high per capita income

2. The chief executive of the American government often refers to an advisory group which possesses neither constitutional nor statutory status under American law. That group is

   (1) the Cabinet
   (2) the Supreme Court
   (3) the Joint Chiefs of Staff
   (4) the Republican National Committee
   (5) the Senate

3. A long-time resident of the state of Connecticut decides to run for the office of United States Senator in New York State. A local journalist writing in opposition to the candidacy derides the man with the term

   (1) carpetbagger
   (2) muckraker
   (3) mugwump
   (4) Bull Moose
   (5) scalawag

4. Candidates for the office of United States president must be natural-born citizens of at least thirty-five years of age and resident in the United States for at least fourteen years. These requirements are set forth by

   (1) the Supreme Court
   (2) the U.S. Constitution
   (3) statutory law
   (4) the Bill of Rights
   (5) Congressional decree

5. In most states governors may exercise the item veto over appropriations bills. The item veto allows the governor to reject certain portions of a bill which is submitted for his signature. The president may not exercise item veto power although some politicians and critics have supported it. To effect this change, what step would be required under American law?

   (1) a message from the President to the House
   (2) a Constitutional Convention
   (3) A decision of the U.S. Supreme Court
   (4) consultation with the Cabinet
   (5) a Constitutional amendment

6. Which statement about the United States Congress is an opinion?

   (1) The Senate is entitled to approve or disapprove appointments to certain offices.
   (2) Congressmen are assigned to committees according to seniority.
   (3) Appropriations bills must originate in the House.
   (4) Congressional legislation has resulted in a very high balance-of-trade deficit for the United States.
   (5) The vice-president is the presiding officer of the Senate.

7. The requirement that a policeman obtain a warrant to conduct a lawful search of your home is based on

   (1) the Bill of Rights
   (2) custom
   (3) the state constitution
   (4) the United States Constitution
   (5) local law

8. The president of the United States has authority over military and foreign policy. Presidential actions, such as the use of the armed forces without declaration of war or congressional authorization, have raised intense controversy in American history. This is especially true where American troops have interfered in the internal affairs of

other nations. Such a situation occurred in the

(1) Civil War
(2) World War I
(3) World War II
(4) Korean Conflict
(5) Falkland Islands War

9. Which choice illustrates the concept of federalism as expressed in the structure of the United States government?

(1) The authority to make and enforce decisions is vested in the judicial branch of government.
(2) Appropriations bills must originate in the House of Representatives.
(3) The Constitution assigns some responsibilities to the federal government, some to the states, while others are shared by the federal and state governments.
(4) The constitutional system of checks and balances concentrates power in the legislative branch of government.
(5) According to the Constitution, political parties are divided between federal, state, and local officials.

Item 10 is based on the public opinion survey below.

10. The information in the chart below indicates that most of the people questioned

(1) favored changes in campaign financing
(2) supported both statements
(3) were unclear about the issues
(4) were divided on the two questions
(5) favored the status quo

11. Which of the following describes an example of lobbying?

(1) A defeated candidate for governor is appointed to the president's cabinet.
(2) Federal contracts are awarded to companies in a particular state in return for certain actions by that state's senators.
(3) Two members of the House agree to support each other's bills.
(4) The United States Chamber of Commerce hires someone to present its views on Capitol Hill.
(5) none of the above

QUESTION	PERCENT OF PUBLIC		
	Agree	Disagree	Not sure
Q: Campaigns for Congress should be supported by public funds only	30	62	8
Q: PAC'S (Political Action Committees) should be prohibited from contributing more than $5,000 to any Congresional campaign	35	53	12

GO ON TO THE NEXT PAGE

12. In a United States presidential election the electoral vote was distributed as follows:

Candidate	W	X	Y	Z
% of electoral vote	36%	36%	18%	10%

Based on this information, which of the following choices would be the most likely outcome of the election?

(1) Candidate W was declared the winner immediately after the election.
(2) Candidate W became president and candidate X became vice-president.
(3) A new presidential election was held with only candidates W and X running for office.
(4) The president was chosen by the members of the House of Representatives.
(5) The president was chosen by a joint resolution of the Senate and the House.

Items 13 to 16 refer to the information below.

In governing their various states, each governor receives administrative assistance from a variety of state officials, both elected and appointed. Most state governments typically include these officials:

Lieutenant governor—presides over the state senate, sits as acting governor when governor leaves the state.
Attorney general——enforces state laws; represents the state in court as chief prosecutor or defense attorney; serves as legal advisor to the state government.
Secretary of state——supervises the state's official business.
State treasurer———collects taxes and pays bills.
Superintendent of public instruction——supervises the administration of public schools and enforces the state education code.

Each of the following items describes a situation where a citizen or citizens would need to call upon the assistance of a state official. Choose the best official to deal with this problem.

---

13. A rapidly growing company decides to change its legal structure and become incorporated. Which official deals with this problem?

(1) Lieutenant governor
(2) Attorney general
(3) Secretary of state
(4) State treasurer
(5) Superintendent of public instruction

14. In the Fort Deeges School District handicapped children are entitled to attend classes along with nonhandicapped children as much as is physically possible. Mr. and Mrs. Jenkin's son, who is confined to a wheelchair, has been denied the right to attend chemistry or physics classes at his high school, despite appeals to the principal and the local school board. To which state official should the Jenkins turn for help?

(1) Lieutenant governor
(2) Attorney general
(3) Secretary of state
(4) State treasurer
(5) Superintendent of public instruction

15. The governor of the state resigns in the middle of his term to run for a seat in the U.S. Senate. Which official deals with this problem?

    (1) Lieutenant governor
    (2) Attorney general
    (3) Secretary of state
    (4) State treasurer
    (5) Superintendent of public instruction

16. A pyramid scheme, supposedly designed to make every participant rich in a short time, has collapsed. Over one hundred people were victimized, and each one lost between $500 and $2,500. To whom should these victims turn for help?

    (1) Lieutenant governor
    (2) Attorney general
    (3) Secretary of state
    (4) State treasurer
    (5) Superintendent of public instruction

Item 17 is based on the quotations below.

"Whenever . . . government becomes destructive to these ends it is the right of the people to alter or abolish it, and to institute new government. . . ."

—Thomas Jefferson

". . . there comes a time when people get tired. We are here this evening to say to those who have mistreated us so long that we are tired —tired of being segregated and humiliated, tired of being kicked about by the brutal feet of oppression. We have no alternative but to protest. . . ."

—Martin Luther King, Jr.

17. Which statement best summarizes the main idea of both quotations?

    (1) Violence is the only effective form of protest.
    (2) Government is harmful to freedom and human dignity.
    (3) Revolution is inevitable in a democratic society.
    (4) The people may ultimately have to force the government to meet their needs.
    (5) The people should ignore laws they do not agree with.

GO ON TO THE NEXT PAGE

Items 18 to 21 are based on the cartoon below.

Goetz gets his man.

18. The cartoon depicts an event that received wide media attention. The central figure, Goetz, was a man who

    (1) wrote graffiti
    (2) was the head of the Transit Union
    (3) sold Mace for protection
    (4) shot four people in a subway car
    (5) mugged a subway rider

19. The cartoonist believes that

    (1) subways are overcrowded
    (2) subways are dirty
    (3) people are helpful to each other on subways
    (4) subways are very fast late at night
    (5) subway riders want more protection

20. The cartoon does NOT imply that

    (1) Goetz was involved in a subway incident
    (2) Goetz was carrying a weapon
    (3) people would arm themselves for protection
    (4) the police would probably protect everyone
    (5) too many people would resort to self-protection

21. Many people approved of Goetz's action because

    (1) they wanted lower train fares
    (2) they had been victims of crimes
    (3) they belonged to the NRA
    (4) they were members of the Transit Union
    (5) they approved of graffiti

Items 22 to 23 refer to the following quotation from the Supreme Court decision in the case of *Brown vs. Board of Education of Topeka, Kansas.*

"We conclude that in the field of public education the doctrine of 'separate but equal' has no place. Separate educational facilities are inherently unequal. Therefore, we hold that the plaintiffs . . . are, by reason of the segregation complained of, deprived of the equal protection of the laws guaranteed by the Fourteenth Amendment."

22. This Supreme Court decision is based on the idea that segregation in education is likely to

    (1) deny individuals the opportunity to make upward social and economic progress
    (2) create unnecessary administrative problems in the nation's schools
    (3) place excessive burdens on school transportation systems
    (4) result in unfair tax increases to support dual school systems
    (5) result in higher educational standards

23. This Supreme Court ruling can most accurately be said to have marked the beginning of the end of

    (1) racial violence
    (2) public education
    (3) legal racial discrimination
    (4) the civil rights movement
    (5) private education

24. The Equal Rights Amendment was ____ after a ten-year struggle for ratification.

    (1) passed
    (2) defeated
    (3) extended
    (4) rewritten
    (5) ratified

25. During the 1960s the United States became deeply involved in a major land war in east Asia. Though America became deeply divided over our interference in another country's affairs, U.S. troops were not completely withdrawn from ____ until 1973.

    (1) China
    (2) Vietnam
    (3) Nicaragua
    (4) El Salvador
    (5) Thailand

26. The first ten amendments to the United States Constitution, otherwise known as the Bill of Rights, guarantee to all citizens all the following EXCEPT

    (1) protection against excessive or unusual punishment
    (2) freedom to assemble peaceably
    (3) the right to vote
    (4) the right to bear arms
    (5) freedom of press and speech

27. At the Constitutional Convention of 1787, various plans of government for the United States were proposed. Sectional jealousies were out in the open. The small states were afraid that the big states, with their larger populations, would overwhelm them in voting power. The question was resolved by the establishment of a Congress which was a bicameral legislature. This resulted in what came to be known as the Senate and the House of Representatives. The House of Representatives now has 435 members.

    (1) which is the same as the number of Senate members
    (2) who are elected for four-year terms
    (3) equally divided among the 50 states
    (4) who are elected by the Electoral College
    (5) who represent the various states in proportion to the state's population

GO ON TO THE NEXT PAGE

Items 28 to 30 are based on the following graph.

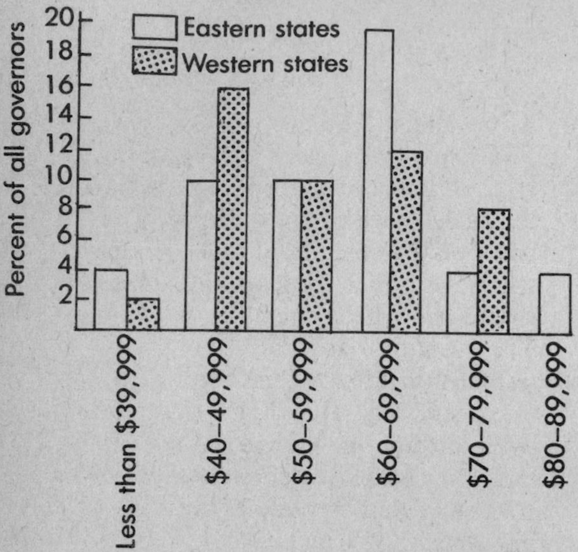

28. In which income bracket was there the *greatest* difference in the percentage of governors from the eastern and western states?

    (1) $30,000–39,999
    (2) $40,000–49,999
    (3) $50,000–59,999
    (4) $60,000–69,999
    (5) $70,000–79,999

29. Which of the following statements about the income of governors in the United States can be correctly inferred from the chart?

    (1) Governors in the western states are likely to earn greater salaries than governors in the eastern states.
    (2) Most governors in the U.S. earn salaries between $40,000 and $69,999 per year.
    (3) Governors in the eastern states are likely to earn greater salaries than governors in the western states.
    (4) Older governors earned more than younger governors.
    (5) Most governors earn less than $55,000 per year.

30. Which of the following diagrams most accurately interprets the information on the chart above?

    (1) Percentage of governors earning less than $50,000 per year.

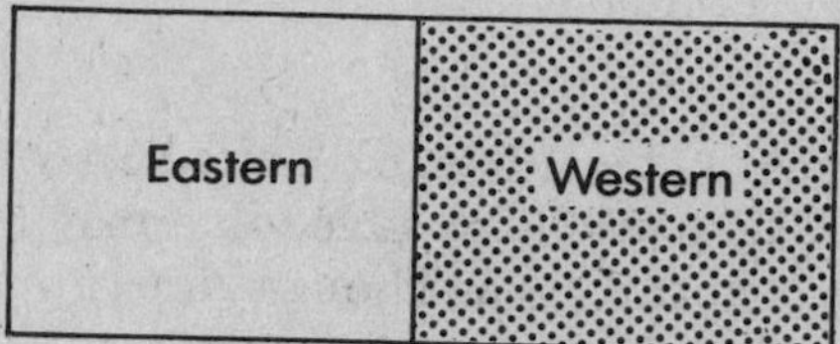

    (2) Percentage of governors earning less than $39,999 per year.

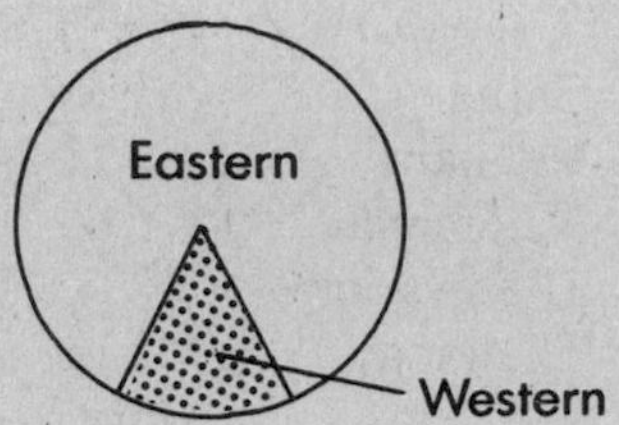

    (3) Percentage of governors earning between $70,000 and $79,999 per year.

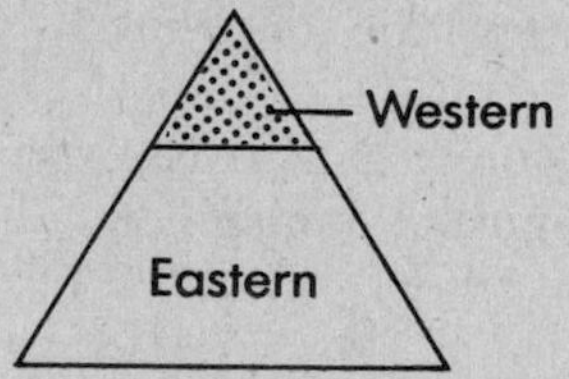

    (4) Percentage of all governors' salaries

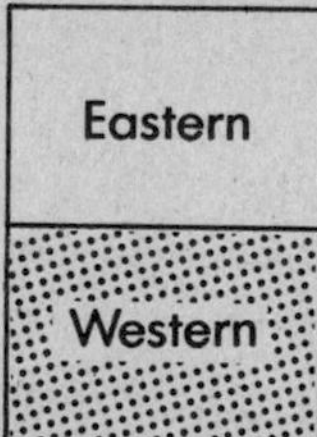

    (5) Percentage of governors earning more than $50,000 per year.

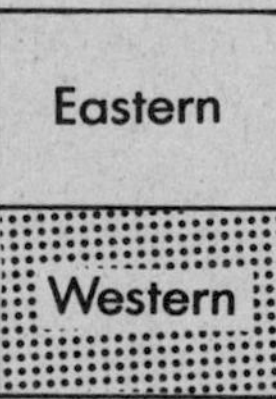

END OF POLITICAL SCIENCE TEST

ANSWER KEY FOR POLITICAL SCIENCE QUESTIONS

1. (4)
2. (1)
3. (1)
4. (2)
5. (5)
6. (4)
7. (1)
8. (4)
9. (3)
10. (5)
11. (4)
12. (4)
13. (3)
14. (5)
15. (1)
16. (2)
17. (4)
18. (4)
19. (5)
20. (4)
21. (2)
22. (1)
23. (3)
24. (2)
25. (2)
26. (3)
27. (5)
28. (4)
29. (2)
30. (3)

EXPLANATIONS FOR POLITICAL SCIENCE QUESTIONS

1. **(4)** A democracy cannot flourish and survive if its citizens cannot read, write, and investigate the positions of candidates for public office.

2. **(1)** The Cabinet exists by custom or tradition. It has no formal legal status and it is not mentioned in the Constitution.

3. **(1)** Carpetbaggers were northerners who moved to the south after the Civil War for certain reasons, including financial gains. A muckraker is a journalist/writer who exposes social evil. Mugwumps are fence-sitters in politics. Bull Moose refers to the political party championed by Theodore Roosevelt after he left office as president. Scalawags were white Southerners who opposed the Confederacy and welcomed Republicans after the Civil War.

4. **(2)** These requirements are set forth in the Constitution. Article II, Section 1 states "No person except a natural born citizen, or a citizen of the United States at the time of the adoption of this Constitution, shall be eligible to the office of president; neither shall any person be eligible to that office who shall not have attained to the age of thirty-five years, and been fourteen years as a resident within the United States."

5. **(5)** Considerable support has been generated for giving the president line item veto power, but to date, no one has taken the essential step of drafting an amendment to the Constitution.

6. **(4)** Choices (1), (2), (3), and (5) concern regulations and/or laws governing the Congress of the U.S. (4) is an opinion statement which requires support.

7. **(1)** The Fourth Amendment, part of the Bill of Rights, states "The right of the people to be secure in their persons, houses, papers, and effects, against unreasonable searches and seizures, shall not be violated, and no warrants shall issue, but upon probable cause, supported by oath or affirmation, and particularly describing the place to be searched, and the persons or things to be seized."

8. **(4)** American troops became involved in the Korean Conflict when President Truman responded to the request of the U. N. Security Council.

9. **(3)** (2) is not an expression of federalism; (1) and (4) related to the system of checks and balances; (5) political parties are not mentioned in the U.S. Constitution. However, (3) is an expression of federalism embodied in the Constitution.

10. **(5)** At the present time, campaigns for Congress are supported by private fortunes, and donations from private citizens, special interest groups, and business interests. A majority of the respondents disagreed quite clearly with both questions (62 to 30 and 53 to 35) thereby eliminating one, two, and four. We do not have any additional information about how or where or to whom these questions were administered, therefore three is not an acceptable answer. (5) is clearly supported by the statistics.

11. **(4)** Lobbying is part of the constitutional guarantee which gives people the right to petition their leaders. Companies and organizations try to influence members of legislatures to vote for or against certain bills which these organizations believe to be in the best interests of their members. In order to accomplish this, they generally hire someone to represent them, that is, a professional lobbyist.

12. **(4)** If no candidate receives a majority of electoral votes, the election is decided by the House of Representatives.

13. **(3)** The secretary of state registers the state's official business including the status of business corporations.

14. **(5)** Education is ultimately a state responsibility, and the state superintendent of public instruction (or his/her equivalent) is usually the final decision-maker in conflicts concerning the application of state education regulations.

15. **(1)** Most states have a lieutenant governor who would fill the job of the governor should he/she retire, resign, die, or be impeached.

16. **(2)** The attorney general, often regarded as the second most important job in state government, is highly visible and "political" as well as responsible for law enforcement within the state.

17. **(4)** Both Thomas Jefferson and Martin Luther King, Jr., supported the notion that a government is for the people and by the people. They believed that it was the people's right to rebel against an oppressive government (Jefferson) or protest against one which discriminated against one group, namely the blacks (King).

18. **(4)** Goetz received a great deal of publicity when he shot four black teenagers in a subway car in December, 1984 and during his trial in 1987.

19. **(5)** The fact that several riders are holding "weapons" indicates that they want protection.

20. **(4)** There are no police officers shown, so the cartoon implies nothing about police protection.

21. **(2)** Many people approved of Goetz because they too had been victims of crime.

22. **(1)** The Supreme Court decision is based upon the idea that segregation in education is "unequal" and likely to deny black children the opportunity to make upward social and economic progress.

23. **(3)** By declaring segregated school systems to be unconstitutional, the Supreme Court ruling can most accurately be said to have marked the beginning of the end of legal racial discrimination.

24. **(2)** The ERA was defeated for lack of ratification by a sufficient number of states under the proper time limits.

25. **(2)** Troops were completely removed from Vietnam by President Nixon in 1973.

26. **(3)** The right to vote is not included in the first ten amendments to the Constitution.

27. **(5)** The number of representatives for each state depends upon the population of that state.

28. **(4)** 20% of the eastern governors in the $60,000 bracket minus 12% of the western governors in the $60,000 bracket equals 8%; other categories yield 2%, 6%, 0%, and 4%.

29. **(2)** This can be checked against the table by adding percentages:

    10 + 16 + 10 + 10 + 20 + 12 = 78% (most)

30. **(3)** In the $70,000 category, there are exactly twice as many western governors as eastern governors. (1) and (5) are incorrect, since percentage earning less than $50,000 is unequal (14%/18%) as is percentage earning over $50,000. (2) is incorrect, because percentage of governors earning less than $39,999 is approximately 4%/2%, while diagram shows a 7/1 ratio. Graph does not support (4).

Geography and Behavioral Science

Directions:

For each question, circle the number of the response that best answers the question or completes the statement. Correct and explanatory answers are provided at the end of the chapter.

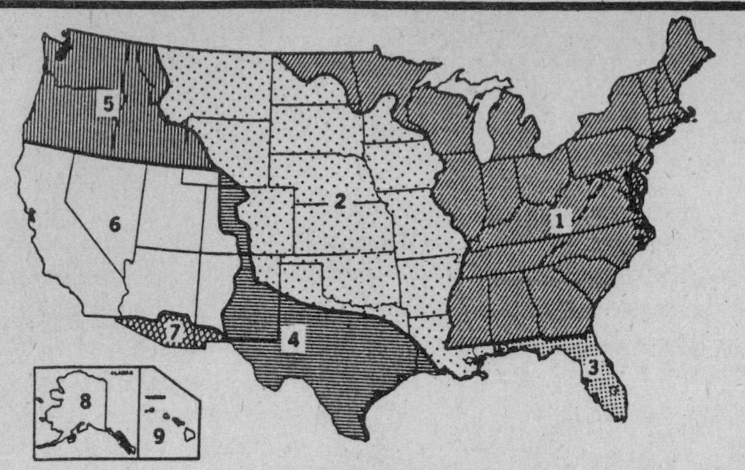

GROSS AREA
Land and Water, square miles

1	Original 13 States 1790.*	888,685
2	Louisianna Purchase 1803	827,192
3	Spanish Cession 1819	72,003
4	Texas Annexed 1845	390,143
5	Oregon Territory 1846	285,580
6	Mexican Cession 1848	529,017
7	Gadsden Purchase 1853	29,640
8	Alaska Purchased 1867	589,757
9	Hawaii Annexed 1898	6,450
	Guam and Puerto Rico 1899	212 and 3,435
	American Samoa 1900	76
	Virgin Islands 1917	133
	Trust Territory of the Pacific Islands and Other 1947	9,087

*Original 13 States and Territories.

Items 1 and 2 refer to the map above.

1. Which of the following represents the largest acquisition of land?

   (1) Texas Annexation
   (2) Spanish Cession
   (3) Oregon Territory
   (4) Louisiana Purchase
   (5) Alaska Purchase

2. Which of the following represents the last addition to the continental United States?

   (1) Alaska Purchase
   (2) Gadsden Purchase
   (3) Hawaii Annexation
   (4) Texas Annexation
   (5) Mexican Cession

Item 3 refers to the following information.

3. The information in the table above is most likely a reflection of which of the following events in United States history?

   (1) sectionalism
   (2) reconstruction
   (3) the rise of industrialism
   (4) a decline in immigration
   (5) the growth of the west

Center of Population: 1790 to 1980

"Center of population" is that point at which an imaginary flat, weightless, and rigid map of the United States would balance if weights of identical value were placed on it so that each weight represented the location of one person on the date of the census.

YEAR	North latitude			West latitude			Approximate location
	°	′	″	°	′	″	
1790 (Aug. 2)	39	16	30	76	11	12	23 miles east of Baltimore, MD
1850 (June 1)	38	59	0	81	19	0	23 miles southeast of Parkersburg, WV
1900 (June 1)	39	9	36	85	48	54	6 miles southeast of Columbus, IN
1950 (Apr. 1)	38	50	21	88	9	33	8 miles north-northwest of Olney, Richland County, IL
1960 (Apr. 1)	38	35	58	89	12	35	In Clinton Co. about 6½ miles northwest of Centralia, IL
1970 (Apr. 1)	38	27	47	89	42	22	5.3 miles east-southeast of the Mascoutah City Hall in St. Clair County, IL
1980 (Apr. 1)	38	8	13	90	34	26	⅛ mile west of De Soto in Jefferson County, MO

Item 4 refers to the following table.

RECENT POPULATION FIGURES FOR COUNTRY X

Year	Birth Rate(1)	Death Rate(1)
1960	35.2	6.7
1970	24.8	6.7
1980	22.8	6.4
1982	21.2	6.6
1983	20.1	6.5

(1) per 1000 population

4. The information shown could be used to support which of the following statements?

(1) The death rate is likely to decline through the 1990's.
(2) The population has increased rapidly.
(3) Population growth has been slowed.
(4) The birth rate will increase slightly.
(5) Population has decreased greatly.

GO ON TO THE NEXT PAGE

Item 5 refers to the diagram below.

5. Based on the diagram below and your knowledge of geography, the tilt of the earth's axis is a major cause of the occurrence of

   (1) tides
   (2) rotation of the earth
   (3) leap years in the calendar
   (4) the change of seasons
   (5) weather

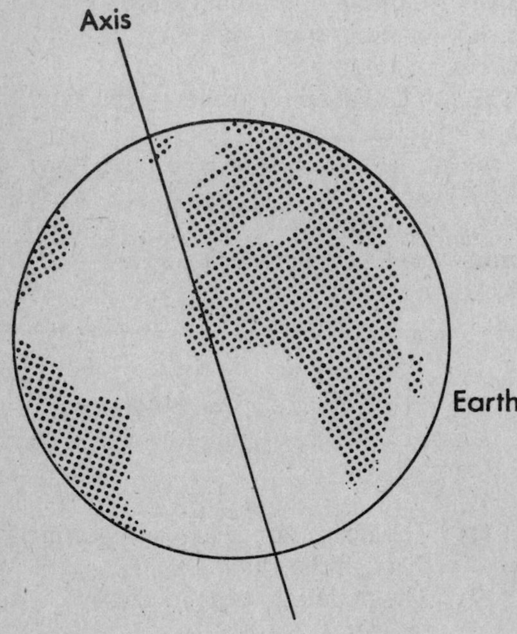

Item 6 refers to the information below.

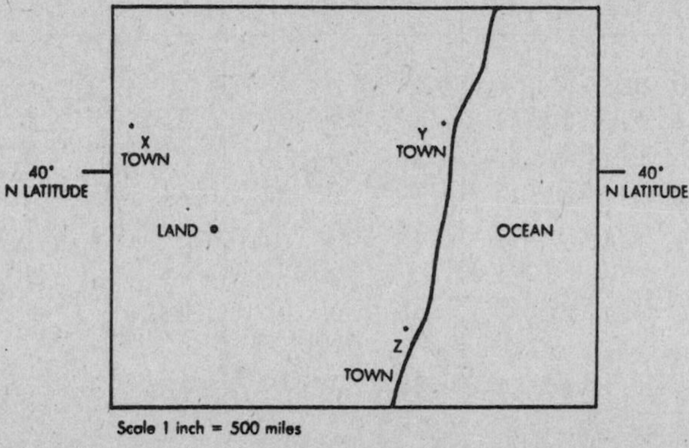

6. The information shown above could most accurately support which of the following statements about climate?

   (1) Z-town will have a milder climate.
   (2) Y-town most likely will have a warmer climate than X-town.
   (3) All three towns will have similar climates.
   (4) X-town and Y-town will experience colder winters than Z-town.
   (5) X-town is likely to have cooler winters than Y-town.

7. Which of the following situations is not matched with the appropriate society?

   (1) Several generations of the same family live together—traditional society
   (2) The birth of many children insures the economic survival of the family—modern technological society
   (3) Children generally follow the occupations of their parents—semi-industrialized society
   (4) Men and women may work at the same jobs—a modern technological society
   (5) Children are educated at home—agricultural society

8. An anthropologist working in a rural Indian village would most like do which of the following activities?

   (1) train farmers to plant new types of crops
   (2) reform the local legal system
   (3) persuade villages to accept family planning programs
   (4) study the relationships/kinship of families and friends
   (5) dig irrigation ditches

9. The cultural development of the United States during the twentieth century may best be described as a

   (1) rebirth of the classical tradition
   (2) return to early American roots
   (3) reflection of a highly industrialized and urbanized society
   (4) reenactment of eastern principles of harmony with nature
   (5) renewal of the European renaissance

Items 10 and 11 refer to the following article.

Self-contained diving suits have made it possible for a diver to explore the depths without the local authorities' knowing very much about it. Should he be lucky enough to discover a wreck, a diver can recover the less cumbersome fragments, bronzes, marble, or bits of statuary, without attracting official attention. Today one can indulge in a secret treasure hunt right down to the seabed with the added advantage that it is far harder to keep a watch on sunken treasure than it is to protect excavations on shore. So the modern despoiler is as great a pest to the serious archaeologist at sea as he is on land. In Egypt and Syria he has deprived us of invaluable data. He nearly always ransacks his objective to take away some portable trophy which he thinks valuable, he keeps his treasure house a secret, and we must blame him for the appearance of various objects impossible to date or catalog.

10. The passage suggests that the author is

    (1) opposed to excavations on shore
    (2) sympathetic to the officials
    (3) sympathetic to the divers
    (4) opposed to investigations in Syria and Egypt
    (5) opposed to the despoilers' cataloging their finds

11. It is to the amateur archeologist's advantage that local authorities

    (1) protect his findings on land
    (2) allow him to keep portable treasures
    (3) provide catalogs of underwater treasures
    (4) are sometimes unaware of his diving activities
    (5) are ignorant of the true value of sunken treasures

12. Which best explains why punishment for actions considered to be criminal differs from one society to another?

    (1) Most societies regard punishment as inherently unjust.
    (2) The death penalty has been abolished all over the world.
    (3) Definitions of justice depend on the values of society.
    (4) Some societies have written constitutions while others rely on common law.
    (5) Punishments are more severe in societies having complex court systems.

GO ON TO THE NEXT PAGE

Items 13 and 14 refer to the following information.

Psychologists divide human memory into three stages: in the *acquisition* stage, information is entered into the memory; the *retention* stage is the period between acquisition and *retrieval*, or recalling the remembered information. At each stage, memory can and does change, sometimes subtly, forgetting small details in the passage of time; at other times, memory shifts radically. New information can be introduced at each and any of the stages. The observer's environment, physical health, background, attitudes, motives, and beliefs all affect what he remembers, how well, and how long he continues to remember.

Under normal circumstances, an individual can recall what he has seen in detail for only a short time after the event. In weeks, the voluntary recall decays; most of the detail is lost and only what seemed important or particularly disturbing at the time is remembered. Under unusual conditions—hypnosis, direct stimulation of the brain, or drug-induced states—it seems possible to recall buried detail. The apparent improvement in recall under hypnosis or the drug sodium pentathol, to take two examples, cannot be verified. Vivid memories may be produced, but who is to say if they are accurate, or whether they have been modified by intervening experiences?

13. A witness testifying at a trial some three years after an accident will be most likely to respond to questioning in which of the following ways?

    (1) The witness will have to testify under the influence of drugs.
    (2) The witness will probably remember only a few striking details.
    (3) The witness will recall the event in great detail.
    (4) The witness will recall the event only if he is in good health.
    (5) The witness will require hypnosis in order to produce accurate details.

14. Based on the information in the passage, psychology has proven that

    (1) the idea of "memory" is only incompletely understood by psychologists
    (2) normal individuals nearly always have excellent memories
    (3) fine details remain the longest in each human memory
    (4) human memory varies greatly from memory in other animals
    (5) the accuracy of memories can be checked by a competent psychologist

Items 15 and 16 refer to the following article.

In the chilly darkness before the dawn of June 21, 1972, John Eddy trudged up the snow-covered slopes of Medicine Mountain in the Bighorn Range of northern Wyoming. He was climbing to a high, windswept plateau where centuries earlier a long-vanished tribe of American Indians had laid out a rudimentary wheel of stones and erected two main cairns, or piles of rock. Reaching the plateau just before sunrise, Eddy crouched behind one cairn. Using it like a cosmic rifle sight, he lined it up with the other cairn built directly in the center of the wheel and looked toward the faint glow in the east. As the rays of the rising sun came streaming over the horizon, Eddy saw that the two cairns were right on target. Immediately, he realized at least one of the purposes of the mysterious wheel was to indicate the dawn of the summer solstice—that moment in the sun's course when it pauses in its northward movement before reversing its direction. It was an extremely important date for the Indians to determine, because the solstice was the time of the Sun Dance for many tribes, an important ceremony marking the passage of a year.

15. This passage appeared in a magazine for scientists who study humans, especially the physical and cultural characteristics, customs and social relationships of humankind. Such scientists are called

    (1) geologists
    (2) psychologists
    (3) historians
    (4) archaeologists
    (5) anthropologists

16. The "dawn of the summer solstice" is still represented in the western calendar. It generally falls around

    (1) March 21
    (2) June 21
    (3) September 21
    (4) December 21
    (5) January 21

Items 17 and 18 are based on the following selection.

Until modern times, high rates of reproduction were necessary to offset high mortality —especially infant mortality. In agricultural societies children were assets in the home and farm-centered economy. Also, before care of the aged became institutionalized, parents had to rely upon their children for care in their old age. Large numbers of children were advantageous. As a result of those factors and of short life expectancy, American women spent most of their adult lives bearing and rearing four or five children.

Long before the tradition of the large family disappeared, some couples had begun to adopt the small family pattern. As a result of declining mortality rates, a diminishing need for child labor in agriculture, increasing costs of raising a child in an industrialized urban society, and improved methods of fertility control, both the number of children desired and the number born declined.

17. In olden times, large families were more desirable because

    (1) many infants died
    (2) old people needed care
    (3) children helped out on the farm
    (4) children were assets
    (5) all of the above

18. Large families were not necessary later because

    (1) more infants survived
    (2) farms were bigger
    (3) juvenile delinquency increased
    (4) life expectancy decreased
    (5) all of the above

GO ON TO THE NEXT PAGE

Items 19 to 22 are based on the information below.

Many of the techniques used to create effective propaganda are known to us in everyday communications and conversation. Each one of us has used or heard these techniques for separating the listener from thorough examination of the idea being conveyed. Listed below are five such techniques and brief descriptions of how each is used.

Plain folks—a speaker tries to convince an audience that we're all just plain folks who think alike and act alike
Glittering generality—a speaker associates his ideas with a "virtue"
Testimonial—a hated or respected person is used to endorse an idea
Card stacking—a speaker uses untrue or illogical statements in order to make the best possible (or worst possible) case for an idea
Bandwagon—attempts to convince the audience that everyone in the group has accepted this idea

Based on the information above, look at the following quotations and situations to determine the propaganda technique in use.

19. At a scientific discussion on the worldwide extinction of the dinosaurs, a supporter leaves out the information that some dinosaurs were still living even after the "massive extinction" of "all" the dinosaurs.

    The propaganda technique in use is

    (1) plain folks
    (2) glittering generality
    (3) testimonial
    (4) card stacking
    (5) bandwagon

20. As you flip on the television set, you see one of America's most famous actresses praising the quality and performance of a luxurious foreign sports car.

    The propaganda technique in use is

    (1) plain folks
    (2) glittering generality
    (3) testimonial
    (4) card stacking
    (5) bandwagon

21. *Vogue, Glamour,* and *Harper's Bazaar* all decree, the fashionable skirt for spring ends just three inches above a woman's knee.

    The propaganda technique in use is

    (1) plain folks
    (2) glittering generality
    (3) testimonial
    (4) card stacking
    (5) bandwagon

22. Taste testers for the cola companies descend upon unsuspecting shoppers in grocery stores and malls and record their results for television and cable audiences.

    The propaganda technique in use is

    (1) plain folks
    (2) glittering generality
    (3) testimonial
    (4) card stacking
    (5) bandwagon

Items 23 and 24 refer to the following quotation.

"An informed public depends on accurate and open reporting by the news media. No individual can obtain for *himself* the information needed for the intelligent discharge of his political responsibilities. . . . The press therefore acts as an agent of the public at large."

23. The quotation most clearly supports the idea that the news media have a responsibility to

(1) report news in an objective fashion
(2) create national agreement on controversial issues
(3) eliminate editorials on controversial news subjects
(4) encourage public participation in newsgathering activities
(5) report every story regardless of its source

24. Which of the following does the speaker believe to be the major reason for keeping abreast of the news?

(1) to demonstrate intelligence
(2) to make sound political judgments
(3) to advance in your job
(4) to increase your store of information
(5) to know what to expect

Items 25 and 26 refer to the following paragraph.

Today there are more than 200 reservations in the United States, established for various tribes of native Americans through special treaties with the federal government. The largest is the Navajo reservation in Arizona, New Mexico, and Utah. Its 15 million acres make it about the size of New England. Many of the 1.4 million native Americans have moved to cities where they have sought to maintain at least a semblance of tribal customs and organization in their new surroundings. Other groups, particularly in the Southwest, still maintain many elements of their ancient heritage.

25. According to this passage, which of the following is true about reservations?

(1) Only the Navajos live on reservations.
(2) All native Americans live on reservations.
(3) The Navajo reservation is in New England.
(4) The largest reservation is in Arizona, New Mexico, and Utah.
(5) There are 1.4 million native Americans living on reservations.

26. The reservations were established

(1) through treaties between the federal government and various tribes
(2) to keep all native Americans in one place
(3) to make the native Americans conform to the white man's ways
(4) through grants by the various state governments
(5) wherever native Americans live

GO ON TO THE NEXT PAGE

Items 27 to 30 refer to the following information.

Americans are members of numerous special interest groups, such as labor unions, professional organizations, business organizations, and others, which exert pressure upon national, state, and local legislators. These special interest groups often employ a specialist in placing pressure, otherwise called a *lobbyist.* Competent lobbyists push for favored treatment for their clients and use a number of techniques in the course of their work. Some of these techniques include

Communications—letter-writing campaigns, personal visits, and telephone calls
Campaign contributions—lobbyists often find contributions for friendly legislators running for reelection
Social contacts—are used to build a network of friendships and obligations
Sanctions—can be applied against a legislator who does not recognize the causes advanced by the lobbyist
Formation of alliances—enables different groups to join together in support of or opposition to a proposed bill

Each of the following items describes the action of a lobby or special interest group. Choose the term which most nearly identifies the technique being used.

27. A proposal to prohibit smoking in public places of assembly, restaurants, elevators, and schools has been brought before the state legislature. The state medical society, the "Right to Fresh Air" Committee, the state nurses association, and several county health departments have jointly endorsed the bill.

    The lobbying technique in use is

    (1) communications
    (2) campaign contributions
    (3) social contacts
    (4) sanctions
    (5) formation of alliances

28. The Friends of Bergen County Public Library have endorsed a bill before the state legislature that will double the amount of state aid to every public library in the state. The bill is tied up in the Education Committee and it seems unlikely that the legislature will have the opportunity to take a vote. The president of the Friends group urges you to send a telegram to the chair of the Education Committee.

    The lobbying technique in use is

    (1) communications
    (2) campaign contributions
    (3) social contacts
    (4) sanctions
    (5) formation of alliances

29. An industry group, the National Association of Television Station Owners, hosts a golf tournament each spring for Congressmen and their staffs, by invitation only.

    The lobbying technique in use is

    (1) communications
    (2) campaign contributions
    (3) social contacts
    (4) sanctions
    (5) formation of alliances

30. Representative Greene took a strong stand against the "gun lobby" in the last two sessions of Congress. Illegal firearms have been the cause of a number of deaths in the suburban district she represents. In her next campaign for reelection she finds herself facing a challenge in the primaries. The candidate who opposes her is funded by several PAC's (political action committees); among them is one funded by members of the National Rifle Association.

    The lobbying technique in use is

    (1) communications
    (2) campaign contributions
    (3) social contacts
    (4) sanctions
    (5) formation of alliances

END OF GEOGRAPHY AND BEHAVIORAL SCIENCE TEST

ANSWER KEY FOR GEOGRAPHY AND BEHAVIORAL SCIENCE QUESTIONS

1. (4)	11. (4)	21. (5)
2. (2)	12. (3)	22. (1)
3. (5)	13. (2)	23. (1)
4. (3)	14. (1)	24. (2)
5. (4)	15. (5)	25. (4)
6. (5)	16. (2)	26. (1)
7. (2)	17. (5)	27. (5)
8. (4)	18. (1)	28. (1)
9. (3)	19. (4)	29. (3)
10. (2)	20. (3)	30. (4)

EXPLANATIONS FOR GEOGRAPHY AND BEHAVIORAL SCIENCE QUESTIONS

1. **(4)** Totalling 827,192 square miles, the Louisiana Purchase (area 2 on the map) nearly doubled the size of the thirteen original colonies.

2. **(2)** The last addition to the continental United States was the Gadsden Purchase (area 7 on the map). Purchased from Mexico in 1853, this land became part of New Mexico and Arizona. Alaska and Hawaii, although added later, are not part of the continental United States.

3. **(5)** The center of population has shifted to the west because more "weight" has been applied to that portion of the country: the western portion has grown in both numbers and percentage of the population.

4. **(3)** The death rate has remained essentially the same and the birth rate has decreased; therefore, population growth has been slowed.

5. **(4)** The northern hemisphere is tilted toward the sun part of the year and away from the sun for the remaining months. In winter the rays strike the northern hemisphere indirectly; in spring the hemisphere is warming; during summer the rays of the sun strike directly; and in the fall the hemisphere cools.

6. **(5)** Though X and Y are the same distance north of the equator, Y's climate will be moderated by the warming effects of the ocean while landlocked X will experience colder weather.

7. **(2)** Large families with many children are often an asset in agricultural societies, but families are generally small in modern technological societies.

8. **(4)** An anthropologist aims to observe other societies without altering them.

9. **(3)** Modern art, dance, and music in the U. S. reflect the dissonance, clamor, crowding, and technology that built the tall skyscrapers and peopled the big cities.

10. **(2)** The passage sounds as if it were written by an archeologist who had a favorite piece of underwater treasure taken by an "irresponsible explorer." He (or she) is undoubtedly sympathetic to the officials.

11. **(4)** Since they cannot easily be traced and found, the amateur archeologists who explore underwater have the advantage over the local authorities.

12. **(3)** The ethics and social values of a society determine what actions are considered criminal. Likewise, a crime that is punishable by death in one part of the world might not be punishable in another part of the world.

13. **(2)** The first sentence of the second paragraph states that recall dims with time. After three years, the witness most likely will remember only a few actual details, and then only those which particularly jolted him.

14. **(1)** Psychologists have a long way to go in proving any hypothesis about memory.

15. **(5)** An anthropologist would most likely study the ancient systems of time-keeping described in the passage.

16. **(2)** Summer begins around June 21.

17. **(5)** Choices (1), (2), (3), and (4) are all stated in the first paragraph.

18. **(1)** Paragraph 2 mentions "declining mortality rates" as one reason for the decrease in family size.

19. **(4)** By conveniently leaving out some facts, the speaker gives his side of the "argument" the strongest support.

20. **(3)** This is an example of a testimonial. The famous actress is associated with the car even though her testimonial may be paid.

21. **(5)** This is an example of the bandwagon technique: everyone is doing it, that is, if your "everyone" includes the group that reads *Vogue, Glamour,* and *Harper's Bazaar.*

22. **(1)** These ordinary people shopping at the supermarket liked X Cola, and being just like them (us), so will you.

23. **(1)** Accurate news reports are for the purpose of informing the public so that individuals can make up their own minds.

24. **(2)** The speaker says that information is needed "for the intelligent discharge of . . . political responsibilities," in other words, to make sound political judgments.

25. **(4)** The second sentence gives this information. All of the other statements are contradicted by information in the article.

26. **(1)** The first sentence states that the reservations were established "through special treaties with the federal government."

27. **(5)** Each of these organizations represents distinct though related interests. By forming an alliance or coalition they are able to convince legislators of the clout behind the advancement of the issue.

28. **(1)** Communications—letter writing, telephone calls, and telegrams—are valuable low-budget tools of lobbying groups as well as individual citizens who wish to express their viewpoints on any issue.

29. **(3)** This is an example of the use of social contacts. Large business and industrial groups frequently sponsor outings and social events for legislators and their staffs and families, especially legislators who sit on key committees that formulate laws restricting or supporting specific industries and types of businesses.

30. **(4)** Though the action involves political campaign contributions, sanctions are being specifically applied against the Congressman.

Part IV

Science Review

ALL ABOUT THE GED SCIENCE TEST

The questions in the GED Science Test are based upon reading passages, graphs, tables, and charts covering material from the fields of biology, chemistry, physics, and earth science. You will be asked to answer four different types of questions:

- **Comprehension** questions which require you to demonstrate an understanding of the meaning of the stimulus. Can you restate, summarize, or identify the implications of the information?
- **Application** questions which ask you to use the information in a context other than the one stated in the reading.
- **Analysis** questions which call for breaking down the information. What are the facts and what are the hypotheses? Were there any assumptions? Can you distinguish between cause and effect?
- **Evaluation** questions which require you to make a judgment based on the facts given. How accurate are the facts presented? Can you differentiate logic from beliefs and values?

The following outline of content areas from which science questions are likely to be drawn is reprinted by permission of the GED Testing Service of the American Council on Education.

I. BIOLOGY
  A. Biology of cells
    1. Chemical basis of life
    2. Energy and the living cell
    3. Photosynthesis and respiration
    4. Cellular organization and processes
  B. Diversity of life
    1. Genetics and inheritance
    2. Variety and classification of organisms
    3. Natural selection and evolution
    4. Plant and animal growth and development
    5. Characteristics and systems of organisms
  C. Population biology
    1. Behavioral complexity, learning, and communication
    2. Ecosystems and communities
    3. Energy and the human race

II. EARTH SCIENCE
  A. Our universe
    1. The solar system
    2. Stars, galaxies, and quasars
  B. The earth
    1. Structure, magnetism, and gravity
    2. Minerals, rocks, and ores
    3. Fossils and the eras of geologic time

- C. The changing earth
    1. The shape of the land, weathering, and erosion
    2. The drifting continents, earthquakes, and volcanoes
    3. The oceans
    4. Mapping and landforms
- D. Air and water
    1. The atmosphere and solar energy
    2. Humidity, air pressure, winds, weather, and climate
- E. Energy and the environment
    1. Geothermal, solar, and nuclear energy
    2. Wind and water power
    3. People and the environment

III. PHYSICS
- A. Mechanics and thermodynamics
    1. Nature of motion
    2. Resolution and composition of forces
    3. Power and simple machines
    4. Heat and work
- B. Nature of waves
    1. Energy transfer
    2. Properties of waves, sound waves, wave nature of light
    3. Reflection, refraction, diffraction, and polarization
- C. Electricity and magnetism
    1. Electric currents and circuits
    2. Generating and transmitting electricity
    3. Magnetic behavior
- D. Nuclear physics
    1. Rays and radiation
    2. Fission and fusion reactions
    3. Particles and accelerators

IV. CHEMISTRY
- A. Structure of matter
    1. Atomic theory, electrons, and clouds
    2. Compounds and equations
    3. Energy changes
- B. Periodicity of elements
    1. Periodic law
    2. Bonding
    3. Kinetic theory
- C. Behavior of matter
    1. Energy and disorder
    2. Solutions
    3. Reaction rate and chemical equilibrium
    4. Acids, bases, and salts
    5. Oxidation—reduction
    6. Electrochemistry
- D. Nuclear and organic chemistry
    1. Radioactivity and half-life
    2. Hydrocarbons
    3. Polymers and oxygen compounds

SOME STRATEGIES FOR ANSWERING SCIENCE QUESTIONS

1. *Read* the passage or study the graphic material carefully. You may want to underline key words and phrases so that you can find them easily as you answer the questions following each reading.

   Some people find it more effective to read the questions first so that they know just what to look for as they read the passage or study the graphs and tables. Try both methods on the practice questions that follow to see which one works best for you.

2. *Reject* an argument or assertion if *one* exception is found to it. Look for the exception or contrary information and that may be your answer.

3. *Draw a quick sketch* where appropriate to help you understand a reading passage. Use very simple diagrams. An arrow or a small dot may help you to change abstract written words to a concrete picture of what is happening.

4. *Formula* problems can be solved by using simple "boxlike" fill-in inserts. For example, Rate × Time = Distance

   R × T = D

   □ × □ = □

   If you travel at 50 miles per hour, how long will it take to cover 200 miles?

5. *Use personal analogies* to reason through a problem. For example, imagine yourself as a bacteria placed in a petri dish. What would you do under the conditions presented in the problem?

6. *Use scrap paper* to jot down your thoughts, but don't let your notes get so jumbled and crowded that they confuse rather than help you.

HOW TO USE THIS SECTION EFFECTIVELY

After you have taken the Diagnostic Exam and filled in the Error Analysis chart as directed, you will see at a glance which science areas need the most study. This section contains many questions based on what is taught in high school science courses. It will serve as a good review of these courses. In addition, it includes many science reading passages for practice in reading and interpreting scientific materials.

This section is divided into four major subject areas:

Biology

Chemistry

Physics

Earth Science

You may wish to give equal study time to all these subjects or to spend more time concentrating on the weaknesses identified by your Diagnostic Test. If you find that you need more study in a particular area, you may want to consult a basic high school text such as:

Prentice-Hall Physical Science, First Edition, 1988 Bacher, Hurd, McLaughlin, and Silver

Prentice-Hall Biology, Fourth Edition, 1987 Gottfried, Madrazo, Motz, Olenchalk, Sinclair, and Skoog

Prentice-Hall Earth Science, First Edition, 1988 Coble, Murray, Rice, and Walla

BIOLOGY

Directions:

Directions: For each question, circle the number of the response that best answers the question or completes the statement. Correct and explanatory answers are provided at the end of the chapter.

1. A biologist could determine that a cell he was viewing under a microscope was a plant cell and not an animal cell because the cell had

   (1) a cell membrane and a nucleus
   (2) a cell wall and chloroplasts
   (3) a contractile vacuole and mitochondria
   (4) cytoplasm and mitochondria
   (5) a cell membrane and cilia

2. The tissues of the human body which cause the legs to move are made up of

   (1) muscle
   (2) nerves
   (3) bone
   (4) cartilage
   (5) skin

3. The nutrients which supply an animal with its main source of energy are

   (1) proteins
   (2) carbohydrates
   (3) water
   (4) lipids
   (5) nucleic acids

4. In a human being, the organ of the body which carries out most of the digestion is the

   (1) mouth
   (2) stomach
   (3) liver
   (4) small intestine
   (5) large intestine

5. John was born with type B blood. Given the choices below, which of them could be his parents?

   (1) I^AI^A and ii
   (2) I^Ai and I^Ai
   (3) I^AI^B and ii
   (4) ii and ii
   (5) I^AI^A and I^AI^A

6. After performing strenuous muscular activity for a period of time, a person's muscles become tired. This fatigue is due to the presence of which one of the following chemicals?

   (1) sugar
   (2) oxygen
   (3) glucose
   (4) lactic acid
   (5) amino acids

7. Which of the following is true of photosynthesis and respiration in green plants?

   (1) Both photosynthesis and respiration take place during the day and at night.
   (2) Photosynthesis takes place only during the day and respiration takes place only at night.
   (3) Photosynthesis takes place only during the day and respiration takes place both day and night.
   (4) Photosynthesis takes place both day and night and respiration takes place only during the day.
   (5) Photosynthesis takes place only during the spring and summer.

8. The part of the brain known as the cerebrum is associated with

   (1) creative thought
   (2) reflex actions such as the knee jerk
   (3) balance and coordination
   (4) instinctive behavior
   (5) choices 2 and 3

9. Which of the following facts is true about the DNA molecule?

   A. It takes the shape of a double helix.
   B. It is associated with chromosomes and reproduction.
   C. It determines the shape and structure of all living things.

   (1) choices A and B only
   (2) choices A and C only
   (3) choices B and C only

(4) choices A, B, and C
(5) choice B only

10. Which of the following is the correct chemical formula for photosynthesis?

(1) $C_6H_{12}O_6 + C_6H_{12}O_6 \rightarrow C_{12}H_{22}O_{11} + H_2O$
(2) $6CO_2 + 12H_2O \rightarrow C_6H_{12}O_6 + 6H_2O + 6O_2$
(3) $NaOH + HCl \rightarrow NaCl + H_2O$
(4) $C_6H_{12}O_6 \rightarrow 2C_2H_5OH + 2CO_2 + H_2O$
(5) $2H_2O \rightarrow 2H_2 + O_2$

11. A decrease in the number of red blood corpuscles will seriously impair the body's ability to

(1) transport oxygen
(2) clot blood
(3) retain water
(4) eliminate waste
(5) retard sunburn

12. If the number of chromosomes in the body cells of an ape is 48, then the number of chromosomes normally found in the ape's sperm cells should be

(1) 15
(2) 20
(3) 24
(4) 48
(5) 96

13. Knee jerk response to a sharp blow is an example of

(1) habit
(2) phototropism
(3) learned response
(4) instinct
(5) reflex

14. After birth, the body is most limited in forming new

(1) nerve cells
(2) blood cells
(3) skin cells
(4) stomach cells
(5) sperm cells

15. A concentration of carbon dioxide in the blood stimulates the breathing center in the

(1) lungs
(2) medulla oblongata
(3) throat
(4) meninges
(5) cerebrum

16. The best substitute for lemons for the treatment of scurvy is

(1) cod-liver oil
(2) vitamin A tablets
(3) orange juice
(4) milk
(5) bread

17. A compound that is quickly absorbed through the walls of the stomach is

(1) alcohol
(2) sugar
(3) fat
(4) protein
(5) kelp

18. Of the following organs, which is specifically a part of the excretory system?

(1) heart
(2) salivary glands
(3) cerebrum
(4) kidney
(5) stomach

19. The use of iodine in the body is most closely related to the function of

(1) the carotid artery
(2) the thyroid gland
(3) the cornea
(4) pancreatic fluid
(5) bile

20. Research indicates that cigarette smoking results in which of the following conditions?

    (1) measles
    (2) cardiovascular stress
    (3) hepatitis
    (4) dandruff
    (5) whooping cough

21. Life processes which take place in most animals include all the following EXCEPT

    (1) using energy for metabolism
    (2) elimination of water and waste
    (3) reproduction
    (4) giving off oxygen
    (5) ingestion and absorption of food

22. Iron is essential in the structure of human

    (1) cartilage
    (2) muscles
    (3) kidneys
    (4) red blood cells
    (5) bones

23. Which of the following lacks a backbone?

    (1) tiger
    (2) jellyfish
    (3) eagle
    (4) alligator
    (5) baby panda

24. Which of the following determines the sex of a human?

    (1) egg cell
    (2) sperm cell
    (3) chromosome
    (4) fibrinogen
    (5) vacuole

25. When a child has appendicitis, its blood will likely show an increase in

    (1) red corpuscles
    (2) white corpuscles
    (3) cytoplasm
    (4) platelets
    (5) hemoglobin

26. Which part of the body would suffer most from a calcium deficiency?

    (1) the skin
    (2) the eyes
    (3) the skeleton
    (4) the digestive system
    (5) the stomach

27. The condition which is most likely to be genetically related is

    (1) syphilis
    (2) tuberculosis
    (3) anemia
    (4) excess teeth
    (5) colitis

28. A family has 7 boys and 1 girl. What is the chance that the next child will be a girl?

    (1) 12.5%
    (2) 25%
    (3) 50%
    (4) 70%
    (5) 100%

29. Pasteurization, a process developed by Louis Pasteur, is most frequently used in the purification of

    (1) coffee
    (2) water
    (3) meat
    (4) malt
    (5) milk

30. Chlorophyll is the green material in plant cells which enables the plant to manufacture

    (1) water
    (2) oxygen
    (3) sugar

(4) carbon monoxide
(5) color

31. Blood in the adult human body makes a complete circulation every

(1) 10 seconds
(2) 1 minute
(3) 30 seconds
(4) 3 minutes
(5) 24 hours

32. The "pacemaker" of the heart is located in the wall of the

(1) left auricle
(2) right auricle
(3) left ventricle
(4) right ventricle
(5) vena cava

33. The most active mixing of many digestive juices occurs in the

(1) stomach
(2) ileum
(3) duodenum
(4) jejunum
(5) rectum

34. Grasses are usually pollinated by

(1) man
(2) birds
(3) water
(4) insects
(5) wind

35. Which of the following is an antiseptic?

(1) aspirin
(2) vitamin A
(3) iodine
(4) potassium permanganate
(5) bakelite

Items 36 and 37 refer to the following passage.

Working a typewriter by touch, like riding a bicycle or strolling on a path, is best done by not giving it a glancing thought. Once you do, your fingers fumble and hit the wrong keys. To do things involving practiced skills, you need to turn loose the systems of muscles and nerves responsible for each maneuver, place them on their own, and stay out of it. There is no real loss of authority in this, since you get to decide whether to do things or not, and you can intervene and embellish the technique any time you like; if you want to ride a bicycle backward, or walk with an eccentric loping gait giving a little skip every fourth step, whistling at the same time, you can do that. But if you concentrate your attention on the details, keeping in touch with each muscle, thrusting yourself into a free fall with each step and catching yourself at the last moment by sticking out the other foot in time to break the fall, you will end up immobilized, vibrating with fatigue.

36. According to the passage, practiced skills such as touch typing and bike riding are best accomplished

(1) by careful attention to detail
(2) by keeping in touch with each muscle
(3) without conscious thought
(4) with concentrated effort
(5) by taking one step at a time

37. The author believes that the result of a carefully thought-out physical response could be

(1) excess energy
(2) overstimulation
(3) excessive fatigue
(4) an attention to detail
(5) wasted effort and time

GO ON TO THE NEXT PAGE

Items 38 to 40 refer to the following article.

Vitamins are organic compounds necessary in small amounts in the diet for the normal growth and maintenance of life of animals, including man.

They do not provide energy, nor do they construct or build any part of the body. They are needed for transforming foods into energy and body maintenance. There are 13 or more of them, and if any is missing a deficiency disease becomes apparent.

Vitamins are similar because they are made of the same elements—carbon, hydrogen, oxygen, and sometimes nitrogen. (Vitamin B_{12} also contains cobalt.) They are different in that their elements are arranged differently, and each vitamin performs one or more specific functions in the body.

Getting enough vitamins is essential to life, although the body has no nutritional use for excess vitamins and some vitamins can be stored only for relatively short periods. Many people, nevertheless, believe in being on the "safe side" and thus take extra vitamins. However, a well-balanced diet will usually meet all the body's vitamin needs.

So-called average or normal eaters probably never need supplemental vitamins, although many think they do. Vitamin deficiency diseases are rarely seen in the U.S. population. People *known* to have deficient diets require supplemental vitamins, as do those recovering from certain illnesses or vitamin deficiencies.

People who are interested in nutrition and good health should become familiar with the initials U.S. RDA. "United States Recommended Daily Allowances" were adopted by FDA for use in nutrition labeling and special dietary foods. They are the highest amounts of vitamins, minerals, and proteins that are needed by most people each day.

38. Which of the following statements about vitamins is NOT true?

    (1) Vitamins contain carbon, hydrogen, and oxygen atoms.
    (2) Vitamins provide energy for growth.
    (3) Vitamins help prevent diseases.
    (4) Only a small amount of a vitamin is needed for it to work.
    (5) Each vitamin performs a different function in the body.

39. According to this article, supplemental vitamins are required for

    (1) everyone interested in nutrition and good health
    (2) people who eat a balanced diet
    (3) people known to have deficient diets
    (4) average or normal eaters
    (5) people who exercise vigorously

40. Recommended Daily Allowances were adopted by the FDA to indicate the

    (1) minimum amount of food a person needs to stay alive
    (2) optimum amount of food needed each day to maintain normal weight
    (3) minimum amount of vitamins necessary to prevent deficiency diseases
    (4) highest amount of vitamins, minerals, and proteins needed by most people each day
    (5) amount of food taken in by average or normal eaters each day

Items 41 to 44 are based on the following information.

Plant survival depends on the plant's ability to disperse its seeds to different areas. If the seeds are too close together, they will compete for the limited land and water and very few will survive. Therefore nature has given plants many allies in spreading their seeds. They are

1. **Wind**——many seeds are able to catch the wind and be carried by it.
2. **Water**——some seeds have the ability to float on water. They will germinate when they are able to anchor into the soil.
3. **Animals**—some seeds attach to the fur of passing animals, while other seeds are eaten by animals and scattered when the animal leaves its waste.
4. **Insects**——pollen attaches to the insect and is carried from one plant to another.
5. **Man**———farmers and scientists are able to spread seeds as they feel would be most advantageous for growth and crop yield.

Each of the following items describes a situation in which a seed is spread by one of the methods of seed dispersal listed above. For each item, choose the one method that best describes the situation. Each of the methods may be used more than once in the following set of items.

41. An explorer on a South Pacific Island found only one coconut tree. The nearest coconut trees were found almost 300 miles away. He reasoned that the coconut seed had been carried by

(1) wind
(2) water
(3) animals
(4) insects
(5) man

42. My lawn has hundreds of dandelions each spring. I see these little seeds with a white puff of silky hairs attached to them. My neighbors sometimes get angry at this because they do not want dandelions on their lawns. Dandelion seeds are spread by

(1) wind
(2) water
(3) animals
(4) insects
(5) man

43. In a field, about ten miles from an apple orchard, may be found a lone apple tree. People seldom travel or camp here, but deer and bears are known to travel through this area. How did the apple seeds travel there?

(1) wind
(2) water
(3) animals
(4) insects
(5) man

44. A cocklebur is an interesting plant. It produces a seed that has stickers or little barbs on the end. In an area untouched by civilization, how would these seeds be dispersed?

(1) wind
(2) water
(3) animals
(4) insects
(5) man

GO ON TO THE NEXT PAGE

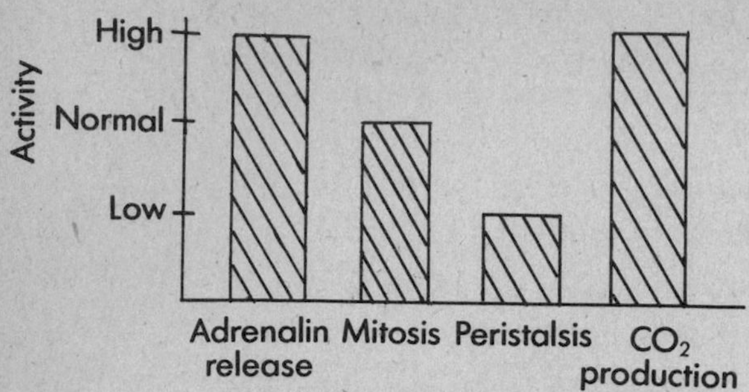

Items 45 to 47 are based on the graph above.

The graph above shows the rate of performance of four activities as they occurred in a man immediately after he had been frightened.

45. From the graph, what can be inferred about the movement of the diaphragm immediately after one has been frightened?

    (1) It becomes more rapid.
    (2) It slows down.
    (3) It ceases for a brief period.
    (4) It is unaffected.
    (5) It becomes more rapid then suddenly slows down.

46. From the graph, one can assume that there was a decrease in activity in which of the following organs?

    (1) thyroid
    (2) kidney
    (3) stomach
    (4) lungs
    (5) brain

47. An analysis of the graph would lead one to assume that which of the following temporarily increased?

    (1) amount of DNA in the nuclei
    (2) synthesis of protein
    (3) storage of glucose in the liver
    (4) production of red blood cells
    (5) concentration of glucose in the blood

Items 48 to 50 refer to the following information.

What is life? Biologists define life as the ability to carry out all of the basic life functions. Some of the life functions are described below.

Regulation—controlling all of the other life processes

Ingestion—taking food in

Digestion—breaking down food

Circulation—moving food to all parts of an organism

Respiration—burning food to make energy

Assimilation—changing food into useful substances

Excretion—removing waste products

Reproduction—making more of the same kind

48. Fire is almost alive, except it cannot carry out which of the following life functions?

(1) regulation
(2) digestion
(3) respiration
(4) excretion
(5) reproduction

49. Which of the following life processes is necessary to ensure the survival of the species?

(1) regulation
(2) circulation
(3) respiration
(4) excretion
(5) reproduction

50. Which of the following describes an organism that carries out all its life functions?

(1) a plant
(2) an animal
(3) incapable of intelligent thought
(4) alive
(5) in danger of extinction

END OF BIOLOGY TEST

ANSWER KEY FOR BIOLOGY QUESTIONS

1. (2)	14. (1)	27. (4)	40. (4)
2. (1)	15. (2)	28. (3)	41. (2)
3. (2)	16. (3)	29. (5)	42. (1)
4. (4)	17. (1)	30. (3)	43. (3)
5. (3)	18. (4)	31. (2)	44. (3)
6. (4)	19. (2)	32. (4)	45. (1)
7. (3)	20. (2)	33. (4)	46. (3)
8. (1)	21. (4)	34. (5)	47. (5)
9. (4)	22. (4)	35. (3)	48. (1)
10. (2)	23. (2)	36. (3)	49. (5)
11. (1)	24. (2)	37. (3)	50. (4)
12. (3)	25. (2)	38. (2)	
13. (5)	26. (3)	39. (3)	

EXPLANATIONS FOR BIOLOGY QUESTIONS

1. **(2)** Only plant cells have a cell wall and chloroplasts.

2. **(1)** Muscles make the legs move.

3. **(2)** Carbohydrates supply the main source of energy to animals.

4. **(4)** In human beings, most digestion takes place in the small intestine.

5. **(3)** Parents with blood types I^AI^B and ii can have children with either type A or type B blood.

6. **(4)** Lactic acid is the chemical that builds up in tired muscles.

7. **(3)** In green plants photosynthesis takes place only during the day when there is sun, but respiration (burning food to make energy) takes place day and night.

8. **(1)** The cerebrum is associated with creative thought and intelligence.

9. **(4)** Choices A, B, and C are true about the DNA molecule.

10. **(2)** This is the formula for photosynthesis. Carbon dioxide and water are changed into sugar and oxygen. Choice (1) is the formula of dehydration synthesis. Choice (3) is the formula for combining sodium hydroxide and hydrochloric acid to form salt and water. Choice (4) is fermentation, changing sugar to alcohol. Choice (5) is electrolysis.

11. **(1)** The major function of the red blood corpuscles is to carry oxygen to various parts of the body.

12. **(3)** The number of chromosomes in the sperm or egg cell of an animal is normally half the number of chromosomes in the general body cell.

13. **(5)** A reflex is an immediate response to a stimulus which takes place without thought or intent.

14. **(1)** Most nerve cells have already been formed by the time a baby is born.

15. **(2)** The medulla oblongata is that part of the brain which controls breathing and circulation.

16. **(3)** Both lemons and oranges contain high concentrations of vitamin C, useful in the treatment of scurvy.

17. **(1)** Alcohol is one of a very few substances very quickly absorbed after being ingested.

18. **(4)** The kidney is the organ in which the body wastes collect. These wastes then form urine and move on to the urinary bladder.

19. **(2)** Iodine is used in the thyroid gland to make thyroxin, the hormone which is the thyroid gland's major product.

20. **(2)** Cigarette smoking is generally associated with cardiovascular stress. The other conditions are produced by specific viruses.

21. **(4)** Most life processes require the utilization of oxygen; it is eliminated only in excess.

22. **(4)** Iron is an important component of hemoglobin.

23. **(2)** A jellyfish is the only one of the possible choices which is an invertebrate.

24. **(2)** The sperm cell contains the particular chromosome which determines the sex of a human embryo.

25. **(2)** White corpuscles produce antibodies, which are useful in fighting potential infection.

26. **(3)** The skeleton, the body's bone structure, depends on calcium for its maintenance.

27. **(4)** Excess teeth (or any other excess body organ) is usually genetically related. The other conditions are acquired after birth.

28. **(3)** Since each sperm can carry the X or the Y chromosome with equal probability, sex determination for each birth is the same, 50% for a boy, and 50% for a girl.

29. **(5)** Milk is the food most often subjected to the pasteurization process in order to eliminate possibly dangerous bacteria.

30. **(3)** Chlorophyll is involved in the manufacture of sugar.

31. **(2)** The blood in the body makes a complete turnover once every minute.

32. **(4)** That part of the heart which sets the pumping action is located in the right ventricle.

33. **(4)** The jejunum is that portion of the small intestine extending from the duodenum to the ileum, where the most active mixing of digestive juices takes place.

34. **(5)** The most common form of pollination of grasses is caused by the wind.

35. **(3)** Iodine is an antiseptic, an item used to clean wounds.

36. **(3)** The third sentence states that to perform practiced skills you need to "turn loose the systems of muscles and nerves responsible for each maneuver, place them on their own, and stay out of it."

37. **(3)** Although wasted time and overstimulation might result, the sense of fatigue or tiredness is the best answer.

38. **(2)** Paragraph 2 states that vitamins "do not provide energy nor do they construct or build any part of the body."

39. **(3)** Paragraph 6 indicates that supplemental vitamins are required for people known to have deficient diets and those recovering from certain illnesses.

40. **(4)** The last sentence defines Recommended Daily Allowances as the highest amounts of vitamins, minerals, and proteins needed by most people each day.

41. **(2)** Coconut seeds float on water and have been known to travel thousands of miles.

42. **(1)** Dandelion seeds catch the wind and travel in the air.

43. **(3)** Animals eat the apples and drop the seeds in their waste as they pass through an area.

44. **(3)** Cockleburs attach to the fur of passing animals and fall off as the animal walks. The passage also specifically says that man is not present in the area.

45. **(1)** The graph shows a high rate of CO_2 production. When the supply of CO_2 in the blood increases, the breathing rate is increased. The brain is stimulated by increased amounts of CO_2 in the blood, and sends impulses to the diaphragm and chest muscles which then move more rapidly. As a result, the rate of breathing is speeded up.

46. **(3)** "Peristalsis" is the term applied to the rhythmic contractions of the smooth muscles in the wall of the alimentary canal. The stomach is one of its organs. The graph shows that there is a low rate of peristalsis, which means there is little digestion going on in the stomach.

47. **(5)** The graph shows a high rate of adrenalin release. One of the effects of adrenalin is to cause a conversion of glycogen, which is stored in the liver, into glucose, which becomes dissolved in the blood. The high concentration of glucose supplies the extra energy that results when large amounts of adrenalin are released.

48. **(1)** Fire is incapable of controlling itself.

49. **(5)** Without the ability to reproduce, an organism will die out.

50. **(4)** If an organism carries out all its basic life functions, it is alive.

CHEMISTRY

Directions:

For each question, circle the number of the response that best answers the question or completes the statement. Correct and explanatory answers are provided at the end of the chapter.

1. All matter has mass and

(1) color
(2) occupies space
(3) is soluble
(4) is solid
(5) odor

2. The smallest particle of gold which still retains its characteristics is

(1) a molecule of gold
(2) a proton
(3) an electron
(4) a gold granule
(5) an atom of gold

3. All atoms contain protons and

(1) neutrons
(2) molecules
(3) electrons
(4) compounds
(5) filled outer shells

4. Brass is

(1) an alloy
(2) a mixture
(3) a mineral
(4) an element
(5) a metaloid

5. This diagram represents the formation of an

(1) atom
(2) isotope
(3) isobar
(4) electron
(5) ion

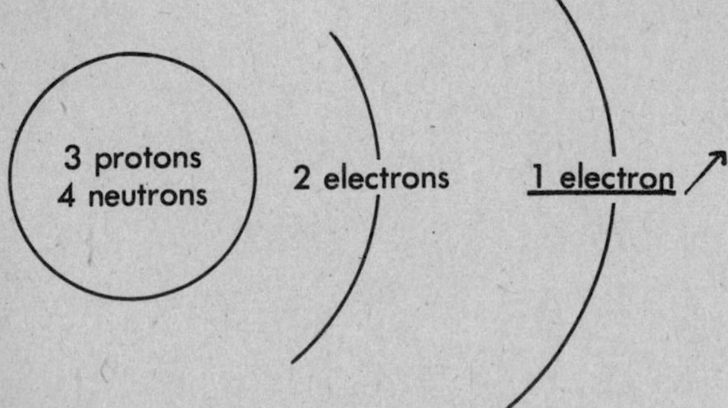

6. A piece of paper is torn. This is an example of a

(1) chemical change
(2) combustion process
(3) nuclear change
(4) physical change
(5) Carnot process

7. Which of the following processes is responsible for clothes drying on the line on a warm summer day?

(1) freezing
(2) condensation
(3) sublimation
(4) evaporation
(5) melting

8. An acid reacts with a base to form water and a salt. This is called

(1) neutralization
(2) esterification
(3) hydrolysis
(4) combustion
(5) deacification

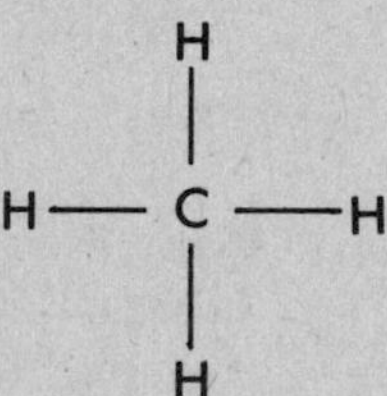

9. In the above compound, methane, four hydrogen atoms are bonded to a carbon atom. The bonds are

(1) electrovalent
(2) ionic
(3) covalent
(4) nuclear
(5) magnetic

10. The following diagram represents

(1) a chemical reaction
(2) a chain reaction
(3) an elastic collision
(4) an inelastic collision
(5) the fusion reaction

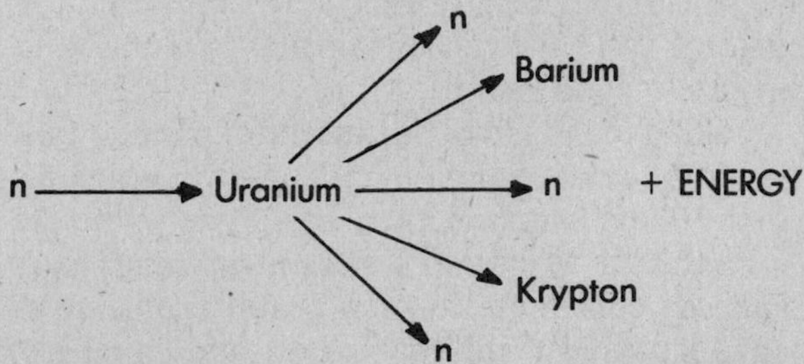

11. Absolute zero is the lowest temperature that it is possible to reach. In terms of the Fahrenheit scale, this is

(1) 0°
(2) minus 273°
(3) minus 459°
(4) minus 820°
(5) minus 1046°

12. Oxygen liquefies at a temperature of

(1) minus 100° Fahrenheit
(2) minus 460° Celsius
(3) minus 297° Fahrenheit
(4) 212° Fahrenheit
(5) 0° Celsius

13. All the following tend to purify water EXCEPT

(1) bacteria
(2) oxidation
(3) sedimentation
(4) chlorination
(5) sunlight

14. In order to effectively make seawater pure enough to drink, that water must first be

(1) chlorinated
(2) distilled
(3) filtered
(4) oxidized
(5) aerated

15. When a fuel is burned, it usually results in the production of

(1) water
(2) hydrogen
(3) calcium
(4) alcohol
(5) oxygen

16. Which of the following compounds is most unstable at room temperature?

(1) H_2SO_4
(2) H_2CO_3
(3) NaCl
(4) HO
(5) $C_6H_{12}O_6$

17. LED is an abbreviation for Light-Emitting Diode. LEDs are most frequently used in

(1) hand-held calculators
(2) manual typewriters
(3) diesel engines
(4) microbiology
(5) cancer medication

18. The number of calories required to change the temperature of 250 grams of water from 22°C to 25°C is

(1) 83.3
(2) 250
(3) 375
(4) 750
(5) 850

GO ON TO THE NEXT PAGE

19. An atom containing 19 protons, 20 neutrons, and 19 electrons has a mass number of

    (1) 19
    (2) 20
    (3) 39
    (4) 58
    (5) 38

20. In the atom of a given element, the proton is found in the

    (1) K-shell
    (2) L-shell
    (3) nucleus
    (4) electron cloud
    (5) M-shell

21. The change from the solid state directly to the gaseous state is called

    (1) sublimation
    (2) evaporation
    (3) condensation
    (4) crystallization
    (5) neutralization

Items 22 to 26 are based on the following selection.

Today's consumers are more aware of the existence of vitamins and minerals than any previous generation. The increasing sales of vitamin-mineral supplements and the considerable interest shown in new FDA regulations on these products attest to this awareness.

While vitamins usually take center stage in any discussion of dietary supplements, minerals also are essential for good health and for growth. Just the right amounts of minerals in our diets are necessary.

Some minerals are needed in relatively large amounts in the diet—calcium, phosphorus, sodium, chloride, potassium, magnesium, and sulfur. "Large" is measured in a range of milligrams to one gram.

Other minerals, called "trace minerals," are needed in small amounts. These are iron, manganese, copper, iodine, zinc, cobalt, fluorine, selenium, and perhaps others.

Some minerals, such as lead, mercury, and cadmium, are regarded as harmful.

Even minerals that the body requires for good health can be harmful if we get too much of them. For example, if all the potassium the body requires in one day is taken in a single, concentrated dose, severe illness can result. Many children under five years of age are hospitalized each year due to iron poisoning caused by accidental ingestion of multiple daily dietary supplements. Some of these children die. Other minerals can cause adverse health effects if an individual takes as little as twice as much as is required to maintain good health.

Taking too much of one essential mineral may upset the balance and function of other minerals in the body. Excess mineral intake can reduce an individual's ability to perform physical tasks and can contribute to such health problems as anemia, bone demineralization and breakage, neurological disease, and fetal abnormalities. The risks are greatest for the very young, pregnant or lactating women, the elderly, and those with inadequate diet or chronic disease.

There are a number of things we do not know about the function of minerals in the body, particularly the trace elements. It is clear, however, that people who take mineral supplements should not use them in amounts greatly in excess of what the body requires.

Mineral elements have two general body functions—building and regulating. Their building functions affect the skeleton and all soft tissues. Their regulating functions include a wide variety of systems, such as heartbeat, blood clotting, maintenance of the internal pressure of body fluids, nerve responses, and transport of oxygen from the lungs to the tissues.

Minerals that are present in relatively large amounts in the body and are required in fairly large amounts in the diet (more than 100 milligrams per day) are generally classified as macrominerals. The others are classified as "trace elements."

22. For proper nutrition of the human body the minerals iron, manganese, and cobalt

    (1) are required in large quantities
    (2) can be identified with a geiger counter
    (3) are needed in small amounts
    (4) can be taken in a single concentrated dose
    (5) are not essential

23. All of the following minerals are necessary for good health EXCEPT

    (1) potassium
    (2) magnesium
    (3) copper
    (4) cadmium
    (5) zinc

24. Mineral elements have two general body functions—building and regulating. Their building functions affect

    (1) skin
    (2) eyes, hair, and teeth
    (3) heart
    (4) bones and all soft tissues
    (5) all of the above

25. Minerals that are required in fairly large amounts in the diet are called

    (1) harmful minerals
    (2) macrominerals
    (3) trace elements
    (4) dietary supplements
    (5) caloric

26. Excess mineral intake can contribute to problems such as

    (1) anemia
    (2) bone breakage
    (3) lack of strength
    (4) all of the above
    (5) choices (1) and (3) only

GO ON TO THE NEXT PAGE

Items 27 to 30 are based on the following selection.

Oral rehydration therapy (ORT) is the most dramatic in a range of low-cost methods now available for protecting the lives and health of children in low-income communities. For the last two years, the *State of the World's Children* report, with the help of the mass media, has drawn worldwide attention to the fact that just four relatively simple and inexpensive methods could now enable parents themselves to halve the rate of child deaths and save the lives of up to 20,000 children each day.

In brief, those methods are:

1. Growth monitoring—which could help mothers to prevent most child malnutrition before it begins. With the help of a 10-cent growth chart, and basic advice on weaning, most mothers could maintain their child's healthy growth—even within their limited resources.
2. Oral rehydration—which could save most of the more than 4 million young children who now die each year from diarrheal dehydration.
3. Breast-feeding—which can ensure that infants have the best possible food and a considerable degree of immunity from common infections during the first six months of life.
4. A full $5 course of immunization —which can protect a child against measles, diphtheria, whooping cough, tetanus, tuberculosis, and polio. At present, these diseases kill an estimated 5 million young children a year, leave 5 million more disabled, and are a major cause of child malnutrition.

27. Following the four methods described can save the lives of many

(1) pregnant women
(2) old people
(3) children
(4) tuberculosis patients
(5) animals

28. According to the passage, newborn infants should consume

(1) cow's milk
(2) pasteurized milk
(3) manufactured milk
(4) dry milk
(5) breast milk

29. The most dramatic low-cost method for protecting the lives and health of children is

(1) growth monitoring
(2) immunization
(3) breast-feeding
(4) oral rehydration therapy (ORT)
(5) vitamin C

30. About how many children would be saved in one year if the four methods were used?

(1) 200,000
(2) 70,000
(3) 20,000
(4) 700,000
(5) 7,000,000

Items 31 to 34 are based on the following selection.

Every day you breathe about 16,000 quarts of air. Almost everywhere in New York state, but especially in heavily populated areas, the air which circulates through your lungs and supplies oxygen to your bloodstream is splotched with unhealthy substances—carbon black, fly ash, soot, silica, metal dust and other organic and nonorganic pollutants.

Air contaminants from industries, incinerators, power plants, automobiles, airplanes, and backyard leaf-and-debris burners stack the odds against us by contributing to staggering death and disease tolls. Medical research shows that air pollution can cause lung cancer. It increases suffering from pneumonia, allergies, asthma, and the common cold, as well as aggravating cases of chronic bronchitis and emphysema.

High concentrations of air pollution—each lasting only a few days—were blamed for sharply increased death rates in Belgium's Meuse Valley in 1930; in Donora, Pa. in 1948; in London in 1952; and in New York City in 1963 and 1966. Air pollution kills.

Air pollution adversely affects all living things, stunting and killing flowers, shrubs, trees, and crops. Spinach, for example, can no longer be grown as an agricultural crop in the Los Angeles basin because of the city's smog problems. Crop damage means higher food prices, amplifying our already inflationary grocery-budget blues.

Pollutants also damage property and materials, soil clothing, discolor paint and even corrode stone, marble, and metal. Again the result can be measured in dollars and cents, in inconvenience and in higher cleaning and maintenance bills for homeowners, businesses, and government alike.

31. Which city has a smog problem that prevents spinach from being grown?

    (1) Meuse Valley
    (2) Los Angeles
    (3) New York
    (4) San Francisco
    (5) Moscow

32. Which is NOT a medical effect of air pollution?

    (1) the common cold
    (2) asthma
    (3) allergies
    (4) polio
    (5) pneumonia

33. The organ of the body most affected by air pollution is the

    (1) brain
    (2) thyroid
    (3) lungs
    (4) intestine
    (5) stomach

34. Air pollution has killed many people in a short time in all of the following locations *except*

    (1) Belgium's Meuse Valley
    (2) Donora, Pa.
    (3) London
    (4) New York City
    (5) Newark

GO ON TO THE NEXT PAGE

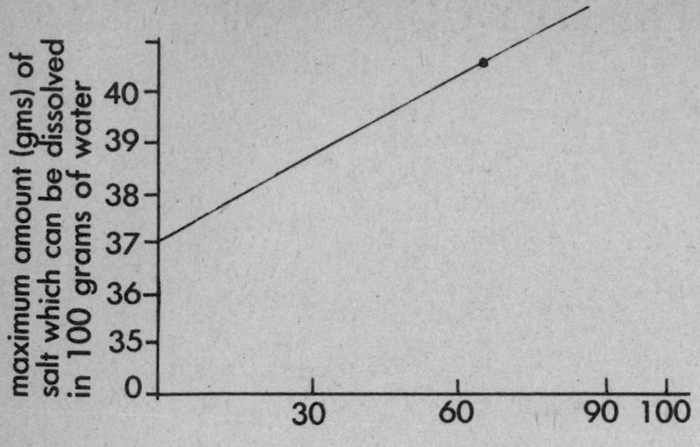

Temperature (°C) of the water

Items 35 to 38 are based on the graph above.

Common salt can be dissolved in water. The hotter the water temperature, the more salt can be dissolved. In the graph above, the line shows the maximum amount (grams) of salt which can be dissolved in 100 grams of water at various temperatures.

35. What is the maximum number of grams of salt that can be dissolved in 100 grams of water at 30° C?

(1) 30
(2) 37
(3) 38
(4) 39
(5) 0

36. At what temperature will the water dissolve a maximum of 39 grams of salt?

(1) 0° C
(2) 30° C
(3) 60° C
(4) 90° C
(5) 100° C

37. At 60° C, 100 grams of water can dissolve any of the following amounts of salt EXCEPT

(1) 30 grams
(2) 37 grams
(3) 38 grams
(4) 39 grams
(5) 40 grams

38. By raising the temperature of the water from 0° C to 100° C, how many more grams of salt can be dissolved?

(1) 0
(2) 1
(3) 2
(4) 3
(5) 4

39. In organic chemistry, the prefix is an important indication of the structure of the compound. For example:

Prefix	Number of carbons
meth-	1
eth-	2
pro-	3
but-	4
pent-	5

Given the compounds $CH_3CH_2CH_2CH_3$ and CH_3CHCH_3 (with a CH_3 group attached to the middle carbon)

$$\begin{array}{c} CH_3\,CH\,CH_3 \\ | \\ CH_3 \end{array}$$

These compounds are both

(1) alkynes
(2) alkenes
(3) isomers of butane
(4) isomers of propane
(5) isomers of pentane

40. A compound has the structural formula:

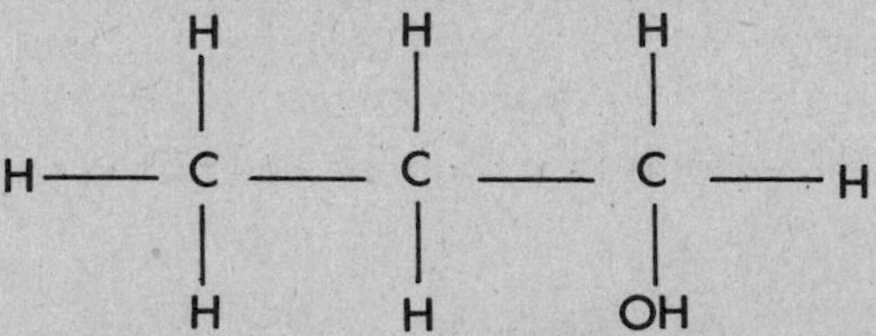

It is classified as an

(1) alkane
(2) alkene
(3) kyne
(4) alcohol
(5) acid

END OF CHEMISTRY TEST

ANSWER KEY FOR CHEMISTRY QUESTIONS

1. (2)	11. (3)	21. (1)	31. (2)
2. (5)	12. (3)	22. (3)	32. (4)
3. (3)	13. (1)	23. (4)	33. (3)
4. (1)	14. (2)	24. (4)	34. (5)
5. (5)	15. (1)	25. (2)	35. (3)
6. (4)	16. (2)	26. (4)	36. (3)
7. (4)	17. (1)	27. (3)	37. (5)
8. (1)	18. (4)	28. (5)	38. (4)
9. (3)	19. (3)	29. (4)	39. (3)
10. (2)	20. (3)	30. (5)	40. (4)

EXPLANATIONS FOR CHEMISTRY QUESTIONS

1. **(2)** This is the definition of matter.

2. **(5)** An atom is the smallest part of an element retaining its properties.

3. **(3)** All atoms have protons, electrons, and neutrons except hydrogen, which has no neutrons.

4. **(1)** Brass is an alloy composed of a combination of copper and zinc.

5. **(5)** An ion is formed when an atom gains or loses electrons.

6. **(4)** The paper is changed physically, not chemically.

7. **(4)** Evaporation is described by the following: Water (liquid) $\rightarrow$ Water (gas)

8. **(1)** Neutralization: Acid + Base $\rightarrow$ Salt + Water

9. **(3)** The bonds are covalent because the electrons are shared.

10. **(2)** In the fission of uranium, a neutron splits up an atom of uranium.

11. **(3)** Absolute zero is the point at which all atomic action apparently stops. On the Fahrenheit scale, this is minus 459°.

12. **(3)** The point at which oxygen turns from its gaseous state to a liquid is minus 297° F.

13. **(1)** The more bacteria in the water, the less pure it is.

14. **(2)** During distillation, the water impurities are removed by vaporizing the water, leaving behind the salts.

15. **(1)** During the "burning" of a fuel, the decomposition of the fuel often results in the release of water (eg. $CH_4 + 20_2 \rightarrow CO_2 + 2H_20$).

16. **(2)** H_2CO_3 (carbonic acid) is an unstable compound which easily breaks down into water (H_2O) and carbon dioxide (CO_2).

17. **(1)** The light in the usual hand-held calculator is generated by a diode.

18. **(4)** It takes one calorie to raise the temperature of one gram of water one degree. Therefore, it takes 750 calories to raise 250 grams of water three degrees (from 22° to 25°).

19. **(3)** The mass number is the total number of neutrons and protons in an atomic nucleus. Therefore, the 19 protons and 20 neutrons result in a mass number of 39.

20. **(3)** The nucleus of the atom contains the protons and neutrons.

21. **(1)** Sublimation is defined as the complete process of a solid passing directly into a vapor state without melting.

22. **(3)** As stated in paragraph 4, iron, manganese, and cobalt are "trace minerals" or minerals needed in small amounts.

23. **(4)** Paragraph 5 mentions cadmium as one of the minerals regarded as harmful.

24. **(4)** As stated in the next-to-last paragraph, the building functions of minerals affect "the skeleton (or bones) and all soft tissues."

25. **(2)** The last paragraph states that minerals required in relatively large amounts are called "macrominerals."

26. **(4)** Choices (1), (2), and (3) are all problems resulting from excess mineral intake. (See paragraph 6.)

27. **(3)** As stated in the first paragraph, following the methods described can "save the lives of up to 20,000 children each day."

28. **(5)** Breast milk is described as "the best possible food" for newborn infants under the heading breast-feeding.

29. **(4)** The first sentence makes this statement.

30. **(5)** According to paragraph 1, these methods can save the lives of 20,000 children each day. 20,000 × 365 = 7,300,000.

31. **(2)** Spinach can no longer be grown in Los Angeles. (See paragraph 4.)

32. **(4)** According to paragraph 2, medical research shows all except polio are effects of pollution.

33. **(3)** The second sentence states that air "circulates through your lungs."

34. **(5)** Of the choices given, only Newark is not mentioned in paragraph 3.

35. **(3)** Find 30°C on the bottom scale. Move up to the line, then move straight across and read the figure from the scale on the left. The answer is 38 grams.

36. **(3)** From 39 grams, move to the right to the line then read the figure below, 60°C.

37. **(5)** At 60°C, the maximum amount which can be dissolved is 39 grams; 40 grams is too much.

38. **(4)** At 0°C, 37 grams can be dissolved. At 100°C, 40 grams can be dissolved. 40 − 37 = 3. Therefore, 3 more grams of salt can be dissolved by raising the temperature of the water from 0° to 100°C.

39. **(3)** Each compound contains 4 carbon atoms. The prefix for 4 carbons is "but-"; therefore, these compounds are isomers of butane.

40. **(4)** The functional group of an alcohol is the OH^-.

PHYSICS

Directions:

For each question, circle the number of the response that best answers the question or completes the statement. Correct and explanatory answers are provided at the end of the chapter.

1. "Opposites attract" is the fundamental law of

   (1) momentum
   (2) forces
   (3) magnetism
   (4) gravitation
   (5) physics

2. In a simple series circuit, if the voltage is doubled and the resistance remains the same, then the

   (1) current halves
   (2) power halves
   (3) power remains the same
   (4) power quadruples
   (5) current doubles

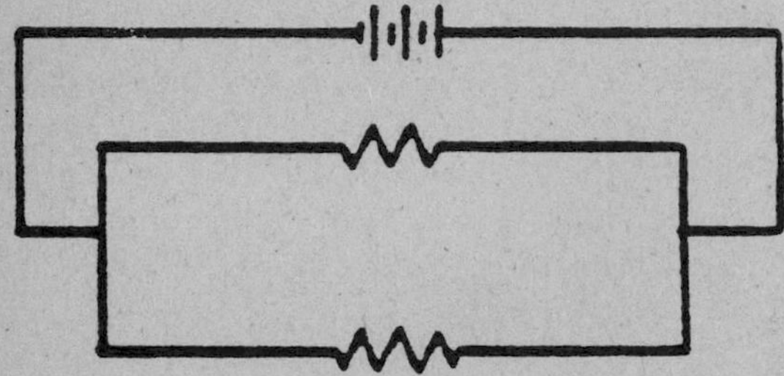

3. In the parallel circuit shown above, the total resistance is

   (1) $\frac{R_1 \times R_2}{R_1 + R_2}$
   (2) $\frac{R_1 + R_2}{R_1 \times R_2}$
   (3) $R_1 + R_2$
   (4) $\frac{R_1 + R_2}{R_1 + R_2}$
   (5) none of the above

4. The diagram below represents a portion of an electrical wire, whose length is (1) and whose thickness is (t).

   The resistance of the wire

   (1) increases with length; increases with thickness
   (2) increases with length; decreases with thickness
   (3) decreases with length; decreases with thickness
   (4) decreases with length; increases with thickness
   (5) is unchanged by changes in length or thickness

5. In the diagram above, a rocket (R) has just left the Earth (E). The attractive force between R and E is

   (1) magnetic
   (2) electrical
   (3) centripetal
   (4) gravitational
   (5) nuclear

6. A 100-pound person weighs about

   (1) 100 kilograms
   (2) 45,000 kilograms
   (3) 45 milligrams
   (4) 45 kilograms
   (5) 450 kilograms

7. In the diagram below, a Weight (W) is pulled a distance (d). If W is doubled, the work required is

   (1) halved
   (2) quadrupled
   (3) doubled
   (4) quartered
   (5) unchanged

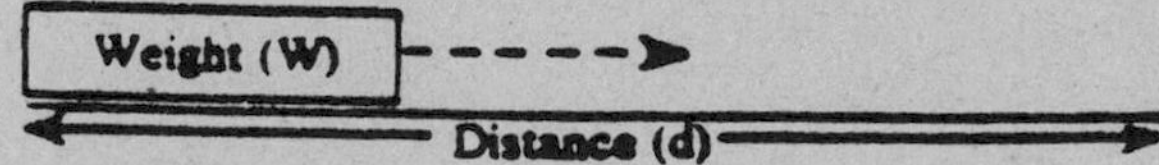

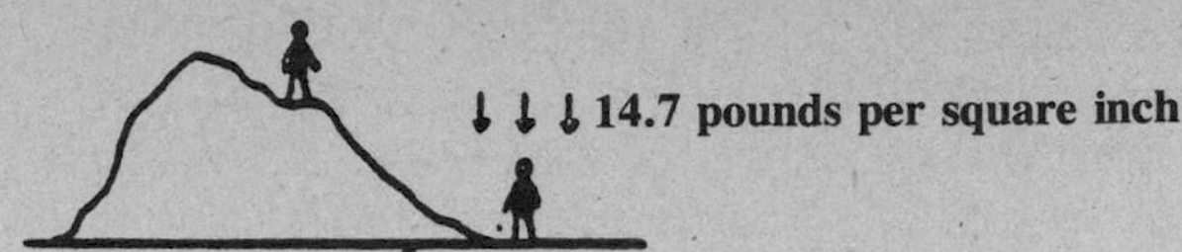

8. The diagram above represents a tall mountain. The atmospheric pressure at the bottom is 14.7 pounds per square inch.

   At the top of the mountain, the atmospheric pressure is

   (1) less because of a smaller amount of atmosphere pushing down
   (2) less because of the greater amount of atmosphere pushing down
   (3) greater since the ambient temperature is lower
   (4) greater since there is a greater proximity to the clouds
   (5) the same

9. How does the heat from the sun reach the earth?

   (1) conduction
   (2) convection
   (3) condensation
   (4) sublimation
   (5) radiation

10. The formula for converting Celsius (C) to Fahrenheit (F) temperature is

    $C = (F - 32) \times \frac{5}{9}$

    If the Fahrenheit temperature is 212°F, then the Celsius temperature is

    (1) 10°
    (2) 32°
    (3) 212°
    (4) 100°
    (5) 200°

11. Sound travels fastest when it moves through

    (1) steel
    (2) water
    (3) light
    (4) air
    (5) a vacuum

12. Which common electrical device contains an electromagnet?

    (1) flatiron
    (2) telephone
    (3) water heater
    (4) toaster
    (5) electrical outlet

13. When all the colors of the spectrum are fused, the resulting light is

    (1) red
    (2) white
    (3) blue
    (4) yellow
    (5) black

14. Isotopes of the same element have the same number of

    (1) protons and electrons
    (2) mesons and neutrons
    (3) neutrons and electrons
    (4) electrons and mesons
    (5) electrons only

15. Which is NOT a form of energy?

    (1) light
    (2) electricity
    (3) temperature
    (4) heat
    (5) radio waves

GO ON TO THE NEXT PAGE

Items 16 to 18 are based on the following selection.

The history of the Frisbee is shrouded in mystery. According to one account, the inventor was a young Yale student named Elihu Frisbie, who one day in 1826 staged a one-man revolt against compulsory attendance at the university chapel. Seizing a collection plate, Elihu boldly sailed it into a stained-glass window, thus inventing the sport and ensuring his expulsion from the college. While that version is purely apocryphal, it does contain a hint of truth. The sport was indeed started at Yale in the 1880s by students who tossed about empty inverted pie tins from the Frisbie Pie Company in nearby Bridgeport, Connecticut. When letting the tin fly, the thrower would yell "Frisbie" as a warning to anyone in its path to watch out, much as a golfer shouts "fore." The fad of flinging about pie tins spread to other Eastern colleges. There are also reports that in Hollywood's early days, cameramen would toss back and forth the metal lids from film containers. But the metal discs had one serious drawback: they could be painful to catch.

For years, Frisbie fell into disuse. Then, in 1947, a man named Fred Morrison, who by trade was a building inspector in Los Angeles, designed a disc made of plastic. Morrison's invention had the unfortunate weakness of tending to shatter when the temperature fell. Nonetheless, the Wham-O company, which at the time was also experimenting with the Hula-Hoop, bought Morrison's idea. Later, while conducting test marketing, Wham-O salesmen learned that college students in the East called the discs "Frisbies." As a result, the company altered the spelling slightly and applied for a trademark for its product under the name of Frisbee.

By the mid-1960s, the Frisbee had developed into perhaps America's most enduring fad. It also quickly spread throughout much of the world. Other companies rushed to produce plastic discs under other trade names and by 1979, some 50 million had been produced.

The Frisbee is an example of a theory that works, but has not yet been fully explained scientifically. Anyone who has seen a Frisbee in flight is well aware that the disc possesses extraordinary aerodynamic characteristics. Furthermore, the shape of the Frisbee, which closely resembles the discus first used by ancient Greek athletes, has a form that can be described as one-third wing, one-third gyroscope, and one-third parachute. Yet no one has established the exact reason a Frisbee flies as it does, or why it can be made to perform such complex aerial maneuvers. The Frisbee, in short, is a theory waiting for verification.

16. The form of a Frisbee is similar to a

(1) wing
(2) parachute
(3) gyroscope
(4) choices (1) and (2) only
(5) choices (1), (2) and (3)

17. Early Frisbees were made of all of the following *except*

(1) pie plates
(2) collection plates
(3) plate glass
(4) lids from film containers
(5) plastic discs

18. The word *aerodynamic* means

(1) moving fast
(2) turning like a dynamo
(3) concerning the motion of the air
(4) concerning airplanes in motion
(5) winglike as in the flight of birds

Items 19 to 21 are based on the following graph.

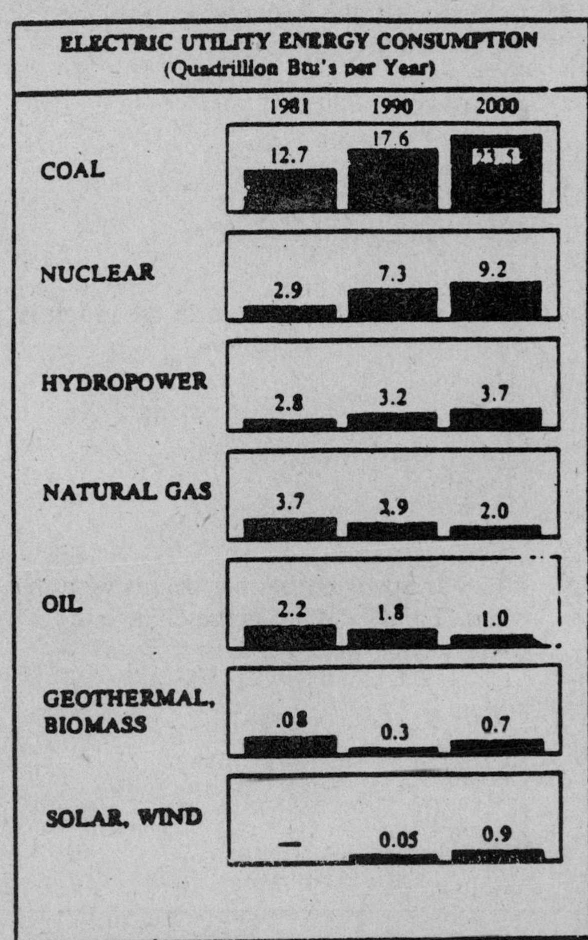

19. The fuel which supplies the greatest amount of energy is

    (1) nuclear
    (2) natural gas
    (3) coal
    (4) hydropower
    (5) solar and wind

20. All of the following fuels are expected to increase in consumption EXCEPT

    (1) coal
    (2) nuclear
    (3) hydropower
    (4) natural gas
    (5) geothermal, biomass

21. Besides coal, the greatest increase in fuel consumption in BTUs is projected for

    (1) nuclear
    (2) hydropower
    (3) natural gas
    (4) oil
    (5) solar, wind

GO ON TO THE NEXT PAGE

Items 22 to 25 are based on the following graph.

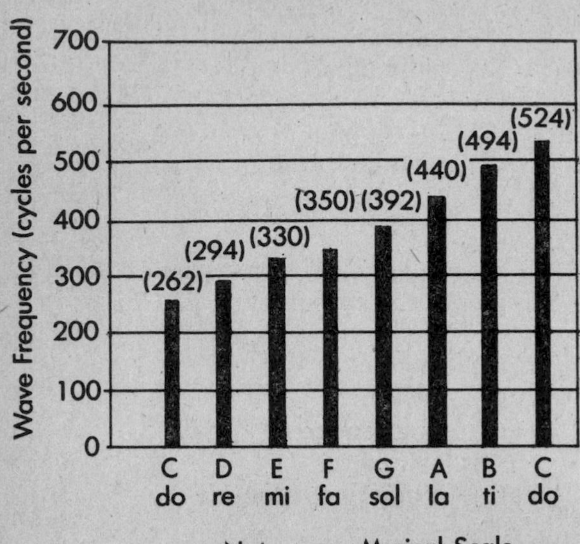

In the above graph, the notes C-D-E-F-G-A-B-C constitute a major scale. The sound frequencies produced by each note are indicated.

22. If a major scale is played, the frequencies

(1) go up by even steps
(2) go up but not evenly
(3) decrease evenly
(4) decrease but not evenly
(5) stay the same

23. Compared to the frequency of the first C, the second C is

(1) twice as much
(2) half as much
(3) four times as much
(4) the same
(5) one-quarter as much

24. The lowest pitch indicated in the graph is

(1) A
(2) B
(3) C
(4) D
(5) E

25. The Star Spangled Banner begins with the notes G and E. What is the change in frequency between these two notes?

(1) 0
(2) 10
(3) 62
(4) 330
(5) 392

Items 26 to 28 are based on the following graph.

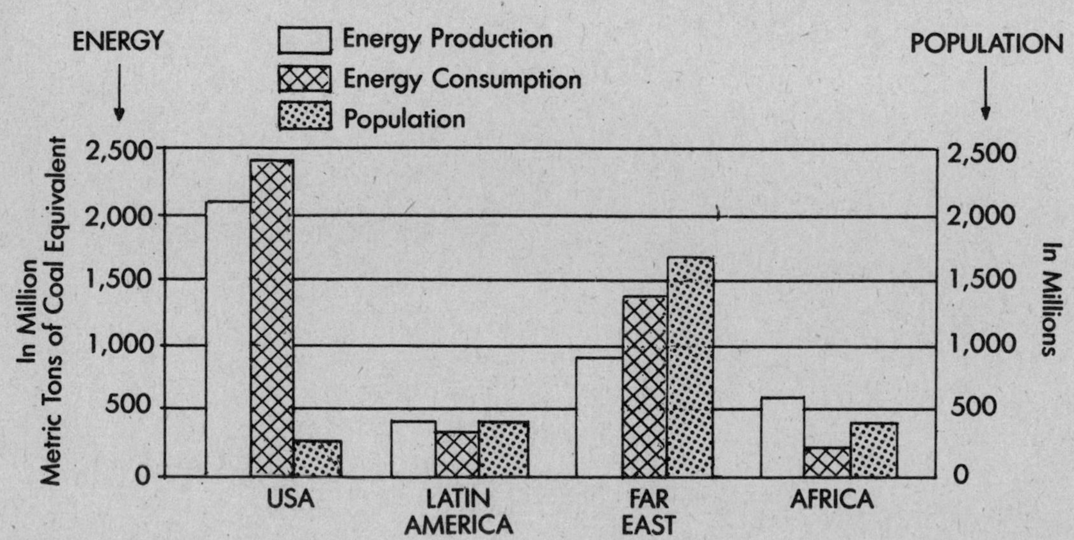

26. Which region used the most energy in 1974?

    (1) USA
    (2) Latin America
    (3) Far East
    (4) Africa
    (5) Impossible to determine from information given.

27. Which area had the smallest population in 1974?

    (1) USA
    (2) Latin America
    (3) Far East
    (4) Africa
    (5) Impossible to determine from information given.

28. If each person uses the same amount of energy to survive, which region would need the most?

    (1) USA
    (2) Latin America
    (3) Far East
    (4) Africa
    (5) Impossible to determine from information given.

Items 29 and 30 are based on the following graph.

The following graph represents the disintegration of a sample of a radioactive element. At time t = 0 the sample has a mass of 4.0 kilograms.

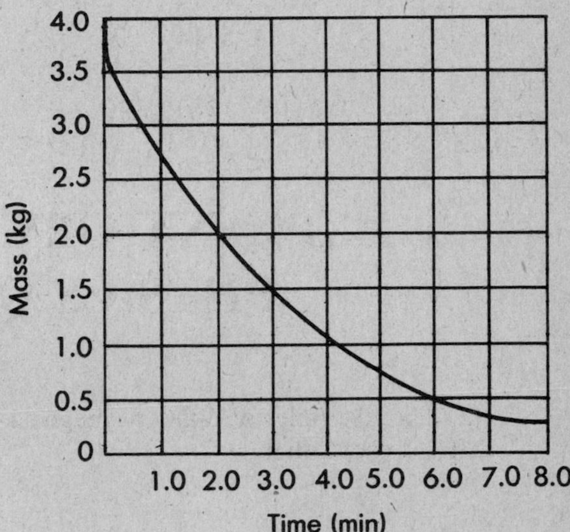

29. What mass of the material remains at 4.0 minutes?

    (1) 1 kg
    (2) 2 kg
    (3) 3 kg
    (4) 4 kg
    (5) 5 kg

30. What is the half-life of the isotope (in minutes)?

    (1) 1.0
    (2) 2.0
    (3) 3.0
    (4) 4.0
    (5) 5.0

END OF PHYSICS TEST

ANSWER KEY FOR PHYSICS QUESTIONS

1. (3)	9. (5)	17. (3)	25. (3)
2. (5)	10. (4)	18. (3)	26. (1)
3. (1)	11. (1)	19. (3)	27. (1)
4. (2)	12. (2)	20. (4)	28. (3)
5. (4)	13. (2)	21. (1)	29. (1)
6. (4)	14. (1)	22. (2)	30. (2)
7. (3)	15. (3)	23. (1)	
8. (1)	16. (5)	24. (3)	

EXPLANATORY ANSWERS FOR PHYSICS QUESTIONS

1. **(3)** The like poles of different magnets repel each other and the unlike poles attract each other.

2. **(5)** Ohm's Law: $E = I \times R$; if E doubles then I must double (R is constant).

3. **(1)** $\frac{1}{R_T} = \frac{1}{R_1} + \frac{1}{R_2} \quad R_T = \frac{1}{\frac{1}{R_1} + \frac{1}{R_2}} = \frac{R_1 \times R_2}{R_1 + R_2}$

4. **(2)** The longer and thinner the wire, the harder for electrons to travel through it.

5. **(4)** Gravity is the attraction between any two objects.

6. **(4)** 1 pound = 454 grams; 1 kilogram = 1000 grams

$$100\ (\cancel{\text{lbs.}}) \times \frac{454(\cancel{\text{gr.}})}{1\ (\cancel{\text{lbs.}})} \times \frac{1 \text{ kilogram}}{1000\ (\cancel{\text{gr.}})} = 45.4 \text{ kg. (about 45 kg.)}$$

7. **(3)** Work = Weight × Distance. Twice as much work moves twice the weight over the same distance.

8. **(1)** The further up the mountain you climb, the less atmosphere is above you. Space has no atmosphere.

9. **(5)** Radiation requires no atmosphere through which to travel.

10. **(4)** By substituting values, $C = (212 - 32) \times \frac{5}{9} = 180 \times \frac{5}{9} = 100°C$

11. **(1)** Steel conducts sound faster than any of the other mediums. Sound does not move at all through a vacuum.

12. **(2)** The telephone is the only one of the five electrical devices which uses an electromagnet, which produces a force field.

13. **(2)** White is the result of the fusion of many colors of the spectrum.

14. **(1)** Isotopes are forms of an element that differ in number of neutrons.

15. **(3)** Energy is defined as the capacity for doing work. Temperature is an indicator of the intensity of heat, but it is not a form of energy.

16. **(5)** As stated in the last paragraph, the form of the Frisbee can be described as "one-third wing, one-third gyroscope, and one-third parachute."

17. **(3)** Pie plates, collection plates, lids from film containers and plastic discs are all mentioned in paragraphs 1 and 2. There is no mention of a Frisbee made of plate glass.

18. **(3)** Aerodynamic means most nearly "concerning the motion of the air."

19. **(3)** Coal shows the highest bar for each year.

20. **(4)** Of the choices given, only natural gas shows a decrease from year to year.

21. **(1)** Nuclear increases the most: 9.2 − 2.9 = 6.3 quadrillion BTUs.

22. **(2)** For each note, the size of the frequency increases, but the amount of increase differs.

23. **(1)** The wave frequency of the second C is exactly twice the frequency of the first C: 2 × 262 = 524.

24. **(3)** Pitch is measured by frequency; therefore, the lowest pitch on the graph is the lowest frequency on the graph, which is C (at 262 cycles/second).

25. **(3)** The difference in frequencies is: 392 (G) − 330 (E) = 62.

26. **(1)** USA consumed the most energy. (It has the highest "energy consumption" bar.)

27. **(1)** USA had the smallest population. (It has the lowest "population" bar.)

28. **(3)** Far East population is the highest. (It has the highest "population" bar.)

29. **(1)** Locate 4.0 minutes on the time axis. Proceed vertically until the function (curve) is reached, then move horizontally toward the mass axis. The value on the mass axis is the quantity remaining after 4.0 minutes.

30. **(2)** By definition, the half-life is the time for fifty percent of the original sample to disintegrate (change). The graph indicates that at 2.0 minutes, 2.0 kg of sample remains. (2.0 kg/4.0 kg) × 100% = 50%.

EARTH SCIENCE

Directions:

For each question, circle the number of the response that best answers the question or completes the statement. Correct and explanatory answers are provided at the end of the chapter.

1. The earth ____ on its axis from west to east.

   (1) revolves
   (2) rotates
   (3) tilts
   (4) rises
   (5) falls

2. During a solar eclipse

   (1) the earth prevents the light of the sun from reaching the moon
   (2) the shadow of the moon falls on the sun
   (3) the moon prevents the light of the sun from reaching the earth
   (4) the sun prevents the reflected moonlight from reaching the earth
   (5) the shadow of the sun falls on the earth

3. The ____ range in size from one to five hundred miles in diameter, and revolve around the sun.

   (1) moons
   (2) comets
   (3) meteors
   (4) satellites
   (5) asteroids

4. Ursa major, Orion, and Andromeda are fixed groups of stars called

   (1) galaxies
   (2) meteors
   (3) constellations
   (4) satellites
   (5) quasars

5. The process by which rocks are broken down into smaller fragments by the atmosphere and other factors in the environment is called

   (1) erosion
   (2) sorting
   (3) wind
   (4) glaciation
   (5) weathering

6. Planting vegetation, terracing, and strip cropping are common practices employed in the prevention of

   (1) mechanical weathering
   (2) soil erosion
   (3) irrigation
   (4) delta formation
   (5) glaciation

7. When air high above the earth's surface is cooled below the dew point it is likely to form

   (1) dew
   (2) clouds
   (3) fog
   (4) hail
   (5) frost

8. Ground water and surface water become polluted by

   (1) runoff from pesticides used on gardens and farms
   (2) improper disposal of chemical wastes
   (3) deposit of untreated sewage into rivers and lakes
   (4) improper disposal of nuclear wastes
   (5) all of the above

9. The instrument used to determine air pressure is called a(n)

   (1) hygrometer
   (2) anemometer
   (3) barometer
   (4) thermometer
   (5) ruler

10. If you fly westward from Los Angeles to Tokyo you will need to adjust your calendar watch for the proper day after you cross the

    (1) Bering Sea
    (2) Alaska
    (3) North Pole
    (4) Atlantic Ocean
    (5) International Date Line

11. Granite, shale, coal, and limestone are commonly known

    (1) minerals
    (2) rocks
    (3) fossils
    (4) sediments
    (5) fuels

12. Sedimentation as a method of water purification results in

    (1) an increase in the bacterial count
    (2) a decrease in the amount of organic matter
    (3) an increase in the amount of hydrogen
    (4) a more rapid water flow
    (5) the destruction of vitamins

13. Mechanical weathering may occur by means of

    (1) plant roots
    (2) temperature changes
    (3) frost action
    (4) all of the above
    (5) none of the above

14. This planet revolves around the sun in an orbit between that of Venus and Mars. It is known to be covered by oceans and some land; it has but a single moon. Name the planet.

    (1) Jupiter
    (2) Saturn
    (3) Earth
    (4) Mercury
    (5) Uranus

15. Tides result from the pull of gravity exerted upon the earth by

    (1) the moon
    (2) the sun
    (3) the moon and the sun
    (4) the Milky Way
    (5) none of the above

16. A group of students working on a science project wish to start some bean plants for an experiment. The best results will probably be obtained if the students locate the plants in a window facing

    (1) the courtyard
    (2) south
    (3) north
    (4) east
    (5) west

17. Cities located along the eastern seaboard consistently record higher temperatures than inland cities in the same states during the winter season. Which of the following statements might explain this situation?

    (1) Eastern cities receive more sun than inland cities.
    (2) The average amount of daylight is greater in the winter than in the summer.
    (3) The angle of the sunlight is greater in inland cities.
    (4) The winter weather along the coast is milder due to the influence of the ocean.
    (5) The winter weather along the coast is milder due to the location of the Appalachian Mountains.

18. Cirrus, dew point, fronts, and isotherm are terms commonly associated with the field of

    (1) meteorology
    (2) archeology
    (3) oceanography
    (4) mineralogy
    (5) seismology

19. Luster, hardness, fracture, and cleavage are properties generally used in describing

    (1) storms
    (2) precipitation
    (3) fossils
    (4) glaciers
    (5) minerals

20. Clay is one of the best materials available for pottery because of its ability to hold water. A geologist would describe this property as

(1) limited erosion
(2) low porosity
(3) high porosity
(4) low permeability
(5) high permeability

21. When air reaches the dew point, its relative humidity is 100%. Cooling the air to a temperature below the dew point causes the water vapor to begin to change back into a liquid or a solid. That process is called

(1) sublimation
(2) condensation
(3) vaporization
(4) precipitation
(5) convection

22. Which of the following metals is a liquid at room temperature?

(1) silver
(2) gold
(3) mercury
(4) iron
(5) lead

23. Which one is unrelated to the other four?

(1) Uranus
(2) Pluto
(3) Polaris
(4) Mars
(5) Venus

24. Which of the following is unrelated to the other four?

(1) wind
(2) soil acidity
(3) tides
(4) wave action
(5) clouds

25. The temperature of the air falls at night because the earth loses heat by

(1) radiation
(2) conduction
(3) convection
(4) rotation
(5) refraction

26. The San Andreas fault is associated most frequently with

(1) tidal waves in Japan
(2) geyser actions in Oregon
(3) volcanoes in Washington
(4) earthquakes in California
(5) hurricanes in Florida

27. The earth rotates 60° in

(1) 1 hour
(2) 2 hours
(3) 3 hours
(4) 4 hours
(5) 6 hours

28. Two places on the same meridian have the same

(1) altitude
(2) longitude
(3) solar time
(4) climatic conditions
(5) tidal motion

29. In which of the following countries would a solar heating device work most effectively?

(1) Greenland
(2) Japan
(3) Australia
(4) Canada
(5) Italy

30. As a passenger balloon rises, its gas bag tends to

(1) become smaller
(2) leak
(3) distort
(4) expand
(5) remain unchanged

Items 31 to 33 are based on the following selection.

The epicenter is located in a sparsely populated area of the San Gabriel Mountains, about 14 km north of San Fernando. The shock was felt in California, Nevada, and Arizona, and as far east as Beryl, Utah. Intensity XI was assigned to the destroyed Olive View Hospital, where three people were killed. In all, 58 people died, 49 of them at the San Fernando Veterans Administration Hospital. Over 2,000 injuries were reported.

Damage to public and private property was estimated at over $500 million. Hundreds of private houses and businesses had to be vacated. Thousands sustained appreciable damage. Collapses of newly built, earthquake-resistive buildings at the Olive View Hospital in the northern Sylmar area reduced this $23.5 million complex to a total loss. Four of its five-story wings pulled away from the main building. Three toppled. The second story of a two-story building in the complex dropped to ground level. This damage resulted from severe ground shaking, not from ground faulting. Older, unreinforced masonry buildings collapsed at the Veterans Administration Hospital. Freeway overpasses collapsed. The near failure of the Lower Van Norman Dam caused authorities to evacuate thousands of residents in the area. Public utilities and facilities of all kinds were damaged, both above and below ground.

31. How many people died in the earthquake?

    (1) 49
    (2) 58
    (3) 235
    (4) 2,000
    (5) 50,000

32. The shock was felt in Utah, Arizona, California and

    (1) New Jersey
    (2) Newark
    (3) Nevada
    (4) New York
    (5) New Mexico

33. Epicenter means

    (1) a sparsely populated area
    (2) furthermost distance of the quake
    (3) part of the earth's surface directly above the origin of the earthquake
    (4) the shopping center destroyed
    (5) the site of the Veterans Hospital

Item 34 refers to the following paragraph.

Early proponents of the theory of continental drift, which was the forerunner of the concept of plate tectonics, did not have an easy time defending their ideas. They were constantly rebuffed by a scientific community that was adamantly committed to the theory of fixed continents. In the sixteenth century, maps began to show that the Western Hemisphere on one hand, and Europe and Asia, on the other, appeared to have been pulled apart since, in interlocking fashion, they appeared to fit nicely into one another. This evidence caused some thinkers to speculate that a sudden, cataclysmic split had occurred between the eastern and western hemispheres. But the idea lay dormant until 1908, when Frank Taylor, an American glacial geologist, put forward the notion that the earth's crust, like a glacier, might be moving infinitesimally slowly in one direction or the other.

34. The term plate tectonics refers to the theory that

    (1) magma can be found deep within the earth's crust
    (2) the continents of the earth are drifting closer together over geological time
    (3) the crust of the earth is made of great moving plates driven by powerful forces within the earth
    (4) glaciers form crevasses as they move over uneven ground
    (5) the earth's center is a very dense core

GO ON TO THE NEXT PAGE

35. On August 10, 1972, a great fireball streaked northward across the bright afternoon skies of the western United States. It was visible to amazed observers for over a minute and a half as it traced a 900-mile path from Utah to Alberta, Canada, leaving behind it a smoky trail which lingered in the air for 20 minutes. In Montana, people heard a sonic boom at the time it passed by. Over Canada, it disappeared.

    This paragraph most likely describes the appearance of

    (1) an F-14 fighter
    (2) the space shuttle
    (3) a disintegrating artificial satellite
    (4) a UFO
    (5) a meteor

Items 36 and 37 relate to the following article.

The principle of balloon flight is simple. The propane is ignited in a burner that is placed directly beneath the opening in the bottom of the balloon. The balloon rises because the air inside the bag is warmer, therefore lighter, than the outside air. If the balloon begins to descend too soon, the crew reignites the burner, sending another blast of lift-producing heat into the bag.

A balloon consists of only three major parts: bag, basket, and burner. The bags (or envelopes, as they are technically called) are made of nylon or polyester. They range in capacity from 33,000 to 100,000 cubic feet, and some reach as high as a seven-story building. The crew basket, constructed from wicker or aluminum, is suspended from the bag by strong tapes. The burner is fixed to a metal platform above the basket.

36. The crew basket on a balloon is usually constructed of wicker or aluminum. What might you predict as an outcome if the crew basket were exchanged for one made of iron or steel?

    (1) The balloon would be harder to control.
    (2) The balloon would rise more easily from the ground.
    (3) The balloon would be unlikely to rise from the ground at all.
    (4) The balloon would be struck by lightning.
    (5) No change would be likely.

37. In the reading above the balloon rises because the air inside the bag is warmer. This occurs because

    (1) when air is heated, its density changes
    (2) the balloon is constructed of light materials
    (3) molecules move more violently in cool air
    (4) cool air always moves towards warm air
    (5) air absorbs heat more rapidly than water

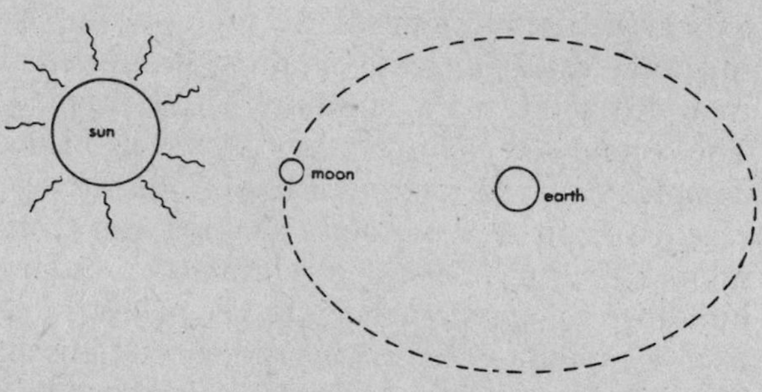

38. The illustration above is an example of

    (1) the phases of the moon
    (2) the seasons of the year
    (3) a lunar eclipse
    (4) a solar eclipse
    (5) radiation

39. The moon rotates once while going around the earth once. As a result,

    (1) the moon follows an elliptical path
    (2) the sun is eclipsed by the moon every seven years
    (3) only one side of the moon faces the earth
    (4) every fourth year is a leap year
    (5) the moon is a satellite of the earth.

Items 40 and 41 are based on the information below.

Few areas in the United States are free from thunderstorms and their attendant hazards, but some areas have more storms than others. The map below shows the incidence of thunderstorm days—days on which thunderstorms are observed—for the United States.

40. Mary and Phil are looking forward to a carefree camping vacation. They would like to avoid the frequent thunderstorms that spoiled their last camping trip. Based on the information in the map below, which region of the country would they be LEAST likely to choose for their next vacation?

(1) California, Oregon, Washington
(2) Florida, Georgia, Alabama
(3) Kentucky, Virginia, West Virginia
(4) Missouri, Iowa, Illinois
(5) Texas, Louisiana, Oklahoma

41. If Mary and Phil should experience a thunderstorm despite their careful planning, they should do any of the following EXCEPT

(1) stay inside a solid building
(2) remain in an all-metal automobile
(3) stand under a tall tree
(4) go to a low place such as a ravine or valley
(5) get off and away from bicycles, motorcycles, and golf carts

Incidence of Thunderstorms

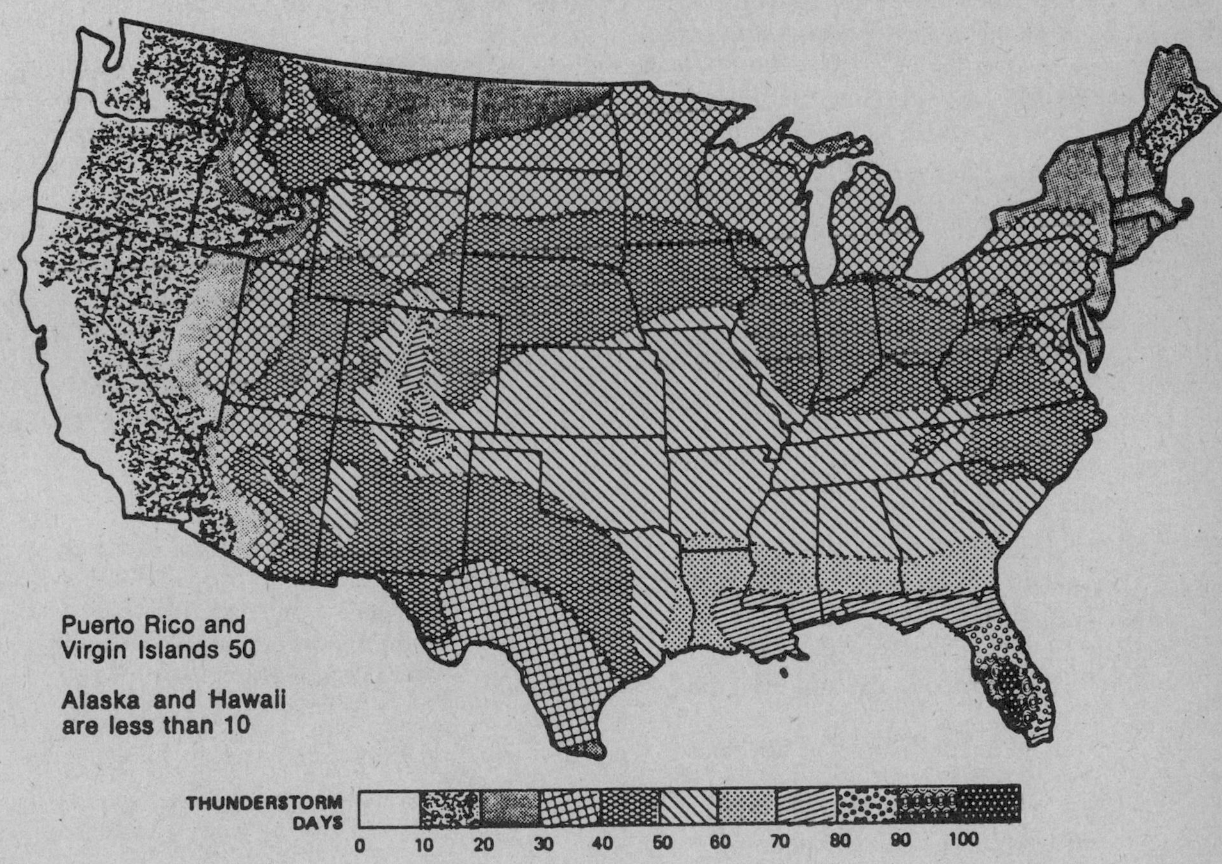

Items 42 to 44 refer to the paragraph below.

It has been fifty years since Clyde W. Tombaugh discovered the planet Pluto. He was a young man from a Kansas farm with only a high school education when he got a job as an astronomer's assistant at the Lowell Observatory in Flagstaff, Arizona, in 1929. There had been a suspicion since the turn of the century that a huge planet, nicknamed Planet X, with a mass seven times greater than Earth existed beyond Uranus and Neptune. The gravitational pull of such a planet, it was believed, would account for observed irregularities in the orbit of Uranus. Using a series of photographs taken of an area of the constellation Gemini, Tombaugh made an unusual observation, which was later determined to be a planet in our own solar system. Other astronomers calculated that Pluto is a mean distance of 3.67 billion miles from the Sun, and takes 248 Earth years to make a complete orbit of the Sun. In 1976, it was finally determined that Pluto was small in both diameter and mass, smaller in fact than Earth's moon. It might be as small as 1750 miles. Astronomers now believe that no Planet X exists anywhere in our solar system.

42. Based on the information given above, one can conclude that

    (1) Planet X does exist but has not yet been found
    (2) the calculations which predicted Planet X were incorrect
    (3) Pluto is a huge planet which affects the orbit of Uranus
    (4) Pluto is in the constellation Gemini
    (5) the planet Pluto must be Planet X

43. It is known from the information given above that

    (1) Pluto is closer to the sun than the Earth
    (2) Mars is farther from the sun than Pluto
    (3) it is impossible to predict the existence of previously unseen planets
    (4) since its discovery, Pluto has not yet made an orbit of the sun
    (5) none of the above

44. The diameter of Pluto is

    (1) equal to that of Planet X
    (2) as large as that of the Earth
    (3) accounts for irregularities in the orbit of Uranus
    (4) less than the size of Earth's moon
    (5) somewhere in the area of the constellation Gemini

Items 45 to 48 relate to the following article.

The Orbiter has only one washroom and toilet. Crew members take turns like a traveling family sharing a motel room. Sanitation facilities are much the same as on the earth. Airflow substitutes for gravity in carrying away the wastes. Plastic sleeves around the hand-wash basin keep spray droplets from floating away into the cabin.

Toilet waste is pushed by airstreams into a container. Some waste may be intentionally saved. Its analysis tells doctors which minerals crew members may lose excessively in weightlessness.

Crew members may use conventional shaving cream and safety razors and disposable towels. For those preferring electric shavers, there is a wind-up shaver operating like an electric model but requiring no plug or battery. It has a built-in vacuum device that sucks up whiskers as the shaving proceeds. For a sponge-bath, the only kind available, there is a watergun adjustable for temperatures from 18 to 35° C (65 to 95°F).

45. How are droplets of water prevented from leaving the sink and entering the cabin?

    (1) The water is frozen.
    (2) Droplets are centrifuged down the drain.
    (3) Droplets are convected by fans.
    (4) Plastic sleeves contain the droplets.
    (5) Water is not used.

46. Why are air streams used to collect toilet waste?

    (1) The wastes are poisonous.
    (2) The wastes are heavy in space.
    (3) The wastes are weightless.
    (4) Astronauts reuse the wastes.
    (5) Wastes must be tested in labs.

47. According to the passage, what floating material could foul up the cabin and harm the crew?

    (1) boots, fuel, wastes
    (2) boots, beds, wastes
    (3) whiskers, bolts, wastes
    (4) landing pods, insulation tiles
    (5) whiskers, water, wastes

48. How much would you weigh while in space?

    (1) twice earth weight
    (2) earth weight
    (3) 50% of earth weight
    (4) 25% of earth weight
    (5) no weight

Items 49 to 50 refer to the information below.

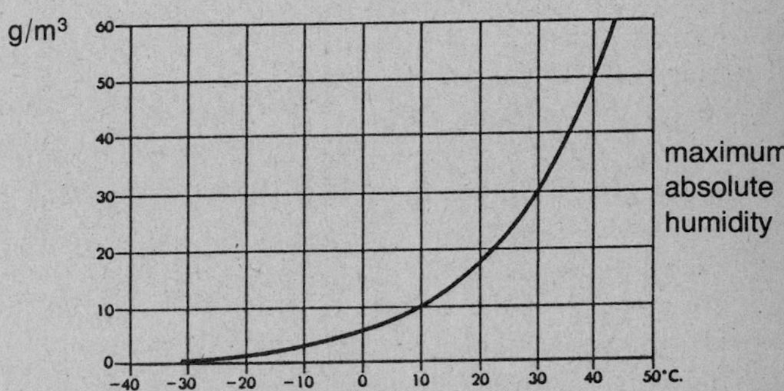

49. Air temperature affects relative humidity, that is, the amount of water vapor in the air compared to the amount of water vapor the air could hold at that temperature. Based on the graph shown above, how much water is needed to saturate each cubic meter of air at 30°C?

    (1) 17 g
    (2) 20 g
    (3) 30 g
    (4) 35 g
    (5) 50 g

50. The cooling of this air will cause it to become saturated with water vapor. The temperature at which the air becomes saturated is called

    (1) break point
    (2) condensation
    (3) dew point
    (4) discomfort index
    (5) relative humidity

END OF EARTH SCIENCE TEST

ANSWER KEY FOR EARTH SCIENCE QUESTIONS

1. (2)	11. (2)	21. (2)	31. (2)	41. (3)
2. (3)	12. (2)	22. (3)	32. (3)	42. (2)
3. (5)	13. (4)	23. (3)	33. (3)	43. (4)
4. (3)	14. (3)	24. (2)	34. (3)	44. (4)
5. (5)	15. (3)	25. (1)	35. (5)	45. (4)
6. (2)	16. (2)	26. (4)	36. (3)	46. (3)
7. (2)	17. (4)	27. (4)	37. (1)	47. (5)
8. (5)	18. (1)	28. (2)	38. (4)	48. (5)
9. (3)	19. (5)	29. (3)	39. (3)	49. (3)
10. (5)	20. (4)	30. (4)	40. (2)	50. (3)

EXPLANATORY ANSWERS FOR EARTH SCIENCE QUESTIONS

1. **(2)** Earth spins or rotates on its axis from west to east, but it revolves around the sun.

2. **(3)** The moon is between the sun and the earth during a solar eclipse, and so prevents the light of the sun from reaching the earth.

3. **(5)** Asteroids, also known as planetoids, are small, usually irregularly shaped bodies that orbit the sun.

4. **(3)** Each is a named constellation in the map of the heavens.

5. **(5)** Weathering occurs when rocks are broken down into smaller fragments.

6. **(2)** The practices named help to prevent soil erosion.

7. **(2)** Clouds are formed high above the earth's surface. Cooler air can't hold as much water as warmer air.

8. **(5)** Choices (1), (2), (3), and (4) are all sources of water pollution.

9. **(3)** Barometers are specifically devised to measure air pressure.

10. **(5)** Add a day to your calendar as you travel toward Tokyo from the United States. You will have crossed an imaginary line known as the international date line.

11. **(2)** Though limestone may contain fossils and coal is used as a fuel, all of these are known as rocks.

12. **(2)** In sedimentation, an amount of organic matter in the water drops to the bottom of the storage area, giving the water a higher degree of purity.

13. **(4)** Choices (1), (2), and (3) are all means of mechanical weathering.

14. **(3)** The only planet with a single moon is earth.

15. **(3)** The moon and the sun both influence tides but the effect of the moon is stronger.

16. **(2)** A southern exposure has the greatest light and warmth.

17. **(4)** Bodies of water are slower to absorb heat, but slower to give it up than is land.

18. **(1)** All these words are associated with weather forecasting, the science of meteorology.

19. **(5)** All of these properties are commonly used in the description of minerals.

20. **(4)** Clay has low permeability, that is, water is not likely to go through it.

21. **(2)** Condensation is the process by which a gas is changed into a liquid; that is, water vapor (gas) has now become water (liquid).

22. **(3)** Mercury is a liquid at room temperature. All the rest are solids.

23. **(3)** Uranus, Pluto, Mars, and Venus are planets that revolve around the sun. Polaris is the north star.

24. **(2)** All the choices except soil acidity are related to the rotation of the earth.

25. **(1)** Radiation is the process by which heat is transferred in space.

26. **(4)** The San Andreas fault is a geological formation in California and is associated with shifts in the earth, better known as earthquakes.

27. **(4)** The earth rotates 360° every 24 hours. A rotation of 60° is equivalent to $\frac{1}{6}$ of a day ($\frac{60}{360} = \frac{1}{6}$, or 4 hours ($\frac{1}{6} \times 24 = 4$).

28. **(2)** A meridian line runs from pole to pole, that is, north to south, and always faces the sun at the same time.

29. **(3)** Australia is the country most likely to use a solar heating device effectively due to its nearness to the equator and its consequent relationship to the sun.

30. **(4)** The gas bag tends to expand as the atmospheric pressure around it tends to decrease. Atmospheric pressure varies inversely with altitude.

31. **(2)** This information is stated in the fourth sentence of paragraph 1.

32. **(3)** This information is stated in the second sentence of paragraph 1.

33. **(3)** The epicenter of an earthquake is the point on the earth's surface that is directly above the origin (or focus) of the earthquake.

34. **(3)** This can be deduced from the paragraph as a whole, especially the reference to a "cataclysmic split" and the comparison of the movement of the earth's crust to that of a glacier.

35. **(5)** The sky show was produced by a meteor, a solid piece of material from outer space which was rushing through the atmosphere, but too large to be completely changed into a gas. Pieces that reach the earth before burning up completely are called meteorites.

36. **(3)** The weight of the basket would be considerably heavier due to the density of the iron or steel.

37. **(1)** When air is heated, molecules are more active, and the density of the air decreases.

38. **(4)** During a solar eclipse the moon travels between the sun and the earth, blocking out the view of the sun totally or partially on at least some part of the earth.

39. **(3)** The moon revolves around the earth over the same amount of time as it rotates. This means that the same side of the moon faces the earth at all times. The side away from us is referred to as the dark side of the moon.

40. **(2)** Based on the map, Florida shows the highest incidence of thunderstorm activity, up to 100 thunderstorm days per year.

41. **(3)** Standing under a tall tree, or telephone pole, or on the top of a hill creates a natural lightning rod. In a forest, seek shelter under a thick growth of small trees. In open areas, go to a low place such as a ravine or valley.

42. **(2)** Obviously, someone was calculating very badly. See the last sentence.

43. **(4)** Since it takes 248 Earth years for Pluto to orbit our Sun, and since it was discovered only 50 years ago, that far-out planet has a long way to go.

44. **(4)** Pluto, being only about 1750 miles in diameter, is smaller in diameter than the earth's moon, which is 2160 miles in diameter.

45. **(4)** The last sentence in paragraph 1 says that "plastic sleeves around the hand-wash basin keep spray droplets from floating away into the cabin."

46. **(3)** From your knowledge about space travel, everything in space is weightless, therefore an external force is necessary to move the wastes.

47. **(5)** Floating material, which are described are whiskers and water (paragraph 4), and wastes (paragraph 3).

48. **(5)** A person in space is too far from Earth's gravitational pull and therefore is weightless.

49. **(3)** The graph indicates that it takes 30 grams of water per cubic meter to saturate air at 30°C.

50. **(3)** The dew point is defined as the temperature at which the air becomes saturated with water. Condensation refers to the process of a gas changing to a liquid.

Part V

Reading Skills Review

HOW TO SHARPEN READING COMPREHENSION SKILLS

GED candidates must be able to read quickly, carefully, and with comprehension. Three of the five tests in the GED test battery depend to a large extent on reading comprehension skill.

The two essential ingredients for successful performance on reading tests are speed and comprehension. This chapter will explain the different kinds of comprehension questions and provide reading passages that will help to sharpen your skills. For best results, follow the simple steps below:

1. Read the section Planning a Strategy to learn about the different kinds of comprehension questions.
2. Read the section Reading: Quick Tips to pick up valuable information on how to increase your reading speed and how to use the principles of paragraph construction to improve your comprehension.
3. Work through the programmed Learning Exercises to gain experience with the various kinds of questions. The questions in this section are presented in boxes called "frames." The reading passages and questions are on the right side of the page and detailed explanations of each response are on the left side of the page. This format enables you to see immediately what the correct answer should be, and why each incorrect answer is wrong. Cover the correct answers with your hand or a piece of paper as you answer each question. As soon as you have chosen an answer to a particular question, uncover the correct answer and check your response against the explanation provided.
4. When you have completed this chapter, practice with the section giving actual GED-type reading questions to familiarize yourself with the variety of reading questions you must face.

PLANNING A STRATEGY

HINTS

1. Read the passage quickly but carefully enough to get the main idea and major supporting details.
2. Read each question and decide what kind it is. *Always* consider each possible answer before making a choice.
3. Eliminate obviously wrong responses immediately. If possible, check confusing answer choices in the passage text.

THE QUESTIONS

Reading comprehension questions are usually one of four kinds. The programmed Learning Exercises are divided into sections offering practice with each of these formats.

Main Idea

This kind of question presents several titles and asks you to choose the one that expresses the main idea or thought of the passage. All of the other ideas in the selection should be related in some way to the main idea and therefore to the title you choose.

Example:

The social standing of a wife in colonial days was determined by the standing of her husband as well as her own ability and resourcefulness. She married not only a husband but also a career. Her position in the community was established in part by the quality of the bread she baked, by the food she preserved for the winter's use, by the whiteness of her washing on the line, by the way her children were clothed, and by her skill in nursing. Doctors were scarce. In case of the illness or death of a neighbor, a woman would put aside her own work to help and she was honored for what she could do.

The title that best expresses the main idea of this selection is

(1) Care of Children in Colonial Times
(2) Community Spirit
(3) Medical Care in Pre-Revolutionary Times
(4) The Colonial Housewife

This selection describes the various homemaking duties a colonial woman was expected to perform. Therefore, the correct response is (4).

Details

Details are the facts and ideas in a selection that explain and support the main idea.

Example:

There are many signs by which people predict the weather. Some of these have a true basis but many have not. There is, for example, no evidence that it is more likely to storm during one phase of the moon than during another. If it happens to rain on Easter, there is no reason to think that it will rain for the next seven Sundays. The groundhog may or may not see his shadow on groundhog day, but it probably won't affect the weather anyway.

Which of the following is NOT listed as a sign of weather phenomenon?

(1) rain on Easter
(2) the phases of the moon

(3) pain in a person's joints
(4) the groundhog's shadow

The correct response is (3). The other choices were mentioned in the passage.

Vocabulary

This kind of question, sometimes called words in context, asks you to choose a synonym for one of the words in the passage.

Example:
The maritime and fishing industries find perhaps 250 applications for rope and cordage. There are hundreds of different sizes, constructions, tensile strengths, and weights in rope and twine. Rope is sold by the pound but ordered by length, and is measured by circumference rather than by diameter.

In this context, the word "application" means

(1) use
(2) description
(3) size
(4) types

The correct response is (1), "use." Try it in the sentence in place of the word "application"; "use" makes sense in that context and keeps the meaning of the sentence intact.

Inference

An inference is a conclusion made from something that is implied. The answer to an inference question will not be found in the passage, therefore, this is the most difficult type of comprehension question to answer. You must read carefully and think logically in order to draw the correct conclusion from the information given.

Example:
The facts, as we see them, on drug use and the dangerous behaviors caused by drugs are that some people do get into trouble while using drugs, and some of those drug users are dangerous to others. Sometimes a drug is a necessary element in order for a person to commit a crime, although it may not be the cause of his or her criminality. On the other hand, the use of a drug sometimes seems to be the only convenient excuse by means of which the observer can account for the undesirable behavior.

The author apparently feels that

(1) the use of drugs always results in crime
(2) drugs and crime are only sometimes related
(3) drug use does not always cause crime
(4) drugs are usually an element in accidents and suicides

The author states that drugs are sometimes a necessary element in a crime, but at other times are just an excuse for criminal behavior. Therefore, (2) is the correct response.

READING: QUICK TIPS

WORDS TO KNOW

Main ideas are the most important thoughts in a paragraph or selection. The main idea is often stated in a topic sentence.

Supporting details are the major thoughts used to explain and expand the main idea.

Skimming is a speed reading technique that is used to extract the main idea and supporting details from a selection.

Scanning is the method used to locate specific information in a selection.

For speed and accuracy in reading and answering comprehension questions, practice and use these skimming and scanning techniques.

To answer main idea and inference questions:

1. Use your index finger as a guide and a pacer, and read the selection through quickly.
2. As you move your finger across each line, concentrate on looking at three or four word phrases, not at one word at a time. Try not to "say" the words in your mind as you go.
3. Follow your finger only with your eyes, not your whole head.
4. Your purpose is to locate the topic sentence, the main idea, and the major supporting details. This information should enable you to answer most main idea and inference questions.

To answer vocabulary and detail questions:

1. Take a key word from the question you want to answer, and "lock" it in your mind.
2. Using your index finger as a guide, scan the lines for that word.
3. *DO NOT READ* when you scan! You are simply looking for the key word.
4. When you find the word, STOP! The answer to your question will usually be in the same sentence.
5. Read the entire sentence carefully before choosing an answer.

The two most important ingredients in a successful reading test performance are accuracy and speed. Both require lots of practice. The tips you have just read should noticeably improve your accuracy and speed if you practice them conscientiously as you do the Learning and Test-type Exercises on the following pages. Keep a record of your time and accuracy; note your progress in both areas.

LEARNING EXERCISES

MAIN IDEA

ANSWER	QUESTION
1. (1) Incorrect This answer suggests the discussion of more than one planet or celestial body. The selection talks only about the moon. (2) Incorrect This response implies a discussion of lifestyles. This is impossible as there is no life on the moon. (3) Incorrect The moon's atmosphere is only one of the subtopics—not the main idea—discussed in this selection. (4) Correct The word "conditions" covers all aspects of the moon discussed in this selection: the moon's size, its terrain, its atmosphere, temperature, etc.	At a distance of approximately 250,000 miles from the earth, the moon is our nearest celestial neighbor. A rugged terrain of mountains, cliffs, plains, and craters covers this globe of 2,000 miles in diameter, but this landscape contains no water. There is no precipitation of any kind on the moon because it lacks an atmosphere. For the same reason, a constant barrage of meteorites and other space debris reaches its surface without hindrance. The beautiful, silvery moon is, in actuality, a barren desert, suffering from great extremes of temperature and devoid of any life as we know it. 1. The title that best expresses the main idea of this selection is (1) Landscapes in Space (2) Life on the Moon (3) The Moon's Atmosphere (4) Conditions on the Moon
2. (1) Incorrect Although all three of these are mentioned in this selection, they are not the *theme* of the selection. (2) Incorrect This topic is mentioned but not discussed. (3) Incorrect This subject is mentioned but not discussed. (4) Correct The selection discusses some of the reasons and remedies for the limitations of language.	The more complicated our thoughts and emotions, the less effective is language as a tool of expression. This is not a simple matter of style or eloquence, for even the finest speakers and writers, using the most sensitive language, would be incapable of putting certain thoughts into words. For this reason, many people use poetry and music instead of prose. These two forms of communication convey subtle yet powerful meanings that cannot be expressed with ordinary words. 2. The title that best expresses the theme of this selection is (1) Words, Poetry, and Music (2) The Hidden Meanings of Words (3) The Eloquence of Fine Speakers (4) Limitations of Language

ANSWER	QUESTION
	The Caribbean sea is to North and South America what the Mediterranean is to the European continent—a central sea. The American body of water is not landlocked. Double strings of islands—the Cuba group and the Bahamas—form an arc at the Atlantic entrance, and this arc is now firmly fortified. Since the Mediterranean of the West is the passage between the Americas, it must be controlled by these countries in order to carry on trade. This sea is as necessary to the Caribbean countries as the Mediterranean is to Italy. The countries of this area produce large quantities of oil, tropical fruits, and vegetables. They are also rich in minerals. This region is capable of supplying the United States with many goods formerly imported from Africa and Asia. In exchange, the countries of this region need the manufactured goods that can be provided only by an industrial nation.
3. (1) Incorrect The selection does not compare the exports of these two areas. (2) Incorrect This subject is not mentioned in the selection. (3) Correct Each of these bodies of water serves the bordering land masses in similar ways. (4) Incorrect Living standards are not discussed in this selection.	3. The Caribbean sea and the Mediterranean are alike with respect to their (1) variety of exports (2) epidemics of serious diseases (3) geographical importance (4) living standards
4. (1) Incorrect The danger of storms is only one of the difficulties affecting migratory birds. (2) Correct Each sentence in this paragraph explains why migration is perilous. (3) Incorrect This topic is mentioned only in the first sentence. (4) Incorrect This subject is not discussed at all in this selection.	The dangers to which migratory birds are subjected during their journeys are but little less than those that would befall them if they remained in unsuitable zones. During long oversea passages, fatigue and hunger weed out the weaklings. Sudden storms and adverse winds strike migrating birds where no land is near, and they are often carried far from the goal they aimed at. Predatory birds accompany them, taking a toll en route, and predatory man waits for the tired wanderers with gun and net. 4. The title that best expresses the main idea of this passage is (1) Dangers of Storms (2) Perils of Migration (3) Unsuitable Environment (4) How Birds Reach Goals

ANSWER	QUESTION
5. (1) Incorrect The selection does not describe the contents, appearance, or uses of the library. It is only mentioned in the first sentence. (2) Incorrect Only one aspect of this topic was mentioned—Jefferson working in his garden. **(3)** Correct The selection describes in detail Jefferson's "full life": his architectural drawings, his love of his estate and gardens, his correspondences, and his "prescription for life." (4) Incorrect This is only one aspect of Jefferson that is discussed in this article.	In his library at Monticello, Jefferson made hundreds of architectural drawings, all of which have been preserved. He must have had a great gift of concentration and a real love for his subject to be able to work in a room with such an outlook. And what energy he had, to find time and will for this precise and exquisite work, at the same time riding over his estate, working in his garden, and carrying on correspondence with everyone from the Marquis de Lafayette to his youngest grandchild. "Something pursued with ardor" was Jefferson's prescription for life, and he got the last ounce of excitement and interest out of everything that came to his notice. 5. The main idea of this selection is expressed in the title (1) The Library of Monticello (2) The Care of the Estate (3) A Full Life (4) Jefferson, the Architect
6. (1) Incorrect Landing areas were referred to with regard to only one kind of lighting. (2) Incorrect Colored lights are just one type of lighting discussed in this selection. (3) Incorrect Just one type of lighting is related to airport identification. **(4)** Correct The selection describes several lighting requirements for airports.	Specific types of lighting are required at first-class airports by the Department of Commerce. To identify an airport, there must be a beacon of light of not less than 100,000 candle power, with a beam that properly distributes light up in the air so that it can be seen all around the horizon from an altitude of from 500 to 2000 feet. All flashing beacons must have a definite Morse code characteristic to aid in identification. Colored lights are required to indicate where safe area for landing ends, red lights being used where landing is particularly dangerous. 6. The best title for this selection is (1) Landing Areas (2) Colored Lights at Airports (3) Identification of Airports (4) Airport Lighting Requirements
	## DETAILS
	Ants are very interesting insects. There are about 8000 different kinds with various ways of finding food. There are hunter ants that capture other insects, shepherd ants that care for aphids from

ANSWER	QUESTION
	which they get sweet honeydew, thief ants that live by stealing, slave-making ants that kidnap the children of other ant nations, and mighty military ants that live by plundering and destroying, driving even men and elephants before them. A city of ant people includes the queen, the workers, the baby ants, and their nurses. Ant babies change their form three times. First, they are small, white eggs. When they hatch, they are little, fat, white worms called larvae. The larvae change into pupae, and the pupae change into adults. The queen is the mother of all the ants in the community. The workers bring food to her and protect her from invaders.
7. **(3)** Correct See paragraph one, sentence three.	7. Hunter ants (1) care for aphids (2) kidnap young ants from other colonies (3) capture other insects (4) plunder and destroy
8. **(1)** Correct See paragraph two, sentence one.	8. A colony of ants (1) includes a queen, workers, babies, and their nurses (2) may have as many as 8000 members (3) is built in a hill (4) protects its members
9. **(4)** Correct See paragraph two, sentence 5.	9. Adult ants (1) hatch from eggs (2) come from larvae (3) are all workers (4) come from pupae
	Commercial interests were quick to recognize the great possibilities of presenting by means of radio what is in effect a person-to-person appeal. At first the novelty made people listen to almost anything, but as the audiences became more accustomed to broadcasts, varied methods of capturing and holding the attention have developed. These vary from the frank interjection of advertising matter in a program of entertainment to the mere sponsoring of the program. Entertainment at first appeared to

ANSWER	QUESTION
	have the greatest appeal, and low comedy and jazz music filled the air. There has come, however, the realization that the radio audience is now as complex as the public and that programs must be set up to attract the attention of as many different types of hearers as possible.
10. **(1)** Correct See the second sentence.	10. When radio was new, (1) people would listen to almost anything (2) advertising was poor (3) advertising was interjected into the programming (4) entertainment was limited
	The part of the ear we see is only a cartilage-and-skin trumpet which catches sound waves. Buried in bone at the base of the skull is the delicate apparatus that makes hearing possible. A passage leads from the outer ear to a membrane called the eardrum. Sound waves striking the eardrum make it vibrate. On the other side of the eardrum lies a space called the middle ear. Across this a chain of three tiny bones carries sound vibrations to another space called the inner ear. Sound messages are conducted along the auditory nerve, located in the inner ear, to the brain for interpretation. The middle ear is connected to the throat by the Eustachian tube. This tube ends near the throat opening of the nose, close to the tonsils. The middle ear also communicates with the mastoid or air cells in the bone behind the ear.
11. **(3)** Correct See paragraph one, sentence one.	11. The outer ear is made of (1) a delicate apparatus (2) a membrane (3) cartilage and skin (4) three tiny bones
12. **(1)** Correct See paragraph two, sentence one.	12. The eardrum is a (1) membrane (2) piece of thin cartilage (3) an air cell (4) a short tube

ANSWER	QUESTION
13. **(3)** Correct See paragraph two, sentence four.	13. Sound vibrations are carried (1) along the auditory nerve (2) through the eardrum (3) to the inner ear across a chain of three tiny bones (4) to the base of the skull
	Track and field events are the only modern sports that would be recognizable in their original form. They can be traced back more than 2500 years to the ancient civilization of Greece. The Greeks held their athletes in high esteem, and champions were looked upon as national heroes. The Greeks began the original Olympic games for the purpose of assembling the greatest athletes of their country. The games were religious pageants as well as peerless athletic events, and were held every four years for more than eight centuries.
14. **(4)** Correct See paragraph one, sentence three.	14. In ancient Greece, athletes were (1) trained as professionals (2) forced to participate in the games (3) usually defeated by the Romans (4) regarded very highly by the public
15. **(1)** Correct See paragraph one, sentence two.	15. The present day Olympics (1) have a 2500-year-old history (2) are religious pageants (3) have been held every four years for eight centuries (4) are completely different from the Greek games
	Observe the people who make an abiding impression of strength and goodness, and you will see that their personal attractiveness and force are rooted in fundamentals of character. They have the physical vitality, endurance, and courage that come from good living. They have the mental stamina and penetration that come from facing up to one's problems, however difficult, and from keeping one's mind on things that really matter. They have the moral power that comes from an active sense of what is right, from doing their part to make truth, justice, and beauty prevail in the world. They have

ANSWER	QUESTION
	the inner peace and grace that are the basics of a truly charismatic personality. People trust them, like to be with them, and depend on them in emergencies. They are the salt of the earth.
16. (1) Incorrect See the second sentence. (2) Incorrect See the sixth sentence. (3) Correct (4) Incorrect See the fifth sentence.	16. A quality NOT mentioned by the author is (1) courage (2) dependability (3) tolerance (4) inner grace
	Although you may still enjoy fairy tales, they probably do not engross you to the degree that they might have a few years ago. Fairy tales belong primarily to a stage in our lives when we are most interested by the world of fantasy. Goblins, wizards, and dwarfs appeal to the young child's wandering imagination and contribute greatly to the development of creativity, but it is a temporary infatuation. As we grow older, real challenges begin to interest us more. The imaginary victories brought about by fairy godmothers lose their power of enchantment and we become absorbed in the stories of real people, real success, and real accomplishment. The fascination of "Jack the Giant Killer" gives way to a keen interest in Commander Byrd's Antarctic exploration, Helen Keller's biography, or the harrowing adventures of spelunkers, deep-sea divers, and mountain climbers. This step marks one of the first great advances in the process of intellectual maturation.
17. (1) Correct See the first paragraph.	17. Young children are primarily interested in (1) fantasy stories (2) horror stories (3) goblins and wizards (4) adventure stories
18. (3) Correct See paragraph two, sentences one and two.	18. People become interested in real-life stories when they (1) are young (2) are adults (3) begin to mature (4) are bored

VOCABULARY

ANSWER	QUESTION
	In May of each year, the ghost of Mark Twain must hover over Angel's Camp, California, while all eyes in this colorful old mining town turn to the tailless, leaping amphibians of the genus Rana. It was just this sort of event that Twain made famous in his early humorous story, "The Celebrated Jumping Frog of Calaveras County." Thousands of spectators gather each year to watch the county's champions hop their way to fame and compete for a $500 first prize. Each frog must undergo a rigid inspection to insure against foul play, such as the loading of the competitor with buckshot, as happened in Twain's tall tale. Back in 1944, Alfred Jermy was the proud owner of Flash, a frog which held the world's championship with a fifteen-foot, ten-inch leap. In 1950, a seven-year-old boy's pet, X-100, stole top honors with three jumps averaging fourteen feet, nine inches. As amazing as these might seem to the novice, these are mere puddle jumps. Half the fun in visiting this Calaveras County contest is to be found in listening to the tales of 600-foot leaps in a favorable wind—well, why not?
19. **(2)** Correct Frogs are a type of amphibian.	19. The amphibians mentioned in the first paragraph are the (1) storytellers (2) frogs (3) citizens of Calveras County (4) human contestants
20. **(4)** Correct The word "novice" means "inexperienced."	20. The word "novice" in the third paragraph means (1) the judges (2) the spectators (3) the owners of the frogs (4) inexperienced readers

	In the year 1799, an officer of the French Army was stationed in a small fortress on the Rosetta River, a mouth of the Nile, near Alexandria, Egypt. He was interested in the ruins of the ancient Egyptian

ANSWER	QUESTION
	civilization, and had seen the Sphinx and the pyramids, those mysterious structures that were erected by men of another era. One day, as a trench was being dug, he found a piece of black slate on which letters had been carved. He had studied Greek in school, and knew this was an inscription written in that language. There were two more lines carved into the stone: one in the Egyptian characters he had seen on other ruins, the other in completely unfamiliar characters. The officer realized the importance of such a find, and relinquished it to scholars who had been puzzling over Egyptian inscriptions. In 1802, a French professor by the name of Champollion began studying the stone in an attempt to decipher the two unknown sets of characters using the Greek letters as a key. He worked with the stone for over 20 years, and in 1823, announced that he had discovered the meaning of the fourteen signs, and in doing so, had unlocked the secret of ancient Egyptian writing. Some 5000 years after an unknown person had made those three inscriptions, the Rosetta Stone became a key, unlocking the written records of Egypt and sharing the history of that civilization with the rest of the world.
21. **(1)** Correct "Decipher" means to break a code and translate the message.	21. The word "decipher" is synonymous with (1) translate (2) encode (3) transcribe (4) transmit
22. **(3)** Correct Other examples of inscriptions are names carved into gravestones, and initials inscribed in jewelry.	22. The word "inscription" means (1) a picture carved in stone (2) a relief sculpture (3) letters carved into a hard substance (4) a written message
23. **(1)** Correct The word "relinquish" means to "let go" or "give up."	23. The word "relinquish" means to (1) give up possession of something (2) lend to someone (3) sell an object (4) study an object

ANSWER	QUESTION
	The impressions that an individual gets from his environment are greatly influenced by his emotional state. When he is happy, objects and people present themselves to him in a favorable aspect; when he is depressed, he views the same things in an entirely different light. It has been said that a person's moods are the lenses that color life with many different hues. Not only does mood affect impression; impression also affects mood. The beauty of a spring morning may dissipate the gloom of a great sorrow, the good-natured chuckle of a fat man may turn anger into a smile, or a telegram may transform a house of mirth into a house of mourning.
24. **(3)** Correct Other synonyms for the word "dissipate" are "scatter," "dissolve," and "evaporate."	24. The word "dissipate" means (1) condense (2) draw out (3) melt away (4) inflate
25. **(1)** Correct When something is changed to something else, it is transformed, or converted.	25. The word "transform" is synonymous with (1) convert (2) conclude (3) interpret (4) convey

INFERENCE

	Intuition is not a quality everyone can understand. As the unimaginative are miserable about a work of fiction until they discover what flesh-and-blood individual served as a model for the hero or heroine, so, too, many scientists scoff at the unscientific notion that intuition as a force exists. They cannot believe that a blind man can see something they cannot see. They rely utterly on the celebrated inductive method of reasoning: expose the facts and conclude from them only what can be proven. Generally speaking, this is a very sound rule, but can we be certain that the really great accomplishments are initiated in this plodding fashion? Dreams are made of quite different stuff, and if any are left in the world who do not know that dreams have remade the world, then perhaps there is little we can teach them.

ANSWER	QUESTION
26. **(1)** Correct	26. The author implies that intuition (1) is the product of imagination (2) relies on factual information (3) is an inductive reasoning process (4) is valueless
	It is exceedingly difficult to draw on a canvas the man whose nature is large and central, without cranks or oddities. The very simplicity of such souls defies an easy summary, for they are as spacious in their effect as daylight or summer. Often we remember friends by a gesture or a trick of expression, or by a favorite phrase. But with Nelson I do not find myself thinking of such idiosyncrasies. His presence warmed and lit up so big a region of life that in thinking of him one is overwhelmed by the multitude of things that he made better by simply existing among them. If you remove a fire from the hearth, you will remember the look, not so much of the blaze itself, as of the whole room in its pleasant glow.
27. **(4)** Correct	27. The phrase "to draw on a canvas" is used in this context to mean (1) to paint a portrait (2) to summarize (3) to make a collage (4) to describe
28. **(1)** Correct	28. The last sentence is a metaphor comparing Nelson to (1) the blaze in a fireplace (2) a hearth (3) fire (4) a pleasant glow
29. **(2)** Correct	29. From the tone of this selection, you might draw the conclusion that the author (1) thinks of Nelson as a strange man (2) is describing a man who has died (3) is overwhelmed by Nelson (4) remembers Nelson only by his gestures
	A glass case in the British Museum houses the mummified remains of two Egyptian kings who lived beside the Nile. The exhibit includes a broken

ANSWER	QUESTION
	plow, a rusted sickle, and two sticks tied together with a leather strap. These were the "bread tools" of Eygptians who lived 4000 years ago during the reigns of the two kings. They are not unlike the tools used by eighteenth-century American farmers, and, in fact, similar sickles may be viewed at Mount Vernon, George Washington's Virginia home.
30. (3) Correct	30. We may conclude from this selection that the ancient Egyptians (1) had only two important kings (2) taught farming techniques to eighteenth-century Americans (3) were relatively advanced in the use of agricultural tools (4) neglected their equipment
	The horn of an automobile is a valuable aid to good driving if properly used. When about to pass another car, it is advisable to notify the driver of the car ahead. Children or animals on the street should be given a warning note. Of course, a courteous driver would not blow his horn unnecessarily in the vicinity of a hospital or a place of worship. He should also be considerate of schools, where quiet is important. The way in which a driver uses his horn is a fairly accurate index to his character, for through the sound he expresses his impatience and his good manners, or the lack of them.
31. (3) Correct	31. The place that a good driver would be least likely to use his horn is (1) St. James Theater (2) Riverdale Apartments (3) Memorial Convalescent Home (4) Yankee Stadium
32. (3) Correct	32. The character of a driver who fails to sound his horn when a dog is crossing the street is (1) noble (2) timid (3) selfish (4) bold

ANSWER	QUESTION
	According to early English history, a small group of people from northeastern Europe, called Easterlings, came by invitation to England to devise and develop a new system of coinage. These people lived in towns that were famous for the accuracy of their coins. The coins that they worked out for England were made of silver and came to be known as the Easterling coins. Later the word "Easterling" was shortened to sterling. The word "sterling" gradually came to be applied to all silver articles of very fine quality.
33. **(1)** Correct	33. The passage implies that the Easterlings (1) had an excellent reputation (2) used silver exclusively (3) were silversmiths (4) coined the word "sterling"
34. (2) Correct	34. The word "sterling" began to be used for high quality silver because (1) it was used to make English coins (2) the Easterlings were known for the quality of their work (3) silver is very expensive (4) the Easterlings were the only people who could make silver coins

THE GED TEST OF INTERPRETING LITERATURE AND THE ARTS

The GED Interpreting Literature and the Arts test consists of excerpts from popular and classical literature and from articles about literature or the arts. There will be ten to twelve excerpts on each test and a total of 45 multiple-choice questions based on these readings.

The excerpts may include fiction, prose nonfiction, poetry, and drama. The distribution of selections for each test is approximately as follows:

Popular Literature—50%

Classical Literature—25%

Commentary—25%

Each excerpt on the Literature Test is followed by two to six questions. These questions fall into one of the following four categories:

1. Comprehension questions—These questions ask you to demonstrate an understanding of specific facts you have read. For example: What color was the house? Who won the ball game? Who surrendered at Saratoga?
2. Inference questions—These questions ask you to draw conclusions from what you have read. For example: If Charles is always late to school, will he arrive on time when he has a test?
3. Application questions—These questions ask you to apply what you have read to a different situation. For example: If you read that cork is a light wood that floats and fishermen use it to support their nets in the water, you might be asked how you could use cork if you were in a shipwreck.
4. Analysis questions—These questions ask you to examine the style and structure of what you have read. For example: From what point of view is a story told? Is the author angry, happy, sarcastic? What techniques does the author use to create a particular effect?

The practice test that follows includes an error analysis that gives you both the content area of each question and the type of skill the question tests. You can use this information to help you determine which type of questions you do well with and which types you will have to work at.

PRACTICE WITH GED-TYPE LITERATURE QUESTIONS

Directions:
For each question circle the number of the response that best answers the question or completes the statement. Correct and explanatory answers are provided at the end of the chapter.

Items 1 to 4 refer to the following excerpt from a play.

WHY WOULD ANYONE WANT TO GO TO SIBERIA?

Luka (pointing to window). He's laughing! *(pause)* Well, children, God be with you! I'll leave you soon . . .

Pepel. Where are you going to?

Luka. To the Ukraine—I heard they discovered a new religion there—I want to seek—yes! People are always seeking—they always want something better—God grant them patience!
Pepel. You think they'll find it?

Luka. The people? They will find it! He who seeks, will find! He who desires strongly, will find!

Natasha. If only they could find something better—invent something better . . .

Luka. They're trying to! But we must help them, girl—we must respect them . . .

Natasha. How can I help them? I am helpless myself!

Pepel (determined). Again—listen—I'll speak to you again, Natasha—here—before him—he knows everything . . . run away with me?

Natasha. Where? From one prison to another?

Pepel. I told you—I'm through with being a thief; so help me God! I'll quit! If I say so, I'll do it! I can read and write—I'll work—He's been telling me to go to Siberia on my own hook—let's go there together, what do you say? Do you think I'm not disgusted with my life? Oh—Natasha—I know . . . I see . . . I console myself with the thought that there are lots of people who are honored and respected—and who are bigger thieves than I! But what good is that to me? It isn't that I repent . . . I've no conscience . . . but I do feel one thing: One must live differently. One must live a better life . . . one must be able to respect one's own self . . .

Luka. That's right, friend! May God help you! It's true! A man must respect himself.

Pepel. I've been a thief from childhood on. Everybody always called me "Vaska—the thief—the son of a thief." Oh—very well—I am a thief—just imagine—now, perhaps, I'm a thief out of spite—perhaps I'm a thief because no one ever called me anything different . . . Well, Natasha . . . ?

Natasha (sadly). Somehow I don't believe in words—and I'm restless today—my heart is heavy . . . as if I were expecting something . . . it's a pity, Vassily, that you talked to me today . . .

Pepel. When should I? It isn't the first time I speak to you . . .

Natasha. And why should I go with you? I don't love you so very much—sometimes I like you—and other times the mere sight of you makes me sick . . . it seems—no—I don't really love you . . . when one really loves, one sees no fault . . . But I do see . . .

Pepel. Never mind—you'll love me after a while! I'll make you care for me . . . if you'll just say yes! For over a year I've watched you . . . you're a decent girl . . . you're kind—you're reliable—I'm very much in love with you . . .

(Vassilisa, in her best dress, appears at window and listens.)

Natasha. Yes—you love me—but how about my sister . . . ?

Pepel (confused). Well, what of her? There are plenty like her . . .

Luka. You'll be all right, girl! If there's no bread, you have to eat weeds . . .

Pepel (gloomily). Please—feel a little sorry for me! My life isn't all roses—it's a hell of a life . . . little swamps were sucking me under . . . and whatever I try to catch and hold on to is rotten . . . it breaks . . . Your sister —Ooh—I thought she was different . . . if she weren't so greedy after money . . . I'd have done anything for her sake, if she were only all mine . . . but she must have someone else . . . and she has to have money—and freedom . . . because she doesn't like the straight and narrow . . . she can't help me. But you're like a young fir tree . . . you bend, but you don't break . . .

—Maxim Gorky, *The Lower Depths*

1. The reader gets the impressions that Luka is

   (1) younger than Pepel and Natasha
   (2) a thief
   (3) Natasha's brother-in-law
   (4) older than Pepel and Natasha
   (5) a police officer

2. Luka seems to be a

   (1) seeker after truth
   (2) hypocrite
   (3) cynic
   (4) pessimist
   (5) priest

3. Pepel wishes to give up his criminal life because

   (1) the police are after him
   (2) he loves Natasha
   (3) he feels he must live differently
   (4) he is sorry he has been a thief
   (5) he wants to become a politician

4. The tone of this section of the play seems to be

   (1) ironic
   (2) satirical
   (3) tragic
   (4) comical
   (5) fearful

GO ON TO THE NEXT PAGE

Items 5 to 8 refer to the following poem.

HOW DOES THIS POET FEEL ABOUT HIS LOVE?

She walks in beauty, like the night
Of cloudless climes and starry skies;
And all that's best of dark and bright
Meet in her aspect and her eyes:
Thus mellow'd to that tender light
Which heaven to gaudy day denies.

One shade the more, one ray the less,
Had half impair'd the nameless grace
Which waves in every raven tress,
Or softly lightens o'er her face;
Where thoughts serenely sweet express
How pure, how dear their dwelling-place.

And on that cheek, and o'er that brow,
So soft, so calm, yet eloquent,
The smiles that win, the tints that glow,
But tell of days in goodness spent,
A mind at peace with all below,
A heart whose love is innocent!

—Gordon Lord Byron, "She Walks In Beauty"

5. Personification is a technique used by writers to ascribe human characteristics to a nonliving object. In the first stanza, what is being personified?

(1) eyes
(2) aspect
(3) night
(4) beauty
(5) walking

6. According to this poem and by using the poet's actual words, what "tell of days in goodness spent"? (line 16)

(1) "the night of cloudless climes" (lines 1–2)
(2) "a heart whose love is innocent" (line 18)
(3) "a mind at peace with all below" (line 17)
(4) "How pure, how dear their dwelling-place." (line 12)
(5) "the smiles that win, the tints that glow" (line 15)

7. The techique used in the poet's comparison of his love to the night (lines 1–2) is called

(1) metaphor
(2) simile
(3) hyperbole
(4) personification
(5) oxymoron

8. The tone of the poet's writing is

(1) worshipful
(2) cynical
(3) scornful
(4) mocking
(5) arrogant

Items 9 to 14 refer to the following excerpt.

WHY IS THIS FIGHT GOING TO TAKE PLACE?

"Johnson," Wolf Larsen said, with an air of dismissing all that had gone before as introductory to the main business in hand, "I understand you're not quite satisfied with those oilskins?"

"No, I am not. They are no good, sir."

"And you've been shooting off your mouth about them."

"I say what I think, sir," the sailor answered courageously, not failing at the same time in ship courtesy, which demanded that "sir" be appended to each speech he made.

It was at this moment that I chanced to glance at Johansen. His big fists were clenching and unclenching, and his face was positively fiendish, so malignantly did he look at Johnson. I noticed a black discoloration, still faintly visible, under Johansen's eye, a mark of the thrashing he had received a few nights before from the sailor. For the first time I began to divine that something terrible was about to be enacted —what, I could not imagine.

"Do you know what happens to men who say what you've said about my slop-chest and me?" Wolf Larsen was demanding.

"I know, sir," was the answer.

"What?" Wolf Larsen demanded, sharply and imperatively.

"What you and the mate there are going to do to me, sir."

"Look at him, Hump," Wolf Larsen said to me, "look at this bit of animated dust, this aggregation of matter that moves and breathes and defies me and thoroughly believes itself to be compounded of something good; that is impressed with certain human fictions such as righteousness and honesty, and that will live up to them in spite of all personal discomforts and menaces. What do you think of him, Hump? What do you think of him?"

"I think that he is a better man than you are," I answered, impelled, somehow, with a desire to draw upon myself a portion of the wrath I felt was about to break upon his head. "His human fictions, as you choose to call them, make for nobility and manhood. You have no fictions, no dreams, no ideals. You are a pauper."

He nodded his head with a savage pleasantness. "Quite true, Hump, quite true. I have no fictions that make for nobility and manhood. A living dog is better than a dead lion, say I with the preacher. My only doctrine is the doctrine of expediency, and it makes for surviving. This bit of the ferment, only dust and ashes, will have no more nobility than any dust and ashes, while I shall still be alive and roaring."

"Do you know what I am going to do?" he questioned. I shook my head.

"Well, I am going to exercise my prerogative of roaring and show you how fares nobility. Watch me."

I cannot give the further particulars of the horrible scene that followed. It was too revolting. It turns me sick even now when I think of it. Johnson fought bravely enough, but he was no match for Wolf Larsen, much less for Wolf Larsen and the mate.

—Jack London, *The Sea Wolf*

9. We can infer that the scene takes place

   (1) in a court of law
   (2) in the street
   (3) in a boxing ring
   (4) on a ship
   (5) on a freight train

10. Wolf Larsen appears to be

    (1) a sailor with the same status as Johnson
    (2) a man who is in authority
    (3) the first mate of the ship
    (4) a policeman
    (5) a mutineer

11. Judging from the selection, Hump is

    (1) a person who has no strong feelings
    (2) a strong person who is able to defeat Larsen
    (3) a man who is able to argue with Larsen
    (4) an out-and-out coward
    (5) a champion of all "underdogs"

GO ON TO THE NEXT PAGE

12. When Hump says, "You are a pauper," he means

 (1) Larsen has no money
 (2) Larsen is too much of an idealist and pays no attention to the realities of life
 (3) Larsen is poor because he has none of the thoughts that make life worth living
 (4) Larsen's oilskins in his slop-chest are worthless
 (5) Larsen once read the book *The Prince and the Pauper*

13. Larsen's idea of the doctrine of expediency is

 (1) not to worry about right or wrong but to survive by any means
 (2) to cheat everyone when possible
 (3) never to admit he was wrong in any situation
 (4) to follow the ideals of nobility only when it suits him to do so
 (5) to sell poor quality merchandise

14. Larsen might be characterized as man who is

 (1) brutal and stupid
 (2) cynical and cruel
 (3) intellectual and lenient
 (4) wise but stern
 (5) arrogant but with a heart of gold

Items 15 to 21 refer to the following short story.

WHY IS GRANDAD GOING AWAY?

Petey hadn't really believed that Dad would be doing it—sending Granddad away.

But here was the blanket that Dad had that day bought for him, and in the morning he'd be going away.

'Now, isn't that a fine blanket!" said the old man, smoothing it over his knees. "And isn't your father a kind man to be giving the old fellow a blanket like that to go away with? It cost something, it did—look at the wool of it! And warm it will be on cold winter nights. There'll be few blankets there the equal of this one!"

It was like Granddad to be saying that. He was trying to make it easier. He'd pretended all along that he wanted to go away to the great brick building—the government place.

"Oh, yes, it's a fine blanket," said Petey, and got up and went into the house. He wasn't the kind to cry, and besides, he was too old for that. He'd just come in to fetch Granddad's fiddle.

It was the last night they'd be having together. There wasn't any need to say, "Play all the old tunes." Granddad tuned up for a minute, and then said, "This is one you'll like to remember."

They didn't hear the two people coming down the gully path. Dad had one arm around the girl with the hard, bright face like a doll's. Dad didn't say anything, but the girl came forward and spoke to Granddad prettily: "I won't be here when you leave in the morning, so I came over to say good-by."

"It's kind of you," said Granddad, with his eyes cast down. "And will you look at this," he said "the fine blanket my son has given me to go away with!"

"Yes," she said, "it's a fine blanket." She felt of the wool and repeated in surprise, "A fine blanket—I'll say it is!" She turned to Dad and said to him coldly, "That blanket really cost something."

He cleared his throat and defended himself: "I wanted him to have the best. . . ."

The girl stood here, still intent on the blanket. "It's double, too," she said, as if accusing Dad.

The boy went suddenly into the house. He was looking for something. He could hear that girl scolding Dad, and Dad becoming angry in his slow way. And now she was suddenly going away in a huff. . . . As Petey came out, she turned and called back, "All the same, he doesn't need a double blanket!" And she ran off up the gully path.

"Oh, she's right," said the boy coldly. "Here, Dad"—and he held out a pair of scissors. "Cut the blanket in two."

"Yes," said the boy harshly, "a single blanket's enough for an old man when he's sent away. We'll save the other half, Dad; it will come in handy later."

"Now, what do you mean by that?" asked Dad.

"I mean," said the boy slowly, "that I'll give it to you, Dad—when you're old and I'm sending you—away."

There was a silence. But Granddad understood, for he put out a hand and laid it on Dad's shoulder. And he heard Granddad whisper, "It's all right, son—I knew you didn't mean it. . . ." And then Petey cried.

But it didn't matter—because they were all three crying together.

—Floyd Dell, "The Blanket"

15. What is the predominant symbol in this story?

    (1) the fiddle
    (2) the blanket
    (3) the scissors
    (4) the young boy
    (5) the old man

16. What does the blanket represent?

    (1) the problems of old age in America
    (2) the problems of divorce and remarriage
    (3) the father's attempt to soothe his guilty conscience
    (4) the difficulty of life in rural America
    (5) the importance of cutting bonds

17. What is the theme of this story?

    (1) When money is scarce, one should not buy expensive items like a blanket.
    (2) The old man got exactly what was his due.
    (3) Unintentionally we all do cruel things at times.
    (4) It can be difficult having old people around when one is planning to remarry.
    (5) Things have changed greatly over the past fifty years.

18. What is the author saying about old age and the difference between generations?

    (1) There is an enormous difference between the three generations.
    (2) Old age is a golden time.
    (3) It is better to be young than old.
    (4) There is no real "generation gap" because we will all be old some day.
    (5) The old are very poorly treated as a general rule.

19. What is the overall tone of this story?

    (1) melancholy
    (2) cheerful
    (3) uplifting
    (4) cruel
    (5) sarcastic

20. What does the scissors represent?

    (1) getting away from an unpleasant duty
    (2) cutting the bonds of love, duty, and respect
    (3) cutting loose from whatever is holding you back
    (4) cutting away dead weight
    (5) assuming new freedom

21. Which of the following best describes Grandad's attitude?

    (1) considerate and understanding
    (2) resentful toward his son's fiancé
    (3) anxious and worried
    (4) bitter but resigned
    (5) angry and humiliated

GO ON TO THE NEXT PAGE

Items 22 to 25 are based on the following passage.

WHAT WERE THE SOLDIERS' FEELINGS AFTER THE BATTLE?

The First Brigade, after pushing its way through the throng at the river with the point of the bayonet, was already forming on the crest of the hill. Now and then we heard the pattering sounds of bullets, stragglers from the leaden storm above, falling upon the roofs of the boats. Our horses were quickly disembarked, and with the First Brigade in columns closed in mass, leaving orders for the rest of the Division to follow as soon as landed, we moved toward the point indicated by the firing. Directly we saw evidence of close and terrible fighting. Artillery horses dead, cannon dismounted, accouterments torn and bloody, appeared everywhere. The first dead soldier we saw had fallen in the road; our artillery had crushed and mangled his limbs, and ground him into the mire. He lay a bloody, loathsome mass, the scraps of his blue uniform furnishing the only distinguishable evidence that a hero there had died. At this sight, I saw a manly fellow gulp down his heart, which swelled too closely into this throat. Near him lay a slender rebel boy—his face in the mud, his brown hair floating in a bloody pool. Soon a dead Major, then a Colonel, then the lamented Wallace, yet alive, were passed in quick and sickening succession. The gray gleaming of the misty morning gave a ghostly pallor to the faces of the dead. The disordered hair, dripping from the night's rain, the distorted and passion-marked faces, the stony, glaring eyes, the blue lips, the glistening teeth, the shriveled and contracted hands, the wild agony of pain and passion in the attitudes of the dead—all the horrid circumstances with which death surrounds the brave when torn from life in the whirlwind of battle—were seen as we marched over the field, the beseeching cries of the wounded from their bloody and miry beds meanwhile saluting our ears and cutting to our hearts.

Daniel McCook, *The Second Division at Shiloh*

22. At the beginning of this selection, the First Brigade

    (1) has just come ashore from landing craft
    (2) is retreating
    (3) has spent the night in battle
    (4) has been wipe out
    (5) has killed some Union soldiers

23. The author's attitude toward the dead soldiers he sees

    (1) reflects pity and sorrow
    (2) shows disgust and hatred
    (3) indicates scorn and revulsion
    (4) is full of humor and delight
    (5) indicates none of the above

24. It is apparent that

    (1) the battle is over
    (2) the battle has just begun
    (3) the First Brigade has been fighting for hours
    (4) the battle has been going on for some time
    (5) the First Brigade is retreating

25. The reader can infer from the author's choice of language that

    (1) he glories in combat
    (2) war disgusts and horrifies him
    (3) he regards battle as a comic adventure
    (4) he wants to desert
    (5) the Union must be preserved

Items 26 to 28 are based on the following article.

DOES THIS CRITIC RECOMMEND RAMEY'S PERFORMANCE?

Samuel Ramey has two strikes against him. First, he is a bass, and most starring operatic roles for men are sewed up by tenors because most composers, from Rossini to Puccini, have opted for the brilliance of the higher male voice.

The second strike is Ramey himself: quiet, taciturn; socially, he borders on the awkward. His sentences run from "Yup" to "Nope" to "I don't know."

But put him onstage and shy Sam Ramey becomes the picture of vigor, as he is currently demonstrating to Metropolitan Opera patrons in Bellini's "I Puritani." His vocal ease in the bel canto opera repertory—the florid style of singing prevalent between the late 17th and 19th centuries—plus his electrifying acting make him one of the compelling reasons for going to the opera these days. As Bernard Holland, a music critic for *The New York Times,* wrote about one Ramey appearance, his voice "was beautifully modulated and admirably sure, and his presence made this performance work. . . ." And so, a country boy from Kansas has won the international stardom enjoyed by only two other basses in this century—Feodor Chaliapin and Ezio Pinza.

Last August, when Ramey tilted at windmills as the title character in Jules Massenet's "Don Quichotte," which was revived especially for him by the New York City Opera, he recreated a role Chaliapin premiered 76 years ago. Until Chaliapin, even the best of basses were barely nourished by a diet of subordinate parts. Except for an occasional binge on such dazzling roles as Rossini's Figaro, Gounod's Méphistophélès, Bioto's Mefistofele and Mozart's Figaro and Don Giovanni, they had to be satisfied with portraying smart old men, stern old men, sweet old men and similar operatic scraps. Many basses still exist on these "graybeard" roles. Ramey himself often has powdered his sand-colored hair white, glued a flowing beard on his square jaw, penciled his broad features with wrinkles —and he's only 44 years old.

In the opera world, tenors and sopranos reign supreme: there is an undeniable gut response to high notes. "Opera's pretty unfair," confides Ramey. "Tenors can begin their careers in starring roles, whereas promising baritones and basses tend to begin with smaller parts. They say the bass voice matures later, so we have to work our way through the secondary roles. If there's one compensation, it's that basses generally stick around longer."

26. It may be determined from this article that Samuel Ramey is

    (1) a guitarist
    (2) a country singer
    (3) an operatic tenor
    (4) an operatic bass
    (5) an actor

27. When the writer says that "Samuel Ramey has two strikes against him," he means that

    (1) Ramey has had two unsuccessful performances
    (2) Ramey's voice and personality are unappealing to critics
    (3) Ramey has the wrong type of voice and too quiet a personality for opera
    (4) Ramey comes from Kansas and has a midwestern accent which fans don't like
    (5) Feodor Chaliapin and Ezio Pinza are competing with Ramey for the starring roles

28. Which of the following best describes Ramey's acting?

    (1) awkward
    (2) electrifying
    (3) taciturn
    (4) vigorous
    (5) forced

GO ON TO THE NEXT PAGE

Items 29 to 33 refer to the following poem.

IS THERE ANY ADVANTAGE TO DYING YOUNG?

The time you won your town the race
We chaired you through the market-place;
Man and boy stood cheering by,
And home we brought you shoulder-high.

Today, the road all runners come,
Shoulder-high we bring you home,
And set you at your threshold down,
Townsman of a stiller town.

Smart lad, to slip betimes away
From fields where glory does not stay,
And early though the laurel grows
It withers quicker than the rose.

Eyes the shady night has shut
Cannot see the record cut,
And silence sounds no worse than cheers
After earth has stopped the ears.

Now you will not swell the rout
Of lads that wore their honors out
Runners whom renown outran
And the name died before the man.

So set, before its echoes fade,
The fleet foot on the sill of shade,
And hold to the low lintel up
The still-defended challenge-cup.

And round that early-laurelled head
Will flock to gaze the strength less dead,
And find unwithered on its curls
The garland briefer than a girl's.

—A. E. Housman, "To An Athlete Dying Young"

29. The athlete in the poem was a

(1) runner
(2) football player
(3) basketball star
(4) girl
(5) tennis champion

30. "Threshold" in line 7 is a metaphor for

(1) the grave
(2) sports
(3) home
(4) life
(5) glory

31. "Stiller town" in line 8 is a metaphor for

(1) a country village
(2) old age
(3) death
(4) love
(5) home

32. The poet praises the athlete for

(1) winning the race
(2) wearing the laurel of victory
(3) breaking a record
(4) returning to his hometown
(5) dying young

33. What advantage does the poet see to the athlete's death at this time?

(1) He was beginning to slow down.
(2) He had been forgotten by his fans.
(3) He had been ill and suffered greatly.
(4) He died while he still had fame.
(5) He has lost all his money.

Items 34 to 38 refer to the following excerpt.

WHAT MAKES A BRAVE MAN?

"Could you see the whites of their eyes?" said the man who was seated on a soapbox.

"Nothing of the kind," replied old Henry warmly. "Just a lot of flitting figures, and I let go at where they 'peared to be the thickest. Bang!"

"Mr. Fleming," said the grocer—his deferential voice expressed somehow the old man's exact social weight—"Mr. Fleming, you never was frightened much in them battles, was you?"

The veteran looked down and grinned. Observing his manner, the entire group tittered. "Well, I guess I was," he answered finally. "Pretty well scared, sometimes. Why, in my first battle I thought the sky was falling down. I thought the world was coming to an end. You bet I was scared."

Everyone laughed. Perhaps it seemed strange and rather wonderful to them that a man should admit the thing, and in the tone of their laughter was probably more admiration than if old Fleming had declared that he had always been a lion. Moreover, they knew that he had ranked as an orderly sergeant, and so their opinion of his heroism was fixed. None, to be sure, knew how an orderly sergeant ranked, but then it was understood to be somewhere just shy of a major general's stars. So when old Henry admitted that he had been frightened, there was a laugh.

"The trouble was," said the old man, "I thought they were all shooting at me. Yes, sir, I thought every man in the other army was aiming at me in particular, and only me. And it seemed so darned unreasonable, you know. I wanted to explain to 'em what an almighty good fellow I was, because I thought then they might quit all trying to hit me. But I couldn't explain, and they kept on being unreasonable—blim-blam!-bang! So I run!"

Two little triangles of wrinkles appeared at the corners of his eyes. Evidently he appreciated some comedy in this recital. Down near his feet, however, little Jim, his grandson, was visibly horror-stricken. His hands were clasped nervously, and his eyes were wide with astonishment at this terrible scandal, his most magnificent grandfather telling such a thing.

When little Jim walked with his grandfather he was in the habit of skipping along on the stone pavement in front of the three stores and the hotel of the town and betting that he could avoid the cracks. But upon this day he walked soberly, with his hand gripping two of his grandfather's fingers.

Then finally he ventured: "Grandpa—now—was that true what you was telling those men?"

"What?" asked the grandfather. "What was I telling them?"

"Oh, about your running."

"Why, yes, that was true enough, Jimmie. It was my first fight, and there was an awful lot of noise, you know."

Jimmie seemed dazed that this idol, of its own will, should so totter. His stout boyish idealism was injured.

—Stephen Crane, "The Veteran"

34. The reader quickly learns that Henry is

(1) a storekeeper
(2) owner of a tannery
(3) an ex-soldier
(4) a major general
(5) a grocer

35. One might say that the old man's leading characteristic is

(1) hypocrisy
(2) pride
(3) honesty
(4) unfriendliness
(5) idealism

36. When Mr. Fleming admitted that he had been afraid in battle, the adult listeners' attitude toward him

(1) turned to amusement because they knew he had never been in a war
(2) turned to bitterness
(3) changed to disgust
(4) remained one of admiration
(5) changed to horror

37. The old man does not seem to be aware that

(1) his grandson is horrified by his admission of fear
(2) little Jim never knew he had fought in a war
(3) the listeners think he is a fool
(4) his grandson is listening
(5) war can be a terrifying experience

38. The most important point that the author wishes the reader to understand is that

(1) the boy doesn't like his grandfather
(2) Henry was afraid in battle
(3) the boy's image of his grandfather as a hero has been destroyed
(4) Henry is highly regarded by his town's people
(5) the boy enjoys the company of the older men

GO ON TO THE NEXT PAGE

Items 39 to 45 refer to the following excerpt from a play.

WHAT HAPPENED TO THE MANUSCRIPT?

Lovborg. To you I can tell the truth, Hedda.

Hedda. The truth?

Lovborg. First promise me—give me your word—that what I now confide to you Thea shall never know.

Hedda. I give you my word.

Lovborg. Good. Then let me tell you that what I said just now was untrue.

Hedda. About the manuscript?

Lovborg. Yes. I have not torn it to pieces—nor thrown it into the fiord.

Hedda. No, n—But—where is it then?

Lovborg. I have destroyed it none the less—utterly destroyed it, Hedda!

Hedda. I don't understand.

Lovborg. Thea said that what I had done seemed to her like a child-murder.

Hedda. Yes, so she said.

Lovborg. But to kill this child—that is not the worst thing a father can do to it.

Hedda. Not the worst?

Lovborg. No. I wanted to spare Thea from hearing the worst.

Hedda. Then what is the worst?

Lovborg. Suppose now, Hedda, that a man—in the small hours of the morning—came home to his child's mother after a night of riot and debauchery, and said: "Listen—I have been here and there—in this place and that. And I have taken our child with me—to this place and to that. And I have lost the child—utterly lost it. The devil knows into what hands it may have fallen—who may have had their clutches on it."

Hedda. Well—but when all is said and done, you know—this was only a book—

Lovborg. Thea's pure soul was in that book.

Hedda. Yes, so I understand.

Lovborg. And you can understand, too, that for her and me together no future is possible.

Hedda. What path do you mean to take then?

Lovborg. None. I will only try to make an end of it all—the sooner the better.

Hedda (a step nearer him). Eilert Lovborg—listen to me. Will you not try to—to do it beautifully?

Lovborg. Beautifully? *(Smiling)* With vine-leaves in my hair, as you used to dream in the old days—?

Hedda. No, no. I have lost my faith in the vine-leaves. But beautifully nevertheless! For once in a way!—Good-bye! You must go now—and do not come here any more.

Lovborg. Good-bye, Mrs. Tesman. And give George Tesman my love. *(He is on the point of going.)*

Hedda. No, wait! I must give you a memento to take with you. *(She goes to the writing-table, opens the drawer and takes out a pistol.)*

Lovborg (looks at her). This? Is this the memento?

Hedda (nodding slowly). Do you recognize it? It was aimed at you once.

Lovborg. You should have used it then.

Hedda. Take it—and do you use it now.

Lovborg (puts the pistol in his breast pocket). Thanks!

Hedda. And beautifully, Eilert Lovborg. Promise me that! *(Hedda listens for a moment at the door. Then she goes up to the writing-table, takes out the packet of manuscript, peeps under the cover, draws a few of the sheets half out, and looks at them. Next she goes over and seats herself in the arm-chair beside the stove, with the packet in her lap. Presently she opens the stove door, and then the packet.)*

Hedda (throws one of the quires into the fire and whispers to herself). Now I am burning your child, Thea!—Burning it, curly-locks! *(Throwing one or two more quires into the stove)* Your child and Eilert Lovborg's. *(Throws the rest in)* I am burning—I am burning your child.

—Henrik Ibsen, *Hedda Gabler*

39. What has Lovborg lost?

(1) a child
(2) his pistol
(3) a jewel
(4) a manuscript
(5) his love

40. Lovborg compares his manuscript to

(1) a child
(2) vine leaves
(3) a memento
(4) his soul
(5) his best friend

41. What does Hedda believe Lovborg will do?

(1) start writing the book again
(2) continue looking for the manuscript
(3) make up with Thea
(4) return to see her soon
(5) commit suicide

42. What does Hedda give to Lovborg?

(1) a book
(2) a letter
(3) vine leaves
(4) a pistol
(5) the manuscript

43. In the end, what does Hedda burn?

(1) old letters
(2) the desk
(3) Lovborg's manuscript
(4) the pistol case
(5) coal

44. When Hedda says, "Will you try to—to do it beautifully?" what does she mean?

(1) She is urging Lovborg to kill Thea.
(2) She wants Lovborg to write a better manuscript next time.
(3) She wants Lovborg to commit suicide in a beautiful way.
(4) She wants Lovborg to dress more colorfully and wear vine leaves on his head.
(5) She is urging Lovborg to return to Thea.

45. The reader can tell from its use in the play that the word "quires" refers to

(1) a book
(2) pistol cases
(3) an entire manuscript
(4) children
(5) sheets of paper

END OF LITERATURE TEST

ANSWER KEY FOR PRACTICE QUESTIONS

1. (4)	10. (2)	19. (1)	28. (2)	37. (1)
2. (1)	11. (3)	20. (2)	29. (1)	38. (3)
3. (3)	12. (3)	21. (1)	30. (1)	39. (4)
4. (3)	13. (1)	22. (1)	31. (3)	40. (1)
5. (3)	14. (2)	23. (1)	32. (5)	41. (5)
6. (5)	15. (2)	24. (4)	33. (4)	42. (4)
7. (2)	16. (3)	25. (2)	34. (3)	43. (3)
8. (1)	17. (3)	26. (4)	35. (3)	44. (3)
9. (4)	18. (4)	27. (3)	36. (4)	45. (5)

ERROR ANALYSIS FOR GED TEST OF INTERPRETING LITERATURE AND THE ARTS

Circle the number of each question you answered incorrectly. Count the number of circles in each content area and write the total number missed in the column headed "Number Incorrect." A large number of incorrect responses in a particular area indicates the need for further study in that area.

		No. Incorrect
Popular Literature	15, 16, 17, 18, 19, 20, 21, 22, 23, 24, 25, 29, 30, 31, 32, 33	
Classical Literature	1, 2, 3, 4, 5, 6, 7, 8, 9, 10, 11, 12, 13, 14, 34, 35, 36, 37, 38, 39, 40, 41, 42, 43, 44, 45	
Commentary	26, 27, 28	

EXPLANATIONS FOR PRACTICE QUESTIONS

1. **(4)** When Pepel and Natasha speak to Luka, it is with respect, and they look to him for advice. Also, he calls them "children." Thus, it can be inferred that he is older than they are. There is no evidence that he is a thief. He is not her brother-in-law, as he says that her sister's "husband . . . is rotten beyond words."

2. **(1)** Luka does not seem to be a hypocrite, for he doesn't say one thing and practice the opposite. He is neither a cynic nor a pessimist, as he speaks his hope for mankind. He is a seeker after truth: he is going to the Ukraine just to observe a new religion.

3. **(3)** Time and time again, Pepel hits at this theme. He says "One must live differently. One must live a better life . . . one must be able to respect one's own self." He is not sorry, though, for what he has done, nor does he say the police are after him. He does love Natasha, it is true, but that is not the reason he wishes to go to Siberia and begin a new life.

4. **(3)** Although the author seems to see Luka as a character of hope, the helplessness and aimlessness of Natasha, on one hand, and Pepel's yearning towards a better life, on the other, mark the selection as tragic.

5. **(3)** The poet said that "she walks in beauty, like the night." The night is being personified because it is given the ability to walk like a living person.

6. **(5)** "The smiles that win, the tints that glow" tell of "days in goodness spent."

7. **(2)** A simile uses the words "like or as" to make a comparison: "She walks . . . , like the night."

8. **(1)** The poet is certainly worshipful.

9. **(4)** There are several hints that this scene takes place on a ship, such as the use of "sir" towards Larsen, the reference to ship courtesy, and Johansen being described as "mate."

10. **(2)** Larsen is the leader, and has authority over Johnson, as Johnson admits. We do not know exactly what rank Larsen has, though, but we can guess he is the captain. He does not act nor talk like a policeman on duty.

11. **(3)** We know that Hump has strong feelings because he has argued bitterly against Larsen. He is not a coward because it is apparently dangerous to argue with Larsen. Yet we can infer Hump is not a strong man since he does not go to Johnson's defense in the fight.

12. **(3)** Hump says that Larsen is a pauper because he has "no dreams, no ideals." Therefore, Larsen cannot be an idealist. We don't know if Larsen has money or not, or if his oilskins are worthless.

13. **(1)** Choice (2) is nearly correct, but is only part of Larsen's system of life. He might admit he was wrong if such a confession didn't threaten him. He certainly has no use for the ideals for nobility. Therefore, it is (1) which sums up what he believes in.

14. **(2)** The other three answers are partly right, but only (2) is completely true. Larsen is brutal, but he is not stupid. He is intellectual, but he is not lenient. He is stern, but not gentle. He has a low opinion of men so he is cynical. That he is cruel is obvious.

15. **(2)** A blanket is a symbol of warmth, comfort, home. Obviously, the symbol is being used here in an ironic manner, as that is what is being denied to Granddad.

16. **(3)** The father feels that by giving Granddad the best blanket he can buy, he will somehow feel better about sending the old man to the government home.

17. **(3)** The father did not really mean to be cruel, as evidenced by the ending which shows his love for his father.

18. **(4)** Petey's line about saving the other half of the blanket for *his* father when he sends *him* away tells us this.

19. **(1)** This is a melancholy, sad story, as we feel the sad music and lonely times bred by misunderstanding and conflict.

20. **(2)** By offering to cut the blanket, Petey is saying that if that is the way you, Dad, treat your father, you can expect me to treat you that way, too.

21. **(1)** We must understand that Granddad is not being sarcastic in what he says; he honestly attempts to see his son's point of view.

22. **(1)** The key word in the third sentence is "disembarked."

23. **(1)** The feeling is that of pity and sorrow for the fallen soldiers of either side.

24. **(4)** The number of dead and the continuing pattern of firing indicates that the battle has been going on for some time.

25. **(2)** The war horrifies and disgusts the writer.

26. **(4)** The second sentence states the Ramey is a bass. The first sentence of the second paragraph tells you that he is currently performing at the Metropolitan Opera.

27. **(3)** The "two strikes" that Samuel Ramey has against him are that he sings in a low bass voice (most operatic leads are tenors) and that he is "socially awkard" (lines 6–7).

28. **(2)** The second sentence of the second paragraph describes Ramey's acting as "electrifying."

29. **(1)** The poet states the athlete "won your town the race" and several times refers to running. The athlete is not a girl because he calls him a "smart lad."

30. **(1)** You know by the title of the poem that the athlete has died. The whole implication of the second stanza is that he is being carried on his funeral day.

31. **(3)** If this is the athlete's funeral day, it becomes obvious that "stiller town" stands for death.

32. **(5)** The poet states that the athlete won the big race in the first stanza, that he broke the record in the fourth stanza, and since he is the champion, the laurel of victory is his. But he does not necessarily praise him for these things. However, he calls him a "smart lad, to slip betimes away" to die.

33. **(4)** (1) and (2) are obviously false. We don't know if (3) is true or not. But the poet states that "Now you will not swell the rout of lads that wore their honors out" and says the athlete is smart to leave "fields where glory does not stay."

34. **(3)** Henry is talking about a battle and war in general. We are not told what job he has in civilian life. We are specifically told that Henry was an "orderly sergeant."

35. **(3)** The old man is honest in the description of his fears; therefore, he is no hypocrite. He does not seem to have pride in himself and is certainly not unfriendly.

36. **(4)** His fellow townsmen just won't believe that Henry is anything less than a hero. There is no indication that they believe him a liar or that they are bitter or disgusted. Jim is the one who is horrified.

37. **(1)** Jim, we are told, is "horror-stricken" at his grandfather's admission that he was afraid in battle. Perhaps Jim didn't know the old man was a soldier, but we are not told so. The probability is that he did know, since his grandfather is his hero. As they walked home together, they probably also came to the store together, and so Henry knew little Jim was present and

listening. The listeners don't regard Henry as a fool; that is obvious from their respectful attitude towards him. Henry is well aware of the terror of war.

38. **(3)** We can eliminate 1, for it is apparent that little Jim worships his grandfather. Choices (2) and (4) are true statements. Henry was afraid in battle and admitted it, and he is highly regarded by his townspeople. But the author focuses his—and our—attention upon Jim's reaction to what his grandfather said.

39. **(4)** In line 9 Hedda reveals that the subject of the conversation is a manuscript.

40. **(1)** In line 17 Lovborg states that Thea thinks destroying the manuscript is "like a child-murder." In other words, the manuscript is compared to a child.

41. **(5)** Lovborg says in line 41 that he will "make an end of it all." Hedda takes out a pistol and gives it to Lovborg. Obviously she thinks he is going to kill himself.

42. **(4)** In line 58, Hedda takes out a pistol from the writing table drawer. In line 64, she hands it to Lovborg.

43. **(3)** In lines 70–77 we are told that Hedda takes out a packet of manuscript and throws it in the fire. We can infer that this is Lovborg's lost manuscript.

44. **(3)** In line 41, Lovborg says he will make an end of it. In lines 44–45, Hedda asks him to "do it beautifully," meaning to commit suicide in a beautiful way.

45. **(5)** In the last 10 lines, the directions state that Hedda takes out a packet of manuscript and begins to throw it in the fire one or two quires at a time. From this information, you can infer that quires are sheets of paper.

Part VI

Math Review for GED Candidates

ALL ABOUT THE GED MATHEMATICS TEST

The questions in the GED Mathematics Test are based on short readings or on graphs, charts, tables, or diagrams.

The questions in the new GED Mathematics Test will stress higher level thinking (applications, analysis, and evaluation) as well as problem-solving ability. More solutions will require multiple-step solutions. Questions will usually be stated in a realistic context instead of in an abstract form.

Sometimes, a problem will not give enough information to solve it. In that case, the answer will be "not enough information is given". At other times, unneeded information will be given, so be sure to read the problem carefully.

Each of the major skills necessary to successfully answer the GED mathematics questions, is presented in this section along with helpful exercises.

FRACTIONS

Fractions and Mixed Numbers

1. A **fraction** is part of a unit.

   a. A fraction has a **numerator** and a **denominator**.

   Example: In the fraction $\frac{3}{4}$, 3 is the numerator and 4 is the denominator.

   b. In any fraction, the numerator is being divided by the denominator.

   Example: The fraction $\frac{2}{7}$ indicates that 2 is being divided by 7.

   c. In a fraction problem, the whole quantity is 1, which may be expressed by a fraction in which the numerator and denominator are the same number.

   Example: If the problem involves $\frac{1}{8}$ of a quantity, then the whole quantity is $\frac{8}{8}$, or 1.

2. A **mixed number** is an integer together with a fraction, such as $2\frac{3}{5}$, $7\frac{3}{8}$, etc. The integer is the integral part, and the fraction is the fractional part.

3. An **improper fraction** is one in which the numerator is equal to or greater than the denominator, such as $\frac{19}{6}$, $\frac{25}{4}$, or $\frac{10}{10}$.

4. To change a mixed number to an improper fraction:

   a. Multiply the denominator of the fraction by the integer.

   b. Add the numerator to this product.

   c. Place this sum over the denominator of the fraction.

   Illustration: Change $3\frac{4}{7}$ to an improper fraction.

   SOLUTION:
   $$7 \times 3 = 21$$
   $$21 + 4 = 25$$
   $$3\tfrac{4}{7} = \tfrac{25}{7}$$

   Answer: $\frac{25}{7}$

5. To change an improper fraction to a mixed number:

   a. Divide the numerator by the denominator. The quotient, disregarding the remainder, is the integral part of the mixed number.

   b. Place the remainder, if any, over the denominator. This is the fractional part of the mixed number.

   Illustration: Change $\frac{36}{13}$ to a mixed number.

   SOLUTION:
   $$13 \overline{)\,36} = 2$$
   $$\underline{26}$$
   $$10 \text{ remainder}$$
   $$\tfrac{36}{13} = 2\tfrac{10}{13}$$

   Answer: $2\frac{10}{13}$

6. The numerator and denominator of a fraction may be changed by multiplying both by the same number, without affecting the value of the fraction.

   Example: The value of the fraction $\frac{2}{5}$ will not be altered if the numerator and the denominator are multiplied by 2, to result in $\frac{4}{10}$.

7. The numerator and the denominator of a fraction may be changed by dividing both by the same number, without affecting the value of the fraction. This process is called **reducing the fraction**. A fraction that has been reduced as much as possible is said to be in **lowest terms**.

   Example: The value of the fraction $\frac{3}{12}$ will not be altered if the numerator and denominator are divided by 3, to result in $\frac{1}{4}$.

   Example: If $\frac{6}{30}$ is reduced to lowest terms (by dividing both numerator and denominator by 6), the result is $\frac{1}{5}$.

8. As a final answer to a problem:

   a. Improper fractions should be changed to mixed numbers.

   b. Fractions should be reduced as far as possible.

Addition of Fractions

9. Fractions cannot be added unless the denominators are all the same.

   a. If the denominators are the same, add all the numerators and place this sum over the common denominator. In the case of mixed numbers, follow the above rule for the fractions and then add the integers.

   Example: The sum of $2\frac{3}{8} + 3\frac{1}{8} + \frac{3}{8} = 5\frac{7}{8}$.

   b. If the denominators are not the same, the fractions, in order to be added, must be converted to ones having the same denominator. To do this, it is first necessary to find the lowest common denominator.

10. The **lowest common denominator** (henceforth called the L.C.D.) is the lowest number that can be divided evenly by all the given denominators. If no two of the given denominators can be divided by the same number, then the L.C.D. is the product of all the denominators.

    Example: The L.C.D. of $\frac{1}{2}$, $\frac{1}{3}$, and $\frac{1}{5}$ is $2 \times 3 \times 5 = 30$.

11. To find the L.C.D. when two or more of the given denominators can be divided by the same number:

    a. Write down the denominators, leaving plenty of space between the numbers.

    b. Select the smallest number (other than 1) by which one or more of the denominators can be divided evenly.

    c. Divide the denominators by this number, copying down those that cannot be divided evenly. Place this number to one side.

    d. Repeat this process, placing each divisor to one side until there are no longer any denominators that can be divided evenly by any selected number.

e. Multiply all the divisors to find the L.C.D.

Illustration: Find the L.C.D. of $\frac{1}{5}$, $\frac{1}{7}$, $\frac{1}{10}$, and $\frac{1}{14}$.

SOLUTION:

$$\begin{array}{r|rrrr} 2 & 5 & 7 & 10 & 14 \\ \hline 5 & 5 & 7 & 5 & 7 \\ \hline 7 & 1 & 7 & 1 & 7 \\ \hline & 1 & 1 & 1 & 1 \end{array}$$

$7 \times 5 \times 2 = 70$

Answer: The L.C.D. is 70.

12. To add fractions having different denominators:

    a. Find the L.C.D. of the denominators.

    b. Change each fraction to an equivalent fraction having the L.C.D. as its denominator.

    c. When all of the fractions have the same denominator, they may be added, as in the example following item 9a.

Illustration: Add $\frac{1}{4}$, $\frac{3}{10}$, and $\frac{2}{5}$.

SOLUTION: Find the L.C.D.:

$$\begin{array}{r|rrr} 2 & 4 & 10 & 5 \\ \hline 2 & 2 & 5 & 5 \\ \hline 5 & 1 & 5 & 5 \\ \hline & 1 & 1 & 1 \end{array}$$

L.C.D. = $2 \times 2 \times 5 = 20$

$$\begin{array}{rcr} \frac{1}{4} & = & \frac{5}{20} \\ \frac{3}{10} & = & \frac{6}{20} \\ +\ \frac{2}{5} & = & +\ \frac{8}{20} \\ \hline & & \frac{19}{20} \end{array}$$

Answer: $\frac{19}{20}$

13. To add mixed numbers in which the fractions have different denominators, add the fractions by following the rules in item 12 above, then add the integers.

Illustration: Add $2\frac{5}{7}$, $5\frac{1}{2}$, and 8.

SOLUTION: L.C.D. = 14

$$\begin{array}{rcr} 2\frac{5}{7} & = & 2\frac{10}{14} \\ 5\frac{1}{2} & = & 5\frac{7}{14} \\ +\ 8 & = & +\ 8 \\ \hline & & 15\frac{17}{14} = 16\frac{3}{14} \end{array}$$

Answer: $16\frac{3}{14}$

Subtraction of Fractions

14. a. Unlike addition, which may involve adding more than two numbers at the same time, subtraction involves only two numbers.

    b. In subtraction, as in addition, the denominators must be the same.

15. To subtract fractions:

    a. Find the L.C.D.

    b. Change both fractions so that each has the L.C.D. as the denominator.

    c. Subtract the numerator of the second fraction from the numerator of the first, and place this difference over the L.C.D.

    d. Reduce, if possible.

    Illustration: Find the difference of $\frac{5}{8}$ and $\frac{1}{4}$.

    SOLUTION: L.C.D. = 8

$$\begin{array}{rcr} \frac{5}{8} & = & \frac{5}{8} \\ -\frac{1}{4} & = & -\frac{2}{8} \\ \hline & & \frac{3}{8} \end{array}$$

    Answer: $\frac{3}{8}$

16. To subtract mixed numbers:

    a. It may be necessary to "borrow," so that the fractional part of the first term is larger than the fractional part of the second term.

    b. Subtract the fractional parts of the mixed numbers and reduce.

    c. Subtract the integers.

    Illustration: Subtract $16\frac{4}{5}$ from $29\frac{1}{3}$.

    SOLUTION: L.C.D. = 15

$$\begin{array}{rcr} 29\frac{1}{3} & = & 29\frac{5}{15} \\ -\ 16\frac{4}{5} & = & -\ 16\frac{12}{15} \end{array}$$

    Note that $\frac{5}{15}$ is less than $\frac{12}{15}$. Borrow 1 from 29, and change to $\frac{15}{15}$.

$$\begin{array}{rcr} 29\frac{5}{15} & = & 28\frac{20}{15} \\ -\ 16\frac{12}{15} & = & -\ 16\frac{12}{15} \\ \hline & & 12\frac{8}{15} \end{array}$$

    Answer: $12\frac{8}{15}$

Multiplication of Fractions

17. a. To be multiplied, fractions need not have the same denominators.

    b. A whole number has the denominator 1 understood.

18. To multiply fractions:

a. Change the mixed numbers, if any, to improper fractions.

b. Multiply all the numerators, and place this product over the product of the denominators.

c. Reduce, if possible.

Illustration: Multiply $\frac{2}{3} \times 2\frac{4}{7} \times \frac{5}{9}$.

SOLUTION:

$$2\frac{4}{7} = \frac{18}{7}$$
$$\frac{2}{3} \times \frac{18}{7} \times \frac{5}{9} = \frac{180}{189}$$
$$= \frac{20}{21}$$

Answer: $\frac{20}{21}$

19. a. **Cancellation** is a device to facilitate multiplication. To cancel means to divide a numerator and a denominator by the same number in a multiplication problem.

Example: In the problem $\frac{4}{7} \times \frac{5}{6}$, the numerator 4 and the denominator 6 may be divided by 2.

$$\frac{\overset{2}{\cancel{4}}}{7} \times \frac{5}{\underset{3}{\cancel{6}}} = \frac{10}{21}$$

b. The word "of" is often used to mean "multiply."

Example: $\frac{1}{2}$ of $\frac{1}{2} = \frac{1}{2} \times \frac{1}{2} = \frac{1}{4}$

20. To multiply a whole number by a mixed number:

a. Multiply the whole number by the fractional part of the mixed number.

b. Multiply the whole number by the integral part of the mixed number.

c. Add both products.

Illustration: Multiply $23\frac{3}{4}$ by 95.

SOLUTION:

$$\frac{95}{1} \times \frac{3}{4} = \frac{285}{4}$$
$$= 71\frac{1}{4}$$
$$95 \times 23 = 2185$$
$$2185 + 71\frac{1}{4} = 2256\frac{1}{4}$$

Answer: $2256\frac{1}{4}$

Division of Fractions

21. The **reciprocal** of a fraction is that fraction inverted.

a. When a fraction is inverted, the numerator becomes the denominator and the denominator becomes the numerator.

Example: The reciprocal of $\frac{3}{8}$ is $\frac{8}{3}$.

Example: The reciprocal of $\frac{1}{3}$ is $\frac{3}{1}$, or simply 3.

b. Since every whole number has the denominator 1 understood, the reciprocal of a whole number is a fraction having 1 as the numerator and the number itself as the denominator.

Example: The reciprocal of 5 (expressed fractionally as $\frac{5}{1}$) is $\frac{1}{5}$.

22. To divide fractions:

    a. Change all the mixed numbers, if any, to improper fractions.

    b. Invert the second fraction and multiply.

    c. Reduce, if possible.

    Illustration: Divide $\frac{2}{3}$ by $2\frac{1}{4}$.

    SOLUTION:

    $$2\tfrac{1}{4} = \tfrac{9}{4}$$
    $$\tfrac{2}{3} \div \tfrac{9}{4} = \tfrac{2}{3} \times \tfrac{4}{9} = \tfrac{8}{27}$$

    Answer: $\frac{8}{27}$

23. A **complex fraction** is one that has a fraction as the numerator, or as the denominator, or as both.

    Example: $\dfrac{\frac{2}{3}}{5}$ is a complex fraction.

24. To clear (simplify) a complex fraction:

    a. Divide the numerator by the denominator.

    b. Reduce, if possible.

    Illustration: Clear $\dfrac{\frac{3}{7}}{\frac{5}{14}}$.

    SOLUTION:

    $$\tfrac{3}{7} \div \tfrac{5}{14} = \tfrac{3}{7} \times \tfrac{14}{5} = \tfrac{42}{35} = \tfrac{6}{5} = 1\tfrac{1}{5}$$

    Answer: $1\frac{1}{5}$

Comparing Fractions

25. If two fractions have the same denominator, the one having the larger numerator is the greater fraction.

    Example: $\frac{3}{7}$ is greater than $\frac{2}{7}$.

26. If two fractions have the same numerator, the one having the larger denominator is the smaller fraction.

    Example: $\frac{5}{12}$ is smaller than $\frac{5}{11}$.

27. To compare two fractions having different numerators and different denominators:

    a. Change the fractions to equivalent fractions having their L.C.D. as their new denominator.

b. Compare, as in the example following item 25.

Illustration: Compare $\frac{4}{7}$ and $\frac{5}{8}$.

SOLUTION: L.C.D. = 7 × 8 = 56

$\frac{4}{7} = \frac{32}{56}$

$\frac{5}{8} = \frac{35}{56}$

Answer: Since $\frac{35}{56}$ is larger than $\frac{32}{56}$, $\frac{5}{8}$ is larger than $\frac{4}{7}$.

Fraction Problems

28. Most fraction problems can be arranged in the form: "What fraction of a number is another number?" This form contains three important parts:

- The fractional part
- The number following "of"
- The number following "is"

a. If the fraction and the "of" number are given, multiply them to find the "is" number.

Illustration: What is $\frac{3}{4}$ of 20?

SOLUTION: Write the question as "$\frac{3}{4}$ of 20 is what number?" Then multiply the fraction $\frac{3}{4}$ by the "of" number, 20:

$$\frac{3}{\cancel{4}_1} \times \overset{5}{\cancel{20}} = 15$$

Answer: 15

b. If the fractional part and the "is" number are given, divide the "is" number by the fraction to find the "of" number.

Illustration: $\frac{4}{5}$ of what number is 40?

SOLUTION: To find the "of" number, divide 40 by $\frac{4}{5}$:

$$40 \div \frac{4}{5} = \frac{\overset{10}{\cancel{40}}}{1} \times \frac{5}{\cancel{4}_1}$$

$$= 50$$

Answer: 50

c. To find the fractional part when the other two numbers are known, divide the "is" number by the "of" number.

Illustration: What part of 12 is 9?

SOLUTION: $9 \div 12 = \frac{9}{12}$

$= \frac{3}{4}$

Answer: $\frac{3}{4}$

Practice Problems Involving Fractions

1. Reduce to lowest terms: $\frac{60}{108}$.
(1) $\frac{1}{48}$
(2) $\frac{1}{3}$
(3) $\frac{30}{59}$
(4) $\frac{10}{18}$
(5) $\frac{5}{9}$

2. Change $\frac{27}{7}$ to a mixed number.
(1) $2\frac{1}{7}$
(2) $3\frac{6}{7}$
(3) $6\frac{1}{3}$
(4) $7\frac{1}{2}$
(5) 8

3. Change $4\frac{2}{3}$ to an improper fraction.
(1) $\frac{10}{3}$
(2) $\frac{11}{3}$
(3) $\frac{14}{3}$
(4) $\frac{42}{3}$
(5) $\frac{49}{3}$

4. Find the L.C.D. of $\frac{1}{6}$, $\frac{1}{10}$, $\frac{1}{18}$, and $\frac{1}{21}$.
(1) 160
(2) 330
(3) 630
(4) 1260
(5) 1420

5. Add $16\frac{3}{8}$, $4\frac{4}{5}$, $12\frac{3}{4}$, and $23\frac{5}{6}$.
(1) $57\frac{91}{120}$
(2) $57\frac{1}{4}$
(3) 58
(4) 59
(5) 60

6. Subtract $27\frac{5}{14}$ from $43\frac{1}{6}$.
(1) 15
(2) $15\frac{7}{21}$
(3) $15\frac{8}{21}$
(4) $15\frac{17}{21}$
(5) 17

7. Multiply $17\frac{5}{8}$ by 128.
(1) 2200
(2) 2205
(3) 2240
(4) 2256
(5) 2400

8. Divide $1\frac{2}{3}$ by $1\frac{1}{9}$.
(1) $\frac{2}{3}$
(2) $1\frac{1}{2}$
(3) $1\frac{23}{27}$
(4) 6
(5) $7\frac{23}{27}$

9. What is the value of $12\frac{1}{6} - 2\frac{3}{8} - 7\frac{2}{3} + 19\frac{3}{4}$?
(1) 21
(2) $21\frac{7}{8}$
(3) $21\frac{8}{9}$
(4) 22
(5) 23

10. Simplify the complex fraction $\frac{\frac{4}{9}}{\frac{2}{5}}$.
(1) $\frac{1}{2}$
(2) $\frac{9}{10}$
(3) $\frac{2}{5}$
(4) $1\frac{8}{9}$
(5) $1\frac{1}{9}$

11. Which fraction is largest?
(1) $\frac{9}{16}$
(2) $\frac{7}{10}$
(3) $\frac{5}{8}$
(4) $\frac{4}{5}$
(5) $\frac{3}{4}$

12. One brass rod measures $3\frac{5}{16}$ inches long and another brass rod measures $2\frac{3}{4}$ inches long. Together their length is
(1) $\frac{9}{16}$
(2) $5\frac{1}{8}$
(3) $6\frac{1}{16}$
(4) $7\frac{1}{16}$
(5) $7\frac{1}{8}$

13. The number of half-pound packages of tea that can be weighed out of a box that holds $10\frac{1}{2}$ lb. of tea is
(1) 5
(2) $10\frac{1}{2}$
(3) $20\frac{1}{2}$
(4) 21
(5) $21\frac{1}{2}$

14. If each bag of tokens weighs $5\frac{3}{4}$ pounds, how many pounds do 3 bags weigh?
(1) $7\frac{1}{4}$
(2) $15\frac{3}{4}$
(3) $16\frac{1}{2}$
(4) $17\frac{1}{4}$
(5) $17\frac{1}{2}$

15. During one week, a man traveled $3\frac{1}{2}$, $1\frac{1}{4}$, $1\frac{1}{6}$, and $2\frac{3}{8}$ miles. The next week he traveled $\frac{1}{4}$, $\frac{3}{8}$, $\frac{9}{16}$, $3\frac{1}{16}$, $2\frac{5}{8}$, and $3\frac{3}{16}$ miles. How many more miles did he travel the second week than the first week?
(1) $1\frac{37}{48}$
(2) $2\frac{1}{2}$
(3) $2\frac{3}{4}$
(4) 3
(5) $3\frac{5}{8}$

16. A certain type of board is sold only in lengths of multiples of 2 feet. The shortest board sold is 6 feet and the longest is 24 feet. A builder needs a large quantity of this type of board in $5\frac{1}{2}$-foot lengths. For minimum waste the lengths to be ordered should be
(1) 6 ft
(2) 12 ft
(3) 22 ft
(4) 24 ft
(5) 26 ft

17. A man spent $\frac{15}{16}$ of his entire fortune in buying a car for $7500. How much money did he possess?
(1) $6000
(2) $6500
(3) $7000
(4) $7500
(5) $8000

18. The population of a town was 54,000 in the last census. It has increased $\frac{2}{3}$ since then. Its present population is
(1) 18,000
(2) 36,000
(3) 72,000
(4) 80,000
(5) 90,000

19. If one third of the liquid contents of a can evaporates on the first day and three fourths of the remainder evaporates on the second day, the fractional part of the original contents remaining at the close of the second day is
(1) $\frac{5}{12}$
(2) $\frac{7}{12}$
(3) $\frac{1}{6}$
(4) $\frac{1}{2}$
(5) $\frac{3}{4}$

20. A car is run until the gas tank is $\frac{1}{8}$ full. The tank is then filled to capacity by putting in 14 gallons. The capacity of the gas tank of the car is
(1) 14
(2) 15
(3) 16
(4) 17
(5) 18

Fraction Problems — Correct Answers

1. **(5)**	6. **(4)**	11. **(4)**	16. **(3)**
2. **(2)**	7. **(4)**	12. **(3)**	17. **(5)**
3. **(3)**	8. **(2)**	13. **(4)**	18. **(5)**
4. **(3)**	9. **(2)**	14. **(4)**	19. **(3)**
5. **(1)**	10. **(5)**	15. **(1)**	20. **(3)**

Problem Solutions — Fractions

1. Divide the numerator and denominator by 12:

$$\frac{60 \div 12}{108 \div 12} = \frac{5}{9}$$

One alternate method (there are several) is to divide the numerator and denominator by 6 and then by 2:

$$\frac{60 \div 6}{108 \div 6} = \frac{10}{18}$$

$$\frac{10 \div 2}{18 \div 2} = \frac{5}{9}$$

Answer: **(5)** $\frac{5}{9}$

2. Divide the numerator (27) by the denominator (7):

$$\begin{array}{r} 3 \\ 7\overline{)27} \\ \underline{21} \\ 6 \end{array} \text{ remainder}$$

$$\frac{27}{7} = 3\frac{6}{7}$$

Answer: **(2)** $3\frac{6}{7}$

3.

$$4 \times 3 = 12$$
$$12 + 2 = 14$$
$$4\frac{2}{3} = \frac{14}{3}$$

Answer: **(3)** $\frac{14}{3}$

4.

2)	6	10	18	21	(2 is a divisor of 6, 10, and 18)
3)	3	5	9	21	(3 is a divisor of 3, 9, and 21)
3)	1	5	3	7	(3 is a divisor of 3)
5)	1	5	1	7	(5 is a divisor of 5)
7)	1	1	1	7	(7 is a divisor of 7)
	1	1	1	1	

L.C.D. $= 2 \times 3 \times 3 \times 5 \times 7 = 630$

Answer: **(3)** 630

5. L.C.D. = 120

$$\begin{array}{rcl} 16\frac{3}{8} & = & 16\frac{45}{120} \\ 4\frac{4}{5} & = & 4\frac{96}{120} \\ 12\frac{3}{4} & = & 12\frac{90}{120} \\ +\ 23\frac{5}{6} & = & +\ 23\frac{100}{120} \\ \hline & & 55\frac{331}{120} = 57\frac{91}{120} \end{array}$$

Answer: **(1)** $57\frac{91}{120}$

6. L.C.D. = 42

$$\begin{array}{rcrcl} 43\frac{1}{6} & = & 43\frac{7}{42} & = & 42\frac{49}{42} \\ -\ 27\frac{5}{14} & = & -\ 27\frac{15}{42} & = & -\ 27\frac{15}{42} \\ \hline & & & & 15\frac{34}{42} = 15\frac{17}{21} \end{array}$$

Answer: **(4)** $15\frac{17}{21}$

7.

$$17\frac{5}{8} = \frac{141}{8}$$

$$\frac{141}{\cancel{8}_{1}} \times \frac{\cancel{128}^{16}}{1} = 2256$$

Answer: **(4)** 2256

8.

$$\begin{aligned} 1\tfrac{2}{3} \div 1\tfrac{1}{9} &= \frac{5}{3} \div \frac{10}{9} \\ &= \frac{\cancel{5}^{1}}{\cancel{3}_{1}} \times \frac{\cancel{9}^{3}}{\cancel{10}_{2}} \\ &= \frac{3}{2} \\ &= 1\tfrac{1}{2} \end{aligned}$$

Answer: **(2)** $1\frac{1}{2}$

9. L.C.D. = 24

$$\begin{array}{rcrcl} 12\frac{1}{6} & = & 12\frac{4}{24} & = & 11\frac{28}{24} \\ -\ 2\frac{3}{8} & = & -\ 2\frac{9}{24} & = & -\ 2\frac{9}{24} \\ \hline \end{array}$$

$$\begin{array}{rcl} 9\frac{19}{24} & = & 9\frac{19}{24} \\ -\ 7\frac{2}{3} & = & -\ 7\frac{16}{24} \\ \hline \end{array}$$

$$\begin{array}{rcl} 2\frac{3}{24} & = & 2\frac{3}{24} \\ +\ 19\frac{3}{4} & = & +\ 19\frac{18}{24} \\ \hline & & 21\frac{21}{24} \end{array}$$

$$21\frac{21}{24} = 21\frac{7}{8}$$

Answer: **(2)** $21\frac{7}{8}$

10. To simplify a complex fraction, divide the numerator by the denominator:

$$\begin{aligned} \frac{4}{9} \div \frac{2}{5} &= \frac{\cancel{4}^{2}}{9} \times \frac{5}{\cancel{2}_{1}} \\ &= \frac{10}{9} \\ &= 1\tfrac{1}{9} \end{aligned}$$

Answer: **(5)** $1\frac{1}{9}$

11. Write all of the fractions with the same denominator. L.C.D. = 80

$$\begin{aligned} \frac{9}{16} &= \frac{45}{80} \\ \frac{7}{10} &= \frac{56}{80} \\ \frac{5}{8} &= \frac{50}{80} \\ \frac{4}{5} &= \frac{64}{80} \end{aligned}$$

Answer: **(4)** $\frac{4}{5}$

12.

$$\begin{array}{rcl} 3\frac{5}{16} & = & 3\frac{5}{16} \\ +\ 2\frac{3}{4} & = & +\ 2\frac{12}{16} \\ \hline & & 5\frac{17}{16} \\ & = & 6\frac{1}{16} \end{array}$$

Answer: **(3)** $6\frac{1}{16}$ in.

13.

$$\begin{aligned} 10\tfrac{1}{2} \div \tfrac{1}{2} &= \frac{21}{2} \div \frac{1}{2} \\ &= \frac{21}{\cancel{2}_{1}} \times \frac{\cancel{2}^{1}}{1} \\ &= 21 \end{aligned}$$

Answer: **(4)** 21

14.

$$\begin{aligned} 5\tfrac{3}{4} \times 3 &= \frac{23}{4} \times \frac{3}{1} \\ &= \frac{69}{4} \\ &= 17\tfrac{1}{4} \end{aligned}$$

Answer: **(4)** $17\frac{1}{4}$

15. First week:
L.C.D. = 24

$$\begin{array}{rcl} 3\frac{1}{2} & = & 3\frac{12}{24} \text{ miles} \\ 1\frac{1}{4} & = & 1\frac{6}{24} \\ 1\frac{1}{6} & = & 1\frac{4}{24} \\ +\ 2\frac{3}{8} & = & +\ 2\frac{9}{24} \\ \hline & & 7\frac{31}{24} = 8\frac{7}{24} \text{ miles} \end{array}$$

Second week:
L.C.D. = 16

$$\begin{array}{rcl} \frac{1}{4} & = & \frac{4}{16} \text{ miles} \\ \frac{3}{8} & = & \frac{6}{16} \\ \frac{9}{16} & = & \frac{9}{16} \\ 3\frac{1}{16} & = & 3\frac{1}{16} \\ 2\frac{5}{8} & = & 2\frac{10}{16} \\ +\ 3\frac{3}{16} & = & +\ 3\frac{3}{16} \\ \hline & & 8\frac{33}{16} = 10\frac{1}{16} \text{ miles} \end{array}$$

L.C.D. = 48

$$\begin{array}{rcl} 10\frac{1}{16} & = & 9\frac{51}{48} \text{ miles second week} \\ -\ 8\frac{7}{24} & = & -\ 8\frac{14}{48} \text{ miles first week} \\ \hline & & 1\frac{37}{48} \text{ miles more traveled} \end{array}$$

Answer: **(1)** $1\frac{37}{48}$

16. Consider each choice:

    Each 6-ft board yields one $5\frac{1}{2}$-ft board with $\frac{1}{2}$ ft waste.
    Each 12-ft board yields two $5\frac{1}{2}$-ft boards with 1 ft waste. ($2 \times 5\frac{1}{2} = 11$; $12 - 11 = 1$ ft waste)
    Each 24-ft board yields four $5\frac{1}{2}$-ft boards with 2 ft waste. ($4 \times 5\frac{1}{2} = 22$; $24 - 22 = 2$ ft waste)
    Each 22 ft board may be divided into four $5\frac{1}{2}$-ft boards with no waste. ($4 \times 5\frac{1}{2} = 22$ exactly)

    Answer: **(3)** 22 ft

17. $\frac{15}{16}$ of fortune is \$7500.
    Therefore, his fortune $= 7500 \div \frac{15}{16}$

    $$= \frac{\overset{500}{\cancel{7500}}}{1} \times \frac{16}{\underset{1}{\cancel{15}}}$$

    $$= 8000$$

    Answer: **(5)** \$8000

18. $\frac{2}{3}$ of $54{,}000 =$ increase

    $$\text{Increase} = \frac{2}{\underset{1}{\cancel{3}}} \times \overset{18{,}000}{\cancel{54{,}000}}$$
    $$= 36{,}000$$
    $$\text{Present population} = 54{,}000 + 36{,}000$$
    $$= 90{,}000$$

    Answer: **(5)** 90,000

19. First day: $\frac{1}{3}$ evaporates
    $\frac{2}{3}$ remains

    Second day: $\frac{3}{4}$ of $\frac{2}{3}$ evaporates
    $\frac{1}{4}$ of $\frac{2}{3}$ remains

    The amount remaining is

    $$\frac{1}{\underset{2}{\cancel{4}}} \times \frac{\overset{1}{\cancel{2}}}{3} = \frac{1}{6} \text{ of original contents}$$

    Answer: **(3)** $\frac{1}{6}$

20. $\frac{7}{8}$ of capacity $= 14$ gal
    therefore, capacity $= 14 \div \frac{7}{8}$

    $$= \frac{\overset{2}{\cancel{14}}}{1} \times \frac{8}{\underset{1}{\cancel{7}}}$$
    $$= 16 \text{ gal}$$

    Answer: **(3)** 16 gal

DECIMALS

1. A **decimal**, which is a number with a decimal point (.), is actually a fraction, the denominator of which is understood to be 10 or some power of 10.

   a. The number of digits, or places, after a decimal point determines which power of 10 the denominator is. If there is one digit, the denominator is understood to be 10; if there are two digits, the denominator is understood to be 100, etc.

   Example: $.3 = \frac{3}{10}$, $.57 = \frac{57}{100}$, $.643 = \frac{643}{1000}$

   b. The addition of zeros after a decimal point does not change the value of the decimal. The zeros may be removed without changing the value of the decimal.

   Example: .7 = .70 = .700 and vice versa, .700 = .70 = .7

   c. Since a decimal point is understood to exist after any whole number, the addition of any number of zeros after such a decimal point does not change the value of the number.

   Example: 2 = 2.0 = 2.00 = 2.000

Addition of Decimals

2. Decimals are added in the same way that whole numbers are added, with the provision that the decimal points must be kept in a vertical line, one under the other. This determines the place of the decimal point in the answer.

   Illustration: Add 2.31, .037, 4, and 5.0017

   SOLUTION:

$$\begin{array}{r} 2.3100 \\ .0370 \\ 4.0000 \\ +\ 5.0017 \\ \hline 11.3487 \end{array}$$

   Answer: 11.3487

Subtraction of Decimals

3. Decimals are subtracted in the same way that whole numbers are subtracted, with the provision that, as in addition, the decimal points must be kept in a vertical line, one under the other. This determines the place of the decimal point in the answer.

   Illustration: Subtract 4.0037 from 15.3

   SOLUTION:

$$\begin{array}{r} 15.3000 \\ -\ 4.0037 \\ \hline 11.2963 \end{array}$$

   Answer: 11.2963

Multiplication of Decimals

4. Decimals are multiplied in the same way that whole numbers are multiplied.

   a. The number of decimal places in the product equals the sum of the decimal places in the multiplicand and in the multiplier.

   b. If there are fewer places in the product than this sum, then a sufficient number of zeros must be added in front of the product to equal the number of places required, and a decimal point is written in front of the zeros.

Illustration: Multiply 2.372 by .012

SOLUTION:

```
   2.372    (3 decimal places)
 ×  .012    (3 decimal places)
 -------
    4744
   2372
 -------
 .028464    (6 decimal places)
```

Answer: .028464

5. A decimal can be multiplied by a power of 10 by moving the decimal point to the *right* as many places as indicated by the power. If multiplied by 10, the decimal point is moved one place to the right; if multiplied by 100, the decimal point is moved two places to the right; etc.

Example:

$.235 \times 10 = 2.35$

$.235 \times 100 = 23.5$

$.235 \times 1000 = 235$

Division of Decimals

6. There are four types of division involving decimals:
   - When the dividend only is a decimal.
   - When the divisor only is a decimal.
   - When both are decimals.
   - When neither dividend nor divisor is a decimal.

   a. When the dividend only is a decimal, the division is the same as that of whole numbers, except that a decimal point must be placed in the quotient exactly above that in the dividend.

Illustration: Divide 12.864 by 32

SOLUTION:

```
       .402
 32 ) 12.864
      12 8
      ----
         64
         64
         --
```

Answer: .402

b. When the divisor only is a decimal, the decimal point in the divisor is omitted and as many zeros are placed to the right of the dividend as there were decimal places in the divisor.

Illustration: Divide 211327 by 6.817

```
                                      31000
SOLUTION:  6.817 ) 211327 = 6817 ) 211327000
           (3 decimal places)        20451        (3 zeros added)
                                       6817
                                       6817
```

Answer: 31000

c. When both divisor and dividend are decimals, the decimal point in the divisor is omitted and the decimal point in the dividend must be moved to the right as many decimal places as there were in the divisor. If there are not enough places in the dividend, zeros must be added to make up the difference.

Illustration: Divide 2.62 by .131

```
                                  20
SOLUTION:  .131 ) 2.62 = 131 ) 2620
                               262
```

Answer: 20

d. In instances when neither the divisor nor the dividend is a decimal, a problem may still involve decimals. This occurs in two cases: when the dividend is a smaller number than the divisor; and when it is required to work out a division to a certain number of decimal places. In either case, write in a decimal point after the dividend, add as many zeros as necessary, and place a decimal point in the quotient above that in the dividend.

Illustration: Divide 7 by 50.

```
                .14
SOLUTION:  50 ) 7.00
                5 0
                2 00
                2 00
```

Answer: .14

Illustration: How much is 155 divided by 40, carried out to 3 decimal places?

```
                 3.875
SOLUTION:  40 ) 155.000
                120
                 35 0
                 32 0
                  3 00
                  2 80
                   200
```

Answer: 3.875

7. A decimal can be divided by a power of 10 by moving the decimal to the *left* as many places as indicated by the power. If divided by 10, the decimal point is moved one place to the left; if divided by 100, the decimal point is moved two places to the left; etc. If there are not enough places, add zeros in front of the number to make up the difference and add a decimal point.

Example: .4 divided by 10 = .04
.4 divided by 100 = .004

Rounding Decimals

8. To round a number to a given decimal place:
   a. Locate the given place.
   b. If the digit to the right is less than 5, omit all digits following the given place.
   c. If the digit to the right is 5 or more, raise the given place by 1 and omit all digits following the given place.

Examples: 4.27 = 4.3 to the nearest tenth
.71345 = .713 to the nearest thousandth

9. In problems involving money, answers are usually rounded to the nearest cent.

Conversion of Fractions to Decimals

10. A fraction can be changed to a decimal by dividing the numerator by the denominator and working out the division to as many decimal places as required.

Illustration: Change $\frac{5}{11}$ to a decimal of 2 places.

SOLUTION: $\frac{5}{11} = 11\overline{)5.00}$ = $.45\frac{5}{11}$

$$\begin{array}{r} .45\frac{5}{11} \\ 11\overline{)5.00} \\ \underline{4.44} \\ 60 \\ \underline{55} \\ 5 \end{array}$$

Answer: $.45\frac{5}{11}$

11. To clear fractions containing a decimal in either the numerator or the denominator, or in both, divide the numerator by the denominator.

Illustration: What is the value of $\frac{2.34}{.6}$?

SOLUTION: $\frac{2.34}{.6} = .6\overline{)2.34} = 6\overline{)23.4}$

$$\begin{array}{r} 3.9 \\ 6\overline{)23.4} \\ \underline{18} \\ 5\,4 \\ \underline{5\,4} \end{array}$$

Answer: 3.9

Conversion of Decimals to Fractions

12. Since a decimal point indicates a number having a denominator that is a power of 10, a decimal can be expressed as a fraction, the numerator of which is the number itself and the denominator of which is the power indicated by the number of decimal places in the decimal.

Example: $.3 = \frac{3}{10}$, $.47 = \frac{47}{100}$

13. When the decimal is a mixed number, divide by the power of 10 indicated by its number of decimal places. The fraction does not count as a decimal place.

Illustration: Change $.25\frac{1}{3}$ to a fraction.

SOLUTION: $.25\frac{1}{3} = 25\frac{1}{3} \div 100$
$= \frac{76}{3} \times \frac{1}{100}$
$= \frac{76}{300} = \frac{19}{75}$

Answer: $\frac{19}{75}$

14. When to change decimals to fractions:

a. When dealing with whole numbers, do not change the decimal.

Example: In the problem $12 \times .14$, it is better to keep the decimal:

$$12 \times .14 = 1.68$$

b. When dealing with fractions, change the decimal to a fraction.

Example: In the problem $\frac{3}{5} \times .17$, it is best to change the decimal to a fraction:

$$\frac{3}{5} \times .17 = \frac{3}{5} \times \frac{17}{100} = \frac{51}{500}$$

15. Because decimal equivalents of fractions are often used, it is helpful to be familiar with the most common conversions.

$\frac{1}{2} = .5$	$\frac{1}{3} = .3333$
$\frac{1}{4} = .25$	$\frac{2}{3} = .6667$
$\frac{3}{4} = .75$	$\frac{1}{6} = .1667$
$\frac{1}{5} = .2$	$\frac{1}{7} = .1429$
$\frac{1}{8} = .125$	$\frac{1}{9} = .1111$
$\frac{1}{16} = .0625$	$\frac{1}{12} = .0833$

Note that the left column contains exact values. The values in the right column have been rounded to the nearest ten-thousandth.

Practice Problems Involving Decimals

1. Add 37.03, 11.5627, 3.4005, 3423, and 1.141.
   (1) 3476.1342
   (2) 3500
   (3) 3524.4322
   (4) 3424.1342
   (5) 3452.4852

2. Subtract 4.64324 from 7.
   (1) 3.35676
   (2) 2.35676
   (3) 2.45676
   (4) 2.36676
   (5) 2.36576

3. Multiply 27.34 by 16.943.
   (1) 463.22162
   (2) 453.52162
   (3) 462.52162
   (4) 462.53162
   (5) 463.52162

4. How much is 19.6 divided by 3.2, carried out to 3 decimal places?
   (1) 6.125
   (2) 6.124
   (3) 6.123
   (4) 5.123
   (5) 5.023

5. What is $\frac{5}{11}$ in decimal form (to the nearest hundredth)?
   (1) .44
   (2) .55
   (3) .40
   (4) .42
   (5) .45

6. What is $.64\frac{2}{3}$ in fraction form?
   (1) $\frac{97}{120}$
   (2) $\frac{97}{150}$
   (3) $\frac{97}{130}$
   (4) $\frac{98}{130}$
   (5) $\frac{99}{140}$

7. What is the difference between $\frac{3}{5}$ and $\frac{9}{8}$ expressed decimally?
   (1) .550
   (2) .425
   (3) .520
   (4) .500
   (5) .525

8. A boy saved up $4.56 the first month, $3.82 the second month, and $5.06 the third month. How much did he save altogether?
   (1) $12.56
   (2) $13.28
   (3) $13.44
   (4) $14.02
   (5) $14.44

9. The diameter of a certain rod is required to be 1.51 ± .015 inches. The rod would not be acceptable if the diameter measured
   (1) 1.490 inches
   (2) 1.500 inches
   (3) 1.510 inches
   (4) 1.525 inches
   (5) 1.511 inches

10. After an employer figures out an employee's salary of $190.57, he deducts $3.05 for social security and $5.68 for pension. What is the amount of the check after these deductions?
    (1) $181.84
    (2) $181.92
    (3) $181.93
    (4) $181.99
    (5) $182.00

11. If the outer diameter of a metal pipe is 2.84 inches and the inner diameter is 1.94 inches, the thickness of the metal is
    (1) .45 inches
    (2) .90 inches
    (3) 1.94 inches
    (4) 2.39 inches
    (5) 2.50 inches

12. A boy earns $20.56 on Monday, $32.90 on Tuesday, $20.78 on Wednesday. He spends half of all that he earned during the three days. How much has he left?
    (1) $29.19
    (2) $31.23
    (3) $34.27
    (4) $37.12
    (5) $38.00

13. The total cost of $3\frac{1}{2}$ pounds of meat at $1.69 a pound and 20 lemons at $.60 a dozen will be
    (1) $6.00
    (2) $6.40
    (3) $6.52
    (4) $6.82
    (5) $6.92

14. A reel of cable weighs 1279 lb. If the empty reel weighs 285 lb and the cable weighs 7.1 lb per foot, the number of feet of cable on the reel is
    (1) 220
    (2) 180
    (3) 140
    (4) 100
    (5) 80

15. 345 fasteners at $4.15 per hundred will cost
    (1) $ .1432
    (2) $1.4320
    (3) $ 14.32
    (4) $143.20
    (5) $149.20

Decimal Problems — Correct Answers

1. (1)	6. (2)	11. (1)
2. (2)	7. (5)	12. (4)
3. (1)	8. (3)	13. (5)
4. (1)	9. (1)	14. (3)
5. (5)	10. (1)	15. (3)

Problem Solutions — Decimals

1. Line up all the decimal points one under the other. Then add:

```
     37.03
     11.5627
      3.4005
   3423.0000
 +    1.141
 -----------
   3476.1342
```

Answer: **(1)** 3476.1342

2. Add a decimal point and five zeros to the 7. Then subtract:

```
   7.00000
 - 4.64324
 ---------
   2.35676
```

Answer: **(2)** 2.35676

3. Since there are two decimal places in the multiplicand and three decimal places in the multiplier, there will be 2 + 3 = 5 decimal places in the product.

```
      27.34
   × 16.943
   --------
       8202
     1 0936
    24 606
   164 04
   273 4
  ---------
  463.22162
```

Answer: **(1)** 463.22162

4. Omit the decimal point in the divisor by moving it one place to the right. Move the decimal point in the dividend one place to the right and add three zeros in order to carry your answer out to three decimal places, as instructed in the problem.

```
              6.125
   3.2. ) 19.6.000
          19 2
          ----
             4 0
             3 2
             ---
              80
              64
              ---
              160
              160
              ---
```

Answer: **(1)** 6.125

5. To convert a fraction to a decimal, divide the numerator by the denominator:

```
        .454
   11 ) 5.000
        4 4
        ---
          60
          55
          --
           50
           44
           --
            6
```

Answer: **(5)** .45 to the nearest hundredth

6. To convert a decimal to a fraction, divide by the power of 10 indicated by the number of decimal places. (The fraction does not count as a decimal place.)

$$64\tfrac{2}{3} \div 100 = \tfrac{194}{3} \div \tfrac{100}{1}$$
$$= \tfrac{194}{3} \times \tfrac{1}{100}$$
$$= \tfrac{194}{300}$$
$$= \tfrac{97}{150}$$

Answer: **(2)** $\frac{97}{150}$

7. Convert each fraction to a decimal and subtract to find the difference:

$\frac{9}{8} = 1.125 \qquad \frac{3}{5} = .60$

$$\begin{array}{r} 1.125 \\ -\ .60 \\ \hline .525 \end{array}$$

Answer: **(5)** .525

8. Add the savings for each month:

$$\begin{array}{r} \$4.56 \\ 3.82 \\ +\ 5.06 \\ \hline \$13.44 \end{array}$$

Answer: **(3)** $13.44

9.

$$\begin{array}{r} 1.51 \\ +\ .015 \\ \hline 1.525 \end{array} \qquad \begin{array}{r} 1.510 \\ -\ .015 \\ \hline 1.495 \end{array}$$

The rod may have a diameter of from 1.495 inches to 1.525 inches inclusive.

Answer: **(1)** 1.490 in.

10. Add to find total deductions:

$$\begin{array}{r} \$3.05 \\ +\ 5.68 \\ \hline \$8.73 \end{array}$$

Subtract total deductions from salary to find amount of check:

$$\begin{array}{r} \$190.57 \\ -\ 8.73 \\ \hline \$181.84 \end{array}$$

Answer: **(1)** $181.84

11. The difference of the two diameters equals the total thickness of the metal on both ends of the inner diameter.

$$\begin{array}{r} 2.84 \\ -1.94 \\ \hline .90 \end{array} \qquad .90 \div 2 = .45 = \text{thickness of metal}$$

Answer: **(1)** .45 in.

12. Add daily earnings to find total earnings:

$$\begin{array}{r} \$20.56 \\ 32.90 \\ +\ 20.78 \\ \hline \$74.24 \end{array}$$

Divide total earnings by 2 to find out what he has left:

$$\begin{array}{r} \$37.12 \\ 2\,\overline{)\,\$74.24} \end{array}$$

Answer: **(4)** $37.12

13. Find cost of $3\frac{1}{2}$ pounds of meat:

$$\begin{array}{r} \$1.69 \\ \times\ 3.5 \\ \hline 845 \\ 5\ 07\ \ \\ \hline \$5.915 \end{array} = \$5.92 \text{ to the nearest cent}$$

Find cost of 20 lemons:

$.60 ÷ 12 = $.05 (for 1 lemon)
$.05 × 20 = $1.00 (for 20 lemons)

Add cost of meat and cost of lemons:

$$\begin{array}{r} \$5.92 \\ +\ 1.00 \\ \hline \$6.92 \end{array}$$

Answer: **(5)** $6.92

14. Subtract weight of empty reel from total weight to find weight of cable:

$$\begin{array}{r} 1279 \text{ lb} \\ -\ 285 \text{ lb} \\ \hline 994 \text{ lb} \end{array}$$

Each foot of cable weighs 7.1 lb. Therefore, to find the number of feet of cable on the reel, divide 994 by 7.1:

```
        14 0.
 7.1. ) 994.0.
        71
        284
        284
          0 0
```

Answer: **(3)** 140

15. Each fastener costs:

$$\$4.15 \div 100 = \$.0415$$

345 fasteners cost:

```
      345
  × .0415
     1725
     345
   13 80
  14.3175
```

Answer: **(3)** $14.32

PERCENTS

1. The **percent symbol** (%) means "parts of a hundred." Some problems involve expressing a fraction or a decimal as a percent. In other problems, it is necessary to express a percent as a fraction or a decimal in order to perform the calculations.

2. To change a whole number or a decimal to a percent:

   a. Multiply the number by 100.

   b. Affix a % sign.

   Illustration: Change 3 to a percent.

   SOLUTION: $3 \times 100 = 300$
   $3 = 300\%$

   Answer: 300%

   Illustration: Change .67 to a percent.

   SOLUTION: $.67 \times 100 = 67$
   $.67 = 67\%$

   Answer: 67%

3. To change a fraction or a mixed number to a percent:

   a. Multiply the fraction or mixed number by 100.

   b. Reduce, if possible.

   c. Affix a % sign.

   Illustration: Change $\frac{1}{7}$ to a percent.

   SOLUTION: $\frac{1}{7} \times 100 = \frac{100}{7}$
   $= 14\frac{2}{7}$
   $\frac{1}{7} = 14\frac{2}{7}\%$

   Answer: $14\frac{2}{7}\%$

   Illustration: Change $4\frac{2}{3}$ to a percent.

   SOLUTION: $4\frac{2}{3} \times 100 = \frac{14}{3} \times 100 = \frac{1400}{3}$
   $= 466\frac{2}{3}$
   $4\frac{2}{3} = 466\frac{2}{3}\%$

   Answer: $466\frac{2}{3}\%$

4. To remove a % sign attached to a decimal, divide the decimal by 100. If necessary, the resulting decimal may then be changed to a fraction.

Illustration: Change .5% to a decimal and to a fraction.

SOLUTION: $.5\% = .5 \div 100 = .005$
$.005 = \frac{5}{1000} = \frac{1}{200}$

Answer: $.5\% = .005$
$.5\% = \frac{1}{200}$

5. To remove a % sign attached to a fraction or mixed number, divide the fraction or mixed number by 100, and reduce, if possible. If necessary, the resulting fraction may then be changed to a decimal.

Illustration: Change $\frac{3}{4}\%$ to a fraction and to a decimal.

SOLUTION: $\frac{3}{4}\% = \frac{3}{4} \div 100 = \frac{3}{4} \times \frac{1}{100}$
$= \frac{3}{400}$

$\frac{3}{400} = 400\overline{)3.0000}$ = .0075

Answer: $\frac{3}{4}\% = \frac{3}{400}$
$\frac{3}{4}\% = .0075$

6. To remove a % sign attached to a decimal that includes a fraction, divide the decimal by 100. If necessary, the resulting number may then be changed to a fraction.

Illustration: Change $.5\frac{1}{3}\%$ to a fraction.

SOLUTION: $.5\frac{1}{3}\% = .005\frac{1}{3}$
$= \frac{5\frac{1}{3}}{1000}$
$= 5\frac{1}{3} \div 1000$
$= \frac{16}{3} \times \frac{1}{1000}$
$= \frac{16}{3000}$
$= \frac{2}{375}$

Answer: $.5\frac{1}{3}\% = \frac{2}{375}$

7. Some fraction-percent equivalents are used so frequently that it is helpful to be familiar with them.

$\frac{1}{25} = 4\%$	$\frac{1}{5} = 20\%$
$\frac{1}{20} = 5\%$	$\frac{1}{4} = 25\%$
$\frac{1}{12} = 8\frac{1}{3}\%$	$\frac{1}{3} = 33\frac{1}{3}\%$
$\frac{1}{10} = 10\%$	$\frac{1}{2} = 50\%$
$\frac{1}{8} = 12\frac{1}{2}\%$	$\frac{2}{3} = 66\frac{2}{3}\%$
$\frac{1}{6} = 16\frac{2}{3}\%$	$\frac{3}{4} = 75\%$

Solving Percent Problems

8. Most percent problems involve three quantities:
   - The rate, R, which is followed by a % sign.
   - The base, B, which follows the word "of."
   - The amount or percentage, P, which usually follows the word "is."

a. If the rate (R) and the base (B) are known, then the percentage (P) = R × B.

Illustration: Find 15% of 50.

SOLUTION:

$$\begin{aligned} \text{Rate} &= 15\% \\ \text{Base} &= 50 \\ P &= R \times B \\ P &= 15\% \times 50 \\ &= .15 \times 50 \\ &= 7.5 \end{aligned}$$

Answer: 15% of 50 is 7.5.

b. If the rate (R) and the percentage (P) are known, then the base (B) = $\frac{P}{R}$.

Illustration: 7% of what number is 35?

SOLUTION:

$$\begin{aligned} \text{Rate} &= 7\% \\ \text{Percentage} &= 35 \\ B &= \frac{P}{R} \\ B &= \frac{35}{7\%} \\ &= 35 \div .07 \\ &= 500 \end{aligned}$$

Answer: 7% of 500 is 35.

c. If the percentage (P) and the base (B) are known, the rate (R) = $\frac{P}{B}$.

Illustration: There are 96 men in a group of 150 people. What percent of the group are men?

SOLUTION:

$$\begin{aligned} \text{Base} &= 150 \\ \text{Percentage (amount)} &= 96 \\ \text{Rate} &= \tfrac{96}{150} \\ &= .64 \\ &= 64\% \end{aligned}$$

Answer: 64% of the group are men.

Illustration: In a tank holding 20 gallons of solution, 1 gallon is alcohol. What is the strength of the solution in percent?

SOLUTION:

$$\begin{aligned} \text{Percentage (amount)} &= 1 \text{ gallon} \\ \text{Base} &= 20 \text{ gallons} \\ \text{Rate} &= \tfrac{1}{20} \\ &= .05 \\ &= 5\% \end{aligned}$$

Answer: The solution is 5% alcohol.

9. In a percent problem, the whole is 100%.

   Example: If a problem involves 10% of a quantity, the rest of the quantity is 90%.

   Example: If a quantity has been increased by 5%, the new amount is 105% of the original quantity.

   Example: If a quantity has been decreased by 15%, the new amount is 85% of the original quantity.

Practice Problems Involving Percents

1. 10% written as a decimal is
   (1) 1.0
   (2) 0.01
   (3) 0.001
   (4) 0.1
   (5) .101

2. What is 5.37% in fraction form?
   (1) $\frac{537}{10.000}$
   (2) $5\frac{37}{10.000}$
   (3) $\frac{537}{1000}$
   (4) $5\frac{37}{100}$
   (5) $\frac{537}{100}$

3. What percent of $\frac{5}{6}$ is $\frac{3}{4}$?
   (1) 75%
   (2) 60%
   (3) 80%
   (4) 85%
   (5) 90%

4. What percent is 14 of 24?
   (1) $62\frac{1}{4}$%
   (2) $58\frac{1}{3}$%
   (3) $41\frac{2}{3}$%
   (4) $33\frac{3}{5}$%
   (5) $73\frac{1}{8}$%

5. 200% of 800 equals
   (1) 2500
   (2) 16
   (3) 1600
   (4) 4
   (5) 2

6. If John must have a mark of 80% to pass a test of 35 items, the number of items he may miss and still pass the test is
   (1) 7
   (2) 8
   (3) 11
   (4) 28
   (5) 30

7. The regular price of a TV set that sold for $118.80 at a 20% reduction sale is
   (1) $148.50
   (2) $142.60
   (3) $138.84
   (4) $ 95.04
   (5) $ 90.04

8. A circle graph of a budget shows the expenditure of 26.2% for housing, 28.4% for food, 12% for clothing, 12.7% for taxes, and the balance for miscellaneous items. The percent for miscellaneous items is
   (1) 31.5
   (2) 79.3
   (3) 20.7
   (4) 68.5
   (5) 80.5

9. Two dozen shuttlecocks and four badminton rackets are to be purchased for a playground. The shuttlecocks are priced at $.35 each and the rackets at $2.75 each. The playground receives a discount of 30% from these prices. The total cost of this equipment is
   (1) $ 7.29
   (2) $11.43
   (3) $13.58
   (4) $18.60
   (5) $20.60

10. A piece of wood weighing 10 ounces is found to have a weight of 8 ounces after drying. The moisture content was
    (1) 25%
    (2) $33\frac{1}{3}$%
    (3) 20%
    (4) 40%
    (5) 60%

11. A bag contains 800 coins. Of these, 10 percent are dimes, 30 percent are nickels, and the rest are quarters. The amount of money in the bag is
    (1) less than $150
    (2) between $150 and $300
    (3) between $301 and $450
    (4) between 451 and 499
    (5) more than $500

12. Six quarts of a 20% solution of alcohol in water are mixed with 4 quarts of a 60% solution of alcohol in water. The alcoholic strength of the mixture is
    (1) 80% (2) 40% (3) 36% (4) 72% (5) 75%
13. A man insures 80% of his property and pays a $2\frac{1}{2}$% premium amounting to $348. What is the total value of his property?
    (1) $17,000 (2) $18,000 (3) $18,400 (4) $17,400 (5) $19,000
14. A clerk divided his 35-hour work week as follows: $\frac{1}{5}$ of his time was spent in sorting mail; $\frac{1}{2}$ of his time in filing letters; and $\frac{1}{7}$ of his time in reception work. The rest of his time was devoted to messenger work. The percent of time spent on messenger work by the clerk during the week was most nearly
    (1) 6% (2) 10% (3) 14% (4) 15% (5) 16%
15. In a school in which 40% of the enrolled students are boys, 80% of the boys are present on a certain day. If 1152 boys are present, the total school enrollment is
    (1) 1440 (2) 2880 (3) 3600 (4) 5400 (5) 5600

Percent Problems — Correct Answers

1. **(4)**	6. **(1)**	11. **(1)**
2. **(1)**	7. **(1)**	12. **(3)**
3. **(5)**	8. **(3)**	13. **(4)**
4. **(2)**	9. **(3)**	14. **(5)**
5. **(3)**	10. **(3)**	15. **(3)**

Problem Solutions — Percents

1. 10% = .10 = .1

   Answer: **(4)** 0.1

2. $5.37\% = .0537 = \frac{537}{10{,}000}$

   Answer: **(1)** $\frac{537}{10{,}000}$

3. Base (number following "of") = $\frac{5}{6}$
   Percentage (number following "is") = $\frac{3}{4}$,

   $$\text{Rate} = \frac{\text{Percentage}}{\text{Base}}$$
   $$= \text{Percentage} \div \text{Base}$$
   $$\text{Rate} = \frac{3}{4} \div \frac{5}{6}$$
   $$= \frac{3}{\cancel{4}_{2}} \times \frac{\cancel{6}^{3}}{5}$$
   $$= \frac{9}{10}$$
   $$\frac{9}{10} = .9 = 90\%$$

   Answer: **(5)** 90%

4. Base (number following "of") = 24
   Percentage (number following "is") = 14

   $$\text{Rate} = \text{Percentage} \div \text{Base}$$
   $$\text{Rate} = 14 \div 24$$
   $$= .58\tfrac{1}{3}$$
   $$= 58\tfrac{1}{3}\%$$

   Answer: **(2)** $58\frac{1}{3}$%

5. 200% of 800 = 2.00 × 800
   = 1600

Answer: **(3)** 1600

6. He must answer 80% of 35 correctly. Therefore, he may miss 20% of 35.

   20% of 35 = .20 × 35
   = 7

Answer: **(1)** 7

7. Since $118.80 represents a 20% reduction, $118.80 = 80% of the regular price.

   Regular price = $\frac{\$118.80}{80\%}$
   = $118.80 ÷ .80
   = $148.50

Answer: **(1)** $148.50

8. All the items in a circle graph total 100%. Add the figures given for housing, food, clothing, and taxes:

```
  26.2%
  28.4%
  12  %
+ 12.7%
-------
  79.3%
```

Subtract this total from 100% to find the percent for miscellaneous items:

```
  100.0%
-  79.3%
--------
   20.7%
```

Answer: **(3)** 20.7%

9. Price of shuttlecocks = 24 × $.35 = $ 8.40
   Price of rackets = 4 × $2.75 = $11.00
   Total price = $19.40

   Discount is 30%, and 100% − 30% = 70%

   Actual cost = 70% of 19.40
   = .70 × 19.40
   = 13.58

Answer: **(3)** $13.58

10. Subtract weight of wood after drying from original weight of wood to find amount of moisture in wood:

```
  10
-  8
----
   2 ounces of moisture in wood
```

Moisture content = $\frac{2 \text{ ounces}}{10 \text{ ounces}}$ = .2 = 20%

Answer: **(3)** 20%

11. Find the number of each kind of coin:

   10% of 800 = .10 × 800 = 80 dimes
   30% of 800 = .30 × 800 = 240 nickels
   60% of 800 = .60 × 800 = 480 quarters

   Find the value of the coins:

80 dimes =	80 × .10 =	$ 8.00
240 nickels =	240 × .05 =	12.00
480 quarters =	480 × .25 =	120.00
	Total	$140.00

Answer: **(1)** less than $150

12. First solution contains 20% of 6 quarts of alcohol.

   Alcohol content = .20 × 6
   = 1.2 quarts

   Second solution contains 60% of 4 quarts of alcohol.

   Alcohol content = .60 × 4
   = 2.4 quarts

   Mixture contains: 1.2 + 2.4 = 3.6 quarts alcohol
   6 + 4 = 10 quarts liquid

   Alcoholic strength of mixture = $\frac{3.6}{10}$ = 36%

Answer: **(3)** 36%

13. $2\frac{1}{2}$% of insured value = $348

   Insured value = $\frac{348}{2\frac{1}{2}\%}$
   = 348 ÷ .025
   = $13,920

   $13,920 is 80% of total value

   Total value = $\frac{\$13{,}920}{80\%}$
   = $13,920 ÷ .80
   = $17,400

Answer: **(4)** $17,400

14. $\frac{1}{5}$ × 35 = 7 hr sorting mail
   $\frac{1}{2}$ × 35 = $17\frac{1}{2}$ hr filing
   $\frac{1}{7}$ × 35 = 5 hr reception
   $29\frac{1}{2}$ hr accounted for

$35 - 29\frac{1}{2} = 5\frac{1}{2}$ hr left for messenger work

% spent on messenger work:

$$\begin{aligned} &= \frac{5\frac{1}{2}}{35} \\ &= 5\tfrac{1}{2} \div 35 \\ &= \tfrac{11}{2} \times \tfrac{1}{35} \\ &= \tfrac{11}{70} \\ &= .15\tfrac{5}{7} \end{aligned}$$

Answer: **(5)** $15\frac{5}{7}$ is most nearly 16%

15. 80% of the boys = 1152

$$\begin{aligned} \text{Number of boys} &= \frac{1152}{80\%} \\ &= 1152 \div .80 \\ &= 1440 \end{aligned}$$

40% of students = 1440

$$\begin{aligned} \text{Total number of students} &= \frac{1440}{40\%} \\ &= 1440 \div .40 \\ &= 3600 \end{aligned}$$

Answer: **(3)** 3600

SHORTCUTS IN MULTIPLICATION AND DIVISION

There are several shortcuts for simplifying multiplication and division. Following the description of each shortcut, practice problems are provided.

Dropping Final Zeros

1. a. A zero in a whole number is considered a "final zero" if it appears in the units column or if all columns to its right are filled with zeros. A final zero may be omitted in certain kinds of problems.

   b. In decimal numbers a zero appearing in the extreme right column may be dropped with no effect on the solution of a problem.

2. In multiplying whole numbers, the final zero(s) may be dropped during computation and simply transferred to the answer.

   Examples:

$$\begin{array}{r} 2310 \\ \times\ 150 \\ \hline 1155 \\ 231 \\ \hline 346500 \end{array} \qquad \begin{array}{r} 129 \\ \times\ 210 \\ \hline 129 \\ 258 \\ \hline 27090 \end{array} \qquad \begin{array}{r} 1760 \\ \times\ 205 \\ \hline 880 \\ 352 \\ \hline 360800 \end{array}$$

Practice Problems

Solve the following multiplication problems, dropping the final zeros during computation.

1. $\begin{array}{r} 230 \\ \times\ 12 \\ \hline \end{array}$

2. $\begin{array}{r} 175 \\ \times\ 130 \\ \hline \end{array}$

3. $\begin{array}{r} 203 \\ \times\ 14 \\ \hline \end{array}$

4. $\begin{array}{r} 621 \\ \times\ 140 \\ \hline \end{array}$

5. $\begin{array}{r} 430 \\ \times\ 360 \\ \hline \end{array}$

6. $\begin{array}{r} 132 \\ \times\ 310 \\ \hline \end{array}$

7. $\begin{array}{r} 350 \\ \times\ 24 \\ \hline \end{array}$

8. $\begin{array}{r} 520 \\ \times\ 410 \\ \hline \end{array}$

9. $\begin{array}{r} 634 \\ \times\ 120 \\ \hline \end{array}$

10. $\begin{array}{r} 431 \\ \times\ 230 \\ \hline \end{array}$

Solutions to Practice Problems

1. $\begin{array}{r} 230 \\ \times\ 12 \\ \hline 46 \\ 23 \\ \hline 2760 \end{array}$

2. $\begin{array}{r} 175 \\ \times\ 130 \\ \hline 525 \\ 175 \\ \hline 22750 \end{array}$

3. $\begin{array}{r} 203 \\ \times\ 14 \\ \hline 812 \\ 203 \\ \hline 2842 \end{array}$
(no final zeros)

4. $\begin{array}{r} 621 \\ \times\ 140 \\ \hline 2484 \\ 621 \\ \hline 86940 \end{array}$

5. $\begin{array}{r} 430 \\ \times\ 360 \\ \hline 258 \\ 129 \\ \hline 154800 \end{array}$

6. $\begin{array}{r} 132 \\ \times\ 310 \\ \hline 132 \\ 396 \\ \hline 40920 \end{array}$

7. $\begin{array}{r} 350 \\ \times\ 24 \\ \hline 140 \\ 70 \\ \hline 8400 \end{array}$

8. $\begin{array}{r} 520 \\ \times\ 410 \\ \hline 52 \\ 208 \\ \hline 213200 \end{array}$

9. $\begin{array}{r} 634 \\ \times\ 120 \\ \hline 1268 \\ 634 \\ \hline 76080 \end{array}$

10. $\begin{array}{r} 431 \\ \times\ 230 \\ \hline 1293 \\ 862 \\ \hline 99130 \end{array}$

Multiplying Whole Numbers by Decimals

3. In multiplying a whole number by a decimal number, if there are one or more final zeros in the multiplicand, move the decimal point in the multiplier to the right the same number of places as there are final zeros in the multiplicand. Then cross out the final zero(s) in the multiplicand.

Examples:

$$\begin{array}{r} 27500 \\ \times \quad .15 \\ \hline \end{array} = \begin{array}{r} 275 \\ \times \;\; 15 \\ \hline \end{array}$$

$$\begin{array}{r} 1250 \\ \times \; .345 \\ \hline \end{array} = \begin{array}{r} 125 \\ \times \; 3.45 \\ \hline \end{array}$$

Practice Problems

Rewrite the following problems, dropping the final zeros and moving decimal points the appropriate number of spaces. Then compute the answers.

1. $\begin{array}{r} 2400 \\ \times \quad .02 \\ \hline \end{array}$

2. $\begin{array}{r} 620 \\ \times \; .04 \\ \hline \end{array}$

3. $\begin{array}{r} 800 \\ \times \; .005 \\ \hline \end{array}$

4. $\begin{array}{r} 600 \\ \times \; .002 \\ \hline \end{array}$

5. $\begin{array}{r} 340 \\ \times \; .08 \\ \hline \end{array}$

6. $\begin{array}{r} 480 \\ \times \quad .4 \\ \hline \end{array}$

7. $\begin{array}{r} 400 \\ \times \; .04 \\ \hline \end{array}$

8. $\begin{array}{r} 5300 \\ \times \quad .5 \\ \hline \end{array}$

9. $\begin{array}{r} 930 \\ \times \quad .3 \\ \hline \end{array}$

10. $\begin{array}{r} 9000 \\ \times \; .001 \\ \hline \end{array}$

Solutions to Practice Problems

The rewritten problems are shown, along with the answers.

1. $\begin{array}{r} 24 \\ \times \;\; 2 \\ \hline 48 \end{array}$

2. $\begin{array}{r} 62 \\ \times \; .4 \\ \hline 24.8 \end{array}$

3. $\begin{array}{r} 8 \\ \times\ .5 \\ \hline .40 \end{array}$

4. $\begin{array}{r} 6 \\ \times\ .2 \\ \hline 1.2 \end{array}$

5. $\begin{array}{r} 34 \\ \times\ .8 \\ \hline 27.2 \end{array}$

6. $\begin{array}{r} 48 \\ \times\ 4 \\ \hline 192 \end{array}$

7. $\begin{array}{r} 4 \\ \times\ 4 \\ \hline 16 \end{array}$

8. $\begin{array}{r} 53 \\ \times\ 50 \\ \hline 2650 \end{array}$

9. $\begin{array}{r} 93 \\ \times\ 3 \\ \hline 279 \end{array}$

10. $\begin{array}{r} 9 \\ \times\ 1 \\ \hline 9 \end{array}$

Dividing by Whole Numbers

4. a. When there are final zeros in the divisor but no final zeros in the dividend, move the decimal point in the dividend to the left as many places as there are final zeros in the divisor, then omit the final zeros.

Example: 2700.) 37523. = 27.) 375.23

b. When there are fewer final zeros in the divisor than there are in the dividend, drop the same number of final zeros from the dividend as there are final zeros in the divisor.

Example: 250.) 45300. = 25.) 4530.

c. When there are more final zeros in the divisor than there are in the dividend, move the decimal point in the dividend to the left as many places as there are final zeros in the divisor, then omit the final zeros.

Example: 2300.) 690. = 23.) 6.9

d. When there are no final zeros in the divisor, no zeros can be dropped in the dividend.

Example: 23.) 690. = 23.) 690.

Practice Problems

Rewrite the following problems, dropping the final zeros and moving the decimal points the appropriate number of places. Then compute the quotients.

1. 600.) 72.
2. 310.) 6200.
3. 7600) 1520.
4. 46.) 920.
5. 11.0) 220.
6. 700.) 84.

7. $90.\overline{)\,8100.}$
8. $8100.\overline{)\,1620.}$
9. $25.\overline{)\,5250.}$
10. $41.0\overline{)\,820.}$
11. $800.\overline{)\,96.}$
12. $650.\overline{)\,1300.}$
13. $5500.\overline{)\,110.}$
14. $36.\overline{)\,720.}$
15. $87.0\overline{)\,1740.}$

Rewritten Practice Problems

1. $6.\overline{)\,.72}$
2. $31.\overline{)\,620.}$
3. $76.\overline{)\,15.2}$
4. $46.\overline{)\,920.}$
5. $11.\overline{)\,220.}$
6. $7.\overline{)\,.84}$
7. $9.\overline{)\,810.}$
8. $81.\overline{)\,16.2}$
9. $25.\overline{)\,5250.}$
10. $41.\overline{)\,820.}$
11. $8.\overline{)\,.96}$
12. $65.\overline{)\,130.}$
13. $55.\overline{)\,1.1}$
14. $36.\overline{)\,720.}$
15. $87.\overline{)\,1740.}$

Solutions to Practice Problems

1. $\begin{array}{r} .12 \\ 6.\overline{)\,.72} \end{array}$

2. $\begin{array}{r} 20 \\ 31.\overline{)\,620.} \\ \underline{62} \\ 00 \end{array}$

3. $\begin{array}{r} .2 \\ 76.\overline{)\,15.2} \\ \underline{15\ 2} \\ 0\ 0 \end{array}$

4. $\begin{array}{r} 20 \\ 46.\overline{)\,920.} \\ \underline{92} \\ 00 \end{array}$

5. $\begin{array}{r} 20 \\ 11.\overline{)\,220.} \\ \underline{22} \\ 00 \end{array}$

6. $\begin{array}{r} .12 \\ 7.\overline{)\,.84} \end{array}$

7. $\begin{array}{r} 90 \\ 9.\overline{)\,810.} \end{array}$

8. $\begin{array}{r} .2 \\ 81.\overline{)\,16.2} \\ \underline{16\ 2} \\ 0\ 0 \end{array}$

9. $\begin{array}{r} 210 \\ 25.\overline{)\,5250.} \\ \underline{50} \\ 25 \\ \underline{25} \\ 00 \end{array}$

10. $\begin{array}{r} 20 \\ 41.\overline{)\,820.} \\ \underline{82} \\ 00 \end{array}$

11. $\begin{array}{r} .12 \\ 8.\overline{)\,.96} \end{array}$

12. $\begin{array}{r} 2 \\ 65.\overline{)\,130.} \\ \underline{130} \\ 00 \end{array}$

13. $\begin{array}{r} .02 \\ 55.\overline{)\,1.10} \\ \underline{1\ 10} \\ 00 \end{array}$

14. $\begin{array}{r} 20 \\ 36.\overline{)\,720.} \\ \underline{72} \\ 00 \end{array}$

15. $\begin{array}{r} 20 \\ 87.\overline{)\,1740.} \\ \underline{174} \\ 00 \end{array}$

Division by Multiplication

5. Instead of dividing by a particular number, the same answer is obtained by multiplying by the equivalent multiplier.

6. To find the equivalent multiplier of a given divisor, divide 1 by the divisor.

   Example: The equivalent multiplier of $12\frac{1}{2}$ is $1 \div 12\frac{1}{2}$ or .08. The division problem $100 \div 12\frac{1}{2}$ may be more easily solved as the multiplication problem $100 \times .08$. The answer will be the same.

7. Common divisors and their equivalent multipliers are shown below:

Divisor	*Equivalent Multiplier*
$11\frac{1}{9}$	.09
$12\frac{1}{2}$	.08
$14\frac{2}{7}$	.07
$16\frac{2}{3}$	.06
20	.05
25	.04
$33\frac{1}{3}$	.03
50	.02

8. A divisor may be multiplied or divided by any power of 10, and the only change in its equivalent multiplier will be in the placement of the decimal point, as may be seen in the following table:

Divisor	*Equivalent Multiplier*
.025	40.
.25	4.
2.5	.4
25.	.04
250.	.004
2500.	.0004

Practice Problems

Rewrite and solve each of the following problems by using equivalent multipliers. Drop the final zeros where appropriate.

1. $100 \div 16\frac{2}{3} =$
2. $200 \div 25 =$
3. $300 \div 33\frac{1}{3} =$
4. $250 \div 50 =$
5. $80 \div 12\frac{1}{2} =$
6. $800 \div 14\frac{2}{7} =$

7. $620 \div 20 =$
8. $500 \div 11\frac{1}{9} =$
9. $420 \div 16\frac{2}{3} =$
10. $1200 \div 33\frac{1}{3} =$
11. $955 \div 50 =$
12. $300 \div 33\frac{1}{3} =$
13. $275 \div 12\frac{1}{2} =$
14. $625 \div 25 =$
15. $244 \div 20 =$
16. $350 \div 16\frac{2}{3} =$
17. $400 \div 33\frac{1}{3} =$
18. $375 \div 25 =$
19. $460 \div 20 =$
20. $250 \div 12\frac{1}{2} =$

Solutions to Practice Problems

The rewritten problems and their solutions appear below:

1. $100 \times .06 = 1 \times 6 = 6$
2. $200 \times .04 = 2 \times 4 = 8$
3. $300 \times .03 = 3 \times 3 = 9$
4. $250 \times .02 = 25 \times .2 = 5$
5. $80 \times .08 = 8 \times .8 = 6.4$
6. $800 \times .07 = 8 \times 7 = 56$
7. $620 \times .05 = 62 \times .5 = 31$
8. $500 \times .09 = 5 \times 9 = 45$
9. $420 \times .06 = 42 \times .6 = 25.2$
10. $1200 \times .03 = 12 \times 3 = 36$
11. $955 \times .02 = 19.1$
12. $300 \times .03 = 3 \times 3 = 9$
13. $275 \times .08 = 22$
14. $625 \times .04 = 25$
15. $244 \times .05 = 12.2$
16. $350 \times .06 = 35 \times .6 = 21$
17. $400 \times .03 = 4 \times 3 = 12$
18. $375 \times .04 = 15$
19. $460 \times .05 = 46 \times .5 = 23$
20. $250 \times .08 = 25 \times .8 = 20$

Multiplication by Division

9. Just as some division problems are made easier by changing them to equivalent multiplication problems, certain multiplication problems are made easier by changing them to equivalent division problems.

10. Instead of arriving at an answer by multiplying by a particular number, the same answer is obtained by dividing by the equivalent divisor.

11. To find the equivalent divisor of a given multiplier, divide 1 by the multiplier.

12. Common multipliers and their equivalent divisors are shown below:

Multiplier	*Equivalent Divisor*
$11\frac{1}{9}$	.09
$12\frac{1}{2}$	.08
$14\frac{2}{7}$	.07
$16\frac{2}{3}$	.06
20	.05
25	.04
$33\frac{1}{3}$	.03
50	.02

Notice that the multiplier-equivalent divisor pairs are the same as the divisor-equivalent multiplier pairs given earlier.

Practice Problems

Rewrite and solve each of the following problems by using division. Drop the final zeros where appropriate.

1. $77 \times 14\frac{2}{7} =$
2. $81 \times 11\frac{1}{9} =$
3. $475 \times 20 =$
4. $42 \times 50 =$
5. $36 \times 33\frac{1}{3} =$
6. $96 \times 12\frac{1}{2} =$
7. $126 \times 16\frac{2}{3} =$
8. $48 \times 25 =$
9. $33 \times 33\frac{1}{3} =$
10. $84 \times 14\frac{2}{7} =$
11. $99 \times 11\frac{1}{9} =$
12. $126 \times 33\frac{1}{3} =$
13. $168 \times 12\frac{1}{2} =$
14. $654 \times 16\frac{2}{3} =$
15. $154 \times 14\frac{2}{7} =$
16. $5250 \times 50 =$
17. $324 \times 25 =$
18. $625 \times 20 =$
19. $198 \times 11\frac{1}{9} =$
20. $224 \times 14\frac{2}{7} =$

Solutions to Practice Problems

The rewritten problems and their solutions appear below:

1. $.07\overline{)77.} = \begin{array}{r}1100.\\ 7\overline{)7700.}\end{array}$
2. $.09\overline{)81.} = \begin{array}{r}900.\\ 9\overline{)8100.}\end{array}$
3. $.05\overline{)475.} = \begin{array}{r}9500.\\ 5\overline{)47500.}\end{array}$
4. $.02\overline{)42.} = \begin{array}{r}2100.\\ 2\overline{)4200.}\end{array}$
5. $.03\overline{)36.} = \begin{array}{r}1200.\\ 3\overline{)3600.}\end{array}$
6. $.08\overline{)96.} = \begin{array}{r}1200.\\ 8\overline{)9600.}\end{array}$
7. $.06\overline{)126.} = \begin{array}{r}2100.\\ 6\overline{)12600.}\end{array}$
8. $.04\overline{)48.} = \begin{array}{r}1200.\\ 4\overline{)4800.}\end{array}$
9. $.03\overline{)33.} = \begin{array}{r}1100.\\ 3\overline{)3300.}\end{array}$
10. $.07\overline{)84.} = \begin{array}{r}1200.\\ 7\overline{)8400.}\end{array}$
11. $.09\overline{)99.} = \begin{array}{r}1100.\\ 9\overline{)9900.}\end{array}$
12. $.03\overline{)126.} = \begin{array}{r}4200.\\ 3\overline{)12600.}\end{array}$
13. $.08\overline{)168.} = \begin{array}{r}2100.\\ 8\overline{)16800.}\end{array}$
14. $.06\overline{)654.} = \begin{array}{r}10900.\\ 6\overline{)65400.}\end{array}$
15. $.07\overline{)154.} = \begin{array}{r}2200.\\ 7\overline{)15400.}\end{array}$
16. $.02\overline{)5250.} = \begin{array}{r}262500.\\ 2\overline{)525000.}\end{array}$
17. $.04\overline{)324.} = \begin{array}{r}8100.\\ 4\overline{)32400.}\end{array}$
18. $.05\overline{)625.} = \begin{array}{r}12500.\\ 5\overline{)62500.}\end{array}$
19. $.09\overline{)198.} = \begin{array}{r}2200.\\ 9\overline{)19800.}\end{array}$
20. $.07\overline{)224.} = \begin{array}{r}3200.\\ 7\overline{)22400.}\end{array}$

POWERS AND ROOTS

1. The numbers that are multiplied to give a product are called the **factors** of the product.

   Example: In $2 \times 3 = 6$, 2 and 3 are factors.

2. If the factors are the same, an **exponent** may be used to indicate the number of times the factor appears.

   Example: In $3 \times 3 = 3^2$, the number 3 appears as a factor twice, as is indicated by the exponent 2.

3. When a product is written in exponential form, the number the exponent refers to is called the **base**. The product itself is called the **power**.

   Example: In 2^5, the number 2 is the base and 5 is the exponent. $2^5 = 2 \times 2 \times 2 \times 2 \times 2 = 32$, so 32 is the power.

4. a. If the exponent used is 2, we say that the base has been **squared**, or raised to the second power.

   Example: 6^2 is read "six squared" or "six to the second power."

   b. If the exponent used is 3, we say that the base has been **cubed**, or raised to the third power.

   Example: 5^3 is read "five cubed" or "five to the third power."

   c. If the exponent is 4, we say that the base has been raised to the fourth power. If the exponent is 5, we say the base has been raised to the fifth power, etc.

   Example: 2^8 is read "two to the eighth power."

5. A number that is the product of a number squared is called a **perfect square**.

   Example: 25 is a perfect square because $25 = 5^2$.

6. a. If a number has exactly two equal factors, each factor is called the **square root** of the number.

   Example: $9 = 3 \times 3$; therefore, 3 is the square root of 9.

   b. The symbol $\sqrt{\ }$ is used to indicate square root.

   Example: $\sqrt{9} = 3$ means that the square root of 9 is 3, or $3 \times 3 = 9$.

7. The square root of the most common perfect squares may be found by using the following table, or by trial and error; that is, by finding the number that, when squared, yields the given perfect square.

Number	*Perfect Square*	*Number*	*Perfect Square*
1	1	10	100
2	4	11	121
3	9	12	144
4	16	13	169
5	25	14	196
6	36	15	225
7	49	20	400
8	64	25	625
9	81	30	900

Example: To find $\sqrt{81}$, note that 81 is the perfect square of 9, or $9^2 = 81$. Therefore, $\sqrt{81} = 9$.

8. To find the square root of a number that is not a perfect square, use the following method:

a. Locate the decimal point.

b. Mark off the digits in groups of two in both directions beginning at the decimal point.

c. Mark the decimal point for the answer just above the decimal point of the number whose square root is to be taken.

d. Find the largest perfect square contained in the left-hand group of two.

e. Place its square root in the answer. Subtract the perfect square from the first digit or pair of digits.

f. Bring down the next pair.

g. Double the partial answer.

h. Add a trial digit to the right of the doubled partial answer. Multiply this new number by the trial digit. Place the correct new digit in the answer.

i. Subtract the product.

j. Repeat steps f–i as often as necessary.

You will notice that you get one digit in the answer for every group of two you marked off in the original number.

Illustration: Find the square root of 138,384.

SOLUTION:

$$\begin{array}{rl} & \;\;3\;\;.\;\;.\;\; \\ & \sqrt{13'83'84.} \\ 3^2 = & \;\;9 \\ \hline & \;\;4\;83 \end{array}$$

$$\begin{array}{rl} & \;\;3\;\;7\;\;2. \\ & \sqrt{13'83'84.} \\ 3^2 = & \;\;9 \\ \hline & \;\;4\;83 \\ 7 \times 67 = & \;\;4\;69 \\ \hline & \;\;\;\;14\;84 \\ 2 \times 742 = & \;\;\;\;14\;84 \\ \hline \end{array}$$

The number must first be marked off in groups of two figures each, beginning at the decimal point, which, in the case of a whole number, is at the right. The number of figures in the root will be the same as the number of groups so obtained.

The largest square less than 13 is 9. $\sqrt{9} = 3$

Place its square root in the answer. Subtract the perfect square from the first digit or pair of digits. Bring down the next pair. To form our trial divisor, annex 0 to this root "3" (making 30) and multiply by 2.

$483 \div 60 = 8$. Multiplying the trial divisor 68 by 8, we obtain 544, which is too large. We then try multiplying 67 by 7. This is correct. Add the trial digit to the right of the doubled partial answer. Place the new digit in the answer. Subtract the product. Bring down the final group. Annex 0 to the new root 37 and multiply by 2 for the trial divisor:

$$2 \times 370 = 740$$
$$1484 \div 740 = 2$$

Place the 2 in the answer.

Answer: The square root of 138,384 is 372.

Illustration: Find the square root of 3 to the nearest hundredth.

SOLUTION:

	1. 7 3 2
	$\sqrt{3.00'00'00}$
$1^2 =$	1
20	2 00
$7 \times 27 =$	1 89
340	11 00
$3 \times 343 =$	10 29
3460	71 00
$2 \times 3462 =$	69 24

Answer: The square root of 3 is 1.73 to the nearest hundredth.

9. To find the square root of a fraction, find the square root of its numerator and of its denominator.

Example: $\sqrt{\frac{4}{9}} = \dfrac{\sqrt{4}}{\sqrt{9}} = \frac{2}{3}$

10. a. If a number has exactly three equal factors, each factor is called the **cube root** of the number.

b. The symbol $\sqrt[3]{}$ is used to indicate the cube root.

Example: $8 = 2 \times 2 \times 2$; therefore, $\sqrt[3]{8} = 2$

Practice Problems Involving Powers and Roots

1. The square of 10 is
   (1) 1
   (2) 2
   (3) 5
   (4) 100
   (5) 105
2. The cube of 9 is
   (1) 3
   (2) 27
   (3) 81
   (4) 99
   (5) 729
3. The fourth power of 2 is
   (1) 2
   (2) 4
   (3) 8
   (4) 16
   (5) 32
4. In exponential form, the product 7 × 7 × 7 × 7 × 7 may be written
   (1) 5^7
   (2) 7^5
   (3) 2^7
   (4) 7^2
   (5) 2^5
5. The value of 3^5 is
   (1) 243
   (2) 125
   (3) 35
   (4) 25
   (5) 15
6. The square root of 1175, to the nearest whole number, is
   (1) 32
   (2) 33
   (3) 34
   (4) 35
   (5) 36
7. Find $\sqrt{503}$ to the nearest tenth.
   (1) 22.4
   (2) 22.5
   (3) 22.6
   (4) 22.7
   (5) 22.8
8. Find $\sqrt{\frac{1}{4}}$.
   (1) 2
   (2) $\frac{1}{2}$
   (3) $\frac{1}{8}$
   (4) $\frac{1}{10}$
   (5) $\frac{1}{16}$
9. Find $\sqrt[3]{64}$.
   (1) 3
   (2) 4
   (3) 8
   (4) 32
   (5) 40
10. The sum of 2^2 and 2^3 is
    (1) 9
    (2) 10
    (3) 12
    (4) 32
    (5) 44

Powers and Roots Problems — Correct Answers

1. **(4)**
2. **(5)**
3. **(4)**
4. **(2)**
5. **(1)**
6. **(3)**
7. **(1)**
8. **(2)**
9. **(2)**
10. **(3)**

Problem Solutions — Powers and Roots

1. $10^2 = 10 \times 10 = 100$

   Answer: **(4)** 100

2. $9^3 = 9 \times 9 \times 9$
   $= 81 \times 9$
   $= 729$

   Answer: **(5)** 729

3. $2^4 = 2 \times 2 \times 2 \times 2$
$= 4 \times 2 \times 2$
$= 8 \times 2$
$= 16$

Answer: **(4)** 16

4. $7 \times 7 \times 7 \times 7 \times 7 = 7^5$

Answer: **(2)** 7^5

5. $3^5 = 3 \times 3 \times 3 \times 3 \times 3$
$= 243$

Answer: **(1)** 243

6. 3 4. 2 = 34 to the nearest whole number
$\sqrt{11'75.00}$

$3^2 =$ 9
2 75
$4 \times 64 =$ 2 56
19 00
$2 \times 682 =$ 13 64
5 36

Answer: **(3)** 34

7. 2 2. 4 2 = 22.4 to the nearest tenth
$\sqrt{5'03.00'00}$

$2^2 =$ 4
1 03
$2 \times 42 =$ 84
19 00
$4 \times 444 =$ 17 76
1 24 00
$2 \times 4482 =$ 89 64
34 36

Answer: **(1)** 22.4

8. $\sqrt{\frac{1}{4}} = \frac{\sqrt{1}}{\sqrt{4}} = \frac{1}{2}$

Answer: **(2)** $\frac{1}{2}$

9. Since $4 \times 4 \times 4 = 64$, $\sqrt[3]{64} = 4$

Answer: **(2)** 4

10. $2^2 + 2^3 = 4 + 8 = 12$

Answer: **(3)** 12

TABLE OF MEASURES

English Measures

Length

1 foot (ft or ′) = 12 inches (in or ″)
1 yard (yd) = 36 inches
1 yard = 3 feet
1 rod (rd) = $16\frac{1}{2}$ feet
1 mile (mi) = 5280 feet
1 mile = 1760 yards
1 mile = 320 rods

Weight

1 pound (lb) = 16 ounces (oz)
1 hundredweight (cwt) = 100 pounds
1 ton (T) = 2000 pounds

Area

1 square foot (ft^2) = 144 square inches (in^2)
1 square yard (yd^2) = 9 square feet

Liquid Measure

1 cup (c) = 8 fluid ounces (fl oz)
1 pint (pt) = 2 cups
1 pint = 4 gills (gi)
1 quart (qt) = 2 pints
1 gallon (gal) = 4 quarts
1 barrel (bl) = $31\frac{1}{2}$ gallons

Dry Measure

1 quart (qt) = 2 pints (pt)
1 peck (pk) = 8 quarts
1 bushel (bu) = 4 pecks

Volume

1 cubic foot (ft^3 or cu ft) = 1728 cubic inches
1 cubic yard (yd^3 or cu yd) = 27 cubic feet
1 gallon = 231 cubic inches

General Measures

Time

1 minute (min) = 60 seconds (sec)
1 hour (hr) = 60 minutes
1 day = 24 hours
1 week = 7 days
1 year = 52 weeks
1 calendar year = 365 days

Angles and Arcs

1 minute (′) = 60 seconds (″)
1 degree (°) = 60 minutes
1 circle = 360 degrees

Counting

1 dozen (doz) = 12 units
1 gross (gr) = 12 dozen
1 gross = 144 units

Table of English—Metric Conversions (Approximate)

English to Metric

1 inch = 2.54 centimeters
1 yard = .9 meters
1 mile = 1.6 kilometers
1 ounce = 28 grams
1 pound = 454 grams
1 fluid ounce = 30 milliliters
1 liquid quart = .95 liters

Metric to English

1 centimeter = .39 inches
1 meter = 1.1 yards
1 kilometer = .6 miles
1 kilogram = 2.2 pounds
1 liter = 1.06 liquid quart

*Table of Metric Conversions**

1 liter = 1000 cubic centimeters (cm^3)
1 milliliter = 1 cubic centimeter
1 liter of water weighs 1 kilogram
1 milliliter of water weighs 1 gram

---

*These conversions are exact only under specific conditions. If the conditions are not met, the conversions are approximate.

THE METRIC SYSTEM

LENGTH

Unit	Abbreviation	Number of Meters
myriameter	mym	10,000
kilometer	km	1,000
hectometer	hm	100
dekameter	dam	10
meter	m	1
decimeter	dm	0.1
centimeter	cm	0.01
millimeter	mm	0.001

AREA

Unit	Abbreviation	Number of Square Meters
square kilometer	sq km *or* km^2	1,000,000
hectare	ha	10,000
are	a	100
centare	ca	1
square centimeter	sq cm *or* cm^2	0.0001

VOLUME

Unit	Abbreviation	Number of Cubic Meters
dekastere	das	10
stere	s	1
decistere	ds	0.10
cubic centimeter	cu cm *or* cm^3 *or* cc	0.000001

CAPACITY

Unit	Abbreviation	Number of Liters
kiloliter	kl	1,000
hectoliter	hl	100
dekaliter	dal	10
liter	l	1
deciliter	dl	0.10
centiliter	cl	0.01
milliliter	ml	0.001

MASS AND WEIGHT

Unit	Abbreviation	Number of Grams
metric ton	MT *or* t	1,000,000
quintal	q	100,000
kilogram	kg	1,000
hectogram	hg	100
dekagram	dag	10
gram	g *or* gm	1
decigram	dg	0.10
centigram	cg	0.01
milligram	mg	0.001

DENOMINATE NUMBERS (MEASUREMENT)

1. A **denominate number** is a number that specifies a given measurement. The unit of measure is called the **denomination**.

   Example: 7 miles, 3 quarts, and 5 grams are denominate numbers.

2. a. The English system of measurement uses such denominations as pints, ounces, pounds, and feet.

   b. The metric system of measurement uses such denominations as grams, liters, and meters.

English System of Measurement

3. To convert from one unit of measure to another, find in the Table of Measures how many units of the smaller denomination equal one unit of the larger denomination. This number is called the **conversion number**.

4. To convert from one unit of measure to a smaller unit, multiply the given number of units by the conversion number.

   Illustration: Convert 7 yards to inches.

   SOLUTION:
   1 yard = 36 inches (conversion number)
   7 yards = 7 × 36 inches
   = 252 inches

   Answer: 252 in

   Illustration: Convert 2 hours 12 minutes to minutes.

   SOLUTION:
   1 hour = 60 minutes (conversion number)
   2 hr 12 min = 2 hr + 12 min
   2 hr = 2 × 60 min = 120 min
   2 hr 12 min = 120 min + 12 min
   = 132 min

   Answer: 132 min

5. To convert from one unit of measure to a larger unit:

   a. Divide the given number of units by the conversion number.

   Illustration: Convert 48 inches to feet.

   SOLUTION: 1 foot = 12 inches (conversion number)

   48 in ÷ 12 = 4 ft

   Answer: 4 ft

   b. If there is a remainder it is expressed in terms of the smaller unit of measure.

   Illustration: Convert 35 ounces to pounds and ounces.

   SOLUTION: 1 pound = 16 ounces (conversion number)

   $$35 \text{ oz} \div 16 = 16\,\overline{)\,35 \text{ oz}}\quad \begin{array}{r} 2 \text{ lb} \\ \underline{32} \\ 3 \text{ oz} \end{array}$$

   = 2 lb 3 oz

   Answer: 2 lb 3 oz

6. To add denominate numbers, arrange them in columns by common unit, then add each column. If necessary, simplify the answer, starting with the smallest unit.

   Illustration: Add 1 yd 2 ft 8 in, 2 yd 2 ft 10 in, and 3 yd 1 ft 9 in.

   SOLUTION:

   $$\begin{array}{rl} & 1 \text{ yd } 2 \text{ ft } 8 \text{ in} \\ & 2 \text{ yd } 2 \text{ ft } 10 \text{ in} \\ + & \underline{3 \text{ yd } 1 \text{ ft } 9 \text{ in}} \\ & 6 \text{ yd } 5 \text{ ft } 27 \text{ in} \\ = & 6 \text{ yd } 7 \text{ ft } 3 \text{ in} \quad (\text{since } 27 \text{ in} = 2 \text{ ft } 3 \text{ in}) \\ = & 8 \text{ yd } 1 \text{ ft } 3 \text{ in} \quad (\text{since } 7 \text{ ft} = 2 \text{ yd } 1 \text{ ft}) \end{array}$$

   Answer: 8 yd 1 ft 3 in

7. To subtract denominate numbers, arrange them in columns by common unit,then subtract each column starting with the smallest unit. If necessary, borrow to increase the number of a particular unit.

   Illustration: Subtract 2 gal 3 qt from 7 gal 1 qt.

   SOLUTION:

   $$\begin{array}{rcr} 7 \text{ gal } 1 \text{ qt} & = & 6 \text{ gal } 5 \text{ qt} \\ -\ 2 \text{ gal } 3 \text{ qt} & = & -\ 2 \text{ gal } 3 \text{ qt} \\ \hline & & 4 \text{ gal } 2 \text{ qt} \end{array}$$

   Note that 1 gal was borrowed from 7 gal.

   1 gal = 4 qt

   Therefore, 7 gal 1 qt = 6 gal 5 qt

   Answer: 4 gal 2 qt

8. To multiply a denominate number by a given number:

   a. If the denominate number contains only one unit, multiply the numbers and write the unit.

   Example: 3 oz × 4 = 12 oz

b. If the denominate number contains more than one unit of measurement, multiply the number of each unit by the given number and simplify the answer, if necessary.

Illustration: Multiply 4 yd 2 ft 8 in by 2.

SOLUTION:

```
     4 yd 2 ft  8 in
×               2
 ------------------
     8 yd 4 ft 16 in
   = 8 yd 5 ft  4 in (since 16 in = 1 ft 4 in)
   = 9 yd 2 ft  4 in (since 5 ft = 1 yd 2 ft)
```

Answer: 9 yd 2 ft 4 in

9. To divide a denominate number by a given number, convert all units to the smallest unit, then divide. Simplify the answer, if necessary.

Illustration: Divide 5 lb 12 oz by 4.

SOLUTION:

```
       1 lb = 16 oz, therefore
5 lb 12 oz = 92 oz
92 oz ÷ 4 = 23 oz
          = 1 lb 7 oz
```

Answer: 1 lb 7 oz

10. Alternate method of division:

a. Divide the number of the largest unit by the given number.

b. Convert any remainder to the next largest unit.

c. Divide the total number of that unit by the given number.

d. Again convert any remainder to the next unit and divide.

e. Repeat until no units remain.

Illustration: Divide 9 hr 21 min 40 sec by 4.

SOLUTION:

```
     2 hr     20 min      25 sec
4 ) 9 hr     21 min      40 sec
    8 hr
    ----
    1 hr =   60 min
             ------
             81 min
             80 min
             ------
              1 min =    60 sec
                         ------
                        100 sec
                        100 sec
                        -------
                          0 sec
```

Answer: 2 hr 20 min 25 sec

Metric Measurement

11. The basic units of the metric system are the meter (m), which is used for length; the gram (g), which is used for weight; and the liter (*l*), which is used for capacity, or volume.

12. The prefixes that are used with the basic units, and their meanings, are:

Prefix	*Abbreviation*	*Meaning*
micro	**m**	one millionth of (.000001)
milli	m	one thousandth of (.001)
centi	c	one hundredth of (.01)
deci	d	one tenth of (.1)
deka	da or dk	ten times (10)
hecto	h	one hundred times (100)
kilo	k	one thousand times (1000)
mega	M	one million times (1,000,000)

13. To convert *to* a basic metric unit from a prefixed metric unit, multiply by the number indicated in the prefix.

Example: Convert 72 millimeters to meters.

72 millimeters = 72 × .001 meters
= .072 meters

Example: Convert 4 kiloliters to liters.

4 kiloliters = 4 × 1000 liters
= 4000 liters

14. To convert *from* a basic unit to a prefixed unit, divide by the number indicated in the prefix.

Example: Convert 300 liters to hectoliters.

300 liters = 300 ÷ 100 hectoliters
= 3 hectoliters

Example: Convert 4.5 meters to decimeters.

4.5 meters = 4.5 ÷ .1 decimeters
= 45 decimeters

15. To convert from any prefixed metric unit to another prefixed unit, first convert to a basic unit, then convert the basic unit to the desired unit.

Illustration: Convert 420 decigrams to kilograms.

SOLUTION: 420 dg = 420 × .1 g = 42 g
42 g = 42 ÷ 1000 kg = .042 kg

Answer: .042 kg

16. To add, subtract, multiply, or divide using metric measurement, first convert all units to the same unit, then perform the desired operation.

Illustration: Subtract 1200 g from 2.5 kg.

SOLUTION:

$$\begin{array}{rcr} 2.5\text{ kg} & = & 2500\text{ g} \\ -\ 1200\text{ g} & = & -\ 1200\text{ g} \\ \hline & & 1300\text{ g} \end{array}$$

Answer: 1300 g or 1.3 kg

17. To convert from a metric measure to an English measure, or the reverse:

a. In the Table of English–Metric Conversions, find how many units of the desired measure are equal to one unit of the given measure.

b. Multiply the given number by the number found in the table.

Illustration: Find the number of pounds in 4 kilograms.

SOLUTION: From the table, 1 kg = 2.2 lb.

$$\begin{aligned} 4\text{ kg} &= 4 \times 2.2\text{ lb} \\ &= 8.8\text{ lb} \end{aligned}$$

Answer: 8.8 lb

Illustration: Find the number of meters in 5 yards.

SOLUTION:

$$\begin{aligned} 1\text{ yd} &= .9\text{ m} \\ 5\text{ yd} &= 5 \times .9\text{ m} \\ &= 4.5\text{ m} \end{aligned}$$

Answer: 4.5 m

Temperature Measurement

18. The temperature measurement currently used in the United States is the degree Fahrenheit (°F). The metric measurement for temperature is the degree Celsius (°C), also called degree Centigrade.

19. Degrees Celsius may be converted to degrees Fahrenheit by the formula:

$$°F = \tfrac{9}{5}°C + 32°$$

Illustration: Water boils at 100°C. Convert this to °F.

SOLUTION:

$$\begin{aligned} °F &= \frac{9}{\cancel{5}_{1}} \times \cancel{100°}^{20} + 32° \\ &= 180° + 32° \\ &= 212° \end{aligned}$$

Answer: 100°C = 212°F

20. Degrees Fahrenheit may be converted to degrees Celsius by the formula:

$$°C = \frac{5}{9}(°F - 32°)$$

In using this formula, perform the subtraction in the parentheses first, then multiply by $\frac{5}{9}$.

Illustration: If normal body temperature is 98.6°F, what is it on the Celsius scale?

SOLUTION:
$$\begin{aligned} °C &= \tfrac{5}{9}(98.6° - 32°) \\ &= \tfrac{5}{9} \times 66.6° \\ &= \tfrac{333}{9}° \\ &= 37° \end{aligned}$$

Answer: Normal body temperature = 37°C.

Practice Problems Involving Measurement

1. A carpenter needs boards for 4 shelves, each 2′9″ long. How many feet of board should he buy?
(1) 11 (2) $11\frac{1}{8}$ (3) 13 (4) $15\frac{1}{2}$ (5) 16

2. The number of half-pints in 19 gallons of milk is
(1) 76 (2) 152 (3) 304 (4) 608 (5) 904

3. The product of 8 ft 7 in multiplied by 8 is
(1) 69 feet 6 inches (2) 68.8 feet (3) $68\frac{2}{3}$ feet (4) 68 feet 2 inches (5) 68 feet 6 inches

4. $\frac{1}{3}$ of 7 yards is
(1) 2 yards (2) 4 feet (3) $3\frac{1}{2}$ yards (4) 5 yards (5) 7 feet

5. Six gross of special drawing pencils were purchased for use in an office. If the pencils were used at the rate of 24 a week, the maximum number of weeks that the six gross of pencils would last is
(1) 6 weeks (2) 12 weeks (3) 24 weeks (4) 36 weeks (5) 42 weeks

6. If 7 ft 9 in is cut from a piece of wood that is 9 ft 6 in, the piece left is
(1) 1 foot 9 inches (2) 1 foot 10 inches (3) 2 feet 2 inches (4) 2 feet 5 inches (5) 2 feet 9 inches

7. Take 3 hours 49 minutes from 5 hours 13 minutes.
(1) 1 hour 5 minutes (2) 1 hour 10 minutes (3) 1 hour 18 minutes (4) 1 hour 20 minutes (5) 1 hour 24 minutes

8. A piece of wood 35 feet 6 inches long was used to make 4 shelves of equal lengths. The length of each shelf was
(1) 8.9 inches (2) 8 feet 9 inches (3) 8 feet $9\frac{1}{2}$ inches (4) 8 feet $10\frac{1}{2}$ inches (5) 8 feet 11 inches

9. The number of yards equal to 126 inches is
(1) 3.5 (2) 10.5 (3) 1260 (4) 1512 (5) 1560

10. If there are 231 cubic inches in one gallon, the number of cubic inches in 3 pints is closest to which one of the following?
(1) 24 (2) 29 (3) 57 (4) 87 (5) 89

11. The sum of 5 feet $2\frac{3}{4}$ inches, 8 feet $\frac{1}{2}$ inch, and $12\frac{1}{2}$ inches is
(1) 14 feet $3\frac{3}{4}$ inches (2) 14 feet $5\frac{3}{4}$ inches (3) 14 feet $9\frac{1}{4}$ inches (4) 15 feet $\frac{1}{2}$ inches (5) 16 feet $\frac{1}{2}$ inches

12. Add 5 hr 13 min, 3 hr 49 min, and 14 min. The sum is
(1) 8 hours 16 minutes (2) 9 hours 16 minutes (3) 9 hours 76 minutes (4) 8 hours 6 minutes (5) 9 hours 26 minutes

13. Assuming that 2.54 centimeters = 1 inch, a metal rod that measures $1\frac{1}{2}$ feet would most nearly equal which one of the following?
(1) 380 centimeters
(2) 46 centimeters
(3) 30 centimeters
(4) 18 centimeters
(5) 10 centimeters

14. A micromillimeter is defined as one millionth of a millimeter. A length of 17 micromillimeters may be represented as
(1) .00017 mm
(2) .0000017 mm
(3) .000017 mm
(4) .00000017 mm
(5) 0.17 mm

15. How many liters are equal to 4200 m*l*?
(1) .42
(2) 42
(3) 420
(4) 420,000
(5) 4.2

16. Add 26 dg, .4 kg, 5 g, and 184 cg.
(1) 215.40 grams
(2) 319.34 grams
(3) 409.44 grams
(4) 849.00 grams
(5) 869.00 grams

17. Four full bottles of equal size contain a total of 1.28 liters of cleaning solution. How many milliliters are in each bottle?
(1) 3.20
(2) 5.12
(3) 320
(4) 512
(5) 620

18. How many liters of water can be held in a 5-gallon jug? (See Conversion Table.)
(1) 19
(2) 38
(3) 40
(4) 50
(5) 60

19. To the nearest degree, what is a temperature of 12°C equal to on the Fahrenheit scale?
(1) 19°
(2) 60°
(3) 57°
(4) 79°
(5) 54°

20. A company requires that the temperature in its offices be kept at 68°F. What is this in °C?
(1) 10°
(2) 15°
(3) 20°
(4) 25°
(5) 30°

Measurement Problems — Correct Answers

1. **(1)**
2. **(3)**
3. **(3)**
4. **(5)**
5. **(4)**
6. **(1)**
7. **(5)**
8. **(4)**
9. **(1)**
10. **(4)**
11. **(1)**
12. **(2)**
13. **(2)**
14. **(3)**
15. **(5)**
16. **(3)**
17. **(3)**
18. **(1)**
19. **(5)**
20. **(3)**

Problem Solutions — Measurement

1.
$$\begin{array}{r} 2\text{ ft }\ 9\text{ in} \\ \times\qquad\quad 4 \\ \hline 8\text{ ft }36\text{ in} = 11\text{ ft} \end{array}$$

Answer: **(1)** 11

2. Find the number of half-pints in 1 gallon:

1 gal = 4 qts
4 qts = 4 × 2 pts = 8 pts
8 pts = 8 × 2 = 16 half-pints

Multiply to find the number of half-pints in 19 gallons:

19 gal = 19 × 16 half-pints
= 304 half-pints

Answer: **(3)** 304

3.
$$\begin{array}{r} 8\text{ ft}\ \ 7\text{ in} \\ \times\qquad\quad 8 \\ \hline 64\text{ ft}\ \ 56\text{ in} = 68\text{ ft}\ \ 8\text{ in} \end{array}$$
(since 56 in = 4 ft 8 in)

$8 \text{ in} = \frac{8}{12} \text{ ft} = \frac{2}{3} \text{ ft}$

$68 \text{ ft } 8 \text{ in} = 68\frac{2}{3} \text{ ft}$

Answer: **(3)** $68\frac{2}{3}$ ft

4. $\frac{1}{3} \times 7 \text{ yd} = 2\frac{1}{3} \text{ yd}$
$= 2 \text{ yd } 1 \text{ ft}$
$= 2 \times 3 \text{ ft} + 1 \text{ ft}$
$= 7 \text{ ft}$

Answer: **(5)** 7 ft

5. Find the number of units in 6 gross:

1 gross = 144 units
6 gross = 6 × 144 units
= 864 units

Divide units by rate of use:

864 ÷ 24 = 36

Answer: **(4)** 36 weeks

6.
$$\begin{array}{rr} 9\text{ ft } 6\text{ in} = & 8\text{ ft}\ \ 18\text{ in} \\ -\ 7\text{ ft } 9\text{ in} = & -\ 7\text{ ft}\ \ \ 9\text{ in} \\ \hline & 1\text{ ft}\ \ \ 9\text{ in} \end{array}$$

Answer: **(1)** 1 ft 9 in

7.
$$\begin{array}{rr} 5\text{ hours } 13\text{ minutes} = & 4\text{ hours } 73\text{ minutes} \\ -\ 3\text{ hours } 49\text{ minutes} = & -\ 3\text{ hours } 49\text{ minutes} \\ \hline & 1\text{ hour } 24\text{ minutes} \end{array}$$

Answer: **(5)** 1 hr 24 min

8.
$$\begin{array}{r} 8\text{ feet}\quad 10\text{ inches} + \frac{2}{4}\text{ inches} = 8\text{ ft } 10\tfrac{1}{2}\text{ in} \\ 4\ \overline{)\ 35\text{ feet}\quad 6\text{ inches}} \\ 32\text{ feet} \\ \hline 3\text{ feet} = 36\text{ inches} \\ 42\text{ inches} \\ 40\text{ inches} \\ \hline 2\text{ inches} \end{array}$$

Answer: **(4)** 8 ft $10\frac{1}{2}$ in

9.
1 yd = 36 in
126 ÷ 36 = 3.5

Answer: **(1)** 3.5

10.
1 gal = 4 qt = 8 pt
Therefore, 1 pt = 231 cubic inches ÷ 8
= 28.875 cubic inches
3 pts = 3 × 28.875 cubic inches
= 86.625 cubic inches

Answer: **(4)** 87

11.
$$\begin{array}{rr} 5\text{ feet} & 2\frac{3}{4}\text{ inches} \\ 8\text{ feet} & \frac{1}{2}\text{ inches} \\ + & 12\frac{1}{2}\text{ inches} \\ \hline 13\text{ feet} & 15\frac{3}{4}\text{ inches} \\ = 14\text{ feet} & 3\frac{3}{4}\text{ inches} \end{array}$$

Answer: **(1)** 14 feet $3\frac{3}{4}$ inches

12.
$$\begin{array}{rr} 5\text{ hr} & 13\text{ min} \\ 3\text{ hr} & 49\text{ min} \\ + & 14\text{ min} \\ \hline 8\text{ hr} & 76\text{ min} \\ = 9\text{ hr} & 16\text{ min} \end{array}$$

Answer: **(2)** 9 hr 16 min

13.
1 foot = 12 inches
$1\frac{1}{2}$ feet = $1\frac{1}{2}$ × 12 inches = 18 inches
1 inch = 2.54 cm

Therefore,
18 inches = 18 × 2.54 cm
= 45.72 cm

Answer: **(2)** 46 cm

14.
1 micromillimeter = .000001 mm
17 micromillimeters = 17 × .000001 mm
= .000017 mm

Answer: **(3)** .000017 mm

15.
4200 ml = 4200 × .001 l
= 4.200 l

Answer: **(5)** 4.2

16. Convert all of the units to grams:

$$\begin{array}{rcrcr} 26\text{ dg} & = & 26 \times .1\text{ g} & = & 2.6\text{ g} \\ .4\text{ kg} & = & .4 \times 1000\text{ g} & = & 400\text{ g} \\ 5\text{ g} & = & & & 5\text{ g} \\ 184\text{ cg} & = & 184 \times .01\text{ g} & = & 1.84\text{ g} \\ \hline & & & & 409.44\text{ g} \end{array}$$

Answer: **(3)** 409.44 g

17. $1.28 \text{ liters} \div 4 = .32 \text{ liters}$

$32 \text{ liters} = .32 \div .001 \text{ m}l$

$= 320 \text{ m}l$

Answer: **(3)** 320

18. Find the number of liters in 1 gallon:

$1 \text{ qt} = .95\ l$

$1 \text{ gal} = 4 \text{ qts}$

$1 \text{ gal} = 4 \times .95\ l = 3.8\ l$

Multiply to find the number of liters in 5 gallons:

$5 \text{ gal} = 5 \times 3.8\ l = 19\ l$

Answer: **(1)** 19

19. $°F = \frac{9}{5} \times 12° + 32°$

$= \frac{108°}{5} + 32°$

$= 21.6° + 32°$

$= 53.6°$

Answer: **(5)** 54°

20. $°C = \frac{5}{9}(68° - 32°)$

$= \frac{5}{\cancel{9}_1} \times \cancel{36}^4°$

$= 20°$

Answer: **(3)** 20°

STATISTICS AND PROBABILITY

Statistics

1. The **averages** used in statistics include the **arithmetic mean**, the **median** and the **mode**.

2. a. The most commonly used average of a group of numbers is the **arithmetic mean**. It is found by adding the numbers given and then dividing this sum by the number of items being averaged.

   Illustration: Find the arithmetic mean of 2, 8, 5, 9, 6, and 12.

   SOLUTION: There are 6 numbers.

$$\text{Arithmetic mean} = \frac{2 + 8 + 5 + 9 + 6 + 12}{6}$$
$$= \frac{42}{6}$$
$$= 7$$

   Answer: The arithmetic mean is 7.

   b. If a problem calls for simply the "average" or the "mean," it is referring to the arithmetic mean.

3. If a group of numbers is arranged in order, the middle number is called the **median**. If there is no single middle number (this occurs when there is an even number of items), the median is found by computing the arithmetic mean of the two middle numbers.

   Example: The median of 6, 8, 10, 12, and 14 is 10.

   Example: The median of 6, 8, 10, 12, 14, and 16 is the arithmetic mean of 10 and 12.

$$\frac{10 + 12}{2} = \frac{22}{2} = 11.$$

4. The **mode** of a group of numbers is the number that appears most often.

   Example: The mode of 10, 5, 7, 9, 12, 5, 10, 5 and 9 is 5.

5. To obtain the average of quantities that are weighted:

   a. Set up a table listing the quantities, their respective weights, and their respective values.

   b. Multiply the value of each quantity by its respective weight.

   c. Add up these products.

   d. Add up the weights.

   e. Divide the sum of the products by the sum of the weights.

Illustration: Assume that the weights for the following subjects are: English 3, History 2, Mathematics 2, Foreign Languages 2, and Art 1. What would be the average of a student whose marks are: English 80, History 85, Algebra 84, Spanish 82, and Art 90?

SOLUTION:

Subject	*Weight*	*Mark*
English	3	80
History	2	85
Algebra	2	84
Spanish	2	82
Art	1	90

English	$3 \times 80 = 240$
History	$2 \times 85 = 170$
Algebra	$2 \times 84 = 168$
Spanish	$2 \times 82 = 164$
Art	$1 \times 90 = 90$
	832

Sum of the weights: $3 + 2 + 2 + 2 + 1 = 10$

$832 \div 10 = 83.2$

Answer: Average = 83.2

Probability

6. The study of probability deals with predicting the outcome of chance events; that is, events in which one has no control over the results.

   Examples: Tossing a coin, rolling dice, and drawing concealed objects from a bag are chance events.

7. The probability of a particular outcome is equal to the number of ways that outcome can occur, divided by the total number of possible outcomes.

   Example: In tossing a coin, there are 2 possible outcomes: heads or tails. The probability that the coin will turn up heads is $1 \div 2$ or $\frac{1}{2}$.

   Example: If a bag contains 5 balls of which 3 are red, the probability of drawing a red ball is $\frac{3}{5}$. The probability of drawing a non-red ball is $\frac{2}{5}$.

8. a. If an event is certain, its probability is 1.

   Example: If a bag contains only red balls, the probability of drawing a red ball is 1.

   b. If an event is impossible, its probability is 0.

   Example: If a bag contains only red balls, the probability of drawing a green ball is 0.

9. Probability may be expressed in fractional, decimal, or percent form.

   Example: An event having a probability of $\frac{1}{2}$ is said to be 50% probable.

10. A probability determined by random sampling of a group of items is assumed to apply to other items in that group and in other similar groups.

Illustration: A random sampling of 100 items produced in a factory shows that 7 are defective. How many items of the total production of 50,000 can be expected to be defective?

SOLUTION: The probability of an item being defective is $\frac{7}{100}$, or 7%. Of the total production, 7% can be expected to be defective.

$$7\% \times 50{,}000 = .07 \times 50{,}000 = 3500$$

Answer: 3500 items

Practice Problems Involving Statistics and Probability

1. The arithmetic mean of 73.8, 92.2, 64.7, 43.8, 56.5, and 46.4 is
(1) 60.6 (2) 61.00 (3) 61.28 (4) 61.48 (5) 62.9

2. The median of the numbers 8, 5, 7, 5, 9, 9, 1, 8, 10, 5, and 10 is
(1) 5 (2) 7 (3) 8 (4) 9 (5) 10

3. The mode of the numbers 16, 15, 17, 12, 15, 15, 18, 19, and 18 is
(1) 15 (2) 16 (3) 17 (4) 18 (5) 19

4. A clerk filed 73 forms on Monday, 85 forms on Tuesday, 54 on Wednesday, 92 on Thursday, and 66 on Friday. What was the average number of forms filed per day?
(1) 60 (2) 72 (3) 74 (4) 92 (5) 94

5. The grades received on a test by twenty students were: 100, 55, 75, 80, 65, 65, 85, 90, 80, 45, 40, 50, 85, 85, 85, 80, 80, 70, 65, and 60. The average of these grades is
(1) 70 (2) 72 (3) 77 (4) 80 (5) 87

6. A buyer purchased 75 six-inch rulers costing 15¢ each, 100 one-foot rulers costing 30¢ each, and 50 one-yard rulers costing 72¢ each. What was the average price per ruler?
(1) $26\frac{1}{8}$¢ (2) $34\frac{1}{3}$¢ (3) 39¢ (4) 42¢ (5) 49¢

7. What is the average of a student who received 90 in English, 84 in Algebra, 75 in French, and 76 in Music, if the subjects have the following weights: English 4, Algebra 3, French 3, and Music 1?
(1) 81 (2) $81\frac{1}{2}$ (3) 82 (4) 83 (5) 84

Items 8 to 11 refer to the following information.

A census shows that on a certain block the number of children in each family is 3, 4, 4, 0, 1, 2, 0, 2, and 2, respectively.

8. Find the average number of children per family.
(1) 2 (2) $2\frac{1}{2}$ (3) 3 (4) $3\frac{1}{2}$ (5) 4

9. Find the median number of children.
(1) 6 (2) 5 (3) 4 (4) 3 (5) 2

10. Find the mode of the number of children.
    (1) 0
    (2) 1
    (3) 2
    (4) 4
    (5) 5

11. What is the probability that a family chosen at random on this block will have 4 children?
    (1) $\frac{4}{9}$
    (2) $\frac{2}{9}$
    (3) $\frac{4}{7}$
    (4) $\frac{2}{1}$
    (5) $\frac{4}{7}$

12. What is the probability that an even number will come up when a single die is thrown?
    (1) $\frac{1}{6}$
    (2) $\frac{1}{5}$
    (3) $\frac{1}{4}$
    (4) $\frac{1}{3}$
    (5) $\frac{1}{2}$

13. A bag contains 3 black balls, 2 yellow balls, and 4 red balls. What is the probability of drawing a black ball?
    (1) $\frac{1}{2}$
    (2) $\frac{1}{3}$
    (3) $\frac{2}{3}$
    (4) $\frac{4}{9}$
    (5) $\frac{4}{5}$

14. In a group of 1000 adults, 682 are women. What is the probability that a person chosen at random from this group will be a man?
    (1) .318
    (2) .682
    (3) .5
    (4) 1
    (5) 1.5

15. In a balloon factory, a random sampling of 100 balloons showed that 3 had pinholes in them. In a sampling of 2500 balloons, how many may be expected to have pinholes?
    (1) 30
    (2) 75
    (3) 100
    (4) 750
    (5) 800

Statistics and Probability Problems — Correct Answers

1. **(5)**	6. **(2)**	11. **(2)**
2. **(3)**	7. **(4)**	12. **(5)**
3. **(1)**	8. **(1)**	13. **(2)**
4. **(3)**	9. **(5)**	14. **(1)**
5. **(2)**	10. **(3)**	15. **(2)**

Problem Solutions — Statistics and Probability

1. Find the sum of the values:

   $73.8 + 92.2 + 64.7 + 43.8 + 56.5 + 46.4 = 377.4$

   There are 6 values.

   $$\text{Arithmetic mean} = \frac{377.4}{6} = 62.9$$

   Answer: **(5)** 62.9

2. Arrange the numbers in order:

   1, 5, 5, 5, 7, 8, 8, 9, 9, 10, 10

   The middle number, or median, is 8.

   Answer: **(3)** 8

3. The mode is that number appearing most frequently. The number 15 appears three times.

   Answer: **(1)** 15

4. $$\text{Average} = \frac{73 + 85 + 54 + 92 + 66}{5} = \frac{370}{5} = 74$$

Answer: **(3)** 74

5. Sum of the grades = 1440.

$$\frac{1440}{20} = 72$$

Answer: **(2)** 72

6.
$$\begin{aligned} 75 \times 15¢ &= 1125¢ \\ 100 \times 30¢ &= 3000¢ \\ \underline{50} \times 72¢ &= \underline{3600¢} \\ 225 \quad & \quad 7725¢ \end{aligned}$$

$$\frac{7725¢}{225} = 34\tfrac{1}{3}¢$$

Answer: **(2)** $34\frac{1}{3}$¢

7.

Subject	*Grade*	*Weight*
English	90	4
Algebra	84	3
French	75	3
Music	76	1

$(90 \times 4) + (84 \times 3) + (75 \times 3) + (76 \times 1)$

$360 + 252 + 225 + 76 = 913$

Weight $= 4 + 3 + 3 + 1 = 11$

$913 \div 11 = 83$ average

Answer: **(4)** 83

8. $$\text{Average} = \frac{3+4+4+0+1+2+0+2+2}{9} = \frac{18}{9} = 2$$

Answer: **(1)** 2

9. Arrange the numbers in order:

0, 0, 1, 2, 2, 2, 3, 4, 4

Of the 9 numbers, the fifth (middle) number is 2.

Answer: **(5)** 2

10. The number appearing most often is 2.

Answer: **(3)** 2

11. There are 9 families, 2 of which have 4 children. The probability is $\frac{2}{9}$.

Answer: **(2)** $\frac{2}{9}$

12. Of the 6 possible numbers, three are even (2, 4, and 6). The probability is $\frac{3}{6}$, or $\frac{1}{2}$.

Answer: **(5)** $\frac{1}{2}$

13. There are 9 balls in all. The probability of drawing a black ball is $\frac{3}{9}$, or $\frac{1}{3}$.

Answer: **(2)** $\frac{1}{3}$.

14. If 682 people of the 1000 are women, $1000 - 682 = 318$ are men. The probability of choosing a man is $\frac{318}{1000} = .318$.

Answer: **(1)** .318

15. There is a probability of $\frac{3}{100} = 3\%$ that a balloon may have a pinhole.

$3\% \times 2500 = 75.00$

Answer: **(2)** 75

GRAPHS

1. **Graphs** illustrate comparisons and trends in statistical information. The most commonly used graphs are **bar graphs**, **line graphs**, **circle graphs**, and **pictographs**.

Bar Graphs

2. **Bar graphs** are used to compare various quantities. Each bar may represent a single quantity or may be divided to represent several quantities.

3. Bar graphs may have horizontal or vertical bars.

Illustration:

Municipal Expenditures, Per Capita

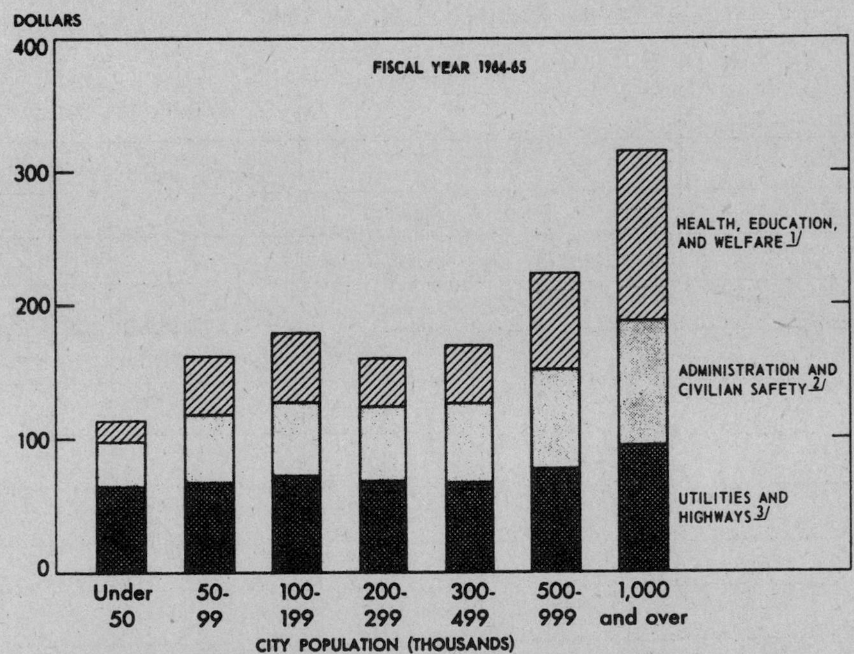

1/PUBLIC WELFARE, EDUCATION, HOSPITALS, HEALTH, LIBRARIES, AND HOUSING AND URBAN RENEWAL.
2/POLICE AND FIRE PROTECTION, FINANCIAL ADMINISTRATION, GENERAL CONTROL, GENERAL PUBLIC BUILDINGS, INTEREST ON GENERAL DEBT, AND OTHER.
3/HIGHWAYS, SEWERAGE, SANITATION, PARKS AND RECREATION, AND UTILITIES.
SOURCE: DEPARTMENT OF COMMERCE.

Question 1: What was the approximate municipal expenditure per capita in cities having populations of 200,000 to 299,000?

Answer: The middle bar of the seven shown represents cities having populations from 200,000 to 299,000. This bar reaches about halfway between 100 and 200. Therefore, the per capita expenditure was approximately $150.

Question 2: Which cities spent the most per capita on health, education, and welfare?

Answer: The bar for cities having populations of 1,000,000 and over has a larger striped section than the other bars. Therefore, those cities spent the most.

Question 3: Of the three categories of expenditures, which was least dependent on city size?

Answer: The expenditures for utilities and highways, the darkest part of each bar, varied least as city size increased.

Line Graphs

4. **Line graphs** are used to show trends, often over a period of time.

5. A line graph may include more than one line, with each line representing a different item.

Illustration:

The graph below indicates at 5 year intervals the number of citations issued for various offenses from the year 1960 to the year 1980.

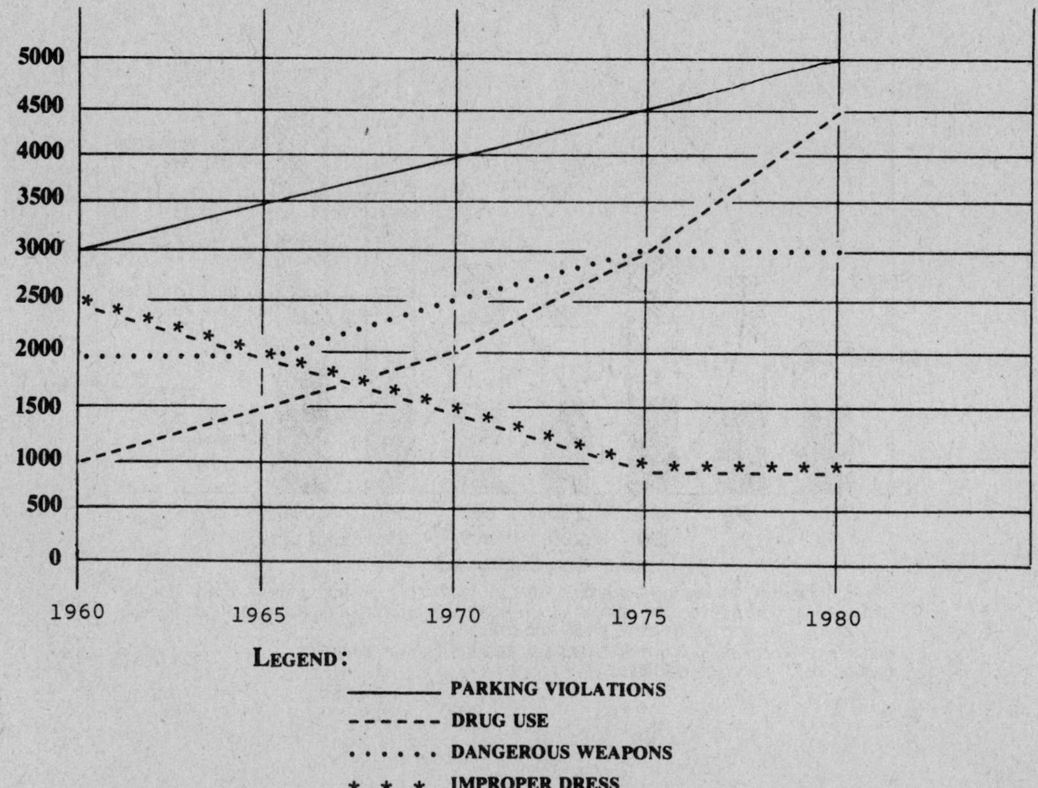

Question 4: Over the 20-year period, which offense shows an average rate of increase of more than 150 citations per year?

Answer: Drug use citations increased from 1000 in 1960 to 4500 in 1980. The average increase over the 20-year period is $\frac{3500}{20} = 175$.

Question 5: Over the 20-year period, which offense shows a constant rate of increase or decrease?

Answer: A straight line indicates a constant rate of increase or decrease. Of the four lines, the one representing parking violations is the only straight one.

Question 6: Which offense shows a total increase or decrease of 50% for the full 20-year period?

Answer: Dangerous weapons citations increased from 2000 in 1960 to 3000 in 1980, which is an increase of 50%.

Circle Graphs

6. **Circle graphs** are used to show the relationship of various parts of a quantity to each other and to the whole quantity.

7. Percents are often used in circle graphs. The 360 degrees of the circle represents 100%.

8. Each part of the circle graph is called a **sector**.

Illustration:

The following circle graph shows how the federal budget of $300.4 billion was spent.

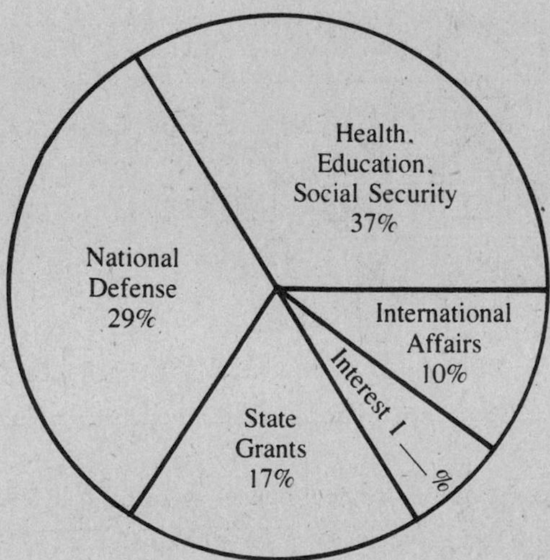

Question 7: What is the value of I?

Answer: There must be a total of 100% in a circle graph. The sum of the other sectors is:

$$17\% + 29\% + 37\% + 10\% = 93\%$$

Therefore, $I = 100\% - 93\% = 7\%$.

Question 8: How much money was actually spent on national defense?

Answer: $29\% \times \$300.4 \text{ billion} = \$87.116 \text{ billion}$
$= \$87{,}116{,}000{,}000$

Question 9: How much more money was spent on state grants than on interest?

Answer: $17\% - 7\% = 10\%$
$10\% \times \$300.4 \text{ billion} = \$30.04 \text{ billion}$
$= \$30{,}040{,}000{,}000$

Pictographs

9. **Pictographs** allow comparisons of quantities by using symbols. Each symbol represents a given number of a particular item.

Illustration:

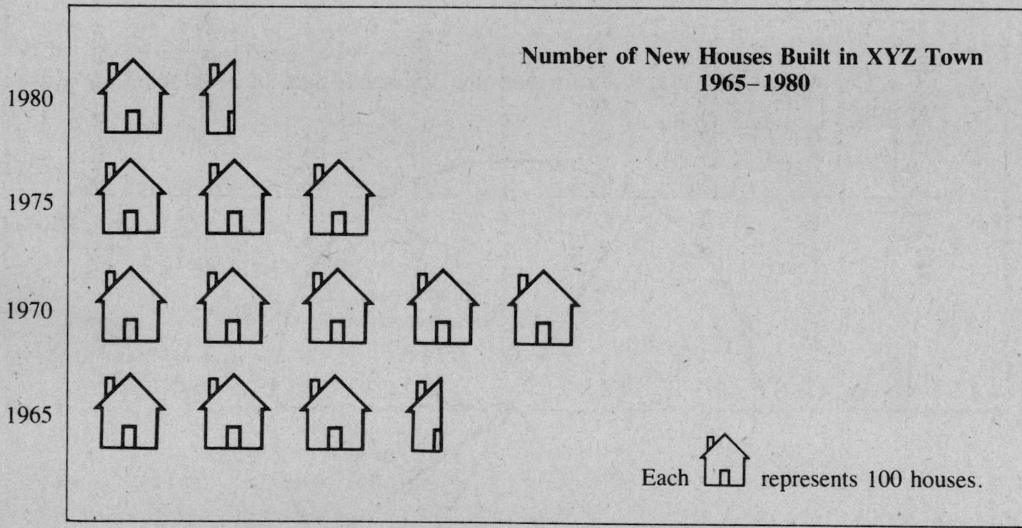

Question 10: How many more new houses were built in 1970 than in 1975?

Answer: There are two more symbols for 1970 than for 1975. Each symbol represents 100 houses. Therefore, 200 more houses were built in 1970.

Question 11: How many new houses were built in 1965?

Answer: There are $3\frac{1}{2}$ symbols shown for 1965; $3\frac{1}{2} \times 100 = 350$ houses.

Question 12: In which year were half as many houses built as in 1975?

Answer: In 1975, $3 \times 100 = 300$ houses were built. Half of 300, or 150, houses were built in 1980.

Practice Problems Involving Graphs

Items 1 to 4 refer to the following graph.

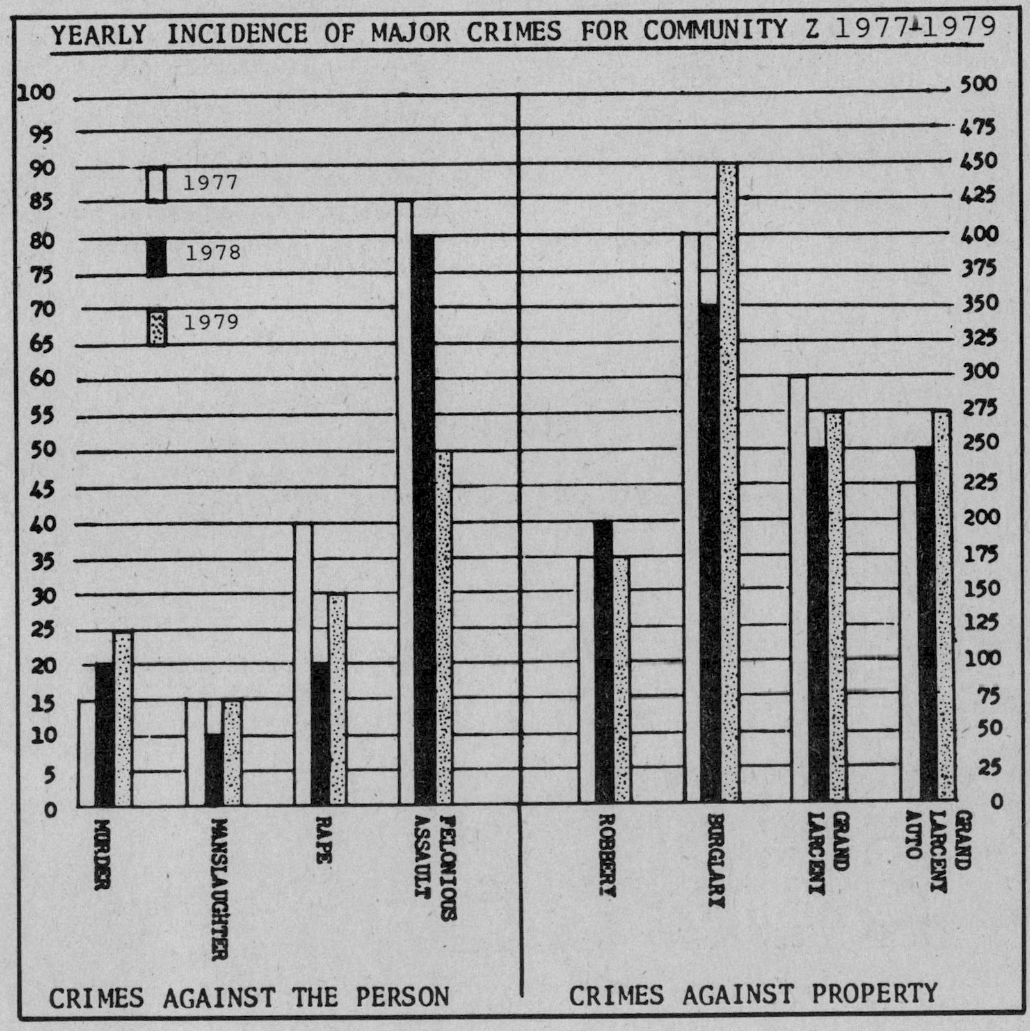

1. In 1979, the incidence of which of the following crimes was greater than in the previous two years?
   (1) grand larceny
   (2) murder
   (3) rape
   (4) robbery
   (5) none of the above

2. If the incidence of burglary in 1980 had increased over 1979 by the same number as it had increased in 1979 over 1978, then the average for this crime for the four-year period from 1977 through 1980 would be most nearly
   (1) 100
   (2) 400
   (3) 425
   (4) 440
   (5) 450

3. The above graph indicates that the *percentage* increase in grand larceny auto from 1978 to 1979 was:
   (1) 5%
   (2) 10%
   (3) 15%
   (4) 20%
   (5) 25%

4. Which of the following cannot be determined because there is not enough information in the above graph to do so?

   (1) For the 3-year period, what percentage of all "Crimes Against the Person" involved murders committed in 1978?
   (2) For the 3-year period, what percentage of all "Major Crimes" was committed in the first six months of 1978?
   (3) Which major crimes followed a pattern of continuing yearly increases for the 3-year period?
   (4) For 1979, what was the ratio of robbery, burglary, and grand larceny crimes?
   (5) none of the above

Items 5 to 7 refer to the following graph.

In the graph below, the lines labeled "A" and "B" represent the cumulative progress in the work of two file clerks, each of whom was given 500 consecutively numbered applications to file in the proper cabinets over a five-day work week.

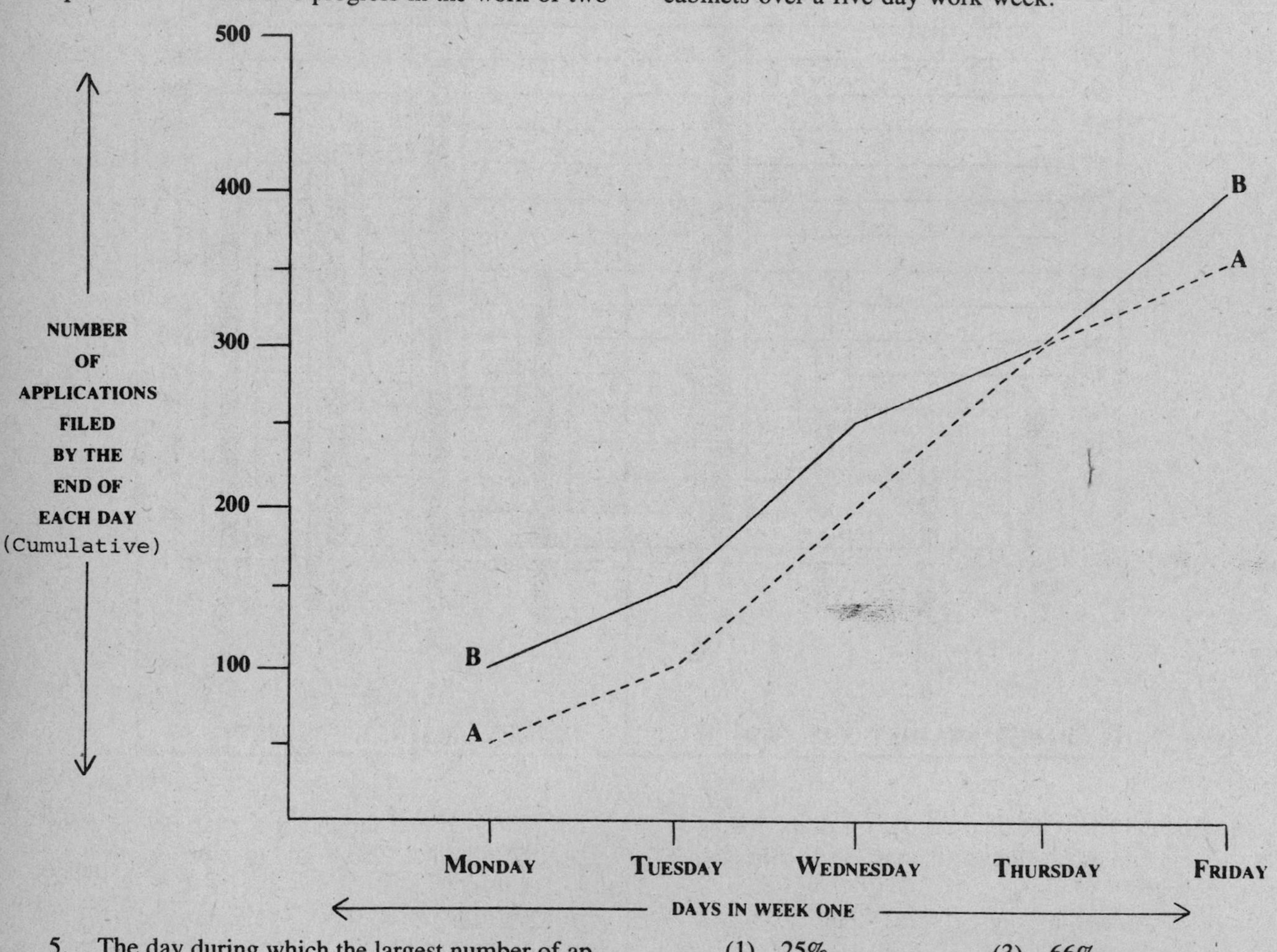

5. The day during which the largest number of applications was filed by both clerks was
   (1) Monday
   (2) Tuesday
   (3) Wednesday
   (4) Thursday
   (5) Friday

6. At the end of the second day, the percentage of applications still to be filed was
   (1) 25%
   (2) 50%
   (3) 66%
   (4) 75%
   (5) 37%

7. Assuming that the production pattern is the same the following week as the week shown in the chart, the day on which Clerk B will finish this assignment will be
   (1) Monday
   (2) Tuesday
   (3) Wednesday
   (4) Thursday
   (5) Friday

Items 8 to 11 refer to the following graph.

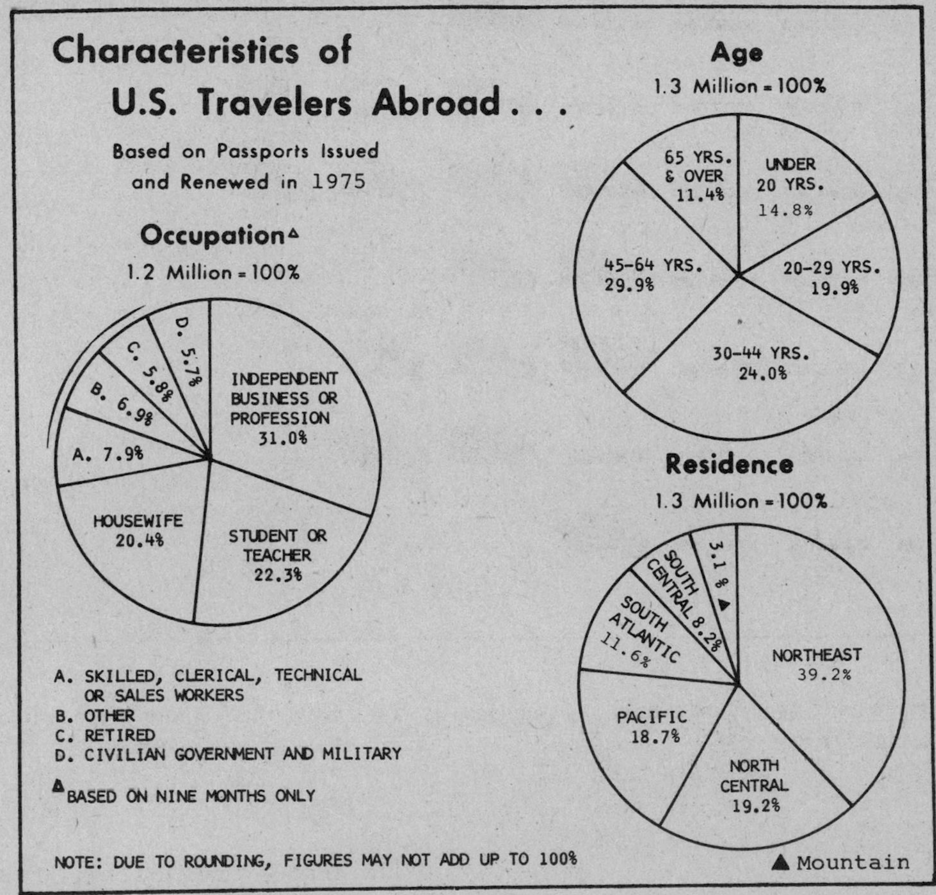

8. Approximately how many persons aged 29 or younger traveled abroad in 1975?
   (1) 175,000
   (2) 245,000
   (3) 385,000
   (4) 400,000
   (5) 450,000

9. Of the people who did *not* live in the Northeast, what percent came from the North Central states?
   (1) 19.2%
   (2) 19.9%
   (3) 26.5%
   (4) 30.00%
   (5) 31.6%

10. The fraction of travelers from the four smallest occupation groups is most nearly equal to the fraction of travelers
    (1) under age 20, and 65 and over, combined
    (2) from the North Central and Mountain states
    (3) between 45 and 64 years of age
    (4) from the Housewife and Other categories
    (5) from the Pacific states

11. If the South Central, Mountain, and Pacific sections were considered as a single classification, how many degrees would its sector include?
    (1) 30°
    (2) 67°
    (3) 108°
    (4) 120°
    (5) 130°

Items 12 to 15 refer to the following graph.

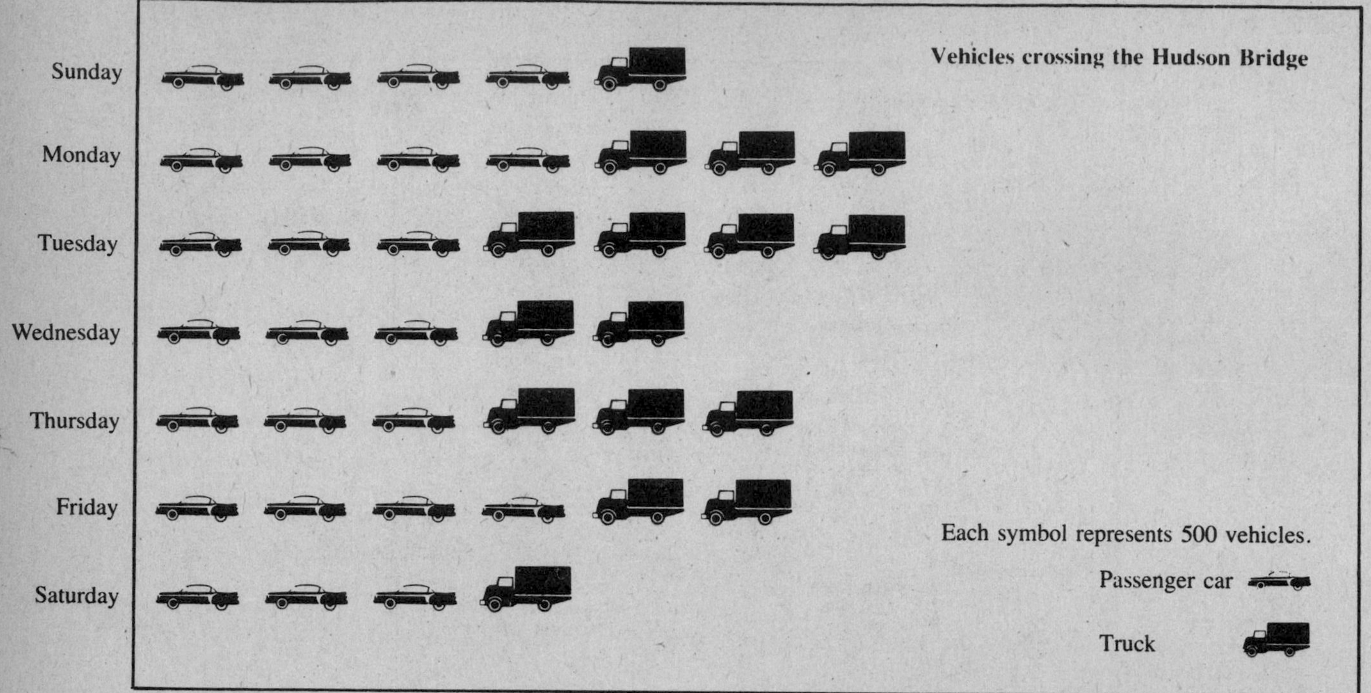

12. What percent of the total number of vehicles on Wednesday were cars?
    (1) 30%
    (2) 60%
    (3) 20%
    (4) 50%
    (5) 75%

13. What was the total number of vehicles crossing the bridge on Tuesday?
    (1) 7
    (2) 700
    (3) 1100
    (4) 3500
    (5) 3700

14. How many more trucks crossed on Monday than on Saturday?
    (1) 200
    (2) 1000
    (3) 1500
    (4) 2000
    (5) 2500

15. If trucks paid a toll of $1.00 and cars paid a toll of $.50, how much money was collected in tolls on Friday?
    (1) $400
    (2) $600
    (3) $1000
    (4) $1500
    (5) $2000

Graphs — Correct Answers

1. **(2)**	6. **(4)**	11. **(3)**
2. **(4)**	7. **(1)**	12. **(2)**
3. **(2)**	8. **(5)**	13. **(4)**
4. **(2)**	9. **(5)**	14. **(2)**
5. **(3)**	10. **(1)**	15. **(5)**

Problem Solutions — Graphs

1. The incidence of murder increased from 15 in 1977 to 20 in 1978 to 25 in 1979.

   Answer: **(2)** murder

2. The incidence of burglary in 1977 was 400; in 1978 it was 350; and in 1979 it was 450. The increase from 1978 to 1979 was 100. An increase of 100 from 1979 gives 550 in 1980.

   The average of 400, 350, 450, and 550 is

   $$\frac{400 + 350 + 450 + 550}{4} = \frac{1750}{4} = 437.5$$

   Answer: **(4)** 440

3. The incidence of grand larceny auto went from 250 in 1978 to 275 in 1979, an increase of 25.

   The percent increase is

   $$\frac{25}{250} = .10 = 10\%$$

   Answer: **(2)** 10%

4. This graph gives information by year, not month. It is impossible to determine from the graph the percentage of crimes committed during the first six months of any year.

   Answer: **(2)**

5. For both A and B, the greatest increase in the cumulative totals occurred from the end of Tuesday until the end of Wednesday. Therefore, the largest number of applications was filed on Wednesday.

   Answer: **(3)** Wednesday

6. By the end of Tuesday, A had filed 100 applications and B had filed 150, for a total of 250. This left 750 of the original 1000 applications.

   $$\frac{750}{1000} = .75 = 75\%$$

   Answer: **(4)** 75%

7. During Week One, Clerk B files 100 applications on Monday, 50 on Tuesday, 100 on Wednesday, 50 on Thursday, and 100 on Friday, a total of 400. On Monday of Week Two, he will file numbers 401 to 500.

   Answer: **(1)** Monday

8. | | |
   |---|---|
   | 20–29 yrs.: | 19.9% |
   | Under 20 yrs.: | +14.8% |
   | | 34.7% |

   $$34.7\% \times 1.3 \text{ million} = .4511 \text{ million} = 451{,}100$$

   Answer: **(5)** 450,000

9. 100% − 39.2% = 60.8% did not live in Northeast.

   19.2% lived in North Central

   $$\frac{19.2}{60.8} = .316 \text{ approximately}$$

   Answer: **(5)** 31.6%

10. Four smallest groups of occupation:

    $$7.9 + 6.9 + 5.8 + 5.7 = 26.3$$

    Age groups under 20 and over 65:

    $$14.8 + 11.4 = 26.2$$

    Answer: **(1)**

11. | | |
    |---|---|
    | South Central: | 8.2% |
    | Mountain: | 3.1% |
    | Pacific: | 18.7% |
    | | 30.0% |

    $$30\% \times 360^\circ = 108^\circ$$

    Answer: **(3)** 108°

12. There are 5 vehicle symbols, of which 3 are cars. $\frac{3}{5} = 60\%$

    Answer: **(2)** 60%

13. On Tuesday, there were 3 × 500 = 1500 cars and 4 × 500 = 2000 trucks. The total number of vehicles was 3500.

    Answer: **(4)** 3500

14. The graph shows 2 more truck symbols on Monday than on Saturday. Each symbols represents 500 trucks, so there were 2 × 500 = 1000 more trucks on Monday.

    Answer: **(2)** 1000

15. On Friday there were

    4 × 500 = 2000 cars
    2 × 500 = 1000 trucks

Car tolls:	2000 × $ .50 =	$1000
Truck tolls:	1000 × $1.00 =	+ $1000
Total tolls:		$2000

    Answer: **(5)** $2000

PAYROLL

1. **Salaries** are computed over various time periods: hourly, daily, weekly, biweekly (every 2 weeks), semimonthly (twice each month), monthly, and yearly.

2. **Overtime** is usually computed as "time and a half"; that is, each hour in excess of the number of hours in the standard workday or workweek is paid at $1\frac{1}{2}$ times the regular hourly rate. Some companies pay "double time," twice the regular hourly rate, for work on Sundays and holidays.

   Illustration: An employee is paid weekly, based on a 40-hour workweek, with time and a half for overtime. If the employee's regular hourly rate is $4.50, how much will he earn for working 47 hours in one week?

   SOLUTION: Overtime hours = 47 − 40 = 7 hours
   Overtime pay = $1\frac{1}{2} \times \$4.50 = \$6.75$ per hour

   Overtime pay for 7 hours:
   $7 \times \$6.75 = \$47.25$

   Regular pay for 40 hours:
   $40 \times \$4.50 = \$180.00$
   Total pay = $47.25 + $180 = $227.25

   Answer: $227.25

3. a. In occupations such as retail sales, real estate, and insurance, earnings may be based on **commission**, which is a percent of the sales or a percent of the value of the transactions that are completed.

   b. Earnings may be from straight commission only, from salary plus commission, or from a commission that is graduated according to transaction volume.

   Illustration: A salesman earns a salary of $200 weekly, plus a commission based on sales volume for the week. The commission is 7% for the first $1500 of sales and 10% for all sales in excess of $1500. How much did he earn in a week in which his sales totaled $3200?

   SOLUTION:

$3200 − $1500 =	$1700	excess sales
.07 × $1500 =	$105	commission on first $1500
.10 × $1700 =	$170	commission on excess sales
	+ $200	weekly salary
	$475	total earnings

   Answer: $475

4. **Gross pay** refers to the amount of money earned whether from salary, commission, or both, before any deductions are made.

5. There are several deductions that are usually made from gross pay:

   a. **Withholding tax** is the amount of money withheld for income tax. It is based on wages, marital status, and number of exemptions (also called allowances) claimed by the employee. The withholding tax is found by referring to tables supplied by the federal, state or city governments.

Example:

Married Persons — Weekly Payroll Period

Wages		Number of withholding allowances claimed				
At least	But less than	0	1	2	3	4
		Amount of income tax to be withheld				
400	410	73.00	67.60	62.30	57.70	53.10
410	420	75.80	70.40	65.00	60.10	55.50
420	430	78.60	73.20	67.80	62.50	57.90
430	440	81.40	76.00	70.60	65.20	60.30
440	450	84.20	78.80	73.40	68.00	62.70
450	460	87.00	81.60	76.20	70.80	65.40
460	470	90.20	84.40	79.00	73.60	68.20
470	480	93.40	87.30	81.80	76.40	71.00
480	490	96.60	90.50	84.60	79.20	73.80
490	500	99.80	93.70	87.50	82.00	76.60

Based on the above table, an employee who is married, claims three exemptions, and is paid a weekly wage of $434.50 will have $65.20 withheld for income tax. If the same employee earned $440 weekly it would be necessary to look on the next line for "at least $440 but less than $450" to find that $68.00 would be withheld.

   b. The FICA (Federal Insurance Contribution Act) tax is also called the Social Security tax. In 1982, the FICA tax was 6.7% of the first $32,400 of annual wages; the wages in excess of $32,400 were not subject to the tax.

   The FICA may be found by multiplying the wages up to and including $32,400 by .067, or by using tables such as the one below.

Example:

Social Security Employee Tax Table

6.7 percent employee tax deductions

Wages			Wages		
At least	But less than	Tax	At least	But less than	Tax
$78.14	$78.28	$5.24	$84.26	$84.40	$5.65
78.29	78.43	5.25	84.41	84.55	5.66
78.44	78.58	5.26	84.56	84.70	5.67
78.59	78.73	5.27	84.71	84.85	5.68
78.74	78.88	5.28	84.86	84.99	5.69
78.89	79.03	5.29	85.00	85.14	5.70
79.04	79.18	5.30	85.15	85.29	5.71
79.19	79.33	5.31	85.30	85.44	5.72
79.34	79.48	5.32	85.45	85.59	5.73
79.49	79.63	5.33	85.60	85.74	5.74
79.64	79.78	5.34	85.75	85.89	5.75
79.79	79.93	5.35			

According to the table above, the Social Security tax, or FICA tax, on wages of \$84.80 is \$5.68. The FICA tax on \$84.92 is \$5.69.

Illustration: Based on 1982 tax figures, what is the total FICA tax on an annual salary of \$30,000?

SOLUTION: .067 × \$30,000 = \$2010.00

Answer: \$2010.00

c. Other deductions that may be made from gross pay are deductions for pension plans, loan payments, payroll savings plans, and union dues.

6. The **net pay**, or **take-home pay**, is equal to gross pay less the total deductions.

Illustration: Mr. Jay earns \$550 salary per week, with the following deductions: federal withholding tax, \$106.70; FICA tax, \$36.85; state tax, \$22.83; pension payment, \$6.42; union dues, \$5.84. How much take-home pay does he receive?

SOLUTION: Deductions:

	\$106.70
	36.85
	22.83
	6.42
	5.84
	\$178.64

Gross pay	=	\$550.00
Deductions	=	− 178.64
Net pay	=	\$371.36

Answer: His take-home pay is \$371.36

Practice Problems Involving Payroll

1. Jane Rose's semimonthly salary is \$750. Her yearly salary is
   (1) \$9000
   (2) \$12,500
   (3) \$18,000
   (4) \$19,500
   (5) \$21,000

2. John Doe earns \$300 for a 40-hour week. If he receives time and a half for overtime, what is his hourly overtime wage?
   (1) \$7.50
   (2) \$9.25
   (3) \$10.50
   (4) \$11.25
   (5) \$15.00

3. Which salary is greater?
   (1) \$50 daily
   (2) \$350 weekly
   (3) \$1378 monthly
   (4) \$17,000 annually
   (5) \$646 biweekly

4. A factory worker is paid on the basis of an 8-hour day, with an hourly rate of \$3.50 and time and a half for overtime. Find his gross pay for a week in which he worked the following hours: Monday, 8; Tuesday, 9; Wednesday, $9\frac{1}{2}$; Thursday, $8\frac{1}{2}$; Friday, 9.
   (1) \$140
   (2) \$154
   (3) \$161
   (4) \$174
   (5) \$231

Questions 5 and 6 refer to the following table:

Single Persons — Weekly Payroll Period

Wages		Number of withholding allowances claimed				
At least	But less than	0	1	2	3	4
		Amount of income tax to be withheld				
370	380	83.60	77.10	70.50	64.50	58.80
380	390	87.00	80.50	73.90	67.50	61.80
390	400	90.40	83.90	77.30	70.80	64.80
400	410	93.80	87.30	80.70	74.20	67.80
410	420	97.20	90.70	84.10	77.60	71.10
420	430	100.60	94.10	87.50	81.00	74.50
430	440	104.10	97.50	90.90	84.40	77.90
440	450	108.00	100.90	94.30	87.80	81.30
450	460	111.90	104.40	97.70	91.20	84.70
460	470	115.80	108.30	101.10	94.60	88.10

5. According to the table above, if an employee is single and has one exemption, the income tax withheld from his weekly salary of $389.90 is
   (1) $90.40
   (2) $87.00
   (3) $83.90
   (4) $83.60
   (5) $80.50

6. According to the table above, if a single person with two exemptions has $90.90 withheld for income tax, his weekly salary could *not* be
   (1) $430.00
   (2) $435.25
   (3) $437.80
   (4) $439.50
   (5) $440.00

7. Sam Richards earns $1200 monthly. The following deductions are made from his gross pay monthly: federal withholding tax, $188.40; FICA tax, $80.40; state tax, $36.78; city tax, $9.24; savings bond, $37.50; pension plan, $5.32; repayment of pension loan, $42.30. His monthly net pay is
   (1) $800.06
   (2) $807.90
   (3) $808.90
   (4) $809.90
   (5) $810.06

8. A salesman is paid a straight commission that is 23% of his sales. What is his commission on $1260 of sales?
   (1) $232.40
   (2) $246.80
   (3) $259.60
   (4) $289.80
   (5) $298.60

9. Ann Johnson earns a salary of $150 weekly plus a commission of 9% of sales in excess of $500 for the week. For a week in which her sales were $1496, her earnings were
   (1) $223.64
   (2) $239.64
   (3) $253.64
   (4) $284.64
   (5) $293.64

10. A salesperson is paid a 6% commission on the first $2500 of sales for the week, and $7\frac{1}{2}$% on that portion of sales in excess of $2500. What is the commission earned in a week in which sales were $3280?
   (1) $150.00
   (2) $196.80
   (3) $208.50
   (4) $224.30
   (5) $246.00

Payroll Problems — Correct Answers

1. (3)
2. (4)
3. (2)
4. (3)
5. (5)
6. (5)
7. (1)
8. (4)
9. (2)
10. (3)

Payroll Problems — Solutions

1. A semimonthly salary is paid twice a month. She receives $750 × 2 = $1500 each month, which is $1500 × 12 = $18,000 per year.

   Answer: **(3)** $18,000

2. The regular hourly rate is
   $300 ÷ 40 = $7.50

   The overtime rate is
   $7.50 × 1½ = $7.50 × 1.5
   = $11.25

   Answer: **(4)** $11.25

3. Write each salary as its yearly equivalent:

   $50 daily = 50 × 5 days
   = $250 weekly
   = $250 × 52 weeks
   = $13,000 yearly

   $350 weekly = $350 × 52 weeks
   = $18,200 yearly

   $1378 monthly = $1378 × 12 months
   = $16,536 yearly

   $17,000 annually = $17,000 yearly

   $646 biweekly = $646 ÷ 2 weeks
   = $323 weekly
   = $323 × 52 weeks
   = $16,796 yearly

   Answer: **(2)** $350 weekly

4. His overtime hours were:

Monday	0
Tuesday	1
Wednesday	1½
Thursday	½
Friday	1
Total	4 hours overtime

   Overtime rate per hour = 1½ × $3.50
   = 1.5 × $3.50
   = $5.25

   Overtime pay = 4 × $5.25
   = $21

   Regular pay for 8 hours per day for 5 days or 40 hours.

   Regular pay = 40 × $3.50 = $140

   Total wages = $140 + $21 = $161

   Answer: **(3)** $161

5. The correct amount is found on the line for wages of at least $380 but less than $390, and in the column under "1" withholding allowance. The amount withheld is $80.50.

   Answer: **(5)** $80.50

6. In the column for 2 exemptions, or withholding allowances, $90.90 is found on the line for wages of at least $430, but less than $440. Choice (D) does not fall within that range.

   Answer: **(5)** $440

7. Deductions:
   $188.40
   80.40
   36.78
   9.24
   37.50
   5.32
   + 42.30
   Total $399.94

   Gross pay = $1200.00
   Total deductions = − 399.94
   $ 800.06

   Answer: **(1)** $800.06

8. 23% of $1260 = .23 × $1260
   = $289.80

   Answer: **(4)** $289.80

9. $1496 − 500 = $996 excess sales
   9% of $996 = .09 × $996
   = $89.64 commission

   $150.00 salary
   + 89.64 commission
   $239.64 total earnings

   Answer: **(2)** $239.64

10. $3280 − $2500 = $780 excess sales

    Commission on $2500:
    .06 × $2500 = $150.00
    Commission on $780:
    .075 × $780 = + 58.50
    Total = $208.50

    Answer: **(3)** $208.50

SEQUENCES

1. A **sequence** is a list of numbers based on a certain pattern. There are three main types of sequences:

   a. If each term in a sequence is being increased or diminished by the same number to form the next term, then it is an **arithmetic sequence**. The number being added or subtracted is called the **common difference**.

   Examples: 2, 4, 6, 8, 10 . . . is an arithmetic sequence in which the common difference is 2.

   14, 11, 8, 5, 2 . . . is an arithmetic sequence in which the common difference is 3.

   b. If each term of a sequence is being multiplied by the same number to form the next term, then it is a **geometric sequence**. The number multiplying each term is called the **common ratio**.

   Examples: 2, 6, 18, 54 . . . is a geometric sequence in which the common ratio is 3.

   64, 16, 4, 1 . . . is a geometric sequence in which the common ratio is $\frac{1}{4}$.

   c. If the sequence is neither arithmetic nor geometric, it is a **miscellaneous sequence**. Such a sequence may have each term a square or a cube, or the difference may be squares or cubes; or there may be a varied pattern in the sequence that must be determined.

2. A sequence may be ascending, that is, the numbers increase; or descending, that is, the numbers decrease.

3. To determine whether the sequence is arithmetic:

   a. If the sequence is ascending, subtract the first term from the second, and the second term from the third. If the difference is the same in both cases, the sequence is arithmetic.

   b. If the sequence is descending, subtract the second term from the first, and the third term from the second. If the difference is the same in both cases, the sequence is arithmetic.

4. To determine whether the sequence is geometric, divide the second term by the first, and the third term by the second. If the ratio is the same in both cases, the sequence is geometric.

5. To find a missing term in an arithmetic sequence that is ascending:

   a. Subtract any term from the one following it to find the common difference.

   b. Add the common difference to the term preceding the missing term.

   c. If the missing term is the first term, it may be found by subtracting the common difference from the second term.

Illustration: What number follows $16\frac{1}{3}$ in this sequence:

$$3,\ 6\tfrac{1}{3},\ 9\tfrac{2}{3},\ 13,\ 16\tfrac{1}{3} \ldots$$

SOLUTION: $6\frac{1}{3} - 3 = 3\frac{1}{3},\ 9\frac{2}{3} - 6\frac{1}{3} = 3\frac{1}{3}$
The sequence is arithmetic; the common difference is $3\frac{1}{3}$.

$$16\tfrac{1}{3} + 3\tfrac{1}{3} = 19\tfrac{2}{3}$$

Answer: The missing term, which is the term following $16\frac{1}{3}$, is $19\frac{2}{3}$.

6. To find a missing term in an arithmetic sequence that is descending:

   a. Subtract any term from the one preceding it to find the common difference.

   b. Subtract the common difference from the term preceding the missing term.

   c. If the missing term is the first term, it may be found by adding the common difference to the second term.

Illustration: Find the first term in the sequence:

$$\_\_\_,\ 16,\ 13\tfrac{1}{2},\ 11,\ 8\tfrac{1}{2},\ 6 \ldots$$

SOLUTION: $16 - 13\frac{1}{2} = 2\frac{1}{2},\ 13\frac{1}{2} - 11 = 2\frac{1}{2}$
The sequence is arithmetic; the common difference is $2\frac{1}{2}$.

$$16 + 2\tfrac{1}{2} = 18\tfrac{1}{2}$$

Answer: The term preceding 16 is $18\frac{1}{2}$.

7. To find a missing term in a geometric sequence:

   a. Divide any term by the one preceding it to find the common ratio.

   b. Multiply the term preceding the missing term by the common ratio.

   c. If the missing term is the first term, it may be found by dividing the second term by the common ratio.

Illustration: Find the missing term in the sequence:

$$2,\ 6,\ 18,\ 54,\ \_\_\_$$

SOLUTION: $6 \div 2 = 3,\ 18 \div 6 = 3$
The sequence is geometric; the common ratio is 3.

$$54 \times 3 = 162$$

Answer: The missing term is 162.

Illustration: Find the missing term in the sequence:

—, 32, 16, 8, 4, 2

SOLUTION: $16 \div 32 = \frac{1}{2}$ (common ratio)

$32 \div \frac{1}{2} = 32 \times \frac{2}{1}$

$= 64$

Answer: The first term is 64.

8. If, after trial, a sequence is neither arithmetic nor geometric, it must be one of a miscellaneous type. Test to see whether it is a sequence of squares or cubes or whether the difference is the square or the cube of the same number; or the same number may be first squared, then cubed, etc.

Practice Problems Involving Sequences

Find the missing term in each of the following sequences:

1. —, 7, 10, 13
2. 5, 10, 20, —, 80
3. 49, 45, 41, —, 33, 29
4. 1.002, 1.004, 1.006, —
5. 1, 4, 9, 16, —
6. 10, $7\frac{7}{8}$, $5\frac{3}{4}$, $3\frac{5}{8}$, —
7. —, 3, $4\frac{1}{2}$, $6\frac{3}{4}$
8. 55, 40, 28, 19, 13, —
9. 9, 3, 1, $\frac{1}{3}$, $\frac{1}{9}$, —
10. 1, 3, 7, 15, 31, —

Sequence Problems — Correct Answers

1. 4
2. 40
3. 37
4. 1.008
5. 25
6. $1\frac{1}{2}$
7. 2
8. 10
9. $\frac{1}{27}$
10. 63

Problem Solutions — Sequences

1. This is an ascending arithmetic sequence in which the common difference is $10 - 7$, or 3. The first term is $7 - 3 = 4$.

2. This is a geometric sequence in which the common ratio is $10 \div 5$, or 2. The missing term is $20 \times 2 = 40$.

3. This is a descending arithmetic sequence in which the common difference is $49 - 45$, or 4. The missing term is $41 - 4 = 37$.

4. This is an ascending arithmetic sequence in which the common difference is $1.004 - 1.002$, or .002. The missing term is $1.006 + .002 = 1.008$.

5. This sequence is neither arithmetic nor geometric. However, if the numbers are rewritten as 1^2, 2^2, 3^2, and 4^2, it is clear that the next number must be 5^2, or 25.

6. This is a descending arithmetic sequence in which the common difference is $10 - 7\frac{7}{8} = 2\frac{1}{8}$. The missing term is $3\frac{5}{8} - 2\frac{1}{8} = 1\frac{4}{8}$, or $1\frac{1}{2}$.

7. This is a geometric sequence in which the common ratio is:

$$4\tfrac{1}{2} \div 3 = \tfrac{9}{2} \times \tfrac{1}{3} = \tfrac{3}{2}$$

The first term is $3 \div \frac{3}{2} = 3 \times \frac{2}{3} = 2$

Therefore, the missing term is 2.

8. There is no common difference and no common ratio in this sequence. However, note the differences between terms:

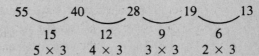

55		40		28		19		13
	15		12		9		6	
	5×3		4×3		3×3		2×3	

The differences are multiples of 3. Following the same pattern, the difference between 13 and the next term must be 1×3, or 3. The missing term is then $13 - 3 = 10$.

9. This is a geometric sequence in which the common ratio is $3 \div 9 = \frac{1}{3}$. The missing term is $\frac{1}{9} \times \frac{1}{3} = \frac{1}{27}$.

10. This sequence is neither arithmetic nor geometric. However, note the difference between terms:

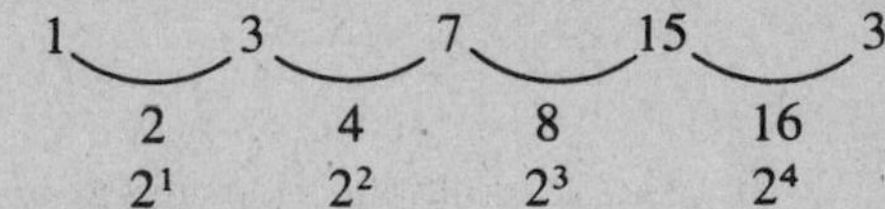

The difference between 31 and the next term must be 2^5, or 32. The missing term is $31 + 32 = 63$.

OPERATIONS WITH ALGEBRAIC EXPRESSIONS

Vocabulary

1. a. In addition, the numbers that are being added are called the **addends**. The solution to an addition problem is the **sum** or **total**.

   b. There are several ways to express an addition problem such as $10 + 2$:

the sum of 10 and 2	2 more than 10
the total of 10 and 2	2 greater than 10
2 added to 10	10 increased by 2

2. a. In subtraction, the number from which something is subtracted is the **minuend**, the number being subtracted is the **subtrahend** and the answer is the **difference**.

   Example: In $25 - 22 = 3$, the minuend is 25, the subtrahend is 22 and the difference is 3.

   b. A subtraction problem such as $25 - 22$ may be expressed as:

25 minus 22	from 25 take 22
25 less 22	25 decreased by 22
the difference of 25 and 22	22 less than 25
subtract 22 from 25	

3. a. In multiplication, the answer is called the **product** and the numbers being multiplied are the **factors** of the product.

   b. In the multiplication $3 \cdot 5 = 15$ [which may also be written as $3(5) = 15$ or $(3)(5) = 15$] all of the following expressions apply:

15 is the product of 3 and 5	15 is a multiple of 3
3 is a factor of 15	15 is a multiple of 5
5 is a factor of 15	

4. a. In division, the number being divided is the **dividend**, the number the dividend is divided by is the **divisor** and the answer is the **quotient**. Any number left over in the division is the **remainder**.

   Example: In $12 \div 2 = 6$, the dividend is 12, the divisor is 2 and the quotient is 6.

   Example: In $3\overline{)22}$ with quotient 7, 21, remainder 1:

$$\begin{array}{r} 7 \\ 3\,\overline{)\,22} \\ \underline{21} \\ 1 \end{array}$$

   22 is the dividend
   3 is the divisor
   1 is the remainder

b. The division problem $12 \div 2$ may be expressed as:

12 divided by 2 — 2 divided into 12

the quotient of 12 and 2

Because $12 \div 2 = 6$ with no remainder, 2 is called a **divisor** of 12, and 12 is said to be **divisible** by 2.

Properties

5. Addition is a **commutative** operation; this means that two numbers may be added in either order without changing their sum:

$$2 + 3 = 3 + 2$$
$$a + b = b + a$$

Multiplication is also commutative:

$$4 \cdot 5 = 5 \cdot 4$$
$$ab = ba$$

6. Subtraction and division problems are *not* commutative; changing the order within a subtraction or division problem may affect the answer:

$$10 - 6 \neq 6 - 10$$
$$8 \div 4 \neq 4 \div 8$$

7. Addition and multiplication are **associative**; that is, if a problem involves only addition or only multiplication, the parentheses may be changed without affecting the answer. Parentheses are grouping symbols that indicate work to be done first.

$$(5 + 6) + 7 = 5 + (6 + 7)$$
$$(2 \cdot 3) \cdot 4 = 2 \cdot (3 \cdot 4)$$
$$(a + b) + c = a + (b + c)$$
$$(ab)c = a(bc)$$

8. Subtraction and division are *not* associative. Work within parentheses *must* be performed first.

$$(8 - 5) - 2 \neq 8 - (5 - 2)$$
$$(80 \div 4) \div 2 \neq 80 \div (4 \div 2)$$

9. a. Multiplication is **distributive** over addition. If a sum is to be multiplied by a number, instead of adding first and then multiplying, each addend may be multiplied by the number and the products added.

$$5(6 + 3) = 5 \cdot 6 + 5 \cdot 3$$
$$a(b + c) = ab + ac$$

b. Multiplication is also distributive over subtraction.

$$8(10 - 6) = 8 \cdot 10 - 8 \cdot 6$$
$$a(b - c) = ab - ac$$

c. The distributive property may be used in both directions.

$$5a + 3a = (5 + 3)a = 8a$$
$$847 \cdot 94 + 847 \cdot 6 = 847(94 + 6) = 847(100) = 84{,}700$$

Signed Numbers

10. a. A **signed number** is a number with a positive (+) or negative (−) sign in front of it. Signed numbers may be represented on a number line as follows:

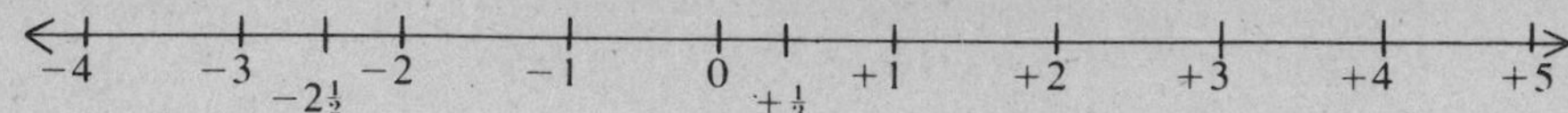

b. If a number (except zero) is written without a sign, it is assumed to be **positive**.

c. Zero is considered a signed number even though it is neither positive nor negative.

d. The magnitude, or **absolute value**, of a signed number is the number without its sign. The symbol used for absolute value is | |.

Examples: The absolute value of −3 is 3.

$|-3| = 3$

The absolute value of +6 is 6.

$|+6| = 6$

11. **Addition:**

a. To add two signed numbers that have the same sign, add their absolute values and give the answer the common sign.

Examples: $(+3) + (+4) = +7$
$(-6) + (-2) = -8$

b. To add two signed numbers that have different signs, subtract their absolute values. Give the answer the sign of the number with the *larger* absolute value.

Examples: $(-4) + (+1) = -3$
$(+5) + (-9) = -4$
$(-6) + (+7) = +1$

12. **Subtraction:**

To subtract two signed numbers, change the sign of the subtrahend. Then use the rules for addition of signed numbers.

Examples: $(-3) - (-5) = (-3) + (+5) = +2$
$(+10) - (-6) = (+10) + (+6) = +16$
$(+8) - (+9) = (+8) + (-9) = -1$
$(-7) - (+3) = (-7) + (-3) = -10$

13. **Multiplication:**

To multiply two signed numbers, multiply their absolute values. If the signed numbers have the same sign, the answer is positive. If the signed numbers have different signs, the answer is negative.

Examples: $(+3)(+4) = +12$
$(-5)(-2) = +10$
$(-6)(+3) = -18$
$(+8)(-1) = -8$

14. **Division:**

To divide two signed numbers, divide their absolute values. If the signed numbers have the same sign, the answer is positive. If the signed numbers have different signs, the answer is negative.

Examples: $(+20) \div (+4) = +5$
$(-18) \div (-9) = +2$
$(-14) \div (+2) = -7$
$(+15) \div (-5) = -3$

15. To evaluate algebraic expressions and formulas:

a. Substitute the given values for the letters in the expression.

b. Perform the arithmetic in the following order:

First, perform the operations within parentheses (if any);

Second, compute all powers and roots;

Third, perform all multiplications and divisions in order from left to right;

Fourth, perform all additions and subtractions in order from left to right.

Illustration: If $P = 2(L + W)$, find P when $L = 10$ and $W = 5$

SOLUTION: Substitute 10 for L and 5 for W:

$P = 2(10 + 5)$ First, add numbers in parentheses.
$= 2(15)$ Then multiply 2 by 15.
$= 30$

Answer: 30

Illustration: Evaluate $5a^2 - 2b$ if $a = 3$ and $b = 10$

SOLUTION: Substitute 3 for a and 10 for b:

$5 \cdot 3^2 - 2 \cdot 10$ First, find 3^2.
$5 \cdot 9 - 2 \cdot 10$ Next, multiply $5 \cdot 9$ and $2 \cdot 10$.
$45 - 20$ Then subtract 20 from 45.
25

Answer: 25

16. a. Algebraic expressions may contain numbers (constants) or letters (variables) or both.

b. In an algebraic expression, if several quantities are being added or subtracted, each of these quantities is called a **term**.

Example: In $4x^2 + 5y + 6$, the terms are: $4x^2$, $5y$, 6.

c. The number factor of each term is called the **coefficient**. The letter part is called the **literal factor**.

Example: In $3x^2$, 3 is the coefficient and x is the literal factor. Note that 2 is the exponent and is part of the literal factor.

d. Any variable appearing without a coefficient is assumed to have a coefficient of 1: $b = 1b$

e. Any variable appearing without an exponent is assumed to have an exponent of 1: $b = b^1$

17. a. If two or more terms have identical literal factors, they are called **like terms**.

Example: $3a$, $6a$ and a are like terms
$2x^4$ and $5x^2$ are *not* like terms

b. Terms may be added (or subtracted) only if they are like terms. Add (or subtract) the coefficients and repeat the literal factor. This is called **combining like terms**.

Examples:

$$3d + 2d = 5d$$
$$6xy + (-4)xy = 2xy$$
$$10z^3 + 5z^3 - 8z^3 = 7z^3$$

c. In most algebraic expressions it is easier to consider the operation that separates terms to be addition only, and the + or − sign immediately preceding each term to be the sign of the coefficient of that term.

Polynomials

18. An expression containing a single term is called a **monomial**. An expression containing more than one term is called a **polynomial**. Special polynomials are **binomials** (two terms) and **trinomials** (three terms).

19. To add (or subtract) two polynomials, add (or subtract) the coefficients of the like terms and repeat the literal factors. The unlike terms may *not* be combined.

Examples: Add

$$\begin{array}{r} 4x^2 - 3x + 2 \\ 2x^2 - 7x - 5 \\ \hline 6x^2 - 10x - 3 \end{array}$$

Subtract

$$\begin{array}{r} 7a - 2b + 4c \\ 9a + 6b - 2c \\ \hline -2a - 8b + 6c \end{array}$$

(Recall that in subtraction the sign of the subtrahend is changed and the rules of addition are used.)

20. To multiply two monomials, multiply their coefficients and add the exponents of like variables.

Examples:

$$2x^5 \cdot 3x^4 = 6x^9$$
$$y^4 \cdot y^{10} = y^{14}$$
$$9b^3 \cdot 2b = 18b^4 \quad \text{(Note that } 2b = 2b^1\text{)}$$
$$(-4a^2b^3)(-3a^{11}b^8) = +12a^{13}b^{11}$$

21. To multiply a polynomial by a monomial, use the distributive property and multiply each term of the polynomial by the monomial.

Examples:

$$3(2x + 4y) = 6x + 12y$$
$$y^2(5y - 3y^5) = 5y^3 - 3y^7$$

22. To multiply a polynomial by a polynomial, multiply each term of the first polynomial by each term of the second polynomial, then add any like terms in the answer.

Examples:

$$(x + 3)(x + 4) = x^2 + 4x + 3x + 12$$
$$= x^2 + 7x + 12$$
$$(a - 1)(b + 5) = ab + 5a - 1b - 5$$
$$(y + 4)(y^2 + 2y - 3) = y^3 + 2y^2 - 3y + 4y^2 + 8y - 12$$
$$= y^3 + 6y^2 + 5y - 12$$

23. To divide two monomials, divide their coefficients and subtract the exponents of like variables.

Examples:

$$\frac{12a^5}{3a^2} = 4a^3$$

$$\frac{ac^7}{ac^5} = c^2 \qquad \text{(Note that } \frac{a}{a} = 1\text{)}$$

$$\frac{-6b^{10}c^7}{+2bc^2} = -3b^9c^5$$

24. To divide a polynomial by a monomial, divide each term of the polynomial by the monomial.

Examples:

$$\frac{15a^2 - 12a}{3} = 5a^2 - 4a$$

$$(12x^3 - 8x^2 + 20x) \div 4x = 3x^2 - 2x + 5$$

Simplifying Algebraic Expressions

25. Algebraic expressions containing parentheses can be simplified by using the following rules:

a. If a positive (+) sign is immediately before the parentheses, the parentheses may simply be omitted.

Example: $3x + (2y + z) = 3x + 2y + z$

b. If a negative (−) sign immediately precedes parentheses, the sign of each term within the parentheses must be changed. The parentheses may then be omitted.

Example: $4 - (2x - y + z) = 4 - 2x + y - z$

c. If a number or letter is indicated as a multiplier immediately before parentheses, the distributive property is used to multiply each term inside the parentheses by the multiplier.

Example: $a - 3(b + c) = a - 3b - 3c$

d. After removing parentheses, combine like terms.

Example: $5z + 2(3z - 4) = 5z + 6z - 8$
$= 11z - 8$

Factoring

26. To **factor** an expression means to find those quantities whose product is the original expression.

27. **Common factors:**

If all of the terms of a polynomial have a common factor, the distributive property may be used.

Examples:

$$ax + ay = a(x + y)$$

$$12d - 8f = 4(3d - 2f)$$

$$x^3 + 2x^2 - 4x = x(x^2 + 2x - 4)$$

28. **Difference of two squares:**

A binomial which is the difference of two squares has as its factors two binomials, one the sum of the square roots, the other the difference of the square roots.

Examples: $x^2 - 9 = (x + 3)(x - 3)$
$25 - y^2 = (5 + y)(5 - y)$

29. **Trinomials:**

a. Quadratic trinomials are of the form: $ax^2 + bx + c$, where a, b and c are constants and $a \neq 0$. Some — but not all — quadratic trinomials can be factored into two binomials, each the sum of an x term and a numerical term.

b. When $a = 1$, the trinomial is written $x^2 + bx + c$. Each binomial factor will be the sum of x and a number. The product of the numbers is c; their sum is b.

Illustration: Factor $x^2 + 7x + 12$

SOLUTION: The product of the numerical parts of the factors must be 12. Pairs of numbers whose product is 12 are:

1 and 12
2 and 6
3 and 4

Of these pairs, the only one whose sum is 7 is 3 and 4. Therefore, the factors are $(x + 3)$ and $(x + 4)$.

Answer: $x^2 + 7x + 12 = (x + 3)(x + 4)$

Illustration: Factor $y^2 + 5y - 6$

SOLUTION: Pairs of numbers whose product is -6 are:

-1 and $+6$
$+1$ and -6
$+2$ and -3
-2 and $+3$

The pair whose sum is $+5$ is -1 and $+6$. Therefore, the factors are $(y - 1)$ and $(y + 6)$.

Answer: $y^2 + 5y - 6 = (y - 1)(y + 6)$

Illustration: Factor $z^2 - 11z + 10$

SOLUTION: The numbers whose product is positive are either both positive or both negative. In this case the sum of the numbers is negative, so consider only the negative pairs. The pairs of negative numbers whose product is $+10$ are:

-1 and -10
-2 and -5

The pair with -11 as its sum is -1 and -10. Therefore the factors are $(z - 1)$ and $(z - 10)$.

Answer: $z^2 - 11z + 10 = (z - 1)(z - 10)$

c. When $a \neq 1$ in the trinomial $ax^2 + bx + c$, the product of the x terms in the binomial factors must be ax^2, the product of the number terms must be c, and when the binomials are multiplied their product must be $ax^2 + bx + c$.

While there will be more than one possible pair of factors in which the product of the number terms is c, the correct pair is the only one whose product is the original trinomial.

Illustration: Factor $3x^2 + 10x + 8$

SOLUTION: The possible pairs of factors to be considered are:

$$(3x + 1)(x + 8)$$
$$(3x + 8)(x + 1)$$
$$(3x + 2)(x + 4)$$
$$(3x + 4)(x + 2)$$

In each case the product of the x terms is $3x^2$ and the product of the number terms is 8. Since the middle term is positive, any negative possibilities are ignored. Multiplying each pair of factors gives:

$$(3x + 1)(x + 8) = 3x^2 + 24x + 1x + 8$$
$$= 3x^2 + 25x + 8$$
$$(3x + 8)(x + 1) = 3x^2 + 3x + 8x + 8$$
$$= 3x^2 + 11x + 8$$
$$(3x + 2)(x + 4) = 3x^2 + 12x + 2x + 8$$
$$= 3x^2 + 14x + 8$$
$$(3x + 4)(x + 2) = 3x^2 + 6x + 4x + 8$$
$$= 3x^2 + 10x + 8$$

Therefore, $3x^2 + 10x + 8$ may be factored as $(3x + 4)(x + 2)$.

30. An expression may require more than one type of factoring before it is factored completely. To factor *completely*:

a. Use the distributive property to remove the highest common factor from each term.

b. If possible, factor the resulting polynomial as the difference of two squares or as a quadratic trinomial.

Examples:

$$3x^2 - 48 = 3(x^2 - 16)$$
$$= 3(x + 4)(x - 4)$$
$$2ay^2 + 12ay - 14a = 2a(y^2 + 6y - 7)$$
$$= 2a(y + 7)(y - 1)$$

Radicals

31. The symbol $\sqrt{x}$ means the positive square root of x. The $\sqrt{\ }$ is called the **radical sign**, and x is called the **radicand**. The symbol $-\sqrt{x}$ means the negative square root of x.

32. Many radicals may be simplified by using the principle $\sqrt{ab} = \sqrt{a} \cdot \sqrt{b}$

Examples:

$$\sqrt{100} = \sqrt{25}\sqrt{4} = 5 \cdot 2 = 10$$
$$\sqrt{18} = \sqrt{9}\sqrt{2} = 3\sqrt{2}$$
$$\sqrt{75} = \sqrt{25}\sqrt{3} = 5\sqrt{3}$$

Note that the factors chosen must include at least one perfect square.

33. a. Radicals with the same radicands may be added or subtracted as like terms.

Examples: $3\sqrt{5} + 4\sqrt{5} = 7\sqrt{5}$

$10\sqrt{2} - 6\sqrt{2} = 4\sqrt{2}$

b. Radicals with different radicands may be combined only if they can be simplified to have like radicands.

Example: $\sqrt{50} + \sqrt{32} - 2\sqrt{2} + \sqrt{3} = \sqrt{25}\sqrt{2} + \sqrt{16}\sqrt{2} - 2\sqrt{2} + \sqrt{3}$

$= 5\sqrt{2} + 4\sqrt{2} - 2\sqrt{2} + \sqrt{3}$

$= 7\sqrt{2} + \sqrt{3}$

34. To multiply radicals, first multiply the coefficients. Then multiply the radicands.

Example: $2\sqrt{3} \cdot 4\sqrt{5} = 8\sqrt{15}$

35. To divide radicals, first divide the coefficients. Then divide the radicands.

Example: $\dfrac{14\sqrt{20}}{2\sqrt{2}} = 7\sqrt{10}$

Summary of Kinds of Numbers

36. The numbers that have been used in this section are called **real numbers** and may be grouped into special categories.

a. The **natural** numbers, or counting numbers, are:

1, 2, 3, 4, 5, 6, 7, 8, 9, 10, 11, 12, . . .

b. A natural number (other than 1) is a **prime** number if it can be exactly divided only by itself and 1. If a natural number has other divisors it is a **composite** number. The numbers 2, 3, 5, 7, and 11 are prime numbers, while 4, 6, 8, 9 and 12 are composites.

c. The **whole** numbers consist of 0 and the natural numbers:

0, 1, 2, 3, . . .

d. The **integers** consist of the natural numbers, the negatives of the natural numbers, and zero:

. . . −3, −2, −1, 0, 1, 2, 3, 4, . . .

Even integers are exactly divisible by 2:

. . . −6, −4, −2, 0, 2, 4, 6, 8, . . .

Odd integers are not divisible by 2:

. . . −5, −3, −1, 1, 3, 5, 7, 9, . . .

e. The **rational** numbers are numbers that can be expressed as the quotient of two integers (excluding division by 0). Rational numbers include integers, fractions, terminating decimals (such as 1.5 or .293) and repeating decimals (such as .333 . . . or .74867676767 . . .).

f. The **irrational** numbers cannot be expressed as the quotient of two integers, but can be written as non-terminating, non-repeating decimals. The numbers $\sqrt{2}$ and π are irrational.

Practice Problems

1. The value of $2(-3) - |-4|$ is
   (1) -10 (2) -2 (3) 2 (4) 10 (5) 12
2. The value of $3a^2 + 2a - 1$ when $a = -1$ is
   (1) -3 (2) 0 (3) 3 (4) 6 (5) 9
3. If $2x^4$ is multiplied by $7x^3$ the product is
   (A) $9x^7$ (B) $9x^{12}$ (3) $9x^{14}$ (4) $14x^{12}$ (5) $14x^7$
4. The expression $3(x - 4) - (3x - 5) + 2(x + 6)$ is equivalent to
   (1) $2x - 15$ (2) $2x + 23$ (3) $2x + 5$ (4) $-2x - 15$ (5) $-2x + 20$
5. The product of $(x + 5)$ and $(x + 5)$ is
   (1) $2x + 10$ (2) $x^2 + 25$ (3) $x^2 + 10x + 25$ (4) $x^2 + 10$ (5) $x^2 + 20$
6. The quotient of $(4x^3 - 2x^2) \div (x^2)$ is
   (1) $4x^3 - 1$ (2) $4x - 2x^2$ (3) $4x^5 - 2x^4$ (4) $4x - 2$ (5) $4x + 2$
7. The expression $(+3x^4)^2$ is equal to
   (1) $6x^8$ (2) $6x^6$ (3) $9x^8$ (4) $9x^6$ (5) $9x^4$
8. If $3x - 1$ is multiplied by $2x$, the product is
   (1) $4x$ (2) $5x^2$ (3) $6x^2 - 1$ (4) $6x^2 - x$ (5) $6x^2 - 2x$
9. One factor of the trinomial $x^2 - 3x - 18$ is
   (1) $x - 9$ (2) $x - 6$ (3) $x - 3$ (4) $x + 9$ (5) $x + 3$
10. The sum of $\sqrt{18}$ and $\sqrt{72}$ is
    (1) $18\sqrt{2}$ (2) $9\sqrt{2}$ (3) $3\sqrt{10}$ (4) 40 (5) 49

Practice Problems — Correct Answers

1. **(1)**
2. **(2)**
3. **(5)**
4. **(3)**
5. **(3)**
6. **(4)**
7. **(3)**
8. **(5)**
9. **(2)**
10. **(2)**

Problem Solutions

1. $$2(-3) - |-4| = -6 - 4$$
   $$= -10$$

   Recall that $|-4|$ means the *absolute value* of -4, which is 4.

   Answer: **(1)** -10

2. If $a = -1$,
   $$3a^2 + 2a - 1 = 3(-1)^2 + 2(-1) - 1$$
   $$= 3(+1) + 2(-1) - 1$$
   $$= 3 - 2 - 1$$
   $$= 0$$

   Answer: **(2)** 0

3. $(2x^4)(7x^3) = 14x^7$ To multiply monomials, multiply coefficients and add exponents of like variables.

   Answer: **(5)** $14x^7$

4. $3(x - 4) - (3x - 5) + 2(x + 6)$
   $= 3x - 12 - 3x + 5 + 2x + 12$
   $= 2x + 5$

   Answer: **(3)** $2x + 5$

5. $(x + 5)(x + 5) = x^2 + 5x + 5x + 25$
   $= x^2 + 10x + 25$

   Answer: **(3)** $x^2 + 10x + 25$

6. $(4x^3 - 2x^2) \div x^2 = 4x^3 \div x^2 - 2x^2 \div x^2$
   $= 4x - 2$

   Answer: **(4)** $4x - 2$

7. $(+3x^4)^2 = (+3x^4)(+3x^4)$
   $= 9x^8$

   Answer: **(3)** $9x^8$

8. $2x(3x - 1) = 2x \cdot 3x - 2x \cdot 1$
   $= 6x^2 - 2x$

   Answer: **(5)** $6x^2 - 2x$

9. Factor $x^2 - 3x - 18$ by finding two numbers whose product is -18 and whose sum is -3. Pairs of numbers whose product is -18 are:

   -1 and $+18$
   $+1$ and -18
   -9 and $+2$
   $+9$ and -2
   -6 and $+3$
   $+6$ and -3

   Of these pairs, the one whose sum is -3 is -6 and $+3$. Therefore, the factors of $x^2 - 3x - 18$ are $(x - 6)$ and $(x + 3)$.

   Answer: **(2)** $x - 6$

10. $\sqrt{18} + \sqrt{72} = \sqrt{9}\sqrt{2} + \sqrt{36}\sqrt{2}$
    $= 3\sqrt{2} + 6\sqrt{2}$
    $= 9\sqrt{2}$

    Answer: **(2)** $9\sqrt{2}$

EQUATIONS, INEQUALITIES AND PROBLEMS IN ALGEBRA

Equations

1. a. An **equation** states that two quantities are equal.

   b. The solution to an equation is a number which can be substituted for the letter, or **variable**, to give a true statement.

   Example: In the equation $x + 7 = 10$,
   if 5 is substituted for x, the equation becomes $5 + 7 = 10$, which is false. If 3 is substituted for x, the equation becomes $3 + 7 = 10$, which is true. Therefore, $x = 3$ is a solution for the equation $x + 7 = 10$.

   c. To **solve an equation** means to find all solutions for the variables.

2. a. An equation has been solved when it is transformed or rearranged so that a variable is isolated on one side of the equal sign and a number is on the other side.

   b. There are two basic principles which are used to transform equations:

      I) The same quantity may be added to, or subtracted from, both sides of an equation.

      Example: To solve the equation $x - 3 = 2$, add 3 to both sides:

$$\begin{array}{rcr} x - 3 & = & 2 \\ +\ 3 & & +3 \\ \hline x & = & 5 \end{array}$$

      Adding 3 isolates x on one side and leaves a number on the other side. The solution to the equation is $x = 5$.

      Example: To solve the equation $y + 4 = 10$, subtract 4 from both sides (adding -4 to both sides will have the same effect):

$$\begin{array}{rcr} y + 4 & = & 10 \\ -\ 4 & & -4 \\ \hline y & = & 6 \end{array}$$

      The variable has been isolated on one side of the equation. The solution is $y = 6$.

II) Both sides of an equation may be multiplied by, or divided by, the same quantity.

Example: To solve $2a = 12$, divide both sides by 2:

$$\frac{2a}{2} = \frac{12}{2}$$
$$a = 6$$

Example: To solve $\frac{b}{5} = 10$, multiply both sides by 5:

$$5 \cdot \frac{b}{5} = 10 \cdot 5$$
$$b = 50$$

3. To solve equations containing more than one operation:

   a. First eliminate any number that is being added to or subtracted from the variable.

   b. Then eliminate any number that is multiplying or dividing the variable.

Illustration: Solve

$$\begin{array}{rcl} 3x - 6 & = & 9 \\ +6 & & +6 \\ \hline 3x & = & 15 \end{array}$$ Adding 6 eliminates −6.

$$\frac{3x}{3} = \frac{15}{3}$$ Dividing by 3 eliminates the 3 which is multiplying the x.

$$x = 5$$ The solution to the original equation is $x = 5$.

4. A variable term may be added to, or subtracted from, both sides of an equation. This is necessary when the variable appears on both sides of the original equation.

Illustration: Solve

$$\begin{array}{rcl} 6y + 9 & = & 2y + 1 \\ -2y & & -2y \\ \hline 4y + 9 & = & +1 \end{array}$$ Eliminate the y term from the right side by subtracting 2y from both sides.

$$\begin{array}{rcl} 4y + 9 & = & +1 \\ -9 & & -9 \\ \hline 4y & = & -8 \end{array}$$ Eliminate 9 from the left side by subtracting 9 from both sides.

$$\frac{4y}{4} = \frac{-8}{4}$$ Divide both sides by 4 to eliminate the multiplication by 4 and isolate the y.

$$y = -2$$

5. It may be necessary to first **simplify** the expression on each side of an equation by removing parentheses or combining like terms.

Illustration: Solve $5z - 3(z - 2) = 8$

$$5z - 3z + 6 = 8$$ Remove parentheses first.

$$2z + 6 = 8$$ Combine like terms.

$$\begin{array}{rcl} -6 & & -6 \end{array}$$ Subtract 6 from both sides.

$$\frac{2z}{2} = \frac{2}{2}$$ Divide by 2 to isolate the z.

$$z = 1$$

6. To check the solution to any equation, replace the variable with the solution in the original equation, perform the indicated operations, and determine whether a true statement results.

   Example: Earlier it was found that $x = 5$ is the solution for the equation $3x - 6 = 9$. To check, substitute 5 for x in the equation:

   $3 \cdot 5 - 6 = 9$ Perform the operations on the left side.

   $15 - 6 = 9$

   $9 = 9$ A true statement results; therefore the solution is correct.

Solving Problems

7. Many types of problems can be solved by using algebra. To solve a problem:

   a. Read it carefully. Determine what information is given and what information is unknown and must be found.

   b. Represent the *unknown* quantity with a letter.

   c. Write an equation that expresses the relationship given in the problem.

   d. Solve the equation.

   Example: If 7 is added to twice a number, the result is 23. Find the number.

   SOLUTION: Let $x =$ the unknown number. Then write the equation:

$$\begin{aligned} 7 + 2x &= 23 \\ -7 \quad & \quad -7 \\ \hline \frac{2x}{2} &= \frac{16}{2} \\ x &= 8 \end{aligned}$$

   Answer: 8

   Example: There are 6 more women than men in a group of 26 people. How many women are there?

   SOLUTION: Let $m =$ the number of men. Then, $m + 6 =$ the number of women.

$$\begin{aligned} (m + 6) + m &= 26 \\ m + 6 + m &= 26 && \text{Remove parentheses.} \\ 2m + 6 &= 26 && \text{Combine like terms.} \\ -6 \quad & \quad -6 \\ \hline \frac{2m}{2} &= \frac{20}{2} \\ m &= 10 \\ m + 6 &= 16 \end{aligned}$$

   Answer: There are 16 women.

   Example: John is 3 years older than Mary. If the sum of their ages is 39, how old is Mary?

SOLUTION: Let m = Mary's age. Then, m + 3 = John's age. The sum of their ages is 39.

$$
\begin{aligned}
m + (m + 3) &= 39 \\
m + m + 3 &= 39 \\
2m + 3 &= 39 \\
-3 &\quad -3 \\
\frac{2m}{2} &= \frac{36}{2} \\
m &= 18
\end{aligned}
$$

Answer: Mary is 18 years old.

Consecutive Integer Problems

8. a. **Consecutive integers** are integers that follow one another.

Example: 7, 8, 9, and 10 are consecutive integers.
−5, −4, −3, −2 and −1 are consecutive integers.

b. Consecutive integers may be represented in algebra as:

$$x, x + 1, x + 2, x + 3, \ldots$$

Example: Find three consecutive integers whose sum is 39.

SOLUTION: Let x = first consecutive integer. Then, x + 1 = second consecutive integer and x + 2 = third consecutive integer.

$$
\begin{aligned}
x + (x + 1) + (x + 2) &= 39 \\
x + x + 1 + x + 2 &= 39 \\
3x + 3 &= 39 \\
-3 &\quad -3 \\
\frac{3x}{3} &= \frac{36}{3} \\
x &= 12
\end{aligned}
$$

Answer: The integers are 12, 13 and 14.

9. Consecutive even and consecutive odd integers are both represented as x, x + 2, x + 4, x + 6, . . .

If x is even, then x + 2, x + 4, x + 6, . . . will all be even.
If x is odd, then x + 2, x + 4, x + 6, . . . will all be odd.

Example: Find four consecutive odd integers such that the sum of the largest and twice the smallest is 21.

SOLUTION: Let x, x + 2, x + 4, and x + 6 be the four consecutive odd integers. Here, x is the smallest and x + 6 is the largest. The largest integer plus twice the smallest is 21.

$$
\begin{aligned}
x + 6 + 2x &= 21 \\
3x + 6 &= 21 \\
-6 &\quad -6 \\
\frac{3x}{3} &= \frac{15}{3} \\
x &= 5
\end{aligned}
$$

Answer: The integers are 5, 7, 9, and 11.

Motion Problems

10. **Motion problems** are based on the following relationship:

Rate · Time = Distance

Rate is usually given in miles per hour. Time is usually given in hours and distance is given in miles.

Example: A man traveled 225 miles in 5 hours. How fast was he traveling (what was his rate)?

SOLUTION: Let r = rate

$$\text{rate} \cdot \text{time} = \text{distance}$$
$$r \cdot 5 = 225$$
$$\frac{5r}{5} = \frac{225}{5}$$
$$r = 45 \text{ miles per hour}$$

Example: John and Henry start at the same time from cities 180 miles apart and travel toward each other. John travels at 40 miles per hour and Henry travels at 50 miles per hour. In how many hours will they meet?

SOLUTION: Let h = number of hours. Then, 40h = distance traveled by John, and 50h = distance traveled by Henry. The total distance is 180 miles.

$$40h + 50h = 180$$
$$\frac{90h}{90} = \frac{180}{90}$$
$$h = 2 \text{ hours}$$

Answer: They will meet in 2 hours.

Perimeter Problems

11. To solve a perimeter problem, express each side of the figure algebraically. The **perimeter** of the figure is equal to the sum of all of the sides.

Example: A rectangle has four sides. One side is the length and the side next to it is the width. The opposite sides of a rectangle are equal. In a particular rectangle, the length is one less than twice the width. If the perimeter is 16, find the length and the width.

SOLUTION:

Let w = width

Then 2w − 1 = length

2w − 1

w w

2w − 1

The sum of the four sides is 16.

$$w + (2w - 1) + w + (2w - 1) = 16$$
$$w + 2w - 1 + w + 2w - 1 = 16$$
$$6w - 2 = 16$$
$$+2 \quad +2$$
$$\frac{6w}{6} = \frac{18}{6}$$
$$w = 3$$
$$2w - 1 = 2(3) - 1 = 5$$

Answer: The width is 3 and the length is 5.

Ratio and Proportion Problems

12. a. A ratio is the quotient of two numbers. The ratio of 2 to 5 may be expressed $2 \div 5$, $\frac{2}{5}$, 2 is to 5, 2:5, or algebraically as $2x:5x$.

The numbers in a ratio are called the terms of the ratio.

Example: Two numbers are in the ratio 3:4. Their sum is 35. Find the numbers.

SOLUTION:

Let $3x$ = the first number
$4x$ = the second number

Note that $\frac{3x}{4x} = \frac{3}{4} = 3:4$

The sum of the numbers is 35.

$$3x + 4x = 35$$
$$\frac{7x}{7} = \frac{35}{7}$$
$$x = 5$$
$$3x = 15$$
$$4x = 20$$

Answer: The numbers are 15 and 20.

b. A ratio involving more than two numbers may also be expressed algebraically. The ratio 2:3:7 is equal to $2x:3x:7x$. The individual quantities in the ratio are $2x$, $3x$, and $7x$.

13. a. A **proportion** states that two ratios are equal.

b. In the proportion $a:b = c:d$ (which may also be written $\frac{a}{b} = \frac{c}{d}$), the inner terms, b and c, are called the **means**; the outer terms, a and d, are called the **extremes**.

Example: In 3:6 = 5:10, the means are 6 and 5; the extremes are 3 and 10.

c. In any proportion, the product of the means equals the product of the extremes. In $a:b = c:d$, $bc = ad$.

Example: In 3:6 = 5:10, or $\frac{3}{6} = \frac{5}{10}$, $6 \cdot 5 = 3 \cdot 10$.

d. In many problems, the quantities involved are in proportion. If three quantities are given in a problem and the fourth quantity is unknown, determine whether the quantities should form a proportion. The proportion will be the equation for the problem.

Example: A tree that is 20 feet tall casts a shadow 12 feet long. At the same time, a pole casts a shadow 3 feet long. How tall is the pole?

SOLUTION: Let p = height of pole. The heights of objects and their shadows are in proportion.

$$\frac{\text{tree}}{\text{tree's shadow}} = \frac{\text{pole}}{\text{pole's shadow}}$$

$$\frac{20}{12} = \frac{p}{3}$$

$$12p = 60$$ The product of the means equals the product of the extremes.

$$\frac{12p}{12} = \frac{60}{12}$$

$$p = 5$$

Answer: The pole is 5 feet tall.

Example: The scale on a map is 3 cm = 500 km. If two cities appear 15 cm apart on the map, how far apart are they actually?

SOLUTION: Let d = actual distance. The quantities on maps and scale drawings are in proportion with the quantities they represent.

$$\frac{\text{first map distance}}{\text{first actual distance}} = \frac{\text{second map distance}}{\text{second actual distance}}$$

$$\frac{3\text{ cm}}{500\text{ km}} = \frac{15\text{ cm}}{d\text{ km}}$$

$$3d = 7500$$ The product of the means equals the product of the extremes.

$$\frac{3d}{3} = \frac{7500}{3}$$

$$d = 2500$$

Answer: The cities are 2500 km apart.

Percent Problems

14. **Percent** problems may be solved algebraically by translating the relationship in the problem into an equation. The word "of" means multiplication, and "is" means equal to.

Example: 45% of what number is 27?

SOLUTION: Let n = the unknown number. 45% of n is 27.

$$.45n = 27$$ Change the % to a decimal (45% = .45)

$$45n = 2700$$ Multiplying both sides by 100 eliminates the decimal.

$$\frac{45n}{45} = \frac{2700}{45}$$

$$n = 60$$

Example: Mr. Jones receives a salary raise from $15,000 to $16,200. Find the percent of increase.

SOLUTION: Let p = percent. The increase is 16,200 − 15,000 = 1,200. What percent of 15,000 is 1,200?

$$p \cdot 15{,}000 = 1{,}200$$

$$\frac{15000p}{15000} = \frac{1200}{15000}$$

$$p = .08$$

$$p = 8\%$$

15. **Interest** is the price paid for the use of money in loans, savings and investments. Interest problems are solved using the formula **I** = **prt**, where:

I = interest
p = principal (amount of money bearing interest)
r = rate of interest, in %
t = time, in years

Example: How long must \$2000 be invested at 6% to earn \$240 in interest?

SOLUTION:

Let t = time
I = \$240
p = \$2000
r = 6% or .06

$$240 = 2000(.06)t$$
$$\frac{240}{120} = \frac{120t}{120}$$
$$2 = t$$

Answer: The \$2000 must be invested for 2 years.

16. a. A **discount** is a percent that is deducted from a marked price. The marked price is considered to be 100% of itself.

Example: If an item is discounted 20%, its selling price is 100% − 20%, or 80%, of its marked price.

Example: A radio is tagged with a sale price of \$42.50, which is 15% off the regular price. What is the regular price?

SOLUTION: Let r = regular price. The sale price is 100% − 15%, or 85%, of the regular price. 85% of r = \$42.50

$$.85r = \$42.50$$
$$\frac{85r}{85} = \frac{4250}{85} \quad \text{Multiply by 100 to eliminate the decimals.}$$
$$r = 50$$

Answer: The regular price was \$50.

b. If two discounts are given in a problem, an intermediate price is computed by taking the first discount on the marked price. The second discount is then computed on the intermediate price.

Example: An appliance company gives a 15% discount for purchases made during a sale, and an additional 5% discount if payment is made in cash. What will the price of a \$800 refrigerator be if both discounts are taken?

SOLUTION: First discount: 100% − 15% = 85%

After the first discount, the refrigerator will cost:

$$85\% \text{ of } \$800 = .85(\$800) = \$680$$

The intermediate price is \$680.

Second discount: 100% − 5% = 95%.

After the second discount, the refrigerator will cost:

$$95\% \text{ of } \$680 = .95(\$680) = \$646$$

Answer: The final price will be \$646.

17. a. **Profit** is the amount of money added to the dealer's cost of an item to find the selling price. The cost price is considered 100% of itself.

Example: If the profit is 20% of the cost, the selling price must be 100% + 20%, or 120% of the cost.

Example: A furniture dealer sells a sofa at $870, which represents a 45% profit over the cost. What was the cost to the dealer?

SOLUTION: Let c = cost price. 100% + 45% = 145%. The selling price is 145% of the cost.

$$145\% \text{ of } c = \$870$$
$$1.45c = 870$$
$$\frac{145c}{145} = \frac{87000}{145}$$
$$c = 600$$

Answer: The sofa cost the dealer $600.

b. If an article is sold at a **loss**, the amount of the loss is deducted from the cost price to find the selling price.

Example: An article that is sold at a 25% loss has a selling price of 100% − 25%, or 75%, of the cost price.

Example: Mr. Charles bought a car for $8000. After a while he sold it to Mr. David at a 30% loss. What did Mr. David pay for the car?

SOLUTION: The car was sold for 100% − 30%, or 70%, of its cost price.

$$70\% \text{ of } \$8000 = .70(\$8000)$$
$$= \$5600$$

Answer: Mr. David paid $5600 for the car.

18. **Tax** is computed by finding a percent of a base amount.

Example: A homeowner pays $2500 in school taxes. What is the assessed value of his property if school taxes are 3.2% of the assessed value?

SOLUTION: Let v = assessed value.

$$3.2\% \text{ of } v = 2500$$
$$.032v = 2500$$
$$\frac{32v}{32} = \frac{2500000}{32} \quad \text{(Multiply by 1000 to eliminate decimals)}$$
$$v = 78125$$

Answer: The value of the property is $78,125.

Inequalities

19. a. The = symbol indicates the relationship between two equal quantities. The symbols used to indicate other relationships between two quantities are:

$\neq$ not equal to
$>$ greater than
$<$ less than
$\geqslant$ greater than or equal to
$\leqslant$ less than or equal to

b. A number is **greater** than any number appearing to its left on the number line. A number is **less** than any number appearing to its right on the number line.

Examples:

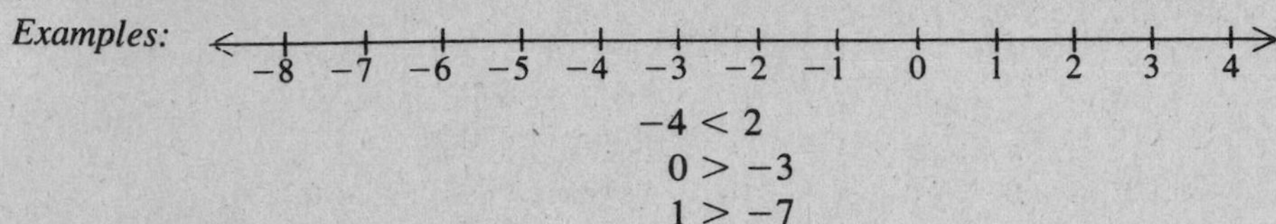

$-4 < 2$
$0 > -3$
$1 > -7$

20. a. An **inequality** states that one quantity is greater than, or less than, another quantity.

b. Inequalities are solved in the same way as equations, except that in multiplying or dividing both sides of an inequality by a negative quantity, the inequality symbol is reversed.

Example: Solve for x:

$3x - 4 > 11$
$\quad + 4 \quad +4$ Add 4 to both sides.
$\frac{3x}{3} > \frac{15}{3}$ Divide both sides by 3. Since 3 is positive, the inequality symbol remains the same.
$x > 5$

The solution x > 5 means that all numbers greater than 5 are solutions to the inequality.

Example: Solve for y:

$2y + 3 > 7y - 2$
$-7y \quad\quad -7y$ Subtract 7y from both sides.
$-5y + 3 > -2$
$\quad - 3 \quad\quad - 3$ Subtract 3 from both sides.
$-5y > -5$ Divide both sides by −5. When dividing both sides by a negative number, reverse the inequality symbol.
$y < 1$

Quadratic Equations

21. a. A **quadratic equation** is an equation in which the variable has 2 as its greatest exponent. Quadratic equations may be put into the form $ax^2 + bx + c = 0$, where a, b and c are constants and $a \neq 0$.

b. The solution of quadratic equations is based on the principle that if the product of two quantities is zero, at least one of those quantities must be zero.
. If one side of a quadratic equation is zero and the other side can be written as the product of two factors, each of those factors may be set equal to zero and the resulting equations solved.

Example: Solve $x^2 - 7x + 10 = 0$

The factors of the trinomial are	$(x - 2)(x - 5) = 0$
Set each factor equal to zero:	$x - 2 = 0; \quad x - 5 = 0$
Solve each equation:	$x = 2 \qquad x = 5$

The solutions of $x^2 - 7x + 10 = 0$ are 2 and 5.

Example: Solve

$$\begin{array}{rcl} x^2 - 5 &=& 4 \\ -4 && -4 \\ \hline x^2 - 9 &=& 0 \end{array}$$

Add −4 to both sides to obtain 0 on the right side.

$$(x + 3)(x - 3) = 0$$

Factor $x^2 - 9$.

$$\begin{array}{rcl|rcl} x + 3 &=& 0 & x - 3 &=& 0 \\ -3 && -3 & +3 && +3 \\ \hline x &=& -3 & x &=& 3 \end{array}$$

Set each factor equal to zero.
Solve each equation.

The solutions of $x^2 - 5 = 4$ are 3 and −3.

Example: Solve

$$3z^2 - 12z = 0$$

$$3z(z - 4) = 0$$

Factor $3z^2 - 12z$.

$$\begin{array}{c|rcl} \frac{3z}{3} = \frac{0}{3} & z - 4 &=& 0 \\ & +4 && +4 \\ \hline z = 0 & z &=& 4 \end{array}$$

Set each factor equal to zero.
Solve each equation.

The solutions of $3z^2 - 12z = 0$ are 0 and 4.

Practice Problems

1. If $6x - (2x + 6) = x + 3$, then $x =$
   (1) −3
   (2) −1
   (3) 1
   (4) 2
   (5) 3

2. If $y^2 - 5y - 6 = 0$, then $y =$
   (1) 6 or −1
   (2) −6 or 1
   (3) −2 or 3
   (4) 2 or −3
   (5) 2 or 3

3. Solve for z: $8z + 5 - 10z > -3$
   (1) $z > 4$
   (2) $z > -4$
   (3) $z < 4$
   (4) $z < -4$
   (5) $z < 16$

4. If $2x^3 + 5x = 4x^3 - 2x^3 + 10$, then $x =$
   (1) −2
   (2) −1
   (3) 1
   (4) 2
   (5) 3

5. One number is three times another number. If their difference is 30, the smaller number is
   (1) 5
   (2) 10
   (3) 15
   (4) 20
   (5) 25

6. The perimeter of the figure below is 41. The length of the longest side is
   (1) 10
   (2) 11
   (3) 12
   (4) 13
   (5) 14

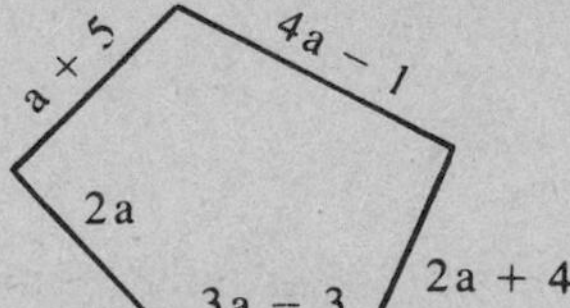

7. The sum of four consecutive even integers is 12. The smallest of the integers is
(1) 4
(2) 3
(3) 2
(4) 1
(5) 0

8. An estate was divided among three heirs, A, B and C, in the ratio 2:3:4. If the total estate was $22,500, what was the smallest inheritance?
(1) $1000
(2) $1250
(3) $2500
(4) $5000
(5) $7500

9. A dealer buys a TV set for $550 and wishes to sell it at a 20% profit. What should his selling price be?
(1) $570
(2) $600
(3) $660
(4) $672
(5) $680

10. Michael earns $50 for 8 hours of work. At the same rate of pay, how much will he earn for 28 hours of work?
(1) $150
(2) $175
(3) $186
(4) $232
(5) $286

11. Mrs. Smith wishes to purchase a freezer with a list price of $500. If she waits for a "15% off" sale and receives an additional discount of 2% for paying cash, how much will she save?
(1) $75.50
(2) $83.50
(3) $85.00
(4) $150.00
(5) $185.00

12. A photograph is 8" wide and 10" long. If it is enlarged so that the new length is 25", the new width will be
(1) $18\frac{1}{2}$"
(2) 20"
(3) 24"
(4) $31\frac{1}{4}$"
(5) 34"

13. Jean sells cosmetics, earning a 12% commission on all sales. How much will she need in sales to earn $300 in commission?
(1) $1800
(2) $1900
(3) $2100
(4) $2300
(5) $2500

14. Mr. Taylor leaves home at 8 AM, traveling at 45 miles per hour. Mrs. Taylor follows him, leaving home at 10 AM and traveling at 55 miles per hour. How long will it take Mrs. Taylor to catch up with Mr. Taylor?
(1) 7 hours
(2) 8 hours
(3) 9 hours
(4) 10 hours
(5) 11 hours

15. Sam buys a jacket marked $85. He pays $90.95 including sales tax. What percent sales tax does he pay?
(1) 4%
(2) 5%
(3) 6%
(4) 7%
(5) 8%

Practice Problems — Correct Answers

1. **(5)**
2. **(1)**
3. **(3)**
4. **(4)**
5. **(3)**
6. **(2)**
7. **(5)**
8. **(4)**
9. **(3)**
10. **(2)**
11. **(2)**
12. **(2)**
13. **(5)**
14. **(3)**
15. **(4)**

Problem Solutions

1. $6x - (2x + 6) = x + 3$

$6x - 2x - 6 = x + 3$ Remove parentheses first.

$4x - 6 = x + 3$ Combine the like terms on the left side.

$\underline{-x \qquad -x}$ Eliminate the x term from the right side.

$3x - 6 = 3$

$\underline{+6 \qquad +6}$ Eliminate the number term from the left side.

$\frac{3x}{3} = \frac{9}{3}$ Divide both sides by 3 to isolate x.

$x = 3$

Answer: **(5)** 3

2. $y^2 - 5y - 6 = 0$

$(y - 6)(y + 1) = 0$ Factor the trinomial side of the quadratic equation.

$y - 6 = 0$	$y + 1 = 0$	Set each factor equal to zero.
$\underline{+6 \quad +6}$	$\underline{-1 \quad -1}$	Solve each equation.
$y = 6$	$y = -1$	

Answer: **(1)** 6 or −1

3. $8z + 5 - 10z > -3$

$-2z + 5 > -3$ Combine the like terms on the left side.

$\underline{-5 \quad -5}$

$-2z > -8$ Divide both sides by −2 and reverse the inequality symbol.

$z < 4$

Answer: **(3)** $z < 4$

4. $2x^3 + 5x = 4x^3 - 2x^3 + 10$

$2x^3 + 5x = 2x^3 + 10$ Combine the like terms on the right side.

$\underline{-2x^3 \qquad -2x^3}$ Subtracting $2x^3$ from both sides leaves a simple equation.

$\frac{5x}{5} = \frac{10}{5}$

$x = 2$

Answer: **(4)** 2

5. Let n = the smaller number. Then 3n = the larger number. The difference of the numbers is 30.

$$3n - n = 30$$

$$\frac{2n}{2} = \frac{30}{2}$$

$$n = 15$$

Answer: **(3)** 15

6. The perimeter is equal to the sum of the sides.

$$a + 5 + 4a - 1 + 2a + 4 + 3a - 3 + 2a = 41$$

$$12a + 5 = 41 \quad \text{Combine like terms.}$$

$$\begin{array}{rcl} 12a + 5 & = & 41 \\ -5 & & -5 \\ \hline \frac{12a}{12} & = & \frac{36}{12} \\ a & = & 3 \end{array}$$

The sides are:

$$a + 5 = 3 + 5 = 8$$
$$4a - 1 = 4 \cdot 3 - 1 = 11$$
$$2a + 4 = 2 \cdot 3 + 4 = 10$$
$$3a - 3 = 3 \cdot 3 - 3 = 6$$
$$2a = 2 \cdot 3 = 6$$

The longest side is 11.

Answer: **(2)** 11

7. Let x, x + 2, x + 4 and x + 6 represent the four consecutive even integers. The sum of the integers is 12.

$$\begin{array}{rcl} x + x + 2 + x + 4 + x + 6 & = & 12 \\ 4x + 12 & = & 12 \\ -12 & & -12 \\ \hline \frac{4x}{4} & = & \frac{0}{4} \\ x & = & 0 \\ x + 2 & = & 2 \\ x + 4 & = & 4 \\ x + 6 & = & 6 \end{array}$$

The smallest integer is 0.

Answer: **(5)** 0

8. Let 2x, 3x and 4x represent the shares of the inheritance. The total estate was $22,500.

$$2x + 3x + 4x = 22500$$
$$\frac{9x}{9} = \frac{22500}{9}$$
$$x = 2500$$
$$2x = 2 \cdot 2500 = 5000$$
$$3x = 3 \cdot 2500 = 7500$$
$$4x = 4 \cdot 2500 = 10{,}000$$

The smallest inheritance was 2x, or $5000.

Answer: **(4)** $5000

9. His selling price will be (100% + 20%) of his cost price.

$$120\% \text{ of } \$550 = 1.20(\$550)$$
$$= \$660$$

Answer: **(3)** $660

10. The amount earned is proportional to the number of hours worked.

Let m = unknown pay

$$\frac{m}{28} = \frac{50}{8}$$

$$8m = 28 \cdot 50$$ The product of the means is equal to the product of the extremes.

$$\frac{8m}{8} = \frac{1400}{8}$$

$$m = 175$$

Answer: **(2)** \$175

11. The selling price after the 15% discount is 85% of list.

$$\text{selling price} = .85(500) = 425$$

The selling price after the additional 2% discount is 98% of 425.

$$\text{new selling price} = .98(425) = 416.50$$

The original price was \$500. Mrs. Smith buys at \$416.50. She saves

$$\$500 - \$416.50 = \$83.50$$

Answer: **(2)** \$83.50

12. The old dimensions and the new dimensions are in proportion. Let w = new width.

$$\frac{\text{new width}}{\text{old width}} = \frac{\text{new length}}{\text{old length}}$$

$$\frac{w}{8} = \frac{25}{10}$$

$$10w = 200$$

$$w = 20$$

Answer: **(2)** 20″

13. Let s = needed sales. 12% of sales will be \$300.

$$\frac{.12s}{.12} = \frac{300}{.12}$$ Divide by .12, or first multiply by 100 to clear the decimal, then divide by 12.

$$s = 2500$$

Answer: **(5)** \$2500

14. Let h = the number of hours needed by Mrs. Taylor. Mr. Taylor started two hours earlier; therefore, he travels h + 2 hours. Mrs. Taylor's distance is 55h. Mr. Taylor's distance is 45(h + 2). When Mrs. Taylor catches up with Mr. Taylor, they will have traveled equal distances.

$$\begin{aligned} 55h &= 45(h+2) \\ 55h &= 45h + 90 \\ -45h &= -45h \\ \hline 10h &= 90 \\ h &= 9 \end{aligned}$$

Answer: **(3)** 9 hours

15. The amount of tax is \$90.95 − \$85 = \$5.95. Find the percent \$5.95 is of \$85. Let p = percent.

$$\frac{p \cdot 85}{85} = \frac{5.95}{85}$$

$$p = .07 = 7\%$$

Answer: **(4)** 7%

GEOMETRY

Angles

1. a. An **angle** is the figure formed by two lines meeting at a point.

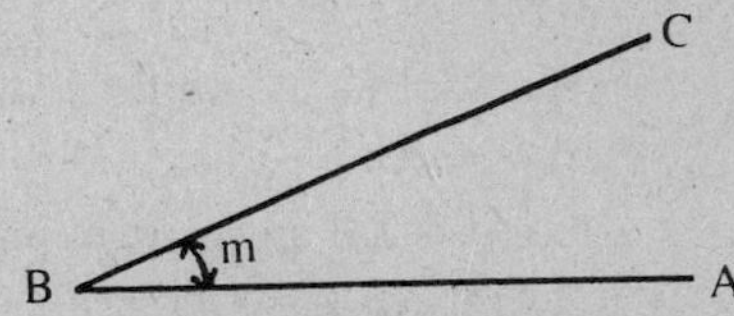

b. The point B is the **vertex** of the angle and the lines BA and BC are the **sides** of the angle.

2. There are three common ways of naming an angle:

   a. By a small letter or figure written within the angle, as $\measuredangle$m.

   b. By the capital letter at its vertex, as $\measuredangle$B.

   c. By three capital letters, the middle letter being the vertex letter, as $\measuredangle$ABC.

3. a. When two straight lines intersect (cut each other), four angles are formed. If these four angles are equal, each angle is a **right angle** and contains 90°. The symbol ⏋is used to indicate a right angle.

Example:

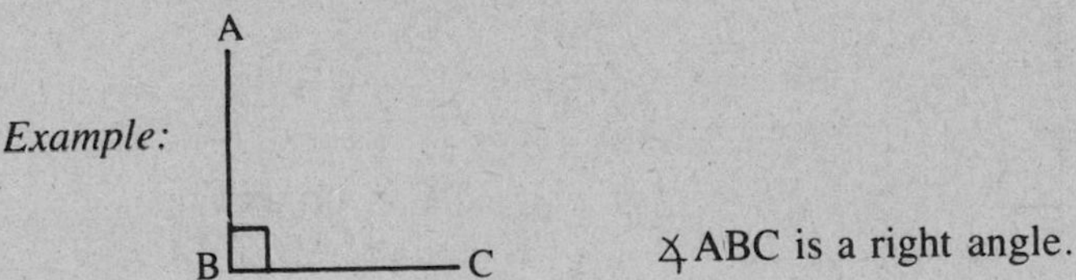

$\measuredangle$ABC is a right angle.

   b. An angle less than a right angle is an **acute angle**.

   c. If the two sides of an angle extend in opposite directions forming a straight line, the angle is a **straight angle** and contains 180°.

   d. An angle greater than a right angle (90°) and less than a straight angle (180°) is an **obtuse angle**.

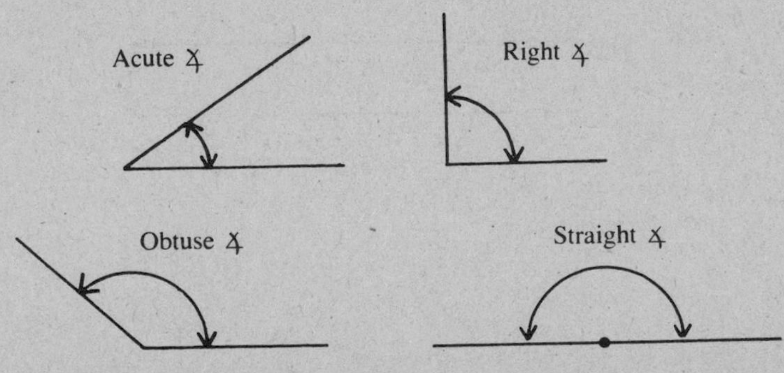

4. a. Two angles are **complementary** if their sum is 90°. To find the complement of an angle, subtract the given number of degrees from 90°.

Example: The complement of 60° = 90° − 60° = 30°.

b. Two angles are **supplementary** if their sum is 180°. To find the supplement of an angle, subtract the given number of degrees from 180°.

Example: The supplement of 60° = 180° − 60° = 120°.

5. When two straight lines intersect, any pair of opposite angles are called **vertical angles** and are equal.

∡a and ∡b are vertical angles
∡a = ∡b

∡c and ∡d are vertical angles
∡c = ∡d

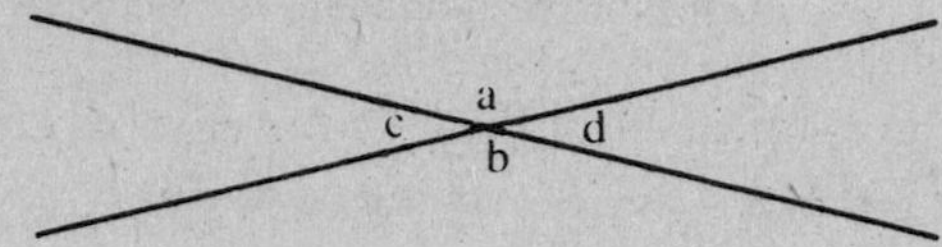

6. Two lines are **perpendicular** to each other if they meet to form a right angle. The symbol ⊥ is used to indicate that the lines are perpendicular.

Example:

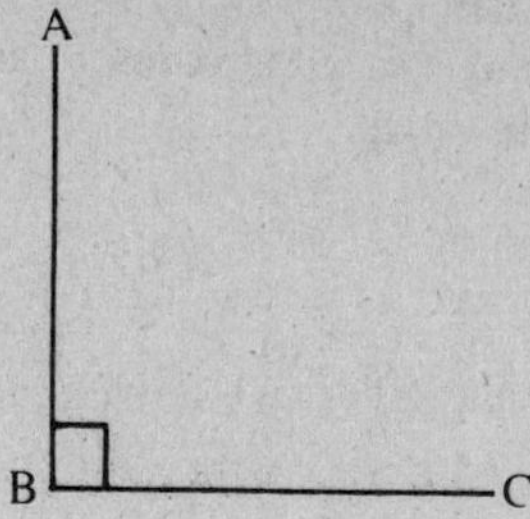

∡ABC is a right angle.
Therefore, AB ⊥ BC.

7. a. Lines that do not meet no matter how far they are extended are called **parallel lines**. The symbol || is used to indicate that two lines are parallel.

Example: AB || CD

b. A line that intersects parallel lines is called a **transversal**. The pairs of angles formed have special names and relationships.

Example:

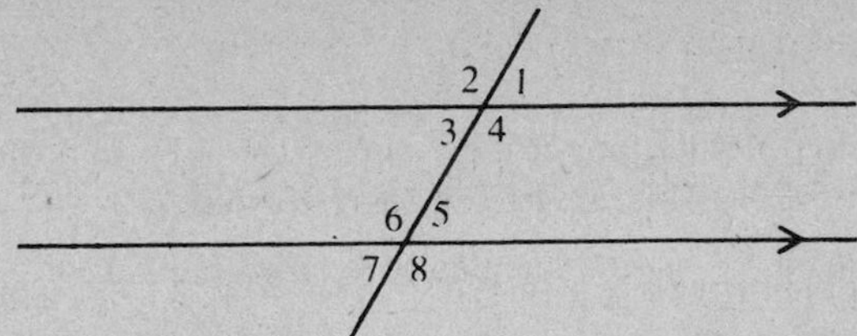

alternate interior angles:

$\angle 3 = \angle 5$
$\angle 4 = \angle 6$

corresponding angles:

$\angle 1 = \angle 5$
$\angle 2 = \angle 6$
$\angle 3 = \angle 7$
$\angle 4 = \angle 8$

Several pairs of angles, such as $\angle 1$ and $\angle 2$, are supplementary. Several pairs, such as $\angle 6$ and $\angle 8$, are vertical angles and are therefore equal.

Triangles

8. A triangle is a closed, three-sided figure. The following figures are triangles.

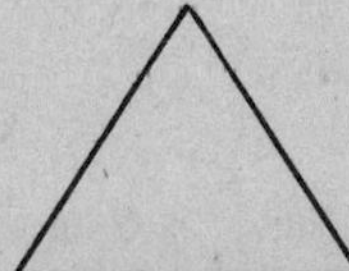

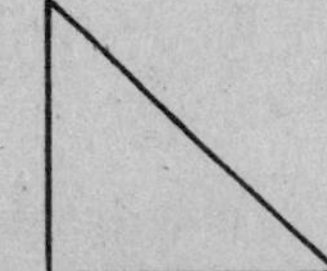

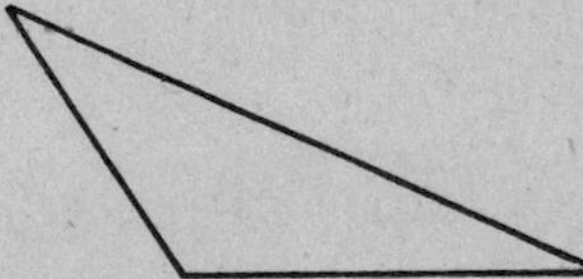

9. a. The sum of the three angles of a triangle is 180°.

   b. To find an angle of a triangle given the other two angles, add the given angles and subtract their sum from 180°.

Illustration: Two angles of a triangle are 60° and 40°. Find the third angle.

SOLUTION: $60° + 40° = 100°$
$180° - 100° = 80°$

Answer: The third angle is 80°.

10. a. A triangle with two equal sides is called an **isosceles triangle**.

    b. In an isosceles triangle, the angles opposite the equal sides are also equal.

Example:

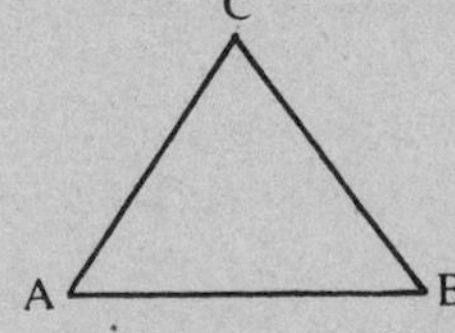

If $AC = BC$, then $\angle A = \angle B$

11. a. A triangle with all three sides equal is called an **equilateral triangle.**

    b. Each angle of an equilateral triangle is 60°.

12. a. A triangle with a right angle is called a **right triangle.**

    b. In a right triangle, the two acute angles are complementary.

    c. In a right triangle, the side opposite the right angle is called the **hypotenuse** and is the longest side. The other two sides are called **legs.**

Example:

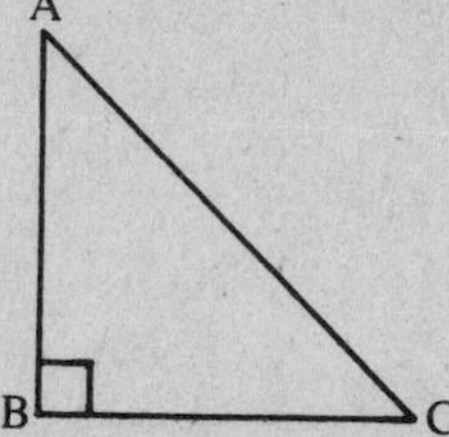

In right triangle ABC, AC is the hypotenuse. AB and BC are the legs.

13. The **Pythagorean Theorem** states that in a right triangle, the square of the hypotenuse equals the sum of the squares of the legs.

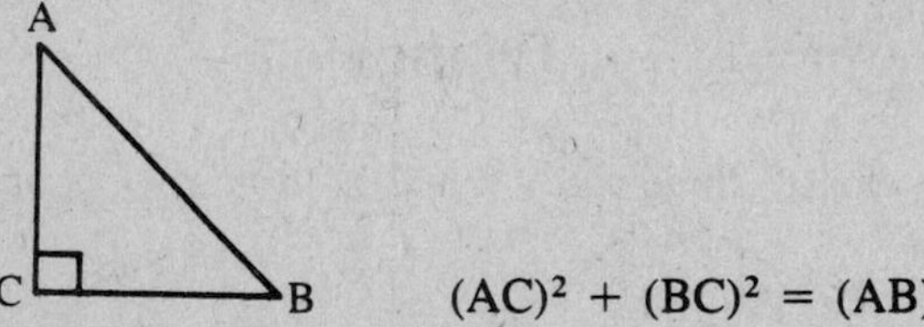

$$(AC)^2 + (BC)^2 = (AB)^2$$

Illustration: Find the hypotenuse (h) in a right triangle that has legs 6 and 8.

SOLUTION:

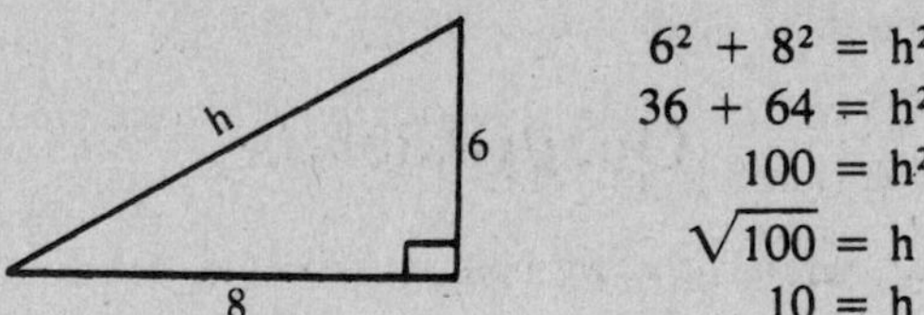

$$\begin{aligned} 6^2 + 8^2 &= h^2 \\ 36 + 64 &= h^2 \\ 100 &= h^2 \\ \sqrt{100} &= h \\ 10 &= h \end{aligned}$$

Illustration: One leg of a right triangle is 5. The hypotenuse is 13. Find the other leg.

SOLUTION: Let the unknown leg be represented by x.

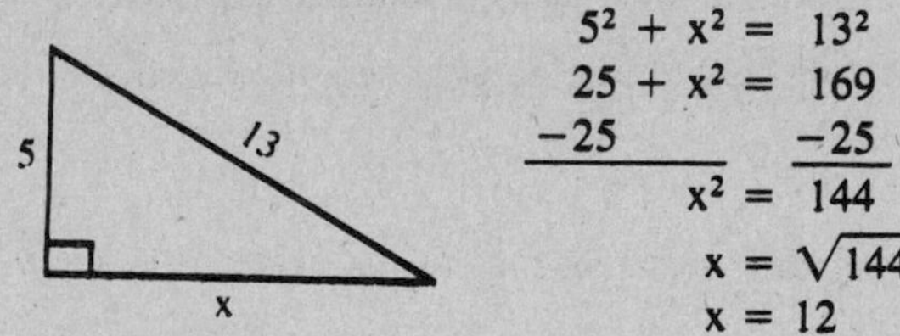

$$\begin{aligned} 5^2 + x^2 &= 13^2 \\ 25 + x^2 &= 169 \\ -25 \quad & \quad -25 \\ x^2 &= 144 \\ x &= \sqrt{144} \\ x &= 12 \end{aligned}$$

Answer: The other leg is 12.

14. a. In a right triangle with equal legs (an isosceles right triangle), each acute angle is equal to 45°. There are special relationships between the legs and the hypotenuse:

$$\text{each leg} = \tfrac{1}{2}(\text{hypotenuse})\sqrt{2}$$
$$\text{hypotenuse} = (\text{leg})\sqrt{2}$$

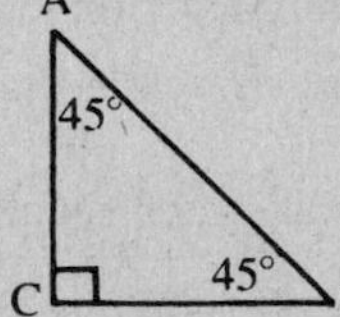

$$AC = BC = \tfrac{1}{2}(AB)\sqrt{2}$$
$$AB = (AC)\sqrt{2} = (BC)\sqrt{2}$$

Example: In isosceles right triangle RST,

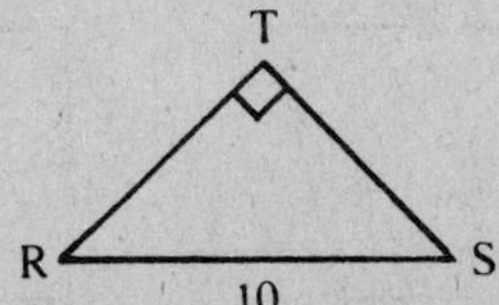

$$RT = \tfrac{1}{2}(10)\sqrt{2}$$
$$= 5\sqrt{2}$$
$$ST = RT = 5\sqrt{2}$$

b In a right triangle with acute angles of 30° and 60°, the leg opposite the 30° angle is one-half the hypotenuse. The leg opposite the 60° angle is one-half the hypotenuse multiplied by $\sqrt{3}$.

Example:

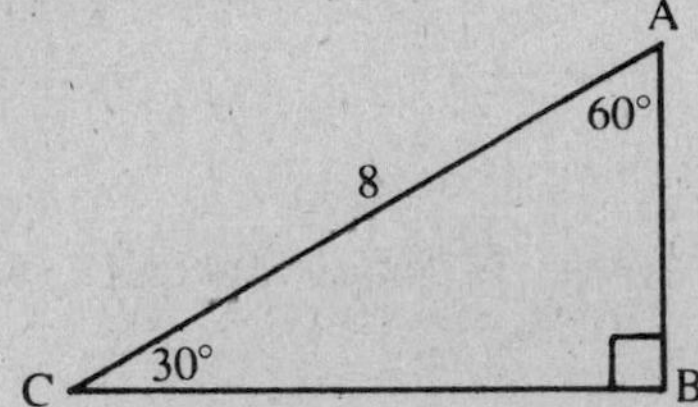

$$AB = \tfrac{1}{2}(8) = 4$$
$$BC = \tfrac{1}{2}(8)\sqrt{3} = 4\sqrt{3}$$

Quadrilaterals

15. a. A **quadrilateral** is a closed, four-sided figure in two dimensions. Common quadrilaterals are the **parallelogram**, **rectangle**, and **square**.

b. The sum of the four angles of a quadrilateral is 360°.

16. a. A **parallelogram** is a quadrilateral in which both pairs of opposite sides are parallel.

b. Opposite sides of a parallelogram are equal.

c. Opposite angles of a parallelogram are equal.

Example:

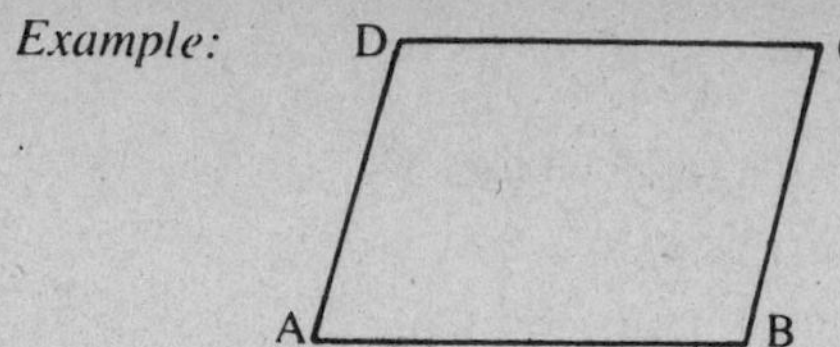

In parallelogram ABCD,
AB || CD, AB = CD, $\angle A = \angle C$
AD || BC, AD = BC, $\angle B = \angle D$

17. a. A **rhombus** is a parallelogram that has all sides equal.

 b. A **rectangle** is a parallelogram that has all right angles.

 c. A **square** is a rectangle that has all sides equal. A square is also a rhombus.

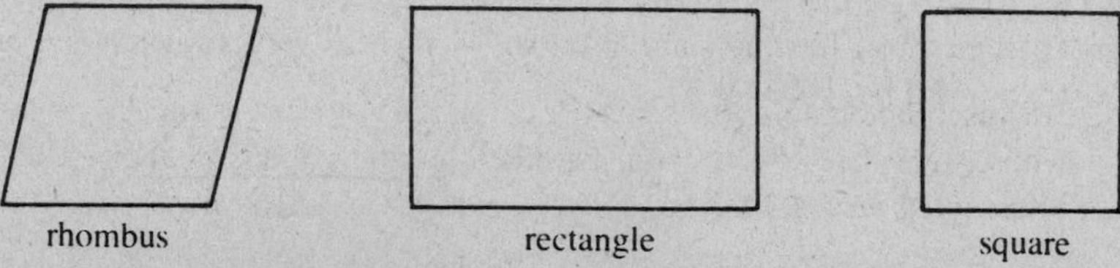

18. A **trapezoid** is a quadrilateral with one and only one pair of opposite sides parallel.

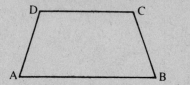

In trapezoid ABCD, AB || CD

Circles

19. A **circle** is a closed plane curve, all points of which are equidistant from a point within called the center.

20. a. A **complete circle** contains 360°.

 b. A **semi-circle** contains 180°.

21. a. A **chord** is a line segment connecting any two points on the circle.

 b. A **radius** of a circle is a line segment connecting the center with any point on the circle.

 c. A **diameter** is a chord passing through the center of the circle.

 d. A **secant** is a chord extended in either one or both directions.

 e. A **tangent** is a line touching a circle at one point and only one.

 f. The **circumference** is the curved line bounding the circle.

g. An **arc** of a circle is any part of the circumference.

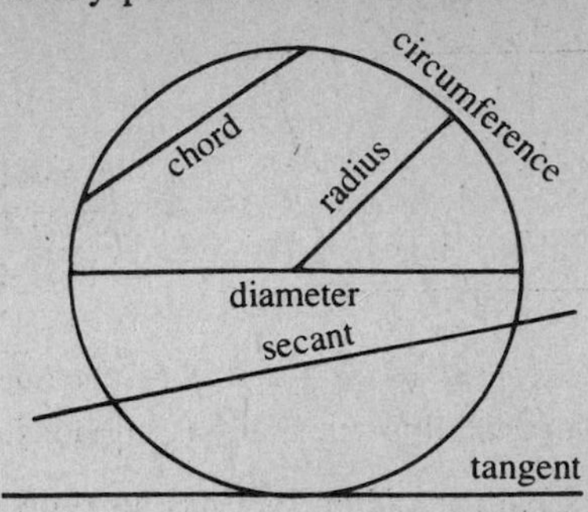

22. a. A **central angle**, as ∡AOB in the figure below, is an angle whose vertex is the center of the circle and whose sides are radii. A central angle is equal in degrees to (or has the same number of degrees as) its intercepted arc.

b. An **inscribed angle**, as ∡MNP, is an angle whose vertex is on the circle and whose sides are chords. An inscribed angle is equal in degrees to one-half its intercepted arc. ∡MNP equals one-half the degrees in arc MP.

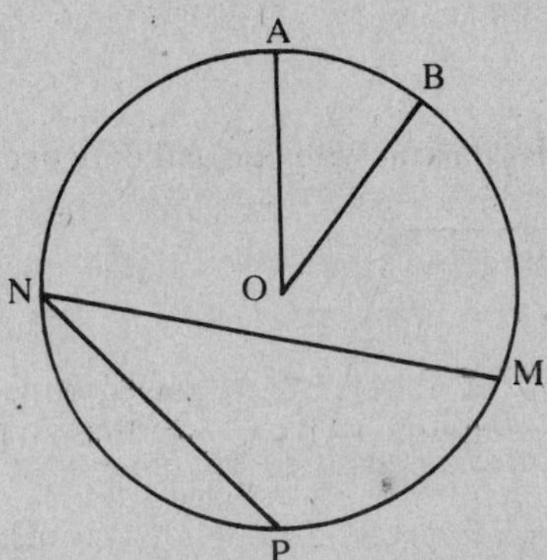

Perimeter

23. The **perimeter** of a two-dimensional figure is the distance around the figure.

Example: The perimeter of the figure below is $9 + 8 + 4 + 3 + 5 = 29$

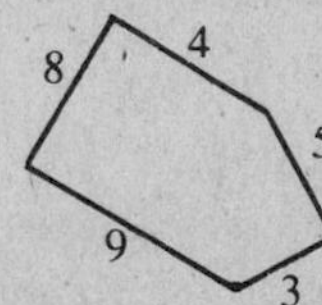

24. a. The perimeter of a triangle is found by adding all of its sides.

Example: If the sides of a triangle are 4, 5 and 7, its perimeter is $4 + 5 + 7 = 16$.

b. If the perimeter and two sides of a triangle are given, the third side is found by adding the two given sides and subtracting this sum from the perimeter.

Illustration: Two sides of a triangle are 12 and 15. The perimeter is 37. Find the other side.

SOLUTION: 12 + 15 = 27
37 − 27 = 10

Answer: The third side is 10.

25. The perimeter of a rectangle equals twice the sum of the length and the width. The length is any side; the width is the side next to the length. The formula is: P = 2(l + w).

Example: The perimeter of a rectangle whose length is 7 feet and width is 3 feet equals 2 × 10 = 20 ft.

26. The perimeter of a square equals one side multiplied by 4. The formula is: P = 4s.

Example: The perimeter of a square one side of which is 5 feet equals 4 × 5 feet = 20 feet.

27. a. The **circumference** of a circle is equal to the product of the diameter multiplied by π. The formula is $C = \pi d$.

b. The number π ("pi") is approximately equal to $\frac{22}{7}$, or 3.14 (3.1416 for greater accuracy). The problem will state which value to use; otherwise, express the answer in terms of "pi," π.

Example: The circumference of a circle whose diameter is 4 inches = 4π inches; or, if it is stated that $\pi = \frac{22}{7}$, then the circumference = $4 \times \frac{22}{7} = \frac{88}{7} = 12\frac{4}{7}$ inches.

c. Since the diameter is twice the radius, the circumference equals twice the radius multiplied by π. The formula is $C = 2\pi r$.

Example: If the radius of a circle is 3 inches, then the circumference = 6π inches.

d. The diameter of a circle equals the circumference divided by π.

Example: If the circumference of a circle is 11 inches, then, assuming $\pi = \frac{22}{7}$,

$$\text{diameter} = 11 \div \frac{22}{7} \text{ inches}$$
$$= \overset{1}{\cancel{11}} \times \frac{7}{\underset{2}{\cancel{22}}} \text{ inches}$$
$$= \frac{7}{2} \text{ inches, or } 3\frac{1}{2} \text{ inches}$$

Area

28. a. In a figure of two dimensions, the total space within the figure is called the **area**.

b. Area is expressed in square denominations, such as **square inches**, **square centimeters** and **square miles**.

c. In computing area, all dimensions must be in the same denomination.

29. The area of a square is equal to the square of the length of any side. The formula is $A = s^2$.

Example: The area of a square one side of which is 6 inches is 6 × 6 = 36 square inches.

30. a. The area of a rectangle equals the product of the length multiplied by the width. The formula is $A = l \times w$.

Example: If the length of a rectangle is 6 feet and its width is 4 feet, then the area is $6 \times 4 = 24$ square feet.

b. If given the area of a rectangle and one dimension, you can find the other dimension by dividing the area by the given dimension.

Example: If the area of a rectangle is 48 square feet and one dimension is 4 feet, then the other dimension is $48 \div 4 = 12$ feet.

31. a. The altitude, or **height**, of a parallelogram is a line drawn from a vertex perpendicular to the opposite side, or **base**.

Example:

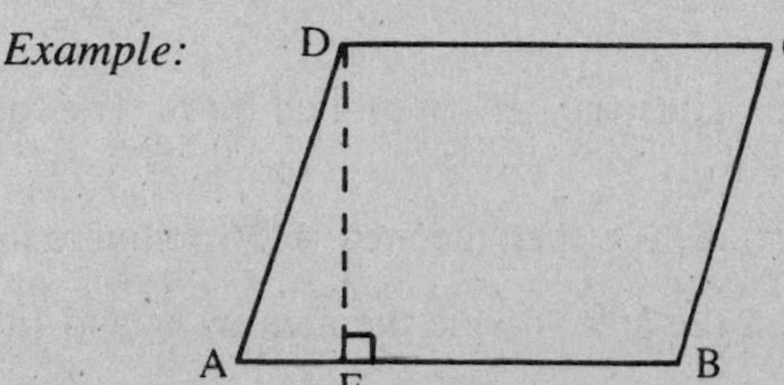

DE is the height
AB is the base

b. The area of a parallelogram is equal to the product of its base and its height. The formula is $A = b \times h$.

Example: If the base of a parallelogram is 10 centimeters and its height is 5 centimeters, its area is $10 \times 5 = 50$ square centimeters.

c. To find the base or the height of a parallelogram given one of these dimensions and given the area, divide the area by the given dimension.

Example: If the area of a parallelogram is 40 square inches and its height is 8 inches, its base is $40 \div 8 = 5$ inches.

32. a. The altitude, or height, of a triangle is a line drawn from a vertex perpendicular to the opposite side, called the base.

b. The area of a triangle is equal to one-half the product of the base and the height. The formula is $A = \frac{1}{2}b \times h$.

Example: The area of a triangle that has a height of 5 inches and a base of 4 inches is $\frac{1}{2} \times 5 \times 4 = \frac{1}{2} \times 20 = 10$ square inches.

c. In a right triangle, one leg may be considered the height and the other leg the base. Therefore, the area of a right triangle is equal to one-half the product of the legs.

Example: The legs of a right triangle are 3 and 4. Its area is $\frac{1}{2} \times 3 \times 4 = 6$ square units.

33. The area of a rhombus is equal to one-half the product of its diagonals. The formula is: $A = \frac{1}{2} \cdot d_1 \cdot d_2$.

Example: If the diagonals of a rhombus are 4 and 6,

$$\text{Area} = \tfrac{1}{2} \cdot 4 \cdot 6$$
$$= 12$$

34. The area of a trapezoid is equal to one-half the product of the height and the sum of the bases.

$$\text{Area} = \tfrac{1}{2}h(\text{base}_1 + \text{base}_2)$$

Example: The area of trapezoid ABCD $= \frac{1}{2} \cdot 4 \cdot (5 + 10)$
$= 2 \cdot 15$
$= 30$

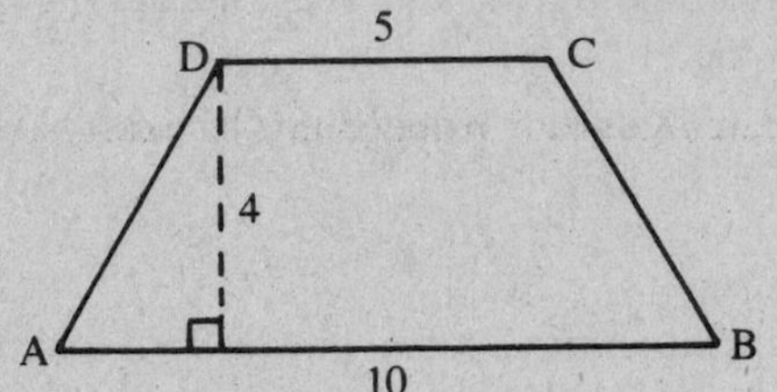

35. a. The area of a circle is equal to the radius squared multiplied by π. The formula is $A = \pi r^2$.

Example: If the radius of a circle is 6 inches, then the area $= 36\pi$ square inches.

b. To find the radius of a circle given the area, divide the area by π and find the square root of the quotient.

Example: To find the radius of a circle of area 100π:

$$\frac{100\pi}{\pi} = 100$$

$$\sqrt{100} = 10 = \text{radius}$$

36. Some figures are composed of several geometric shapes. To find the area of such figures, it is necessary to find the area of each of their parts.

Illustration: Find the area of the figure below:

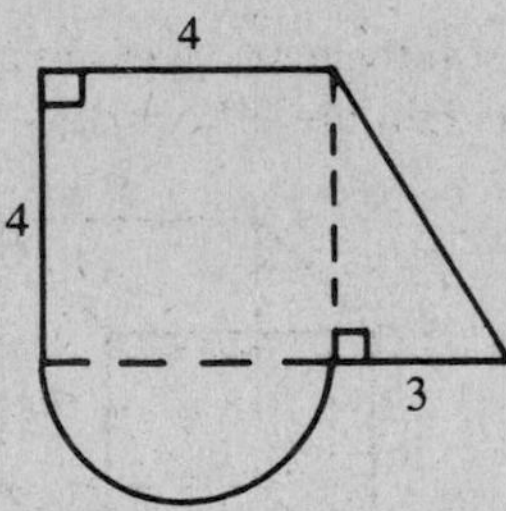

SOLUTION: The figure is composed of three parts: a square of side 4, a semi-circle of diameter 4 (the lower side of the square), and a right triangle with legs 3 and 4 (the right side of the square).

$$\text{Area of square} = 4^2 = 16$$

$$\text{Area of triangle} = \tfrac{1}{2} \times 3 \times 4 = 6$$

$$\text{Area of semi-circle is } \tfrac{1}{2} \text{ area of circle} = \tfrac{1}{2}\pi r^2$$

$$\text{Radius} = \tfrac{1}{2} \times 4 = 2$$

$$\text{Area} = \tfrac{1}{2}\pi r^2$$

$$= \tfrac{1}{2}\pi 2^2 = 2\pi$$

$$\text{Total area} = 16 + 6 + 2\pi = 22 + 2\pi$$

Three-Dimensional Figures

37. a. In a three dimensional figure, the total space contained within the figure is called the **volume** and is expressed in cubic denominations.

    b. The total outside surface is called the **surface area** and it is expressed in square denominations.

    c. In computing volume and surface area, all dimensions must be expressed in the same denomination.

38. a. A rectangular solid is a figure of three dimensions having six rectangular faces meeting each other at right angles. The three dimensions are **length**, **width**, and **height**. The figure below is a rectangular solid; "l" is the length, "w" is the width, and "h" is the height.

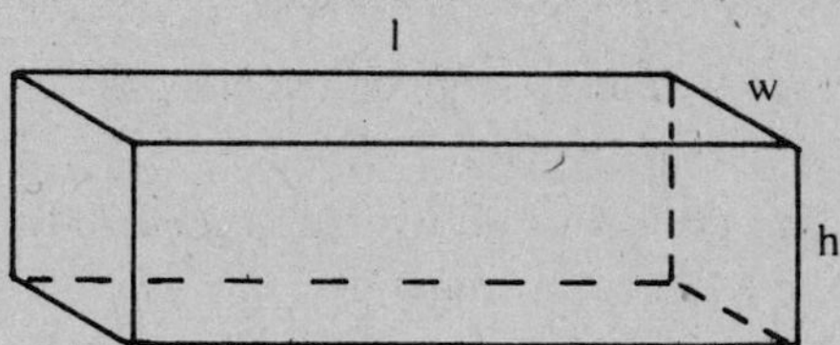

    b. The volume of a rectangular solid is the product of the length, width, and height; $V = l \times w \times h$.

    Example: The volume of a rectangular solid whose length is 6 ft, width 3 ft, and height 4 ft is $6 \times 3 \times 4 = 72$ cubic ft.

39. a. A **cube** is a rectangular solid whose edges are equal. The figure below is a cube; the length, width, and height are all equal to "e."

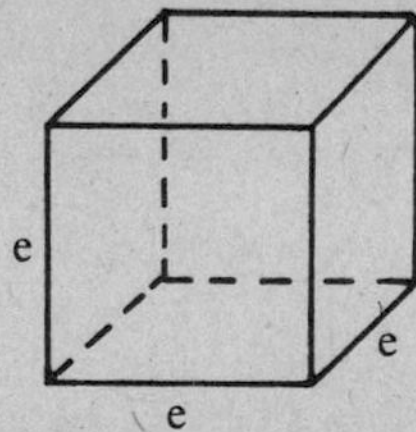

    b. The volume of a cube is equal to the edge cubed; $v = e^3$.

    Example: The volume of a cube whose height is 6 inches equals $6^3 = 6 \times 6 \times 6 =$ 216 cubic inches.

    c. The surface area of a cube is equal to the area of any side multiplied by 6.

    Example: The surface area of a cube whose length is 5 inches $= 5^2 \times 6 = 25 \times 6 = 150$ square inches.

40. The volume of a circular cylinder is equal to the product of π, the radius squared, and the height.

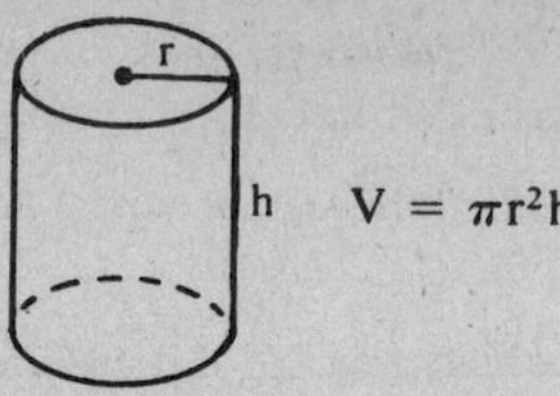

Example: A circular cylinder has a radius of 7 inches and a height of $\frac{1}{2}$ inch. Using $\pi = \frac{22}{7}$, its volume is:

$$\frac{22}{7} \times 7 \times 7 \times \frac{1}{2} = 77 \text{ cubic inches}$$

41. The volume of a sphere is equal to $\frac{4}{3}$ the product of π and the radius cubed.

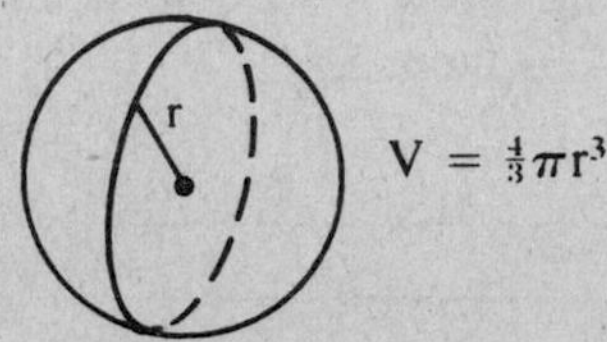

Example: If the radius of a sphere is 3 cm, its volume in terms of π is:

$$\frac{4}{3} \times \pi \times 3 \times 3 \times 3 = 36\pi \text{ cubic centimeters}$$

42. The volume of a cone is given by the formula $V = \frac{1}{3}\pi r^2 h$, where r is the radius and h is the height.

Example: In the cone shown below, if h = 9 cm, r = 10 cm and $\pi = 3.14$, then the volume is:

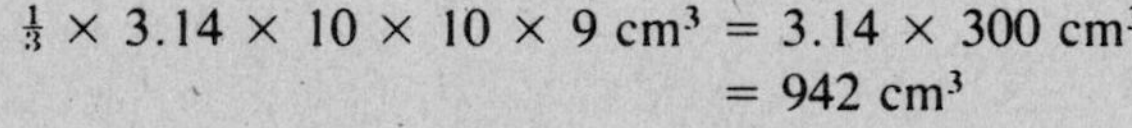

$$\frac{1}{3} \times 3.14 \times 10 \times 10 \times 9 \text{ cm}^3 = 3.14 \times 300 \text{ cm}^3$$
$$= 942 \text{ cm}^3$$

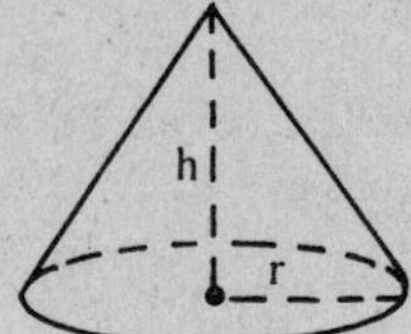

43. The volume of a pyramid is given by the formula $V = \frac{1}{3}Bh$, where B is the area of the base and h is the height.

Example: In the pyramid shown below, the height is 10 inches and the side of the base is 3 inches. Since the base is a square,

$$B = 3^2 = 9 \text{ square inches}$$
$$V = \frac{1}{3} \times 9 \times 10 = 30 \text{ cubic inches}$$

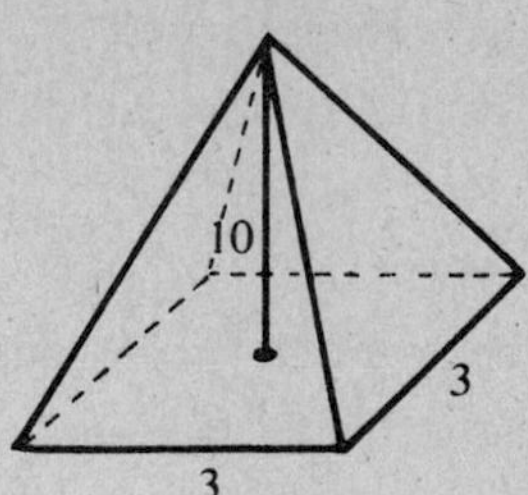

Summary of Geometric Formulas

Perimeter

Any 2-dimensional figure	P = sum of all the sides
Rectangle	$P = 2(l + w)$
Square	$P = 4s$
Circle	Circumference $= 2\pi r = \pi d$

Area

Square	$A = s^2$
Rectangle	$A = l \cdot w$
Parallelogram	$A = b \cdot h$
Triangle	$A = \frac{1}{2} \cdot b \cdot h$
Right triangle	$A = \frac{1}{2} \cdot leg_1 \cdot leg_2$
Rhombus	$A = \frac{1}{2} \cdot d_1 \cdot d_2$
Trapezoid	$A = \frac{1}{2} \cdot h(b_1 + b_2)$
Circle	$A = \pi r^2$

Volume

Rectangular solid	$V = l \cdot w \cdot h$
Cube	$V = e^3$
Circular cylinder	$V = \pi r^2 h$
Sphere	$V = \frac{4}{3}\pi r^3$
Cone	$V = \frac{1}{3}\pi r^2 h$
Pyramid	$V = \frac{1}{3} \cdot B \cdot h$ (B = area of base)

Practice Problems Involving Geometry

1. If the perimeter of a rectangle is 68 yards and the width is 48 feet, the length is
   (1) 10 yards (2) 18 yards (3) 20 feet (4) 56 feet (5) 60 feet
2. The total length of fencing needed to enclose a rectangular area 46 feet by 34 feet is
   (1) 26 yards 1 foot (2) $26\frac{2}{3}$ yards (3) 52 yards 2 feet (4) $53\frac{1}{3}$ yards (5) 54 yards
3. An umbrella 50″ long can lie on the bottom of a trunk whose length and width are, respectively
   (1) 36 inches, 30 inches (2) 42 inches, 24 inches (3) 42 inches, 36 inches (4) 39 inches, 30 inches (5) 44 inches, 24 inches
4. A road runs 1200 ft. from A to B, and then makes a right angle going to C, a distance of 500 ft. A new road is being built directly from A to C. How much shorter will the new road be?
   (1) 400 feet (2) 609 feet (3) 850 feet (4) 1300 feet (5) 1350 feet
5. A certain triangle has sides that are, respectively, 6 inches, 8 inches, and 10 inches long. A rectangle equal in area to that of the triangle has a width of 3 inches. The perimeter of the rectangle, expressed in inches, is
   (1) 11 (2) 16 (3) 18 (4) 20 (5) 22
6. If AB || DE, ∡C = 50° and ∡1 = 60°, then ∡A =
   (1) 30° (2) 60° (3) 70° (4) 50° (5) 80°

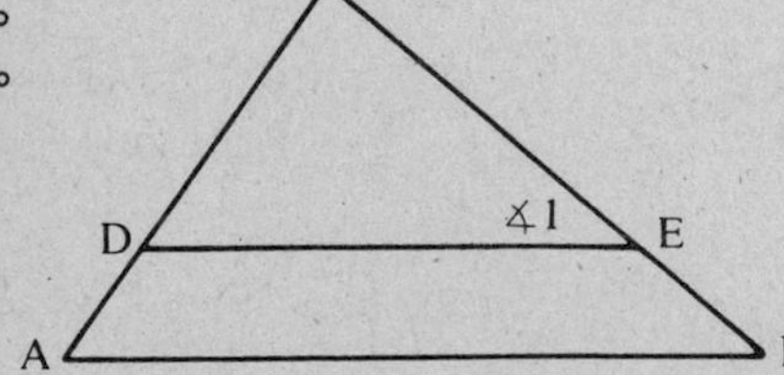

7. A rectangular bin 4 feet long, 3 feet wide, and 2 feet high is solidly packed with bricks whose dimensions are 8 inches, 4 inches, and 2 inches. The number of bricks in the bin is
   (1) 54 (2) 648 (3) 1296 (4) 1300 (5) none of these
8. If the cost of digging a trench is $2.12 a cubic yard, what would be the cost of digging a trench 2 yards by 5 yards by 4 yards?
   (1) $21.20 (2) $40.00 (3) $64.00 (4) $84.80 (5) $90.00
9. A piece of wire is shaped to enclose a square, whose area is 121 square inches. It is then reshaped to enclose a rectangle whose length is 13 inches. The area of the rectangle, in square inches, is
   (1) 64 (2) 96 (3) 117 (4) 144 (5) 169
10. The area of a 2-foot-wide walk around a garden that is 30 feet long and 20 feet wide is
    (1) 104 square feet (2) 120 square feet (3) 180 square feet (4) 200 square feet (5) 216 square feet
11. The area of a circle is 49π. Find its circumference, in terms of π.
    (1) 14π (2) 28π (3) 49π (4) 98π (5) 100π
12. In two hours, the minute hand of a clock rotates through an angle of
    (1) 90° (2) 180° (3) 360° (4) 720° (5) 900°
13. A box is 12 inches in width, 16 inches in length, and 6 inches in height. How many square inches of paper would be required to cover it on all sides?
    (1) 192 (2) 360 (3) 720 (4) 1440 (5) 2000

14. If the volume of a cube is 64 cubic inches, the sum of its edges is
(1) 4 inches
(2) 8 inches
(3) 16 inches
(4) 24 inches
(5) 48 inches

15. The diameter of a conical pile of cement is 30 feet and its height is 14 feet. If $\frac{3}{4}$ cubic yard of cement weighs 1 ton, the number of tons of cement in the cone to the nearest ton is
(Volume of a cone = $\frac{1}{3}\pi r^2 h$; use $\pi = \frac{22}{7}$)
(1) 92
(2) 163
(3) 489
(4) 652
(5) 689

Geometry Problems — Correct Answers

1. **(2)**
2. **(4)**
3. **(3)**
4. **(1)**
5. **(5)**
6. **(3)**
7. **(2)**
8. **(4)**
9. **(3)**
10. **(5)**
11. **(1)**
12. **(4)**
13. **(3)**
14. **(5)**
15. **(2)**

Problem Solutions — Geometry

1. Perimeter = 2(l + w). Let the length be x yards.

$$\begin{aligned} \text{Each width} &= 48 \text{ ft} \\ &= 16 \text{ yd} \\ 2(x + 16) &= 68 \\ 2x + 32 &= 68 \\ -32 &\quad -32 \\ \frac{2x}{2} &= \frac{36}{2} \\ x &= 18 \end{aligned}$$

Answer: **(2)** 18 yards

2. $$\begin{aligned} \text{Perimeter} &= 2(l + w) \\ &= 2(46 + 34) \text{ feet} \\ &= 2 \times 80 \text{ feet} \\ &= 160 \text{ feet} \end{aligned}$$

$$160 \text{ feet} = 160 \div 3 \text{ yards} = 53\tfrac{1}{3} \text{ yards}$$

Answer: **(4)** $53\frac{1}{3}$ yards

3. The umbrella would be the hypotenuse of a right triangle whose legs are the dimensions of the trunk. According to the Pythagorean Theorem, in any right triangle the square of the hypotenuse equals the sum of the squares of the legs. Therefore, the sum of the dimensions squared must at least equal the length of the umbrella squared: $(50)^2 = 2500$.

The only set of dimensions that fills this condition is (3):

$$\begin{aligned} (42)^2 + (36)^2 &= 1764 + 1296 \\ &= 3060 \end{aligned}$$

Answer: **(3)** 42″, 36″

4. The new road is the hypotenuse of a right triangle whose legs are the old road.

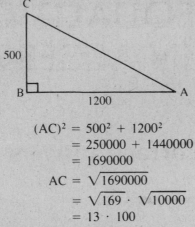

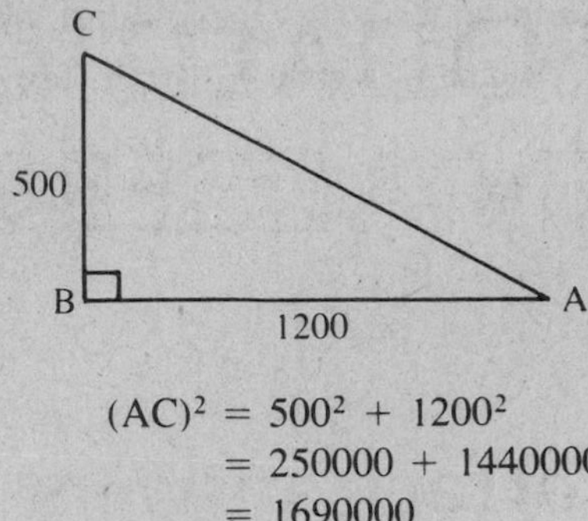

$$\begin{aligned}(AC)^2 &= 500^2 + 1200^2\\ &= 250000 + 1440000\\ &= 1690000\\ AC &= \sqrt{1690000}\\ &= \sqrt{169}\cdot\sqrt{10000}\\ &= 13 \cdot 100\\ &= 1300\end{aligned}$$

$$\begin{aligned}\text{Old road} &= 500 \text{ ft} + 1200 \text{ ft}\\ &= 1700 \text{ ft}\\ \text{New road} &= 1300 \text{ ft}\\ \text{Difference} &= 400 \text{ ft}\end{aligned}$$

Answer: **(1)** 400 feet

5. Since $6^2 + 8^2 = 10^2$, or $36 + 64 = 100$, the triangle is a right triangle. Its area is $\frac{1}{2} \times 6 \times 8 = 24$ sq. in. (area of a triangle $= \frac{1}{2} \cdot b \cdot h$). Therefore, the area of the rectangle is also 24 square inches. If the width of the rectangle is 3 inches, the length is $24 \div 3 = 8$ inches. Then, the perimeter of the rectangle is $2(3 + 8) = 2 \times 11 = 22$ inches.

Answer: **(5)** 22

6. ∡B and ∡1 are corresponding angles formed by the parallel lines AB and DE and the transversal BC. Therefore, ∡1 = ∡B = 60°.

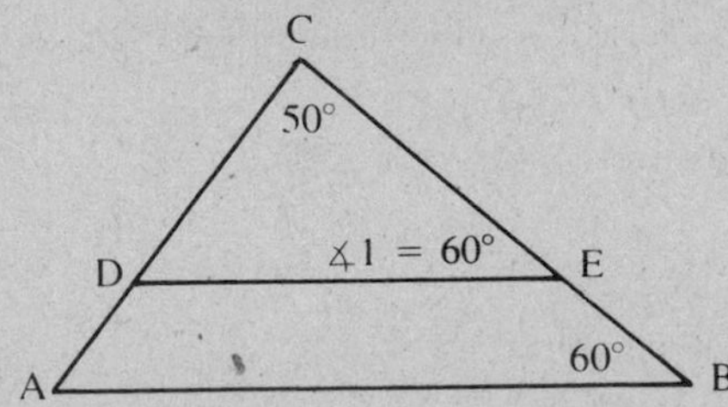

The sum of the angles of a triangle is 180°.

$$\begin{aligned}\measuredangle A + \measuredangle B + \measuredangle C &= 180^\circ\\ \measuredangle A + 60^\circ + 50^\circ &= 180^\circ\\ \measuredangle A + 110^\circ &= 180^\circ\\ -110^\circ &\quad -110^\circ\\ \measuredangle A &= 70^\circ\end{aligned}$$

Answer: **(3)** 70°

7. Convert the dimensions of the bin to inches:

4 feet = 48 inches
3 feet = 36 inches
2 feet = 24 inches

Volume of bin = $48 \times 36 \times 24$ cubic inches
= 41,472 cubic inches

Volume of each brick = $8 \times 4 \times 2$ cubic inches
= 64 cubic inches

$41472 \div 64 = 648$ bricks

Answer: **(2)** 648

8. The trench contains:

$2 \text{ yd} \times 5 \text{ yd} \times 4 \text{ yd} = 40$ cubic yards

$40 \times \$2.12 = \$84.80$

Answer: **(4)** $84.80

9. If the area of the square is 121 square inches, each side is $\sqrt{121} = 11$ inches and the perimeter is $4 \times 11 = 44$ inches. The perimeter of the rectangle is then 44 inches. If the two lengths are each 13 inches, their total is 26 inches. $44 - 26 = 18$ inches remain for the two widths. Therefore, each width is equal to $18 \div 2 = 9$ inches.

The area of a rectangle with length 13 inches and width 9 inches is $13 \times 9 = 117$ square inches.

Answer: **(3)** 117

10. The walk consists of:

a) 2 rectangles of length 30 ft and width 2 ft.
Area of each = $2 \times 30 = 60$ sq ft
Area of both = 120 sq ft

b) 2 rectangles of length 20 ft and width 2 ft.
Area of each = $2 \times 20 = 40$ sq ft
Area of both = 80 sq ft

c) 4 squares, each having a side of 2 ft.
Area of each square = $2^2 = 4$ sq ft
Area of 4 squares = 16 sq ft

Total area of walk = $120 + 80 + 16$
= 216 sq ft

Alternatively, you may solve this problem by finding the area of the garden and the area of the garden plus the walk, then subtracting to find the area of the walk alone:

Area of garden = $20 \times 30 = 600$ sq ft

Area of garden + walk:
$(20 + 2 + 2) \times (30 + 2 + 2) = 24 \times 34$
= 816 sq ft

Area of walk alone:
$816 - 600 = 216$ sq ft

Answer: **(5)** 216 sq ft

11. Area of a circle = πr^2. If the area is 49π, the radius is $\sqrt{49} = 7$.

Circumference = $2\pi r$
= $2 \times \pi \times 7$
= 14π

Answer: **(1)** 14π

12. In one hour, the minute hand rotates through 360°. In two hours it rotates through $2 \times 360° = 720°$.

Answer: **(4)** 720°

13. 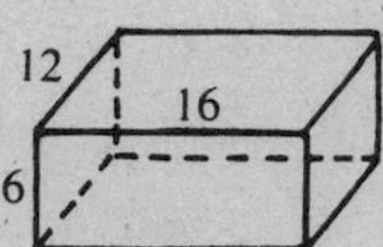

Area of top = $12 \times 16 = 192$ sq in.
Area of bottom = $12 \times 16 = 192$ sq in.
Area of front = $6 \times 16 = 96$ sq in.
Area of back = $6 \times 16 = 96$ sq in.
Area of right side = $6 \times 12 = 72$ sq in.
Area of left side = $6 \times 12 = 72$ sq in.

Total surface area:
$192 + 192 + 96 + 96 + 72 + 72 = 720$ sq in.

Answer: **(3)** 720

14. For a cube, $V = e^3$. If the volume is 64 cubic inches, each edge is $\sqrt[3]{64} = 4$ inches.

A cube has 12 edges. If each edge is 4 inches, the sum of the edges is $4 \times 12 = 48$ inches.

Answer: **(5)** 48 inches

15. If diameter = 30, radius = 15.

$$V = \frac{1}{\cancel{3}_1} \times \frac{22}{\cancel{7}_1} \times \cancel{15}^5 \times 15 \times \cancel{14}^2$$

= 3300 cubic feet

27 cubic feet = 1 cubic yard
3300 cu ft ÷ 27 cu ft = $122\frac{2}{9}$ cu yd

$122\frac{2}{9} \div \frac{3}{4} = \frac{1100}{9} \times \frac{4}{3} = \frac{4400}{27}$
= 163 tons to the nearest ton

Answer: **(2)** 163

COORDINATE GEOMETRY

1. a. **Coordinate geometry** is used to locate and to graph points and lines on a plane.

   b. The coordinate system is made up of two number lines that are perpendicular and that intersect at 0.

   The horizontal number line is called the **x-axis**.

   The vertical number line is called the **y-axis**.

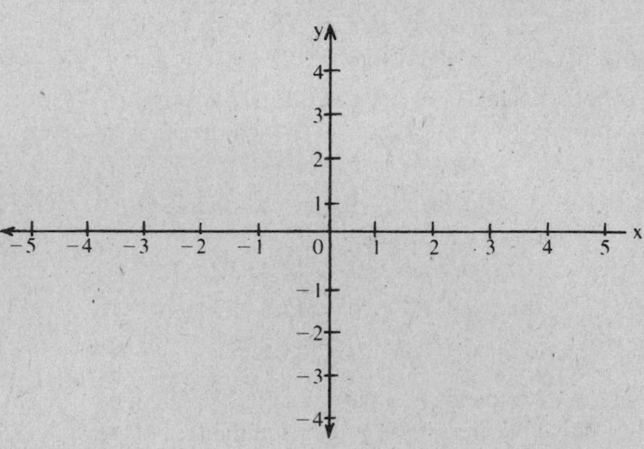

Graphing Points

2. a. Any point on the plane has two numbers **(coordinates)**, which indicate its location. The **x-coordinate (abscissa)** is found by drawing a vertical line from the point to the x-axis. The number on the x-axis where the vertical line meets it is the x-coordinate of the point.

   The **y-coordinate (ordinate)** is found by drawing a horizontal line from the point to the y-axis. The number on the y-axis where the horizontal line meets it is the y-coordinate of the point. The two coordinates are always given in the order (x,y).

Example:

The x-coordinate of point A is 3.

The y-coordinate of point A is 2.

The coordinates of point A are given by the ordered pair (3,2).

Point B has coordinates (−1,4).

Point C has coordinates (−4,−3).

Point D has coordinates (2,−3).

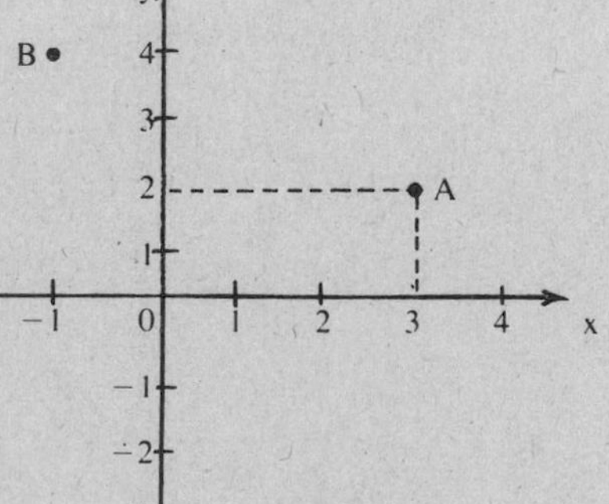

b. The point at which the x-axis and the y-axis meet has coordinates (0,0) and is called the **origin**.

c. Any point on the y-axis has 0 as its x-coordinate. Any point on the x-axis has 0 as its y-coordinate.

3. To graph a point whose coordinates are given, first locate the x-coordinate on the x-axis. From that position, move vertically the number of spaces indicated by the y-coordinate.

Example: To graph $(4,-2)$, locate 4 on the x-axis. Then move -2 spaces vertically (2 spaces down) to find the given point.

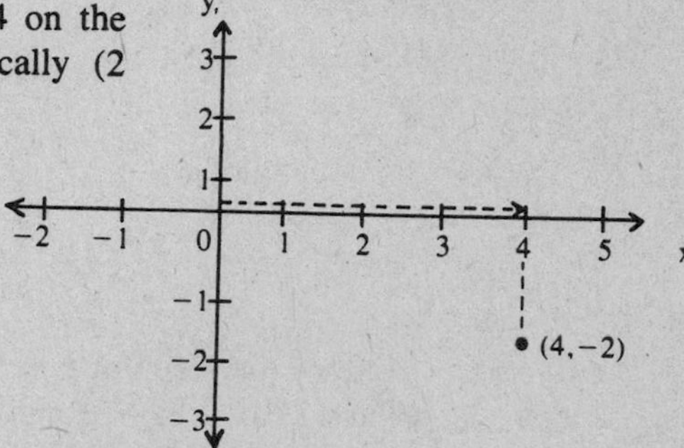

Graphing Equations

4. a. For any equation in x or y or both, ordered pairs (x,y) may be found which are solutions for (or which "satisfy") the equation.

Example: (3,4), (1,6) and (7,0) are solutions to the equation $x + y = 7$, since $3 + 4 = 7$, $1 + 6 = 7$ and $7 + 0 = 7$.

Example: (2,0), (2,1), (2,3) and (2,10) all satisfy the equation $x = 2$. Note that the value of y is irrelevant in this equation.

Example: $(-3,1)$, (4,1) and (12,1) all satisfy the equation $y = 1$.

b. To find ordered pairs that satisfy an equation, it is usually easiest to substitute any value for x and solve the resulting equation for y.

Example: For the equation $y = 2x - 1$:

$$\text{if } x = 3,\ y = 2(3) - 1 = 6 - 1 = 5$$

Therefore, (3,5) is a solution to the equation.

$$\text{if } x = -2,\ y = 2(-2) - 1 = -4 - 1 = -5$$

Therefore, $(-2,-5)$ is a solution to the equation.

$$\text{if } x = 0,\ y = 2(0) - 1 = 0 - 1 = -1$$

Therefore, $(0,-1)$ is a solution to the equation.

c. If two or more ordered pairs that satisfy a given equation are graphed and the points are connected, the resulting line is the graph of the given equation.

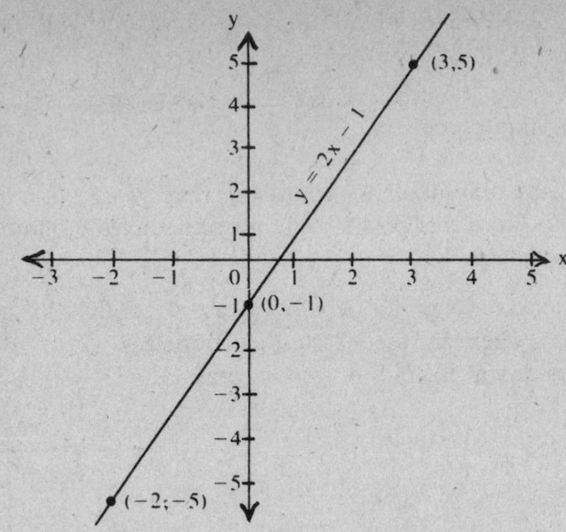

Example: To draw the graph of $y = 2x - 1$, graph the points $(3,5)$, $(-2,-5)$ and $(0,-1)$. Then draw the line passing through all of them.

5. Any equation that can be written in the form $y = mx + b$, where m and b remain constant, is called a **linear equation** and has a straight line as its graph.

   Example: $y = x$ may be written $y = 1x + 0$ and has a straight line graph.

   Example: The equation $y - 3 = 2x$ may be rewritten:

$$\begin{array}{rcl} y - 3 &=& 2x \\ \underline{+\ 3} && \underline{+\ 3} \\ y &=& 2x + 3 \end{array}$$

   Therefore, the graph of $y - 3 = 2x$ is a straight line.

6. a. Any line parallel to the x-axis has the equation $y = a$, where a is constant.

   b. Any line parallel to the y-axis has the equation $x = b$, where b is constant.

   Example: The graph of $y = 5$ is parallel to the x-axis and passes through the y-axis at 5.

   The graph of $x = -1$ is parallel to the y-axis and passes through the x-axis at -1.

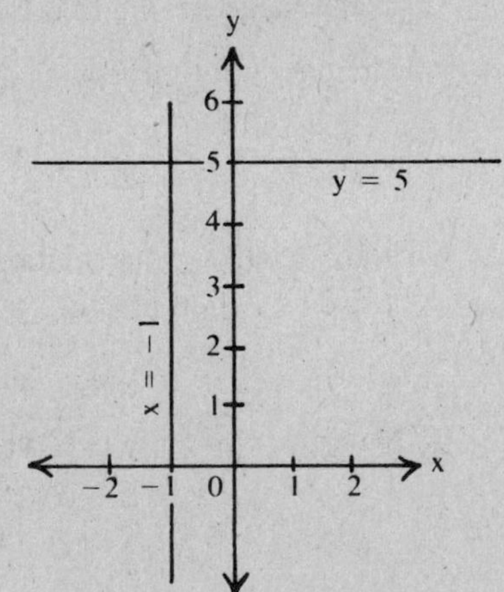

7. a. The coordinates of any point on a straight line must satisfy the equation of that line.

   b. If a point lies on more than one line, its coordinates must satisfy the equation of each of the lines.

Example: Any point on the graph of y = 2 must have 2 as its y-coordinate. Any point on the graph of y = x must have its x-coordinate equal to its y-coordinate.

The point where the two lines meet must have coordinates which satisfy both equations. Its coordinates are (2,2).

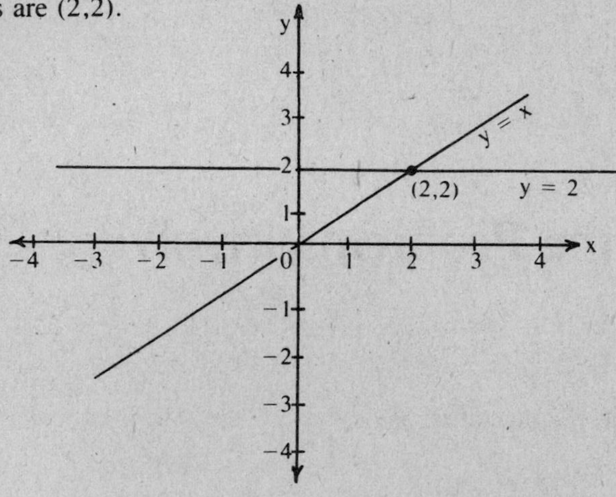

Solving Pairs of Equations

8. To find the ordered pair that is a solution to a pair of equations, graph both equations and find the point at which their corresponding lines meet.

Example: Solve the pair of equations:

$$x + y = 5$$
$$y = x + 1$$

Graph both equations:

The pairs (0,5), (1,4) and (5,0) are solutions for x + y = 5.

The pairs (0,1), (1,2) and (3,4) are solutions for y = x + 1.

The lines meet at the point (2,3). The pair (2,3) is a solution to both equations.

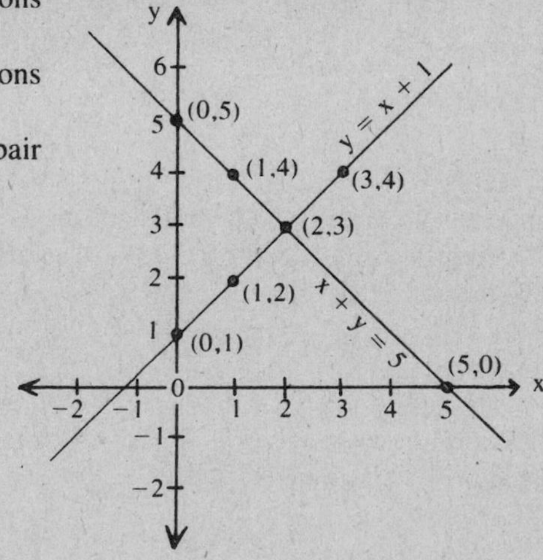

Distance Between Two Points

9. The distance d between any two points (x_1,y_1) and (x_2,y_2) is given by the formula:

$$d = \sqrt{(x_1 - x_2)^2 + (y_1 - y_2)^2}$$

Example: The distance between the points (13,5) and (1,0) is:

$$\begin{aligned} d &= \sqrt{(13 - 1)^2 + (5 - 0)^2} \\ &= \sqrt{(12)^2 + (5)^2} \\ &= \sqrt{144 + 25} \\ &= \sqrt{169} \\ &= 13 \end{aligned}$$

Practice Problems Involving Graphs

1. In the graph below, the coordinates of point A are
   (1) (−1,3)
   (2) (−3,1)
   (3) (1,−3)
   (4) (3,−1)
   (5) 1,3)

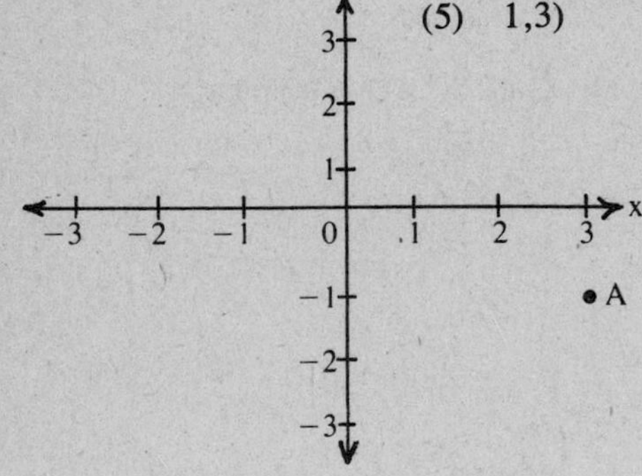

2. A circle has its center at (0,0) and diameter AB. If the coordinates of A are (−4,0), then the coordinates of B are
   (1) (4,0)
   (2) (0,4)
   (3) (0,−4)
   (4) (4,−4)
   (5) (4,4)

3. Point R lies on the graph of $y = 3x - 4$. If the abscissa of R is 1, the ordinate of R is
   (1) 3
   (2) 2
   (3) 1
   (4) 0
   (5) −1

4. The lines $y = 4$ and $x = 7$ intersect at the point
   (1) (4,7)
   (2) (7,4)
   (3) (3,0)
   (4) (0,3)
   (5) (3,3)

5. The distance from point A to point B in the graph below is
   (1) 3
   (2) 4
   (3) 5
   (4) 6
   (5) 7

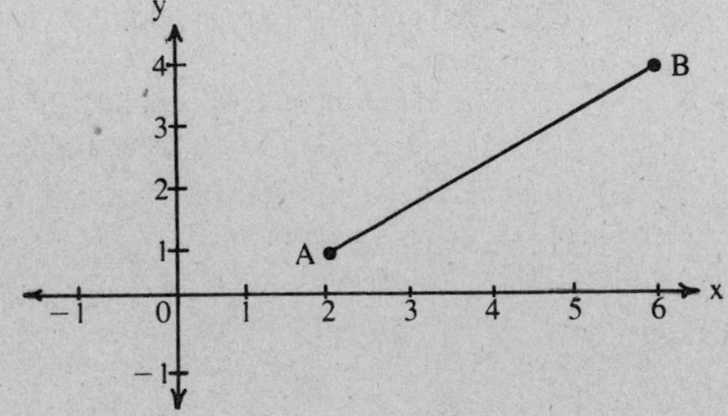

6. The line shown in the graph below has which of the following equations?
(1) $x = 2$
(2) $y = -2$
(3) $y = x + 2$
(4) $x = y + 2$
(5) $y = x$

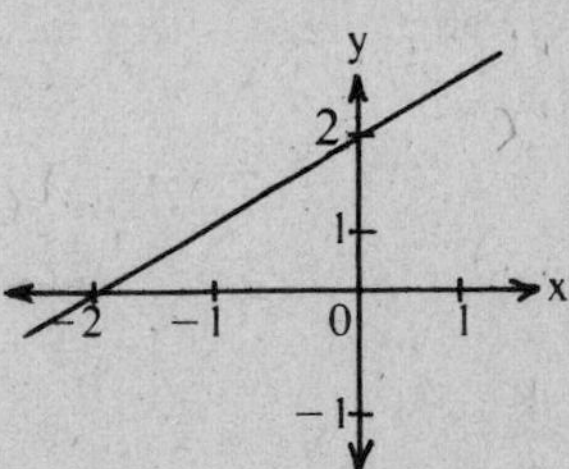

7. The graph of $x + 2y = 6$ intersects the y-axis at the point
(1) (0,3)
(2) (0,−3)
(3) (3,0)
(4) (−3,0)
(5) (3,3)

8. The graphs of $y = 2x$ and $y = x + 1$ intersect at the point
(1) (1,2)
(2) (0,1)
(3) (2,1)
(4) (1,0)
(5) (0,2)

9. The distance from (−1,0) to (5,−2) is
(1) $4\frac{1}{2}$
(2) $5\frac{1}{2}$
(3) $\sqrt{10}$
(4) $2\sqrt{10}$
(5) $3\sqrt{10}$

10. A triangle has vertices A(1,2), B(11,2) and C(4,5). How many square units are in the area of triangle ABC?
(1) 40
(2) 30
(3) 25
(4) 20
(5) 15

Graph Problems — Correct Answers

1. **(4)**
2. **(1)**
3. **(5)**
4. **(2)**
5. **(3)**
6. **(3)**
7. **(1)**
8. **(1)**
9. **(4)**
10. **(5)**

Problem Solutions — Graphs

1. A vertical line through A meets the x-axis at 3; therefore, the x-coordinate is 3.
 A horizontal line through A meets the y-axis at −1; therefore, the y-coordinate is −1.
 The coordinates of point A are (3, −1).

Answer: **(4)** (3, −1)

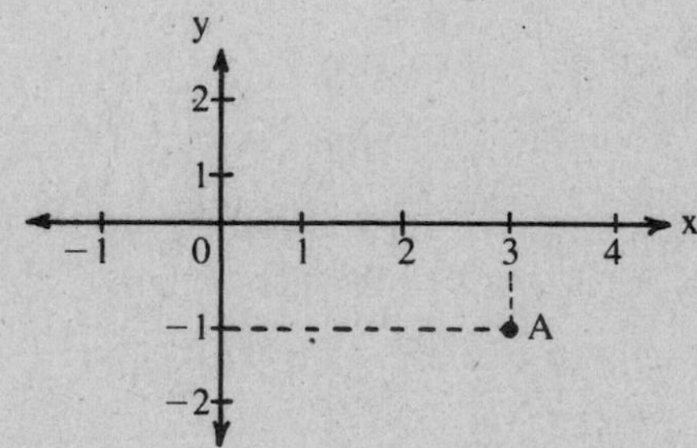

2. The diameter of a circle is a straight line passing through the center of the circle. The endpoints of the diameter are the same distance from the center.

   The center of the given circle is on the x-axis, at the origin. Point A is also on the x-axis, 4 units from the center. Point B must be on the x-axis, 4 units from the center.

   The coordinates of B are (4,0).

   Answer: **(1)** (4,0)

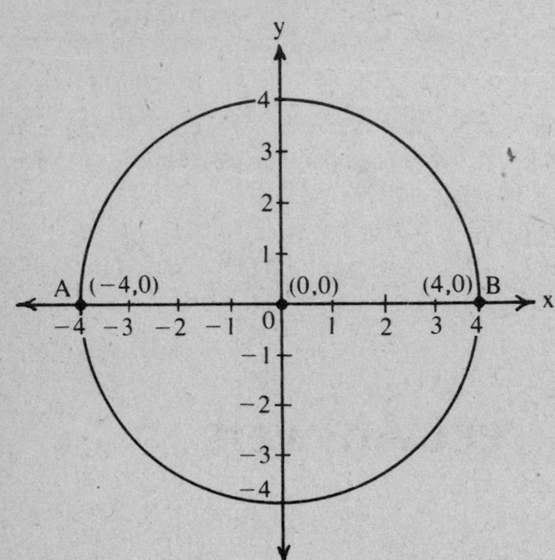

3. Substitute 1 for x in the equation:

$$y = 3 \cdot 1 - 4$$
$$= 3 - 4$$
$$= -1$$

   Answer: **(5)** −1

4. The coordinates of the point of intersection must satisfy both equations. Choice B has x-coordinate = 7 and y-coordinate = 4.

   Answer: **(2)** (7,4)

5. Point A has coordinates (2,1) and point B has coordinates (6,4). Using the distance formula,

$$d = \sqrt{(6 - 2)^2 + (4 - 1)^2}$$
$$= \sqrt{(4)^2 + (3)^2}$$
$$= \sqrt{16 + 9}$$
$$= \sqrt{25}$$
$$= 5$$

   An alternate solution is to consider the right triangle formed by AB and the lines of the graph paper, with the right angle vertex at (6,1). Find the lengths of the legs by counting the spaces on the graph. The horizontal leg is 4 and the vertical leg is 3.

   Using the Pythagorean Theorem,

$$(AB)^2 = 3^2 + 4^2$$
$$= 9 + 16$$
$$= 25$$
$$AB = \sqrt{25} = 5$$

   Answer: **(3)** 5

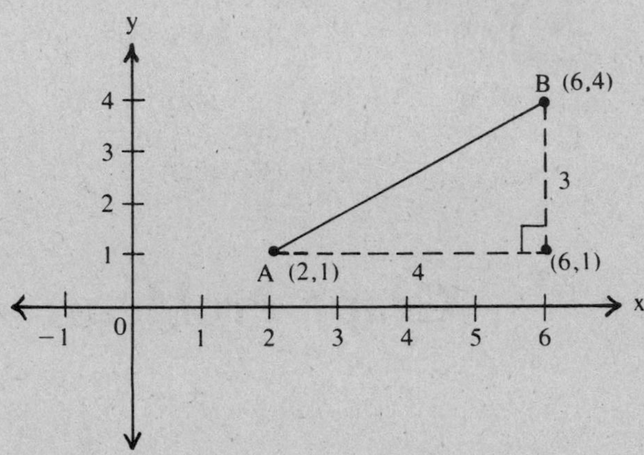

6. The line passes through the points (−2,0) and (0,2). Choice C is the only equation which is satisfied by both ordered pairs.

$$(-2,0):\quad y = x + 2$$
$$0 = -2 + 2$$
$$(0,2):\quad y = x + 2$$
$$2 = 0 + 2$$

   Answer: **(3)** y = x + 2

7. Any point on the y-axis has its x-coordinate equal to 0. Substituting 0 for x in the equation,

$$x + 2y = 6$$
$$0 + 2y = 6$$
$$2y = 6$$
$$y = 3$$

   Answer: **(1)** (0,3)

8. Graph both lines on the same set of axes. To find points on the graph of each line, choose any value for x and find the corresponding y.

For $y = 2x$:

if $x = 0$,	$y = 2 \cdot 0 = 0$	(0,0)
if $x = 3$,	$y = 2 \cdot 3 = 6$	(3,6)
if $x = -1$,	$y = 2(-1) = -2$	(−1,−2)

For $y = x + 1$:

if $x = -1$,	$y = -1 + 1 = 0$	(−1,0)
if $x = 2$,	$y = 2 + 1 = 3$	(2,3)
if $x = 0$,	$y = 0 + 1 = 1$	(0,1)

The point of intersection of the two lines is (1,2).

An alternate solution is to determine which of the given choices satisfies both equations.

Answer: **(1)** (1,2)

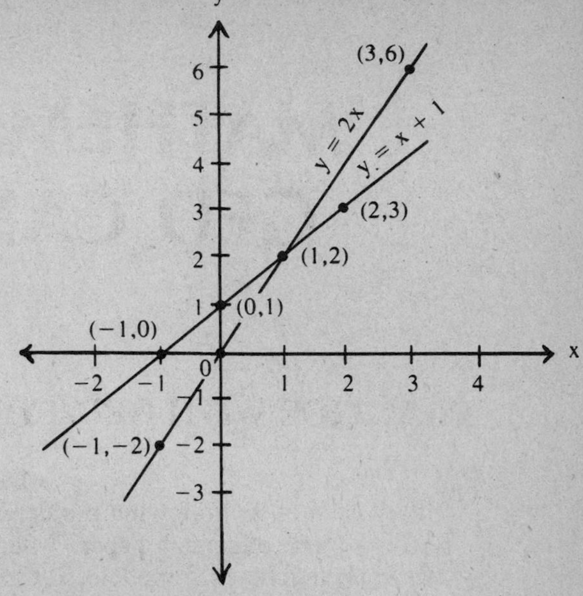

9. Using the distance formula,

$$d = \sqrt{(x_1 - x_2)^2 + (y_1 - y_2)^2}$$
$$d = \sqrt{[(-1) - 5]^2 + [0 - (-2)]^2}$$
$$= \sqrt{(-6)^2 + (+2)^2}$$
$$= \sqrt{36 + 4}$$
$$= \sqrt{40}$$
$$= \sqrt{4}\sqrt{10}$$
$$= 2\sqrt{10}$$

Answer: **(4)** $2\sqrt{10}$

10. Base AB = 10

Height = 3

$$\text{Area} = \tfrac{1}{2}(\text{base})(\text{height})$$
$$= \tfrac{1}{2} \cdot 10 \cdot 3$$
$$= 15$$

Answer: **(5)** 15

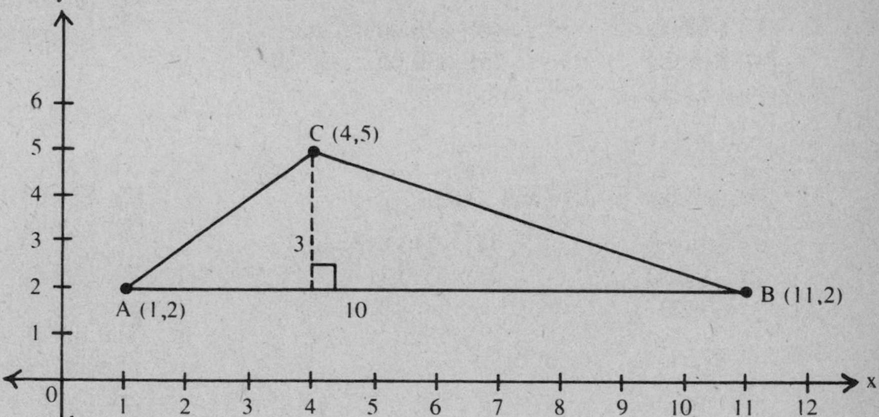

MATHEMATICS FOR GED CANDIDATES

PRACTICE WITH GED-TYPE MATHEMATICS QUESTIONS

Directions:
Study each of the following problems and work out your answers in the margins or on a piece of scratch paper. After each problem you will find five suggested answers, numbered from 1 to 5. Circle the number of the answer you have figured out to be correct. Solutions for each problem appear at the end of the examination.

1. The difference between three hundred four thousand eight hundred two and two hundred twelve thousand eight hundred ten is

(1) 91,992
(2) 96,592
(3) 182,328
(4) 209,328
(5) 210,972

2. Joan earns $4.00 per hour. On a day that she works from 9:30 AM to 3:00 PM, how much will she earn?

(1) $14.00
(2) $18.00
(3) $22.00
(4) $26.00
(5) $30.00

3. The product of .010 and .001 is

(1) .01100
(2) .10100
(3) .00001
(4) .01000
(5) .01010

4. If $2x + y = 7$, what is the value of y when $x = 3$?

(1) 1
(2) 3
(3) 5
(4) 7
(5) 9

5. Paul received a bonus of $750, which was 5% of his annual salary. His annual salary was

(1) $37,500
(2) $25,000
(3) $22,500
(4) $15,000
(5) $7,500

6. The value of $(-6) + (-2)(-3)$ is

(1) -24
(2) -12
(3) 0
(4) 12
(5) 24

7. Round 825.6347 to the nearest hundredth.

(1) 800
(2) 825.63
(3) 825.64
(4) 825.635
(5) 825.645

8. The coordinates of point P on the graph are

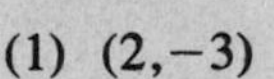

(1) (2,−3)
(2) (−3,2)
(3) (−2,3)
(4) (3,−2)
(5) (−2,−3)

y
P
1
0
1

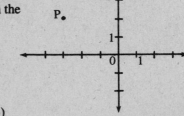

9. A boy buys oranges at 3 for 30¢ and sells them at 5 for 60¢. How many oranges must he sell in order to make a profit of 50¢?

(1) 12
(2) 25
(3) 50
(4) 75
(5) 100

10. The formula for the volume of a right circular cone is $V = \frac{1}{3}\pi r^2 h$, where r is the radius and h is the height. Find the approximate volume of a right circular cone which has radius 3 inches and height 14 inches (π is approximately $\frac{22}{7}$).

(1) 33 cubic inches
(2) 132 cubic inches
(3) 396 cubic inches
(4) 686 cubic inches
(5) 1188 cubic inches

11. Of the following, the number which is nearest in value to 5 is

(1) 4.985
(2) 5.005
(3) 5.01
(4) 5.1
(5) 5.105

12. If a rope four yards long is cut into three equal pieces, how long will each piece be?

(1) 4 feet
(2) $3\frac{1}{2}$ feet
(3) $3\frac{1}{3}$ feet
(4) 3 feet
(5) $2\frac{1}{4}$ feet

13. The number of square units in the area of triangle ABC is

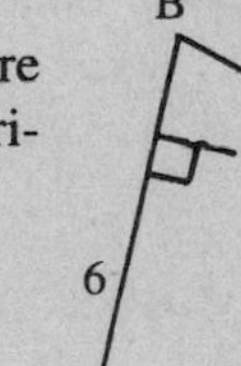

(1) 35
(2) 28
(3) 24
(4) 14
(5) 12

14. The cost of 30 sandwich rolls at \$1.50 per dozen is

(1) \$3.00
(2) \$3.45
(3) \$3.75
(4) \$4.50
(5) \$4.80

15. If $P = 2(a + b)$, find P when $a = 3$ and $b = 4$.

(1) 9
(2) 10
(3) 14
(4) 24
(5) 28

16. Two angles of a triangle measure 30° and 50°. The number of degrees in the third angle is

(1) 10
(2) 40
(3) 50
(4) 90
(5) 100

17. A map is drawn to the scale $1\frac{1}{2}$ inches = 50 miles. What is the actual distance between two towns which are $4\frac{1}{2}$ inches apart on the map?

(1) 45 miles
(2) 90 miles
(3) 120 miles
(4) 150 miles
(5) 300 miles

18. The numbers in the sequence 1, 4, 9, 16, 25, . . . follow a particular pattern. If the pattern is continued, what number should appear after 25?

(1) 28
(2) 30
(3) 34
(4) 36
(5) 40

19. If shipping charges to a certain point are \$1.24 for the first five ounces and 16 cents for each additional ounce, the weight of a package for which the charges are \$3.32 is

(1) 13 ounces
(2) 15 ounces
(3) $1\frac{1}{8}$ pounds
(4) $1\frac{1}{4}$ pounds
(5) $1\frac{1}{2}$ pounds

20. If a recipe for a cake calls for $2\frac{1}{2}$ cups of flour, and Mary wishes to make three such cakes, the number of cups of flour she must use is

(1) 5
(2) $6\frac{1}{2}$
(3) $7\frac{1}{2}$
(4) 9
(5) $9\frac{1}{2}$

21. The equation of the line passing through the points (−2,2) and (3,−3) is

(1) $x + y = 5$
(2) $x - y = 5$
(3) $y - x = 5$
(4) $y = x$
(5) $y = -x$

22. What will it cost to carpet a room 12 feet wide and 15 feet long if carpeting costs \$20.80 per square yard?

(1) \$334.60
(2) \$374.40
(3) \$416.00
(4) \$504.60
(5) \$560.00

23. If a five pound mixture of nuts contains two pounds of cashews and the rest peanuts, what percent of the mixture is peanuts?

(1) 20
(2) 30
(3) 40
(4) 50
(5) 60

Items 24 to 26 refer to the graph below.

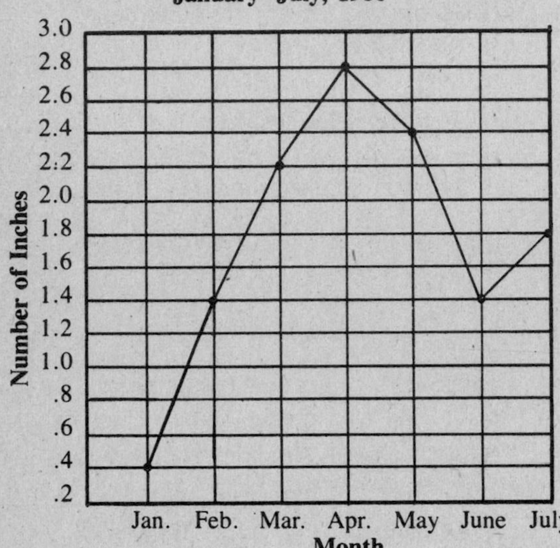

24. The total rainfall for the months January, February and March was, in inches,

(1) 2.2
(2) 3.4
(3) 4.0
(4) 4.8
(5) 7.6

25. The average monthly rainfall, in inches, for April, May and June was

(1) 2.0
(2) 2.1
(3) 2.2
(4) 2.3
(5) 2.4

26. Which statement about the information given in the graph is *false*?

(1) The rainfall in April was twice the rainfall in February.
(2) June had greater rainfall than February.
(3) The month with the least rainfall was January.
(4) March had .4 inches greater rainfall than July.
(5) May had more rain than March.

27. How long will the shadow of a five foot tall person be at the same time that an eight foot high pole casts a shadow 24 feet long?

(1) 1 foot
(2) 8 feet
(3) 15 feet
(4) $32\frac{1}{2}$ feet
(5) 72 feet

28. George has a five dollar bill and a ten dollar bill. If he buys one item costing $7.32 and another item costing $1.68, how much money will he have left?

(1) $1.10
(2) $5.64
(3) $6.00
(4) $9.00
(5) $9.90

29. If one card is picked at random from a deck of cards, the probability that it is a club is

(1) 1
(2) $\frac{1}{52}$
(3) $\frac{1}{13}$
(4) $\frac{1}{10}$
(5) $\frac{1}{4}$

30. Jack can ride his bicycle 6 miles in 48 minutes. At the same rate, how long will it take him to ride 15 miles?

(1) 1 hour 20 minutes
(2) 2 hours
(3) 2 hours 12 minutes
(4) 3 hours
(5) 3 hours 12 minutes

31. If $2x - 7 = 3$, then $3x + 1 =$

(1) 4
(2) 5
(3) 7
(4) 12
(5) 16

32. Over a four year period, the sales of the Acme Company increased from $13,382,675 to $17,394,683. The average yearly increase was

(1) $4,012,008
(2) $3,146,014
(3) $2,869,054
(4) $1,060,252
(5) $1,003,002

33. The perimeter of figure ABCDE is

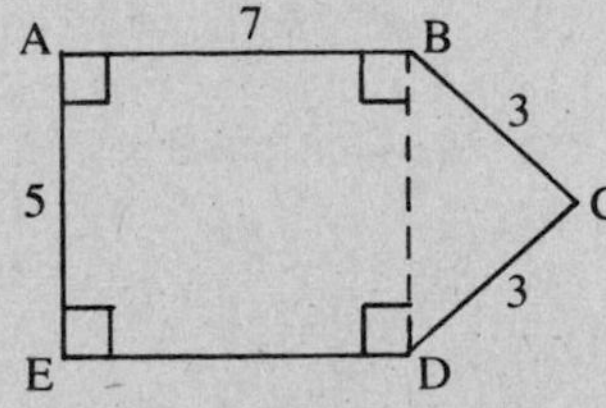

(1) 18
(2) 25
(3) 38
(4) 44
(5) 45

34. Of the following, the unit which would most likely be used to measure the distance from New York to Albany is the

(1) liter
(2) kilometer
(3) centigram
(4) millimeter
(5) degree Celsius

35. The simple interest on $200 at 12% for 2 years is

(1) $6
(2) $12
(3) $24
(4) $48
(5) $120

Items 36 to 38 refer to the picture graph below.

The picture graph represents how many men (man), women (woman), boys (○), and girls (△) visited a museum one particular week. Each figure represents 100.

Mon.	*Tues.*	*Wed.*	*Thurs.*	*Fri.*
man	man	man	woman	woman
man	woman	woman	woman	woman
woman	△	woman	△	man
○	△	○	△	man
○	○	△	○	○
△		△	○	△
			○	

36. Over the five-day period, the ratio of men visitors to women visitors was

(1) 3:4
(2) 4:3
(3) 3:7
(4) 4:7
(5) 7:3

37. If the admission price was 50¢ per child and $1.50 per adult, the combined revenue on Monday and Thursday was

(1) $11.50
(2) $260
(3) $1150
(4) $2600
(5) $11,500

38. The total number of visitors to the museum during the week was

(1) 3000
(2) 2200
(3) 1400
(4) 300
(5) 30

39. A man spent exactly one dollar in the purchase of 3-cent stamps and 5-cent stamps. The number of 5-cent stamps which he could *not* have purchased under the circumstances is

(1) 5
(2) 8
(3) 9
(4) 11
(5) 14

40. The number of grams in one kilogram is

(1) .001
(2) .01
(3) .1
(4) 10
(5) 1000

41. An appliance store gives a 15% discount off the list price of all of its merchandise. An additional 30% reduction of the store price is made for the purchase of a floor model. A television set which has a list price of $300 and is a floor model sells for

(1) $210.00
(2) $228.50
(3) $178.50
(4) $165.00
(5) $135.00

42. Mrs. Jones wishes to buy 72 ounces of canned beans for the least possible cost. Which of the following should she buy?

(1) Six 12-ounce cans at 39¢ per can
(2) Seven 10-ounce cans at 34¢ per can
(3) Three 24-ounce cans at 79¢ per can
(4) Two 25-ounce cans at 62¢ per can
(5) Five 13-ounce cans at 37¢ per can

43. The distance from point A to point B is

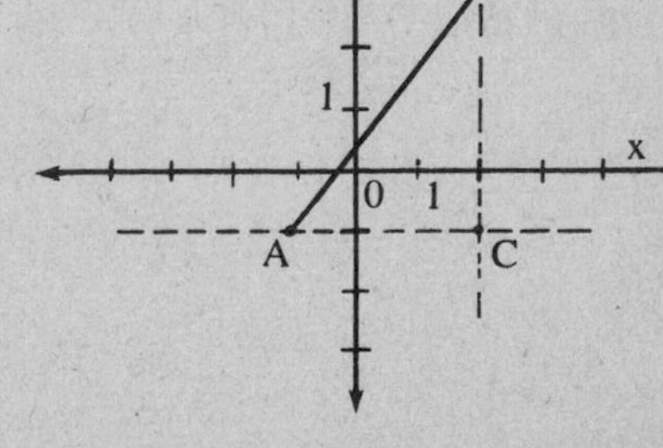

(1) 3
(2) 5
(3) 6
(4) $\sqrt{5}$
(5) $\sqrt{7}$

44. If $x^2 - x - 6 = 0$, then x is equal to

(1) 3 only
(2) −2 only
(3) −3 or 2
(4) 3 or −2
(5) −3 or −2

45. Which quantity is *not* equal to $75(32 + 88)$?

(1) $75 \cdot 32 + 75 \cdot 88$
(2) $(75 \cdot 32) + 88$
(3) $75(88 + 32)$
(4) $(88 + 32) \cdot 75$
(5) $88 \cdot 75 + 32 \cdot 75$

46. In a certain boys' camp, 30% of the boys are from New York State and 20% of these are from New York City. What percent of the boys in the camp are from New York City?

(1) 60
(2) 50
(3) 20
(4) 10
(5) 6

47. If 1 ounce is approximately equal to 28 grams, then 1 pound is approximately equal to

(1) 250 grams
(2) 350 grams
(3) 450 grams
(4) 550 grams
(5) 650 grams

48. Which fraction is equal to .25%?

(1) $\frac{1}{400}$
(2) $\frac{1}{40}$
(3) $\frac{1}{4}$
(4) $\frac{5}{2}$
(5) $\frac{50}{2}$

Items 49 and 50 refer to the table below.

VALUE OF PROPERTY STOLEN — 1977 and 1978
LARCENY

	1977		1978	
CATEGORY	**Number of Offenses**	**Value of Stolen Property**	**Number of Offenses**	**Value of Stolen Property**
Pocket-picking	20	$ 1,950	10	$ 950
Purse-snatching	175	5,750	120	12,050
Shoplifting	155	7,950	225	17,350
Automobile thefts	1040	127,050	860	108,000
Thefts of automobile accessories	1135	34,950	970	24,400
Bicycle thefts	355	8,250	240	6,350
All other thefts	1375	187,150	1300	153,150

49. Of the total number of larcenies reported in 1977, automobile thefts accounted for, most nearly,

(1) 5%
(2) 15%
(3) 25%
(4) 50%
(5) 65%

50. Of the following, the category which had the largest reduction in value of stolen property from 1977 to 1978 was

(1) pocket-picking
(2) automobile thefts
(3) shoplifting
(4) bicycle thefts
(5) purse-snatching

Items 51 to 54 refer to the following information.

Mike is starting a new job on April 15. His working hours are 8:30 to 4:30 from Monday through Friday and his starting pay is $18,500 per year. To get to this job, Mike will have to take a train each day. The railroad offers only the following types of tickets:

1. A monthly ticket which is good from the first to the last day of each month and costs $129.00
2. A weekly ticket which is good from Saturday morning to Friday night each week and costs $40.00
3. A one-way ticket which costs $6.25

The calendar for the month in which Mike starts to work is shown below.

APRIL						
S	M	T	W	T	F	S
	1	2	3	4	5	6
7	8	9	10	11	12	13
14	15	16	17	18	19	20
21	22	23	24	25	26	27
28	29	30				

51. Based on the fare schedule and the calendar shown, which is the least costly method for Mike to get to work from April 15 through April 30?

    (1) Buying one-way tickets for the first 3 days, a weekly ticket for the next week and then one-way tickets for the last 4 days
    (2) Buying 1 monthly ticket
    (3) Buying one-way tickets for the first 3 days and then buying 2 weekly tickets
    (4) Buying 3 weekly tickets
    (5) Buying one-way tickets for each trip

52. What is the total difference in cost between buying one-way tickets for each trip everyday from April 15–April 30 and buying 3 weekly tickets?

    (1) $5
    (2) $10
    (3) $20
    (4) $25
    (5) $30

53. Mike wants to take an apartment closer to his new job so that he can decrease his transportation expense. He has determined that he cannot afford to pay more than 30% of his salary for rent. What is the greatest monthly rental Mike can afford if he is to stay within his own budget guidelines?

    (1) $555
    (2) $462
    (3) $384
    (4) $355
    (5) Not enough information is given.

54. If Mike eliminates his train fare by moving closer to his job, what effect will this have on his available cash?

    (1) He will have $129 more cash each month
    (2) He will have $40 more cash each week
    (3) He will have $1584 more cash each year
    (4) He will have 10% more available cash
    (5) Not enough information is given.

55. During a ten day museum exhibit the number of visitors doubled each day. If the exhibit opened on Tuesday and the attendance on Friday of the same week was 1000, what was the attendance on opening day?

    (1) 1000
    (2) 500
    (3) 250
    (4) 125
    (5) 100

56. If the daily attendance at the museum continued the same trend, how many visitors should they expect on the following Monday?

    (1) 250
    (2) 500
    (3) 2000
    (4) 4000
    (5) 8000

CORRECT ANSWERS FOR GED-TYPE MATHEMATICS QUESTIONS

1. **(1)**	11. **(2)**	21. **(5)**	31. **(5)**	41. **(3)**	51. **(3)**
2. **(3)**	12. **(1)**	22. **(3)**	32. **(5)**	42. **(1)**	52. **(5)**
3. **(3)**	13. **(5)**	23. **(5)**	33. **(2)**	43. **(2)**	53. **(2)**
4. **(1)**	14. **(3)**	24. **(3)**	34. **(2)**	44. **(4)**	54. **(5)**
5. **(4)**	15. **(3)**	25. **(3)**	35. **(4)**	45. **(2)**	55. **(4)**
6. **(3)**	16. **(5)**	26. **(2)**	36. **(1)**	46. **(5)**	56. **(5)**
7. **(2)**	17. **(4)**	27. **(3)**	37. **(3)**	47. **(3)**	
8. **(2)**	18. **(4)**	28. **(3)**	38. **(1)**	48. **(1)**	
9. **(2)**	19. **(3)**	29. **(5)**	39. **(3)**	49. **(3)**	
10. **(2)**	20. **(3)**	30. **(2)**	40. **(5)**	50. **(2)**	

SOLUTIONS FOR GED-TYPE MATHEMATICS QUESTIONS

1.
$$\begin{array}{r} 304{,}802 \\ -\ 212{,}810 \\ \hline 91{,}992 \end{array}$$

Answer: **(1)** 91,992

2. From 9:30 AM to 3 PM is $5\frac{1}{2}$ hours.

$$\$4 \cdot 5\tfrac{1}{2} = \$22$$

Answer: **(3)** $22.00

3.
$$\begin{array}{rl} .010 & \text{(3 decimal places)} \\ \times\ .001 & \text{(3 decimal places)} \\ \hline .000010 & \text{(6 decimal places)} \end{array}$$

The final zero may be dropped:

$$.000010 = .00001$$

Answer: **(3)** .00001

4. When $x = 3$, $2x + y = 7$ becomes

$$2 \cdot 3 + y = 7$$

Solve for y:

$$\begin{array}{rcl} 6 + y &=& 7 \\ -6 \quad & & -6 \\ \hline y &=& 1 \end{array}$$

Answer: **(1)** 1

5. Let s = Paul's annual salary

$$5\% \text{ of } s = \$750$$
$$.05s = \$750$$
$$\frac{.05s}{.05} = \frac{\$750}{.05}$$
$$s = \$15{,}000$$

Answer: **(4)** $15,000

6. $(-6) + (-2)(-3) = (-6) + (+6)$
$= 0$

First multiply, then add.

Answer: **(3)** 0

7. To round 825.6347 to the nearest hundredth, consider 4, the digit in the thousandths place. Since it is less than 5, drop all digits to the right of the hundredths place.

   825.6347 = 825.63 to the nearest hundredth

   Answer: **(2)** 825.63

8. Point P has coordinates $x = -3$ and $y = 2$.

   Answer: **(2)** $(-3,2)$

9. The boy buys oranges for 10¢ each (30¢ ÷ 3). He sells them for 12¢ each (60¢ ÷ 5). Therefore his profit is 2¢ per orange. He must sell 50¢ ÷ 2¢ = 25 oranges for a 50¢ profit.

   Answer: **(2)** 25

10. $V = \frac{1}{3}\pi r^2 h$, $r = 3''$, $h = 14''$

    $V = \frac{1}{3} \cdot \frac{22}{7} \cdot 3 \cdot 3 \cdot 14$

    $V = \frac{22 \cdot 3 \cdot 2}{1}$

    $V = 132$

    Answer: **(2)** 132 cubic inches

11. Find the difference between each choice and 5:

5.000	5.005	5.01	5.1	5.105
−4.985	−5.000	−5.00	−5.0	−5.000
.015	.005	.01	.1	.105
		= .010	= .100	

    The smallest difference is .005, therefore 5.005 is closer than the other choices to 5.

    Answer: **(2)** 5.005

12. 4 yards = 4 · 3 feet = 12 feet
    12 feet ÷ 3 = 4 feet per piece

    Answer: **(1)** 4 feet

13. Area of a triangle = $\frac{1}{2}$ · base · height

    The height, which is 4, is drawn to base AB, which is 6.

    $$\begin{aligned}\text{Area} &= \tfrac{1}{2} \cdot 6 \cdot 4 \\ &= 3 \cdot 4 \\ &= 12\end{aligned}$$

    Answer: **(5)** 12

14. If 1 dozen rolls costs \$1.50, each roll costs

    \$1.50 ÷ 12 = \$.125

    Then 30 rolls will cost

    30(\$.125) = \$3.75

    Answer: **(3)** \$3.75

15. $P = 2(a + b)$

    If $a = 3$ and $b = 4$,

    $$\begin{aligned}P &= 2(3 + 4) \\ &= 2(7) \\ &= 14\end{aligned}$$

    Answer: **(3)** 14

16. The sum of the angles of a triangle is 180°. The two given angles total 80°.

    180° − 80° = 100°

    The third angle is 100°.

    Answer: **(5)** 100

17. Let x represent the actual distance between towns, then write a proportion:

    $$\frac{x}{50} = \frac{4\frac{1}{2}}{1\frac{1}{2}}$$

    $$\frac{x}{50} = 3 \qquad (\text{Since } 4\tfrac{1}{2} \div 1\tfrac{1}{2} = 3)$$

    $$x = 150$$

    Answer: **(4)** 150 miles

18. Each of the numbers in the sequence is a perfect square:

    1, 4, 9, 16, 25, . . .
    $1^2, 2^2, 3^2, 4^2, 5^2, \ldots$

    The next number is 6^2, or 36.

    Answer: **(4)** 36

19.

\$3.32	total charge
− 1.24	charge for first five ounces
\$2.08	charge for additional weight at \$.16 per ounce

    2.08 ÷ .16 = 13

    5 ounces + 13 ounces = 18 ounces
    = 1 pound 2 ounces
    = $1\frac{1}{8}$ pound

    Answer: **(3)** $1\frac{1}{8}$ pound

20. $2\frac{1}{2} \cdot 3 = \frac{5}{2} \cdot 3$
$= \frac{15}{2}$
$= 7\frac{1}{2}$

Answer: **(3)** $7\frac{1}{2}$

21. Substitute the coordinates of each point in each equation. Only $y = -x$ is satisfied by the coordinates of the points:

$(-2,2)$: $2 = -(-2)$
$(3,-3)$: $-3 = -(3)$

Answer: **(5)** $y = -x$

22. 12 feet = 4 yards
15 feet = 5 yards
4 yards · 5 yards = 20 square yards

$20.80 per square yard
× 20 square yards
$416.00

Answer: **(3)** $416.00

23. There are three pounds of peanuts.

$\frac{3}{5} = .60 = 60\%$

Answer: **(5)** 60

24. January: .4
February: 1.4
March: 2.2
Total: 4.0

Answer: **(3)** 4.0

25. April: 2.8
May: 2.4
June: 1.4
Total: 6.6
Average: $6.6 \div 3 = 2.2$

Answer: **(3)** 2.2

26. The rainfall in June was 1.4 inches, the same as the rainfall in February.

Answer: **(2)**

27. Let x represent the person's height, and write a proportion:

$\frac{5}{x} = \frac{8}{24}$

$\frac{5}{x} = \frac{1}{3}$

$x = 15$ (Cross multiply)

person 5′ x′ pole 8′ 24′

Answer: **(3)** 15 feet

28. George has $15.00. His total purchase is:

$7.32
+ 1.68
$9.00

He will have $15.00 − $9.00 = $6.00 left.

Answer: **(3)** $6.00

29. There are 52 cards in a deck, of which 13 are clubs. The probability of picking a club is $\frac{13}{52} = \frac{1}{4}$.

Answer: **(5)** $\frac{1}{4}$

30. It takes Jack 48 minutes ÷ 6 miles = 8 minutes for each mile. At that rate it will take him 15 · 8 = 120 minutes for 15 miles.

120 minutes = 2 hours

Answer: **(2)** 2 hours

31.
$$\begin{aligned} 2x - 7 &= 3 \\ +7 &\quad +7 \\ 2x &= 10 \\ x &= 5 \end{aligned}$$

If $x = 5$, $3x + 1 = 3 \cdot 5 + 1 = 16$

Answer: **(5)** 16

32. The increase in sales was

$17,394,683
− 13,382,675
$ 4,012,008

The average yearly increase over 4 years was

$4,012,008 ÷ 4 = $1,003,002

Answer: **(5)** $1,003,002

33. The perimeter is the sum of all the sides of the figure. ABED is a rectangle, so side ED = 7.

Perimeter = 7 + 5 + 7 + 3 + 3 = 25

Answer: **(2)** 25

34. Kilometer is used to measure long distances.

Answer: **(2)** kilometer

35. I = p · r · t, where I = interest, p = principal, r = rate, t = time in years.

If p = \$200, r = 12%, and t = 2 years,

I = (\$200)(12%)(2)
= (\$200)(.12)(2)
= \$48.00

Answer: **(4)** \$48

36. There are 6 symbols representing men and 8 symbols representing women. The ratio is 6:8, or 3:4.

Answer: **(1)** 3:4

37.

Monday:	300 children	300 adults
Thursday:	500 children	200 adults
Total:	800 children	500 adults

Total revenue = 800(\$.50) + 500(\$1.50)
= \$400 + \$750
= \$1150

Answer: **(3)** \$1150

38. There are 30 symbols in all. Each symbol represents 100 people.

30 · 100 = 3000

Answer: **(1)** 3000

39. Try each choice:

(1) 5 5¢ stamps = 25¢
100¢ − 25¢ = 75¢
= exactly 25 3¢ stamps

(2) 8 5¢ stamps = 40¢
100¢ − 40¢ = 60¢
= exactly 20 3¢ stamps

(3) 9 5¢ stamps = 45¢
100¢ − 45¢ = 55¢
= 18 3¢ stamps and 1¢ change

(4) 11 5¢ stamps = 55¢
100¢ − 55¢ = 45¢
= exactly 15 3¢ stamps

(5) 14 5¢ stamps = 70¢
100¢ − 70¢ = 30¢
= exactly 10 3¢ stamps

In choice (3), exactly \$1.00 cannot be spent.

Answer: **(3)** 9

40. 1 kilogram = 1000 grams

Answer: **(5)** 1000

41. The price after the 15% discount is

85% of \$300 = .85(\$300)
= \$255

The price after the 30% discount is

70% of \$255 = .70(\$255)
= \$178.50

Answer: **(3)** \$178.50

42. Only choices (1) and (3) represent 72 ounces.

Choice (1): 6(\$.39) = \$2.34
Choice (3): 3(\$.79) = \$2.37

Answer: **(1)** Six 12-ounce cans at 39¢ per can.

43. ABC is a right triangle.
$AC = 3$
$BC = 4$

Using the Pythagorean Theorem,

$$(AB)^2 = 3^2 + 4^2$$
$$= 9 + 16$$
$$= 25$$
$$AB = \sqrt{25} = 5$$

Note that ABC is a 3-4-5 right triangle.

Answer: **(2)** 5

44.
$$x^2 - x - 6 = 0$$
$$(x - 3)(x + 2) = 0$$
$$x - 3 = 0 \qquad x + 2 = 0$$
$$x = 3 \qquad x = -2$$

An alternate method is to substitute each given answer into the equation to determine which are solutions. For example, in choice (3), $x = -3$

$$(-3)^2 - (-3) - 6 = 9 + 3 - 6 = 6 \neq 0$$

Therefore $x = -3$ is not a solution of $x^2 - x - 6 = 0$.

Answer: **(4)** 3 or −2

45. Choices (1), (3), (4) and (5) are all examples of the commutative and distributive properties. The quantity in choice (2) is not equal to $75(32 + 88)$.

Answer: **(2)** $(75 \cdot 32) + 88$

46.
$$20\% \text{ of } 30\% = (.20)(.30)$$
$$= .06$$
$$= 6\%$$

Answer: **(5)** 6%

47.
$$1 \text{ pound} = 16 \text{ ounces}$$
$$(16)(28) = 448$$

Answer: **(3)** 450 grams

48.
$$.25\% = .0025$$
$$= \frac{25}{10000}$$
$$= \frac{1}{400}$$

Answer: **(1)** $\frac{1}{400}$

49. Total larcenies in 1977:

$$\begin{array}{r} 20 \\ 175 \\ 155 \\ 1040 \\ 1135 \\ 355 \\ +\ 1375 \\ \hline 4255 \end{array}$$

$$\frac{\text{Auto thefts}}{\text{Total}} = \frac{1040}{4255} = .24 \text{ (approximately)}$$
$$= 24\%$$

Answer: **(3)** 25%

50. Pocket-picking:
$$\begin{array}{r} 1950 \\ -\ 950 \\ \hline 1000 \end{array} \text{ reduction}$$

Auto thefts:
$$\begin{array}{r} 127{,}050 \\ -\ 108{,}000 \\ \hline 19{,}050 \end{array} \text{ reduction}$$

Shoplifting: increased

Bicycle thefts:
$$\begin{array}{r} 8250 \\ -\ 6350 \\ \hline 1900 \end{array} \text{ reduction}$$

Purse-snatching: increased

Answer: **(2)** automobile thefts

51. Calculate the cost of each combination of tickets.

    1. One-way tickets for the first 3 days = \$6.25 × 2 × 3 = \$37.50
       1 weekly ticket = \$40.00
       One-way tickets for 4 days = \$6.25 × 2 × 4 = \$50.00
       Total Cost = \$37.50 + \$40 + \$50 = \$127.50
    2. 1 monthly ticket = \$129
    3. One-way tickets for 3 days = \$6.25 × 2 × 3 = \$37.50
       2 weekly tickets = \$40 × 2 = \$80
       Total Cost = \$37.50 + \$80 = \$117.50
    4. 3 weekly tickets = \$40 × 3 = \$120
    5. One-way tickets for each trip = \$6.25 × 2 × 12 = \$150

    Comparing the total costs, you can see that option 3 is the least expensive.

    Answer: **(5)** Buying one-way tickets for the first 3 days and then buying 2 weekly tickets.

52. Using the calculations you have just made in question 1, you know that the cost of one-way tickets for each trip = \$150. The cost of 3 weekly tickets = \$40 × 3 = \$120. The difference between these costs is \$150 − \$120 = \$30.

    Answer: **(5)** \$30

53. First find out how much money Mike makes each month.
    \$18,500 ÷ 12 = \$1541.67 per month
    To find 30% of his monthly income, multiply \$1541.67 by .30
    \$1541.67 × .30 = \$462.50

    Answer: **(2)** \$462.50

54. Although you know that Mike will no longer have to pay train fare, you do not know whether or not he will have to pay bus or subway fare, or parking fees. Nor do you know what other expenses he will have in connection with the apartment.

    Answer: **(5)** Not enough information is given.

55. Counting backward and halving each new attendance, we get

Friday	1000
Thurs.	500
Wed.	250
Tues.	125

    Answer: **(4)** 125

56. Counting forward, we double attendances and get

Friday	1000
Sat.	2000
Sun.	4000
Mon.	8000

    Answer: **(5)** 8000

Part VII

Two Complete Sample Tests

Directions:

Each Sample Exam has five separate tests: Writing Skills, Social Studies, Science, Interpreting Literature and the Arts, and Mathematics.

1. Read and follow the directions given at the start of each test.
2. Stick to the time limits given for each test.
3. Enter your answers on the tear-out answer sheets provided for the test.
4. When you have completed the entire exam, compare your answers with the correct answers given at the end of the test battery.
5. Count the total number of correct answers for each of the five tests and enter this number in the space provided on your answer sheet.
6. Add the five subtotals to obtain your total score for the test battery.
7. Use the Error Analysis Chart following each exam to see where you are weak and where you are strong.
8. Consult the Explanatory Answers for explanations of all questions you missed.

Answer Sheet GED Sample Test

TEST 1: WRITING SKILLS - PART 1

Number correct ☐

1 ① ② ③ ④ ⑤
2 ① ② ③ ④ ⑤
3 ① ② ③ ④ ⑤
4 ① ② ③ ④ ⑤
5 ① ② ③ ④ ⑤
6 ① ② ③ ④ ⑤
7 ① ② ③ ④ ⑤
8 ① ② ③ ④ ⑤
9 ① ② ③ ④ ⑤
10 ① ② ③ ④ ⑤
11 ① ② ③ ④ ⑤
12 ① ② ③ ④ ⑤
13 ① ② ③ ④ ⑤
14 ① ② ③ ④ ⑤
15 ① ② ③ ④ ⑤
16 ① ② ③ ④ ⑤
17 ① ② ③ ④ ⑤
18 ① ② ③ ④ ⑤
19 ① ② ③ ④ ⑤
20 ① ② ③ ④ ⑤
21 ① ② ③ ④ ⑤
22 ① ② ③ ④ ⑤
23 ① ② ③ ④ ⑤
24 ① ② ③ ④ ⑤
25 ① ② ③ ④ ⑤
26 ① ② ③ ④ ⑤
27 ① ② ③ ④ ⑤
28 ① ② ③ ④ ⑤
29 ① ② ③ ④ ⑤
30 ① ② ③ ④ ⑤
31 ① ② ③ ④ ⑤
32 ① ② ③ ④ ⑤
33 ① ② ③ ④ ⑤
34 ① ② ③ ④ ⑤
35 ① ② ③ ④ ⑤
36 ① ② ③ ④ ⑤
37 ① ② ③ ④ ⑤
38 ① ② ③ ④ ⑤
39 ① ② ③ ④ ⑤
40 ① ② ③ ④ ⑤
41 ① ② ③ ④ ⑤
42 ① ② ③ ④ ⑤
43 ① ② ③ ④ ⑤
44 ① ② ③ ④ ⑤
45 ① ② ③ ④ ⑤
46 ① ② ③ ④ ⑤
47 ① ② ③ ④ ⑤
48 ① ② ③ ④ ⑤
49 ① ② ③ ④ ⑤
50 ① ② ③ ④ ⑤
51 ① ② ③ ④ ⑤
52 ① ② ③ ④ ⑤
53 ① ② ③ ④ ⑤
54 ① ② ③ ④ ⑤
55 ① ② ③ ④ ⑤

GO ON TO WRITING SKILLS-PART II

TEST 2: SOCIAL STUDIES

Number correct ☐

1 ① ② ③ ④ ⑤
2 ① ② ③ ④ ⑤
3 ① ② ③ ④ ⑤
4 ① ② ③ ④ ⑤
5 ① ② ③ ④ ⑤
6 ① ② ③ ④ ⑤
7 ① ② ③ ④ ⑤
8 ① ② ③ ④ ⑤
9 ① ② ③ ④ ⑤
10 ① ② ③ ④ ⑤
11 ① ② ③ ④ ⑤
12 ① ② ③ ④ ⑤
13 ① ② ③ ④ ⑤
14 ① ② ③ ④ ⑤
15 ① ② ③ ④ ⑤
16 ① ② ③ ④ ⑤
17 ① ② ③ ④ ⑤
18 ① ② ③ ④ ⑤
19 ① ② ③ ④ ⑤
20 ① ② ③ ④ ⑤
21 ① ② ③ ④ ⑤
22 ① ② ③ ④ ⑤
23 ① ② ③ ④ ⑤
24 ① ② ③ ④ ⑤
25 ① ② ③ ④ ⑤
26 ① ② ③ ④ ⑤
27 ① ② ③ ④ ⑤
28 ① ② ③ ④ ⑤
29 ① ② ③ ④ ⑤
30 ① ② ③ ④ ⑤
31 ① ② ③ ④ ⑤
32 ① ② ③ ④ ⑤
33 ① ② ③ ④ ⑤
34 ① ② ③ ④ ⑤
35 ① ② ③ ④ ⑤
36 ① ② ③ ④ ⑤
37 ① ② ③ ④ ⑤
38 ① ② ③ ④ ⑤
39 ① ② ③ ④ ⑤
40 ① ② ③ ④ ⑤
41 ① ② ③ ④ ⑤
42 ① ② ③ ④ ⑤
43 ① ② ③ ④ ⑤
44 ① ② ③ ④ ⑤
45 ① ② ③ ④ ⑤
46 ① ② ③ ④ ⑤
47 ① ② ③ ④ ⑤
48 ① ② ③ ④ ⑤
49 ① ② ③ ④ ⑤
50 ① ② ③ ④ ⑤
51 ① ② ③ ④ ⑤
52 ① ② ③ ④ ⑤
53 ① ② ③ ④ ⑤
54 ① ② ③ ④ ⑤
55 ① ② ③ ④ ⑤
56 ① ② ③ ④ ⑤
57 ① ② ③ ④ ⑤
58 ① ② ③ ④ ⑤
59 ① ② ③ ④ ⑤
60 ① ② ③ ④ ⑤
61 ① ② ③ ④ ⑤
62 ① ② ③ ④ ⑤
63 ① ② ③ ④ ⑤
64 ① ② ③ ④ ⑤

STOP

TEST 3: SCIENCE

Number correct ☐

1 ① ② ③ ④ ⑤
2 ① ② ③ ④ ⑤
3 ① ② ③ ④ ⑤
4 ① ② ③ ④ ⑤
5 ① ② ③ ④ ⑤
6 ① ② ③ ④ ⑤
7 ① ② ③ ④ ⑤
8 ① ② ③ ④ ⑤
9 ① ② ③ ④ ⑤
10 ① ② ③ ④ ⑤
11 ① ② ③ ④ ⑤
12 ① ② ③ ④ ⑤
13 ① ② ③ ④ ⑤
14 ① ② ③ ④ ⑤
15 ① ② ③ ④ ⑤
16 ① ② ③ ④ ⑤
17 ① ② ③ ④ ⑤
18 ① ② ③ ④ ⑤
19 ① ② ③ ④ ⑤
20 ① ② ③ ④ ⑤

TEST 3: SCIENCE (Con't)

21 ① ② ③ ④ ⑤
22 ① ② ③ ④ ⑤
23 ① ② ③ ④ ⑤
24 ① ② ③ ④ ⑤
25 ① ② ③ ④ ⑤
26 ① ② ③ ④ ⑤
27 ① ② ③ ④ ⑤
28 ① ② ③ ④ ⑤
29 ① ② ③ ④ ⑤
30 ① ② ③ ④ ⑤
31 ① ② ③ ④ ⑤
32 ① ② ③ ④ ⑤
33 ① ② ③ ④ ⑤
34 ① ② ③ ④ ⑤
35 ① ② ③ ④ ⑤
36 ① ② ③ ④ ⑤
37 ① ② ③ ④ ⑤
38 ① ② ③ ④ ⑤
39 ① ② ③ ④ ⑤
40 ① ② ③ ④ ⑤
41 ① ② ③ ④ ⑤
42 ① ② ③ ④ ⑤
43 ① ② ③ ④ ⑤
44 ① ② ③ ④ ⑤
45 ① ② ③ ④ ⑤
46 ① ② ③ ④ ⑤
47 ① ② ③ ④ ⑤
48 ① ② ③ ④ ⑤
49 ① ② ③ ④ ⑤
50 ① ② ③ ④ ⑤
51 ① ② ③ ④ ⑤
52 ① ② ③ ④ ⑤
53 ① ② ③ ④ ⑤
54 ① ② ③ ④ ⑤
55 ① ② ③ ④ ⑤
56 ① ② ③ ④ ⑤
57 ① ② ③ ④ ⑤
58 ① ② ③ ④ ⑤
59 ① ② ③ ④ ⑤
60 ① ② ③ ④ ⑤
61 ① ② ③ ④ ⑤
62 ① ② ③ ④ ⑤
63 ① ② ③ ④ ⑤
64 ① ② ③ ④ ⑤
65 ① ② ③ ④ ⑤
66 ① ② ③ ④ ⑤

STOP

TEST 4: INTERPRETING LITERATURE AND THE ARTS

Number correct ☐

1 ① ② ③ ④ ⑤
2 ① ② ③ ④ ⑤
3 ① ② ③ ④ ⑤
4 ① ② ③ ④ ⑤
5 ① ② ③ ④ ⑤
6 ① ② ③ ④ ⑤
7 ① ② ③ ④ ⑤
8 ① ② ③ ④ ⑤
9 ① ② ③ ④ ⑤
10 ① ② ③ ④ ⑤
11 ① ② ③ ④ ⑤
12 ① ② ③ ④ ⑤
13 ① ② ③ ④ ⑤
14 ① ② ③ ④ ⑤
15 ① ② ③ ④ ⑤
16 ① ② ③ ④ ⑤
17 ① ② ③ ④ ⑤
18 ① ② ③ ④ ⑤
19 ① ② ③ ④ ⑤
20 ① ② ③ ④ ⑤
21 ① ② ③ ④ ⑤
22 ① ② ③ ④ ⑤
23 ① ② ③ ④ ⑤
24 ① ② ③ ④ ⑤
25 ① ② ③ ④ ⑤
26 ① ② ③ ④ ⑤
27 ① ② ③ ④ ⑤
28 ① ② ③ ④ ⑤
29 ① ② ③ ④ ⑤
30 ① ② ③ ④ ⑤
31 ① ② ③ ④ ⑤
32 ① ② ③ ④ ⑤
33 ① ② ③ ④ ⑤
34 ① ② ③ ④ ⑤
35 ① ② ③ ④ ⑤
36 ① ② ③ ④ ⑤
37 ① ② ③ ④ ⑤
38 ① ② ③ ④ ⑤
39 ① ② ③ ④ ⑤
40 ① ② ③ ④ ⑤
41 ① ② ③ ④ ⑤
42 ① ② ③ ④ ⑤
43 ① ② ③ ④ ⑤
44 ① ② ③ ④ ⑤
45 ① ② ③ ④ ⑤

STOP

TEST 5: MATHEMATICS

Number correct ☐

1 ① ② ③ ④ ⑤
2 ① ② ③ ④ ⑤
3 ① ② ③ ④ ⑤
4 ① ② ③ ④ ⑤
5 ① ② ③ ④ ⑤
6 ① ② ③ ④ ⑤
7 ① ② ③ ④ ⑤
8 ① ② ③ ④ ⑤
9 ① ② ③ ④ ⑤
10 ① ② ③ ④ ⑤
11 ① ② ③ ④ ⑤
12 ① ② ③ ④ ⑤
13 ① ② ③ ④ ⑤
14 ① ② ③ ④ ⑤
15 ① ② ③ ④ ⑤
16 ① ② ③ ④ ⑤
17 ① ② ③ ④ ⑤
18 ① ② ③ ④ ⑤
19 ① ② ③ ④ ⑤
20 ① ② ③ ④ ⑤
21 ① ② ③ ④ ⑤
22 ① ② ③ ④ ⑤
23 ① ② ③ ④ ⑤
24 ① ② ③ ④ ⑤
25 ① ② ③ ④ ⑤
26 ① ② ③ ④ ⑤
27 ① ② ③ ④ ⑤
28 ① ② ③ ④ ⑤
29 ① ② ③ ④ ⑤
30 ① ② ③ ④ ⑤
31 ① ② ③ ④ ⑤
32 ① ② ③ ④ ⑤
33 ① ② ③ ④ ⑤
34 ① ② ③ ④ ⑤
35 ① ② ③ ④ ⑤
36 ① ② ③ ④ ⑤
37 ① ② ③ ④ ⑤
38 ① ② ③ ④ ⑤
39 ① ② ③ ④ ⑤
40 ① ② ③ ④ ⑤
41 ① ② ③ ④ ⑤
42 ① ② ③ ④ ⑤
43 ① ② ③ ④ ⑤
44 ① ② ③ ④ ⑤
45 ① ② ③ ④ ⑤
46 ① ② ③ ④ ⑤
47 ① ② ③ ④ ⑤
48 ① ② ③ ④ ⑤
49 ① ② ③ ④ ⑤
50 ① ② ③ ④ ⑤
51 ① ② ③ ④ ⑤
52 ① ② ③ ④ ⑤
53 ① ② ③ ④ ⑤
54 ① ② ③ ④ ⑤
55 ① ② ③ ④ ⑤
56 ① ② ③ ④ ⑤

STOP

GED SAMPLE TEST I

TEST 1. WRITING SKILLS

This test has two parts. Part I measures your ability to recognize errors in written material. Part II tests your ability to write a short essay.

PART I. RECOGNIZING AND CORRECTING ERRORS

Time: 75 Minutes—55 Questions

Directions:

This test consists of several paragraphs in which each sentence is numbered. Some of the sentences within each paragraph contain errors in sentence structure, usage, or mechanics. Other sentences are correct as written. Following each paragraph are questions based upon it. Read the paragraph first, then answer the questions about it. For each item, choose the answer that would result in the most effective writing of the sentence. The best answer must be consistent with the meaning and tone of the paragraph. Record your answers in the Writing Skills section of the answer sheet.

FOR EXAMPLE:

Often their are two equally effective ways to solve a problem.

What correction should be made to this sentence?

(1) replace their with there
(2) change are to is
(3) change two to too
(4) insert a comma after equally
(5) no change is necessary

In this example, the word *their,* which means "belonging to them," is incorrectly substituted for the word *there.* To indicate this correction, mark answer space 1 on your answer sheet.

Items 1 to 10 are based on the following paragraph.

(1) Exposure to sum industrial agents increases cancer risks. (2) The kinds of workplace substances that cause cancer can be divided into three broad groups: chemicals, metals, and dusts and fibers. (3) Only a small number of agents in these categories truely cause cancer. (4) They do damage by acting alone or, probably more often, by acting in combination with another workplace carcinogen (cancer-causing agent) or cigarette smoke. (5) For example, studies showing that breathing in asbestos fibers creates an especially high risk of lung disease and cancer. (6) These risk is extremely high for workers who smoke. (7) In fact, some scientists suggest that the main Carcinogen in the workplace is the cigarette. (8) Regulatory agencies, industries, and organized labor have developed health and safety meassures related to hazardous exposures in the workplace. (9) Industries will have been taking a number of steps to reduce or eliminate risks to workers. (10) Individuals can also take steps. (11) Health and safety rules of the workplace ought to be known and followed.

1. Sentence 1: **Exposure to sum industrial agents increases cancer risks.**

   Which of the following is the best way to write the underlined portion of this sentence? If you think the original is the best way to write the sentence, choose option (1).

   (1) Exposure to sum
   (2) Exposure because some
   (3) Exposure to some
   (4) Exposure while some
   (5) Expozure to sum

2. Sentence 2: **The kinds of workplace substances that cause cancer can be divided into three broad groups: chemicals, metals, and dusts and fibers.**

   What correction should be made to this sentence?

   (1) capitalize substances
   (2) capitalize cancer
   (3) omit the colon after groups
   (4) change the colon after groups to a semicolon.
   (5) no correction is necessary

3. Sentence 3: **Only a small number of agents in these categories truely cause cancer.**

   What correction should be made to this sentence?

   (1) change these to those
   (2) change the spelling of categories to catagories
   (3) change the spelling of truely to truly
   (4) change cancer to Cancer
   (5) no correction is necessary

4. Sentence 4: **They do damage by acting alone or, probably more often, by acting in combination with another workplace carcinogen (cancer-causing agent) or cigarette smoke.**

   If you rewrote sentence 4 beginning with Agents acting alone or in combination the next words should be

   (1) do damage
   (2) act alone
   (3) probably acting
   (4) or workplace
   (5) and smoke

5. Sentence 5. **For example, studies showing that breathing in asbestos fibers creates an especially high risk of lung disease and cancer.**

   Which of the following is the best way to write the underlined portion of this sentence? If you think that the original is the best way to write write the sentence, choose option (1).

   (1) For example, studies showing that breathing
   (2) For example studies showing that breathing
   (3) For example studies shown that breathing
   (4) For example, studies have shown that breathing
   (5) For example, studies showing breathing

6. Sentence 6: **These risk is extremely high for workers who smoke.**

   What correction should be made to this sentence?

   (1) change These to The
   (2) change *is* to are
   (3) change the spelling of extremely to extremly
   (4) change who to whose
   (5) change smoke to smokes

7. Sentence 7: **In fact, some scientists suggest that the main Carcinogen in the workplace is the cigarette.**

   What correction should be made to this sentence?

   (1) delete the comma after fact
   (2) change the comma after fact to a semicolon
   (3) change suggest to suggests
   (4) change Carcinogen to carcinogen
   (5) change the period after cigarette to a comma

8. Sentence 8: **Regulatory agencies, industries, and organized labor have developed health and safety meassures related to hazardous exposures in the workplace.**

   What correction should be made to this sentence?

   (1) change spelling of agency to Agencies
   (2) insert a comma after labor
   (3) change spelling of meassures to measures
   (4) insert a colon after meassures
   (5) no correction is necessary

9. Sentence 9: **Industries will have been taking a number of steps to reduce or eliminate risks to workers.**

   Which of the following is the best way to write the underlined portion of this sentence? If you think the original is the best way to write the sentence, choose option (1).

   (1) will have been taking
   (2) can have been taking
   (3) taked
   (4) can take
   (5) taking

10. Sentence 11: **Health and safety rules of the workplace ought to be known and followed.**

    If you rewrote sentence 11 beginning with Workplace health and safety rules the next word should be

    (1) follow
    (2) ought
    (3) yet
    (4) know
    (5) work

GO ON TO THE NEXT PAGE

Items 11 to 19 are based on the following paragraph.

(1) Chronic use of alcohol can caused changes in the liver that speed up the metabolism of some drugs, such as anticoagulants, anticonvulsants, and diabetes drugs. (2) They become less effective because they do not stay in the body long enough. (3) Prolonged alcohol abused can also damage the liver, decreasing its ability to metabolize or process certain drugs. (4) In that case, the drugs stay in the system too long. (5) This is particularly serious when the drugs are antipsychotic drugs, who can cause further liver damage.

(6) Alcohol is a central nervous system depressant. (7) Alcohol taken along with another central nervous system depressant drug can affect performance skills, judgment, and alertness. (8) If the mixture include overdoses of barbiturates, Valium, or Darvon, the result can be fatal.

(9) A person whom has developed a tolerance to the sedative effects of alcohol may need larger doses of tranquilizers or sleeping pills to get the desired effect. (10) This led to an overdose without the person being aware of it.

11. Sentence 1: **Chronic use of alcohol can caused changes in the liver that speed up the metabolism of some drugs, such as anticoagulants, anticonvulsants, and diabetes drugs.**

    Which of the following is the best way to write the underlined portion of this sentence? If you think the original is the best way to write the sentence, choose option (1).

    (1) can caused changes
    (2) had caused changes
    (3) causing changes
    (4) having caused changes
    (5) can cause changes

12. Sentence 2: **They become less effective because they do not stay in the body long enough.**

    What correction should be made to this sentence?

    (1) change become to became
    (2) change less to least
    (3) change because to nor
    (4) insert a colon after because
    (5) no correction is necessary

13. Sentence 3: **Prolonged alcohol abused can also damage the liver, decreasing its ability to metabolize or process certain drugs.**

    What correction should be made to this sentence?

    (1) capitalize Alcohol
    (2) change abused to abuse
    (3) change the comma after liver to a semicolon
    (4) change spelling of its to it's
    (5) no correction is necessary

14. Sentence 5: **This is particularly serious when the drugs are antipsychotic drugs, who can cause further liver damage.**

    Which of the following is the best way to write the underlined portion of this sentence? If you think the original is the best way to write the sentence, choose option (1).

    (1) who can cause
    (2) which can cause
    (3) who have caused
    (4) whose cause
    (5) who caused

15. Sentence 5: **This is particularly serious when the drugs are antipsychotic drugs, who can cause further liver damage.**

    If you rewrote sentence 5 beginning with
    With antipsychotic drugs
    the next word should be

    (1) this
    (2) particularly
    (3) when
    (4) who
    (5) can

Items 20 to 29 are based on the following paragraph.

(1) More and more people have microwave ovens at home today and find themselves facing a throughly different method of cooking. (2) Let's look, then, at how microwave ovens work, and how that effects their use with perishable goods, particularly meat and poultry. (3) Microwaves were extra-short radio waves produced in the oven. (4) The movement (friction) is caused inside the food by these waves they actually do the cooking. (5) The air in the oven usually doesn't heat up very much. (6) The waves bounce around inside the oven, passing through the food repeatedly. (7) This causes cooking beginning just below the food's surface. (8) Full cooking is achieved as the heat starts to spread through the rest of the food. (9) While microwaving is quick, it does not always cook food evenly. (10) Before new microwave owners master their ovens, they often find that some spots in a food will overcook, while others are still not thoroughly cooked. (11) To complete cooking of the whole food unless overcooking these high-heat spots, many microwave recipes call for a 10 to 15-minute standing time following power cooking. (12) That allows cooking to continue after you take the food out of the oven as the heat spreads evenly througout the food.

20. Sentence 1: **More and more people have microwave ovens at home today and find themselves facing a throughly different method of cooking.**

What correction should be made to this sentence?

(1) capitalize Microwave
(2) add a semicolon after today
(3) change the spelling of throughly to thoroughly
(4) change the spelling of different to diffirent
(5) no correction necessary

21. Sentence 2: **Let's look, then, at how microwave ovens work, and how that effects their use with perishable goods, particularly meat and poultry.**

What correction should be made to this sentence?

(1) change work to works
(2) change effects to affects
(3) change use to used
(4) change the spelling of particularly to particulary
(5) insert a comma after meat

22. Sentence 3: **Microwaves were extra-short radio waves produced in the oven.**

What correction should be made to this sentence?

(1) change microwaves to microwave
(2) change were to are
(3) capitalize the words radio waves
(4) change produced to producing
(5) no correction is necessary

23. Sentence 4: **The movement (friction) is caused inside the food by these waves they actually do the cooking.**

Which of the following is the best way to write the underlined portion of this sentence? If you think the original is the best way to write the sentence, choose option (1).

(1) waves they
(2) waves, they
(3) waves who
(4) waves. They
(5) waves' they

24. Sentence 5: **The air in the oven usually doesn't heat up very much.**

What correction should be made to this sentence?

(1) insert a comma after air
(2) insert a semicolon after oven
(3) change the spelling of usually to usualy
(4) change doesn't to don't
(5) no correction is necessary

16. Sentence 7: **Alcohol taken along with another central nervous system depressant drug can affect performance skills, judgment and alertness.**

What correction should be made to this sentence?

(1) insert a comma after alcohol
(2) insert a colon after drug
(3) insert a comma after drug
(4) insert a colon after affect
(5) no correction is necessary

17. Sentence 8: **If the mixture include overdoses of barbiturates, Valium, or Darvon, the result can be fatal.**

What correction should be made to this sentence?

(1) change If to When
(2) change include to includes
(3) change barbiturates to Barbiturates
(4) change result to results
(5) no correction is necessary

18. Sentence 9: **A person whom has developed a tolerance to the sedative effects of alcohol may need larger doses of tranquilizers or sleeping pills to get the desired effect.**

What correction should be made to this sentence?

(1) change whom to who
(2) change has developed to developing
(3) change tolerance to tolerances
(4) insert a comma after alcohol
(5) no correction is necessary

19. Sentence 10: **This led to an overdose without the person being aware of it.**

Which of the following is the best way to write the underlined portion of this sentence? If you think the original is the best way to write the sentence, choose option (1).

(1) This led to
(2) This, led to
(3) These led to
(4) This can lead to
(5) There should lead to

GO ON TO THE NEXT PAGE

25. Sentence 6: **The waves bounce around inside the oven, passing through the food repeatedly.**

If you rewrote sentence 6 beginning with
Inside the oven
the next words should be

(1) passing through
(2) around waves
(3) to pass
(4) the waves
(5) to bounce

26. Sentence 7: **This causes cooking beginning just below the food's surface.**

Which of the following is the best way to write the underlined portion of the sentence? If you think that the original is the best way to write the sentence, choose option (1).

(1) cooking beginning just
(2) cooking to begin just
(3) cooking just
(4) beginning cooking just
(5) cooking began just

27. Sentence 8: **Full cooking is achieved as the heat starts to spread through the rest of the food.**

If you rewrote sentence 8 beginning with
As the heat starts to spread
the next words should be

(1) through starting
(2) full cooking
(3) after achieving
(4) on the cooking
(5) the rest of

28. Sentence 11: **To complete cooking of the whole food unless overcooking these high-heat spots, many microwave recipes call for a 10 to 15-minute standing time following power cooking.**

Which of the following is the best way to write the underlined portion of this sentence? If you think the original is the best way to write the sentence, choose option (1).

(1) food unless overcooking
(2) food on overcooking
(3) food without overcooking
(4) food. Unless overcooking
(5) food, overcook

29. Sentence 12: **That allows cooking to continue after you take the food out of the oven as the heat spreads evenly througout the food.**

What correction should be made to this sentence?

(1) change That to Than
(2) change allows to allowed
(3) change the spelling of continue to conttinue
(4) change the spelling of spreads to spreds
(5) change the spelling of througout to throughout

GO ON TO THE NEXT PAGE

Items 30 to 39 are based on the following passage.

(1) For parents, it is a challenge to recognize and keep a balanced perspective on they're teenager's emotional roller coaster ride. (2) As their children bounce back and forth between childhood and adulthood, alternating irresponsibility with responsibility, blatantly, testing parental authority one moment and depending on it the next, parents often do not know what to expect. (3) They must maintain needed discipline, yet they understood their teenager's growing need for independent action, even for rebellion.

(4) It is easy to understand, why many parents and adolescents find this such a difficult period to "survive." (5) But once it is over, even the most rebellious child often becomes appreciative, affectionate, and devoted. (6) With maturity comes the realization that much of their parents' behavior, once so irritated, was motivated by feelings of love for them. (7) Also, having children of their own bring understanding of the pressures their parents faced.

(8) Parents should also been aware of their own imperfections. (9) At times, lack of knowledge, poor advice, community pressures, or their own stresses can cause them to overreact and teenage behaviors. (10) To avoid making the same mistakes as their parents, or to make up for what they missed in their childhood, parents sometimes make mistakes themselves. (11) Adolescence was a trying period, but it is also an exciting one. (12) If parents and teenagers keep tuned in to each other, this period may seem less trying and more fun for everyone.

30. Sentence 1: **For parents, it is a challenge to recognize and keep a balanced perspective on they're teenager's emotional roller coaster ride.**

What correction should be made to this sentence?

(1) change the spelling of recognize to reckonize
(2) change the spelling of balanced to balansed
(3) change they're to their
(4) change the spelling of teenager's to teenagers
(5) no correction is necessary

31. Sentence 2: **As their children bounce back and forth between childhood and adulthood, alternating irresponsibility with responsibility, blatantly, testing parental authority one moment and depending on it the next, parents often do not know what to expect.**

Which of the following is the best way to write the underlined portion of this sentence? If you think the original is the best way to write the sentence, choose option (1).

(1) with responsibility, blatantly, testing
(2) with responsibility; blatantly testing
(3) with responsibility. Blatantly testing
(4) with responsibility, blatantly testing
(5) with responsibility. Blatantly, testing

32. Sentence 3: **They must maintain needed discipline, yet they understood their teenager's growing need for independent action, even for rebellion.**

What correction should be made to this sentence?

(1) change maintain to have maintained
(2) change understood to understand
(3) change their to there
(4) change the spelling of independent to independant
(5) change the spelling of rebellion to rebelion

33. Sentence 4: **It is easy to understand, why many parents and adolescents find this such a difficult period to "survive."**

Which of the following is the best way to write the underlined portion of this sentence? If you think the original is the best way to write the sentence, choose option (1).

(1) It is easy to understand,
(2) It is easy to understand
(3) Easy to understand
(4) Easiest to understand,
(5) To try to understand

34. Sentence 5: **But once it is over, even the most rebellious child often becomes appreciative, affectionate, and devoted.**

Which of the following is the best way to write the underlined portion of this sentence? If you think the original is the best way to write the sentence, choose option (1).

(1) becomes appreciative, affectionate,
(2) becomes appreciating, affectionate
(3) becomes apreciattive, affectionate
(4) becomes appreciative, afecttionate
(5) becomes appreciating nor affectionate

35. Sentence 6: **With maturity comes the realization that much of their parents' behavior, once so irritated, was motivated by feelings of love for them.**

What correction should be made to this sentence?

(1) change comes to come
(2) change the spelling of realization to realazation
(3) change parents' to parents
(4) change irritated to irritating
(5) change love to loving

36. Sentence 7: **Also, having children of their own bring understanding of the pressures their parents faced.**

What correction should be made to this sentence?

(1) change having to had
(2) change their to they're
(3) change bring to brings
(4) change parents to parents'
(5) no correction is necessary

37. Sentence 8: **Parents should also been aware of their own imperfections.**

What correction should be made to this sentence?

(1) change parents to parents'
(2) delete also
(3) insert have after also
(4) change been to be
(5) no correction is necessary

38. Sentence 9: **At times, lack of knowledge, poor advice, community pressures, or their own stresses can cause them to overreact and teenage behaviors.**

Which of the following is the best way to write the underlined portion of this sentence? If you think the original is the best way to write the sentence, choose option (1).

(1) overreact and teenage
(2) overreact to teenage
(3) overreact for teenage
(4) overreact because teenage
(5) overreact before teenage

39. Sentence 11: **Adolescence was a trying period, but it is also an exciting one.**

Which of the following is the best way to write the underlined portion of this sentence? If you think the original is the best way to write the sentence, choose option (1).

(1) Adolsecence was
(2) Adolescence is
(3) Adolescence to be
(4) Adolescence keeps
(5) Adolescence had been

GO ON TO THE NEXT PAGE

Items 40 to 47 are based on the following passage.

(1) Hypothermia means low body temperature. (2) It is caused by exposure to cold. (3) Hypothermia developed when body heat is lost to a cool or cold environment faster than it can be replaced. (4) This heat loss causes the body temperature to fall below the normal 98.6°F (37°C), resulting in a life-threatening physical and mental deterioration. (5) Without medical treatment and rewarming, the victim of hypothermia will die. (6) Hypothermia is a serious public health problem in winter, although older Americans are its most frequent victims, infants and people with certain diseases are also especially at risk. (7) Although most people associate hypothermia with exposure to severe outdoor cold, indoor cold exposure is considered by experts to be the most common cause of hypothermia in the United States. (8) Indoor temperatures having to fall below freezing to cause hypothermia; in fact, most elderly victims become ill at temperatures between 50°F (10°C) and 65°F (18°C), as a result of mild cold exposure that would only produce discomfort in younger people. (9) The most important defense against hypothermia for vulnerable people living in cool or cold homes is personal insulation. (10) Dressed warmly during the day and sleeping with plenty of bedcovers at night is very important. (11) Several layers of loose clothing provide more insulation for the body than tight clothing. (12) Good nutrition is also important because food provides the energy that the body used to produce heat.

40. Sentence 3: **Hypothermia developed when body heat is lost to a cool or cold environment faster than it can be replaced.**

    What correction should be made to this sentence?

    (1) change developed to develops
    (2) insert a comma after developed
    (3) insert a comma after cool
    (4) change the spelling of environment to enviromment
    (5) no correction is necessary

41. Sentence 4: **This heat loss causes the body temperature to fall below the normal 98.6°F (37°C), resulting in a life-threatening physical and mental deterioration.**

    If you rewrote sentence 4 beginning with Life-threatening physical and mental deterioration
    the next words should be

    (1) body temperature
    (2) can result
    (3) falls below
    (4) lost heat
    (5) causes normal

42. Sentence 5: **Without medical treatment and rewarming, the victim of hypothermia will die.**

    What correction should be made to this sentence?

    (1) change medical to medecal
    (2) insert a comma after treatment
    (3) remove the comma after rewarming
    (4) replace will die with died
    (5) no correction is necessary

43. Sentence 6: **Hypothermia is a serious public health problem in winter, although older Americans are its most frequent victims, infants and people with certain diseases are also especially at risk.**

    Which of the following is the best way to write the underlined portion of this sentence? If you think the original is the best way to write the sentence, choose option (1).

    (1) in winter, although older
    (2) in winter, because older
    (3) in winter; and all though older
    (4) in winter. Although older
    (5) in winter, and older

44. Sentence 7: **Although most people associate hypothermia with exposure to severe outdoor cold, indoor cold exposure is considered by experts to be the most common cause of hypothermia in the United States.**

Which of the following is the best way to write the underlined portion of this sentence? If you think the original is the best way to write the sentence, choose option (1).

(1) Although most people
(2) Because most people
(3) After most people
(4) Otherwise most people
(5) Having most people

45. Sentence 8: **Indoor temperatures having to fall below freezing to cause hypothermia; in fact, most elderly victims become ill at temperatures between 50°F (10°C) and 65°F (18°C), as a result of mild cold exposure that would only produce discomfort in younger people.**

Which of the following is the best way to write the underlined portion of this sentence? If you think the original is the best way to write the sentence, choose option (1).

(1) temperatures having to fall
(2) temperatures having fallen
(3) temperatures to fall
(4) temperatures falling
(5) temperatures do not have to fall

46. Sentence 10: **Dressed warmly during the day and sleeping with plenty of bedcovers at night is very important.**

What correction should be made to this sentence?

(1) replace Dressed with Dressing
(2) insert a comma after warmly
(3) insert a comma after day
(4) change night to nights
(5) no correction is necessary

47. Sentence 12: **Good nutrition is also important because food provides the energy that the body used to produce heat.**

What correction should be made to this sentence?

(1) replace is with was
(2) insert a period after important
(3) insert a comma after energy
(4) replace used with uses
(5) change the spelling of produce to produse

GO ON TO THE NEXT PAGE

Items 48 to 55 are based on the following paragraph.

(1) United States consumers have learned a very basic fact of life, the days of unlimited low cost energy are over. (2) This does not mean we have to go back to the horse and buggy days or even gave up all our timesaving, energy-powered appliances. (3) What it does mean is that we have to be more conscious of how we "spend" our energy resources and to making a commitment to become more efficient energy consumers. (4) Many Americans have all ready realized that saving energy means saving money. (5) It also means preserving our limited domestic energy resources for future generations. (6) According to the United States department of Energy, seventy percent of residential energy expenditures are used for heating and cooling our homes, twenty percent for heating water, and the remaining ten percent for lighting, cooking and operating small appliances. (7) Each of us can makes a positive contribution to solving America's energy dilemma. (8) We looked for ways to use energy more efficiently in our homes and in our cars. (9) By avoiding waste, we can also help to reduce our dependence on high priced foreign oil. (10) Remember, the energy we conserved today can serve us tomorrow.

48. Sentence 1: **United States consumers have learned a very basic fact of life, the days of unlimited low cost energy are over.**

    Which of the following is the best way to write the underlined portion of this sentence? If you think the original is the best way to write the sentence, choose option (1).

    (1) fact of life, the days
    (2) fact of life. The days
    (3) fact of life; The days
    (4) fact of life, and the days
    (5) fact of life for the days

49. Sentence 2: **This does not mean we have to go back to the horse and buggy days or even gave up all our timesaving, energy-powered appliances.**

    What correction should be made to this sentence?

    (1) change have to had
    (2) capitalize Horse and Buggy
    (3) insert a period after days
    (4) change gave to give
    (5) change energy-powered to energy, powered

50. Sentence 3: **What it does mean is that we have to be more conscious of how we "spend" our energy resources and to making a commitment to become more efficient energy consumers.**

    What correction should be made to this sentence?

    (1) change have to had
    (2) change the spelling of conscious to conscience
    (3) change to making to make
    (4) change commitment to committment
    (5) change the spelling of efficient to eficient

51. Sentence 4: **Many Americans have all ready realized that saving energy means saving money.**

    What correction should be made to this sentence?

    (1) change have to had
    (2) change all ready to already
    (3) change the spelling of realized to reallized
    (4) insert a colon after that
    (5) no correction is necessary

52. Sentence 6: **According to the United States department of Energy, seventy percent of residential energy expenditures are used for heating and cooling our homes, twenty percent for heating water, and the remaining ten percent for lighting, cooking and operating small appliances.**

Which of the following is the best way to write the underlined portion of the sentence? If you think the original is the best way to write the sentence, choose option (1).

(1) United States department of Energy
(2) United States department of energy
(3) United States Department of energy
(4) United states department of energy
(5) United States Department of Energy

53. Sentence 7: **Each of us can makes a positive contribution to solving America's energy dilemma.**

What correction should be made to this sentence?

(1) change can to may
(2) change makes to make
(3) insert a comma after contribution
(4) change America's to Americas
(5) change the spelling of dilemma to dillema

54. Sentence 8: **We looked for ways to use energy more efficiently in our homes and in our cars.**

Which of the following is the best way to write the underlined portion of this sentence? If you think the original is the best way to write the sentence, choose option (1).

(1) We looked for
(2) We have looked for
(3) We looks for
(4) We had looked for
(5) We can look for

55. Sentence 10: **Remember, the energy we conserved today can serve us tomorrow.**

What correction should be made to this sentence?

(1) delete the word Remember
(2) change energy to energies
(3) change conserved to conserve
(4) change serve to serves
(5) change the spelling of tomorrow to tommorrow

END OF WRITING SKILLS TEST—PART I

PART II. ESSAY

Time: 45 Minutes–1 Essay

Directions:

This part of the GED is designed to find out how well you write. You will be given one question which asks you to explain something or to present an opinion on an issue. In constructing your answer for this part of the exam, you should take the following steps:

1. Before you begin to write your answer, read all of the material accompanying the question.
2. Carefully plan what you will say before you begin to write.
3. Use the blank pages in the test booklet (or scratch paper provided for you) to make notes to plan your essay.
4. Write your answer on the separate answer sheet.
5. Carefully read over what you have written and make any changes that will improve your work.
6. Check your paragraphing, sentence structure, spelling, punctuation, capitalization, and usage, and correct any errors.

You will have 45 minutes to write a response to the question you are given. Write clearly with a ballpoint pen so the evaluators can read what you have written. Any notes you make on the blank pages or scratch paper will not be included in your evaluation.

Your essay will be scored by at least two trained readers who will evaluate the paper according to its overall impact. They will be concerned with how clearly you made your main points, how thoroughly your ideas are supported, and how effective and correct your writing is throughout the entire composition. You will receive no credit for writing on a topic other than the one assigned.

SAMPLE TOPIC

Over 85% of households in America clip and redeem supermarket coupons and refund offers. Write a composition of about 200 words in which you explain why you think people take the time to do this. Be specific, and use examples to support your view.

USE THIS PAGE FOR NOTES.

TEST 2. SOCIAL STUDIES

85 Minutes—64 Questions

Directions:

The Social Studies Test consists of multiple-choice questions intended to measure your knowledge of general concepts in history, economics, geography, and political and behavorial science. The questions are based on reading passages, maps, graphs, charts, and cartoons. For each question, first study the information given and then answer the questions about it. You may refer to the readings or graphs as often as necessary in order to answer the questions. Record your answers in the Social Studies section of your answer sheet.

FOR EXAMPLE:

Which medium most regularly presents opinions and interpretations of the news?

(1) national television news programs
(2) local television news programs
(3) newspaper editorial pages
(4) teletype news agency reports
(5) radio news broadcasts

The correct answer is "newspaper editorial pages." Therefore, you should mark answer space 3 on your answer sheet.

Items 1 to 5 refer to the following selection:

Labor conditions in the South differed markedly from those in the North. For one thing, until well after the beginning of the twentieth century, the South failed to attract immigrant labor, or even the children of immigrants. Whites from the poorer lands of the Piedmont and from the mountains supplied the bulk of the labor for the textile mills and such others as required skilled operatives, while a preponderance of blacks did the harder work of the mines, the blast furnaces, and the lumber industry. Only in rare instances were the two races employed side by side at the same tasks; industries that used both blacks and whites took care to maintain a division of labor between the races, regularly assigning the inferior position to the blacks.

In the textile mills, the employment of women and children was practically universal, although the extent to which young children were exploited has probably been exaggerated. Nevertheless, the opportunity for the whole family to be gainfully employed was one of the chief attractions of the mills to the rural whites. Wages were low, at first far lower than wages paid in the Northern mills. With the mother and children and the father all at work, however, the total income was much larger than that from a rundown farm, and the temptation to leave that farm for the factory was almost irresistible.

1. Based on the information in this article, which phrase most clearly describes the economic condition of Southern farmers at the beginning of the twentieth century?

   (1) poor but encouraging
   (2) comparatively worse than the condition of mill workers
   (3) unaffected by racial tensions
   (4) determined by prices paid in Northern cities
   (5) attractive to immigrant labor

2. Early in this century, who was most likely to have received training for skilled jobs in Southern factories?

   (1) blacks and whites alike
   (2) white children only
   (3) educated whites
   (4) immigrant labor
   (5) white men

3. From this selection, what can be inferred about early twentieth-century rural life in the South?

   (1) Higher education did not play a major role.
   (2) There were few racial barriers.
   (3) It was far better than life in the North.
   (4) It was marked by rapid technological change.
   (4) It depended on immigrant labor.

4. Why did whites gradually move toward work in factories and mills?
   (1) Cotton was king in the south.
   (2) Land was not economically productive.
   (3) More money could be made there by the whole family.
   (4) Blacks were taking over the farms.
   (5) Northern competition was intense.

5. Based on the information in this article. which of the following reasons best explains why industries did not exploit child labor to a greater extent?

   (1) There were not enough children available.
   (2) The children were in school half the day.
   (3) It was not economically practical.
   (4) Parents refused to allow their young children to work.
   (5) The children rebelled against the work.

Items 6 to 8 are based on the following map.

AFGHANISTAN

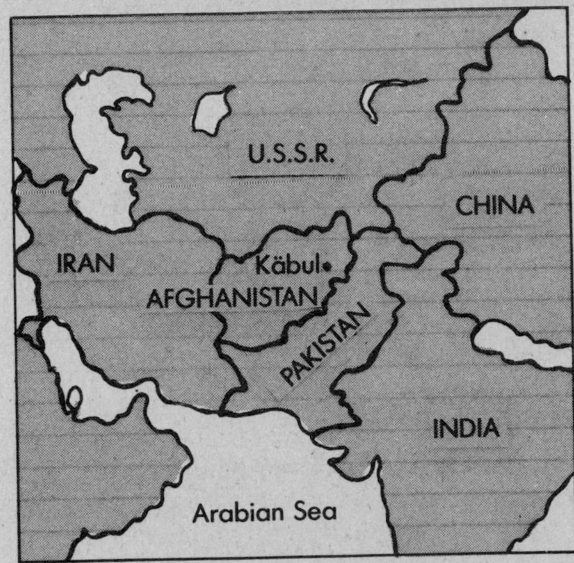

6. Which of the following statements most likely explains why Afghanistan has had difficulty getting its exports to market?

   (1) It does not produce enough.
   (2) It is a primitive country.
   (3) It is hated by its neighbors.
   (4) It has a low literacy rate among its inhabitants.
   (5) It has no access to the sea.

7. The people of Afghanistan are divided into various ethnic groups including Pushtuns, Tajiks, Uzbeks, and Hazaras. About 50 percent of its 19,500,000 people speak Pushtu, another 35 percent speak Persian, and 11 percent speak Turkic languages, while the remaining people speak a variety of different languages. The country is about one-fifth the physical size of the United States. Only about ten percent of the people are literate in any language. Based on this information,which conclusion is most likely?

   (1) Afghanistan is a rich, well-run nation.
   (2) Afghanistan has heavy industry and technologically advanced corporations.
   (3) Afghanistan is essentially an agricultural economy.
   (4) The capital of Afghanistan is a major Asian city.
   (5) Afghanistan cannot support its own army.

8. Which of the following statements is best supported by the map?

   (1) Freshwater fish makes up the main part of the Afghan diet.
   (2) Russia would most likely seek to annex Afghanistan.
   (3) Afghanistan is a strategic middle European port.
   (4) Afghanistan was once a part of Pakistan.
   (5) Afghanistan is bordered by mountains.

GO ON TO THE NEXT PAGE

Items 9 to 14 are based on the following selection

Certain kinds of deceptive advertising appeals and claims appear over and over again despite continued efforts to halt them. Advertisers who make such claims generally have found them so successful that they can make a great deal of profit before any action can be taken to force them to stop. Listed below are five types of deceptive advertising practices:

1. **meaningless claims**——ads that appear to supply useful facts but upon closer examination, the information is meaningless
2. **misrepresentation**——ads that exaggerate or make false claims about a product
3. **"bait and switch"**——an insincere offer to sell a product or service that the advertiser does not really wish or intend to sell. When the shopper shows interest in the product, the advertiser offers another, of higher price
4. **referral sales schemes**—ads that offer purchasers bonuses for providing the seller with names of other prospective buyers
5. **fictitious pricing**——overstatement of the "list price" in order to convince shoppers that advertised prices offer special pricing

Each of the following statements illustrates a type of deceptive advertising. Choose the deceptive practice being used in each situation. The categories may be used more than once in the set of items but no one question has more than one best answer.

9. "You may never need to buy another pair of socks again—unless the laundry loses them! We guarantee it!"

(1) meaningless claim
(2) misrepresentation
(3) "bait and switch"
(4) referral sales scheme
(5) fictitious pricing

10. "Scientific studies prove that Cleer detergent is absolutely guaranteed to last 40% longer or your money will be cheerfully refunded."

(1) meaningless claim
(2) misrepresentation
(3) "bait and switch"
(4) referral sales scheme
(5) fictitious pricing

11. The Simmons family arrives at Giant Furniture in response to the following ad: "Three rooms of furniture—only $200!" At Giant, the Simmonses are shown a bed, a sofa, and a dining room table, all scratched and in poor condition. The salesman diverts them to more expensive items in better condition.

(1) meaningless claim
(2) misrepresentation
(3) "bait and switch"
(4) referral sales scheme
(5) fictitious pricing

12. Television City claims that the manufacturer's suggested price on the 19-inch color television is $500, and the $400 Television City special sale price therefore represents a $100 savings over list. In actuality, the manufacturer's suggested price is $398.99.

    (1) meaningless claim
    (2) misrepresentation
    (3) "bait and switch"
    (4) referral sales scheme
    (5) fictitious pricing

13. "It's official! CHATTERING TEDDY BEARS sold by competitive companies are now outselling virtually every other toy in America! Demand is so great that even models introduced one year ago still sell for much more in the stores! But we are able to offer these adorable toys at far, far less, through this special introductory mail offer."

    (1) meaningless claim
    (2) misrepresentation
    (3) "bait and switch"
    (4) referral sales scheme
    (5) fictitious pricing

14. A builder of swimming pools offers a pool buyer $50 for each prospective purchaser he refers to the builder. In order for the prospective buyer to collect the $50, the person who was referred must purchase the pool.

    (1) meaningless claim
    (2) misrepresentation
    (3) "bait and switch"
    (4) referral sales scheme
    (5) fictitious pricing

GO ON TO THE NEXT PAGE

Items 15 to 18 refer to the following maps:

North America in 1763

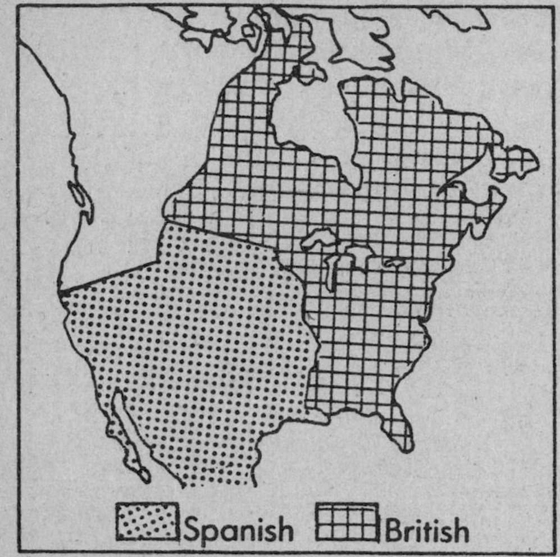

North America in 1689

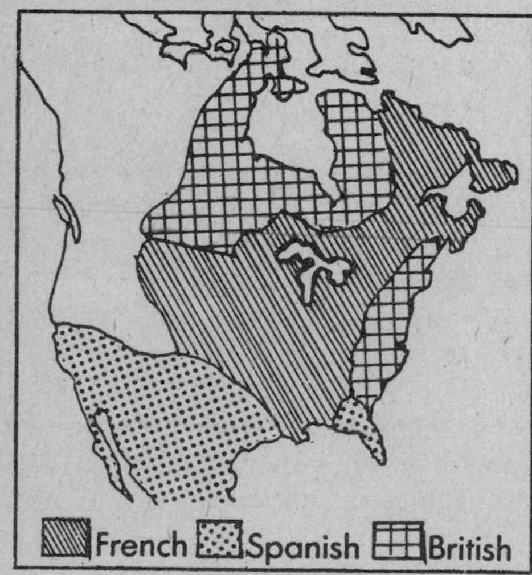

15. Which of the following choices best explains the changes between the two maps?

    (1) The French defeated the British in the French and Indian Wars, 1754–1763.
    (2) The Spanish diverted their forces to do battle in Mexico.
    (3) The British made the colonies bear their part in the cost of maintaining the British Empire.
    (4) The Treaty of France eliminated France as a colonial power in North America.
    (5) The American colonists gained valuable military experience.

16. According to the map, which power controlled British Columbia in 1689?

    (1) France
    (2) Spain
    (3) England
    (4) England and France
    (5) none of the above

17. According to the map, which power controlled Louisiana in 1689?

    (1) France
    (2) England and France
    (3) Spain
    (4) England
    (5) France and Spain

18. Based on the map, which power controlled the Mississippi River in 1763?

    (1) Spain
    (2) England
    (3) Spain and England
    (4) Spain and France
    (5) France

19. How far are we from the day when a plastic card will replace cash? We have not yet reached the point where cash is obsolete, but the tremendous growth in the use of credit cards during the past three decades has been nothing short of phenomenal. A recent survey estimated that there were more credit cards in circulation than there are people in the United States.

    Which of the following statements wou best explain the reason for the enor popularity of credit cards?

    (1) Most cards do not ch interest payments smarter to use
    (2) Most credi ceiling.
    (3) Mer o
    (4) Ca when
    (5) Credit relatively

Items 20 to 25 refer to the following cartoon:

This Doonesbury cartoon was published in a number of American newspapers shortly before the 1980 election—and rejected by a number of other newspapers.

DOONESBURY **by Garry Trudeau**

20. How is Ronald Reagan portrayed in this cartoon?

    (1) warm-hearted and kindly
    (2) slightly stupid and belligerent
    (3) cerebral and discriminating
    (4) cautious and suspicious
    (5) brainy and unprejudiced

21. What are the final two words of the cartoon most likely meant to introduce?

    (1) an important story about Ronald Reagan
    (2) a message from the Republican National Committee
    (3) another reporter
    (4) a commercial
    (5) a new show

22. In the second panel, what does the speaker see in Reagan's mind?

    (1) visions of life in America in the 1930's
    (2) clips from old movies
    (3) memories from life in America in the 1950's
    (4) thoughts of old friends
    (5) regretful memories

23. What is the cartoonist criticizing in the third panel?

    (1) what he sees as Reagan's mistakes
    (2) Reagan's too-frequent vacations
    (3) the national debt
    (4) newspapers' prying
    (5) television's invasion of Reagan's privacy

24. What other aspects of contemporary American life is the cartoonist criticizing throughout the cartoon?

    (1) foreign correspondents
    (2) well-to-do Americans
    (3) explorers
    (4) radio
    (5) television

25. Based on the content of the cartoon, what is the most likely reason why some newspapers accepted it for publication while others rejected it?

    (1) anger over being held up to ridicule
    (2) fear of losing network advertising
    (3) belief that it was too wordy and no one would bother to read it
    (4) belief that few would understand it
    (5) belief that it would offend people

GO ON TO THE NEXT PAGE

Items 26 to 29 refer to the following article.

You *need* stress in your life! Does that surprise you? Perhaps so, but it is quite true. Without stress, life would be dull and unexciting. Stress adds flavor, challenge, and opportunity to life. Too much stress, however, can seriously affect your physical and mental well-being. A major challenge in this stress-filled world of today is to make the stress in your life work *for* you instead of against you.

Stress is with us all the time. It comes from mental or emotional activity and physical activity. It is unique and personal to each of us. So personal, in fact, that what may be relaxing to one person may be stressful to another. For example, if you're an executive who likes to keep busy all the time, "taking it easy" at the beach on a beautiful day may feel extremely frustrating, nonproductive, and upsetting. You may be emotionally distressed from "doing nothing." Too much emotional stress can cause physical illness such as high blood pressure, ulcers, or even heart disease; physical stress from work or exercise is not likely to cause such ailments. The truth is that physical exercise can help you to relax and to handle your mental or emotional stress.

26. The author feels that stress

(1) can be easily removed
(2) is necessary for daily living
(3) affects only a few people
(4) is caused by physical illness
(5) is a result of emotional activity

27. How does the author of this article picture life without stress?

(1) challenging
(2) full of opportunity
(3) relaxing
(4) dull and unexciting
(5) emotionally exhausting

28. Which of the following statements can be inferred from the information in the article?

(1) Stress can easily be eliminated.
(2) Some people function well under stress.
(3) Executives have more stress than people in less demanding jobs.
(4) Stress can rarely work in your favor.
(5) Physical stress is likely to cause emotional illnesses.

29. Which of the following slogans would the author of this article most likely endorse?

(1) Stress: Get Rid of it Now!
(2) Stress: The Cure-All!
(3) Stress: It Can Work for You!
(4) Executive Stress: The Worst.
(5) Stress: Your Worst Enemy!

Items 30 to 33 refer to the following article.

Consumers can sometimes save more than 200 percent on prescription drugs if, before buying, they telephone for price information which most druggists are ready and willing to provide, according to a survey by the New York State Consumer Protection Board.

The Board telephoned eighty pharmacies in the Albany, Syracuse, New York City, and Long Island areas and requested prices for ninety 5-milligram tablets of Valium, a commonly-prescribed tranquilizer, and forty 250-milligram capsules of tetracycline, a commonly-prescribed antibiotic. Only nine of the eighty pharmacies refused to quote prices over the phone.

The greatest price differences were in Manhattan where the Valium prescription could be filled for prices ranging from \$10.80 to \$21.50—a \$10.70 or 99 percent spread. The tetracycline prices ranged from \$2.50 to \$7.95—a \$5.45 or 218 percent spread.

In the Syracuse area, the Valium prices ranged from \$9.74 to \$14.00—a \$4.25 or 44 percent spread—and the tetracycline prices ranged from \$2.25 to \$5.50—a \$3.25 or 144 percent spread.

In the Albany area, Valium ranged from \$9.74 to \$13.50—a 39 percent spread, while tetracycline ranged from \$1.99 to \$4.00—a \$2.01 or 101 percent spread.

30. Of the areas mentioned in the selection above, where can tetracycline be obtained at the lowest cost?

    (1) Manhattan
    (2) Syracuse
    (3) Albany
    (4) Long Island
    (5) New York City

31. If you lived in one of the areas named above, what would be the best way to get information on Valium prices?

    (1) ask your doctor
    (2) ask a friend
    (3) telephone several pharmacies
    (4) visit a drugstore
    (5) call a hospital

32. Based on this article, which of the areas named below would have the highest cost of living?

    (1) Manhattan
    (2) Syracuse
    (3) Albany
    (4) Buffalo
    (5) Long Island

33. What is the author showing the consumer in this article?

    (1) Comparison shopping pays off.
    (2) Druggists are cheats.
    (3) Living in New York is expensive.
    (4) Drugs are addictive.
    (5) Antibiotics and tranquilizers are harmful.

GO ON TO THE NEXT PAGE

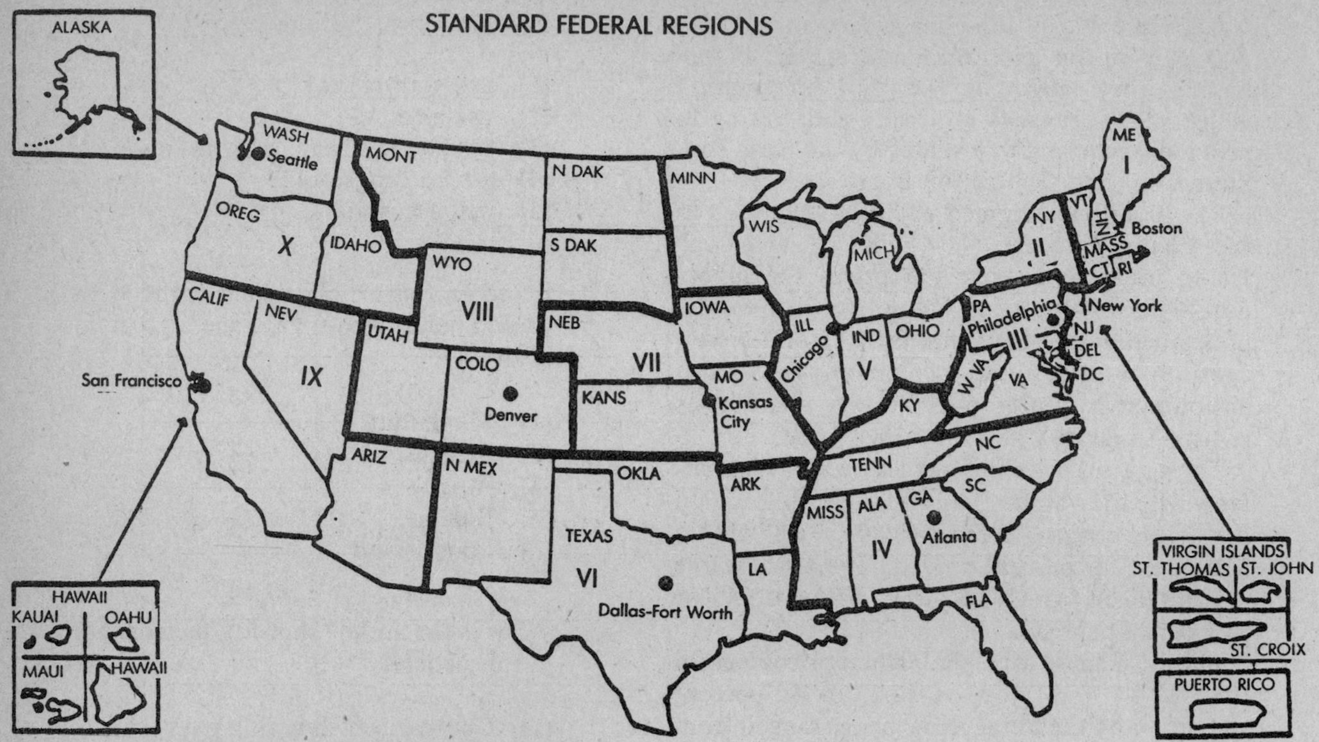

Items 34 to 37 are based on the map above and the following selection.

In order to make the federal government more accessible to the people who need its services, the Executive Branch is divided into ten geographical regions as shown on the map above. The dots in each region locate the regional headquarters city.

34. If you are a resident of Salt Lake City, where is the regional headquarters for your area?

(1) Seattle
(2) Chicago
(3) Atlanta
(4) Denver
(5) Kansas City

35. If you are a resident of Puerto Rico, where is the regional headquarters for your area?

(1) Atlanta
(2) Miami
(3) Philadelphia
(4) New York City
(5) Boston

36. What states does Region VII include?

(1) South Dakota, Iowa, Kansas, Missouri
(2) Arkansas, Illinois, Missouri, Iowa
(3) Iowa, Missouri, Kansas, Nebraska
(4) Iowa, Colorado, Missouri, Kansas
(5) Arkansas, Oklahoma, Kansas, Nebraska

37. From the information presented on the map, which of the following best explains why Region II is so small?

(1) It is close to Washington, DC.
(2) It is densely populated.
(3) It receives a great deal of federal assistance.
(4) It has powerful Congressmen and Senators.
(5) It lacks a headquarter city.

Items 38 to 40 are based on the following chart.

		Urban Population		Rural Population	
Year	Total United States Population		% of Total Population		% of Total Population
1790	3,929,000	202,000	5%	3,728,000	95%
1820	9,618,000	693,000	7	8,945,000	93
1850	23,261,000	3,544,000	15	19,648,000	85
1880	50,262,000	14,130,000	28	36,026,000	72
1910	92,407,000	41,999,000	45	49,973,000	55
1940	132,122,000	74,424,000	56	57,245,000	44
1970	203,810,000	149,325,000	73	54,054,000	27

38. A net loss in rural population is evident in which period?

(1) 1790–1820
(2) 1820–1850
(3) 1880–1910
(4) 1910–1940
(5) 1940–1970

39. Which statement is best supported by the data in the chart?

(1) The number of people living in rural areas in 1970 was less than the number living in rural areas in 1880.
(2) The percentage of the total population living in rural areas increased during the 1900's.
(3) The number of people living in urban areas declined during the 19th century.
(4) A majority of the people were living in urban areas by 1940.
(5) The number of people living in rural areas decreased steadily from 1880 to 1970.

40. Which explanation best accounts for the change in urban population during the late 1800's and early 1900's?

(1) decrease in farm production
(2) increase in industrial jobs
(3) expansion of immigration quotas
(4) improvements in transportation
(5) decrease in birth rate

GO ON TO THE NEXT PAGE

Items 41 to 43 refer to the following table.

Population by State

State	1980	1970	Percent change, 1970–80	Pop. rank, 1980
Alabama	3,893,888	3,444,354	+13.1	22
Alaska	401,851	302,583	+32.8	50
Arizona	2,718,425	1,775,399	+53.1	29
Arkansas	2,286,435	1,923,322	+18.9	33
California	23,667,565	19,971,069	+18.5	1
Colorado	2,889,735	2,209,596	+30.8	28
Connecticut	3,107,576	3,032,217	+2.5	25
Delaware	594,317	548,104	+8.4	47
D.C.	638,432	756,668	−15.6	—
Florida	9,746,324	6,791,418	+43.5	7
Georgia	5,463,105	4,587,930	+19.1	13
Hawaii	964,691	769,913	+25.3	39
Idaho	944,038	713,015	+32.4	41
Illinois	11,426,518	11,110,285	+2.8	5
Indiana	5,490,260	5,195,392	+5.7	12
Iowa	2,913,808	2,825,368	+3.1	27
Kansas	2,364,236	2,249,071	+5.1	32
Kentucky	3,660,257	3,220,711	+13.7	23
Louisiana	4,206,312	3,644,637	+15.4	19
Maine	1,125,027	993,722	+13.2	38
Maryland	4,216,975	3,923,897	+7.5	18
Massachusetts	5,737,037	5,689,170	+0.8	11
Michigan	9,262,078	8,881,826	+4.3	8
Minnesota	4,075,970	3,806,103	+7.1	21
Mississippi	2,520,638	2,216,994	+13.7	31
Missouri	4,916,759	4,677,623	+5.1	15
Montana	786,690	694,409	+13.3	44
Nebraska	1,569,825	1,485,333	+5.7	35
Nevada	800,493	488,738	+63.8	43
New Hampshire	920,610	737,681	+24.8	42
New Jersey	7,364,823	7,171,112	+2.7	9
New Mexico	1,302,981	1,017,055	+28.1	37
New York	17,558,072	18,241,391	−3.7	2
North Carolina	5,881,813	5,084,411	+15.7	10
North Dakota	652,717	617,792	+5.7	46
Ohio	10,797,624	10,657,423	+1.3	6
Oklahoma	3,025,290	2,559,463	+18.2	26
Oregon	2,633,149	2,091,533	+25.9	30
Pennsylvania	11,863,895	11,800,766	+0.5	4
Rhode Island	947,154	949,723	−0.3	40
South Carolina	3,121,833	2,590,713	+20.5	24
South Dakota	690,768	666,257	+3.7	45
Tennessee	4,591,120	3,926,018	+16.9	17
Texas	14,229,288	11,198,655	+27.1	3
Utah	1,461,037	1,059,273	+37.9	36
Vermont	511,456	444,732	+15.0	48
Virginia	5,346,818	4,651,448	+14.9	14
Washington	4,132,180	3,413,244	+21.1	20
West Virginia	1,950,279	1,744,237	+11.8	34
Wisconsin	4,706,521	4,417,821	+6.5	16
Wyoming	469,567	332,416	+41.3	49
Total U.S.	226,546,965	293,362,635	+11.4	—

41. Which of the following states had the greatest percentage change in population from 1970 to 1980?

(1) Alaska
(2) Arizona
(3) California
(4) Nevada
(5) Texas

42. Which state had the greatest increase in total population from 1970 to 1980?

(1) Alaska
(2) Arizona
(3) California
(4) Nevada
(5) Texas

43. From the data shown, where did the greatest growth take place?

(1) The South and Middle Atlantic States
(2) The South and Western States
(3) The Mid-Central States
(4) The Pacific Northwest
(5) New England

Items 44 to 46 refer to the following article.

Can an inkblot reveal personality traits? The Rorschach test, which uses the inkblot, is still not fully accepted as a valuable diagnostic tool by professionals in the field of psychology. If properly interpreted, a Rorschach test, in one hour, could provide personality data that would take weeks or months of ordinary interviews to reveal. The test consists of ten cards, each of which contains an inkblot intended to elicit a response from the subject. Test result analysis is a complex computation of many variables, including what colors, designs, and images are reported by the subject. Normal subjects usually respond to the whole design, while disturbed subjects are more likely to focus on individual details. Highly excitable subjects often show intense response to color, while depressed subjects may not mention color at all. Lack of reliability is the major reason for the limited use of the Rorschach test.

44. According to the article, which of the following best explains the Rorschach test?

(1) a universally accepted method of diagnosing a state of mind
(2) a psychological test with limited reliability
(3) a set of fifteen inkblots which subjects are asked to describe
(4) a quick and easy new test which is used to diagnose behavior
(5) a series of tests which puzzle its proponents and its subjects

45. According to Rorschach standards, what is a highly emotional and excited person most likely to do?

(1) see whole designs in the inkblots
(2) focus on details rather than designs
(3) respond to color
(4) respond to card size
(5) not respond at all

46. According to the article, which of the following statements best explains the popularity of the Rorschach test?

(1) It creates interesting data.
(2) It is highly reliable.
(3) It is popular with patients.
(4) It takes weeks or months to administer.
(5) It saves valuable diagnostic time.

GO ON TO THE NEXT PAGE

Items 47 to 49 refer to the following article.

Can you spot a criminal by his physical characteristics? When the science of criminology was founded in the nineteenth century, an imaginative Italian observer decided that criminals are born that way and are distinguished by certain physical marks. They are, he claimed, "a special species, a subspecies having distinct physical and mental characteristics. In general, all criminals have long, large, protruding ears, abundant hair, a thin beard, prominent frontal sinuses, a protruding chin, large cheekbones." Rapists, he argued, have "brilliant eyes, delicate faces" and murderers may be distinguished by "cold, glassy eyes, nose always large and frequently aquiline; jaws strong; cheekbones large, hair curly, dark and abundant."

Around the turn of the century, a British physician made a detailed study of the faces of three thousand convicts and compared them with a like number of English college students, measuring the noses, ears, eyebrows, and chins of both groups. He could find no correlation between physical types and criminal behavior.

But the myth doesn't die easily. During the 1930s, a German criminologist, Gustav Aschaffenburg, declared that stout, squat people with large abdomens are more likely to be occasional offenders, while slender builds and slight muscular development are common among habitual offenders. In the 1940s, according to writer Jessica Mitford, a group of Harvard sociologists decided that criminals are most likely to be "mesomorphs, muscular types with large trunks who walk assertively, talk noisily, and behave aggressively. Watch out for those."

47. What did the earliest criminologist mentioned in this selection believe?

    (1) Bald men do not commit crimes.
    (2) Rapists have strong, immobile facial expressions.
    (3) Large-nosed people are apt to be murderers.
    (4) Criminals have distinct physical characteristics.
    (5) A protruding chin is a sign of mental illness.

48. Which of the following descriptions is most likely to fit habitual criminals, according to the German criminologist?

    (1) quick-witted and glassy-eyed
    (2) a scholarly English sort
    (3) marked by aggressive behavior
    (4) short and squat
    (5) slight and underdeveloped

49. According to the article, how long has the "scientific" attempt to discover whether criminals are a specific physical type been going on?

    (1) since the 1940s
    (2) since the turn of the century
    (3) since criminology began
    (4) since the 1930s
    (5) since Biblical times

Items 50 to 56 are based on the following selection.

The Equal Pay Act prohibits pay discrimination because of sex. Men and women performing work in the same establishment under similar conditions must receive the same pay if their jobs require equal skill, effort, and responsibility. Differentials in pay based on a seniority or merit system, a system that measures earnings by quantity or quality of production, or any other factor other than sex are permitted.

Employers may not reduce the wage rate of any employee in order to eliminate illegal differentials. Labor organizations are prohibited from causing or attempting to cause employers to violate the act.

The act was approved in 1963 as an amendment to the Fair Labor Standards Act and applies to most workers in both the public and private sectors, including executive, administrative, and professional employees and outside sales personnel.

The Labor Department officially interpreted the provisions of the act to apply to "wages," which includes all remuneration for employment. Thus, the act prohibits discrimination in all employment-related payments, including overtime, uniforms, travel, retirement, and other fringe benefits. The Supreme Court has upheld the position that jobs of men and women need be only "substantially equal"—not identical—for purposes of comparison under the law.

50. John is a sewing machine operator and Mary is a clerk. They both work in the same factory. Which of the following explains how John and Mary are to be treated under the law?

    (1) They must earn the same pay because they work in the same place.
    (2) John must earn more because he has a harder job.
    (3) Mary must earn more because she has a more important job.
    (4) John's pay would have to be reduced if it were higher than Mary's.
    (5) Neither one may be discriminated against because of his or her sex.

51. Which of the following groups of people are covered by the Fair Labor Standards Act?

    (1) office workers
    (2) office bookkeepers
    (3) lawyers
    (4) all of the above
    (5) none of the above

52. Susan and Martha are both piece workers (they are paid according to how much they produce). Susan can make 10 widgets an hour; Martha can make 12. Which of the following best explains how Susan and Martha are to be treated under the law?

    (1) Both women should earn the same salary.
    (2) It is illegal to pay Susan for overtime work.
    (3) Martha can be paid more than Susan.
    (4) Disagreements should be sent to the union grievance committee.
    (5) Piece workers are not protected by the Fair Labor Standards Act.

53. The term *wages* includes which of the following?

    (1) regular salary
    (2) overtime
    (3) fringe benefits
    (4) working clothes
    (5) all of the above

54. According to the information in the passage, which of the following best explains why Paul and Nancy receive the same salary, even though their jobs have different titles?

    (1) Their jobs require equal expertise and responsibility.
    (2) They were both hired at the same time.
    (3) They work the same number of hours.
    (4) Nancy is better liked and received more overtime than Paul.
    (5) Paul had his salary decreased to eliminate illegal differences.

55. According to the provisions of the act, which of the following must be true in order for jobs to require equal pay for men and women?

    (1) The jobs must be exactly alike.
    (2) The jobs must be in the same level.
    (3) The jobs must be equal but not necessarily identical.
    (4) Salaries may not be based on seniority or merit.
    (5) Salary scales must be the same in the public and private sectors.

56. Which of the following statements is the most likely reason why this law was enacted?

    (1) People had been discriminated against on the basis of age.
    (2) Managers were having a difficult time attracting workers.
    (3) Wages were unequal because of differences in educational level.
    (4) Women doing the same types of jobs as men were receiving less pay.
    (5) People were being discriminated against on the basis of nationality.

GO ON TO THE NEXT PAGE

Items 57 to 59 are based on the following graph.

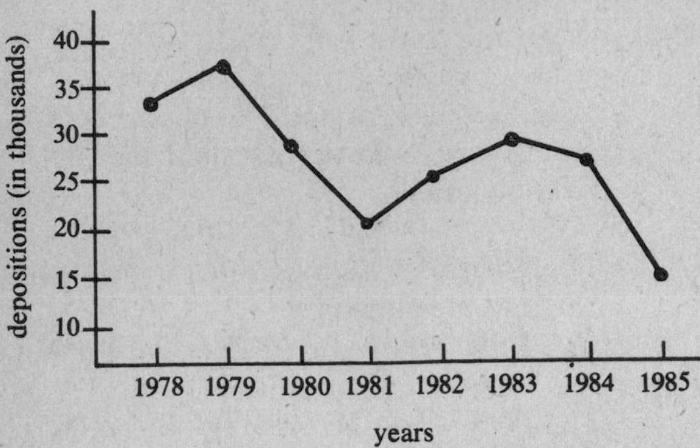

57. In which year did the XYZ Savings Bank have the greatest number of depositors?

    (1) 1978
    (2) 1979
    (3) 1981
    (4) 1982
    (5) 1985

58. In 1984 the bank had approximately how many depositors?

    (1) 3
    (2) 30
    (3) 35
    (4) 25,000
    (5) 35,000

59. Which of the following statements about the bank's depositors is FALSE?

    (1) The number of depositors increased slightly in 1982.
    (2) The lowest number of depositors is recorded in 1985.
    (3) The number of depositors decreased slightly in 1983.
    (4) The number of depositors continues to rise each year.
    (5) The number of depositors varies from year to year.

Items 60 and 61 refer to the following graph.

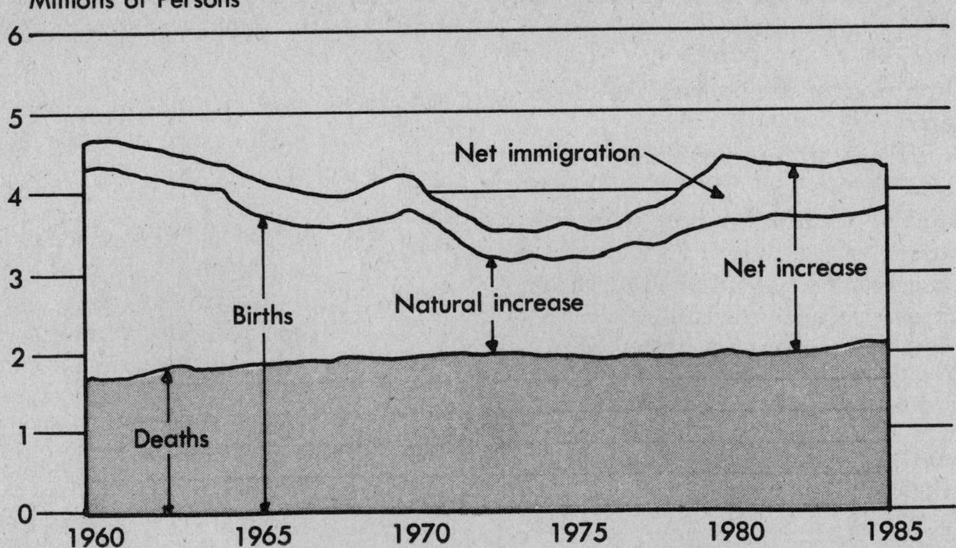

60. According to the chart above, what outcomes could be supported in describing the United States population between 1960 and 1985?

    (1) The birth rate declined sharply in the 1970's.
    (2) Immigration has decreased considerably in the 1980's.
    (3) The rate of population growth will continue to decline.
    (4) The birth rate will soon become the highest ever recorded in the nation.
    (5) The death rate continues to decrease.

61. Based on the information recorded in the graph, what portion of the net population increase in the 1980's is due to immigration?

    (1) 4%
    (2) 12%
    (3) 16%
    (4) 25%
    (5) 45%

Items 62 to 64 are based on the following selection.

As early as 1928 the American market was considered saturated. A used-car market began cutting into new-car sales. To fight it, automakers began introducing fresh models every year, a practice that came to be known as "planned obsolescence." Car stylists began to hold more clout than engineers.

Eventually even flashy chrome and fins could not cover up the realities of poor workmanship. Writer Jerry Flint summarizes what he calls the end of "the golden age of the auto" in his book *The Dream Machine:* "Nineteen-hundred-sixty-five was the peak, and the cars—even the country—seemed to go downhill from then. The engines got bigger, not better, the paint became wilder, and the knobs fell off the dash."

Noel Grove, "Swing Low, Sweet Chariot," *National Geographic,* Vol. 164, No. 1, July, 1983.

62. Which of the following best explains why new cars became difficult to sell by 1928?

    (1) Workmanship was shoddy.
    (2) Too many cars were available.
    (3) Too many cars were being imported.
    (4) Cars cost too much.
    (5) Cars were too flashy.

63. According to the passage, what does planned obsolescence mean?

    (1) production of more efficient gasoline engines
    (2) manufacturing more durable cars
    (3) superior quality of foreign cars
    (4) increased production of more expensive cars
    (5) manufacturing poor quality goods that quickly became old and outmoded

64. According to the information in the passage, who would be most hurt by automobiles that last for many years?

    (1) the manufacturers
    (2) the petroleum industry
    (3) the public
    (4) the pedestrian
    (5) the gasoline station

END OF SOCIAL STUDIES TEST

TEST 3. SCIENCE

95 Minutes—66 Questions

Directions:

The Science Test consists of multiple-choice questions intended to measure general concepts in biology, earth science, physics, and chemistry. Some of the questions are based on short readings. Others are based on graphs, charts, tables, or diagrams. For each question, study the information given and then answer the question or questions based upon it. Refer to the information as often as necessary in answering the questions. Record your answer in the Science section of your answer sheet.

FOR EXAMPLE:

A physical change may alter the state of matter, but does not change its chemical composition. Which of the following is NOT a physical change?

(1) boiling water
(2) dissolving salt in water
(3) shaving wood
(4) rusting metal
(5) breaking glass

When metal rusts a new substance is formed. This is a chemical, not a physical, change. Therefore, answer space 4 should be marked on your answer sheet.

Items 1 to 5 relate to the following information.

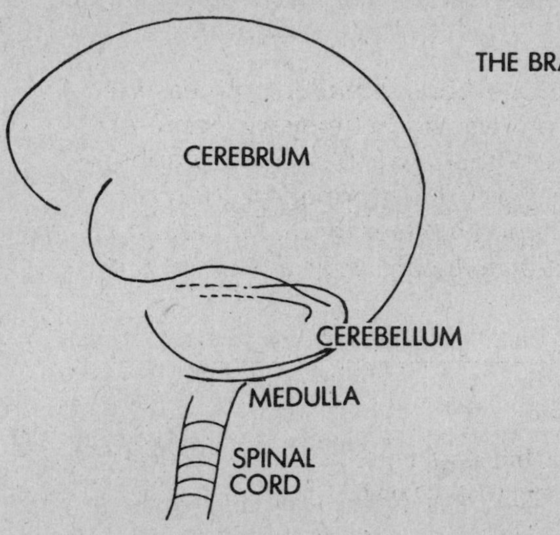

Part	Function
Cerebrum	memory, creativity, intelligence
Cerebellum	balance and coordinating controllable actions
Medulla	reflexes for the upper part of the body and control over heart and respiratory system
Spinal Cord	lower body reflexes

1. If the cerebellum of an eagle was destroyed, which of the following would the bird be unable to do?

   (1) build a nest
   (2) fly
   (3) find food
   (4) reproduce
   (5) breathe

2. Which of the following does the cerebrum allow people to do?

   (1) cough
   (2) sneeze
   (3) bite your nails
   (4) take this test
   (5) walk a tightrope

3. Which of the following parts of the brain controls the action when your knee jumps as the doctor hits it just below the knee cap?

   (1) cerebrum
   (2) cerebellum
   (3) medulla
   (4) spinal cord
   (5) cerebrum and cerebellum

4. Which part of the brain increases a person's breathing and heart rate while he is running a race?

   (1) cerebellum
   (2) cerebellum and cerebrum
   (3) spinal cord
   (4) medulla
   (5) spinal cord and cerebrum

5. How does the human brain differ from that of a cat?

   (1) A cat has a better spinal cord.
   (2) A human has a more developed cerebrum.
   (3) A human has a more developed cerebellum.
   (4) A cat has a more developed cerebellum.
   (5) A cat has a more developed cerebrum.

GO ON TO THE NEXT PAGE

Items 6 to 10 refer to the following information.

The study of the damage done during and after the accident at the nuclear generating plant at Three Mile Island in Pennsylvania has taken on some unusual scientific aspects. One way of determining the extent of nuclear contamination has been through the study of bees in the area. One Cornell University toxicologist collected honey within six miles of the plant, studied it, and showed that the honey was free of radioactive material. Beekeepers in the study area each sent two- and three-pound samples of honey to Cornell, where these samples were analyzed with a gamma spectrometer designed to detect various expected radioisotopes. None of the samples showed unusual amounts of radioactivity. One possible explanation is that the radioactive dust from the power plant settled on leaves and flowers, but was washed into the ground by rain soon after the accident. Another possible explanation is that the radiation from the plant was gaseous and floated away, landing far from the immediate vicinity of the nuclear facility.

6. According to the passage, what can we assume happened to the power plant at Three Mile Island?

   (1) There was a major meltdown.
   (2) Nothing.
   (3) It was switched from nuclear to coal capability.
   (4) A bad shipment of nuclear material was processed.
   (5) Radioactivity was released.

7. What does the study of the honey produced near Three Mile Island prove?

   (1) There was no contamination in the area.
   (2) Bees are not susceptible to radioactivity.
   (3) The honey showed no unusual contamination.
   (4) Analytical methods to determine radioactivity are inexact.
   (5) The experimental methods were faulty.

8. When you are not sure about the solution to a problem, make a hypothesis or guess for a first step. What hypothesis explained the absence of radioactivity in the honey?

   (1) The plant released no radiation.
   (2) The radiation combined to make a neutral particle.
   (3) The radioactive dust washed into the soil.
   (4) The release was stopped just in time.
   (5) Bees can destroy radiation.

9. Which of the following statements can be inferred from the paragraph?

   (1) Honey has been tested in this manner for at least fifty years.
   (2) The radioactive dust did not travel very far.
   (3) Radioactive dust could not have settled on leaves and flowers.
   (4) Cornell University is located in Pennsylvania.
   (5) The beekeepers were unwilling to cooperate.

10. Which of the following substances can we infer could have been tested in similar ways?

    (1) milk
    (2) metals
    (3) cheese
    (4) flour
    (5) clothing

Items 11 to 14 are based on the following table.

BLIZZARD OF 1978

	Massachusetts	Rhode Island	New Hampshire	Maine	New Jersey
DEATHS	73	26	0	0	0
INJURED OR ILL	4,324	232	28	3	0
HOSPITALIZED	483	50	1	0	0
SINGLE FAMILY HOUSES DESTROYED	301	0	13	22	3
PERSONS SHELTERED	23,520	9,150	483	0	155

11. Which state suffered the greatest damage during the blizzard of 1978?

    (1) Rhode Island
    (2) New Hampshire
    (3) Massachusetts
    (4) Maine
    (5) New Jersey

12. Which two states lost the greatest number of homes?

    (1) New Jersey and Maine
    (2) Massachusetts and New Hampshire
    (3) Massachusetts and Maine
    (4) Rhode Island and New Jersey
    (5) Rhode Island and Maine

13. How many people died in the blizzard of 1978?

    (1) 483
    (2) 232
    (3) 99
    (4) 26
    (5) 73

14. Which of the following professions compiles tables such as this one?

    (1) psychologists
    (2) professors
    (3) doctors
    (4) podiatrists
    (5) actuaries

GO ON TO THE NEXT PAGE

PERIODIC TABLE OF THE ELEMENTS

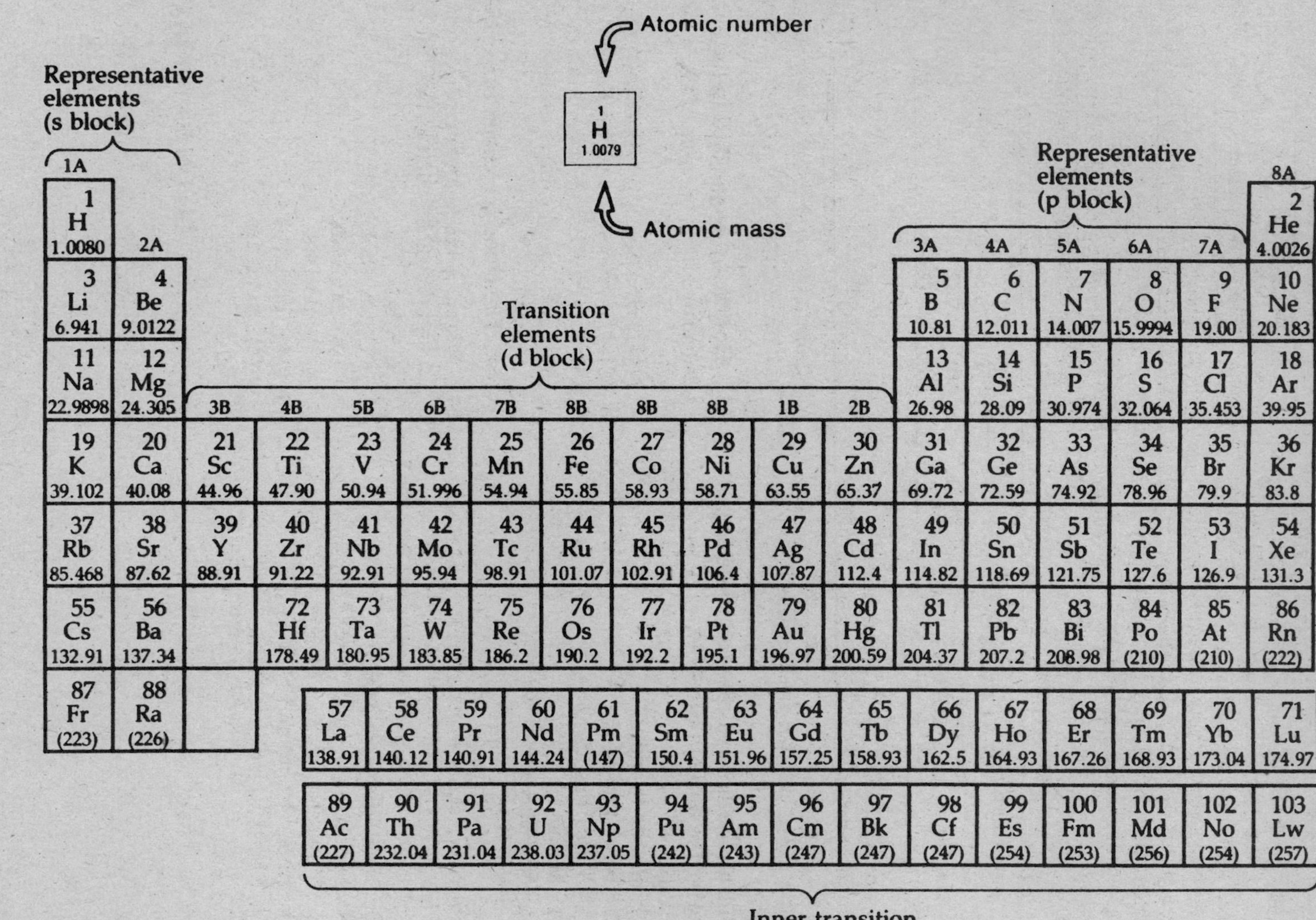

Key: 1 / H / 1.0079 — Atomic number (top), Atomic mass (bottom)

Representative elements (s block): 1A, 2A
Transition elements (d block): 3B–2B
Representative elements (p block): 3A–8A

1A	2A	3B	4B	5B	6B	7B	8B	8B	8B	1B	2B	3A	4A	5A	6A	7A	8A
1 H 1.0080																	2 He 4.0026
3 Li 6.941	4 Be 9.0122											5 B 10.81	6 C 12.011	7 N 14.007	8 O 15.9994	9 F 19.00	10 Ne 20.183
11 Na 22.9898	12 Mg 24.305											13 Al 26.98	14 Si 28.09	15 P 30.974	16 S 32.064	17 Cl 35.453	18 Ar 39.95
19 K 39.102	20 Ca 40.08	21 Sc 44.96	22 Ti 47.90	23 V 50.94	24 Cr 51.996	25 Mn 54.94	26 Fe 55.85	27 Co 58.93	28 Ni 58.71	29 Cu 63.55	30 Zn 65.37	31 Ga 69.72	32 Ge 72.59	33 As 74.92	34 Se 78.96	35 Br 79.9	36 Kr 83.8
37 Rb 85.468	38 Sr 87.62	39 Y 88.91	40 Zr 91.22	41 Nb 92.91	42 Mo 95.94	43 Tc 98.91	44 Ru 101.07	45 Rh 102.91	46 Pd 106.4	47 Ag 107.87	48 Cd 112.4	49 In 114.82	50 Sn 118.69	51 Sb 121.75	52 Te 127.6	53 I 126.9	54 Xe 131.3
55 Cs 132.91	56 Ba 137.34		72 Hf 178.49	73 Ta 180.95	74 W 183.85	75 Re 186.2	76 Os 190.2	77 Ir 192.2	78 Pt 195.1	79 Au 196.97	80 Hg 200.59	81 Tl 204.37	82 Pb 207.2	83 Bi 208.98	84 Po (210)	85 At (210)	86 Rn (222)
87 Fr (223)	88 Ra (226)																

Inner transition elements (f block)

57 La 138.91	58 Ce 140.12	59 Pr 140.91	60 Nd 144.24	61 Pm (147)	62 Sm 150.4	63 Eu 151.96	64 Gd 157.25	65 Tb 158.93	66 Dy 162.5	67 Ho 164.93	68 Er 167.26	69 Tm 168.93	70 Yb 173.04	71 Lu 174.97
89 Ac (227)	90 Th 232.04	91 Pa 231.04	92 U 238.03	93 Np 237.05	94 Pu (242)	95 Am (243)	96 Cm (247)	97 Bk (247)	98 Cf (247)	99 Es (254)	100 Fm (253)	101 Md (256)	102 No (254)	103 Lw (257)

Items 15 to 19 are based on the periodic table on page 538.

15. The periodic table consists of horizontal rows called periods and vertical columns called groups. Those elements which have similar chemical properties appear in the same group. Which of the following elements is most similar to magnesium (Mg) in its chemical properties?

(1) sodium (Na)
(2) chlorine (Cl)
(3) potassium (K)
(4) calcium (Ca)
(5) zinc (Zn)

16. The atoms of different elements have different numbers of electrons and protons, corresponding to their atomic numbers. The number of electrons or protons in a neutral atom is called the atomic number of that element. Which of the following elements has the greatest number of electrons?

(1) argon (Ar)
(2) boron (B)
(3) cobalt (Co)
(4) phosphorus (P)
(5) fluorine (F)

17. The most reactive elements are the ones with only one electron or seven electrons in their outermost shells. The least reactive are the ones with 8 electrons in their outermost shells. The group number suggests the number of electrons in the outermost shell of an atom. Which group contains the most reactive metals?

(1) I A
(2) III B
(3) IV B
(4) VII A
(5) VIII A

18. The noble gases have 8 electrons in their outermost shells. These elements tend not to react with other elements to form compounds. Which of the following elements belongs to the group of noble gases?

(1) oxygen (O)
(2) neon (Ne)
(3) sulfur (S)
(4) hydrogen (H)
(5) nitrogen (N)

19. The elements in the modern periodic table are arranged by atomic

(1) radius
(2) mass
(3) charge
(4) energy
(5) radiation

20. One half of the moon's surface is always illuminated by the sun. Yet from earth the moon appears to change its shape as it goes through a cycle of phases. Which of the following explains why an observer on earth sees the phases of the moon?

(1) The moon revolves around the sun.
(2) The moon rotates on its axis.
(3) The earth revolves around the sun.
(4) The moon revolves around the earth.
(5) The moon can change its shape.

Item 21 is based on the diagram below.

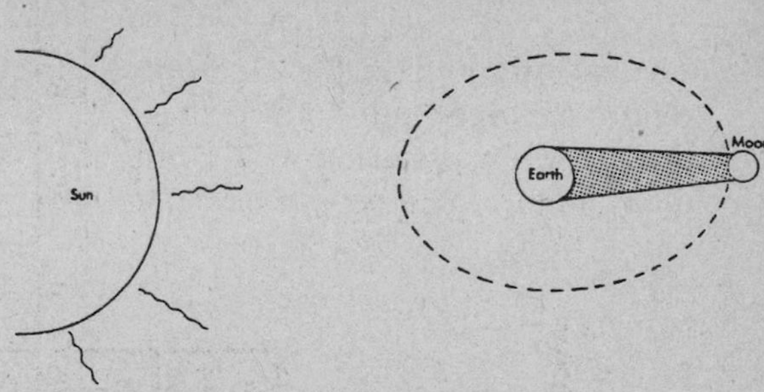

21. The illustration above depicts which one of the following?

(1) seasons of the year
(2) solar eclipse
(3) lunar eclipse
(4) sunspots
(5) the effect of tides

GO ON TO THE NEXT PAGE

Items 22 to 26 are based on the following experiment.

Below is a graph describing the results of an experiment that was done by a biologist. He put live bacteria and growth medium (food for bacteria to live on) into a closed container. He then counted the number of live bacteria every half-hour for a 16 hour period.

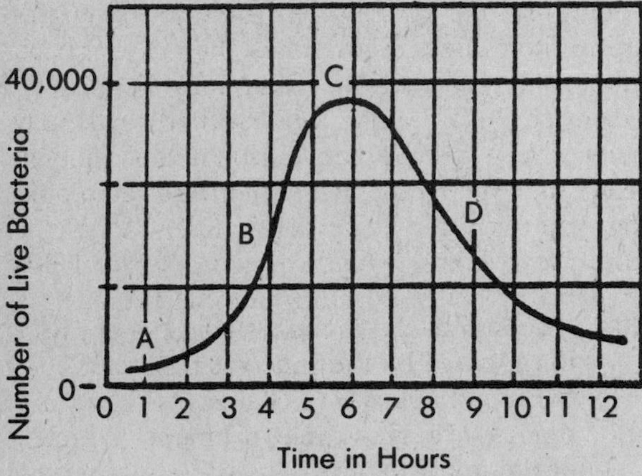

22. Which of the following choices correctly describes the process by which the bacteria grew?

    (1) fission
    (2) sporing
    (3) vegetative propagation
    (4) meiosis
    (5) sexual reproduction

23. The bacteria used in the experiment reproduce every half-hour. If the experiment was started with 1 cell, how many would there be 4 hours later?

    (1) 8
    (2) 16
    (3) 256
    (4) 512
    (5) 40,000

24. What is happening at point "B" on the graph?

    (1) The temperature is increasing rapidly.
    (2) The number of bacteria is increasing rapidly.
    (3) The bacteria are getting larger.
    (4) The number of bacteria is decreasing slowly.
    (5) Cannot be determined from the information given.

25. Why did the number of live bacteria decrease at point "D"?

    (1) The temperature decreased.
    (2) The bacteria ran out of food.
    (3) The bacteria got larger.
    (4) High temperature killed all of the bacteria.
    (5) The bacteria were poisoned by their own waste products.

26. Which of the following can be inferred from the results of this experiment?

    (1) Bacteria can grow anywhere, anytime.
    (2) Bacteria can be easily eliminated with cleaners.
    (3) It takes a very long time for bacteria to grow.
    (4) It is important to store leftover food correctly.
    (5) Bacteria pose a very real threat to people.

Items 27 to 29 are based on the diagram below.

The diagram represents resistors R_1 and R_2, connected to a constant power source of 40 volts.

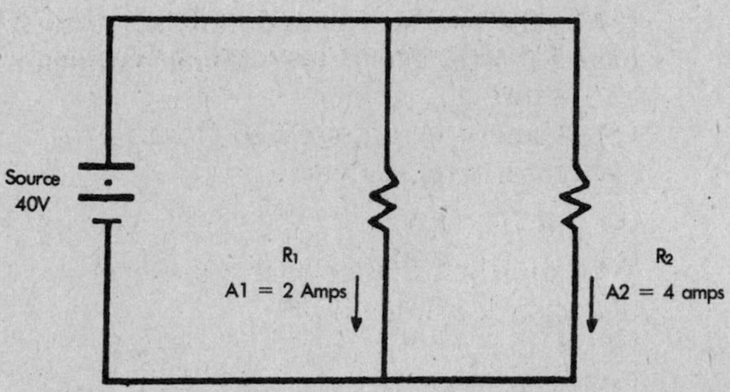

27. The voltage drop across R_1 is

    (1) 10
    (2) 12
    (3) 15
    (4) 40
    (5) 50

28. The power (P = Volts × Current) supplied to the circuit, in watts, is

    (1) 80
    (2) 120
    (3) 160
    (4) 240
    (5) 300

29. Stanley wants to increase the current in A2. Which of the following will achieve this result?

    (1) increase the resistance of R_2
    (2) increase the resistance of R_1
    (3) decrease the voltage of the source
    (4) add another resistor
    (5) it can't be done

Items 30 to 32 are based on the following information.

Microwave ovens use a principle of heating different from that employed by ordinary ovens. The key part of a microwave oven is its magnetron, which generates the microwaves that then go into the oven. Some of these energy waves hit the food directly, while others bounce around the oven until they find their way into the food. Sometimes the microwaves intersect, strengthening their effect. Sometimes they cancel each other out. Parts of the food may be heavily saturated with energy, while other parts may receive very little. In conventional cooking, you select the oven temperature. In microwave cooking, you select the power level. The walls of the microwave oven are made of metal, which helps the microwaves bounce off them. However, this turns to a disadvantage for the cook who uses metal cookware.

30. There are both advantages and disadvantages to microwave cooking. Based on the information given, which of the following is probably the greatest disadvantage of microwaving?

    (1) overcooked food
    (2) radioactive food
    (3) unevenly cooked food
    (4) expensive costs of preparing food
    (5) cold food

31. In a conventional oven, the temperature selection would be based upon degrees. In a microwave oven, the power selection would probably be based upon

    (1) wattage
    (2) voltage
    (3) lumens
    (4) solar units
    (5) ohms

32. What is the source of the microwaves in the oven?

    (1) reflected energy
    (2) convection currents
    (3) the magnetron
    (4) short waves and bursts of energy
    (5) the food itself

GO ON TO THE NEXT PAGE

Items 33 to 35 relate to the following information.

Since each parent contributes one-half of the genetic material to the offspring, the genes occur in pairs. Different forms of the same gene are called alleles. In human beings multiple alleles determine blood type. These alleles are designated I^A, I^B, and i. The chart below indcates the possible combinations for each blood type.

Blood Type	Genotype
A	I^AI^A or I^Ai
B	I^BI^B or I^Bi
AB	I^AI^B
O	ii

33. John has type B blood. Which of the choices below could represent the genes of John's parents?

Father		*Mother*
(1) I^AI^A	and	ii
(2) I^Ai	and	I^Ai
(3) I^AI^B	and	ii
(4) ii	and	ii
(5) I^AI^B	and	I^AI^A

34. A person with type AB blood is sometimes called a universal recipient because he can receive blood from anyone. A person with type O blood is sometimes called a universal donor because he can give blood to anyone.

If Martha is a universal donor, what must have been the blood type of her parents?

Father		*Mother*
(1) I^AI^A	and	ii
(2) ii	and	I^BI^B
(3) ii	and	ii
(4) I^AI^A	and	I^AI^B
(5) I^AI^B	and	I^AI^B

35. Baby Jay has type AB blood. Which of the following had to be his parents?

Father		*Mother*
(1) I^AI^A	and	I^AI^A
(2) I^Ai	and	I^Ai
(3) I^AI^B	and	ii
(4) I^Ai	and	I^Bi
(5) I^Bi	and	I^BI^B

Items 36 and 37 refer to the following graph.

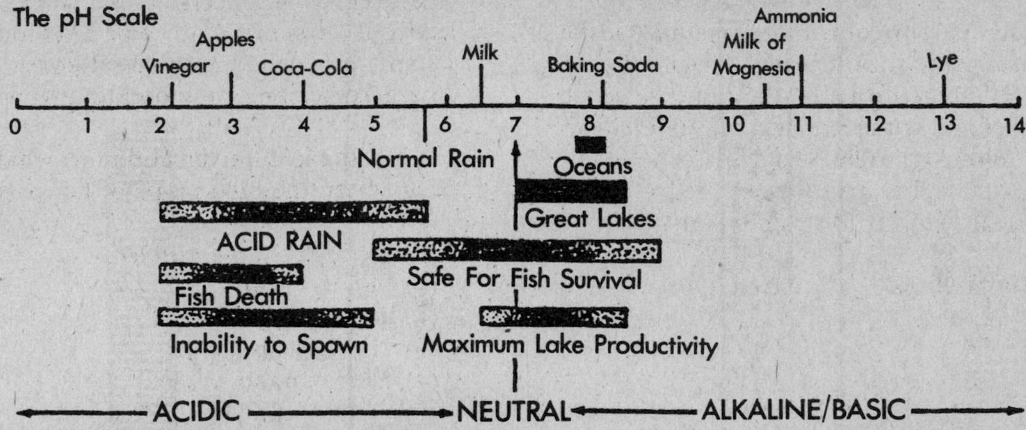

pH values of common acid and alkaline substances; a lower value denotes a higher acid content.

36. According to the graph, which of the following best defines acid rain?

(1) precipitation having a pH less than normal rain
(2) precipitation having a pH between 6 and 7
(3) precipitation which has a pH greater than the pH of ocean water
(4) precipitation which always results in death to fish
(5) precipitation that results in maximum lake productivity

37. Which of the following best describes the pH of normal rain?

(1) extremely acidic
(2) slightly acidic
(3) neutral
(4) slightly alkaline
(5) extremely alkaline

GO ON TO THE NEXT PAGE

Items 38 to 41 are based on the following two graphs.

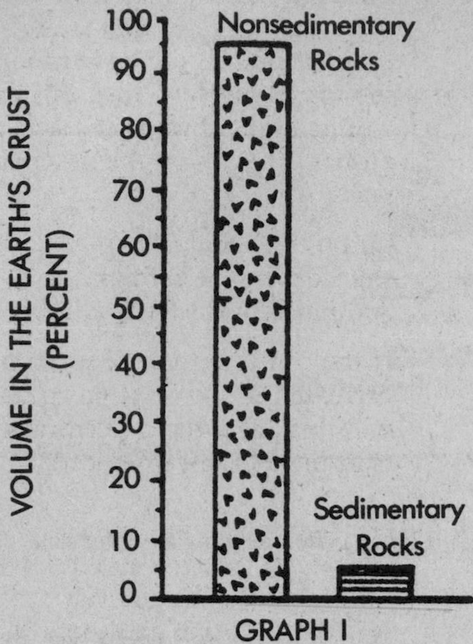

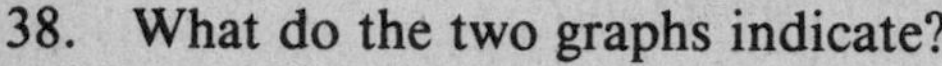

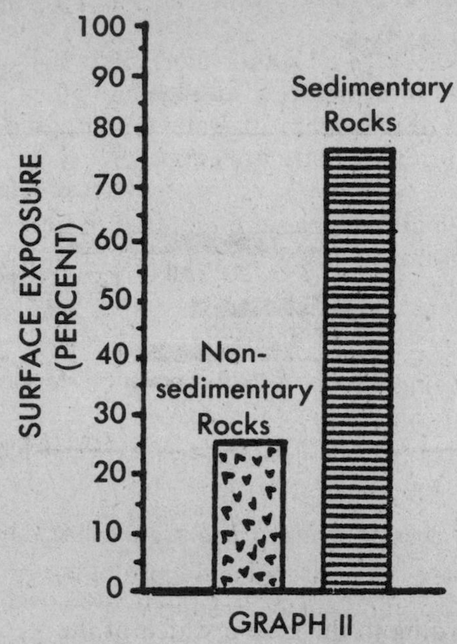

GRAPH II

38. What do the two graphs indicate?

(1) the arrangement of materials on the earth's surface
(2) the advantage of sedimentary rocks
(3) the contents of nonsedimentary rocks
(4) the contents of the earth's core
(5) the composition of the earth's crust

39. According to the graphs, approximately what percentage of the earth's crust is composed of sedimentary rock?

(1) 25%
(2) 75%
(3) 5%
(4) 95%
(5) 45%

40. All of the rocks represented in graph I must contain which of the following?

(1) minerals
(2) fossils
(3) outcrops
(4) sediments
(5) shale

41. Which of the following statements can be inferred from the data shown on the graphs?

(1) The crust of the earth is composed mostly of sedimentary rocks.
(2) Rock outcrops on the earth's surface are chiefly of the nonsedimentary type.
(3) Most nonsedimentary rocks are composed of the melted remains of sedimentary rocks.
(4) Most sedimentary rock is found at or near the surface of the earth.
(5) Most sedimentary rocks are found deep within the earth's core.

Items 42 and 43 are based on the following information.

Energy is needed to heat water. Our gas or electric bill indicates this at the end of each month. To heat 1 gram of water 1 centigrade degree requires 1 calorie of energy.

42. How many calories are required to heat 200 grams of water for tea from 20°C to 100°C?

    (1) 200
    (2) 1000
    (3) 1600
    (4) 4000
    (5) 16,000

43. Suppose that you had enough fuel left in your camping heater to supply 180,000 calories of heat. If the water was supplied from a stream at 10°C, how many grams of water could be heated to boiling (100°C)?

    (1) 200
    (2) 800
    (3) 1000
    (4) 2,000
    (5) 20,000

44. Chemicals act like people. When they are put under stress, they tend to do anything they can to reduce that stress. When more chemicals are added to one side of the reaction below, then this excess stress will be used up when it reacts to form more chemicals on the other side of the reaction.

    Chlorine is obtained from salt (sodium chloride) by the formula:
    Sodium Chloride ↔ Sodium + Chlorine

    If the concentration of sodium is increased in the reaction container, how will this affect the concentration of chlorine and salt produced?

    (1) more chlorine and salt
    (2) more chlorine and less salt
    (3) less chlorine and salt
    (4) less chlorine and more salt
    (5) no change

GO ON TO THE NEXT PAGE

Items 45 to 50 are based on the following graph.

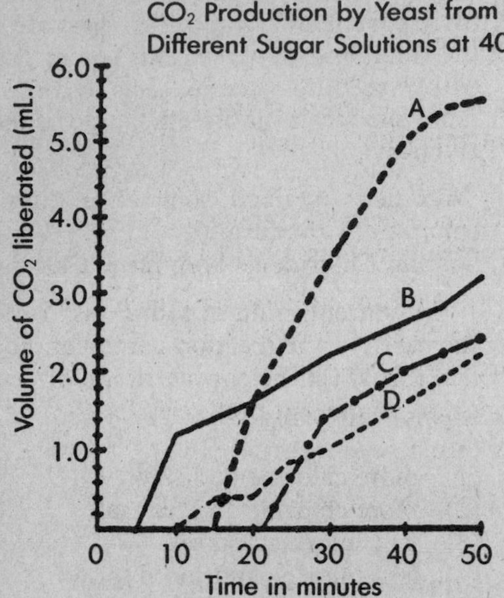

45. What does this graph measure?

    (1) The O_2 produced by CO_2 in a yeast culture.
    (2) The waste products of sugar solutions infused with CO_2.
    (3) The CO_2 produced from yeast culture placed in a water solution of four different sugars of the same concentration.
    (4) The water produced from yeast culture placed in four different salt solutions.
    (5) The CO_2 produced from a yeast culture placed in a yeast solution of four different sugar solutions at 55°C.

46. What was the volume of CO_2 liberated from solution B after 30 minutes?

    (1) 2.2 microns
    (2) 2.2 millimeters
    (3) 2.2 liters
    (4) 3.0 millimeters
    (5) 2.2 milliliters

47. From which solution was CO_2 liberated first?

    (1) A
    (2) B
    (3) C
    (4) D
    (5) a tie between C and D

48. In how many minutes was the same volume of CO_2 liberated from solution A and solution B?

    (1) 1.1
    (2) 1.6
    (3) 6
    (4) 20
    (5) 16

49. From which solution was the most CO_2 liberated at the end of 30 minutes?

    (1) A
    (2) B
    (3) C
    (4) D
    (5) cannot be determined

50. Which of the following processes could this graph be recording?

    (1) respiration
    (2) circulation
    (3) bread production
    (4) photosynthesis
    (5) candy production

Items 51 to 54 are based on the following information.

Farmers and scientists are able to make use of the fact that many plants and animals are able to reproduce asexually, that is, without the need for two parents. Some of the methods used by plants and animals are described below.

1. Budding———a plant is able to pinch off a little piece of itself. This little piece will develop into an entire organism that is exactly like the parent.
2. Sporing———a plant is able to produce thousands of little "seeds" called spores. Each spore is capable of growing into an entire plant.
3. Grafting———farmers are able to take a twig from a plant and attach it to the stem of another plant. In this way a farmer is able to mix the most desirable features from both plants.
4. Tubers———thick fleshy underground stems with many "eyes" or buds. Each bud is able to grow into a new organism.
5. Regeneration—some plants and animals are able to regrow lost parts.

Each of the following items describes one of the methods of asexual reproduction listed above. For each item, choose the one method of reproduction described by the situation. Each of the methods may be used more than once in the following set of items.

51. One of the enemies of the clam fisherman is the starfish. A particular fisherman had the habit of cutting up the starfish that he caught and throwing the pieces back into the water. However, he noticed that each year he found fewer and fewer clams. This was probably due to the fact that the starfish is able to reproduce by

(1) budding
(2) sporing
(3) grafting
(4) tubers
(5) regeneration

52. Mrs. Johnson noticed that if she left bread in her bread box for several days a small spot of mold would develop on one side of the loaf. She also noticed that if she didn't throw the bread out, in a day or two the entire loaf of bread was covered with mold. This is because mold reproduces by

(1) budding
(2) sporing
(3) grafting
(4) tubers
(5) regeneration

53. Potato farming is a large industry in many parts of the United States. Farmers are able to take one potato, cut it into many parts, and each part will become a new potato plant producing many potatoes. The potato reproduces by

(1) budding
(2) sporing
(3) grafting
(4) tubers
(5) regeneration

54. A recent ad in a magazine advertised a special tree that produces Bosc, Anjou, and Bartlett pears. This tree was made possible by

(1) budding
(2) sporing
(3) grafting
(4) tubers
(5) regeneration

GO ON TO THE NEXT PAGE

Item 55 is based on the following diagram.

The diagram below shows the discharge measured at a point in a stream during a period of one year.

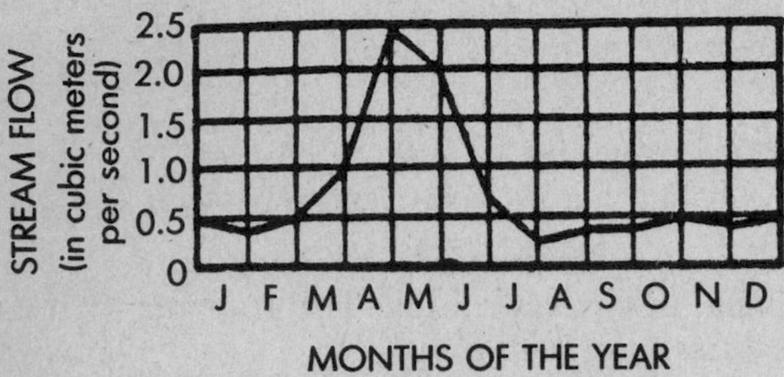

55. According to the diagram, when does the greatest change in stream flow occur?

    (1) January 1 to March 1
    (2) March 1 to May 1
    (3) May 1
    (4) May 1 to July 1
    (5) October 1 to December 1

Items 56 to 59 are based on the following selection.

It seems that not a season goes by without at least one diet book high on the best-seller list. Some diets advocated by these books are simply variations of a basic, safe 1,000- to 1,200-calorie balanced diet. But others may be downright dangerous, as they emphasize one food or food group and the elimination of others—in other words, they advocate diets that are unbalanced.

Some of these diets fraudulently claim that certain foods have the ability to "burn fat." No food can do that. Body fat is "burned" or gotten rid of only by using more energy than is supplied by the food you eat.

One extreme form of this type of diet—a liquid protein diet containing less than 400 calories a day—was linked to 17 deaths in 1977 and 1978. Scientists who studied the deaths found that the dieters had died of irregular heart rhythms and cardiac arrest.

The Food and Drug Administration now requires warning labels on weight-reduction products when more than 50 percent of the product's calories come from protein.

Other very-low-calorie liquid and powdered products have appeared on the market recently with a lower proportion of protein. But consumers should be aware that any diet of fewer than 800 calories a day is potentially dangerous and should be undertaken only under medical supervision.

56. Under which of the following conditions will body fat be burned?

    (1) when you stop exercising
    (2) when you eat a high-protein diet
    (3) when you eat certain foods
    (4) only if you consume a high carbohydrate diet
    (5) when you use more calories than you consume

57. According to the reading, which of the following is the reason that liquid protein diets may be dangerous?

    (1) Ketones are burned.
    (2) Dieters may suffer cardiac arrest.
    (3) Carbohydrates are excreted.
    (4) Body fat is burned.
    (5) Fat deposits are broken down more quickly than carbohydrates.

58. According to this passage a person on a diet of 600 calories a day could expect to

    (1) die from an irregular heart rhythm
    (2) gain weight first and then lose weight slowly
    (3) lose weight first and then gain it back
    (4) lose a pound of fat each day
    (5) lose weight fairly rapidly

59. An average daily balanced diet for people who wish to lose weight should contain how many calories?

    (1) between 400 and 800
    (2) between 800 and 1000
    (3) between 1000 and 1200
    (4) between 1500 and 2000
    (5) between 2000 and 3000

Items 60 to 64 are based on the following experiment.

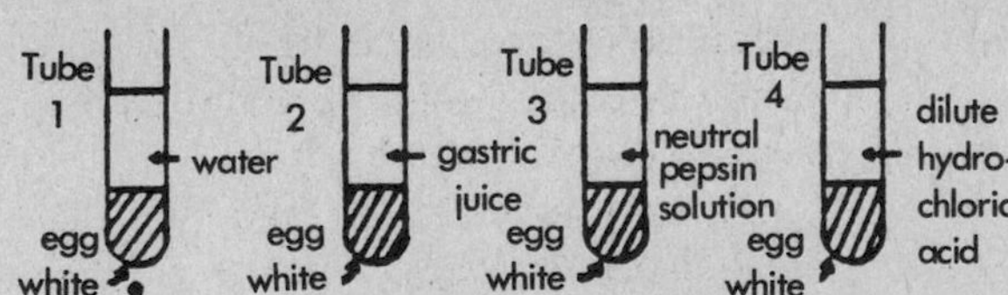

60. What does the experiment above measure?

    (1) The rate at which egg white dissolves in the same solutions.
    (2) The rate at which egg white dissolves in different solutions.
    (3) The ability of different substances to create protein.
    (4) The rate at which different solutions turn egg white into egg yolk.
    (5) The ability of egg white to dissolve different substances.

61. For the experiment to be valid, which of the following must be true?

    (1) All four test tubes must have varying temperatures.
    (2) The same person must handle the test tubes.
    (3) The substances must be added to the test tubes at precisely the same moment.
    (4) All four test tubes must be kept at a constant temperature.
    (5) The test tubes must be kept in the same position.

62. Which nutrient is being acted upon in this experiment?

    (1) sugar
    (2) starch
    (3) protein
    (4) fat
    (5) liquid

63. In which test tube would the egg white dissolve most rapidly?

    (1) 1
    (2) 2
    (3) 3
    (4) 4
    (5) 1 and 2

64. Which process does this experiment most closely resemble?

    (1) respiration
    (2) excretion
    (3) ingestion
    (4) circulation
    (5) digestion

GO ON TO THE NEXT PAGE

65. Diets high in saturated fat and cholesterol have been linked to heart disease and a diet high in fat to some cancers. If you wish to cut down on saturated fats and cholesterol in your diet, which of the following foods should you avoid?

    (1) fish
    (2) poultry
    (3) dry beans and peas
    (4) cheese
    (5) spaghetti

66. What is the air pressure indicated on diagram of the barometer?

    (1) 108.1 mb
    (2) 1028.5 mb
    (3) 1029.5 mb
    (4) 1031.0 mb
    (5) 130.0 mb

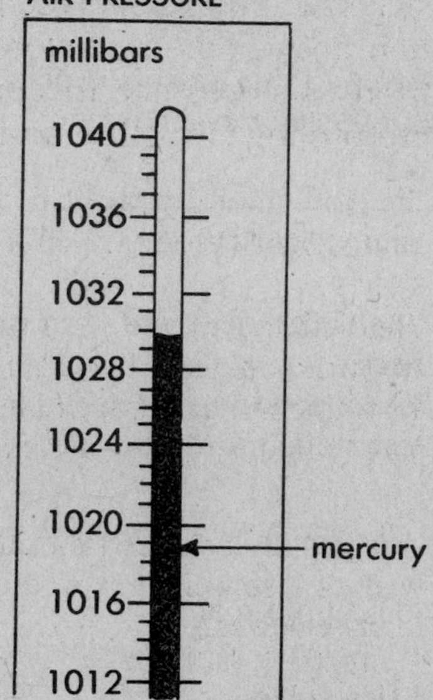

END OF SCIENCE TEST

TEST 4. INTERPRETING LITERATURE AND THE ARTS

Time: 65 Minutes—45 Questions

Directions:

This test consists of multiple-choice questions based on a variety of excerpts from popular and classical literature and articles about literature or the arts. Each selection is followed by a number of questions. Read each selection and then answer the questions based upon it. You may refer to the reading as often as necessary to answer the questions. Record your answers in the Interpreting Literature and the Arts section of your answer sheet.

FOR EXAMPLE:

He died at eventide . . . I saw his breath beat quicker and quicker, pause, and then his little soul leapt like a star that travels in the night and left a world of darkness in its train. The day changed not . . . Only in the chamber of death writhed the world's most piteous thing—a childless mother.

The reader can infer that death has come to

(1) an old man
(2) a favorite dog
(3) a child
(4) a mother
(5) a soldier

The correct answer is "a child"; therefore, you should blacken answer space 3 on your answer sheet.

Items 1 to 4 are based on the following poem.

WHY IS THE SPEAKER SENT TO EAT IN THE KITCHEN?

I, Too

I, too, sing America
I am the darker brother
They send me to eat in the kitchen
when company comes,
But I laugh
And eat well
And grow strong
Tomorrow,
I'll be at the table
When company comes
Nobody'll dare
say to me
"Eat in the Kitchen,"
Then.
Besides
They'll see how beautiful I am
and be ashamed—
I, too, am America

1. Which of the following choices best expresses the tone of this poem?

(1) angry but hopeful
(2) cheerful and optimistic
(3) totally pessimistic
(4) mockingly antagonistic
(5) sensitive but desperate

2. Which of the following phrases best describes the poem's speaker?

(1) a household servant
(2) an illiterate field hand
(3) a young woman
(4) black America
(5) an ugly child

3. What does the speaker mean by the word "sing" in the sentence "I, too, sing America"?

(1) decry
(2) praise
(3) criticize
(4) chant
(5) think about

4. The phrase, "I, too, sing America" is an example of which of the following literary devices?

(1) personification
(2) rhyme
(3) illusion
(4) metaphor
(5) allusion

Items 5 to 7 are based on the following selection.

HOW DOES SHAW FEEL ABOUT HIS WORK?

As I lie here, helpless and disabled, or, at best, nailed by one foot to the floor like a doomed Strasburg goose, a sense of injury grows on me. For nearly four years—to be precise, since New Year 1895—I have been a slave of the theatre. It has tethered me to the mile radius of foul and sooty air which has its centre in the Strand, as a goat is tethered in the little circle of cropped and trampled grass that makes the meadow ashamed. Every week it clamors for its tale of written words; so that I am like a man fighting a windmill: I have hardly time to stagger to my feet from the knockdown blow of one sail, when the next strikes me down. Now I ask, is it reasonable to spend my life in this way? For just consider my position. Do I receive any spontaneous recognition for the prodigies of skill and industry I lavish on an unworthy institution and a stupid public? Not a bit of it: half my time is spent telling people what a clever man I am. It is no use merely doing clever things in England. The English do not know what to think until they are coached, laboriously and insistently for years, in the proper and becoming opinion.

from "Valedictory" by Bernard Shaw, used by permission of The Society of Authors on behalf of the Bernard Shaw Estate.

5. What position is Shaw giving up in this essay?

   (1) playwright
   (2) stage director
   (3) drama critic
   (4) animal trainer
   (5) publicist

6. Based on the information given, when was this essay probably written?

   (1) in England during the Second World War
   (2) in England at the end of the nineteenth century
   (3) in America during the Roaring Twenties
   (4) in America at the start of the twentieth century
   (5) in England after the First World War

7. What impression is Shaw giving in this essay?

   (1) He thinks highly of the British theatre.
   (2) He feels his efforts have been appreciated.
   (3) He does not like his job.
   (4) He has been physically injured in his work.
   (5) He is aware that he has a perceptive audience.

GO ON TO THE NEXT PAGE

Items 8 to 12 refer to the following selection.

WHAT IS ON GEORGIANA'S CHEEK?

The crimson hand, which at first had been strongly visible upon the marble paleness of Georgiana's cheek, now grew more faintly outlined. She remained not less pale than ever; but the birthmark, with every breath that came and went, lost somewhat of its former distinctness. Its presence had been awful; its departure was more awful still. Watch the stain of the rainbow fading out of the sky, and you will know how the mysterious symbol passed away.

"By Heaven! it is well-nigh gone!" said Aylmer to himself, in almost irrepressible ecstasy. "I can scarcely trace it now. Success! Success! And now it is like the faintest rose color. The lightest flush of blood across her cheek would overcome it. But she is so pale!"

He drew aside the window curtain and suffered the light of natural day to fall into the room and rest upon her cheek. At the same time he heard a gross, hoarse chuckle, which he had long known as his servant Aminadab's expression of delight.

"Ah, clod! ah, earthly mass!" cried Aylmer, laughing in a sort of frenzy. "You have served me well! Matter and spirit—earth and heaven—have both done their part in this! Laugh, thing of the senses! You have earned the right to laugh."

These exclamations broke Georgiana's sleep. She slowly unclosed her eyes and gazed into the mirror which her husband had arranged for that purpose. A faint smile flitted over her lips when she recognized how barely perceptible was now that crimson hand which had once blazed with such disastrous brilliancy as to scare away all their happiness. But then her eyes sought Aylmer's face with a trouble and anxiety that he could by no means account for.

"My poor Aylmer!" murmured she.

"Poor? Nay, richest, happiest, most favored!" exclaimed he. "My peerless bride, it is successful! You are perfect!"

"My poor Aylmer," she repeated with a more than human tenderness, "you have aimed loftily; you have done nobly. Do not repent that with so high and pure a feeling, you have rejected the best the earth could offer. Aylmer, dearest Aylmer, I am dying!"

from "The Birthmark" by Nathaniel Hawthorne

8. Which of the following statements about Aylmer can be inferred from the selection?

(1) He does not love Georgiana.
(2) He is trying to kill his wife.
(3) He is disappointed at the result.
(4) He has performed some operation on his wife.
(5) He has caused his wife to commit suicide.

9. Which of the following best describes the form of the birthmark?

(1) a crimson hand
(2) a pale rose
(3) a rainbow
(4) a butterfly
(5) an all-over flush

10. Which of the following statements correctly describes what happens to the mysterious symbol on Georgiana's cheek?

(1) It does not change.
(2) Its color deepens.
(3) It begins to fade.
(4) It is completely obliterated.
(5) Its shape changes.

11. How does Aylmer regard Georgiana in the end of the passage?

(1) humorous
(2) flawless
(3) amusing
(4) unappreciative
(5) moody

12. Which of the following choices best explains the main idea of this selection?

(1) perfection cannot be achieved on earth
(2) birthmarks should be removed
(3) leave well enough alone
(4) beauty is in the eye of the beholder
(5) love conquers all

Items 13 to 17 are based on the following poem.

WHO IS BEING WELCOMED?

The New Colossus

Not like the brazen giant of Greek fame
With conquering limbs astride from land to land
Here at our sea-washed, sunset gates shall stand
A mighty woman with a torch, whose flame
Is the imprisoned lightning, and her name
Mother of Exiles. From her beacon hand
Glows world-wide welcome; her mild eyes command
The air-bridged harbor that twin cities frame.

"Keep, ancient lands, your storied pomp!" cries she
with silent lips. "Give me your tired, your poor,
Your huddled masses yearning to breathe free,
The wretched refuse of your teeming shore.
Send these, the homeless, tempest-tost, to me.
I lift my lamp beside the golden door!"

Emma Lazarus

13. Which of the following statements best describes the purpose of this poem?

(1) to memorialize the poet's mother
(2) to insult European governments
(3) to glorify the Greek myths
(4) to describe America
(5) to provide spiritual uplift to incoming refugees

14. What does the title of the poem seem to imply?

(1) The United States is a giant new country.
(2) There was a similar statue in ancient times.
(3) Italian refugees are particularly welcome.
(4) New York City is a great modern place.
(5) The old Colossus of Rhodes has been replaced.

15. What is the form of this poem?

(1) a sonnet
(2) blank verse
(3) free verse
(4) a ballad
(5) a rondel

16. What does the phrase "the wretched refuse of your teeming shore" suggest?

(1) America is for rich people only.
(2) Only poor people want to come here.
(3) All immigrants are political refugees.
(4) Americans look up to Europeans.
(5) America is wide open and empty.

17. What is the tone of this poem?

(1) sorrowful
(2) scornful
(3) delightful
(4) bewildered
(5) exalted

GO ON TO THE NEXT PAGE

Items 18 and 19 are based on the following selection.

WHAT IS NATURE?

The stars awaken a certain reverence, because although always present, they are inaccessible; but all natural objects make a kindred impression, when the mind is open to their influence. Nature never wears a mean appearance. Neither does the wisest man extort her secret, and lose his curiosity by finding out all her perfection. Nature never became a toy to a wise spirit. The flowers, the animals, the mountains, reflected the wisdom of his best hour, as much as they had delighted the simplicity of his childhood.

from "Nature" by Ralph Waldo Emerson

18. Which of the following words best describes how the author characterizes Nature?

    (1) flawed
    (2) beautiful
    (3) unknowable
    (4) perfect
    (5) unchanging

19. According to the passage, what does the phrase "Nature never wears a mean appearance" mean?

    (1) Beauty is in the eye of the beholder.
    (2) A thing of beauty is a joy forever.
    (3) Something is ugly only when we say it is.
    (4) There is no such thing as perfection in nature.
    (5) Everything in nature has beauty.

Items 20 to 23 refer to the following passage.

WHEN DID THE SHORT STORY BECOME POPULAR?

As we know the short story today, it is largely a product of the nineteenth and twentieth centuries, and its development parallels the rapid development of industrialism in America. We have been a busy people, busy principally in evolving a production system supremely efficient. Railroads and factories have blossomed almost overnight; mines and oil fields have been discovered and exploited; mechanical inventions by the thousands have been made and perfected. Speed has been an essential element in our endeavors, and it has affected our lives, our very natures. Leisurely reading has been, for most Americans, impossible. As with our meals, we have grabbed bits of reading standing up, cafeteria style, and gulped down cups of sentiment on the run. We have had to read while hanging on to a strap in a swaying trolley car or in a rushing subway or while tending to a clamoring telephone switchboard. Our popular magazine has been our literary automat and its stories have often been no more substantial than sandwiches.

20. According to the passage, the short story today owes its popularity primarily to its

    (1) setting
    (2) plot
    (3) style
    (4) length
    (5) characters

21. The author believes the short story has developed because of the American

    (1) reaction against the classics
    (2) need for reassurance
    (3) lack of culture
    (4) lack of education
    (5) taste for speed

22. From this selection one can assume that the author's attitude toward short stories is one of

    (1) approval
    (2) regret
    (3) indifference
    (4) contempt
    (5) impartiality

23. Which of the following titles best expresses the ideas of this paragraph?

    (1) "Quick-lunch" Literature
    (2) Life in the Machine Age
    (3) Culture in Modern Life
    (4) Reading While Traveling
    (5) The Development of Industrialization

GO ON TO THE NEXT PAGE

Items 24 to 28 are based on the following selection.

HOW DID THE NORTHMEN EXPLAIN THE CREATION OF THE WORLD?

The peoples of the northland were allied in blood and language to those of the peninsulas of Greece and Rome; and consequently there are numerous resemblances between the myths of the North and of the South.

Yet, although the resemblances are striking, the gods of the North in a good many respects differed from those of the South. The latter were more joyous and sunny; the former reflected the gloom and the hard conditions of life in the forests and waters of northern Europe. The stories told about them likewise differed.

For the Northmen believed that at the beginning for long ages existed *Niflheim,* a world of mist and ice. In the midst of Niflheim was a deep well, and from this well flowed ten rivers. To the south lay *Muspellsheim,* which glowed with fire. Gradually, in the course of time, the warmer airs from Muspellsheim melted the frost of the North, and out of the clouds that resulted sprang the giant *Ymir* and a whole race of other giants. The ground became visible, and on it lay masses of stones. From the frost itself sprang the cow *Audhumla,* and her milk nourished Ymir. The cow herself, by licking the salty, frost-covered stones, created the gods. On the first day she licked the stones a man's hair came forth, on the next day a man's head, and on the third day a whole man came forth. He was named *Buri,* and he was fair and tall. Then a female being was created, and from her and Buri came *Bor* and a number of goddesses. Bor's sons were the gods *Odin, Vili,* and *Ve;* and from them were descended the other gods.

These three gods slew the giant Ymir, and out of his body formed the heavens and the earth: from his flesh the earth, from his blood the sea, from his bones the mountains, from his hair the trees, and from his skull the sky. *Midgard* was the name given the earth, and over it the sky was made fast at its four corners. At each corner sat a dwarf.

From the sparks that Muspellsheim sent forth the three gods made stars to illumine the earth, and set them in the sky; and there too they placed the sun and the moon and set a course for them. Around the earth flowed the great sea, and on its coast lived the giants, at *Jotunnheim.* Among the giants were Nor, with his daughter *Nat* and his grandson *Dag.* Nat was dark and swarthy, Dag was light and handsome; and them Odin took into the heavens to rule over the night and the day. Nat or Night drives first the horse *Hrimfaxi,* from whose bit the foam flies down over the earth and becomes dew. In her wake comes Dag or Day with his steed, *Skinfa,* and his mane throws radiance over land and water.

from *Myths and Their Meaning* by May J. Herzberg.

24. How did the gods of the North differ from the gods of the South?

    (1) The Northern gods were larger.
    (2) The Southern gods were older.
    (3) The Southern gods had better dispositions.
    (4) The Northern gods had more children.
    (5) The Southern gods were gloomy.

25. According to the Northmen legend, how were the first gods created?

    (1) They sprang from the deep well of Niflheim.
    (2) They were the offspring of the giant Ymir.
    (3) They sprang forth from the mist and ice.
    (4) They sprang from the fires of Muspellsheim.
    (5) They were created by Audhumla the cow who licked the frost-covered stones.

26. What was made from the giant Ymir?

    (1) earth
    (2) four dwarves
    (3) the goddess Bor
    (4) another body
    (5) Audhumla, the cow

27. Who ruled night and day?

    (1) Midgard
    (2) Muspellsheim
    (3) Odin
    (4) Jotunnheim
    (5) descendants of Nor

28. From this story, what can we infer was the reason this myth was created?

    (1) to excuse the gods' behavior
    (2) to amuse people during long winter nights
    (3) to link the North and South
    (4) to explain the difference between the North and South
    (5) to quiet children at the end of a long day

GO ON TO THE NEXT PAGE

Items 29 to 32 refer to the following selection.

DID LEWY CLEMENT HAVE A NICE LIFE?

Lewy Clement's life was not terrifically tossed. Saltless, rather. Or like an unmixed batter. Lumpy.

Little Clement's mother had grown listless after the desertion. She looked as though she had been scrubbed, up and down, on the washing board, doused from time to time in gray and noisome water. But little Clement looked alert, he looked happy, he was always spirited. He was in second grade. He did his work, and had always been promoted. At home he sang. He recited little poems. He told his mother little stories wound out of the air by himself. His mother glanced at him once in a while. She would have been proud of him if she had had the time.

She started toward her housemaid's work each morning at seven. She left a glass of milk and a bowl of dry cereal and a dish of prunes on the table, and set the alarm clock for eight. At eight little Clement punched off the alarm, stretched, got up, washed, dressed, combed, brushed, ate his breakfast. It was quiet in the apartment. He hurried off to school. At noon he returned from school, opened the door with his key. It was quiet in the apartment. He poured himself a second glass of milk, got more prunes, and ate a slice—"just one slice," his mother had cautioned—of bread and butter. He went back to school. At three o'clock he returned from school, opened the door with his key. It was quiet in the apartment. He got a couple of graham crackers out of the cookie can. He drew himself a glass of water. He changed his clothes. Then he went out to play, leaving behind him the two rooms. Leaving behind him the brass beds, the lamp with the faded silk tassel and frayed cord, the hooked oven door, the cracks in the walls and the quiet. As he played, he kept a lookout for his mother, who usually arrived at seven or near that hour. When he saw her rounding the corner, his little face underwent a transformation. His eyes lashed into brightness, his lips opened suddenly and became a smile, and his eyebrows climbed toward his hairline in relief and joy.

He would run to his mother and almost throw his little body at her. "Here I am, mother! Here I am! Here I am!"

from "Neighbors" by Gwendolyn Brooks

29. Why is the author's introductory paragraph effective in capturing the reader's interest?

    (1) It relies on the author's personal experience.
    (2) It refers to ideas about maturity which are familiar to most readers.
    (3) It explains the advantages and disadvantages of Lewy's upbringing.
    (4) It has a variety of sentence lengths and descriptive words.
    (5) It explains why Lewy behaves the way he does.

30. Which of the following choices is especially effective in describing Lewy's home life?

    (1) "glass of milk," "bowl of dry cereal"
    (2) "faded silk tassel," "cracks in the wall"
    (3) "hurried off to school," "returned from school"
    (4) "glass of water," "changed his clothes"
    (5) "punched the alarm," "rounding the corner"

31. How does Lewy feel about his mother?

    (1) He resents her for working such long hours.
    (2) He blames her for his father's desertion.
    (3) He is indifferent to her.
    (4) He adores her.
    (5) He wishes she was proud of him.

32. Which of the following words best describes the author's attitude toward Mrs. Clement?

    (1) admiring
    (2) bitter
    (3) indignant
    (4) neutral
    (5) worshipful

GO ON TO THE NEXT PAGE

Items 33 to 36 refer to the following article.

IS THERE REALLY A NEW DRUG EPIDEMIC?

Last week a debate heated up about whether the media have collectively hyped the nation's drug problem, especially the threat posed by crack, a potent form of cocaine. At the forefront was an unlikely critic of media warnings about illegal narcotics: the Federal Drug Enforcement Administration.

Crack has dominated media attention during the recent surge in drug coverage. A CBS report televised in early September, *48 Hours on Crack Street,* drew the highest viewership of any network documentary in six years. NBC has aired more than 400 reports on drug abuse since the beginning of March; ABC two weeks ago highlighted drugs on all its news programs. Cocaine and crack have been front-page news in dailies ranging from city tabloids to the *Wall Street Journal,* which last week reported abuse was "rife" in rural Oklahoma. Crack has repeatedly reached Page One of the New York *Times* and Washington *Post,* and the drug crisis rated two cover stories within three months at *Newsweek.* The magazine's editor in chief, Richard Smith, wrote in the June 16 issue: "An epidemic is abroad in America, as pervasive and dangerous in its way as the plagues of medieval times." TIME has given cover attention to drug use in the workplace and the antidrug crusade led by President and Mrs. Reagan. But the DEA, after a city-by-city survey of crack's availability, asserted in a report that the result of media attention "has been a distortion of the public perception of the extent of crack use."

The DEA said the drug "generally is not available" in some major cities, including Chicago, Philadelphia and New Orleans, and is not widely available in many other metropolitan areas. In addition, contrary to some news reports, the DEA found little evidence that crack use had spread from inner cities to many suburbs. The study concluded, "Crack presently appears to be a secondary rather than primary problem in most areas."

33. Which of the following statements would the author of this article support?

    (1) "Crack is the most serious problem facing America today."
    (2) "Crack is killing more of our young people than all other factors combined."
    (3) "Unless something is done soon to combat the crack plague, we will sacrifice a generation."
    (4) "The media has greatly distorted the extent to which crack is used."
    (5) "Very few people really use crack."

34. Which of the following groups does the author place in the vanguard of this controversy?

    (1) the DEA
    (2) the EPA
    (3) the White House
    (4) the public television stations
    (5) radio stations

35. Which of the following techniques does the author use to make his point?

    (1) cause and effect
    (2) advantages and disadvantages
    (3) reasons and causes
    (4) process analysis
    (5) examples

36. The media compares today's use of crack to which of the following?

    (1) an invasion
    (2) the plague
    (3) the Seven Years' War
    (4) an automobile collision
    (5) a wound

Items 37 to 41 refer to the following poem.

WHAT HAPPENED TO OZYMANDIAS?

Ozymandias

I met a traveler from an antique land
Who said: "Two vast and trunkless legs of stone
Stand in the desert. Near them, on the sand,
Half sunk, a shattered visage lies, whose frown
And wrinkled lip, and sneer of cold command,
Tell that its sculptor well those passions read
Which yet survive, stamped on these lifeless things,
The hand that mocked them, and the heart that fed:
And on the pedestal these words appear:
'My name is Ozymandias, king of kings:
Look on my works, ye Mighty, and despair!'
Nothing beside remains. Round the decay
Of that colossal wreck, boundless and bare
The lone and level sands stretch far away."

Percy Bysshe Shelley

37. Which of the following is Shelley NOT writing about in this poem?

(1) the sin of pride
(2) an ancient pharaoh or king
(3) the healing process
(4) a wrecked statue in the desert
(5) a tale told by a tourist

38. Who can the reader assume Ozymandias was?

(1) the kind and benevolent ruler
(2) Alexander the Great
(3) a sculptor of ancient Greece
(4) a haughty king of ancient times
(5) a traveler in the desert

39. What is the "shattered visage" the author writes about?

(1) a broken promise
(2) a torn sheet of papyrus
(3) a shattered head
(4) a smashed statue
(5) none of the above

40. The repetition of sounds in "boundless and bare/ The lone and level sands stretch far away." (lines 13 and 14) provide an example of which of the following?

(1) simile
(2) alliteration
(3) onomatopoeia
(4) personification
(5) metaphor

41. Which of the following best describes the meaning of this poem?

(1) Time wounds all heels.
(2) Here today, gone tomorrow.
(3) The bigger they are, the harder they fall.
(4) Even the mighty are mortal.
(5) Pride goeth before a fall.

GO ON TO THE NEXT PAGE

Items 42 to 45 refer to the following selection.

WHO ARE BINNIE AND MRS. TEENIE THOMPSON?

There was an insane youth of twenty, twice released from Dunning. He had a smooth tan face, overlaid with oil. His name was Binnie. Or perhaps it was Bennie, or Benjamin. But his mother lovingly called him "Binnie." Binnie strode the halls, with huge eyes, direct and annoyed. He strode, and played "catch" with a broken watch, which was attached to a long string wound around his left arm. There was no annoyance in his eyes when he spoke to Maud Martha, though, and none in his nice voice. He was very fond of Maud Martha. Once, when she answered a rap on the door, there he was, and he pushed in before she could open her mouth. He had on a new belt, he said. "My Uncle John gave it to me," he said. "So my pants won't fall down." He walked about the apartment, after closing the door with a careful sneer. He touched things. He pulled a petal from a pink rose with savage anger, then kissed it with a tenderness that was more terrible than the anger; briskly he rapped on the table, turned suddenly to stare at her, to see if she approved of what he was doing—she smiled uncertainly; he saw the big bed, fingered it, sat on it, got up, kicked it. He opened a dresser drawer, took out a ruler. "This is ni-ice—but I won't take it" (with firm decision, noble virtue). "I'll put it back." He spoke of his aunt, his Uncle John's wife Octavia. "She's ni-ice—you know, she can even call me, and I don't even get mad." With another careful sneer, he opened the door. He went out.

Mrs. Teenie Thompson. Fifty-three; and pepper whenever she talked of the North Shore people who had employed her as housemaid for ten years. "She went to huggin' and kissin' of me—course I got to receive it—I got to work for 'em. But they think they got me thinkin' they love me. Then I'm supposed to kill my silly self slavin' for 'em. To be worthy of their love. These old whi' folks. They jive you, honey. Well, I jive 'em back.

from "Neighbors" by Gwendolyn Brooks

42. What was one of Binnie's favorite games?

(1) bouncing on beds
(2) snapping his belt
(3) knocking on doors and then hiding
(4) playing catch with his watch
(5) calling his Aunt Octavia and hanging up

43. How did Maud feel while Binnie was in her apartment?

(1) exhausted
(2) frightened
(3) happy
(4) annoyed
(5) flattered

44. Which of the following best describes the "North Shore people" Mrs. Teenie Thompson speaks about in lines 33-43?

(1) young
(2) Southern
(3) rich
(4) affectionate
(5) poor

45. Why is the phrase describing Mrs. Teenie Thompson as "pepper whenever she spoke of the North Shore people who had employed her" especially effective?

(1) It succinctly describes her anger at her employers.
(2) It clearly describes her admiration for her employers.
(3) It describes her love of her job.
(4) It describes how she treats Binnie.
(5) It explains her relationship with Binnie.

END OF LITERATURE TEST

TEST 5. MATHEMATICS

90 Minutes—56 Questions

Directions:

The Mathematics Test consists of multiple-choice questions covering the areas of arithmetic, algebra, and geometry. The problems emphasize the practical aspects of mathematics necessary to the solution of everyday problems. A page of formulas is provided for reference in solving the problems presented. However, you will have to determine which formula (if any) is needed to solve a particular problem. Read each problem carefully and then work out the solution on your own before looking at the answer choices. Work quickly, but carefully, answering as many questions as you can. If a problem is too difficult for you, skip it and come back to it after you have completed all of the problems you know how to solve. Record your answers in the Mathematics section of your answer sheet.

FOR EXAMPLE:

Jill's drug store bill totals $8.68. How much change should she get if she pays with a $10.00 bill?

(1) $2.32
(2) $1.42
(3) $1.32
(4) $1.28
(5) $1.22

The correct answer is "$1.32." Therefore, you should mark answer space 3 on your answer sheet.

FORMULAS

Description	Formula
AREA (A) of a:	
square	$A=s^2$; where s=side
rectangle	$A=lw$; where l=length, w=width
parallelogram	$A=bh$; where b=base, h=height
triangle	$A=\frac{1}{2}bh$; where b=base, h=height
circle	$A=\pi r^2$; where $\pi=3.14$, r=radius
PERIMETER (P) of a:	
square	$P=4s$; where s=side
rectangle	$P=2l+2w$; where l=length, w=width
triangle	$P=a+b+c$; where a, b, and c are the sides
circumference (C) of a circle	$C=\pi d$; where π=3.14, d=diameter
VOLUME (V) of a:	
cube	$V=s^3$; where s=side
rectangular container	$V=lwh$; where l=length, w=width, h=height
cylinder	$V=\pi r^2h$; where π=3.14, r=radius, h=height
Pythagorean relationship	$c^2=a^2+b^2$; where c=hypotenuse, a and b are legs of a right triangle
distance (d) between two points in a plane	$d=\sqrt{(x_2-x_1)^2+(y_2-y_1)^2}$; where (x_1, y_1) and (x_2, y_2) are two points in a plane
slope of a line (m)	$m=\frac{y_2-y_1}{x_2-x_1}$; where (x_1, y_1) and (x_2, y_2) are two points in a plane
mean	mean$=\frac{x_1+x_2+\cdots+x_n}{n}$; where the x's are the values for which a mean is desired, and n=number of values in the series
median	median=the point in an ordered set of numbers at which half of the numbers are above and half of the numbers are below this value
simple interest (i)	$i=prt$; where p=principal, r=rate, t=time
distance (d) as function of rate and time	$d=rt$; where r=rate, t=time
total cost (c)	$c=nr$; where n=number of units, r=cost per unit

Items 1 to 4 refer to the data below.

Attendance at Sports Events (in millions)

Activity	1960	1965	1970	1974	1975	1976	1977	1978
Baseball, major leagues:								
Regular season	19.9	22.4	28.7	30.0	29.8	31.3	38.7	40.6
American League	9.2	8.9	12.1	13.0	13.2	14.7	19.6	20.5
National League	10.7	13.6	16.7	17.0	16.6	16.7	19.1	20.1
Basketball, professional, NBA	2.0	2.8	5.1	6.9	7.9	8.5	11.0	10.9
Football, collegiate	20.4	24.7	29.5	31.2	31.7	32.0	32.9	34.3
Football, professional, NFL	3.2	4.7	10.0	10.7	10.7	11.6	11.6	13.4
Horseracing	46.9	62.9	69.7	74.9	78.7	79.3	76.0	76.0
Greyhound racing	7.9	10.9	2.7	16.3	17.5	19.0	20.0	20.1
Hockey, NHL	2.4	2.8	6.0	8.6	9.5	9.1	8.6	8.5

1. In which year did attendance at American Baseball League games first exceed attendance at National League games?

   (1) 1960
   (2) 1970
   (3) 1975
   (4) 1977
   (5) 1978

2. Which sporting event was the most popular during 1965?

   (1) baseball
   (2) horseracing
   (3) football
   (4) hockey
   (5) Not enough information is given.

3. In 1978, what percentage of the people who attended Major League ball games (basketball, baseball, and football) went to baseball games?

   (1) 17
   (2) 21
   (3) 63
   (4) 65
   (5) 71

4. In 1977, which sporting activity netted the LEAST revenue?

   (1) hockey
   (2) football
   (3) greyhound racing
   (4) baseball
   (5) Not enough information is given.

5. If the perimeter of a rectangular swimming pool is 68 yards and the width is 48 feet, the length is

   (1) 10 yards
   (2) 18 yards
   (3) 20 feet
   (4) 56 feet
   (5) 60 feet

6. If fencing costs \$9.00 per yard, what would be the total cost of the fencing needed to enclose a rectangular area measuring 46 feet by 34 feet?

   (1) \$34
   (2) \$46
   (3) \$160
   (4) \$480
   (5) \$640

GO ON TO THE NEXT PAGE

7. Which quantity is NOT equal to 75 (32 + 88)?

   (1) $75 \cdot 32 + 75 \cdot 88$
   (2) $(75 \cdot 32) + 88$
   (3) $75(88 + 32)$
   (4) $(88 + 32) \cdot 75$
   (5) $88 \cdot 75 + 32 \cdot 75$

8. It takes 8 boards laid end-to-end to make a walkway from the parking lot to the entrance to the school. If each board is 8 feet 7 inches long, how long will the walkway be?

   (1) 69 feet 6 inches
   (2) 68.8 feet
   (3) $68\frac{2}{3}$ feet
   (4) 68 feet 2 inches
   (5) Not enough information is given.

9. The Little League ordered a 6-foot-long sandwich for their annual picnic. If the sandwich is to be cut into 40 equal pieces, how long will each piece be?

   (1) 3 feet
   (2) 24 inches
   (3) .3 feet
   (4) $2\frac{1}{2}$ inches
   (5) $1\frac{4}{5}$ inches

Items 10 to 11 refer to the following information.

The owner of a bookstore places the following order for books from a publisher.

TITLE	PRICE	DISCOUNT	QUANTITY	COST
A New You	17.95	40%	20	10.77
Puff Pastry	21.00	40%	10	12.60
Caring for Your Dog	8.95	20%	15	7.16
Auto Repair for Beginners	16.00	20%	18	12.80

10. The bookstore owner already has a \$147.60 credit with the publisher from an earlier order. Taking this credit into account, how much will the publisher bill the bookstore?

    (1) \$147.60
    (2) \$531.60
    (3) \$679.20
    (4) \$772.65
    (5) \$920.25

11. The bookstore sold everything in the order except for nine copies of *Puff Pastry*. How much money did the bookstore make on the order?

    (1) \$236.45
    (2) \$271.68
    (3) \$565.80
    (4) \$679.20
    (5) Not enough information is given.

12. An umbrella 50 inches long can lie on the bottom of a rectangular trunk whose length and width are, respectively

    (1) 36 inches, 30 inches
    (2) 42 inches, 24 inches
    (3) 42 inches, 36 inches
    (4) 39 inches, 30 inches
    (5) 39 inches, 36 inches

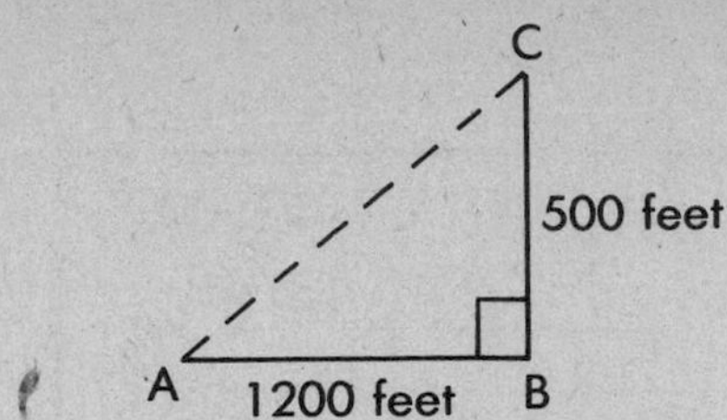

13. A road runs 1200 feet from A to B, and then makes a right angle going to C, a distance of 500 feet. A new road is being built directly from A to C. How much shorter will the new road be?

(1) 400 feet
(2) 609 feet
(3) 850 feet
(4) 1300 feet
(5) 1500 feet

14. A recent survey shows that .25% of smokers find it easy to stop. Which of the following fractions is equal to .25%?

(1) $\frac{1}{400}$
(2) $\frac{1}{40}$
(3) $\frac{1}{4}$
(4) $\frac{5}{2}$
(5) $\frac{50}{2}$

15. Six gross of special drawing pencils were purchased for use in an office. If the pencils were used at the rate of 24 a week, the maximum number of weeks that the six gross of pencils would last is

(1) 6 weeks
(2) 12 weeks
(3) 24 weeks
(4) 36 weeks
(5) 40 weeks

16. If 7 feet 9 inches is cut from a piece of wood that is 9 feet 6 inches, how long is the remaining piece?

(1) 1 foot 9 inches
(2) 1 foot 10 inches
(3) 2 feet 2 inches
(4) 2 feet 5 inches
(5) 3 feet

17. John is three times his son's age. If the difference between their ages is 30, how old is the son?

(1) 5
(2) 10
(3) 15
(4) 20
(5) 25

18. The perimeter of the figure below is 41. The length of the longest side is

(1) 10
(2) 11
(3) 12
(4) 13
(5) 14

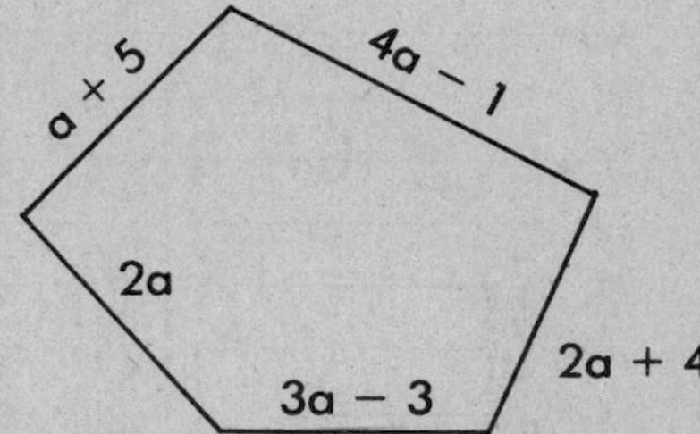

19. A certain triangle has sides that are, respectively, 6 inches, 8 inches, and 10 inches long. A rectangle equal in area to this triangle has a width of 3 inches. The perimeter of the rectangle, expressed in inches, is

(1) 11
(2) 16
(3) 18
(4) 20
(5) 22

20. A pill contains 0.2 grams of a medicine. How many pills can be made from 1 kilogram (1000 grams) of the medicine?

(1) 20
(2) 200
(3) 500
(4) 5000
(5) 10,000

GO ON TO THE NEXT PAGE

Items 21 to 23 refer to the following graph.

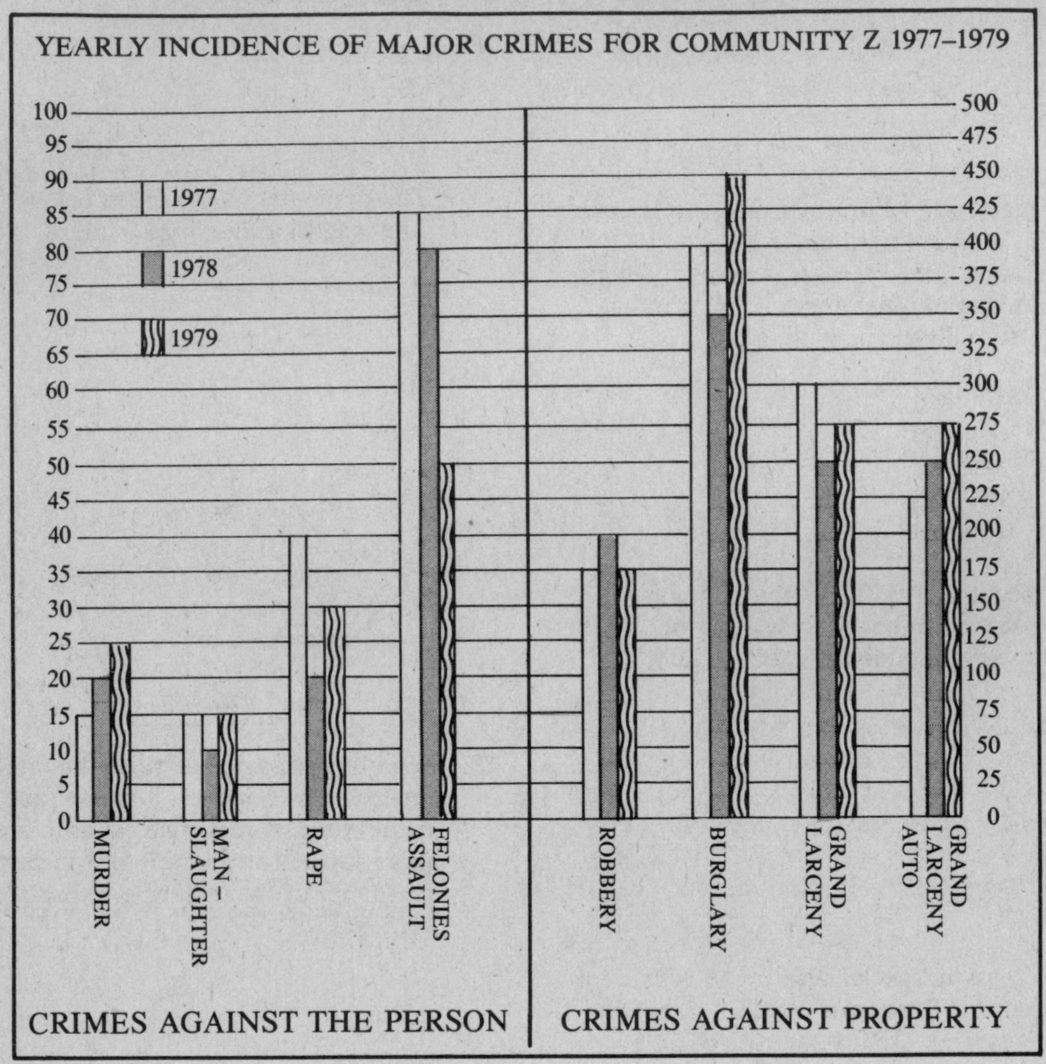

21. In 1979, the incidence of which of the following crimes was greater than in the previous two years?

(1) grand larceny
(2) murder
(3) rape
(4) robbery
(5) burglary

22. If the incidence of burglary in 1980 had increased over 1979 by the same number as it had increased in 1979 over 1978, then the average for this crime for the 4-year period from 1977 through 1980 would be most nearly

(1) 100
(2) 400
(3) 425
(4) 430
(5) 440

23. The above graph indicates that the *percentage* increase in grand larceny auto from 1978 to 1979 was

(1) 5%
(2) 10%
(3) 15%
(4) 20%
(5) 65%

24. Working alone, Jane put the first coat of paint on her living room walls in 5 hours 13 minutes. Four friends came to help with the second coat, and together they finished in 3 hours 49 minutes. How much time was saved by using her friends to help paint the room?

(1) 1 hour 5 minutes
(2) 1 hour 10 minutes
(3) 1 hour 18 minutes
(4) 1 hour 24 minutes
(5) 1 hour 30 minutes

25. A piece of wood 35 feet 6 inches long was used to make 4 shelves of equal lengths. The length of each shelf was

(1) 8.9 inches
(2) 8 feet 9 inches
(3) 8 feet $9\frac{1}{2}$ inches
(4) 8 feet $10\frac{1}{2}$ inches
(5) 8 feet 11 inches

26. Mrs. Symonds bought 12 raffle tickets at a lodge bazaar. Her husband bought 3 tickets. If 500 tickets were sold all together, and only one prize will be awarded, what is the probability that Mr. and Mrs. Symonds will win?

(1) $\frac{500}{12}$
(2) $\frac{495}{12}$
(3) $\frac{3}{100}$
(4) $\frac{15}{485}$
(5) $\frac{1}{500}$

27. An estate was divided among three heirs, A, B, and C, in the ratio 2:3:4. If the total estate was $22,500, what was the smallest inheritance?

(1) $1000
(2) $1250
(3) $2500
(4) $4000
(5) $5000

28. A triangular sign was cut out of wood (see below). If AB || DE, ∡ C = 50° and ∡ 1 = 60°, then ∡ A =

(1) 30°
(2) 60°
(3) 70°
(4) 50°
(5) 45°

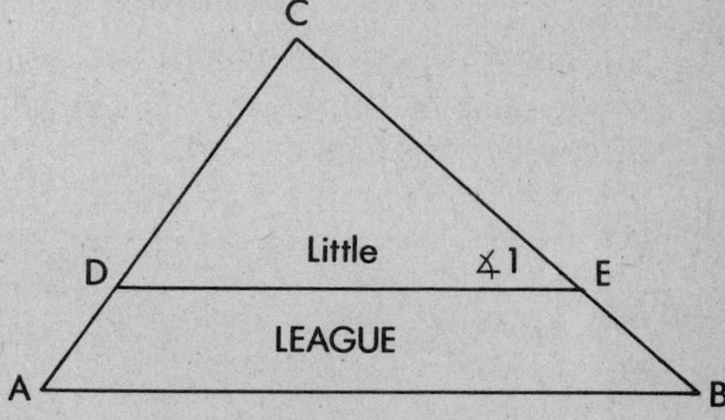

29. If 1 ounce is approximately equal to 28 grams, then how many grams are in a 1-pound box of candy?

(1) 250 grams
(2) 350 grams
(3) 450 grams
(4) 550 grams
(5) 650 grams

30. The number of yards in a 126-inch length of rope is

(1) 3.5
(2) 10.5
(3) 42
(4) 1512
(5) 1600

31. If there are 231 cubic inches in one gallon of gasoline, the number of cubic inches in 3 pints is closest to which one of the following?

(1) 24
(2) 29
(3) 57
(4) 84
(5) 187

GO ON TO THE NEXT PAGE

32. A dealer buys a TV set for $550 and wishes to sell it at a 20% profit. What should his selling price be?

    (1) $570
    (2) $600
    (3) $620
    (4) $640
    (5) $660

33. Michael earns $50 for 8 hours of work. At the same rate of pay, how much will he earn for 28 hours of work?

    (1) $150
    (2) $175
    (3) $186
    (4) $232
    (5) $250

34. A rectangular bin 4 feet long, 3 feet wide, and 2 feet high is solidly packed with bricks whose dimensions are 8 inches, 4 inches, and 2 inches. The number of bricks in the bin is

    (1) 64
    (2) 648
    (3) 1296
    (4) 4147
    (5) None of these

35. If one card is picked at random from a deck of cards, the probability that it is a club is

    (1) 1
    (2) $\frac{1}{52}$
    (3) $\frac{1}{13}$
    (4) $\frac{1}{10}$
    (5) $\frac{1}{4}$

Items 36 and 37 refer to the following graph.

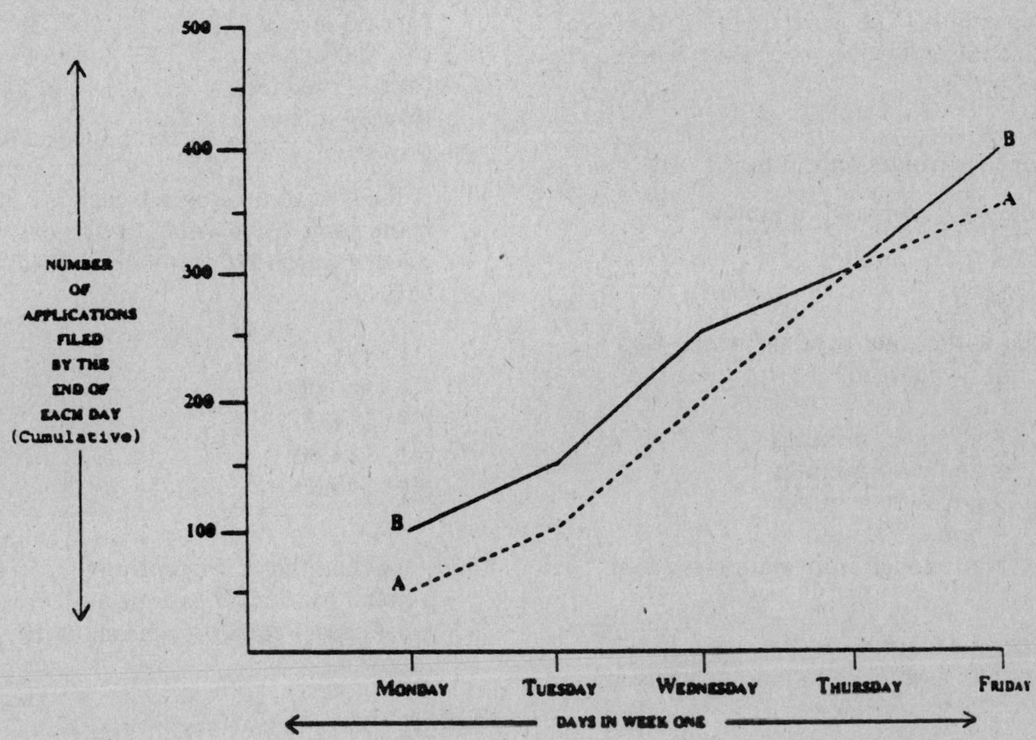

In the graph above, the lines labeled "A" and "B" represent the cumulative progress in the work of two file clerks, each of whom was given 500 consecutively numbered applications to file in the proper cabinets over a 5-day work week.

36. The day during which the largest number of applications was filed by both clerks was

    (1) Monday
    (2) Tuesday
    (3) Wednesday
    (4) Thursday
    (5) Friday

37. At the end of the second day, the percentage of applications still to be filed was

    (1) 25%
    (2) 50%
    (3) 66%
    (4) 75%
    (5) 85%

GO ON TO THE NEXT PAGE

Items 38 and 39 refer to the following information.

Al's Garage charges $25 per hour to service domestic cars and $30 per hour for foreign cars. Bob brought his 3-year-old Chevrolet to the garage for repairs. The work sheet for Bob's car shows that the following mechanics worked on Bob's car:

Carl for 5 hours 16 minutes

Anne for 3 hours 49 minutes

Ed for 25 minutes

38. What is the total time for which Bob should be charged?

(1) 8 hours 10 minutes
(2) 8 hours 30 minutes
(3) 9 hours 10 minutes
(4) 9 hours 30 minutes
(5) Not enough information is given.

39. If the bill for new parts totaled $84.25, what will Bob have to pay for parts and labor for this servicing?

(1) $237.50
(2) $279.25
(3) $321.75
(4) $325.50
(5) Not enough information is given.

40. Mrs. Smith wishes to purchase a freezer with a list price of $500. If she waits for a "15% off" sale and receives an additional discount of 2% for paying cash, how much will she save?

(1) $75.50
(2) $83.50
(3) $85.00
(4) $150.00
(5) $200.00

41. A photograph is 8 inches wide and 10 inches long. If it is enlarged so that the new length is 25 inches the new width will be

(1) $18\frac{1}{2}$ inches
(2) 20 inches
(3) 24 inches
(4) $31\frac{1}{4}$ inches
(5) 34 inches

42. If the cost of digging a trench is $2.12 a cubic yard, what would be the cost of digging a trench 2 yards by 5 yards by 4 yards?

(1) $21.20
(2) $40.00
(3) $64.00
(4) $84.80
(5) $90.00

43. Assuming that 2.54 centimeters = 1 inch, a metal rod that measures $1\frac{1}{2}$ feet would most nearly equal which one of the following?

(1) 380 centimeters
(2) 246 centimeters
(3) 30 centimeters
(4) 18 centimeters
(5) 46 centimeters

44. A micromillimeter is defined as one millionth of a millimeter. A length of 17 micro millimeters may be represented by

(1) .00017 millimeters
(2) .0000017 millimeters
(3) .000017 millimeters
(4) .00000017 millimeters
(5) .017 millimeters

45. Jean sells cosmetics, earning a 12% commission on all sales. How much will she need in sales to earn $300 in commission?

    (1) $1800
    (2) $2500
    (3) $3600
    (4) $4000
    (5) $4400

46. Mr. Taylor leaves home at 8 AM, traveling at 45 miles per hour. Mrs. Taylor follows him, leaving home at 10 AM and traveling at 55 miles per hour. How long will it take Mrs. Taylor to catch up with Mr. Taylor?

    (1) 7 hours
    (2) 8 hours
    (3) 9 hours
    (4) 10 hours
    (5) 11 hours

47. A piece of wire is shaped to enclose a square, whose area is 121 square inches. It is then reshaped to enclose a rectangle whose length is 13 inches. The area of the rectangle, in square inches, is

    (1) 64
    (2) 96
    (3) 117
    (4) 144
    (5) 150

48. How many liters of blood are equal to 4200 cubic centimeters (1 milliliter = 1 cubic centimeter)?

    (1) .42
    (2) 4.2
    (3) 420
    (4) 420,000
    (5) 4,200,000

49. Sam buys a jacket marked $85. He pays $90.95 including sales tax. What percent sales tax does he pay?

    (1) 4%
    (2) 5%
    (3) 6%
    (4) 7%
    (5) 8%

50. The area of a 2-foot-wide walk around a garden that is 30 feet long and 20 feet wide is

    (1) 104 square feet
    (2) 216 square feet
    (3) 680 square feet
    (4) 704 square feet
    (5) 716 square feet

51. In the movie set for *The Wizard of Oz,* the length of the Yellow Brick Road was 200 yards, and its width was 1.5 yards. How many square feet of yellow flooring material was necessary to cover the road?

    (1) 600
    (2) 1000
    (3) 1700
    (4) 2700
    (5) 3000

52. If the yellow flooring material in problem 51 cost $18.00 per square yard, what will be the cost of enough of the flooring to cover 500 square feet of the road?

    (1) $10
    (2) $50
    (3) $100
    (4) $500
    (5) $1000

GO ON TO THE NEXT PAGE

53. Suppose a graph was drawn to represent the actual distance covered in an army maneuver, where each coordinate point represented 1 mile [for example, (1,0) was one mile, along the x-axis from the origin, (0,0)].

How many miles would a soldier have to walk to go from: (0,0) to (4,0) to (4,3) to (0,3) and finally to (0,0)?

(1) 7
(2) 10
(3) 14
(4) 17
(5) 20

54. In electrical theory, a formula used is:

$$I_1 = \frac{R_2}{R_1 + R_2} \times I_2$$

Find the value for I_1, if:

$R_1 = 4$
$R_2 = 4$
$I_2 = 17$

(1) 4
(2) 5.5
(3) 7.0
(4) 8.5
(5) 10.0

55. At the Apex company, five employees earn $15,000 per year, three employees earn $17,000 per year and one employee earns $18,000 per year. What is the average yearly salary of these employees?

(1) $16,667
(2) $16,000
(3) $17,000
(4) $16,448
(5) $16,025

56. Income tax in a certain state is figured at 2% of the first $1000, 3% of the next $2000, 4% of the next $3000 and 5% thereafter. Find the tax on an income of $25,000.

(1) $1150
(2) $1015
(3) $950
(4) $200
(5) $187

END OF MATHEMATICS TEST

ANSWER KEY FOR GED SAMPLE TEST I

After completing the Practice Test Battery, check your answers against the key answers that follow. Enter the total number of correct answers for each test in the box provided on your Answer Sheet. Then turn to the Error Analysis on page 579 to see how well you did.

TEST 1. WRITING SKILLS—PART I

1. (3)
2. (5)
3. (3)
4. (1)
5. (4)
6. (1)
7. (4)
8. (3)
9. (4)
10. (2)
11. (5)
12. (5)
13. (2)
14. (2)
15. (1)
16. (5)
17. (2)
18. (1)
19. (4)
20. (3)
21. (2)
22. (2)
23. (4)
24. (5)
25. (4)
26. (2)
27. (2)
28. (3)
29. (5)
30. (3)
31. (4)
32. (2)
33. (2)
34. (1)
35. (4)
36. (3)
37. (4)
38. (2)
39. (2)
40. (1)
41. (2)
42. (5)
43. (4)
44. (1)
45. (5)
46. (1)
47. (4)
48. (2)
49. (4)
50. (3)
51. (2)
52. (5)
53. (2)
54. (5)
55. (3)

TEST 2. SOCIAL STUDIES

1. (2)
2. (5)
3. (1)
4. (3)
5. (3)
6. (5)
7. (3)
8. (2)
9. (2)
10. (1)
11. (3)
12. (5)
13. (1)
14. (4)
15. (4)
16. (5)
17. (1)
18. (3)
19. (5)
20. (2)
21. (4)
22. (3)
23. (1)
24. (5)
25. (5)
26. (2)
27. (4)
28. (2)
29. (3)
30. (3)
31. (3)
32. (1)
33. (1)
34. (4)
35. (4)
36. (3)
37. (2)
38. (5)
39. (4)
40. (2)
41. (4)
42. (3)
43. (2)
44. (2)
45. (3)
46. (5)
47. (4)
48. (5)
49. (3)
50. (5)
51. (4)
52. (3)
53. (5)
54. (1)
55. (3)
56. (4)
57. (2)
58. (4)
59. (4)
60. (1)
61. (4)
62. (2)
63. (5)
64. (1)

TEST 3. SCIENCE

1. (2)	15. (4)	29. (2)	43. (4)	57. (2)
2. (4)	16. (3)	30. (3)	44. (4)	58. (5)
3. (4)	17. (1)	31. (1)	45. (3)	59. (3)
4. (4)	18. (2)	32. (3)	46. (5)	60. (2)
5. (2)	19. (2)	33. (3)	47. (2)	61. (4)
6. (5)	20. (4)	34. (3)	48. (4)	62. (3)
7. (3)	21. (3)	35. (4)	49. (1)	63. (2)
8. (3)	22. (1)	36. (1)	50. (3)	64. (5)
9. (2)	23. (3)	37. (2)	51. (5)	65. (4)
10. (1)	24. (2)	38. (5)	52. (2)	66. (3)
11. (3)	25. (5)	39. (3)	53. (4)	
12. (3)	26. (4)	40. (1)	54. (3)	
13. (3)	27. (4)	41. (4)	55. (2)	
14. (5)	28. (4)	42. (5)	56. (5)	

TEST 4. INTERPRETING LITERATURE AND THE ARTS

1. (1)	10. (3)	19. (5)	28. (4)	37. (3)
2. (4)	11. (2)	20. (4)	29. (4)	38. (4)
3. (2)	12. (1)	21. (5)	30. (2)	39. (3)
4. (5)	13. (5)	22. (2)	31. (4)	40. (2)
5. (3)	14. (1)	23. (1)	32. (1)	41. (5)
6. (2)	15. (1)	24. (3)	33. (4)	42. (4)
7. (3)	16. (2)	25. (5)	34. (1)	43. (2)
8. (4)	17. (5)	26. (1)	35. (5)	44. (3)
9. (1)	18. (3)	27. (5)	36. (2)	45. (1)

TEST 5. MATHEMATICS

1. (4)	13. (1)	25. (4)	37. (4)	49. (4)
2. (2)	14. (1)	26. (3)	38. (4)	50. (2)
3. (3)	15. (4)	27. (5)	39. (3)	51. (4)
4. (5)	16. (1)	28. (3)	40. (2)	52. (5)
5. (2)	17. (3)	29. (3)	41. (2)	53. (3)
6. (4)	18. (2)	30. (1)	42. (4)	54. (4)
7. (2)	19. (5)	31. (4)	43. (5)	55. (2)
8. (3)	20. (4)	32. (5)	44. (3)	56. (1)
9. (5)	21. (2)	33. (2)	45. (2)	
10. (2)	22. (5)	34. (2)	46. (3)	
11. (1)	23. (2)	35. (5)	47. (3)	
12. (3)	24. (4)	36. (3)	48. (2)	

ERROR ANALYSIS FOR GED SAMPLE TEST I

Circle the number of each question you answered incorrectly. Count the number of circles in each content area and write the total number missed in the column headed "Number Incorrect." A large number of incorrect responses in a particular area indicates the need for further study in that area.

Subject Area	Questions	No. Incorrect
TEST 1. WRITING SKILLS	55	
Sentence Structure	2, 4, 5, 10, 12, 15, 16, 23, 24, 25, 27, 32, 35, 41, 42, 43, 44, 45, 46, 48, 50, 55	
Usage	6, 9, 11, 13, 14, 17, 18, 19, 22, 26, 28, 36, 37, 38, 39, 40, 47, 49, 53, 54	
Capitalization	7, 52	
Punctuation	31, 33	
Spelling/Possessives/ Contractions	1, 3, 8, 20, 21, 29, 30, 34, 51	
TEST 2. SOCIAL STUDIES	64	
History	1, 2, 3, 5, 15, 16, 17, 18, 20, 21, 22, 23, 24, 25, 38, 39, 40, 41, 42, 43	
Economics	1, 2, 4, 5, 6, 9, 10, 11, 12, 13, 14, 19, 30, 31, 32, 33, 50, 51, 52, 53, 55, 56, 57, 58, 59, 62, 63, 64	
Geography	6, 7, 8, 34, 35, 36, 37, 38, 39, 40, 41, 42, 43, 60, 61	
Political Science	34, 35, 36, 37, 47, 48, 49, 50, 51, 52, 54, 55, 56, 60, 61	
Behavorial Science	3, 7, 9, 10, 11, 12, 13, 14, 25, 26, 27, 28, 29, 44, 45, 46, 47, 48, 49, 56	
TEST 3. SCIENCE	66	
Biology	1, 2, 3, 4, 5, 22, 23, 24, 25, 26, 33, 34, 35, 45, 46, 47, 48, 49, 50, 51, 52, 53, 54, 56, 57, 58, 59, 60, 61, 62, 63, 64, 65	
Chemistry	15, 16, 17, 18, 19, 44	
Earth Science	13, 14, 15, 16, 20, 21, 36, 37, 38, 39, 40, 41, 55, 66	
Physics	6, 7, 8, 9, 10, 27, 28, 29, 30, 31, 32, 42, 43	
TEST 4. INTERPRETING LITERATURE AND THE ARTS	45	
Popular Literature	9, 10, 11, 12, 13, 14, 15, 16, 17, 18, 19, 20, 21, 22, 23, 24, 25	
Classical Literature	1, 2, 3, 4, 5, 6, 7, 8, 29, 30, 31, 32, 33, 34, 35, 36, 37, 38, 39, 40, 41, 42, 43, 44, 45	
Commentary	26, 27, 28	
TEST 5. MATHEMATICS	56	
Measurement	8, 9, 15, 16, 24, 25, 30, 31, 38, 39, 43, 44, 48, 52	
Algebra	10, 11, 17, 18, 27, 32, 33, 40, 41, 45, 46, 49, 51, 54, 56	
Geometry	5, 6, 12, 13, 19, 28, 34, 42, 47, 50	
Numeration	7, 14, 20, 29	
Statistics	1, 2, 3, 4, 21, 22, 23, 26, 35, 36, 37, 53, 55	

EXPLANATORY ANSWERS FOR GED SAMPLE TEST I

TEST 1. WRITING—PART I

1. **(3)** *Exposure to some. Sum* refers to a quantity or number; it's a noun. Some refers to an unspecified number or part; it's an adjective.

2. **(5)** No correction is necessary.

3. **(3)** Change *truely* to *truly.*

4. **(1)** *do damage*. Agents acting alone or in combination do damage. This is the only choice that leads to a logical sentence.

5. **(4)** *For example, studies have shown that breathing.* The original sentence lacks a verb following the subject *studies.*

6. **(1)** Change *These* to *The. Risk* is singular; these is plural.

7. **(4)** Change *Carcinogen* to *carcinogen.* Carcinogen is not a proper name and it should not be capitalized.

8. **(3)** Change the spelling of *meassures* to *measures.*

9. **(4)** *Can take.* Clues in the paragraph, especially in sentence 10, indicate the tense to be used.

10. **(2)** *ought*. Workplace health and safety rules ought to be known and followed.

11. **(5)** *can cause changes.* Entire passage is in present tense.

12. **(5)** No correction is necessary.

13. **(2)** Change *abused* to *abuse. Abused* is the past tense of a verb; abuse is a noun.

14. **(2)** *which can cause.* This is a case of incorrect pronoun reference: *who* refers to a person; *which* refers to a thing.

15. **(1)** *this.* The sentence would read: With antipsychotic drugs this can be particularly serious, since these drugs can cause further liver damage.

16. **(5)** No correction is necessary.

17. **(2)** change *include* to *includes. Mixture,* a singular subject, requires a singular verb *(includes).*

18. **(1)** change *whom* to *who. Who* is needed as the subject of the verb *has developed.*

19. **(4)** *This can lead to.* Clues may be found by looking at the verb tense in other sentences of the paragraph.

20. **(3)** change *throughly* to *thoroughly.*

21. **(2)** change *effects* to *affects. Effect* (noun) means an influence; as a verb it means to bring about. *Affect* (verb) means to influence.

22. **(2)** change *were* to *are.* The verb tense must agree with the subject as well as with the sense of the paragraph.

23. **(4)** *waves. They.* A period is needed to correct the original run-on sentence.

24. **(5)** No correction is necessary.

25. **(4)** *the waves. Waves* is the subject of the sentence; it should be placed after the phrase for correct sentence structure and clarity.

26. **(2)** *cooking to begin just.* Infinitive is required here.

27. **(2)** *full cooking.* This is the only choice which maintains sense and clarity. As the heat starts to spread full cooking is achieved.

28. **(3)** *food without overcooking. Unless* as a connector has the meaning except, or except for. *Without* is a better word choice for this sentence.

29. **(5)** Change the spelling of *througout* to *throughout.*

30. **(3)** Change *they're* to *their*. The two words are homonyms. *They're* is a contraction for they are; this sentence calls for the possessive *their.*

31. **(4)** *with responsibility, blatantly testing.* Commas have been overused here and they obscure the meaning of the sentence.

32. **(2)** Change *understood* to *understand.* The two verbs should be parallel in form and tense: maintain/understand.

33. **(2)** *It is easy to understand.* Comma does not add sense or clarity to sentence.

34. **(1)** *becomes appreciative, affectionate.* Spelling is correct. No correction is necessary.

35. **(4)** change *irritated* to *irritating.* As given, the meaning of the sentence is ambiguous. The behavior of the parents was not being irritated; it was Mom and Dad who were irritating the kids!

36. **(3)** change *bring* to *brings.* Subject and verb must be in agreement.

37. **(4)** change *been* to *be. Be* is the proper verb form.

38. **(2)** *overreact to teenage.* Proper coordination and clarity are provided by the use of *to.*

39. **(2)** *Adolescence is.* The paragraph is written in the present tense.

40. **(1)** change *developed* to *develops.* Paragraph is written in present tense.

41. **(2)** *can result.* Life-threatening physical and mental determination can result from heat loss which causes the body temperature to fall below the normal 98.6°F.

42. **(5)** No correction is necessary. Commas are used correctly.

43. **(4)** *in winter. Although older.* The original run-on sentence needs to be divided.

44. **(1)** *Although most people.* No correction is necessary.

45. **(5)** *temperatures do not have to fall.* This choice changes 8 from a sentence fragment to a complete and understandable sentence that makes sense in the context of the paragraph.

46. **(1)** replace *Dressed* with *Dressing.* For parallel sentence structure, use *dressing* and *sleeping.*

47. **(4)** replace *used* with *uses.* Sequence of tenses in the sentence; food cannot provide the body with something the body has already used.

48. **(2)** *fact of life. The days.* This choice corrects a run-on sentence.

49. **(4)** Change *gave* to *give.* Sense of the sentence requires *give* for the proper sequence of tenses.

50. **(3)** Change *to making* to *make.* Parallel sentence structure: to be more conscious/to make a commitment.

51. **(2)** Change *all ready* to *already. All ready* means everybody or everything ready; *already* means previously.

52. **(5)** *United States Department of Energy.* This is the only choice that is properly capitalized.

53. **(2)** Change *makes* to *make.* The correct verb form is each *can make.*

54. **(5)** *We can look for.* The original sentence makes no sense in the context of the paragraph which is written in present tense.

55. **(3)** Change *conserved* to *conserve.* As written, the sentence lacks clarity; if we are in the process of conserving today, the present tense should be used in the sentence.

TEST 1. WRITING—PART II

SAMPLE ESSAY RESPONSE

There are two main reasons why people take the time to cut out coupons and mail in refund offers. First, they can save a lot of money. Second, people like to try new products, especially when they cost less. Using coupons can save people money.

The main reason why people use coupons and refund offers is that they can save money in the supermarket. The savings are best on name-brand items. When bought with coupons, a cart full of name-brand frozen vegetables, cereal, and juices costs less than a cart full of store brands. Using coupons on name-brand foods brings their cost below store brands. Some supermarkets double coupons, which saves even more. People also save money with refund offers. There are often refund offers on pet foods and cereals. Some refunds offer free items, too, such as t-shirts, hats, and toys, another form of savings. Coupons and refunds are a good way of saving money at the food store.

Manufacturers offer coupons and refunds to make people buy their products. People enjoy trying new things, especially when they can save money at the same time. There are often coupons that save money on new snack foods, such as cookies and granola bars. Coupons encourage people to try frozen dinners. Refund offers make new shampoos and toothpastes less expensive. People like trying new things. Coupons and refunds save money on these items.

Over 85% of Americans use coupons and refund offers, adding up to big savings at the checkout counter. Coupons also give people a chance to sample new products for less money. That's why so many people redeem them.

TEST 2. SOCIAL STUDIES

1. **(2)** The last sentence of the article describes the farms as "rundown." Thus, they offer only the barest subsistence to their workers. Because they were worse off than the mill workers, poor farmers left their land to work in the mills, hoping to do better.

2. **(5)** The answer can be found in the third sentence: "whites . . . supplied the bulk of the labor for the textile mills and such others as required skilled operators, while a preponderance of blacks did the harder work of the mines." Further, we can infer that white adults, rather than children (2), would have supplied the main part of the work force.

3. **(1)** People were employed regardless of their educational level. We know that (2) is false because blacks "did the harder work of the mines." (3) is false, as shown in such sentences as "Wages were low, at first far lower than wages paid in the Northern mills." (4) is false, for conditions were static. (5) is false because the article specifically says the South failed to attract immigrants.

4. **(3)** In the mills, whole families could work for money. Although their wages were usually low, since the entire family was involved, they could make more than they could on the farms.

5. **(3)** Since the article indicates all able-bodied people worked, we can infer that it was not economically practical to employ greater numbers of children.

6. **(5)** The only conclusion that can be drawn from the information given on the map is that Afghanistan has no access to the sea.

7. **(3)** Based on the fact that there is a wide variety of different languages and only 10% of the people are literate, it follows that Afghanistan is agriculturally, not technologically, based.

8. **(2)** We know from the map that choices (1) and (3) cannot be true, for Pakistan blocks any access to the sea. We cannot determine (4) and (5) from the map. Therefore, based on its proximity to Russia, we can conclude that it is not unlikely Russia seeks to annex Afghanistan.

9. **(2)** misrepresentation. The company exaggerates the strength of its socks.

10. **(1)** meaningless claim. Cleer is guaranteed to last 40% longer than what?

11. **(3)** bait and switch. The seller has no intention of selling the advertisied product. Instead, the Simmons' are offered a higher priced model.

12. **(5)** fictitious pricing. Television City overstated the list price to convince the buyer that the advertised price represents a savings.

13. **(1)** meaningless claim. While the ad may seem to be an example of misrepresentation, there are no real facts here to be exaggerated. The first sentence in particular makes no sense. Why would CHATTERING TEDDY BEARS sold by *competitive companies* outsell other toys? This would make sense only if the CHATTERING TEDDY BEARS *sold by the company that is advertising* outsold other toys. Thus, we have what appears to be useful information which upon closer examination turns out to be meaningless.

14. **(4)** referral sales scheme. The purchaser is offered $50 to give the pool builder names of prospective buyers. Here, they must actually buy pools for the prospective buyer to collect his money.

15. **(4)** France was eliminated as a power, thus vanishing from the map. (1) makes no sense; if France defeated England, England should vanish from the map. (2) is the same as (1); if Spain diverted her forces, she should have lost control of her land in America and thus vanished from the map. (3) and (5) have nothing to do with the question.

16. **(5)** British Columbia, in the extreme northwest portion of the map, has no shading, indicating it is not controlled by any country listed here.

17. **(1)** Louisiana is in the southern part of the area controlled by France.

18. **(3)** According to the map, the Mississippi River divides the land controlled by Spain from the land controlled by England. We can assume, therefore, they share control of the river.

19. **(5)** People recognize that cards make purchases, especially unplanned ones, easier. In addition, cards are relatively safe. (1) and (2) are not true. (3) is true, but not sufficient reason to explain credit cards' enormous popularity. (4) is not true. It is against the law to send unsolicited cards to people.

20. **(2)** The sarcasm of "images of idyllic America" and "impulses to send U.S. forces to . . . " implies both stupidity and belligerence.

21. **(4)** On television, "now this" is a phrase used to move to a commercial during a broadcast.

22. **(3)** "5¢ Cokes," "Burma Shave signs," and "hardworking white people" are all images from the 1950s. (1) can be omitted, because the 1930s was the time of the Great Depression and the images would be of hardship. There is nothing to indicate that (2) or (4) is true. (5) makes no sense; why would anyone regret an "idyllic" life?

23. **(1)** The cartoonist sees sending troops into the countries he mentioned as an example of "human aggression."

24. **(5)** He is making fun of the tone and style of television.

25. **(5)** The newspapers were concerned that people would find this criticism of their president offensive.

26. **(2)** The author states that stress is necessary for daily living.

27. **(4)** As stated in sentence 4: "Without stress life would be dull and unexciting."

28. **(2)** Some people, such as that busy executive, work well under what others might consider excessive stress.

29. **(3)** In the last line of the first paragraph, the author states that stress can work for you.

30. **(3)** The last line of the paragraph indicates that tetracycline can be bought in Albany for $1.99, the lowest price mentioned.

31. **(3)** No single indicated source has enough information. Therefore, several calls are probably necessary to get a complete picture. This may be inferred from the way the Consumer Protection Board did it.

32. **(1)** Because the highest prices for drugs are in New York City, it can be inferred that prices for other things are also very high.

33. **(1)** The paragraph implies that the only way to get a bargain is to search for it.

34. **(4)** Denver is the headquarters for Region VIII, which includes Utah, where Salt Lake City is located.

35. **(4)** New York City is headquarters for Region II, which includes Puerto Rico.

36. **(3)** Region VII includes Iowa, Missouri, Kansas, and Nebraska.

37. **(2)** It has a great many people in need of government services.

38. **(5)** The next-to-last column shows the actual number of people in rural communities for each census year. The number continued to grow until 1940, then decreased in the period 1940–1970.

39. **(4)** The fourth column shows the total percentage of United States population living in urban areas for each census year. By 1940, more than 50% of the United States population was living in urban areas. (1) Although the actual percentage of people living in rural areas decreased relative to the total population, 36 million people lived in rural areas in 1880, and 54 million in 1970. (2) The percentage of people living in rural areas dropped from 55% in 1910, to 44% in 1940, and to 27% in 1970. (3) By reading the third column, it can be seen that the number of people living in urban areas increased during the 19th century. (5) The fifth column shows that the number of people living in rural areas increased from 1880 until 1940, then decreased between 1940 and 1970.

40. **(2)** The availability of factory and other industrial jobs in urban areas attracted farm workers as well as immigrants. (1) Farm production had to increase to meet the needs of a growing urban population. Farm machinery freed rural workers for industrial employment. (3) Immigration quotas were first imposed in the 1920's. (4) Although transportation improved, this was not the most significant factor in urban development. (5) A decreasing birth rate would not explain urban growth.

41. **(4)** The fourth column shows that the greatest percent of change in population was an increase of 63.8% for Nevada.

42. **(3)** Comparing the figures in columns two and three shows that the greatest increase in total population occurred in California, which grew from nearly 20 million in 1970 to over 23.6 million in 1980.

43. **(2)** The greatest growth in population was in the South and the West, sometimes referred to as the Sun Belt.

44. **(2)** According to the passage, the Rorschach test is a psychological test which can provide a great deal of information about a person but which lacks reliability.

45. **(3)** The next-to-last sentence states that highly excitable subjects often show intense response to color.

46. **(5)** In one hour the Rorschach test can provide data that would take weeks to reveal through other methods.

47. **(4)** As stated in the first paragraph, the Italian criminologist believed that criminals were ". . . a subspecies having distinct physical and mental characteristics."

48. **(5)** Aschaffenberg believed that habitual offenders were slender and had slight muscular development.

49. **(3)** Criminology began in the nineteenth century and attempts to find common criminal characteristics have been going on since that time.

50. **(5)** The Act prohibits discrimination based upon sex.

51. **(4)** The Act covers all of the workers listed.

52. **(3)** It is not discriminatory to pay more to a worker who produces more. (See paragraph 1, sentence 3.)

53. **(5)** "Wages" include regular salary, overtime, fringe benefits, and work clothes as stated in paragraph 4.

54. **(1)** Workers whose jobs require the same skill, effort, and responsibility must receive the same pay, as stated in the second sentence of paragraph 1.

55. **(3)** According to the Supreme Court ruling mentioned in the last sentence, jobs of men and women need not be identical, only "substantially equal," to qualify for equal pay.

56. **(4)** The purpose of the act was to prevent pay discrimination because of sex.

57. **(2)** The highest point of the graph is 1979.

58. **(4)** Use your pencil or the edge of a piece of paper to see where the dot for 1984 meets the scale for number of depositors. There were approximately 25,000 depositors in 1984.

59. **(4)** The number of depositors has risen and fallen over the period shown, so (4) is false.

60. **(1)** The line representing births takes a dip in the 1970's with only a slight rise at the end of the decade. (2), (3), (4), and (5) are unsupported. The immigration rate seems to have increased; there is no discernible increase or decrease overall during the period 1980–1985. The highest number of births appear in the earliest years shown on the chart, but there is no indication of an actual rate of births/thousand. The number of deaths shows a slight increase through the period.

61. **(4)** About 75% of the net increase is represented as a natural increase on the chart; remaining 25% is represented as net immigration.

62. **(2)** The market was saturated and too many cars were available.

63. **(5)** Manufacturing poor-quality cars created planned obsolescence.

64. **(1)** Manufacturers would not be able to sell as many cars if the ones they made lasted a very long time.

TEST 3. SCIENCE

1. **(2)** The cerebellum controls balance which is necessary for flight.

2. **(4)** Your cerebrum allows you to think.

3. **(4)** The knee jerk reflex is controlled by the spinal cord.

4. **(4)** The medulla controls heart rate and respiration.

5. **(2)** A human has a more highly developed cerebrum.

6. **(5)** The first sentence refers to an "accident at the nuclear generating plant." We can assume radioactive material was released. (4) is incorrect, for we have no way of knowing from the passage what caused the accident. (1) is too extreme.

7. **(3)** The study shows only that honey produced in the Three Mile Island vicinity was not contaminated by radioactivity.

8. **(3)** As stated in the passage, "One possible explanation is that the radioactive dust . . . was washed into the ground by rain."

9. **(2)** Since bees travel, we can assume the radioactive dust did not contaminate a wide area. Choice (1) is wrong because there is nothing in the paragraph to support it. Nuclear energy was harnessed in the 1940's. There is nothing to support choice (4); Cornell is located in New York.

10. **(1)** Like honey, the composition of milk is affected by what the cow eats. Choice (3) is incorrect because cheese has a very long shelf life and might not have been affected by the radioactivity.

11. **(3)** Massachusetts has the highest number in all five categories.

12. **(3)** Massachusetts lost the largest number of homes (301), followed by Maine with 22 lost.

13. **(3)** Total 73 (Massachusetts) and 26 (Rhode Island) to find this answer.

14. **(5)** Actuaries compile tables and compute statistical information. (4) Podiatrists treat ailments of the feet.

15. **(4)** Magnesium (Mg) and calcium (Ca) are both in Group IIA. Elements in the same group have similar chemical properties.

16. **(3)** Cobalt has an atomic number of 27 which means it has 27 electrons and 27 protons. This is more electrons than any other element listed.

17. **(1)** The elements in Group IA, the metals, have only one electron in their outermost shells. Therefore, they are the most reactive.

18. **(2)** The noble gases all belong to Group VIIIA. (The group number tells that there are 8 electrons in the outermost shell.)

19. **(2)** The elements are arranged in order of mass, going from the lightest, hydrogen (H), to the heaviest natural element, uranium (U).

20. **(4)** As the moon changes its position in its orbit around the earth, different amounts of the illuminated side are visible from the earth.

21. **(3)** During a lunar eclipse the shadow of the earth is cast upon the moon.

22. **(1)** Bacteria reproduce by a process called binary fission. One cell splits into two cells, then each of the two cells divides to form four cells . . . and so on.

23. **(3)** Start with 1; 1/2 hour later there are 2; 1 hour later there are 4; then 8, 16, 32, 64, 128, then 256 at the end of 4 hours.

24. **(2)** The number of bacteria is increasing rapidly, as indicated by the sharply rising line on the graph.

25. **(5)** The bacteria, in a closed container, have no more room in which to live and are being poisoned by their own waste products.

26. **(4)** The bacteria flourished in a growth medium (food). In the same way, we can infer that incorrectly stored food provides a breeding ground for bacteria. While (5) is true, it cannot be inferred from this experiment.

27. **(4)** The voltage across each branch of a parallel circuit is the same. Since the source supplies 40 volts, the potential difference, voltage through R_1 is also 40 volts.

28. **(4)** The power is calculated by $p = V \times I = 40(\text{volts}) \times 6(\text{amp})$; $p = 240$ watts.

29. **(2)** The greater the resistance in R_1, the more current will be diverted to R_2.

30. **(3)** The uneven saturation of energy would probably result in unevenly cooked food.

31. **(1)** Electrical power in the home is measured in watts or kilowatts. As the degree is a measure of heat energy, the watt is a measure of electrical energy.

32. **(3)** The magnetron within the microwave oven generates the energy.

33. **(3)** To have type B blood, John must have received at least one I^B gene with no I^A gene.

34. **(3)** For type O blood, Martha had to receive a recessive gene (i) from each parent.

35. **(4)** To have type AB blood, a child must receive an I^A gene from one parent and an I^B gene from the other parent.

36. **(1)** According to the graph, the pH of acid rain is between 2 and 5.6. The pH of normal rain is indicated as 5.6. Therefore, the best definition of acid rain is precipitation having a pH less than normal rain.

37. **(2)** The pH of normal rain is approximately 5.6 on the scale. This is best described as slightly acidic.

38. **(5)** The two graphs indicate the contents of the earth's crust. They do not indicate how these materials are arranged, choice (1), nor the advantage of certain types of rocks, choice (2).

39. **(3)** Graph 1 shows that most of the earth's crust is composed of nonsedimentary rocks. According to this graph, sedimentary rocks make up 5% of the total crust.

40. **(1)** All rocks are composed of minerals.

41. **(4)** Graph 1 shows that sedimentary rocks make up a very small percentage of the total volume of the earth's crust. Graph 2 suggests that there is a lot of sedimentary rock exposed at the earth's surface. Using both graphs, it may be inferred that there is very little sedimentary rock, but that much of what is present is at the earth's surface.

42. **(5)** The temperature of the water must be raised from 20°C to 100°C or 80 Centigrade degrees. It takes one calorie to raise one gram of water one Centigrade degree. It must take *more* calories to raise *200* grams of water, *80* Centigrade degrees. $200 \times 80 = 16{,}000$ calories.

43. **(4)** This problem is similar to the previous one with the unknown being the amount of water instead of the amount of energy. Therefore, X grams $\times(100-10)$ Centigrade degrees $=$ 180,000 calories. The result is 2000 grams.

44. **(4)** More products on the right side of an equation indicate a greater chance of reactants on the right. Therefore, the more sodium, the more salt is produced, and the more chlorine is used up.

45. **(3)** As indicated on the top of the graph, this is a measurement of the CO_2 produced from yeast cultured in sugar solutions.

46. **(5)** Select the curve for solution B, the solid line. Then, draw a vertical line upward from 30 minutes until it intersects the curve. Now, draw a horizontal line to the left until it intersects the scale for column of CO_2 liberated. This will be at 2.2 ml. "ml" stands for "milliliters."

47. **(2)** The curve for solution B (the solid line) shows that CO_2 was liberated after about five minutes, well before any of the other solutions showed CO_2 production.

48. **(4)** The curves for solution A and solution B intersect at a point before 20 minutes. At this point, 1.6 ml. of CO_2 was liberated by both solutions. This can be determined by drawing a line horizontally from the point of intersection to the scale at the left.

49. **(1)** At the end of 30 minutes, the most CO_2 was liberated from solution A. Draw a horizontal line from this point to the scale at the left. The volume of liberated CO_2 is 3.4 ml.

50. **(3)** Yeast is fermented to produce bread.

51. **(5)** Starfish have the ability to regrow lost arms. In this example, many of the cut pieces were able to grow into new starfish.

52. **(2)** Bread mold reproduces by sporing. Each tiny mold is able to produce thousands of tiny spores.

53. **(4)** Potatoes reproduce by tubers. Each stem with a bud will grow into a potato plant.

54. **(3)** Grafting can produce seedless grapes, sturdy apple and orange trees, and in this case, a pear tree that bears different types of pears.

55. **(2)** On March 1, the discharge of the stream is 0.5 cubic meters per second. On May 1, the discharge has increased to 2.5 cubic meters per second. This represents a greater change in stream flow than occurred during any of the other periods listed.

56. **(5)** The passage states that body fat is burned "only by using more energy than is supplied by the food you eat."

57. **(2)** Scientists who studied the deaths of people on liquid protein diets found that "the dieters had died of irregular heart rhythms and cardiac arrest."

58. **(5)** While a diet of 600 calories a day may not be healthy, a person on such a diet will lose weight fairly rapidly.

59. **(3)** The second sentence indicates that a basic, safe diet consists of 1000 to 1200 calories per day.

60. **(2)** This experiment measures the rate at which egg white dissolves in four different solutions.

61. **(4)** The test tubes must be kept at the same temperature for the experiment to be valid. Choice (2) is incorrect, for it would not matter who put the material into the tubes. Choice (3) is incorrect, as the experiment would be valid as long as time charts were kept. Choice (5) is incorrect, as it would not matter if the tubes were in different positions in the lab.

62. **(3)** The white of an egg is composed of albumen, which is a protein. Pepsin is an enzyme which digests proteins.

63. **(2)** Gastric juice is formed in the stomach. It contains the enzymes pepsin and rennin, hydrochloric acid, and water. Pepsin, in the presence of hydrochloric acid, digests proteins, of which egg white is an example.

64. **(5)** Digestion is the breaking down of food in the body. Egg white, a food, is being broken down in this experiment by enzymes found in the stomach.

65. **(4)** Milk and milk products such as cheese and yogurt (unless made from skim or low-fat milk) are high in saturated fat and cholesterol.

66. **(3)** In the diagram, the level of mercury is between 1028 mb and 1032 mb. Since there are four divisions between these two values, each marking represents an increase of one millibar. The mercury is halfway between 1029 mb and 1030 mb, making its value 1029.5 mb.

TEST 4. INTERPRETING LITERATURE AND THE ARTS

1. **(1)** There is anger here (line 3) and hope, "Tomorrow/I'll be at the table," (lines 8 and 9).

2. **(4)** The "darker brother" symbolizes black America.

3. **(2)** The speaker is saying that he, too, praises America, even though he feels he has been denied his proper place in American life.

4. **(5)** The phrase is an allusion, a reference, to Walt Whitman's poem "I Hear America Singing." The other choices do not fit. Personification (1) is giving human qualities to nonliving things. Rhyme, (2), is incorrect, because two sentences are necessary for rhyme, and (3), an illusion, means mirage. (4), Metaphor, is a comparison, and there is nothing being compared here.

5. **(3)** In line 5, he calls himself "a slave of the theater." In the last sentence, he mentions coaching the English people "in the proper and becoming opinion." These two things point toward a position as a drama critic.

6. **(2)** The author states that he has been a slave of the theater for four years, since New Year 1895. Therefore, the selection was written in 1899, the last year of the nineteenth century. The last two sentences indicate that the essay was written in England.

7. **(3)** The tone of the entire passage clearly indicates that the author does not like his job. He feels "helpless . . . disabled . . . doomed." He regards the public for whom he writes as "stupid" and the theater as "unworthy."

8. **(4)** The key words, "Success! Success!" indicate that something has been attempted and completed. The fifth paragraph tells us that the "crimson hand which had once blazed" is now "barely perceptible," so we know that Aylmer has done something to try to remove it.

9. **(1)** The first sentence describes the birthmark as a "crimson hand."

10. **(3)** Again, the first sentence tells us the birthmark is beginning to fade. The fifth paragraph, however, informs us the mark never completely vanishes.

11. **(2)** In the seventh paragraph, Aylmer describes his wife as "perfect."

12. **(1)** By trying to perfect his wife, Aylmer destroyed her. Perfection cannot be achieved by man, the author is saying.

13. **(5)** The phrases "Mother of Exiles," "world-wide welcome," and "send these, the homeless . . . to me" tell us the poem is intended to welcome incoming refugees. It appears on the base of the Statue of Liberty in New York Harbor.

14. **(1)** America is a *new* colossus, symbolized by "a mighty woman with a torch," the Statue.

15. **(1)** This is a sonnet, a 14-line poem with a specific rhyme scheme.

16. **(2)** The phrase suggests that only poor people seek refuge. The idea that immigrants to America are wretched or unwanted in their own countries is certainly not always true.

17. **(5)** The tone is exalted, uplifting, ringing.

18. **(3)** The third sentence states that not even the wisest man can extort the secret of Nature and find out all her perfection. This means that nature is unknowable.

19. **(5)** The line means that Nature can never be unattractive. From the very first line Emerson says we should worship Nature because all her aspects inspire us. "The stars awaken a certain reverence," he begins.

20. **(4)** In lines 7–10, the author says that speed has been an essential element in our lives and leisurely reading has been impossible for most Americans. We are forced to grab "bits of reading" on the run. From this we can infer that the short story is popular because of its length.

21. **(5)** As stated in the first sentence, the development of the short story parallels the development of industrialism in America. Industrialization made speed an essential part of American life. There is no mention of choices (1), (2), or (4) and the author distinctly attributes the development of the short story to the need for speed, rather than the lack of culture.

22. **(2)** The entire selection conveys an attitude of regret, especially the last sentence in which the author calls the popular short story "no more substantial than sandwiches."

23. **(1)** The main idea of the passage is that we read as we often eat lunch: quickly, between other activities, "cafeteria style." In other words, reading is like a quick lunch. Choices (2), (3), and (5) are much too broad and choice (4) is too narrow to cover the ideas expressed in the passage.

24. **(3)** As stated in the second paragraph, the gods of the North were gloomy, while the gods of the South were joyous and sunny.

25. **(5)** As stated in paragraph three, the cow Audhumla licked the stones and thereby created the gods.

26. **(1)** According to paragraph four, out of Ymir's body came the heavens and the earth.

27. **(5)** Nat and Dag were the daughter and grandson of Nor. Odin took these two into heaven to rule the night and day.

28. **(4)** Since the North and South were so different, we can infer the myth was created to explain the differences between the two.

29. **(4)** The author uses short sentences, long sentences, and descriptive words such as "saltless" and "lumpy" to get the reader's attention. (1) is incorrect because we have no way of knowing whether or not this story is based on the author's own experience. (2) is wrong because most readers may not have had a childhood like Lewy's. The opening does not explain the advantages or disadvantages of Lewy's life (choice 3) or explain Lewy's behavior (choice 5).

30. **(2)** describes Lewy's life most effectively. The "faded silk tassel" indicates how his mother tried to bring some beauty into the home, but it has faded with the father's departure. "Cracks in the wall" describes their present poverty.

31. **(4)** The final paragraph indicates Lewy's love for his mother.

32. **(1)** The author admires Mrs. Clement for doing such a fine job raising her son despite her own sorrow at the breakup of her marriage (see paragraph 2). Even though she works long hours, she has managed to keep her son well-fed, clean, and happy.

33. **(4)** Despite all the media coverage, the DEA survey indicates "there has been a distortion of the public perception of the extent of crack use."

34. **(1)** The DEA, the Federal Drug Enforcement Administration, issued the report the author discusses.

35. **(5)** The author provides a series of examples to make his point, citing various television stations, newspapers, and magazines that have focused attention on crack.

36. **(2)** According to a quote from the June 16 issue of *Newsweek,* the crack epidemic is as dangerous as the plagues of medieval times.

37. **(3)** There is no mention of healing in this poem.

38. **(4)** The phrase "sneer of cold command," and the inscription on the base of the statue describe a proud king. The statue, destroyed by the passage of time, lies in an "ancient land." This tells us Ozymandias lived long ago.

39. **(3)** A "visage" is either a face or a head.

40. **(2)** The poem is a sonnet.

41. **(5)** The author is saying that no one should be haughty, for in the end we are all the same.

42. **(4)** The first paragraph describes how he "played catch with a broken watch."

43. **(2)** Binnie "sneers," and shows "savage anger" in Maud's apartment. She smiles at him "uncertainly," indicating that she is frightened of him.

44. **(3)** The North Shore people are best described as rich, as they have been able to afford a housemaid for ten years. Although they hug and kiss her, (4) is a poor choice, since their show of affection is solely designed to get her to work harder for them.

45. **(1)** "Pepper" is biting and sharp, best describing her anger at the North Shore people who employ her.

TEST 5. MATHEMATICS

1. **(4)** Look across the chart on the two baseball league lines. The first time that the American League overtook the attendance figures was in 1977 when the American League =19.6 million and National League = 19.1.

2. **(2)** The most popular sporting event in 1965 can be found by looking down the column for 1965. The largest attendance was 62.9 million, for horseracing.

3. **(3)**

   40.6 million—baseball, regular season

   10.9 million—basketball, NBA

   13.4 million—football, NFL

   64.9 million—Total

   $\% \text{ baseball} = \frac{40.6}{64.9} \times 100 = 62.56$
   $= 63\%$

4. **(5)** The chart, *Attendance at Sports Events,* does not mention any data on cash revenues but only on attendance at events. Therefore, choice (5) is the correct choice.

5. **(2)** From the Formula Page, P = 21 + 2w

   Each width = 48 ft or $\frac{48}{3}$ = 16 yd

   Substituting in the formula

   $$68 = 21 + 2(16)$$
   $$68 = 21 + 32$$
   $$68 - 32 = 11$$
   $$36 = 21$$
   $$18 = 1$$

6. **(4)** The perimeter is twice the width plus twice the length, or (2 × 46) + (2 × 34) = 160 feet. If the cost is \$9.00 per yard, it would be $\frac{9}{3}$ or \$3.00 per foot (1 yard is 3 feet). The total cost is 160 ft × 3 \$/ft = \$480.

7. **(2)** Choices (1), (3), (4), and (5) are all examples of the commutative and distributive properties. The quantity in choice (2) is not equal to 75(32 +88).

8. **(3)** 8 ft 7 in

$$\begin{array}{r} 8 \text{ ft } 7 \text{ in} \\ \times \quad 8 \\ \hline 64 \text{ ft } 56 \text{ in} \end{array} = 68 \text{ ft } 8 \text{ in (since 56 in = 4 ft 8 in)}$$

$$8 \text{ in} = \tfrac{8}{12} \text{ ft} = \tfrac{2}{3} \text{ ft}$$

$$68 \text{ ft } 8 \text{ in} = 68\tfrac{2}{3} \text{ ft}$$

9. **(5)** 6 feet = 6 × 12 = 72 inches
   72 ÷ 40 = $1\frac{4}{5}$ inches

10. **(2)** To determine the total cost of the order calculate the amount paid for *all* the books:

$$\begin{array}{rr} 20 \times 10.77 = & 215.40 \\ 10 \times 12.60 = & 126.00 \\ 15 \times \ \ 7.16 = & 107.40 \\ 18 \times 12.80 = & \underline{230.40} \\ \text{Total} & \$679.20 \\ \text{Deduct the amount of the credit} & \underline{-147.60} \\ & \$531.60 \end{array}$$

11. **(1)** To answer this question you need to calculate the difference between the price paid for each book and the price at which each book was sold, then total the increase for all the books sold. Remember, only one copy of *Puff Pastry* was sold. Your worksheet will look like this:

$$\begin{array}{rr} 20 \times (17.95 - 10.77) = (7.18 \times 20) = & 143.60 \\ 1 \times (21.00 - 12.60) = (8.40 \times \ \ 1) = & 8.40 \\ 15 \times \ \ (8.95 - \ \ 7.16) = (1.79 \times 15) = & 26.85 \\ 18 \times (16.00 - 12.80) = (3.20 \times 18) = & \underline{57.60} \\ & \$236.45 \end{array}$$

12. **(3)** The umbrella would be the hypotenuse of a right triangle whose legs are the dimensions of the trunk. According to the Pythagorean Theorem, in any right triangle the square of the hypotenuse equals the sum of the squares of the legs. Therefore, the sum of the dimensions squared must at least equal the length of the umbrella squared: $(50)^2 = 2500$.

    The only set of dimensions that fills this condition is (3):

$$\begin{aligned} (42)^2 + (36)^2 &= 1764 + 1296 \\ &= 3060 \end{aligned}$$

    Answer: 42 inches, 36 inches

13. **(1)** The new road is the hypotenuse of a right triangle whose legs are the old road.

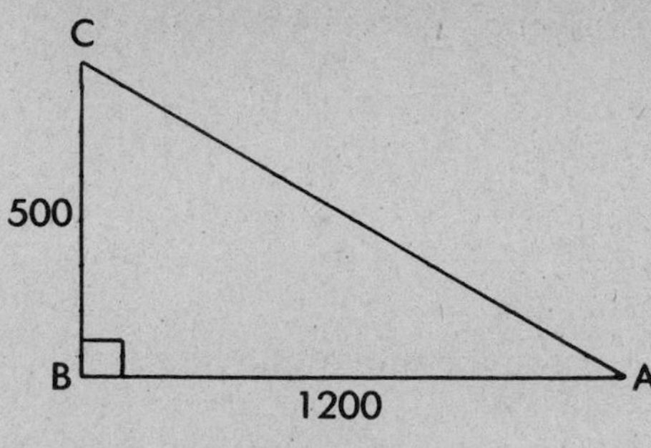

$$\begin{aligned}(AC)^2 &= 500^2 + 1200^2\\ &= 250000 + 1440000\\ &= 1690000\\ AC &= \sqrt{1690000}\\ &= \sqrt{169} \cdot \sqrt{10000}\\ &= 13 \cdot 100\\ &= 1300\end{aligned}$$

If you remember the 5-12-13 right triangle, you can see right away that the new road will be 1300 feet.

$$\begin{aligned}\text{Old road} &= 500 \text{ ft} + 1200 \text{ ft}\\ &= 1700 \text{ ft}\\ \text{New road} &= 1300 \text{ ft}\\ \text{Difference} &= 400 \text{ ft}\end{aligned}$$

14. **(1)** $.25\% = .0025$

$$= \frac{25}{10000}$$
$$= \frac{1}{400}$$

15. **(4)** Find the number of units in 6 gross:

$$\begin{aligned}1 \text{ gross} &= 144 \text{ units}\\ 6 \text{ gross} &= 6 \times 144 \text{ units}\\ &= 864 \text{ units}\end{aligned}$$

Divide units by rate of use:

$$864 \div 24 = 36 \text{ weeks}$$

16. **(1)**

$$\begin{array}{rcr} 9 \text{ ft } 6 \text{ in} & = & 8 \text{ ft } 18 \text{ in}\\ \underline{-7 \text{ ft } 9 \text{ in}} & = & \underline{-7 \text{ ft } \;\; 9 \text{ in}}\\ & & 1 \text{ ft } \;\; 9 \text{ in}\end{array}$$

17. **(3)** Let n = the son's age. Then 3n = the father's age. The difference of the numbers is 30.

$$3n - n = 30$$
$$\frac{2n}{2} = \frac{30}{2}$$
$$n = 15$$

18. **(2)** The perimeter is equal to the sum of the sides.

$$a + 5 + 4a - 1 + 2a + 4 + 3a - 3 + 2a = 41$$
$$12a + 5 = 41 \quad \text{Combine like terms.}$$
$$\underline{\quad -5 \quad -5}$$
$$\frac{12a}{12} = \frac{36}{12}$$
$$a = 3$$

The sides are:

$$a + 5 = 3 + 5 = 8$$
$$4a - 1 = 4 \cdot 3 - 1 = 11$$
$$2a + 4 = 2 \cdot 3 + 4 = 10$$
$$3a - 3 = 3 \cdot 3 - 3 = 6$$
$$2a = 2 \cdot 3 = 6$$

The longest side is 11.

19. **(5)** Since $6^2 + 8^2 = 10^2$, or $36 + 64 = 100$, the triangle is a right triangle. Its area is $\frac{1}{2} \times 6 \times 8 = 24$ sq. in. (area of a triangle $= \frac{1}{2} \cdot b \cdot h$). Therefore, the area of the rectangle is also 24 square inches. If the width of the rectangle is 3 inches, the length is $24 \div 3 = 8$ inches. Then, the perimeter of the rectangle is $2(3 + 8) = 2 \times 11 = 22$ inches.

20. **(4)** 1 kilogram = 1000 grams
1000/.2 = 5000 pills

21. **(2)** The incidence of murder increased from 15 in 1977 to 20 in 1978 to 25 in 1979.

22. **(5)** The incidence of burglary in 1977 was 400; in 1978 it was 350; and in 1979 it was 450. The increase from 1978 to 1979 was 100. An increase of 100 from 1979 gives 550 in 1980.
The average of 400, 350, 450, and 550 is

$$\frac{400 + 350 + 450 + 550}{4} = \frac{1750}{4}$$
$$= 437.5 \text{ which is closest to } 440.$$

23. **(2)** The incidence of grand larceny auto went from 250 in 1978 to 275 in 1979, an increase of 25.
    The percent increase is

$$\frac{25}{250} = .10 = 10\%$$

24. **(4)**

$$\begin{array}{rcr} 5 \text{ hours } 13 \text{ minutes} & = & 4 \text{ hours } 73 \text{ minutes} \\ -\underline{3 \text{ hours } 49 \text{ minutes}} & = & -\underline{3 \text{ hours } 49 \text{ minutes}} \\ & & 1 \text{ hour } \ 24 \text{ minutes} \end{array}$$

25. **(4)**

$$\begin{array}{r} 8 \text{ feet} \quad 10 \text{ inches} + \frac{2}{4} \text{ inches} = 8 \text{ ft } 10\tfrac{1}{2} \text{ in} \\ 4\overline{)35 \text{ feet} \quad 6 \text{ inches}} \\ \underline{32 \text{ feet}} \\ 3 \text{ feet} = \underline{36 \text{ inches}} \\ 42 \text{ inches} \\ \underline{40 \text{ inches}} \\ 2 \text{ inches} \end{array}$$

26. **(3)** In order to determine Mr. and Mrs. Symonds' chance of winning we need to know the total number of tickets sold and the number of tickets bought by Mr. and Mrs. Symonds.

$$\frac{\text{no. of tickets bought}}{\text{total number sold}} = \frac{(12 + 3)}{500} = \frac{15}{500} = \frac{3}{100}$$

27. **(5)** Let 2x, 3x, and 4x represent the shares of the inheritance. The total estate was $22,500.

$$2x + 3x + 4x = 22500$$

$$\frac{9x}{9} = \frac{22500}{9}$$

$$x = 2500$$

$$2x = 2 \cdot 2500 = 5000$$

$$3x = 3 \cdot 2500 = 7500$$

$$4x = 4 \cdot 2500 = 10{,}000$$

The smallest inheritance was 2x, or $5000.

28. **(3)** ∡ B and ∡ 1 are corresponding angles formed by the parallel lines AB and DE and the transversal BC. Therefore, ∡ 1 = ∡ B = 60°.

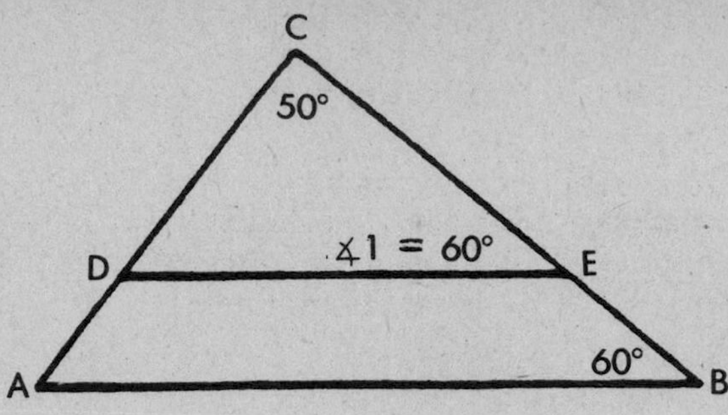

The sum of the angles of a triangle is 180°

$$\begin{aligned} \measuredangle A + \measuredangle B + \measuredangle C &= 180^\circ \\ \measuredangle A + 60^\circ + 50^\circ &= 180^\circ \\ \measuredangle A + 110^\circ &= 180^\circ \\ -110^\circ \quad & \quad -110^\circ \\ \hline \measuredangle A \quad &= 70^\circ \end{aligned}$$

29. **(3)** 1 pound = 16 ounces
(16)(28) = 448 (approximately 450 grams)

30. **(1)** 1 yd = 36 in
126 ÷ 36 = 3.5

31. **(4)** 1 gal = 4 qt = 8 pt
Therefore, 1 pt = 231 cubic inches ÷ 8
= 28.875 cubic inches
3 pts = 3 × 28.875 cubic inches
= 86.625 cubic inches (closest to 84)

32. **(5)** His selling price will be (100% + 20%) of his cost price.
120% of \$550 = 1.20(\$550)
= \$660

33. **(2)** The amount earned is proportional to the number of hours worked.
Let m = unknown pay

$8m = 28 \times 50$ The product of the means is equal to the product of the extremes.

$$\frac{8m}{8} = \frac{1400}{8}$$

$$m = 175$$

34. **(2)** Convert the dimensions of the bin to inches:

4 feet = 48 inches
3 feet = 36 inches
2 feet = 24 inches

Volume of bin = 48 × 36 × 24 cubic inches
= 41,472 cubic inches

Volume of
each brick= 8 × 4 × 2 cubic inches
=64 cubic inches

41472 ÷ 64 =648 bricks

35. **(5)** There are 52 cards in a deck, of which 13 are clubs. The probability of picking a club is $\frac{13}{52} = \frac{1}{4}$.

36. **(3)** For both A and B, the greatest increase in the cumulative totals occurred from the end of Tuesday until the end of Wednesday. Therefore, the largest number of applications was filed on Wednesday.

37. **(4)** By the end of Tuesday, A had filed 100 applications and B had filed 150, for a total of 250. This left 750 of the original 1000 applications.

$$\frac{750}{1000} = .75 = 75\%$$

38. **(4)** Add the items for each of the mechanics:

5 hr 16 min
3 hr 49 min
25 min
8 hr 90 min = 9 hr 30 min

39. **(3)** The charge for labor on a domestic car is $25 per hour.

$$\$25 \times 9\tfrac{1}{2} = \$237.50$$

Add the cost of parts; $237.50 + $84.25 = $321.75

40. **(2)** The selling price after the 15% discount is 85% of list.

selling price = .85(500)
= $425

The selling price after the additional 2% discount is 98% of $425.

new selling price = .98(425)
= $416.50

The original price was $500. Mrs. Smith buys at $416.50. She saves
$500 − $416.50 = $83.50

41. **(2)** The old dimensions and the new dimensions are in proportion. Let w = new width.

$$\frac{\text{new width}}{\text{old width}} = \frac{\text{new length}}{\text{old length}}$$

$$\frac{w}{8} = \frac{25}{10}$$

$$10w = 200$$

$$w = 20$$

42. **(4)** The trench contains

$$2 \text{ yd} \times 5 \text{ yd} \times 4 \text{ yd} = 40 \text{ cubic yards}$$

$$40 \times \$2.12 = \$84.80$$

43. **(5)** 1 foot = 12 inches

$1\frac{1}{2}$ feet = $1\frac{1}{2} \times 12$ inches = 18 inches

1 inch = 2.54 cm

Therefore,

18 inches = 18×2.54 cm

= 45.72 cm

44. **(3)** 1 micromillimeter = .000001 mm

17 micromillimeters = $17 \times .000001$ mm

= .000017 mm

45. **(2)** Let s = needed sales. 12% of sales will be \$300.

$$\frac{.12s}{.12} = \frac{\$300}{.12}$$

Divide by .12, or first multiply by 100 to clear the decimal, then divide by 12.

s= \$2500

46. **(3)** Let h = the number of hours needed by Mrs. Taylor. Mr. Taylor started two hours earlier; therefore, he travels h + 2 hours. Mrs. Taylor's distance is 55h. Mr. Taylor's distance is 45(h +2). When Mrs. Taylor catches up with Mr. Taylor, they will have traveled equal distances.

$$\begin{aligned} 55h &= 45(h + 2) \\ 55h &= 45h + 90 \\ -45h &= -45h \\ \hline 10h &= 90 \\ h &= 9 \end{aligned}$$

47. **(3)** If the area of the square is 121 square inches, each side is $\sqrt{121} = 11$ inches and the perimeter is $4 \times 11 = 44$ inches. The perimeter of the rectangle is then 44 inches. If the two lengths are each 13 inches, their total is 26 inches. $44 - 26 = 18$ inches remain for the two widths. Therefore, each width is equal to $18 \div 2 = 9$ inches.

    The area of a rectangle with length 13 inches and width 9 inches is $13 \times 9 = 117$ square inches.

48. **(2)** $4200 \text{ m}l = 4200 \times .001\ l$
$= 4.200\ l$

49. **(4)** The amount of tax is $90.95 − $85 = $5.95. Find the percent $5.95 is of $85. Let p = percent.

$$\frac{p \cdot 85}{85} = \frac{5.95}{85}$$

$$p = .07 = 7\%$$

50. **(2)**

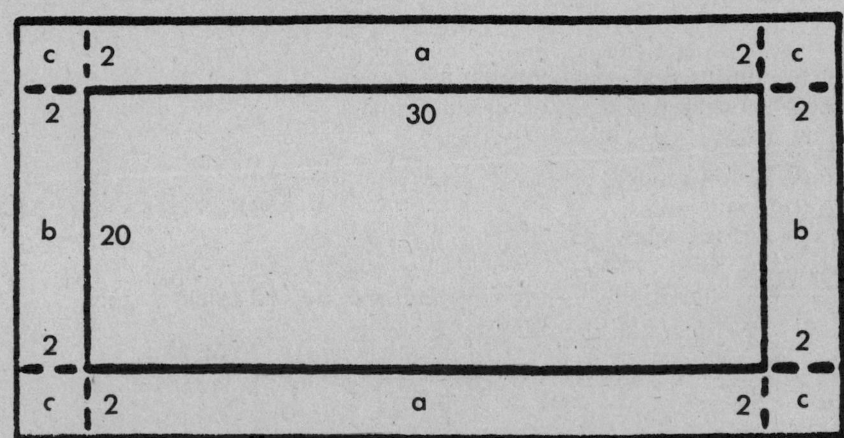

The walk consists of:

a) 2 rectangles of length 30 ft and width 2 ft.
Area of each $= 2 \times 30 = 60$ sq ft.
Area of both $= 120$ sq ft.

b) 2 rectangles of length 20 ft and width 2 ft.
Area of each $= 2 \times 20 = 40$ sq ft
Area of both $= 80$ sq ft

c) 4 squares, each having a side of 2 ft
Area of each square $= 2^2 = 4$ sq ft
Area of 4 squares $= 16$ sq ft

Total area of walk $= 120 + 80 + 16 = 216$ sq ft

Alternatively, you may solve this problem by finding the area of the garden and the area of the garden plus the walk, then subtracting to find the area of the walk alone:

Area of garden = 20 × 30 = 600 sq ft
Area of garden + walk:
(20 + 2 + 2) × (30 + 2 + 2) = 24 × 34
= 816 sq ft

Area of walk alone:
816 − 600 = 216 sq ft

51. **(4)** Change the dimensions to what is asked for . . . feet. Therefore,
200 yards × 1.5 yards becomes
600 feet × 4.5 feet when we multiply each yard by 3 to get feet.

"Square feet" tells you that you are looking for the area of the Yellow Brick Road. From the Formula Page, area of a rectangle = length × width. Therefore the area of the road is
600 × 4.5 = 2700 square feet

52. **(5)** \$18/square yard is \$18/(9 square feet), since there are 3 · 3 square feet in a square yard.
\$18/9 = \$2 per square foot, and
for 500 square feet, it would be 500 square feet · \$2.00/square foot = \$1000.

53. **(3)** Plot the points and connect them as shown.
(0,0) to (4,0) = 4 miles
(4,0) to (4,3) = 3 miles
(4,3) to (0,3) = 4 miles
(0,3) to (0,0) = 3 miles

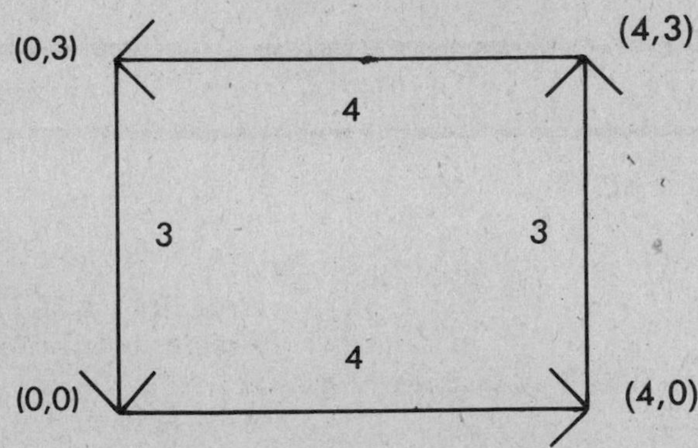

The graph traces a rectangular figure whose perimeter is 14 miles.

54. **(4)** In this problem, just substitute the number values for the letters:

$$I_1 = \frac{4}{4+4} \cdot 17$$

Solving for the values, we find,
$I_1 = 8.5$

55. **(2)** Find the total wages paid and divide by the number of employees:
Total Wages: $5 \times \$15{,}000 = \$75{,}000$
$3 \times \$17{,}000 = \$51{,}000$
$1 \times \$18{,}000 = \underline{\$18{,}000}$
$\$144{,}000$
Number of employees $= 5 + 3 + 1 = 9$
Average Wage $= \$144{,}000 \div 9 = \$16{,}000$

56. **(1)** 2% of \$1000 = $\$1000 \times .02 = \$20$
3% of \$2000 = $\$2000 \times .03 = \$60$
4% of \$3000 = $\$3000 \times .04 = \$120$
5% of (\$25,000 − \$6000) = 5% of \$19,000 = $\$19{,}000 \times .05 = \$950$
Total tax = \$20 + \$60 + \$120 + \$950 = \$1150

Answer Sheet GED Sample Test

TEST 1: WRITING SKILLS - PART 1 Number correct ☐

1 ① ② ③ ④ ⑤	15 ① ② ③ ④ ⑤	29 ① ② ③ ④ ⑤	43 ① ② ③ ④ ⑤
2 ① ② ③ ④ ⑤	16 ① ② ③ ④ ⑤	30 ① ② ③ ④ ⑤	44 ① ② ③ ④ ⑤
3 ① ② ③ ④ ⑤	17 ① ② ③ ④ ⑤	31 ① ② ③ ④ ⑤	45 ① ② ③ ④ ⑤
4 ① ② ③ ④ ⑤	18 ① ② ③ ④ ⑤	32 ① ② ③ ④ ⑤	46 ① ② ③ ④ ⑤
5 ① ② ③ ④ ⑤	19 ① ② ③ ④ ⑤	33 ① ② ③ ④ ⑤	47 ① ② ③ ④ ⑤
6 ① ② ③ ④ ⑤	20 ① ② ③ ④ ⑤	34 ① ② ③ ④ ⑤	48 ① ② ③ ④ ⑤
7 ① ② ③ ④ ⑤	21 ① ② ③ ④ ⑤	35 ① ② ③ ④ ⑤	49 ① ② ③ ④ ⑤
8 ① ② ③ ④ ⑤	22 ① ② ③ ④ ⑤	36 ① ② ③ ④ ⑤	50 ① ② ③ ④ ⑤
9 ① ② ③ ④ ⑤	23 ① ② ③ ④ ⑤	37 ① ② ③ ④ ⑤	51 ① ② ③ ④ ⑤
10 ① ② ③ ④ ⑤	24 ① ② ③ ④ ⑤	38 ① ② ③ ④ ⑤	52 ① ② ③ ④ ⑤
11 ① ② ③ ④ ⑤	25 ① ② ③ ④ ⑤	39 ① ② ③ ④ ⑤	53 ① ② ③ ④ ⑤
12 ① ② ③ ④ ⑤	26 ① ② ③ ④ ⑤	40 ① ② ③ ④ ⑤	54 ① ② ③ ④ ⑤
13 ① ② ③ ④ ⑤	27 ① ② ③ ④ ⑤	41 ① ② ③ ④ ⑤	55 ① ② ③ ④ ⑤
14 ① ② ③ ④ ⑤	28 ① ② ③ ④ ⑤	42 ① ② ③ ④ ⑤	**GO ON TO WRITING SKILLS-PART II**

TEST 2: SOCIAL STUDIES Number correct ☐

1 ① ② ③ ④ ⑤	18 ① ② ③ ④ ⑤	35 ① ② ③ ④ ⑤	52 ① ② ③ ④ ⑤
2 ① ② ③ ④ ⑤	19 ① ② ③ ④ ⑤	36 ① ② ③ ④ ⑤	53 ① ② ③ ④ ⑤
3 ① ② ③ ④ ⑤	20 ① ② ③ ④ ⑤	37 ① ② ③ ④ ⑤	54 ① ② ③ ④ ⑤
4 ① ② ③ ④ ⑤	21 ① ② ③ ④ ⑤	38 ① ② ③ ④ ⑤	55 ① ② ③ ④ ⑤
5 ① ② ③ ④ ⑤	22 ① ② ③ ④ ⑤	39 ① ② ③ ④ ⑤	56 ① ② ③ ④ ⑤
6 ① ② ③ ④ ⑤	23 ① ② ③ ④ ⑤	40 ① ② ③ ④ ⑤	57 ① ② ③ ④ ⑤
7 ① ② ③ ④ ⑤	24 ① ② ③ ④ ⑤	41 ① ② ③ ④ ⑤	58 ① ② ③ ④ ⑤
8 ① ② ③ ④ ⑤	25 ① ② ③ ④ ⑤	42 ① ② ③ ④ ⑤	59 ① ② ③ ④ ⑤
9 ① ② ③ ④ ⑤	26 ① ② ③ ④ ⑤	43 ① ② ③ ④ ⑤	60 ① ② ③ ④ ⑤
10 ① ② ③ ④ ⑤	27 ① ② ③ ④ ⑤	44 ① ② ③ ④ ⑤	61 ① ② ③ ④ ⑤
11 ① ② ③ ④ ⑤	28 ① ② ③ ④ ⑤	45 ① ② ③ ④ ⑤	62 ① ② ③ ④ ⑤
12 ① ② ③ ④ ⑤	29 ① ② ③ ④ ⑤	46 ① ② ③ ④ ⑤	63 ① ② ③ ④ ⑤
13 ① ② ③ ④ ⑤	30 ① ② ③ ④ ⑤	47 ① ② ③ ④ ⑤	64 ① ② ③ ④ ⑤
14 ① ② ③ ④ ⑤	31 ① ② ③ ④ ⑤	48 ① ② ③ ④ ⑤	**STOP**
15 ① ② ③ ④ ⑤	32 ① ② ③ ④ ⑤	49 ① ② ③ ④ ⑤	
16 ① ② ③ ④ ⑤	33 ① ② ③ ④ ⑤	50 ① ② ③ ④ ⑤	
17 ① ② ③ ④ ⑤	34 ① ② ③ ④ ⑤	51 ① ② ③ ④ ⑤	

TEST 3: SCIENCE Number correct ☐

1 ① ② ③ ④ ⑤	6 ① ② ③ ④ ⑤	11 ① ② ③ ④ ⑤	16 ① ② ③ ④ ⑤
2 ① ② ③ ④ ⑤	7 ① ② ③ ④ ⑤	12 ① ② ③ ④ ⑤	17 ① ② ③ ④ ⑤
3 ① ② ③ ④ ⑤	8 ① ② ③ ④ ⑤	13 ① ② ③ ④ ⑤	18 ① ② ③ ④ ⑤
4 ① ② ③ ④ ⑤	9 ① ② ③ ④ ⑤	14 ① ② ③ ④ ⑤	19 ① ② ③ ④ ⑤
5 ① ② ③ ④ ⑤	10 ① ② ③ ④ ⑤	15 ① ② ③ ④ ⑤	20 ① ② ③ ④ ⑤

TEST 3: SCIENCE (Con't)

21 ① ② ③ ④ ⑤
22 ① ② ③ ④ ⑤
23 ① ② ③ ④ ⑤
24 ① ② ③ ④ ⑤
25 ① ② ③ ④ ⑤
26 ① ② ③ ④ ⑤
27 ① ② ③ ④ ⑤
28 ① ② ③ ④ ⑤
29 ① ② ③ ④ ⑤
30 ① ② ③ ④ ⑤
31 ① ② ③ ④ ⑤
32 ① ② ③ ④ ⑤
33 ① ② ③ ④ ⑤
34 ① ② ③ ④ ⑤
35 ① ② ③ ④ ⑤
36 ① ② ③ ④ ⑤
37 ① ② ③ ④ ⑤
38 ① ② ③ ④ ⑤
39 ① ② ③ ④ ⑤
40 ① ② ③ ④ ⑤
41 ① ② ③ ④ ⑤
42 ① ② ③ ④ ⑤
43 ① ② ③ ④ ⑤
44 ① ② ③ ④ ⑤
45 ① ② ③ ④ ⑤
46 ① ② ③ ④ ⑤
47 ① ② ③ ④ ⑤
48 ① ② ③ ④ ⑤
49 ① ② ③ ④ ⑤
50 ① ② ③ ④ ⑤
51 ① ② ③ ④ ⑤
52 ① ② ③ ④ ⑤
53 ① ② ③ ④ ⑤
54 ① ② ③ ④ ⑤
55 ① ② ③ ④ ⑤
56 ① ② ③ ④ ⑤
57 ① ② ③ ④ ⑤
58 ① ② ③ ④ ⑤
59 ① ② ③ ④ ⑤
60 ① ② ③ ④ ⑤
61 ① ② ③ ④ ⑤
62 ① ② ③ ④ ⑤
63 ① ② ③ ④ ⑤
64 ① ② ③ ④ ⑤
65 ① ② ③ ④ ⑤
66 ① ② ③ ④ ⑤

STOP

TEST 4: INTERPRETING LITERATURE AND THE ARTS

Number correct ☐

1 ① ② ③ ④ ⑤
2 ① ② ③ ④ ⑤
3 ① ② ③ ④ ⑤
4 ① ② ③ ④ ⑤
5 ① ② ③ ④ ⑤
6 ① ② ③ ④ ⑤
7 ① ② ③ ④ ⑤
8 ① ② ③ ④ ⑤
9 ① ② ③ ④ ⑤
10 ① ② ③ ④ ⑤
11 ① ② ③ ④ ⑤
12 ① ② ③ ④ ⑤
13 ① ② ③ ④ ⑤
14 ① ② ③ ④ ⑤
15 ① ② ③ ④ ⑤
16 ① ② ③ ④ ⑤
17 ① ② ③ ④ ⑤
18 ① ② ③ ④ ⑤
19 ① ② ③ ④ ⑤
20 ① ② ③ ④ ⑤
21 ① ② ③ ④ ⑤
22 ① ② ③ ④ ⑤
23 ① ② ③ ④ ⑤
24 ① ② ③ ④ ⑤
25 ① ② ③ ④ ⑤
26 ① ② ③ ④ ⑤
27 ① ② ③ ④ ⑤
28 ① ② ③ ④ ⑤
29 ① ② ③ ④ ⑤
30 ① ② ③ ④ ⑤
31 ① ② ③ ④ ⑤
32 ① ② ③ ④ ⑤
33 ① ② ③ ④ ⑤
34 ① ② ③ ④ ⑤
35 ① ② ③ ④ ⑤
36 ① ② ③ ④ ⑤
37 ① ② ③ ④ ⑤
38 ① ② ③ ④ ⑤
39 ① ② ③ ④ ⑤
40 ① ② ③ ④ ⑤
41 ① ② ③ ④ ⑤
42 ① ② ③ ④ ⑤
43 ① ② ③ ④ ⑤
44 ① ② ③ ④ ⑤
45 ① ② ③ ④ ⑤

STOP

TEST 5: MATHEMATICS

Number correct ☐

1 ① ② ③ ④ ⑤
2 ① ② ③ ④ ⑤
3 ① ② ③ ④ ⑤
4 ① ② ③ ④ ⑤
5 ① ② ③ ④ ⑤
6 ① ② ③ ④ ⑤
7 ① ② ③ ④ ⑤
8 ① ② ③ ④ ⑤
9 ① ② ③ ④ ⑤
10 ① ② ③ ④ ⑤
11 ① ② ③ ④ ⑤
12 ① ② ③ ④ ⑤
13 ① ② ③ ④ ⑤
14 ① ② ③ ④ ⑤
15 ① ② ③ ④ ⑤
16 ① ② ③ ④ ⑤
17 ① ② ③ ④ ⑤
18 ① ② ③ ④ ⑤
19 ① ② ③ ④ ⑤
20 ① ② ③ ④ ⑤
21 ① ② ③ ④ ⑤
22 ① ② ③ ④ ⑤
23 ① ② ③ ④ ⑤
24 ① ② ③ ④ ⑤
25 ① ② ③ ④ ⑤
26 ① ② ③ ④ ⑤
27 ① ② ③ ④ ⑤
28 ① ② ③ ④ ⑤
29 ① ② ③ ④ ⑤
30 ① ② ③ ④ ⑤
31 ① ② ③ ④ ⑤
32 ① ② ③ ④ ⑤
33 ① ② ③ ④ ⑤
34 ① ② ③ ④ ⑤
35 ① ② ③ ④ ⑤
36 ① ② ③ ④ ⑤
37 ① ② ③ ④ ⑤
38 ① ② ③ ④ ⑤
39 ① ② ③ ④ ⑤
40 ① ② ③ ④ ⑤
41 ① ② ③ ④ ⑤
42 ① ② ③ ④ ⑤
43 ① ② ③ ④ ⑤
44 ① ② ③ ④ ⑤
45 ① ② ③ ④ ⑤
46 ① ② ③ ④ ⑤
47 ① ② ③ ④ ⑤
48 ① ② ③ ④ ⑤
49 ① ② ③ ④ ⑤
50 ① ② ③ ④ ⑤
51 ① ② ③ ④ ⑤
52 ① ② ③ ④ ⑤
53 ① ② ③ ④ ⑤
54 ① ② ③ ④ ⑤
55 ① ② ③ ④ ⑤
56 ① ② ③ ④ ⑤

STOP

GED SAMPLE TEST II

TEST 1. WRITING SKILLS

This test has two parts. Part I measures your ability to recognize errors in written material. Part II tests your ability to write a short essay.

PART I. RECOGNIZING AND CORRECTING ERRORS

Time: 75 Minutes—55 Questions

Directions:

This test consists of several paragraphs in which each sentence is numbered. Some of the sentences within each paragraph contain errors in sentence structure, usage, or mechanics. Other sentences are correct as written. Following each paragraph are questions based upon it. Read the paragraph first, then answer the questions about it. For each item, choose the answer that would result in the most effective writing of the sentence. The best answer must be consistent with the meaning and tone of the paragraph. Record your answers in the Writing Skills section of the answer sheet.

FOR EXAMPLE:

Often their are two equally effective ways to solve a problem.

What correction should be made to this sentence?

(1) replace <u>their</u> with <u>there</u>
(2) change <u>are</u> to <u>is</u>
(3) change <u>two</u> to <u>too</u>
(4) insert a <u>comma</u> after <u>equally</u>
(5) no change is necessary

In this example, the word <u>their</u>, which means "belonging to them," is incorrectly substituted for the word <u>there</u>. To indicate this correction, mark answer space 1 on your answer sheet.

Items 1 to 10 are based on the following passages.

(1) Asthmatics simply are born with extra-sensitive bronchial tissue they can develop this extra sensitive tissue, too. (2) An asthmatic attack ocurrs when some irritant stimulates the autonomic (or involuntary) nervous system, which controls the muscles of the body's breathing apparatus. (3) Or some irritants can directly cause a chemical reaction in certain cells that line the bronchial tubes. (4) Either way, the bands of smooth muscle around the bronchi and bronchioles contract; and the mucous membranes lining the bronchial tubes swell and increase their production of thick mucus. (5) All three actions narrow the airway and left the sufferer gasping for breath.

(6) Asthma attacks vary widely in severity and length from person to person and even for the same persons at different times. (7) They can begin slowly, with increasing severity, or they can come on abruptly. (8) They often occur in the middle of the night. (9) Usually they were mild and brief, subsiding within a few minutes, sometimes even without therapy. (10) Or they may persist for several hours or even days. (11) Between attacks they are free of symptoms. (12) Others have mild coughing much of the time, punctuated by episodes of struggling for breath.

1. Sentence 1: **Asthmatics simply are born with extra-sensitive bronchial tissue they can develop this extra-sensitive tissue, too.**

   Which of the following is the best way to write the underlined portion of this sentence? If you think the original is the best way to write the sentence, choose option (1).

   (1) tissue they can
   (2) tissue, they can
   (3) tissue; They can
   (4) tissue since they can
   (5) tissue. They can

2. Sentence 2: **An asthmatic attack ocurrs when some irritant stimulates the autonomic (or involuntary) nervous system, which controls the muscles of the body's breathing apparatus.**

   What correction should be made to this sentence?

   (1) change the spelling of ocurrs to occurs
   (2) insert a period after system
   (3) change the spelling of muscles to mussels
   (4) change the spelling of body's to bodies
   (5) change the spelling of apparatus to aparratus

3. Sentence 3: **Or some irritants can directly cause a chemical reaction in certain cells that line the bronchial tubes.**

   If you rewrote sentence 3 beginning with In certain cells that line the bronchial tubes
   the next words would be

   (1) directly cause
   (2) become irritated
   (3) chemicals react
   (4) some irritants
   (5) or cause

4. Sentence 4: **Either way, the bands of smooth muscle around the bronchi and bronchioles contract; and the mucous membranes lining the bronchial tubes swell and increase their production of thick mucus.**

   Which of the following is the best way to write the underlined portion of this sentence? If you think the original is the best way to write the sentence, choose option (1).

   (1) swell and increase
   (2) swells and increases
   (3) swells and increasing
   (4) swell and to increase
   (5) swollen and increased

5. Sentence 5: **All three actions narrow the airway and left the sufferer gasping for breath.**

   What correction should be made to this sentence?

   (1) change three to 3
   (2) change narrow to narrowed
   (3) change left to leave
   (4) change the spelling of breath to breathe
   (5) no correction is necessary

6. Sentence 6: **Asthma attacks vary widely in severity and length from person to person and even for the same persons at different times.**

   What correction should be made to this sentence:

   (1) insert a comma after severity
   (2) change the spelling of length to lenth
   (3) insert a semicolon after length
   (4) change same persons to same person
   (5) change times to time

7. Sentence 7: **They can begin slowly, with increasing severity, or they can come on abruptly.**

   Which of the following is the best way to write the underlined portion of this sentence? If you think the original is the best way to write the sentence, choose option (1).

   (1) slowly, with increasing severity,
   (2) slowly, each increasing severity,
   (3) slowly, climb increasing severity
   (4) slowly beyond increasing severity,
   (5) slowly, with increasing severity

8. Sentence 9: **Usually they were mild and brief, subsiding within a few minutes, sometimes even without therapy.**

   What correction should be made to this sentence?

   (1) change the spelling of usually to usualy
   (2) change were to are
   (3) change the comma after brief to a period/capitalize subsiding
   (4) change sometimes to some times
   (5) no correction is necessary

9. Sentence 11: **Between attacks they are free of symptoms.**

   Which of the following is the best way to write the underlined portion of this sentence? If you think the original is the best way to write the sentence, choose option (1).

   (1) Between attacks they
   (2) Between attacks we
   (3) Between attacks some asthmatics
   (4) Between attacks minutes
   (5) Between attacks ones

10. Sentence 12: **Others have mild coughing much of the time, punctuated by severe episodes of struggling for breath.**

    If you rewrote sentence 12 beginning with Often severe episodes of struggling for breath
    the next word(s) should be

    (1) and coughing
    (2) mildly
    (3) others
    (4) punctuate
    (5) punctuates

GO ON TO THE NEXT PAGE

Items 11 to 19 are based on the following paragraph.

(1) Coffee is the most important food imported between the United States. (2) As one of the world's biggest coffee drinkers, we buy nearly half the world's supply. (3) Over three billion dollars a year are spent to supply each of us with an average of 750 cups annually. (4) The United States imports two major kinds of coffee—the milder flavored Arabica varieties, primarily growth in Central and South America, and the more strongly flavored Robusta varieties from Africa and Asia. (5) Beans generally as green beans must be blended, roasted, and ground before they reach the consumer. (6) A dark roast is preferred in the south, a light roast along the Pacific Coast, and a medium roast elsewhere in the United States. (7) Robusta varieties were largely used in instant coffees. (8) But recently, increasing quantities are being used in roasted blends, these blends make a strong coffee. (9) Coffee drinking became a popular pastime in the mid-seventeenth century in London when literary, scientific, religious, and political matters were discussed by the intellectuals of the time over steaming mugs of the imported brew.

11. Sentence 1: **Coffee is the most important food imported between the United States.**

Which of the following is the best way to write the underlined portion of this sentence? If you think the original is the best way to write the sentence, choose option (1).

(1) imported between
(2) imported after
(3) imported also
(4) imported into
(5) imported on

12. Sentence 2: **As one of the world's biggest coffee drinkers, we buy nearly half the world's supply.**

If you rewrote sentence 2 beginning with Almost half the world's coffee supply the next word should be

(1) biggest
(2) is
(3) as
(4) buys
(5) nearly

13. Sentence 3: **Over three billion dollars a year are spent to supply each of us with an average of 750 cups annually.**

What correction should be made to this sentence?

(1) change three billion to 3,000,000
(2) change dollars to $
(3) insert a comma after year
(4) change annually to anually
(5) no correction is necessary

14. Sentence 4: **The United States imports two major kinds of coffee–the milder flavored Arabica varieties, primarily growth in Central and South America, and the more strongly flavored Robusta varieties from Africa and Asia.**

Which of the following is the best way to write the underlined portion of this sentence? If you think the original is the best way to write the sentence, choose option (1).

(1) primarily growth
(2) primarily growed
(3) primarily grown
(4) primarily. Grown
(5) primarily to grow

15. Sentence 5: **Beans generally as green beans that must be blended, roasted, and ground before they reach the consumer.**

Which of the following is the best way to write the underlined portion of this sentence? If you think the original is the best way to write the sentence, choose option (1).

(1) Beans generally as
(2) Beans, generally,
(3) Beans which generally as
(4) Beans that generally as
(5) Beans are generally imported as

16. Sentence 6: **A dark roast is preferred in the south, a light roast along the Pacific Coast, and a medium roast elsewhere in the United States.**

    What correction should be made to this sentence?

    (1) change the spelling of preferred to prefered
    (2) change south to South
    (3) change Pacific Coast to pacific coast
    (4) change the United States to The United States
    (5) no correction is necessary

17. Sentence 7: **Robusta varieties were largely used in instant coffees.**

    What correction should be made to this sentence?

    (1) change varieties to Varieties
    (2) change were to are
    (3) change used to in use
    (4) change coffees to Coffees
    (5) no correction is necessary

18. Sentence 8: **But recently, increasing quantities are being used in roasted blends, these blends make a strong coffee.**

    Which of the following is the best way to write the underlined portion of this sentence? If you think the original is the best way to write the sentence, choose option (1).

    (1) blends, these blends
    (2) blends; These blends
    (3) blends, the blends
    (4) blends. These blends
    (5) blends these blends

19. Sentence 9: **Coffee drinking became a popular pastime in the mid-seventeenth century in London when literary, scientific, religious, and political matters were discussed by the intellectuals of the time over steaming mugs of the imported brew.**

    What correction should be made to this sentence?

    (1) insert a period after century
    (2) insert a period after London
    (3) change the spelling of scientific to sceintific
    (4) change the spelling of political to poletical
    (5) no correction is necessary

GO ON TO THE NEXT PAGE

Items 20 to 27 are based on the following passage.

(1) Employment interviewers serve individuals and businesses, they take information and requests and provide services and help. (2) Services provided by several other occupations, such as personnel officer and counselor, are similar to these, yet have important differences. (3) Personnel officers work for a single firm and may help in the hiring of new employees but do not act as brokers for different organizations and never represent individual jobseekers, personnel officers may also have additional duties in areas such as payroll or benefits management.

(4) College carrer counselors are similar to employment interviewers in that they operate to help people find jobs. (5) However, their primary duties being in student development, helping new students choose their major and arrange a proper class schedule. (6) A master's degree is usually the minimum educational requirement for a position as a college career counselor.

(7) Counselors in community organizations and vocational rehabilitation facilities also helped clients find jobs, but their primary duties are usually something other than being a job finder. (8) Individuals seeking assistence from these organizations usually have more than employability problems and need help for conditions like drug abuse or alcohol dependency.

20. Sentence 1: **Employment interviewers serve individuals and businesses, they take information and requests and provide services and help.**

    What correction should be made to this sentence?

    (1) change the comma to a period after businesses. Capitalize *They*.
    (2) change the spelling of businesses to busineses
    (3) change the comma to a colon after businesses
    (4) insert for between businesses and they
    (5) no correction is necessary

21. Sentence 2: **Services provided by several other occupations, such as personnel officer and counselor, are similar to these, yet have important differences.**

    What correction should be made to this sentence?

    (1) change provided to providing
    (2) change the spelling of personnel to personal
    (3) change counselor to councilor
    (4) change the spelling of similar to similer
    (5) no correction is necessary

22. Sentence 3: **Personnel officers work for a single firm and may help in the hiring of new employees but do not act as brokers for different organizations and never represent individual jobseekers, personnel officers may also have additional duties in areas such as payroll or benefits management.**

    Which of the following is the best way to write the underlined portion of this sentence? If you think the original is the best way to write the sentence choose option 1.

    (1) individual jobseekers, personnel officers
    (2) individual jobseekers, personnal officers
    (3) individual job seekers; personnal officers
    (4) individual jobseekers. Personnel officers
    (5) individual jobseekers; personal officers

23. Sentence 4: **College carrer counselors are similar to employment interviewers in that they operate to help people find jobs.**

What correction should be made to this sentence?

(1) change carrer to Carrer
(2) change spelling of carrer to career
(3) change counselors to councilors
(4) change the spelling of similar to similer
(5) change the spelling of operate to opperate

24. Sentence 5: **However, their primary duties being in student development, helping new students choose their major and arrange a proper class schedule.**

What correction should be made to this sentence?

(1) change duties to duty
(2) change being to are
(3) change helping to to help
(4) change choose to chose
(5) change the spelling of arrange to arange

25. Sentence 6: **A master's degree is usually the minimum educational requirement for a position as a college career counselor.**

What correction should be made to this sentence?

(1) change master's to masters'
(2) change is to was
(3) change the spelling of career to carrer
(4) change counselor to councilor
(5) no correction is necessary

6. Sentence 7: **Counselors in community organizations and vocational rehabilitation facilities also helped clients find jobs, but their primary duties are usually something other than being a job finder.**

Which of the following is the best way to write the underlined portion of this sentence? If you think the original is the best way to write the sentence, choose option (1).

(1) also helped clients
(2) also helped to clients
(3) also, helped clients
(4) also to help
(5) also help clients

27. Sentence 8: **Individuals seeking assistence from these organizations usually have more than employability problems and need help for conditions like drug abuse or alcohol dependency.**

What correction should be made to this sentence?

(1) change the spelling of Individuals to Individuels
(2) change the spelling of assistence to assistance
(3) change these to those
(4) change the spelling of usually to usally
(5) change than to then

GO ON TO THE NEXT PAGE

Items 28 to 37 are based on the following passage.

(1) To become a construction or building inspector, severel years of experience as a construction contractor, supervisor, or craft worker are generally required. (2) Most employers also required an applicant to have a high school diploma. (3) High school preparation should include courses in drafting, algebra, geometry, and english.

(4) Workers who want to become inspectors should have a thorough knowledge of construction materials and practices in either a general area like structural or heavy construction, nor in a specialized area such as electrical or plumbing systems, reinforced concrete, or structural steel. (5) A significant number of construction and building inspectors have recent experience as carpenters, electricians, plumbers, or pipefitters.

(6) Many employers prefer inspectors who have graduated from an apprenticeship program, and have studied engineering or architecture for at least two years, inspectors might have a degree from a community or junior college, with courses in construction technology, blueprint reading, mathematics, and building inspection.

(7) Construction building inspectors must be in good physical condition in order to walk and climbing about construction sites. (8) They must also have a motor vehicle operator's license. (9) In addition, federal, state, and many local governments usually requires that inspectors pass a civil service examination. (10) Construction and building inspectors usually receive most of their training on the job. (11) During the first couple of weeks, working with an experienced inspector, they learn about inspection techniques; codes, ordinances, and regulations; contract specifications; and recordkeeping and reporting duties. (12) They began by inspecting less complex types of construction such as residential buildings, then gradually, the difficulty of their assignments is increased.

28. Sentence 1: **To become a construction or building inspector, severel years of experience as a construction contractor, supervisor, or craft worker are generally required.**

    What correction should be made to this sentence?

    (1) change the spelling of become to becomme
    (2) add a comma between construction and or
    (3) change the spelling of severel to several
    (4) change the spelling of experience to experiense
    (5) change the spelling of generally to generelly

29. Sentence 2: **Most employers also required an applicant to have a high school diploma.**

    What correction should be made to this sentence?

    (1) change employers to employees
    (2) insert are between also and required
    (3) change required to require
    (4) change to have to having
    (5) no correction is necessary

30. Sentence 3: **High school preparation should include courses in drafting, algebra, geometry, and english.**

    What correction should be made to this sentence?

    (1) change the spelling of preparation to preperation
    (2) change include to included
    (3) capitalize the word drafting
    (4) change the spelling of geometry to Geometry
    (5) change the spelling of english to English

31. Sentence 4: **Workers who want to become inspectors should have a thorough knowledge of construction materials and practices in either a general area like structural or heavy construction, nor in a specialized area such as electrical or plumbing systems, reinforced concrete, or structural steel.**

    What correction should be made to this sentence?

(1) change thorough to through
(2) change the spelling of materials to materiels
(3) insert a colon after practices
(4) change nor to or
(5) no correction is necessary

32. Sentence 6: **Many employers prefer inspectors who have graduated from an apprenticeship program, and have studied engineering or architecture for at least two years, inspectors might have a degree from a community or junior college, with courses in construction technology, blueprint reading, mathematics, and building inspection.**

Which of the following is the best way to write the underlined portion of this sentence? If you think the original is the best way to write the sentence, choose option (1).

(1) two years, inspectors
(2) two years even though, inspectors
(3) two years. Inspectors
(4) two years, Inspectors
(5) two years inspectors

33. Sentence 7: **Construction building inspectors must be in good physical condition in order to walk and climbing about construction sites.**

Which of the following is the best way to write the underlined portion of this sentence? If you think the original is the best way to write the sentence, choose option (1).

(1) to walk and climbing about
(2) to walking and climbing about
(3) to walking and climb about
(4) to walk and climb about
(5) to walking and climbing about

34. Sentence 8: **They must also have a motor vehicle operator's license.**

Which of the following is the best way to write the underlined portion of this sentence? If you think the original is the best way to write the sentence, choose option (1).

(1) must also have
(2) to also have
(3) did also have
(4) had also have
(5) must of also

35. Sentence 9: **In addition, federal, state, and many local governments usually requires that inspectors pass a civil service examination.**

What correction should be made to this sentence?

(1) capitalize local
(2) change the spelling of governments to goverments
(3) change requires to require
(4) change pass to passed
(5) no correction is necessary

36. Sentence 10: **Construction and building inspectors usually receive most of their training on the job.**

If you rewrote sentence 10 beginning with Most training of inspectors the next word should be

(1) receives
(2) they
(3) and
(4) occurs
(5) on

37. Sentence 12: **They began by inspecting less complex types of construction such as residential buildings, then gradually, the difficulty of their assignments is increased.**

Which of the following is the best way to write the underlined portion of this sentence? If you think the original is the best way to write the sentence, choose option (1).

(1) They began
(2) They begin
(3) They beginning
(4) They will begin
(5) They, to begin

GO ON TO THE NEXT PAGE

Items 38 to 45 are based on the following passage.

(1) Broadcast technicians operate and maintain the electronic equipment used to record and transmit radio and television programs. (2) They work with microphones, sound, and videotape recorders, light and sound effects, television cameras, transmitters, and other equipment.

(3) In the control room of the radio or broadcast studio, these technicians operate equipment that regulates the signal strength, clarity, and range of sounds and colors in the material been recorded or broadcast. (4) These technicians also operate panels that select the source of the broadcasted material. (5) Technicians may switch from one camera or studio to annother, from film to live programming, or from national to local programs. (6) By means of hand signals and, in television, by use of telefone headsets, they give technical directions to personnel in the studio. (7) When events outside the studio are to be broadcast, technicians go to the site and set up, test, and operate the remote equipment. (8) After the broadcast, they dismantled the equipment and return it to the station. (9) As a rule, broadcast technicians in small stations perform a variety of duties. (10) In large stations and at networks on the other hand technicians are more specialized, although specific job assignments may change from day to day.

38. Sentence 1: **Broadcast technicians operate and maintain the electronic equipment used to record and transmit radio and television programs.**

What correction should be made to this sentence?

(1) change technicians to technician's
(2) change the spelling of operate to operrate
(3) change maintain to maintenance
(4) change record to recording
(5) no correction is necessary

39. Sentence 2: **They work with microphones, sound, and videotape recorders, light and sound effects, television cameras, transmitters, and other equipment.**

Which of the following is the best way to write the underlined portion of this sentence? If you think the original is the best way to write the sentence, choose option (1).

(1) with microphones, sound, and videotape
(2) with microphones, sound and videotape
(3) with: microphones, sound, and videotape
(4) with; microphones, sound, and videotape
(5) with microphones sound, and videotape

40. Sentence 3: **In the control room of the radio or broadcast studio, these technicians operate equipment that regulates the signal strength, clarity, and range of sounds and colors in the material been recorded or broadcast.**

What correction should be made to this sentence?

(1) change these to where
(2) change the spelling of signal to signel
(3) change the spelling of strength to strenth
(4) add a comma after sounds
(5) change been to being

41. Sentence 5: **Technicians may switch from one camera or studio to annother, from film to live programming, or from national to local programs.**

    Which of the following is the best way to write the underlined portion of this sentence? If you think the original is the best way to write the sentence, choose option (1).

    (1) studio to annother, from film to live
    (2) studio to annother, of films to live
    (3) studio to annother, from films to life
    (4) studio to another, from film to live
    (5) studio to another; from film to live

42. Sentence 6: **By means of hand signals and, in television, by use of telefone headsets, they give technical directions to personnel in the studio.**

    What correction should be made to this sentence?

    (1) change spelling of signals to signels
    (2) change use to used
    (3) change spelling of telefone to telephone
    (4) change give to gave
    (5) change personnel to personal

43. Sentence 7: **When events outside the studio are to be broadcast, technicians go to the site and set up, test, and operate the remote equipment.**

    What correction should be made to this sentence?

    (1) change When to Where
    (2) change go to going
    (3) change site to sight
    (4) change the spelling of operate to operrate
    (5) no correction is necessary

44. Sentence 8: **After the broadcast, they dismantled the equipment and return it to the station.**

    Which of the following is the best way to write the underlined portion of the sentence? If you think the original is the best way to write the sentence, choose option (1).

    (1) they dismantled
    (2) they requested to dismantle
    (3) they order dismantling
    (4) they have dismantled
    (5) they dismantle

45. Sentence 10: **In large stations and at networks on the other hand technicians are more specialized, although specific job assignments may change from day to day.**

    Which of the following is the best way to write the underlined portion of this sentence? If you think the original is the best way to write the sentence, choose option (1).

    (1) networks on the other hand
    (2) networks, on the other hand
    (3) networks, on the other hand,
    (4) networks; on the other hand
    (5) networks: on the other hand,

GO ON TO THE NEXT PAGE

Items 46 to 55 are based on the following passage.

(1) The success of any retail establishment depended largely on its sales workers. (2) Courtous and efficient service from behind the counter or on the sales floor does much to please customers and build a store's reputation.

(3) Weather selling furniture, electrical appliances, or clothing, a sales worker's primary job is to interest customers in the merchandise. (4) This is done by describing the product's construction, demonstrating its use, and to show various models and colors. (5) For expensive "big ticket" items, special knowledge or skills are needing. (6) Personal computer sales workers, for example, must have sufficient knowledge of electronics to explain to customers the features of various brands and models and the meaning of manufacturer's specifications.

(7) In addition to selling, most retail sales workers make out sales checks, receive cash payments, and give change and reciepts. (8) More and more stores are installing point-of-sale terminals that register sales, adjusting inventory figures, and perform simple calculations. (9) This equipment increases workers' productivity—enabling them to provide better customer service. (10) They also handles returns and exchanges of merchandise and keep their work areas neat. (11) In addition, they may help stack shelves, or racks, mark price tags, take inventory, and prepare displays. (12) However, in jobs selling standardized articles such as food, hardware, linens, and housewares, sales workers often do little more than take payments and wrap purchases.

46. Sentence 1: **The success of any retail establishment depended largely on its sales workers.**

    Which of the following is the best way to write the underlined portion of this sentence? If you think the original is the best way to write the sentence, choose option (1).

    (1) depended largely
    (2) to depend largely
    (3) has depends largely
    (4) depends largely
    (5) to depending largely

47. Sentence 2: **Courtous and efficient service from behind the counter or on the sales floor does much to please customers and build a store's reputation.**

    What correction should be made to this sentence?

    (1) change the spelling of courtous to courteous
    (2) change the spelling of efficient to eficient
    (3) change the spelling of please to pleese
    (4) change the spelling of store's to stores'
    (5) no correction is necessary

48. Sentence 3: **Weather selling furniture, electrical appliances, or clothing, a sales worker's primary job is to interest customers in the merchandise.**

    What correction should be made to this sentence?

    (1) change Weather to Whether
    (2) delete the comma after appliances
    (3) change the spelling of clothing to clotthing
    (4) change the spelling of worker's to workers'
    (5) change the spelling of interest to intirest

49. Sentence 4: **This is done by describing the product's construction, demonstrating its use, and to show various models and colors.**

    Which of the following is the best way to write the underlined portion of the sentence? If you think the original is the best way, choose option (1).

    (1) use, and to show various
    (2) use, and to show varies
    (3) use. And to show various
    (4) use; and showing various
    (5) use, and showing various

50. Sentence 5: **For expensive "big ticket" items, special knowledge or skills are needing.**

What correction should be made to this sentence?

(1) change the spelling of expensive to espensive
(2) capitalize "Big Ticket"
(3) change the spelling of knowledge to knoweledge
(4) change needing to needed
(5) no correction is necessary

51. Sentence 7: **In addition to selling, most retail sales workers make out sales checks, receive cash payments, and give change and reciepts.**

What correction should be made to this sentence?

(1) delete the comma after selling
(2) change sales to sale's
(3) change make to made
(4) add a comma after change
(5) change the spelling of reciepts to receipts

52. Sentence 8: **More and more stores are installing point-of-sale terminals that register sales, adjusting inventory figures, and perform simple calculations.**

Which of the following is the best way to write the underlined portion of this sentence? If you think the original is the best way, choose option (1).

(1) register sales, adjusting
(2) registered sales, adjusting
(3) register sales, adjust
(4) register sales; adjusting
(5) register sales, adjusted

53. Sentence 9: **This equipment increases workers' productivity—enabling them to provide better customer service.**

If you rewrote sentence 9 beginning with One benefit of this equipment is the next word should be

(1) product
(2) before
(3) benefits
(4) to
(5) them

54. Sentence 10: **They also handles returns and exchanges of merchandise and keep their work areas neat.**

Which of the following is the best way to write the underlined portion of this sentence? If you think the original is the best way to write the sentence, choose option (1).

(1) They also handles returns
(2) They handles returns also
(3) They also handle returns,
(4) They handle returns also
(5) They also handle returns

55. Sentence 11: **In addition, they may help stack shelves, or racks, mark price tags, take inventory, and prepare displays.**

What correction should be made to this sentence?

(1) delete the comma after shelves
(2) delete the comma after racks
(3) change take to taking
(4) change prepare to preparing
(5) no correction is necessary

END OF WRITING SKILLS TEST PART I

PART II. ESSAY TEST

Time: 45 Minutes—1 Essay

Directions:

This part of the GED is designed to find out how well you write. You will be given one question which asks you to explain something or to present an opinion on an issue. In constructing your answer for this part of the exam, you should take the following steps:

1. Before you begin to write your answer, read all of the material accompanying the question.
2. Carefully plan what you will say before you begin to write.
3. Use the blank pages in the test booklet (or scratch paper provided for you) to make notes to plan your essay.
4. Write your answer on the separate answer sheet.
5. Carefully read over what you have written and make any changes that will improve your work.
6. Check your paragraphing, sentence structure, spelling, punctuation, capitalization, and usage, and correct any errors.

You will have 45 minutes to write a response to the question you are given. Write clearly with a ballpoint pen so the evaluators can read what you have written. Any notes you make on the blank pages or scratch paper will not be included in your evaluation.

Your essay will be scored by at least two trained readers who will evaluate the paper according to its overall impact. They will be concerned with how clearly you make your main points, how thoroughly your ideas are supported, and how effective and correct your writing is throughout the entire composition. You will receive no credit for writing on a topic other than the one assigned.

SAMPLE TOPIC

Computers have certainly been responsible for many changes in America. Some of these changes have made our lives better, while some have made our lives more difficult.

Write a composition of about 200 words describing the effect of computers on modern life. You may describe the positive effects, the negative effects, or both. Be as specific as possible, and use examples to support your view.

WRITING SKILLS - PART II

TEST 2. SOCIAL STUDIES

Time: 85 Minutes—64 Questions

Directions:

The Social Studies Test consists of multiple-choice questions intended to measure your knowledge of general concepts in history, economics, geography, and political and behavioral science. The questions are based on reading passages, maps, graphs, charts, and cartoons. For each question, first study the information given and then answer the question about it. You may refer to the readings or graphs as often as necessary in order to answer the questions. Record your answers in the Social Studies section of your answer sheet.

FOR EXAMPLE:

Which medium most regularly presents opinions and interpretations of the news?

(1) national television news programs
(2) local television news programs
(3) newspaper editorial pages
(4) teletype news agency reports
(5) radio news broadcasts

① ② ● ④ ⑤

The correct answer is "newspaper editorial pages." Therefore, you should mark answer space 3 on your answer sheet.

1. Which of the following conclusions is supported by the graph below?

   (1) All women work in paid employment.
   (2) Most women work part-time.
   (3) Three out of every four women work part-time.
   (4) For every woman employed part-time, there are three women employed full-time.
   (5) All women work at least part-time.

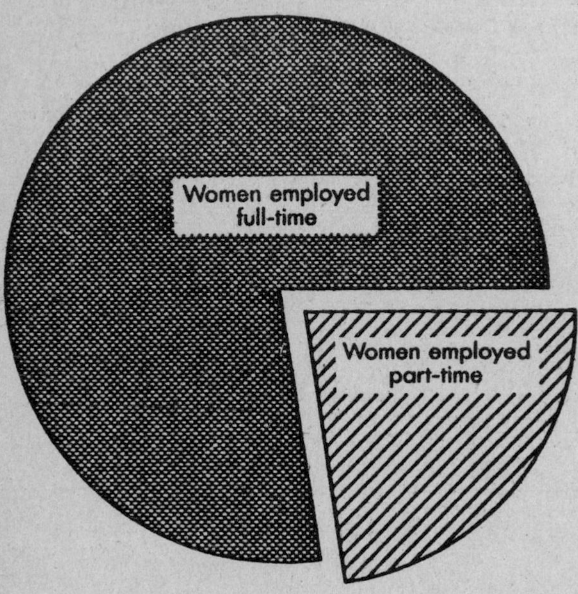

Employed women by full- or part-time status, 1982

Items 2 to 5 are based on the following selection.

Although the poll takers are most widely known for their political surveys, the greatest part of their work is on behalf of American businesses. There are three kinds of commercial surveys. One is public relations research, such as that done for banks, which finds out how the public feels about a company. Another is employee-attitude research, which learns from rank-and-file workers how they really feel about their jobs and their bosses, and which can avert strikes by getting to the bottom of grievances quickly. The third, and probably most spectacular, is marketing research, the testing of public receptivity to new products and designs. The investment a company must make for a new product is enormous—$10,000.000 to $20,000,000, for instance, for just one new product.

Through surveys, a company can discover in advance what objections the public has to competing products, and whether it really wants or needs a new one. These surveys are actually a new set of signals permitting better communications between business and the general public—letting them talk to each other. Such communication is vital in a complex society. Without it, we would have not only tremendous waste but also the industrial anarchy of countless new, unwanted products appearing and disappearing.

2. According to the passage, polls can benefit industry by

   (1) reducing waste
   (2) establishing fair prices
   (3) strengthening people's faith in business
   (4) saving small businesses
   (5) serving as a new form of advertising

3. What method is used to develop the ideas in this selection?

   (1) cause and effect
   (2) contrast
   (3) examples
   (4) anecdotes
   (5) vivid description

4. Which is NOT mentioned as an area in which polls have been conducted?

   (1) new products
   (2) new designs
   (3) employee attitudes
   (4) labor-management relationships
   (5) family relationships

5. Which of the following best describes the use of surveys for business purposes?

   (1) overrated
   (2) too widely used
   (3) often deceptive
   (4) necessary
   (5) costly

GO ON TO THE NEXT PAGE

Items 6 to 9 are based on the following selection.

The stock market collapse began in October 1929 when banks in Great Britain raised their interest rates to 6½ percent in order to bring home needed capital that had been attracted to the United States by the speculation for high profits. As a result, many European holdings were thrown on the market, and the prices of stocks began to fall. Frightened by declining stock prices and no longer able to borrow at will, American speculators also began to unload. Frantic selling followed, and the value of stocks listed on the New York Stock Exchange plummeted from $87,000,000,000 to $55,000,000,000 or about 37 percent. This, however, was only the beginning. Despite repeated assurances from high government and financial authorities that prosperity was just around the corner, nine similar declines to new low levels were recorded during the next three years. By the first of March, 1933, all stocks listed on the New York Stock Exchange were worth only about $19,000,000,000.

It was soon apparent that a period of unparalleled depression had begun. The prices of goods dropped sharply; foreign trade fell off; factories curtailed production or, frequently, simply closed their doors; real estate values (but not mortgages) declined; new construction practically stopped; banks failed. Worst of all, wages were cut drastically and unemployment began to mount. By the end of 1930, about six or seven million workers were out of jobs; two years later, the number had doubled. The United States was not alone in its distress. It was soon visible to all that whatever seriously affected one great nation would eventually affect the world.

6. Which of the following statements is best supported by evidence presented in this selection?

   (1) All governments are corrupt.
   (2) All great nations are tied together by economics.
   (3) When many people lose their jobs, unemployment develops.
   (4) The Depression could have been avoided by clever people.
   (5) If America was ruled by a dictator, the stock market crash would not have happened.

7. Which of the following is a hypothesis supported by this selection?

   (1) Inflation goes hand-in-hand with unemployment.
   (2) Mortgage rates drop during a depression.
   (3) Land values go up when real estate declines.
   (4) Unemployment rises when prices drop.
   (5) Government can prevent a depression by assuring people.

8. Which of the following occurred when the Depression began?

   (1) Factories decreased output.
   (2) Foreign trade increased.
   (3) Confidence was restored.
   (4) Prices of goods increased.
   (5) Wages were unaffected.

9. According to the information in the passage, what set off the stock market collapse?

   (1) England tried to bring more money into the country.
   (2) America attempted to correct a foreign trade imbalance.
   (3) Wages were cut sharply and unemployment rose.
   (4) American stockholders were frightened.
   (5) Mortgages dropped quickly; real estate prices fell off.

Items 10 and 11 refer to the following information.

The Constitution provides for a separation of power between federal and state governments and a system of checks and balances to regulate the three branches of government. The three most important powers of government are lodged mainly in three separate branches: The legislative branch which has the power to make laws, the executive branch which has the power to enforce laws, and the judicial branch which has the power to interpret laws.

10. Which of the following statements best explains the reason for the system of checks and balances?

    (1) It allows the government to use checks to pay bills.
    (2) It allows the president to choose the best possible advisors.
    (3) It permits Congressional committees to conduct investigations.
    (4) It diffuses power so that no one branch of government becomes too strong.
    (5) It gives the U.S. greater stature as leader of the free world.

11. Which of the following is an example of the system of checks and balances in action?

    (1) The Bill of Rights guarantees freedom of speech.
    (2) States are responsible for the health and safety of their citizens.
    (3) The president vetoes legislation passed by Congress.
    (4) The vice-president takes over if the president is unable to fulfill the duties of his office.
    (5) Members of Congress are free from arrest for anything said on the floor of Congress.

Items 12 to 14 are based on the following graph.

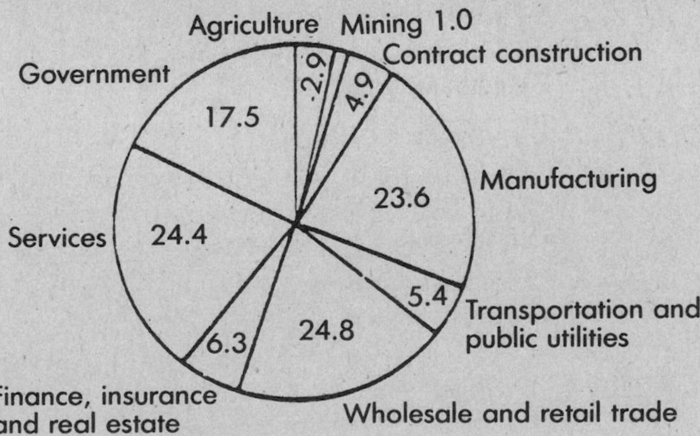

[1]*Wage and salary workers, except for agriculture, which includes self-employed and unpaid family workers.*

Source: Bureau of Labor Statistics

12. The graph above projects the number and kinds of jobs, which are expected to be available in 1990. It includes farm workers, some of whom are either self-employed or unpaid family workers. According to the information in this graph, what is the total number of workers expected to be in 1990?

    (1) 95,000,000
    (2) 100,000,000
    (3) 103,000,000
    (4) 107,000,000
    (5) 111,000,000

13. Generally speaking, government regulations will be carried out by workers on the federal, state, and local levels. According to the graph, government workers will be nearly three times as numerous as workers in which one of the following categories?

    (1) the service industries
    (2) the finance, insurance, and real estate fields
    (3) the mining industries
    (4) agriculture
    (5) manufacturing

14. What is this type of graph called?

    (1) bar graph
    (2) line graph
    (3) "pie" graph
    (4) chart
    (5) diagram

GO ON TO THE NEXT PAGE

Items 15 to 18 are based on the following selection.

Genocide is the systematic destruction and eradication of a racial, political, or cultural group. Its aim is total annihilation of that group, of its history and of all memories of it. Genocide is not a new concept. Over the ages, the group in power has tried to eliminate peoples weaker than itself. While genocide in practice involves the cooperation of many, it is usually the idea of one strong leader.

Carthage was established in 850 B.C. at a sheltered point on the Gulf of Tunis. Because of its strategic location and fine harbor, the colony grew to be the center of Phoenician trade. Carthage became one of the largest and richest cities of ancient times with a population estimated at more than 1,000,000.

In time the ambitions of Carthage collided with those of other nations. It was with Rome that the great struggle occurred in a series of three long and bitter wars extending intermittently from 264 B.C. to 146 B.C. with the Romans finally victorious. Because their leaders insisted that Carthage must be destroyed if the Romans were ever to have peace, the Romans killed or enslaved the Carthaginians, burned their city and plowed under the site.

It has been said that in the long run only religion, art, and wisdom insure immortality. The Carthaginians apparently were more successful at trade than at any of these, for there are today few traces of their civilization.

15. According to the information in the passage, which of the following is an example of genocide?

    (1) Carthage had a population estimated at more than 1,000,000.
    (2) The wars lasted more than 100 years and the Romans were victorious.
    (3) The Romans killed or enslaved the Carthaginians, burned their city, and plowed under the site.
    (4) The ambitions of Carthage collided with those of other nations.
    (5) The Phoenicians were very successful at trade.

16. According to the passage, which of the following statements shows that the Romans were successful in their genocide?

    (1) The Romans needed to destroy Carthage in order to have peace.
    (2) There are few traces of the civilization of Carthage remaining today.
    (3) Carthage was one of the largest and richest cities of ancient times.
    (4) Carthage was established about 850 B.C.
    (5) Traces of Roman civilization may be found throughout northern Africa.

17. According to the passage, which of the following insures immortality?

    (1) great wealth
    (2) celebrated victories
    (3) harsh laws
    (4) sound economy
    (5) fine art

18. According to the passage, why did the Romans want to destroy Carthage?

    (1) They were jealous because Carthage was such a wealthy city.
    (2) They objected to the religion of the Carthaginians.
    (3) They feared the strength of the Carthaginians.
    (4) They wanted to take over Phoenician trade.
    (5) They had traditionally hated the Carthaginians.

Items 19 to 22 refer to the following speakers.

Economists *A, B, C, D,* and *E* represent five points of view on what each believes the relationship of big business and government should be.

Economist A: As this nation has industrialized, much business has grown so large that only the federal government is capable of regulating it. The government must protect the consumer against trusts, for, after all, the government exists to help the individuals do what they cannot do by themselves.

Economist B: This country's amazing economic growth rests upon private enterprise which should be allowed to function freely. The government's role should be only to provide an economic climate conducive to the development of business.

Economist C: Major industry has become so large that the individual citizen is at the mercy of the big corporations. The only way to solve the problem is for the government to assume ownership of the nation's basic industries.

Economist D: Ours is a market economy where the consumer is king. Leave business alone, and it will provide consumers with what they want at the cheapest prices possible.

Economist E: Combinations in business are not necessarily an evil, but government must regulate their diverse activities to assure the welfare of various economic groups.

19. Which economist would be considered a socialist?

(1) A
(2) B
(3) C
(4) D
(5) E

20. Which economist is most likely to favor such measures as the Truth in Packaging Act and the Truth in Lending Act?

(1) A
(2) B
(3) C
(4) D
(5) E

21. Which economist best represents the policies followed by the United States government during the period of great economic growth experienced through most of the nineteenth century?

(1) A
(2) B
(3) C
(4) D
(5) E

22. According to the theory of *laissez-faire* economics advocated by Economist D, prices should be determined chiefly by

(1) government regulations
(2) supply and demand
(3) leaders of business and industry
(4) negotiations between labor and management
(5) lobbyists working for a variety of special interest groups

Item 23 refers to the following quotation.

"To whom does this land belong? I believe it belongs to me. If you asked me for a piece of it I would not give it. I cannot spare it and I like it very much . . . I hope you will listen to me"

23. This quotation most likely represents the point-of-view of a member of which of the following groups?

(1) a European immigrant in the 1890's
(2) a civil rights advocate in the 1960's
(3) a professional worker in the 1980's
(4) an American Indian in the 1860's
(5) a southern sharecropper during Reconstruction

Items 24 and 25 are based on the following cartoon.

Drawing by Chas. Addams; © 1979 The New Yorker Magazine, Inc.

24. The cartoonist is commenting on something that he feels concerns Americans deeply. Which of the following does the cartoonist feel preoccupies Americans?

    (1) home hobbies
    (2) urban crime
    (3) the do-it-yourself craze
    (4) locksmithing as a vocation
    (5) urban decay

25. Which of the following best expresses the main idea of the cartoon?

    (1) No one is absolutely safe.
    (2) Locks and door devices are foolish.
    (3) The more locks you have, the safer you are.
    (4) Crime does not pay.
    (5) Cities are inherently unsafe.

Items 26 to 30 are based on the following information.

Taxes are classified according to the way they are paid and the way they relate to the taxpayer's income. Listed below are five types of taxation and a brief description of how each works.

1. **Negative income taxes**—federal payments to families with income below a stipulated level
2. **Value added taxes**—added at each stage of the processing of a raw material or the production and distribution of a commodity
3. **Progressive taxes**—based on the taxpayer's income; the more he earns, the more he is required to pay
4. **Regressive taxes**—take a higher percentage of income from the poor than the rich
5. **Surtax**—a tax on a tax

Each of the following statements describes one type of taxation. Choose the category in which the taxation described would most likely occur. The categories may be used more than once in the set of items but no one question has more than one best answer.

26. Taxes are paid on all tobacco products at each step in the production process, including harvesting, drying, processing, and the finished cigarettes, pipe tobacco, etc. These taxes are best described as

    (1) negative income taxes
    (2) value added taxes
    (3) progressive taxes
    (4) regressive taxes
    (5) surtaxes

27. Below is a table of tax rates.

Income	*Tax*
$0–6,000	0%
6,001–16,000	15%
16,001–28,000	25%
28,001–60,000	30%

The tax shown on the table above is best described as

    (1) negative income tax
    (2) value added tax
    (3) progressive tax
    (4) regressive tax
    (5) surtax

28. The federal government has determined that it requires $9,000 a year to support a family of four. The Dittmeir family, made up of a father, mother, and two children, earns a total of $8,500 per year. The federal government gives the family $500 per year. This payment is an example of

    (1) negative income tax
    (2) value added tax
    (3) progressive tax
    (4) regressive tax
    (5) surtax

29. If a man earns $200 a month, and he buys $50 worth of goods upon which there is a 10% tax, that tax takes $2\frac{1}{2}$% of his income for that month. Another man, who earns $1,000 a month, may buy the same goods at $50. He will pay only $\frac{1}{2}$ of 1% of his income in taxes. Which type of tax is illustrated by this example?

    (1) negative income tax
    (2) value added tax
    (3) progressive tax
    (4) regressive tax
    (5) surtax

30. The federal government needs an additional 1 million dollars of income for this fiscal year. To raise the money, the government adds 4¢ a gallon to the 15¢ a gallon gasoline tax. This tax is an example of

    (1) negative income tax
    (2) value added tax
    (3) progressive tax
    (4) regressive tax
    (5) surtax

GO ON TO THE NEXT PAGE

Items 31 to 34 are based on the following information.

Petroleum consumption has been a significant factor in the economy of both industrialized and developing countries. The following graphs show the petroleum consumption patterns of selected industrialized countries for the calendar year 1983.

International Petroleum Consumption for Major Noncommunist Industrialized Countries

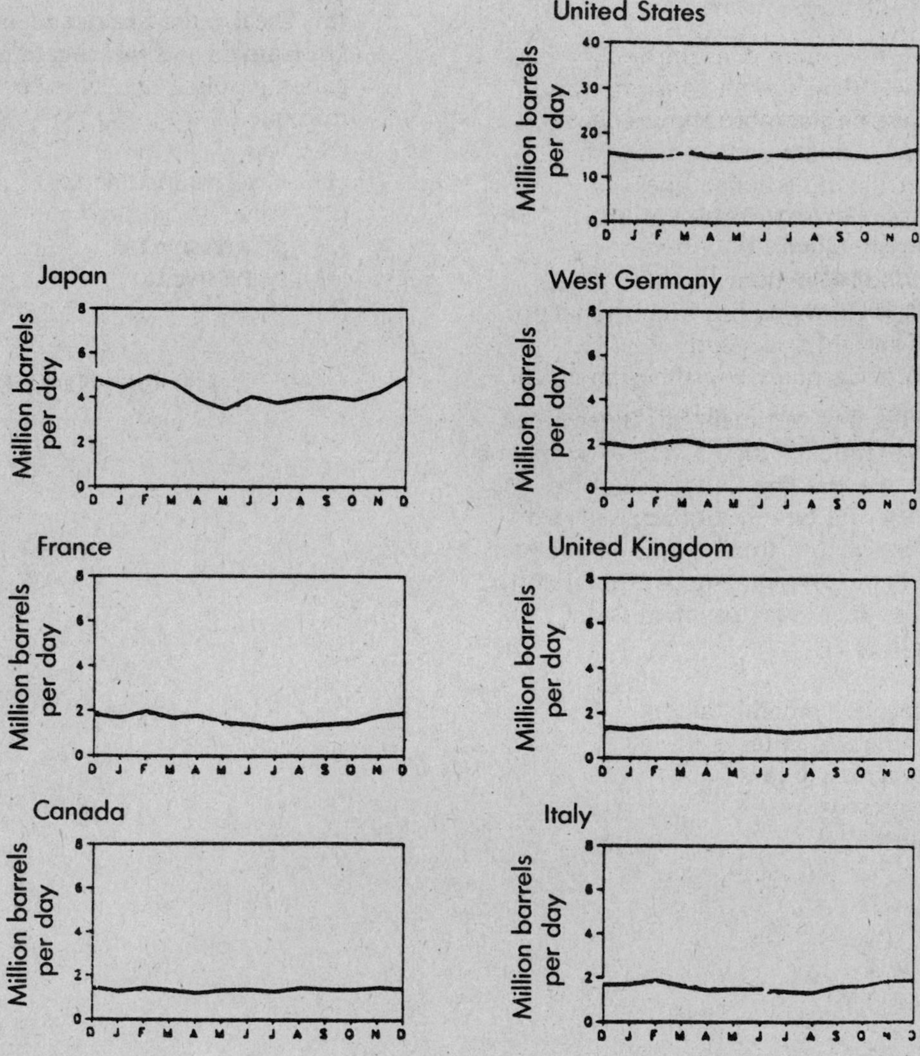

31. One of the countries on this chart appears to have a voracious appetite for fuel consumption. According to the information above, which nation has the highest daily consumption?

    (1) Canada
    (2) France
    (3) West Germany
    (4) Japan
    (5) United States

32. Based on the information shown above, which of the following is the most accurate statement that could be made about petroleum consumption in West Germany?

    (1) West German consumption is much lower than Italian consumption.
    (2) West Germany consumes approximately twice as much petroleum as Japan does.
    (3) West German consumption is slightly higher than that of the United Kingdom.
    (4) West Germany has been the victim of an OPEC boycott.
    (5) West Germany consumes about the same amount of petroleum as the United States does.

33. Of all the nations shown above, which country has the greatest variation in consumption from month to month?

    (1) West Germany
    (2) United Kingdom
    (3) United States
    (4) Canada
    (5) Japan

34. Which two countries consume the greatest amount of petroleum?

    (1) The United States and Japan
    (2) The United States and West Germany
    (3) The United States and France
    (4) The United States and Italy
    (5) Canada and the United Kingdom

GO ON TO THE NEXT PAGE

Items 35 to 38 are based on the following selection.

In 1979, Americans consumed about eight billion pounds of red meat that had been cured with nitrites and/or nitrates. Smaller amounts of poultry and fish contained these preservatives, which are now the subject of bitter legal, public relations, and regulatory battles being fought between the meat industry and some consumer groups. The controversy was sparked by the disclosure that nitrosamines, which are suspected of causing cancer, formed in some cured meats under certain conditions, including frying bacon with very high heat. Since then, government and industry have taken a number of steps to lessen the danger from these preformed nitrosamines. These steps include lowering the level of nitrite used, and adding sodium ascorbate or sodium erythorbate, both of which are believed to retard the formation of nitrosamines from nitrites.

Both industry and government believe that the use of nitrites is an important protection against botulism, the most deadly food-borne toxin. Some consumer groups say the botulism threat is overstated, and that the toxin will not form in meats which are properly processed and kept under refrigeration. Consumer activists contend that the talk of botulism is a smoke screen to protect the industry reliance on long shelf life Food scientists point out that the botulism spore (the inactive stage of the bacteria's life) is notoriously difficult to kill. Heat sufficient to destroy it would alter the flavor and texture of meat products.

35. Which of the following is the best title for this passage?

    (1) The Problem of Nitrosamines—the Consumer's Dilemma
    (2) Big Business Wins Again
    (3) Cancer and the Problem of Big Business
    (4) Botulism: A Deadly Poison
    (5) Protecting the Meat-Eater

36. According to the information in the passage, what is "botulism"?

    (1) a bacterial food poisoning
    (2) a form of cancer
    (3) a food spoilage retardant
    (4) sodium erythorbate
    (5) an antitoxin produced by the body

37. According to the passage, what is the problem with using heat to destroy the botulism spore in meat products?

    (1) excessive cost
    (2) danger to workers' lives
    (3) lower profits for processors
    (4) change in the flavor and texture of the meat
    (5) encourages cancer cells to grow

38. According to the passage, why do consumer groups believe processors are really using nitrites?

    (1) to keep products on store shelves for a longer time
    (2) to allow processors to use cheap meat
    (3) to change the flavor and texture of meat
    (4) to allow the substitution of cheap meat for more expensive
    (5) to allow canned meat into the country

39. The geography of an area determines how the land will be used. Colonists found the land in the Northern colonies was rocky and good soil was scarce. In the Southern colonies, they found an abundance of good soil. Which of the following was a result of these conditions?

    (1) Many large plantations could be found in Connecticut.
    (2) Virginia could only have small farms.
    (3) North Carolina was forced to develop large industrial factories to support the people.
    (4) It was difficult to grow rice and tobacco in Georgia.
    (5) Fur trading and fishing were the major industries of New Hampshire.

Items 40 to 42 are based on the following bill.

SW **Valley Water Company** INCORPORATED
360 West End Road • Redwood, New York 10994

BILLING DATE		SERVICE ADDRESS	
JUN 03 86		15 Jones AVE	45-110-13

METER NUMBER	FOR THE PERIOD FROM	TO	NO. OF DAYS IN PERIOD	RATE CODE	METER READINGS PREVIOUS	PRESENT	CONSUMPTION IN 100 CU. FT.	BILLING CODE	AMOUNT
05445074	0221	0331	38		1355	1364	9		
30669921	0331	0522	52		0000	0022	22		
					SUMMER RATE				31.19
					WINTER RATE				62.71

BUDGET PAYMENT PLAN	
COST FOR WATER CONSUMED THIS PERIOD	BALANCE IN PLAN AFTER PAYMENT OF AMOUNT DUE

ONE HUNDRED CUBIC FEET EQUALS 748 GALLONS. YOUR CONSUMPTION FOR THE CURRENT BILLING PERIOD WAS 23,188 GALLONS.

AMOUNT DUE $93.90

PAYABLE ON OR BEFORE JUN 20 86

40. Based on this bill, how many gallons of water were used from February 21 to March 31?

 (1) 1,364
 (2) 6,732
 (3) 16,456
 (4) 28,424
 (5) cannot be determined from the information given

41. How much does 100 cubic feet of water cost in the winter given the fact that the winter rate ends on March 31?

 (1) $1.42
 (2) $1.46
 (3) $3.02
 (4) $3.47
 (5) $6.97

42. Based on an average cost, how much did each gallon of water cost?

 (1) $.004
 (2) $.01
 (3) $.40
 (4) $1.29
 (5) $3.12

Item 43 refers to the following passage.

New England merchants sold lumber, meat, and fish to the West Indies in exchange for molasses and money. The molasses was distilled into rum. The rum was then sold in Africa in exchange for slaves and gold. The merchants also sold raw materials to England. They used the money they earned to buy finished goods from England. This was called the "Triangular Trade."

43. Which of the following statements best explains one of the reasons for the establishment of the "Triangular Trade," according to the information presented in the paragraph?

 (1) New England colonists used rum as a medicine.
 (2) Slaves were needed to run factories in England.
 (3) England needed a market for the goods it manufactured.
 (4) The people in the West Indies paid high wages to their slaves.
 (5) African nations had a well-developed merchant marine fleet.

GO ON TO THE NEXT PAGE

Items 44 to 48 are based on the following selection.

The events of the period from 1920 to 1930 in the United States have been consolidated by historians into a special area of study. The era of the 1920's lends itself to study as a unit in regard to the pervading temperament and interests of the decade. The twenties have been called the "Jazz Age," the age of flappers, Lindbergh, and frivolous nonsense. The 1920's, however, had a serious side as well which reflected the needs and shortcomings of a nation that was trying to adjust to the aftermath of a world war.

Historical and literary works of this period are abundant. Some of the major themes of these works on the 1920's dealt with the Red Scare, immigration, urbanization, the farmer, and the change in morals in the United States. In general, the 1920's was a period in which the United States was transformed from a rural nation into a world power with far-reaching responsibilities. The historiographical and popular writings, both contemporary and modern, suggest that the era of the twenties was overwhelmed by the pressures of the new machine age. Thus, the 1920's represented a period of transition, a reaction to the coming of the modern American way of life.

44. Based on the information in the article, which of the following statements best describes the 1920's?

    (1) It was time of frivolous nonsense.
    (2) It was marked by depression and hard times.
    (3) There was great change.
    (4) Many great works were produced, especially movies.
    (5) There were many great inventions.

45. According to the passage, what might a person see if he had a time machine and could go back to the 1920's?

    (1) many machines doing farm work
    (2) soldiers coming home from war
    (3) early space flight
    (4) a stock market crash
    (5) a sober nation suffering economic hardship

46. Based on the passage, what do the terms "Jazz Age" and "flappers" represent?

    (1) fads of the 1920's
    (2) the names of political parties of the 1920's
    (3) terms used before 1900
    (4) an omen of things yet to come
    (5) immigrants who arrived during the 1920's

47. Which of the following statements best explains the reasons why historians treat the 1920's as a special area of study?

    (1) There were a great many literary and historical works produced.
    (2) The United States transformed from a rural to industrial nation.
    (3) It had a mood all its own.
    (4) It was the first machine age.
    (5) The 1920's were a great deal like the present age.

48. Which of the following statements can be inferred based on the information in the article?

    (1) 1920–1930 was a period of great happiness.
    (2) The "Jazz Age" was a unique era in American life.
    (3) The twenties represented an era of unparalleled change.
    (4) There were no Communists in the twenties.
    (5) Historians group eras on the basis of different characteristics.

Items 49 and 50 are based on the following cartoon.

49. What does the cartoonist see happening when inflation increases very rapidly?

    (1) Unskilled workers will not know how to sail a ship.
    (2) Unskilled workers will be unlikely to survive.
    (3) Skilled workers will have a better captain.
    (4) The seas will be very rough for all workers.
    (5) Skilled workers will be better able to compensate for the ravages of inflation than unskilled workers.

50. According to the information in the cartoon, what would be the best course for an individual to take when inflation strikes?

    (1) learn to swim
    (2) get training in a job skill
    (3) move to a different country
    (4) have a savings account
    (5) join the armed services

GO ON TO THE NEXT PAGE

Items 51 to 55 are based on the following passage.

Many organizations have established group meal programs for the elderly, who might not otherwise eat properly because they cannot afford to buy proper food or do not know what foods make up a balanced diet. Often the elderly are not physically able to shop or prepare meals. Many, because of loneliness and isolation, may decide it is too much trouble to prepare a meal to eat alone. One of the most important aspects of the group meal program is the companionship it provides, which reduces loneliness.

Through group meal programs, older Americans are provided with a hot meal once a day (usually lunch), five days a week, at thousands of sites throughout the country, including senior centers, churches, schools, public housing and other community facilities. In all of these settings, the programs provide not only a nutritious and inexpensive meal but also social and recreational activities that older people otherwise might not have.

The Older Americans Act provides for a national nutrition program for the elderly and authorizes the federal government to pay up to ninety percent of the cost, with state and local governments paying at least ten percent. The states allocate these funds to local sponsoring agencies, called grantees, that employ persons to operate the nutrition projects. In 1975, there were over 4,200 sites in the federal program, providing almost a quarter of a million meals each day to older Americans. Since participation in the federal program does not meet all the nutritional needs of the elderly, many senior centers and other publicly and privately funded agencies also provide low-cost meals.

51. Which of the following titles best expresses the main idea of this article?

    (1) Feeding Americans
    (2) Providing an Adequate Diet for the Elderly
    (3) Eating Well and Keeping Fit
    (4) The Loneliness of the Aged
    (5) Meals: Nutritious and Inexpensive

52. According to the article, how many meals are served every day to the elderly with the support of the federal government?

    (1) 2500
    (2) 4000
    (3) 100,000
    (4) 250,000
    (5) 2,500,000

53. Which of the following does the author feel the elderly should be guaranteed?

    (1) financial support
    (2) mental stimulation
    (3) psychological assistance
    (4) adequate exercise
    (5) proper nutrition

54. According to the information presented in the article, which of the following statements is the most likely explanation for the large number of elderly who participate in the nutrition program?

    (1) With today's variety of lifestyles, more of the elderly are living on their own.
    (2) There are few supermarkets near elderly people.
    (3) The elderly enjoy eating by themselves.
    (3) These centers are near public transportation.
    (5) Older Americans enjoy cooking for themselves.

55. Which of the following statements is best supported by evidence presented in this article?

    (1) There are adequate federal resources to support the nutrition program.
    (2) The nutrition program was designed only to feed the elderly.
    (3) The program satisfies an elderly person's total daily nutritional needs.
    (4) Some elderly people suffer as much from isolation as from inadequate nutrition.
    (5) The program needs to be extended to meet the needs of younger Americans.

Items 56 and 57 refer to the following map

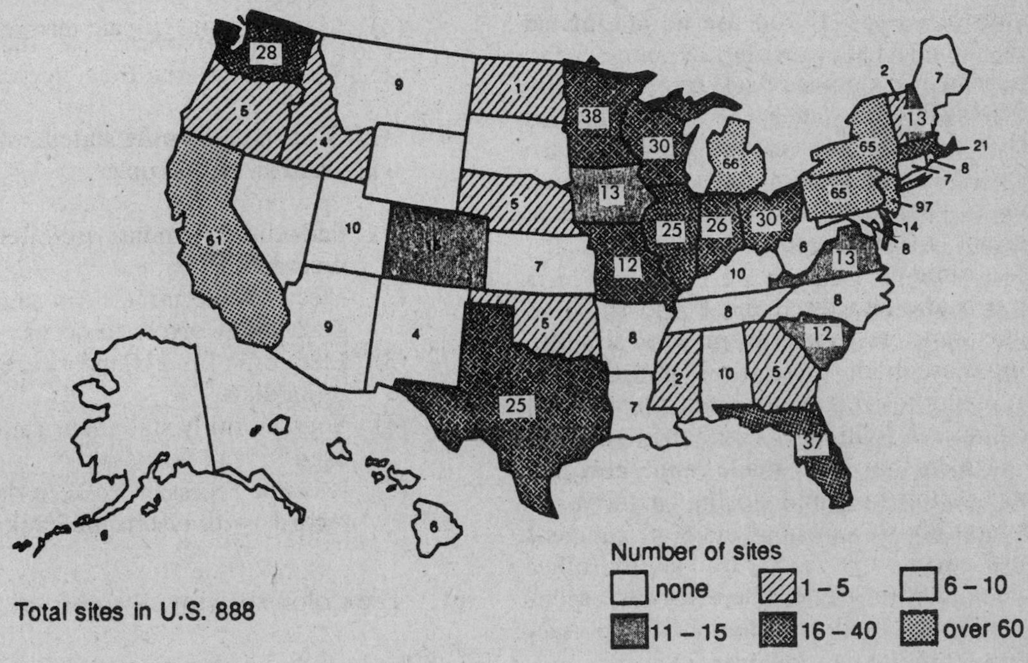

56. Based on this map, in which of the following states are residents LEAST likely to be exposed to toxic wastes?

    (1) Nevada
    (2) Texas
    (3) California
    (4) Florida
    (5) Missouri

57. According to this map, an administrator allocating funding to the clean-up of hazardous waste sites would probably choose which area in order to improve the environment of the greatest number of people?

    (1) Maine, Vermont, New Hampshire
    (2) New York, New Jersey, Pennsylvania
    (3) Washington and Oregon
    (4) Georgia, Alabama, Florida
    (5) Texas and Oklahoma

GO ON TO THE NEXT PAGE

Items 58 to 60 are based on the following selection.

A cancelled check is permanent proof that a payment has been made. Can an electronic terminal give this proof?

The answer is yes. If you use an automated teller machine (ATM) to withdraw money or to make deposits, or a point-of-sale terminal to pay for a purchase, you can get a written receipt —much like the sales receipt you get with a cash purchase—showing the amount of the transfer, the date it was made, and other information. This receipt is your record of transfers initiated at an electronic terminal.

Your periodic statement must also show all electronic transfers to and from your account, including those made at electronic terminals, or under a preauthorized arrangement, or ordered by telephone. It will also name the party to whom payment has been made, and show any fees and your opening and closing balances.

Your monthly statement is proof of payment to a third party, your record for tax and other purposes, and your way of checking and reconciling electronic fund transfer (EFT) transactions with your account balance.

Remember when you're paying bills that electronic fund transfer transactions may take place *immediately.* When you write a check you enter the amount on your checkbook stub and deduct it to keep a running account of your balance. Be sure to keep the same kind of accurate, day-to-day record of your electronic fund transfer transactions.

58. According to the information in the passage, which of the following provides proof that payment has been made?

    (1) a cancelled check
    (2) an automated teller machine
    (3) a point-of-sale terminal
    (4) a telephone order
    (5) word of mouth

59. According to the information in the passage, why is it important for the consumer to keep an accurate record of each transaction made?

    (1) to prevent additional charges on the account
    (2) to discourage fraud
    (3) to prove payment
    (4) to know how much money is left in the account
    (5) to use a point-of-sale terminal properly

60. Which of the following statements is supported by this article?

    (1) Periodic statements are often incomplete.
    (2) Electronic terminals can cause a great many errors to occur.
    (3) Electronic fund transfers are immediate.
    (4) Your monthly statement cannot be used for tax purposes
    (5) It is not necessary to keep day-to-day records with electronic banking.

61. The Colonists wrote these words in 1776:

"The history of the present King of Great Britain is a history of repeated injuries and usurpations, all having in direct object the establishment of an absolute Tyranny over these States. To prove this, let Facts be submitted to a candid world."

Why would these words be written?

    (1) to justify a revolution against the king
    (2) to thank the king for ruling fairly
    (3) to send an ambassador to meet with the king
    (4) to set up an American Constitution
    (5) to force the king to abdicate

62. Sulfur dioxide emissions from industrial plants combine with water in the atmosphere to form a poisonous rain or snow. What is this called?

    (1) water pollution
    (2) air pollution
    (3) sulfur pollution
    (4) acid rain
    (5) industrial accidents

Item 63 refers to the chart below.

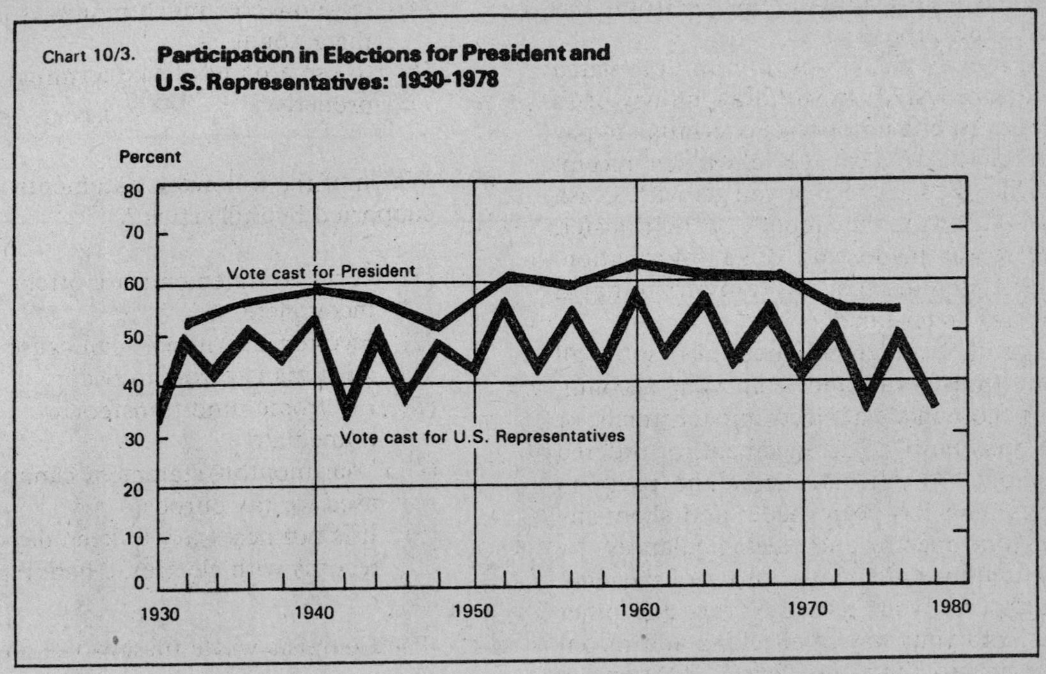

63. The chart shown above pictures the behavior of American voters in national elections from the 1930's through the 1970's. Based on this information, what could the student of American history conclude?

    (1) The end of World War II discouraged voters' interest in the 1948 presidential election.
    (2) Candidates for the House of Representatives receive fewer votes in "off-year" elections.
    (3) Candidates for President receive a higher number of votes in "off-year" elections.
    (4) President Eisenhower's popularity drew the highest number of voters to the polls during the time period 1930–1977.
    (5) Domestic dissension over the Vietnamese Conflict encouraged intense voter participation in the 1966 presidential election.

GO ON TO THE NEXT PAGE

Item 64 refers to the graph below.

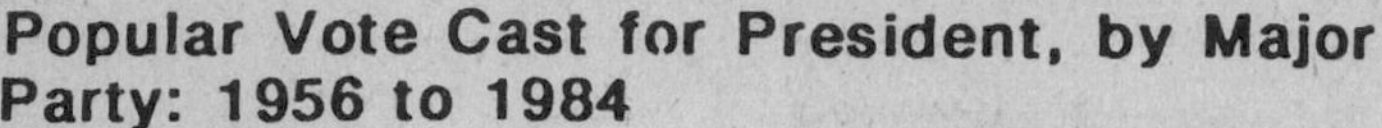

Popular Vote Cast for President, by Major
Party: 1956 to 1984

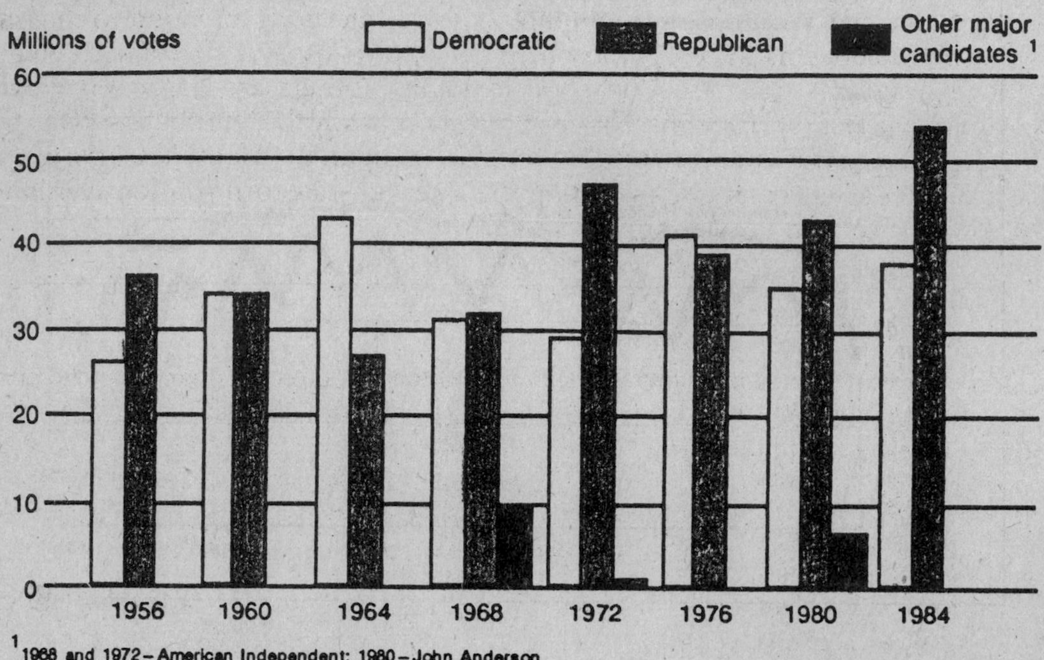

Statistical Abstract p. 229

64. The size of the popular vote usually determines the outcome of a presidential election, which is officially certified by the Electoral College. Using the information shown in the chart above, a student of American history could infer that.

    (1) The Republican party is larger than the Democratic party.
    (2) Democratic candidates are more popular than Republican presidential candidates.
    (3) The Electoral College determined the winner in 1960.
    (4) Ronald Reagan was officially certified as president-elect on December 15, 1980.
    (5) A "third-party candidate" rarely influences the outcome of recent presidential elections.

END OF SOCIAL STUDIES TEST

TEST 3. SCIENCE

Time: 95 Minutes—66 Questions

Directions:

The Science Test consists of multiple-choice questions intended to measure general concepts in biology, earth science, physics, and chemistry. Some of the questions are based on short readings. Others are based on graphs, charts, tables, or diagrams. For each question, study the information given and then answer the question or questions based upon it. Refer to the information as often as necessary in answering the questions. Record your answer in the Science section of your answer sheet.

FOR EXAMPLE:

A physical change may alter the state of matter, but does not change its chemical composition. Which of the following is NOT a physical change?

(1) boiling water
(2) dissolving salt in water
(3) shaving wood
(4) rusting metal
(5) breaking glass

When metal rusts a new substance is formed. This is a chemical, not a physical, change. Therefore, answer space 4 should be marked on your answer sheet.

Items 1 to 4 are based on the following schematic diagram.

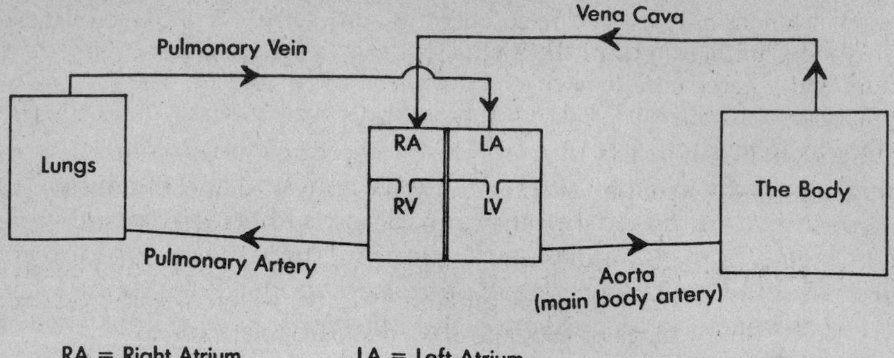

The above diagram indicates how blood circulates in the human body.

1. According to the diagram, in which direction do arteries carry blood?

   (1) to the heart
   (2) away from the heart
   (3) both to and from the heart
   (4) only to the body
   (5) between the body and lungs

2. To which of the following does the left ventricle pump blood?

   (1) the pulmonary artery
   (2) the vena cava
   (3) the pulmonary vein
   (4) the left atrium
   (5) all parts of the body

3. The blood found in the pulmonary vein has just left the lungs. Which of the following statements is true about this blood?

   (1) It is rich in iron.
   (2) It is poor in oxygen.
   (3) It is rich in oxygen.
   (4) It has no blood cells.
   (5) It lacks the ability to fight germs.

4. Which of the following sequences shows the actual flow of blood?

   (1) lungs, the heart, right atrium, right ventricle
   (2) the body, the lungs, vena cava, aorta
   (3) vena cava, right atrium, left ventricle, aorta
   (4) right ventricle, pulmonary artery, lungs, pulmonary vein
   (5) right ventricle, right atrium, vena cava, the lungs

Items 5 to 8 are based on the following information.

The animal kingdom is divided into several groups called Phyla. One of these Phyla is called the Chordates. All of the animals of this group have a backbone-like structure and a nerve cord located at the back of the organism. The Phylum Chordata can be further divided into five groups called classes. These classes are described as follows:

1. **Fish**————cold-blooded organisms with two-chambered hearts, gills, fins, and either a cartilagenous or bony skeleton.
2. **Amphibians**—cold-blooded organisms with a three-chambered heart. They can live either on land or in the water. They have either lungs or gills and have a slimy moist skin.
3. **Reptiles**———cold-blooded organisms with three-chambered hearts. They have lungs and a dry skin. Some reptiles have a four-chambered heart.
4. **Birds**————warm-blooded organisms with a four-chambered heart. They all have lungs and are covered with feathers.
5. **Mammals**——warm-blooded organisms with four-chambered hearts. They nourish their young with milk. They all have lungs.

Each of the following items describes a class of vertebrates that refers to one of the five classes listed above. For each item, choose the one class that best describes the animal. Each of the classes above may be used more than once in the following set of items.

5. This cold-blooded animal is greatly feared. It has a cartilagenous skeleton, gill openings, and a mouth on its underside. It has been known to attack man. This animal belongs to which of the following classes?

(1) fish
(2) amphibians
(3) reptiles
(4) birds
(5) mammals

6. The platypus is a small aquatic animal with webbed feet, a tail like a beaver's and a bill like a duck's. It lays eggs from which the young hatch. The mother feeds her young milk. Scientists classify this animal in which of the following groups?

(1) fish
(2) amphibians
(3) reptiles
(4) birds
(5) mammals

7. This warm-blooded animal can fly. It has the ability to navigate in total darkness by the use of a built-in sonar unit. This animal cares for its young, but it has no feathers. To which of the following classes does this animal belong?

(1) fish
(2) amphibians
(3) reptiles
(4) birds
(5) mammals

8. Ancient scientists thought that these animals simply came from the mud. This was because there were none of these animals in the water one day and on the next day there were thousands of them. A few weeks later the water was clear again, and those animals that were left alive were living on the land. These animals belonged to which of the following classes?

(1) fish
(2) amphibians
(3) reptiles
(4) birds
(5) mammals

GO ON TO THE NEXT PAGE

Items 9 and 10 refer to the following information.

NORMAL TEMPERATURE DURING JANUARY
FOR SELECTED CITIES

	MAXIMUM	MINIMUM
San Francisco, CA	55	42
Los Angeles, CA	67	48
Phoenix, AZ	65	39
Denver, CO	43	16
Miami, FL	75	59
Atlanta, GA	51	33
Chicago, IL	29	14
New Orleans, LA	62	43
Boston, MA	36	23
St. Paul, MN	20	2
New York City, NY	37	26
Portland, OR	44	34
Philadelphia, PA	39	24
Houston, TX	62	41

9. As a travel agent, Sam uses the chart above to advise his clients about weather conditions in the cities they plan to visit. Based on this temperature chart and the travel plans that follow, which of Sam's clients can expect to experience the widest range of temperatures on the trip scheduled?

(1) Pat, who will spend the week of January 12 in New York, Chicago, and Denver
(2) Julie, who will spend the first two weeks of January in Miami, Atlanta, and New Orleans
(3) Joe, who will tour New Orleans, Phoenix, and Houston the last week of January
(4) Mike, whose travel plans include visits to Phoenix, Los Angeles, and San Franscisco in mid-January
(5) Sue, who will make a trip to Portland, San Franscisco, and Denver at the end of January

10. Which of the five travelers would be most likely to experience the coldest weather on the trip planned?

(1) Pat
(2) Julie
(3) Joe
(4) Mike
(5) Sue

11. When Charles turned on the radio on Labor Day the announcer was talking about a deep tropical depression 50 miles east of the Bahamas. The announcer was most likely referring to conditions which would generate

(1) spreading of the seabed
(2) a tornado
(3) mineral deposits
(4) continental shelf
(5) a hurricane

Item 12 refers to this diagram of a rock.

12. Which description most nearly represents the process by which the rock shown here was formed?

(1) Magma is intruded into a sill or a dike.
(2) Batholiths become exposed as a mountain is worn away.
(3) Volcanic ash piles up on the ground and forms rock when squeezed together.
(4) Gravel and other large particles settle out of water and eventually become cemented together.
(5) Heat and pressure have transformed sediments into a new kind of rock.

GO ON TO THE NEXT PAGE

Item 13 refers to the following graph.

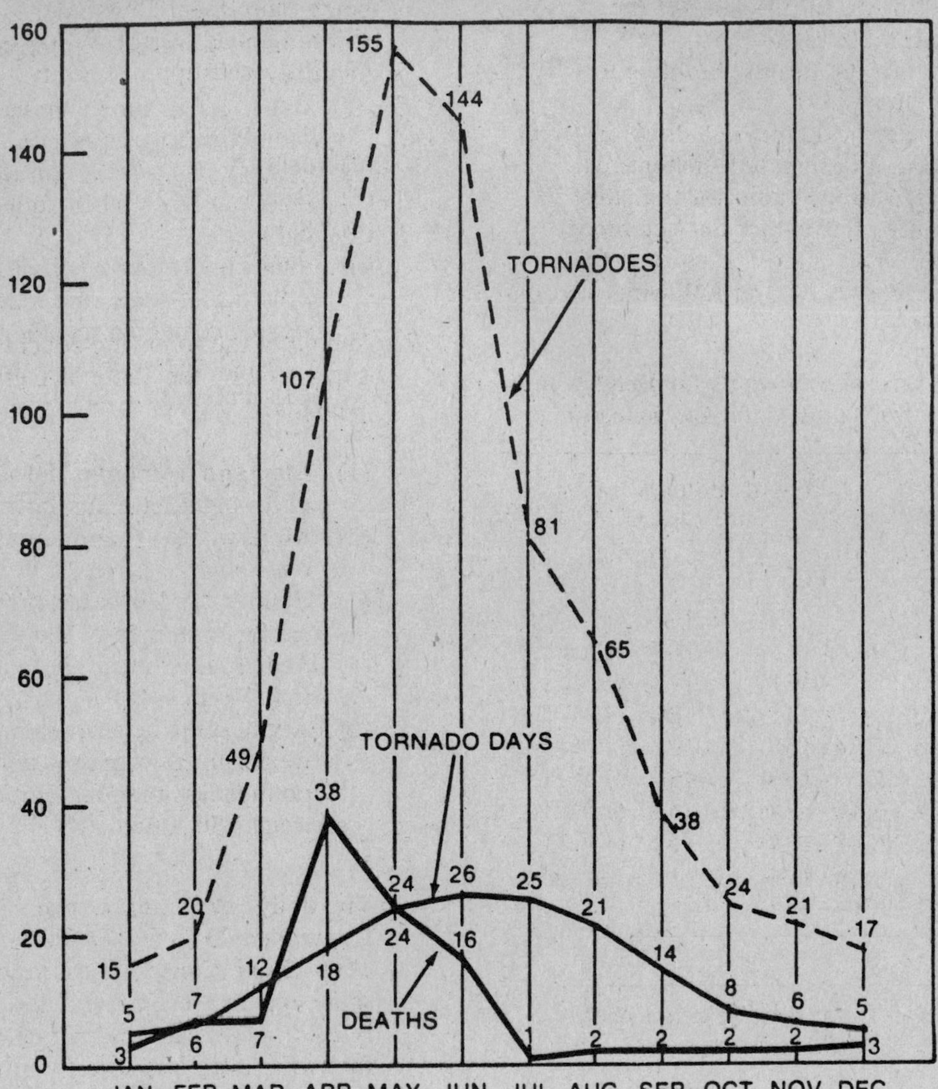

13. Which of the following conclusions is supported by the graph?

(1) The greatest number of tornadoes and the greatest number of tornado deaths occur in the same month.
(2) Although tornadoes can occur in any month, the greatest number of tornadoes occur in May.
(3) Fall tornadoes result in more tornado deaths than spring tornadoes.
(4) Winter tornadoes tend to be more severe than spring or summer tornadoes.
(5) There are more than 700 tornadoes each year.

14. If a traveler does sight a tornado, he should do any of the following, EXCEPT

(1) get down on the floor of the automobile
(2) run to the nearest building for shelter
(3) lie flat in the nearest ditch or ravine
(4) go to a designated shelter area
(5) listen to the radio for the latest National Weather Service report

Items 15 to 18 refer to the following information.

Suggested Desirable Weights for Heights and Ranges for Adult Males and Females

Height (inches)	Weight (pounds) Men		Women	
58			102	(92–119)
60			107	(96–125)
62	123	(112–141)	113	(102–131)
64	130	(118–148)	120	(108–138)
66	136	(124–156)	128	(114–146)
68	145	(132–166)	136	(122–154)
70	154	(140–174)	144	(130–163)
72	162	(148–184)	152	(138–173)
74	171	(156–194)		
76	181	(164–204)		

Heights and Weights of Selected Adults

Jane	5′4″	150 lb
Jeff	6′	165 lb
Bill	5′8″	130 lb
Sara	5′8″	130 lb
Paul	5′6″	156 lb

15. Based on the Table of Desirable Weights, which of the following adults should gain some weight?

(1) Jane
(2) Jeff
(3) Bill
(4) Sara
(5) Paul

16. Medically, to be overweight is to weigh 10 to 20% more than is recommended foı one's height. Obesity is the condition of being more than 20% above recommended weight. Who fits the medical definition of obesity?

(1) Jane
(2) Jeff
(3) Bill
(4) Sara
(5) Paul

17. Which of the following conclusions is supported by the Table of Desirable Weights?

(1) Men and women of the same height and weight have similar builds.
(2) More women than men are overweight.
(3) Women tend to reach maturity earlier than men of the same weight.
(4) At the same height, men are stronger than women.
(5) At the same height, recommended weight for a woman is about 10 pounds less than recommended weight for a man.

18. The daily calorie intake recommended for women 23 to 50 years old is 1600–2400 calories. For a man of the same age, the recommended daily intake is 2300–2700 calories. Which of the following is an important application of this information?

(1) Women should eat only half as much as men regardless of size.
(2) Men exercise more vigorously than women and so they can eat more without gaining weight.
(3) Women must be more careful in their food choice in order to obtain all the necessary nutrients without gaining weight.
(4) Height and weight are the only factors in weight control.
(5) Only women need to worry about weight control.

GO ON TO THE NEXT PAGE

Item 19 refers to the information below.

Jane can push with a force of 40 newtons. A graph describing her ability to do work is shown below.

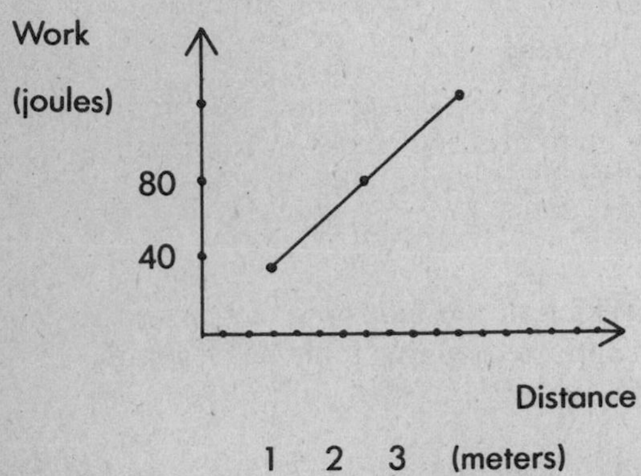

The amount of force necessary to move an object along a flat surface is:
W(work) = F(force) × D(distance)

19. If Jane pushes a block with a horizontal force of 40 newtons, at a constant speed of 2 meters per second, then how much work, in joules, is done on the block in 6 seconds?

(1) 80
(2) 120
(3) 240
(4) 480
(5) 500

Items 20 to 23 refer to the following article.

A knowledge of the spine can help in understanding the hows and whys of backache.

The spine is made up of 33 or 34 vertebrae (bones), the total depending on whether an individual has four or five vertebrae in the coccyx (tailbone), a normal variation. The vertebrae are separated and cushioned by oval pads called discs. For medical diagnostic purposes, the vertebrae are divided into five sections: the cervical (neck) region, containing seven vertebrae; the thoracic or dorsal (mid-back) region, containing 12 vertebrae; the lumbar (lower back) region, containing five vertebrae; the sacrum (back of the pelvis), which is one bone; and the coccyx (tailbone), with its four or five vertebrae. The most flexible regions—the neck and lower back—are the sites of most back problems.

Physicians often talk about vertebrae and discs with letter and number designations that are abbreviations for the section of the back and distance from the top of the spine. For example, the second vertebra down in the lumbar area is called L2.

Each disc is designated by the vertebrae above and below it. For instance, the L2–L3 disc is between the L2 and L3 vertebrae. The T12–L1 disc is between the lowest thoracic vertebra and the hightest lumbar vertebra. Discs under heavy mechanical stress, and thus the ones most likely to cause problems, are C5–C6, L3–L4, and L5–S1. Nerves in and around the spine are designated in the same manner as the vertebrae.

The back also contains ligaments, thick strong strands of tissue that attach one bone to another, and tendons, which are structures similar to ligaments but which attach muscles to bones.

The ligaments attached to the spine may rupture if the back flexes suddenly. This can be a source of localized pain for long periods. The remedy for a ruptured spinal ligament is usually surgery.

20. Most back problems seem to occur in which area of the spine?

(1) neck and lower back
(2) fused areas
(3) tailbone
(4) mid-back
(5) pelvic region

21. The back contains which of the following parts?

    I. ligaments
    II. tendons
    III. bones
    IV. vertebrae
    V. discs
    VI. nerves

    (1) I, II, and IV only
    (2) II, III, V, and VI only
    (3) I, II, and III only
    (4) II, IV, V, and VI only
    (5) I, II, III, IV, V, and VI

22. What is the function of the discs?

    (1) to separate the five regions of the spine
    (2) to provide a means for numbering the vertebrae
    (3) to attach muscles to bones
    (4) to separate and cushion the vertebrae
    (5) to make up for variations in the number of vertebrae

23. If you twist suddenly and experience a sharp pain in your back, you may have torn a

    (1) vertebra
    (2) ligament
    (3) coccyx
    (4) sacra
    (5) dorsal bone

24. The diagram below represents a section of undisturbed rock and the general location of fossils of several closely related species. According to current accepted evolutionary theory, which is the most probable correct assumption to be made concerning species *A, B, C,* and *D*?

species C & D
species C
species A & B & C
species A & B
species A

    (1) A is the ancestor of of B, C, and D.
    (2) B was already extinct when C evolved.
    (3) C evolved more recently than A, B, and D.
    (4) D is the ancestor of A, B, and C.
    (5) C and D represent the oldest species.

25. If line *A* in the diagram below represents a population of hawks in a community, then what would most likely be represented by line *B*?

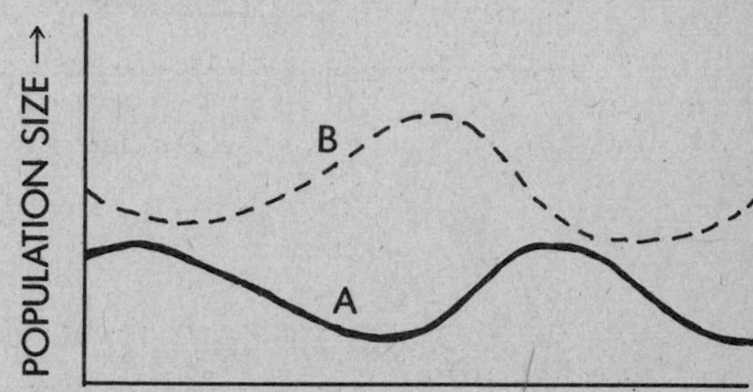

    (1) the dominant trees in that community
    (2) a population with which the hawks have a mutualistic relationship
    (3) variations in the numbers of producers in that community
    (4) a population on which the hawks prey
    (5) a population of hawk parasites

26. Occasionally hospitals have outbreaks of staphylococcus bacteria infections which resist treatment with antibiotics that were once effective. What is the most acceptable explanation for this condition?

    (1) Due to selective forces, new staphylococcus strains have become more abundant.
    (2) Newer antibiotics are weaker than those used in the past.
    (3) Laboratory strains of staphylococcus have been weakened.
    (4) Patients have become less susceptible to bacterial infection.
    (5) Staphylococci are weakened by age.

GO ON TO THE NEXT PAGE

Items 27 to 29 refer to the following graph.

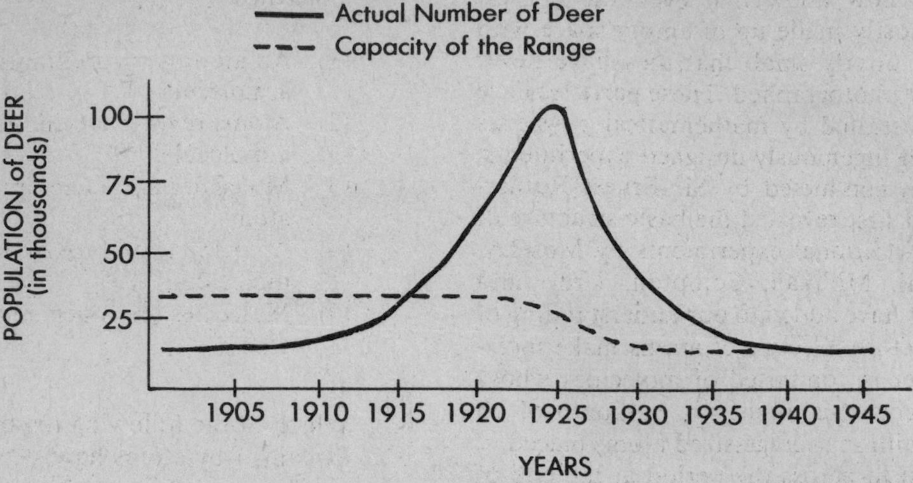

The graph above represents the relationship between the capacity of the range (number of deer that could be supported by the range), the number of deer actually living on the range, and time.

27. In what year was the number of deer living on the range equal to the capacity of the range?

    (1) 1905
    (2) 1915
    (3) 1920
    (4) 1930
    (5) 1945

28. What is the most likely reason why the capacity of the range to support deer decreased between 1920 and 1930?

    (1) The deer population became too large.
    (2) The number of predators increased between 1915 and 1925.
    (3) The deer population decreased in 1919.
    (4) An unusually cold winter occurred in 1918.
    (5) There was a decrease in rainfall in 1920.

29. What might be one reason why the number of deer began to increase in 1910?

    (1) The deer's natural enemies were killed.
    (2) The capacity of the range increased.
    (3) The available vegetation of the area decreased.
    (4) The winter was longer than normal in 1905.
    (5) The human population of the area increased.

Items 30 to 32 refer to the following passage.

Scientists now know that even the densest matter is mostly made up of empty space with particles so utterly small that they have never been seen or photographed. These particles have been demonstrated by mathematical physicists in a series of ingeniously designed experiments. Experiments conducted by Sir Ernest Rutherford in 1911 first revealed the basic structure of the atom. Additional experiments by Moseley, Bohr, Fermi, Millikan, Compton, Urey, and many others have added to our understanding of atomic structure. Groups of atoms make molecules. Matter is composed of molecules whose average diameter is about $\frac{1}{125}$ millionth of an inch. Five million average-sized atoms placed in a row would fit across the period at the end of this sentence. Although indivisible by ordinary chemical means, atoms are now known to be composed of a nucleus with protons (positively charged particles) and neutrons (electrically neutral particles), and electrons (negatively charged particles) which revolve at incredible speed around the atomic nucleus.

30. According to the passage, atoms are composed of which of the following particles?

    I. protons
    II. neutrons
    III. electrons
    IV. molecules

    (1) I and II only
    (2) II only
    (3) IV only
    (4) I, II, and III only
    (5) I, II, III, and IV

31. Which of the following best describes the relationship between atoms and molecules?

    (1) An atom is $\frac{1}{125}$ millionth the size of a molecule.
    (2) Atoms revolve around the nucleus of a molecule.
    (3) Molecules are made up of groups of atoms.
    (4) Atoms may be broken down into molecules.
    (5) Molecules are much smaller than atoms.

32. Which of the following reasons best explains why atoms have never been seen?

    (1) They are too small to be seen.
    (2) They revolve too quickly to be seen.
    (3) They are mostly empty space.
    (4) They do not really exist.
    (5) They are indivisible by ordinary chemical means.

GO ON TO THE NEXT PAGE

Items 33 to 35 refer to the following information.

Medical assistance should generally be given only by properly trained persons. However, you may find yourself in a situation where immediate assistance is unavailable, and you may have to help the injured victims. In these cases, remember these basic first aid rules:

Unless absolutely necessary because of the danger of fire or other hazard, avoid moving the injured person. If he must be moved, get help and try not to change the position in which he was found. If possible, cover him with coats or blankets to keep him warm.

Never lift a victim by holding him under the shoulders (armpits) and knees.

If a victim appears to have a broken back or broken neck, and you bend him forward or sit him up, you may cut his spinal cord and paralyze him permanently. Such a victim should only be lifted on a rigid board or lying on his stomach with the head supported. In turning such a victim over, be sure not to double him, let his neck fall forward, or twist his head.

Control excessive bleeding with thick cloth pads, as clean as possible, applied with pressure by hand or by bandaging.

Cover burns with clean cloths to reduce the pain. Apply no ointments.

Do not offer the injured anything to drink.

If the injured person does not seem to be breathing, attempt to revive breathing by administering "artificial respiration."

33. Jimmy dashed into the burning house and saw his grandfather lying on the floor, a wooden beam across his back. According to the basic first aid rules, what should Jimmy do with his injured grandfather?

(1) Move him out of the house without changing his position.
(2) Sit him up and drag him out of the house.
(3) Put him over his shoulder and carry him out of the house.
(4) Make him stand and walk out of the house.
(5) Leave him where he is.

34. Bleeding should usually be stopped by

(1) applying a bandage to the wound
(2) waiting for it to stop on its own
(3) administering artificial respiration
(4) a doctor
(5) applying pressure to the wound

35. Why does the author believe that everyone should know proper first aid?

(1) No doctor may be available.
(2) The victim may experience compounded injuries if he is improperly treated at the scene of the accident.
(3) The victim might die if he is not attended to.
(4) Choices (1), (2), and (3)
(5) Choices (1) and (3) only

36. If a doctor describes his patient as dehydrated, he is saying that the person

(1) has a contagious disease
(2) needs insulin
(3) cannot manufacture chlorophyll
(4) has lost a great deal of water
(5) has just been inoculated

Items 37 to 39 relate to the following information.

The number of protons remains the same for an atom of a given element, but the number of neutrons may vary. When this happens, we have two different varieties of the same element, or two isotopes of the element. One isotope is heavier than the other, but chemically they behave the same way. Isotopes of the same element have the same atomic number but different atomic mass.

37. Based on the information above, which is true of isotopes of an element?

    (1) They have the same number of protons, but a different number of electrons.
    (2) They have the same atomic number, but different atomic weight.
    (3) They have more protons than electrons.
    (4) They react more readily to form compounds.
    (5) They are exactly alike.

38. Which pair of atoms represents different isotopes of the same element?

    (1) $^{12}_{6}C$ and $^{13}_{6}C$
    (2) $^{12}_{6}C$ and $^{12}_{7}C$
    (3) $^{12}_{6}C$ and $^{13}_{7}C$
    (4) $^{14}_{7}N$ and $^{14}_{8}N$
    (5) $^{235}_{92}U$ and $^{235}_{93}Np$

39. In one half-life, half of a radioactive mass disintegrates. Strontium 90 has a half-life of 20 years. A sample originally weighing 8 grams, at the end of 40 years, will weigh

    (1) 1 gram
    (2) 2 grams
    (3) 4 grams
    (4) 16 grams
    (5) 32 grams

Items 40 and 41 refer to the following passage.

For the past six or seven years, a group of scientists has been attempting to make fortunes by breeding "bugs"—microorganisms that will manufacture valuable chemicals and drugs. This budding industry is called genetic engineering, and out of this young program, at least one company has induced a lowly bacterium to manufacture human interferon, a rare and costly substance that fights virus infections by "splicing" human genes into their natural hereditary material. But there are dangers in this activity, including the accidental development of a mutant bacterium which may change the whole life pattern on earth. There are also legal questions about whether a living organism can be patented, and what new products can be marketed from living matter. The Congressional agency which oversees these new developments says that it will be about seven years before any new product developed by genetic engineering will be allowed to be placed on the market.

40. Which of the following possibilities is one of the potential problems of genetic engineering?

    (1) an oversupply of bacteria
    (2) dangerous mutations
    (3) overpopulation
    (4) excess food
    (5) too many engineers

41. Human interferon can be used to fight viral infections. This means that interferon may be helpful in curing

    (1) diseases that are responsible for deformities
    (2) diseases that are genetic in origin
    (3) problems related to psychological stress
    (4) the common cold
    (5) diseases caused by drugs and alcohol

GO ON TO THE NEXT PAGE

Items 42 to 47 refer to the following information.

The ear is so complicated that its operation is not well understood. Certainly it is extremely sensitive. At the threshold of audibility, the power requirement is inconceivably tiny. If all the people in the United States were listening simultaneously to a whisper (20 decibels), the power received by their collective eardrums would total only a few millionths of a watt—far less than the power generated by a single flying mosquito.

This aural organ is also remarkable for its ability to distinguish among various pitches and their qualities of sound. In the range of frequencies where the ear is most sensitive (between 500 and 4000 vibrations per second), changes in pitch of only .3% can be detected.

The normal ear can respond to frequencies ranging from 20 to 20,000 vibrations per second. In this range, it is estimated that the ear can distinguish more than half a million separate pure tones. Above the audible range, air vibrations similar to sound are called supersonic vibrations. These may be generated and detected by electrical devices and are useful particularly for depth sounding at sea. Supersonic vibrations apparently can be heard by some animals—notably bats. It is believed that bats are guided during flight by supersonic sounds which are reflected back to their ears.

Humans can tell approximately where a sound comes from because we have two ears, not one. The sound arriving at one ear a split second before or after its arrival at the second ear gives the brain information, which the latter organ interprets to note the direction from which the sound originally came.

42. Which of the following statements about human hearing is true?

(1) All ear vibrations occur at frequencies between 2,000 and 20,000 vibrations per second.
(2) All human beings can hear sounds if the vibrations are within a range of between 2 and 20,000 vibrations per second.
(3) All human beings are able to hear sounds of 500,000 vibrations per second.
(4) Vibrations below 20 or above 20,00 per second cannot be detected by the normal human ear.
(5) The human ear is sensitive to changes in pitch as long as the change exceeds 3%.

43. If a musical instrument had the ability to make a sound at 1,000 vibrations per second, most people would consider the sound

(1) inaudible
(2) high pitched
(3) ultrasonic
(4) low pitched
(5) medium pitched

44. Which of the following occurs when a sound comes from a person's left side?

(1) It hits the left ear first.
(2) It hits both ears at the same time.
(3) It hits the right ear first.
(4) It cannot be perceived unless it is a pure tone.
(5) It tells how far away a moving object is.

45. Which of the following statements is true, based on the information in the passage?

    (1) Thanks to modern medical advances, scientists now completely understand how the ear functions.
    (2) If a singer trying to reach the octave above middle C (512 vibrations per second) is off key by 1.5 vibrations, the fault can be detected.
    (3) The human ear can distinguish over 1 million differences in frequency or loudness.
    (4). Humas can tell approximately where a sound comes from because our ears are located near the front of our heads.
    (5) Supersonic vibrations occur in the middle of the audible range.

46. We can infer from the passage that our ability to perceive supersonic vibrations would be useful in which of the following situations?

    (1) listening to a concert
    (2) telling where a sound comes from
    (3) measuring depth at sea
    (4) hearing bats
    (5) distinguishing pitches

47. According to the passage, bats are guided during flight in which of the following ways?

    (1) by listening to the sounds mosquitoes emit
    (2) by distinguishing an exceptionally wide variety of pitches
    (3) by judging the way waves travel
    (4) by using the stereo function of their ears
    (5) by supersonic sounds that function as a natural radar

GO ON TO THE NEXT PAGE

Items 48 to 53 are based on the following information:

Listed below are five types of chemical reactions and brief descriptions of the characteristics of each reaction.

1. **Combination reaction**—two or more substances combine to form a more complex substance
2. **Decomposition reaction**—a substance is broken down to form two or more simpler substances often accomplished by the addition of heat
3. **Single replacement reaction**—one element of a compound is replaced by another element
4. **Double replacement reaction**—two compounds react by exchanging their positive ions, often producing a solid which is called a precipitate
5. **Atomic fission**—the nucleus of an atom of a heavy element is split to release energy and two lighter elements

Each of the following items describes a chemical reaction that may be classified as one of the types of chemical reactions defined above. For each item, choose the category which best describes the reaction given. Each of the categories above *may* be used more than once in the following set of items.

48. Sulfur reacts with oxygen to form sulfur dioxide, a common cause of air pollution:

$S + O_2 \rightarrow SO_2$

This reaction may be classified as

(1) a combination reaction
(2) a decomposition reaction
(3) single replacement reaction
(4) double replacement reaction
(5) atomic fission

49. Aluminum reacts with hydrochloric acid to yield aluminum chloride and hydrogen gas:

$2Al + 6HCl \rightarrow 2AlCl_3 + 3H_2$

This reaction may be classified as:

(1) a combination reaction
(2) a decomposition reaction
(3) single replacement reaction
(4) double replacement reaction
(5) atomic fission

50. Neutrons penetrate the nuclei of uranium^{235} to form barium and krypton plus an enormous amount of energy

This reaction may be classified as

(1) a combination reaction
(2) a decomposition reaction
(3) single replacement reaction
(4) double replacement reaction
(5) atomic fission

51. Magnesium hydroxide neutralizes hydrochloric acid in the stomach by forming magnesium chloride and water:

$Mg(OH)_2 + 2HCl \rightarrow MgCl_2 + 2H_2O$

This reaction is an example of

(1) a combination reaction
(2) a decomposition reaction
(3) single replacement reaction
(4) double replacement reaction
(5) atomic fission

52. Sulfurous acid when heated yields water and sulfur dioxide:

$$H_2SO_3 \xrightarrow{\text{Heat}} H_2O + SO_2$$

This reaction may be classified as

(1) a combination reaction
(2) a decomposition reaction
(3) single replacement reaction
(4) double replacement reaction
(5) atomic fission

53. Sodium reacts with chloride to yield sodium chloride (salt):

$$2Na + Cl_2 \rightarrow 2NaCl$$

This reaction may be classified as

(1) a combination reaction
(2) a decomposition reaction
(3) single replacement reaction
(4) double replacement reaction
(5) atomic fission

Item 54 is based on the following graph.

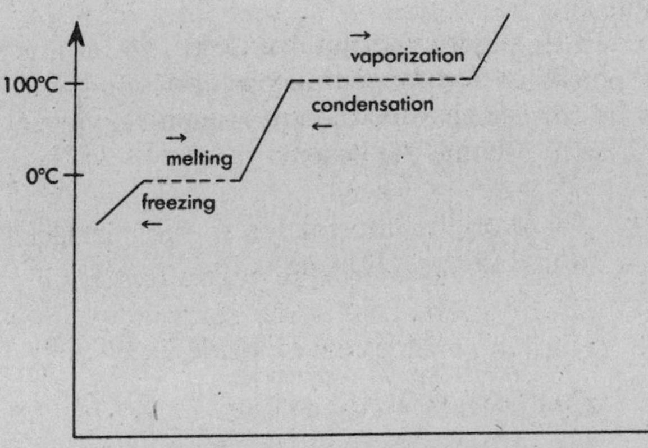

Heating/Cooling Curve for Water

54. The Heating/Cooling Curve describes the two special temperatures at which the phases of water change. When water boils, each gram gains an amount of heat equal to the heat of which of the following?

(1) fusion
(2) vaporization
(3) sublimination
(4) reaction
(5) molecules

55. The force necessary to move a mass is equal to its mass times its acceleration. Two blocks are to be moved along a flat surface:

Block	Mass	Acceleration
1	2 kg	3 m/sec^2
2	4 kg	6 m/sec^2

Compared to block 1, the force necessary to move block 2 is

(1) one half as much
(2) the same
(3) twice as much
(4) three times as much
(5) four times as much

56. The force of gravity accelerates an object through space at 9.8 m/sec^2. An object, initially at rest, falls freely near the earth's surface. How long, in seconds, does it take the object to attain a speed of 98 meters per second?

(1) 1
(2) 10
(3) 98
(4) 980
(5) 1000

GO ON TO THE NEXT PAGE

Items 57 to 59 refer to the following information

SARSAT—Search Satellite Aided Tracking—is a project designed to demonstrate the use of satellites to save lives by reducing the time required to locate and rescue air and maritime distress victims.

This system can be used for regional or global coverage and will be able to locate the distress site within 1 to 3 miles. When the system is fully operational, it will be capable of detecting and locating 200–300 distress signals at a time.

Satellites were used to track a Japanese adventurer while he trekked by dogsled across the Greenland ice cap to the North Pole. They tracked a number of sailboats during a European race in 1979 and tracked both the successful and unsuccessful "Double Eagle" transatlantic balloon flights.

57. SARSAT can pinpoint the locations of disaster victims to within a range of how many miles?

    (1) 1/2 to 1 mile
    (2) 1 to 3 miles
    (3) 5 to 10 miles
    (4) 100 to 150 miles
    (5) 200 to 300 miles

58. Who is most likely to benefit from SARSAT?

    I. victims of plane crashes
    II. victims of accidents at sea
    III. victims of disasters in space
    IV. lost or injured explorers

    (1) I and III only
    (2) II and III only
    (3) I, II, and III only
    (4) I, II, and IV only
    (5) I, II, III, and IV

59. What are the advantages of SARSAT to air rescue efforts?

    (1) saves time and increases accuracy
    (2) saves time and reduces cost
    (3) saves time and is easy to use
    (4) increases accuracy and reduces cost
    (5) always works

60. Cyclic changes are changes that occur at a definite rate and are repeated regularly. All of the following are examples of cyclic changes EXCEPT

    (1) change from day to night
    (2) change of seasons
    (3) tides
    (4) eclipses
    (5) earthquakes

Items 61 to 65 refer to the following information.

The genetic material is now known to be deoxyribonucleic acid (DNA). The two general functions of DNA are (1) to replicate for the propagation of life, and (2) to serve as a template for protein synthesis. It is this second function that we shall outline here. The initial step is the assemblage of messenger ribonucleic acid (m-RNA) by DNA. This process is known as transcription. The m-RNA then acts as a complement of the genetic code in the DNA molecule that assembled it. The m-RNA then directs the assembly of a protein from an available pool of protein building blocks, amino acids. This process is known as translation. Therefore, we can summarize protein synthesis as transcription and translation. A second kind of RNA, known as transfer ribonucleic acid (t-RNA), is responsible for directing the correct amino acid to its correct place in the amino acid sequence that is to become the protein.

61. Based on the information in the passage, which of the following is true?

    (1) DNA is directly responsible for the synthesis of a protein.
    (2) m-RNA makes DNA.
    (3) Transcription follows translation.
    (4) Proteins are assemblages of amino acids.
    (5) None of the above.

62. Which of the following best describes "transcription"?

    (1) the assembly of DNA from a protein model
    (2) DNA manufacture of m-RNA
    (3) m-RNA manufacture of a protein
    (4) replication
    (5) m-RNA manufacture of t-RNA

63. Relative to DNA, m-RNA could be considered which of the following?

    (1) complement of DNA
    (2) replicate of DNA
    (3) duplicate of DNA
    (4) nucleotide
    (5) protein

64. This article describes a portion of the knowledge scientists now possess concerning DNA and RNA. Based on this description, which of the following can we infer scientists are able to do?

    (1) synthesize new proteins
    (2) cure cancer
    (3) replace defective genetic material
    (4) create exact reproductions of people
    (5) create models of DNA and RNA

65. From the passage, we can infer that DNA directs which of the following things?

    (1) weather
    (2) eye color
    (3) hair length
    (4) taste in clothing
    (5) hair style

66. Conductors are materials through which electrons can flow freely. Most metals make good electrical conductors, but of all, silver is the best. Next to silver, copper is a good conductor, with aluminum following closely behind.

    Which of the following best explains why copper is the metal most widely used in electrical wiring?

    (1) It is the best conductor of electricity.
    (2) It has a high resistance to electricity.
    (3) It is cheaper than aluminum.
    (4) It is a better conductor than aluminum and cheaper than silver.
    (5) It is the most flexible metal.

END OF SCIENCE TEST

TEST 4. INTERPRETING LITERATURE AND THE ARTS

Time: 65 Minutes—45 Questions

Directions:

This test consists of multiple-choice questions based on a variety of excerpts from popular and classical literature and articles about literature or the arts. Each selection is followed by a number of questions. Record your answers in the Interpreting Literature and the Arts section of your answer sheet.

FOR EXAMPLE:

He died at eventide . . . I saw his breath beat quicker and quicker, pause, and then his little soul leapt like a star that travels in the night and left a world of darkness in its train. The day changed not . . . Only in the chamber of death writhed the world's most piteous thing—a childless mother.

The reader can infer that death has come to

(1) an old man
(2) a favorite dog
(3) a child
(4) a mother
(5) a soldier

The correct answer is "a child"; therefore, you should blacken answer space 3 on your answer sheet.

Items 1 to 3 refer to the following selection.

WHERE DOES THE AUTHOR LIVE?

We were of the city, but somehow not in it. Whenever I went off on my favorite walk to Highland Park in the "American" district to the north, on the border of Queens, and climbed the hill to the old reservoir from which I could look straight across to the skyscrapers of Manhattan, I saw New York as a foreign city. There, brilliant and unreal, the city had its life, as Brownsville was ours. That the two were joined in me I never knew then—not even on those glorious summer nights of my last weeks in high school when, with what an ache, I would come back into Brownsville along Liberty Avenue, and, as soon as I could see blocks ahead of me the Labor Lyceum, the malted milk and Fatima signs over the candy stores, the old women in their house-dresses sitting in front of the tenements like priestesses of an ancient cult, I knew I was home.

1. Which of the following phrases best describes the author at this time in his life?

   (1) angry with the world he knows
   (2) excited about graduating from high school
   (3) young and apparently the child of immigrants
   (4) living in a slum and hating it
   (5) preparing to go to college in New York

2. In the phrase "the malted milk and Fatima signs over the candy stores," what does "Fatima" most likely refer to?

   (1) a religious shrine
   (2) a brand of cigarettes
   (3) an advertisement for a travel agency
   (4) a movie theater
   (5) a massage parlor

3. Which of the following best describes what the author was like when he wrote this selection?

   (1) an outsider hating his neighborhood
   (2) an unhappy loner
   (3) a self-indulgent immigrant
   (4) a naive college freshman
   (5) a happy and sensitive high school senior

GO ON TO THE NEXT PAGE

Items 4 to 8 refer to the following selection.

HOW DOES UNDERSHAFT FEEL ABOUT THE SALVATION ARMY?

Undershaft: One moment, Mr. Lomax. I am rather interested in the Salvation Army. Its motto might be my own: Blood and Fire.

Lomax (shocked): But not your sort of blood and fire, you know.

Undershaft: My sort of blood cleanses: my sort of fire purifies.

Barbara: So do ours. Come down tomorrow to my shelter—the West Ham Shelter—and see what we are doing. We're going to march to a great meeting in the Assembly at Mile End. Come and see the shelter and then march with us: It will do you a lot of good. Can you play anything?

Undershaft: In my youth I earned pennies, and even shillings occasionally, in the streets and in public house parlors by my natural talent for stepdancing. Later on, I became a member of the Undershaft Orchestra Society, and performed passably on the tenor trombone.

Lomax (scandalized—putting down the concertina): Oh I say!

Barbara: Many a sinner has played himself into heaven on the trombone, thanks to the Army.

Lomax (to Barbara, still rather shocked): Yes; but what about the cannon business, don't you know? *(to Undershaft)* Getting into heaven is not exactly in your line, is it?

Lady Britomart: Charles!!!

Lomax: Well; but it stands to reason, don't it? The cannon business may be necessary and all that; we can't get along without cannons; but it isn't right, you know. On the other hand, there may be a certain amount of tosh about the Salvation Army—I belong to the Established Church myself—but still you can't deny that it's religion; and you can't go against religion, can you? At least unless you're downright immoral, don't you know.

4. Which of the following can be inferred from this selection?

   (1) Undershaft is a professional trombone player
   (2) Lomax is forthright and determined
   (3) Lady Britomart is the wife of Lomax.
   (4) Undershaft is a munitions manufacturer.
   (5) Lomax does not believe in organized religion.

5. Which of the following words best describes the tone of Lomax's statement, "We can't get along without cannons, but it isn't right, you know"?

   (1) cynical
   (2) idealistic
   (3) sarcastic
   (4) hypocritical
   (5) bitter

6. What does Undershaft's description of himself lead the reader to believe?

   (1) He is sorry for his mistakes.
   (2) He should give more to charity.
   (3) He hates the Salvation Army.
   (4) He was poor as a young man.
   (5) He comes from a wealthy family.

7. What does Lomax mean when he describes the Salvation Army as "tosh"? (Line 37)

   (1) It is not good to join the Salvation Army.
   (2) A lot of nonsense is associated with the Salvation Army.
   (3) The Salvation Army gives away tosh, a kind of English candy.
   (4) The Salvation Army consists of many wealthy people.
   (5) The Salvation Army does a lot for the average person.

8. From the description of Barbara in the selection, which of the following is she most likely seeking?

   (1) to enjoy life
   (2) to punish her father
   (3) to do good for people
   (4) to make even more money
   (5) to marry Lomax

Items 9 to 11 refer to the following poem.

WHAT IS WEIR LIKE?

The skies they were ashen and sober;
  The leaves they were crisped and sere—
The leaves they were withering and sere:
  It was night in the lonesome October
Of my most immemorial year;
  It was hard by the dim lake of Auber,
In the misty mid region of Weir—
  It was down by the dank tarn of Auber
In the ghoul-haunted woodland of Weir

from "Ulalume" by Edgar Allen Poe

9. Which of the following pairs of words best describes the atmosphere of this poem?

   (1) mysterious and horrifying
   (2) quiet and tranquil
   (3) silent and lonely
   (4) frivolous and high spirited
   (5) quiet and contemplative

10. What does the author mean when he says "my most immemorial year"?

    (1) the year he remembers most easily
    (2) his most important year
    (3) the year he cannot remember
    (4) the most horrifying year of his life
    (5) the year he traveled to Weir

11. Why does the author use the words "ashen," "sere," and "dank"?

    (1) to show his hatred of Ulalume
    (2) to underscore his love of Auber
    (3) to exhibit his distrust of October
    (4) to establish the mood of the country
    (5) to reassure the reader

GO ON TO THE NEXT PAGE

Items 12 to 15 are based on the following selection.

WHAT IS WINTER LIKE IN THE YUKON?

Day had broken cold and gray, exceedingly cold and gray, when the man turned aside from the main Yukon trail and climbed the high earth bank, where a dim and little-traveled trail led eastward through the fat spruce timberland. It was nine o'clock. There was no sun or hint of sun, though there was not a cloud in the sky. It was a clear day, and yet there seemed an intangible pall over the face of things, a subtle gloom that made the day dark, and that was due to the absence of sun.

But all this—the mysterious, far-reaching hairline trail, the absence of sun from the sky, the tremendous cold, and the strangeness and weirdness of it all—made no impression on the man. It was not because he was long used to it. He was a newcomer to the land, a cheechako, and this was his first winter. The trouble with him was that he was without imagination. That there should be anything more to it than that was a thought that never entered his head.

As he turned to go, he spat speculatively. There was a sharp, explosive crackle that startled him. He spat again. And again, in the air, before it could fall to the snow, the spittle crackled. He knew that at fifty below spittle crackled in the snow, but his spittle had crackled in the air. Undoubtedly it was colder than fifty below—how much colder he did not know.

At the man's heels trotted a dog, a big native husky, the proper wolf dog, gray-coated and without any visible or temperamental difference from its brother, the wild wolf. The animal was depressed by the tremendous cold. It knew that it was not time for traveling. Its instinct told it a truer tale than was told to the man by the man's judgment.

adapted from "To Build a Fire" by Jack London

12. Which of the following does the author use to emphasize the extreme cold?

   (1) the spittle crackling
   (2) the "subtle gloom" and "little traveled trail"
   (3) the absence of sun
   (4) "the strangeness and weirdness of it all"
   (5) "the mysterious, far-reaching hairline trail"

13. Which of the following can be inferred from the selection?

   (1) The man is jealous of the dog.
   (2) The man is unusually perceptive and wise.
   (3) It is impossible to build a fire.
   (4) The dog is wiser than the man.
   (5) The extreme cold will kill them both.

14. What is the temperature of the Yukon in the story?

   (1) −30 degrees
   (2) −10 degrees
   (3) zero degrees
   (4) −65 degrees
   (5) −50 degrees

15. Which words and phrases in the first sentence are especially successful in establishing the story's mood?

   (1) "main Yukon trail," "high earth bank"
   (2) "led eastward," "fat spruce timberland"
   (3) "cold and gray," "dim"
   (4) "man turned aside," "led eastward"
   (5) "Day had broken," "little-traveled trail"

Items 16 to 22 refer to the following address:

WHAT DOES MR. MINOW THINK ABOUT TELEVISION?

This is my first public address since I took over my new job. I seem to have detected a certain nervous apprehension about what I might say or do when I emerged from that locked office for this, my maiden station break. It may also come as a surprise to some of you, but I want you to know that you have my admiration and respect. Anyone who is in the broadcasting business has a tough row to hoe.

Let's talk . . . of television today. The percentage increase of total revenues from 1959 to 1960 was 9 percent, and the percentage of increase of profit was 9.7 percent. This, despite a recession. For your investors, the price has indeed been right.

I have confidence in your health.

But not in your product.

It is with this and much more in mind that I come before you today.

I am in Washington to help broadcasting, not to harm it; to strengthen it, not weaken it; to reward it, not punish it; to encourage it, not threaten it; to stimulate it, not censor it.

Above all, I am here to uphold and protect the public interest.

What do we mean by "the public interest"? Some say the public interest is merely what interests the public. I disagree.

So does . . . Governor Collins. In a recent speech, he said, "Broadcasting, to serve the public interest, must have a soul and a conscience. a burning desire to excel, as well as to sell; the urge to build the character . . . and stature of the people . . ."

Like everybody, I wear more than one hat. I am the chairman of the FCC. I am also a television viewer . . . I have seen a great many television programs that seem to me eminently worthwhile, and I am not talking about the much-bemoaned good old days of "Playhouse 90" and "Studio One."

But when television is bad, nothing is worse. I invite you to sit down in front of your television set . . . and stay there without a book, magazine, or newspaper . . . to distract you—and keep your eyes glued to that set until the station signs off. I can assure you that you will observe a vast wasteland.

Newton N. Minow, excerpted from *EQUAL TIME: the Private Broadcaster and the Public Interest,* edited by Lawrence Laurent.

16. Which of the following choices best defines the phrase "my maiden station break"?

    (1) the broadcasting company's administrative offices
    (2) the health of the television industry
    (3) a rumor regarding conflict of interest
    (4) the narrator's speech
    (5) the Federal Communications Commission

17. Which of the following words best describes the audience's mood?

    (1) relaxed
    (2) amused
    (3) apprehensive
    (4) hostile
    (5) favorable

18. Which of the following techniques is Minow using in the paragraph that begins: "I am in Washington to help broadcasting, not to harm it . . ."?

    (1) comparison and contrast
    (2) examples
    (3) advantages and disadvantages
    (4) analysis of a process
    (5) chronological order

19. What is the author's paramount interest?

    (1) to retain his position as chairman
    (2) to maintain television's high profit level
    (3) to attain public office
    (4) to schedule new and different television shows
    (5) to serve public interest

GO ON TO THE NEXT PAGE

20. Judging from his remarks, what does Minow believe is true about "Playhouse 90" and "Studio One"?

    (1) They should be revised.
    (2) They were excellent shows.
    (3) They are the best television currently offers.
    (4) They have potential for the movie industry.
    (5) They are not as popular as current shows.

21. The phrase "A tough row to hoe" is an example of which of the following?

    (1) metaphor
    (2) simile
    (3) personification
    (4) cliche
    (5) redundancy

22. The author would agree with which of the following statements?

    (1) Television needs extensive government intervention.
    (2) The people who work in television are underpaid.
    (3) Television is profitable but presents inferior material.
    (4) Television is a necessary evil.
    (5) Fewer people will watch television in the future.

Items 23 to 27 are based on the following poem.

DO GOOD FENCES MAKE GOOD NEIGHBORS?

Something there is that doesn't love a wall,
That sends the frozen ground swell under it.
The work of hunters is another thing:
I have come after them and made repair
Where they have left not one stone on a stone,
But they would have the rabbit out of hiding.
The gaps I mean,
No one has seen them made or heard them made,
But at spring mending time we find them there.
I let my neighbor know beyond the hill;
And on a day we meet
And set the wall between us once again.
There is where we do not need the wall:
He is all pine and I am apple orchard.
My apples trees will never get across
And eat the cones under his pine, I tell him.
He only says, "Good fences make good neighbors."
Spring is the mischief in me, and I wonder
If I could put a notion in his head:
"*Why* do they make good neighbors?
Before I built a wall I'd ask to know
What I was walling in or walling out.
Something there is that doesn't love a wall.
That wants it down."
I see him there
Bringing a stone grasped firmly by the top
In each hand, like an old stone savage armed.
He moves in darkness as it seems to me.
He says again, "Good fences make good neighbors."

23. According to the author, which of the following destroys walls?

    (1) hunters and farmers
    (2) hunters and nature
    (3) orchards and bad weather
    (4) rabbits and hunters
    (5) his neighbor and animals

24. Which of the following sentences best expresses the neighbor's view of walls?

    (1) "Something there is that doesn't love a wall."
    (2) "He is all pine and I am apple orchard."
    (3) "*Why* do they make good neighbors?"
    (4) "Good fences make good neighbors."
    (5) "He moves in darkness it seems to me."

25. Which of the following statements would the speaker agree with?

    (1) Walls are necessary to keep hunters from the cows.
    (2) Walls are important to isolate apple orchards from pine trees.
    (3) Walls help neighbors stay close.
    (4) It is important to keep fences well repaired.
    (5) Walls between people are unnecessary.

26. Which of the following choices best defines the sentence: "He moves in darkness as it seems to me"?

    (1) Night is falling and they still have a lot of wall to repair.
    (2) His neighbor has a vision problem.
    (3) His neighbor has never questioned the importance of walls.
    (4) Good neighbors are made slowly, over the years.
    (5) Acts of kindness are usually not rewarded.

27. Which of the following choices best expresses the tone of this poem?

    (1) resigned yet questioning
    (2) angry and despairing
    (3) hopeful and eager
    (4) proud and haughty
    (5) nonchalant

GO ON TO THE NEXT PAGE

Items 28 to 31 are based on the following article.

WHAT ARE THE DIFFERENCES BETWEEN THE JAPANESE AND THE AMERICANS?

I will confess that this distinction—between different and wrong—sometimes eludes me in Japan. Child psychologists and family therapists have told me that the Japanese parent's way of persuading his children to stop doing something is not to say "It's wrong" or "It's unfair" but rather to tell the child, "people will laugh at you." This is not my idea of a wholesome child-rearing philosophy, but I'm not preparing my children for membership in a society that places such stress on harmonious social relations. Several American psychologists have recently claimed that the Japanese approach may in fact equip children for more happiness in life than American practices do.

From what I have seen, a tight-knit, almost tribal society like Japan is better set up for straightforward productive competition than is the West. It places less emphasis on profit than on ensuring that every company and every worker will retain a place in the economic order.

From bureaucrats at the Ministry of Foreign Affairs (who, I am told, average six hours of overtime a *day)* to department-store package-wrappers, the Japanese seem immune against the idea that discharging their duty to others must be considered "just a job."

Recently, everyone was working, Japan was taking a proud place in the world, there were no serious domestic divisions, and the drugs, dissoluteness, and similar discords that blight the rest of the world barely existed here.

from "The Japanese Are Different From You and Me" by James Fallows, 1986 as first published in *The Atlantic Monthly*, September 1986, Vol. 258, No. 3

28. According to the article, which of the following is a major goal in Japan?

(1) good social relations
(2) surpassing American manners
(3) training children to excel
(4) becoming industrially independent
(5) increasing exports

29. Based on the article, which of the following statements would a Japanese parent be most likely to say?

(1) "Take art lessons so you will draw better than the others."
(2) "Arrive in class early so you stand out."
(3) "Don't wear that jacket because your friends will ridicule you."
(4) "I will tell the teacher she was unfair to give you that test."
(5) "Get good grades to show that you are better than the other students."

30. Which of the following aspects of Japanese life does the author praise?

(1) emphasis on profit
(2) drub rehabilitation programs
(3) worker's belief that a job is just a job
(4) sense of individualness
(5) efforts to give every worker a place

31. Which of the following does the author think benefits Japanese society?

(1) serious political divisions
(2) a national purpose
(3) increased imports
(4) high prices
(5) increased profits

Items 32 to 35 are based on the following selection.

WHY WAS RICHARD WRIGHT'S SPEECH CHANGED?

The school term ended. I was selected as valedictorian of my class and assigned to write a paper to be delivered at one of the public auditoriums. One morning the principal summoned me to his office.

"Well, Richard Wright, here's your speech," he said with smooth bluntness and shoved a stack of stapled sheets across his desk.

"What speech?" I asked as I picked up the papers.

"The speech you're to say the night of graduation," he said.

"But, professor, I've written my speech already," I said.

He laughed confidently, indulgently.

"Listen, boy, you're going to speak to both *white* and colored people that night. What can you alone think of saying to them? You have no experience . . . "

He stared at me, then left. The principal's speech was simpler and clearer than mine, but it did not say anything; mine was cloudy, but it said what I wanted to say. What could I do? I had half a mind not to show up at the graduation exercises. I was hating my environment more each day. As soon as school was over, I would get a job, save money, and leave.

The news of my clash with the principal had spread through the school and the students were openly critical of me.

The night of graduation I was nervous and tense; I rose and faced the audience and my speech rolled out. When my voice stopped there was some applause. I did not care if they liked it or not; I was through. Immediately, even before I left the platform, I tried to shunt all memory of the event from me. A few of my classmates managed to shake my hand as I pushed toward the door, seeking the street. Somebody invited me to a party and I did not accept. I did not want to see any of them again. With almost seventeen years of baffled living behind me, I faced the world in 1925.

32. Which of the following is true about the principal's speech?

    (1) It had been delivered two years earlier.
    (2) Richard Wright added his own comments to it.
    (3) It was not appreciated by the graduation audience.
    (4) It did not have much substance.
    (5) Richard Wright liked it better than his own.

33. Which of the following can you infer as the reason the principal gave Richard Wright a different speech to deliver?

    (1) He wanted to make sure Wright did not offend the white audience.
    (2) He was afraid Wright did not know how to compose a speech.
    (3) He wanted to steal Wright's limelight.
    (4) He was hoping Wright would let a white student be the valedictorian.
    (5) Wright had asked him to write the speech.

34. Why did Richard insist on delivering his own speech?

    (1) He was rebelling against authority.
    (2) He felt he had his own story to tell.
    (3) He hated the principal
    (4) He felt that he was far superior to his fellow students.
    (5) He wanted to condemn racial prejudice.

35. At the end of the story, what does Wright do?

    (1) enjoys the applause
    (2) decides to become a hobo
    (3) isolates himself
    (4) goes off to college
    (5) becomes friends with the principal

GO ON TO THE NEXT PAGE

Items 36 to 41 are based on the following essay.

WHAT IS JONATHAN SWIFT SUGGESTING BE DONE TO CHILDREN?

It is a melancholy Object to those, who walk through this great Town, or travel in the Country; when they see the *Streets,* the *Roads,* and *Cabbin-doors* crowded with *Beggars* of the Female Sex, followed by three, four, or six children, *all in Rags,* and importuning every *Passenger* for an *Alms.* These *Mothers,* instead of being able to work for their honest Lively-hood, are forced to employ all their Time in strolling to beg Sustenance for their *helpless Infants;* who, as they grow up, either turn *Thieves* for want of Work; or leave their *dear Native Country, to fight for the Pretender in* Spain, or sell themselves to the Barbadoes.

I SHALL now therefore humbly propose my own Thoughts; which I hope will not be liable to the least Objection.

I have been assured by a very knowing *American* of my Acquaintance in *London;* that a young healthy Child, well nursed, is at a Year old, a most delicious, nourishing, and wholesome Food; whether *Stewed, Roasted, Baked, or Broiled;* and, I make no doubt, that it will equally serve in a *Fricasie,* or *Ragout.*

I DO therefore humbly offer it to *publick Consideration,* that of the Hundred and Twenty Thousand Children, already computed, Twenty thousand may be reserved for Breed; whereof only one Fourth part be Males; which is more than we allow to *Sheep, back Cattle, or Swine;* and my Reason is, that these Children are seldom the Fruits of Marriage, a *Circumstance not much regarded by our Savages;* therefore, one Male will be sufficient to serve *Four Females.* That of the remaining Hundred thousand, may, at a Year old, be offered in Sale to the *Persons of Quality and Fortune,* through the Kingdom; always advising the Mother to let them suck plentifully in the last Month, so as to render them plump, and fat for a good Table.

I GRANT this food will be somewhat dear, and therefore very *proper for landlords;* who, as they have already devoured most of the Parents, seem to have the best Title to the Children.

from "A Modest Proposal" by Jonathan Swift

36. What problem is Swift describing in this essay?

    (1) what abjectly poor people are forced to do to survive
    (2) a national shortage of skilled laborers
    (3) an international food shortage
    (4) how foreign wars have depleted the national treasury
    (5) the necessity of finding new ways to breed animals

37. What solution does Swift propose to the problem he describes?

    (1) import greater amounts of food
    (2) train people to work as skilled laborers
    (3) cook and eat children
    (4) stop allowing citizens to work as hired soldiers
    (5) license landlords

38. Which of the following words best describes the tone of this selection?

    (1) grave
    (2) fanciful
    (3) worshipful
    (4) factual
    (5) mocking

39. Why does Swift compare the children to animals?

    (1) to prove that he likes animals and children equally well
    (2) to show that people consider poor children little more than animals
    (3) to help improve animal care in Ireland
    (4) because there are more animals than children
    (5) to show how well regarded both are

40. "I GRANT this food will be somewhat dear, and therefore very *proper for landlords;* who, as they have already devoured most of their Parents, seem to have the best Title to the children." Which of the following statements best explains what Swift is saying about landlords?

    (1) Because they cannot afford proper food, landlords are forced to go hungry.
    (2) Swift admires them because they treat their tenants well.
    (3) They are very dear to their tenants.
    (4) They treat the children of their tenants very well.
    (5) Having taken all the parents own, they might as well take their children, too.

41. Which of the following would Swift most likely support?

    (1) aid to starving landlords
    (2) jails for those in debt
    (3) aid to mothers and children
    (4) laws to treat animals better
    (5) increased foreign aid

GO ON TO THE NEXT PAGE

Items 42 and 43 are based on the following article.

HOW HAVE COMICS CHANGED?

It may seem a long way from the countercultural underground "comix" of the sixties and early seventies, with their explicit criticism of American society, to the violence and hedonism of today's comics—a retreat from "relevance" to mere entertainment. But the comic books of the eighties are probably more diverse and more geared to an adult audience than those of any previous era. The growth of comic-book "specialty stores" in the past eight years or so has made it possible for companies like First, Pacific, and Fantagraphics to compete with the majors (DC and Marvel) in distribution.

Even what most people think of as an American comic book—the colorful, energetic adventures of ultra-powered beings like Superman and Spiderman, who fight their way across the roofs of skyscrapers to the accompaniment of boldly lettered *Zaps* and *Pows*—even these superhero comics have been reclaimed for adults and made more sophisticated. Generally—and accurately—denounced for its stupidity, male-adolescent outlook, sameness, and sheer junkiness, the superhero genre has nonetheless produced a trio of uneven but fascinating talents: Frank Miller (Daredevil, Dark Knight), Dave Sim (Cerebus), and Howard Chaykin (American Flagg!).

from "Comic Books for Grownups" by Lloyd Rose, 1986 as first published in *The Atlantic Monthly*, August 1986, Vol. 258, No. 2

42. Which of the following does the author believe characterized comics of the past?

(1) weak draftmanship
(2) production by a number of small, independent companies
(3) stereotyped heroes that appeal to males
(4) violence and hedonism
(5) distribution by specialty stores

43. Which of the following statements would the author most likely agree with?

(1) Comics of the past were better than comics of the present.
(2) It's better to have comics distributed by large companies.
(3) Today's comics present relevant social criticism.
(4) Comics today are generally the same as comics of the past.
(5) Comics have produced some intriguing new talent.

Items 44 and 45 are based on the following selection.

WHAT ARE THE GODS OF THE NORTH LIKE?

Originally there were three chief gods, but in time all the power came into the hands of Odin, king of gods and men. He and the other gods dwelt in Asgard, which lay at the end of Bifrost, the rainbow. Here were many palaces of gold and silver, but the most beautiful of them was Valhalla, the dwelling place of Odin.

Upon the shoulders of Odin, the All–Father, sat the ravens Hugin and Munin—Thought and Memory. They flew each day over the whole world, and brought back to him reports of all that was happening.

Thor, son of Odin and Frigg, was the thunderer, the god of war. He was the strongest of gods and men. Another son was Balder. He was the best of the gods, and in him all was perfect. He shone with such radiance that light came from him. Frey governed the rain and sunshine, and made all things of the earth grow. His sister, Freya, was the goddess of love and music and flowers.

Of a different sort was Loki, the god of evil. He liked to bring about quarrels, and originated all frauds and deceits, and was the disgrace of the gods. He was handsome to look upon, but malicious in disposition and very fickle.

from *Myths and Their Meaning* by May J. Herzberg.

44. From the passage, which of the following can be inferred?

(1) Odin was not well-informed about world events.
(2) Odin was the most perfect god.
(3) There were other gods responsible for other characteristics.
(4) Odin was not married.
(5) Loki was Odin's favorite son.

45. Loki was all of the following except:

(1) a disgrace
(2) ugly
(3) clever
(4) evil
(5) fickle

END OF LITERATURE TEST

TEST 5. MATHEMATICS

Time: 90 Minutes—56 Questions

Directions:

The Mathematics Test consists of multiple-choice questions covering the areas of arithmetic, algebra, and geometry. The problems emphasize the practical aspects of mathematics necessary to the solution of everyday problems. A page of formulas is provided for reference in solving the problems presented. However, you will have to determine which formula (if any) is needed to solve a particular problem. Read each problem carefully and then work out the solution on your own before looking at the answer choices. Work quickly, but carefully, answering as many questions as you can. If a problem is too difficult for you, skip it and come back to it after you have completed all of the problems you know how to solve. Record your answers in the Mathematics section of your answer sheet.

FOR EXAMPLE:

Jill's drug store bill totals $8.68. How much change should she get if she pays with a $10.00 bill?

(1) $2.32
(2) $1.42
(3) $1.32
(4) $1.28
(5) $1.22

The correct answer is "$1.32." Therefore, you should mark answer space 3 on your answer sheet.

FORMULAS

Description	Formula
AREA (A) of a:	
square	$A=s^2$; where s=side
rectangle	$A=lw$; where l=length, w=width
parallelogram	$A=bh$; where b=base, h=height
triangle	$A=\frac{1}{2}bh$; where b=base, h=height
circle	$A=\pi r^2$; where $\pi=3.14$, r=radius
PERIMETER (P) of a:	
square	$P=4s$; where s=side
rectangle	$P=2l+2w$; where l=length, w=width
triangle	$P=a+b+c$; where a, b, and c are the sides
circumference (C) of a circle	$C=\pi d$; where $\pi=3.14$, d=diameter
VOLUME (V) of a:	
cube	$V=s^3$; where s=side
rectangular container	$V=lwh$; where l=length, w=width, h=height
cylinder	$V=\pi r^2 h$; where $\pi=3.14$, r=radius, h=height
Pythagorean relationship	$c^2=a^2+b^2$; where c=hypotenuse, a and b are legs of a right triangle
distance (d) between two points in a plane	$d=\sqrt{(x_2-x_1)^2+(y_2-y_1)^2}$; where (x_1, y_1) and (x_2, y_2) are two points in a plane
slope of a line (m)	$m=\frac{y_2-y_1}{x_2-x_1}$; where (x_1, y_1) and (x_2, y_2) are two points in a plane
mean	mean $=\frac{x_1+x_2+\cdots+x_n}{n}$; where the x's are the values for which a mean is desired, and n=number of values in the series
median	median = the point in an ordered set of numbers at which half of the numbers are above and half of the numbers are below this value
simple interest (i)	$i=prt$; where p=principal, r=rate, t=time
distance (d) as function of rate and time	$d=rt$; where r=rate, t=time
total cost (c)	$c=nr$; where n=number of units, r=cost per unit

Items 1 to 4 are based upon the information provided by the graphs below.

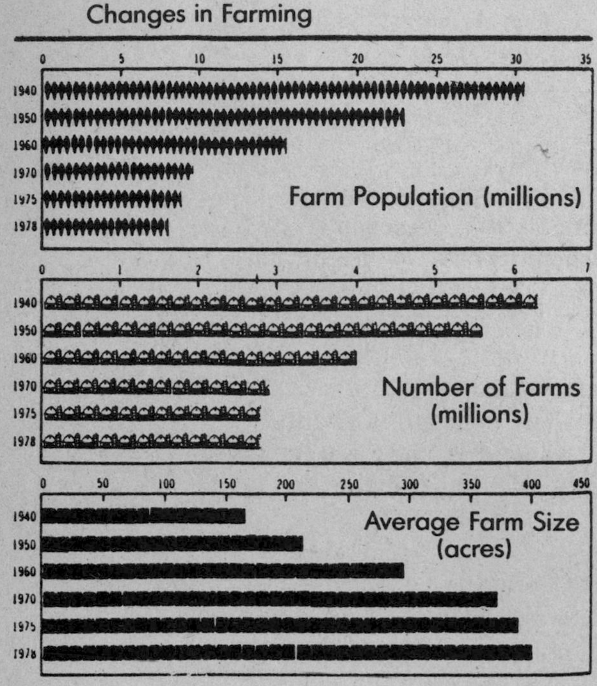

1. Which of the following statements is true about the changes in farming between 1940 and 1978?

   (1) Farm population, number of farms, and average farm size all increased.
   (1) Farm population and number of farms have increased but average farm size decreased.
   (3) Farm population and number of farms decreased but average farm size increased.
   (4) Farm population decreased, but the number of farms and average farm size increased.
   (5) Farm population, number of farms, and average farm size all decreased.

2. The average population on each farm during 1975 was most nearly

   (1) 1
   (2) 2
   (3) 3
   (4) 4
   (5) Not enough information is given.

3. The percent of increase in average farm size from 1940 to 1978 is most nearly

   (1) 50%
   (2) 75%
   (3) 100%
   (4) 150%
   (5) Not enough information is given.

4. The average population of cattle per farm in 1975 was most nearly

   (1) 10
   (2) 100
   (3) 150
   (4) 1000
   (5) Not enough information is given.

5. Between 9 a.m. and noon, how many degrees does the hour hand of a clock move?

   (1) 30
   (2) 60
   (3) 90
   (4) 180
   (5) 360

6. 30% of the senior class are women. 60% of the class have blue eyes. What percentage of the women in the senior class have blue eyes?

   (1) 18
   (2) 20
   (3) 30
   (4) 40
   (5) Not enough information is given.

7. Jack's allowance is $30 per month. In April, Jack sponsored two friends in a walkathon for a total contribution of $7.50. What percent of Jack's April allowance does this contribution represent?

   (1) 7.5
   (2) 10.0
   (3) 20.0
   (4) 25
   (5) 30

8. A rectangular swimming pool is to be filled with water to a depth of 10 feet. If the pool is 30 feet long by 20 feet wide, how many cubic feet of water will be needed to fill the pool?

   (1) 500
   (2) 600
   (3) 2000
   (4) 5000
   (5) 6000

9. A 10-foot cylinder is full of radioactive liquid waste. If the diameter of the cylinder is 1 foot, how many cubic feet of liquid can it contain?

   (1) $1\ \pi$
   (2) $1.5\ \pi$
   (3) $2\ \pi$
   (4) $2.5\ \pi$
   (5) $3\ \pi$

10. In the year 2525, an archeologist found a cornerstone in Chicago with the following date:

    M CM L X I X.

    In Roman numerals it represents which number?

    (1) 964
    (2) 1131
    (3) 1931
    (4) 1969
    (5) 2509

11. How many years will it take for $2000 invested at 6% to earn $240 in interest?

    (1) 1
    (2) 2
    (3) 3
    (4) 4
    (5) 5

12. A radio has a sale price of $42.50, which is 15% off the regular price. Which of the following is equal to the regular price of the radio?

    (1) $42.50 × .15
    (2) $42.50 ÷ .15
    (3) $42.50 + .15
    (4) $42.50 × .85
    (5) $42.50 ÷ .85

13. Jane made up a total of 1.28 liters of her special cleaning solution. If she divides the solution equally among 4 bottles to give to 4 friends, how many milliliters of the solution will be in each bottle?

    (1) 3.20
    (2) 5.12
    (3) 320
    (4) 512
    (5) 1280

GO ON TO THE NEXT PAGE

14. The Browns have a 250-gallon storage tank for heating oil. When the gauge showed that the tank was only $\frac{1}{4}$ full, Mrs. Brown ordered a delivery of fuel oil. The delivery truck arrived within an hour of Mrs. Brown's call and the tank was filled. Assuming that the gauge is accurate, how many gallons of heating oil were needed to fill the tank?

(1) 62.5
(2) 187.5
(3) 200
(4) 225.5
(5) 250

15. A machine is able to produce 3500 parts an hour. However, the plant engineer has determined that the machine is most efficient when run at 80% of maximum speed. At its most efficient speed, how many parts can this machine produce in a 40-hour work week?

(1) 11,200
(2) 14,000
(3) 35,000
(4) 112,000
(5) 140,000

16. A man got married at 32 and retired at 64. He was 94 years old when he died in 1973. In what year was he born?

(1) 1876
(2) 1879
(3) 1881
(4) 1886
(5) 1893

17. Multiply $(x + 3)(x + 4)(x + 2)$ to get

(1) $x^3 + 9x^2 + 26x + 24$
(2) $x^3 + 14x^2 + 24$
(3) $x^3 + 14x^2 + 26x$
(4) $x^2 + 14x + 24$
(5) $x^2 + 26x + 24$

Item 18 is based on the picture below.

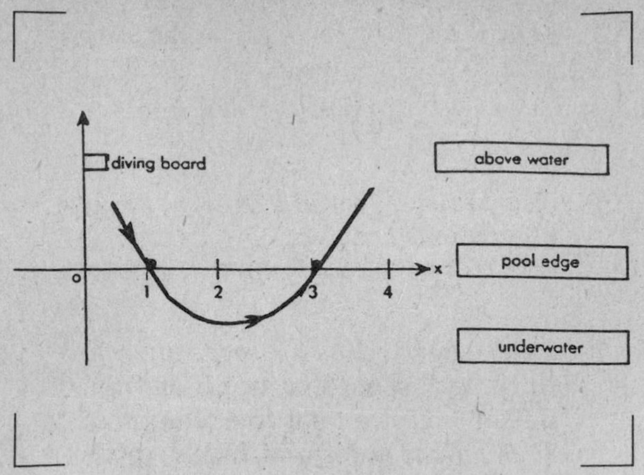

18. Dan the diver dove into the pool at line 1 (see picture), made a parabolic path under water, and resurfaced at line 3. The formula for the curve is y =

(1) $(x - 1)(x + 3)$
(2) $(x + 1)(x - 3)$
(3) $(x + 1)(x + 3)$
(4) $(x - 1)(x - 3)$
(5) $(3x)(x)$

19. A box for playing cards has the dimensions

L = 3 inches

W = 2 inches

Thickness = $\frac{1}{2}$ inch

If each card measures 3 inches × 2 inches, and has a thickness of $\frac{1}{100}$ inch, how many cards can fit into the box?

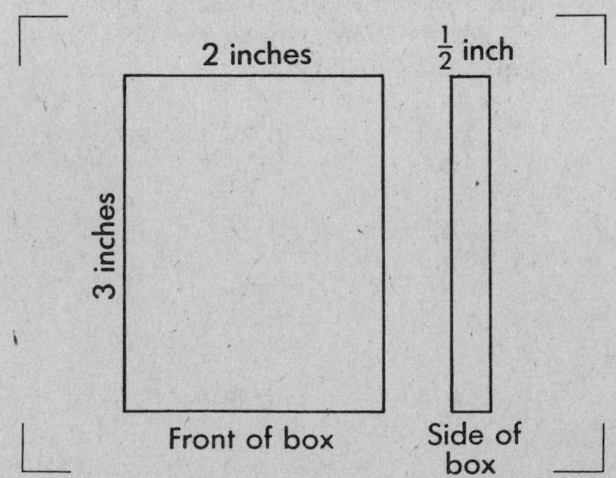

(1) 20
(2) 30
(3) 40
(4) 50
(5) 100

20. The area of a wheel is 2.25 π. What is the radius of the wheel in feet?

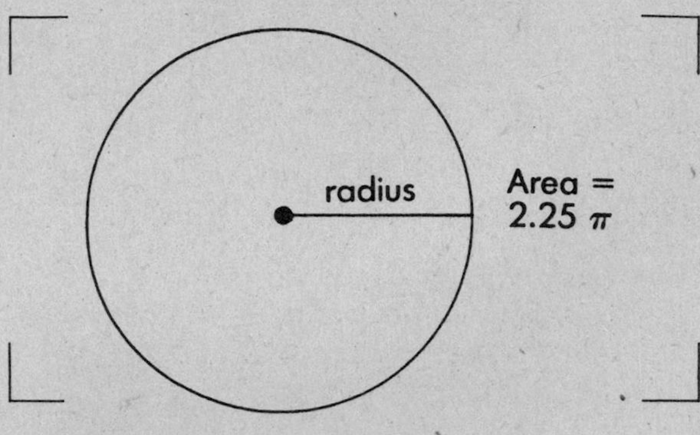

(1) 1
(2) $1\frac{1}{2}$
(3) $2\frac{1}{2}$
(4) 4
(5) 5

21. Jim loaded parcels at the Express Motor Company for 3 hours on Thursday night, 4 hours on Friday night, and 8 hours on Saturday, for a pay rate of $7.00 an hour. On Monday and Tuesday he worked the usual 4 hours each afternoon in the college bookstore at $4.50 an hour. Which of the following expressions represents the number of dollars Jim earned in the past week?

(1) 7 (15) + 4.5 (8)
(2) 3 (4 + 8 + 7) + 4.5 (4)
(3) 7 (15) × 18
(4) 7 (8) × 4.5 (15)
(5) Not enough information is given.

22. A packer for a knitting yarn company must organize his work so the boxes with the greatest weight are placed in the bottom of the shipping crate and lighter boxes are placed on the top. Five boxes must be packed for the next shipment. The boxes have the following weights:

Yarn D—216 ounces

Yarn E—5.7 pounds

Yarn F—35 pounds

Yarn G—77.4 ounces

Yarn H—10.3 pounds

Which of the following sequences correctly lists the order in which boxes should be packed?

(1) E, H, F, G, D
(2) G, E, H, D, F
(3) D, E, F, G, H
(4) F, D, H, E, G
(5) F, E, H, G, D.

23. A storage closet has seven shelves, each $3\frac{1}{2}$ feet long and 1 foot wide. All of the shelves are to be decorated with plastic edging. The edging comes packaged in 9-foot lengths. How many packages of edging are needed to trim all seven shelves without any seams?

(1) 1
(2) 2
(3) 3
(4) 4
(5) 5

24. The batting average of a baseball player is the ratio of the number of hits to the number of times at bat. At the middle of the season, Sam Brown's batting average was 0.271. If at that point in the season, Brown has been at bat 85 times, how many hits did he have?

(1) 12
(2) 22
(3) 23
(4) 27
(5) 36

GO ON TO THE NEXT PAGE

25. Mary looks out the window and sees that the outdoor temperature is 12° Centigrade. She wants to convert the Centigrade temperature to Fahrenheit temperature so that Mark will understand.
    The conversion formula is:

    $F = (\frac{9}{5}C) + 32.$

    Find the Fahrenheit temperature.

    (1) 19°
    (2) 54°
    (3) 57°
    (4) 79°
    (5) 90°

26. What is the cost of buying a triangular plot of land that measures 122 feet along the base and 124 feet deep in an area where the price of land is $2.00 per square foot?

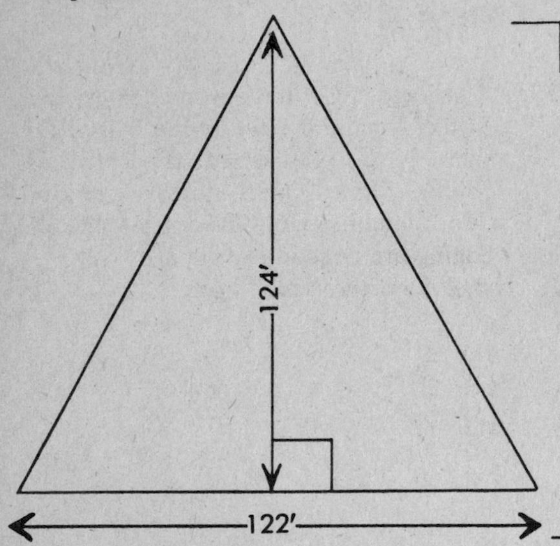

    (1) $30,256
    (2) $15,128
    (3) $7,564
    (4) $3,258
    (5) Not enough information is given.

27. A certain copying machine can make 8 copies in 12 seconds. How many copies can this same machine make in 7 minutes?

    (1) 630
    (2) 672
    (3) 336
    (4) 224
    (5) 280

28. Simplify

    $$\frac{\frac{x}{y}+2}{\frac{x}{y}-2}$$

    (1) $\frac{x+y}{x-y}$

    (2) $\frac{2x+y}{2x-y}$

    (3) $\frac{x+2y}{x+2y}$

    (4) $\frac{x+2y}{x-2y}$

    (5) $\frac{x}{yy}$

Items 29 and 30 are based on the following information:

June Hansen made a series of deposits and withdrawals from her checking account during the month of September. They were

September 2	$375 deposit
September 6	$150 withdrawal
September 10	$35 withdrawal
September 12	$42 deposit
September 19	$140 withdrawal
September 26	$28 withdrawal

29. According to Hansen's August statement, she started the month of September with a balance of \$257. What was her checkbook balance on October 1?

(1) \$165
(2) \$185
(3) \$321
(4) \$331
(5) \$465

30. On December 1, Hansen had a balance of \$421 and wrote a check for \$193.47. How much money must she deposit in order to bring her checkbook balance to a total of \$600?

(1) \$127.59
(2) \$362.41
(3) \$372.47
(4) \$500.00
(5) \$627.59

31. Memorial Park is bounded by A and B Streets and First and Second Avenues as shown below. To walk around the park starting at A Street and First Avenue, you walk 1200 feet west on A Street, make a right angle turn and walk 100 feet north on First Avenue, make another right angle turn and walk 1200 feet east on B Street, then turn and walk 100 feet south on First Avenue. What is the area of Memorial Park in square feet?

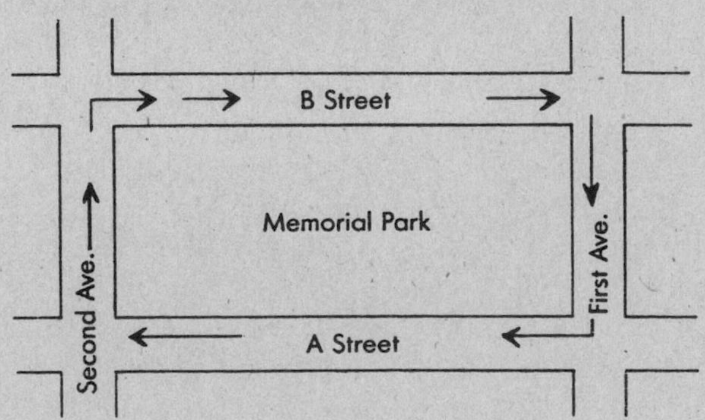

(1) 50,000
(2) 75,000
(3) 80,000
(4) 100,000
(5) 120,000

32. Factor to simplest terms
$m^4 - 81 =$

(1) $(m^2 + 9)(m^2 - 9)$
(2) $(m^2 + 9)(m + 9)(m - 9)$
(3) $(m^2 - 9)(m + 3)(m - 3)$
(4) $(m^2 + 9)(m + 3)(m - 3)$
(5) $(m + 3)^2(m - 3)^2$

33. Bill wants a new stereo receiver but he can save only \$35.00 from his paycheck each week. The receiver will amount to a total of \$750.00. Bill's brother has agreed to lend him \$100.00 toward the stereo. How many weeks will Bill have to wait before he has enough money to pay for the stereo?

(1) 8
(2) 18
(3) 19
(4) 21
(5) 22

GO ON TO THE NEXT PAGE

34. On their first trip to Big City, Linda and her friends set off on a sightseeing tour. They took a cab from the hotel and rode 3 miles west to see the Riverside statute. Then they turned south along Broadway for 8 miles to see the office towers, apartment houses, and stores. After lunch, they took another cab 3 miles west to explore the restored Union Station. How many miles is the trip from Union Station back to the hotel if they return via Hill Street as shown on the map below?

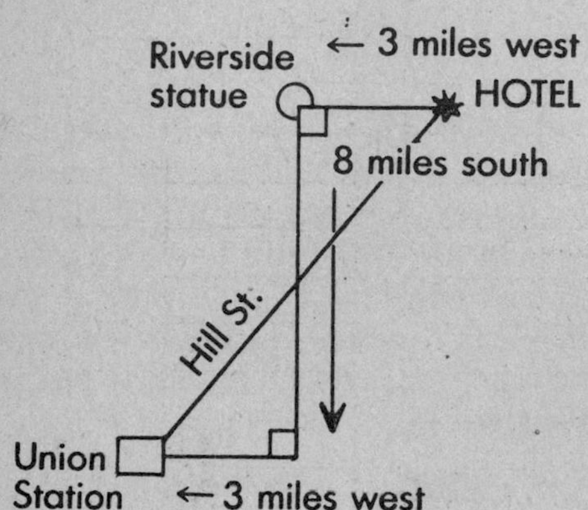

(1) 4
(2) 7
(3) 10
(4) 11
(5) 14

35. The wage rate in a certain trade is \$8.60 an hour for a 40-hour week and $1\frac{1}{2}$ times the base pay for overtime. An employee who works 48 hours in a week earns

(1) \$412.80
(2) \$447.20
(3) \$498.20
(4) \$582.80
(5) \$619.20

36. Jane Michaels borrowed \$200 on March 31 at the simple interest rate of 8% per year. If she wishes to repay the loan and the interest on May 15, what is the total amount she must pay?

(1) \$200
(2) \$201
(3) \$202
(4) \$208
(5) \$216

Items 37 to 40 refer to the following information.

Equipment, supplies, and salaries were the only three categories for which the bureau spent money.

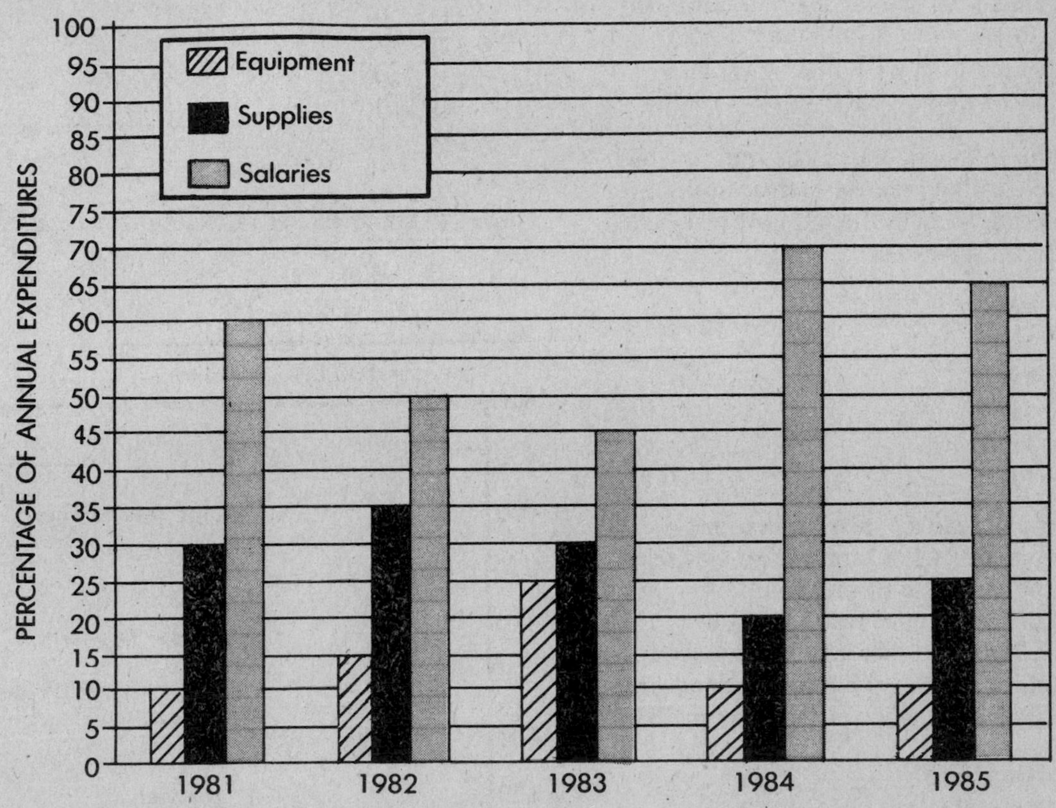

The bureau's annual expenditures for the years 1981–1985 are shown in the following table.

Year	Expenditures
1981	$ 800,000
1982	1,200,000
1983	1,500,000
1984	1,000,000
1985	1,200,000

37. If the percentage of expenditures for salaries in one year is added to the percentage of expenditures for equipment in that year, a total of the two percentages for that year is obtained. The two years for which this total is the same are

(1) 1981 and 1983
(2) 1981 and 1984
(3) 1982 and 1984
(4) 1982 and 1985
(5) 1983 and 1985

GO ON TO THE NEXT PAGE

38. Of the following, the year in which the bureau spent the greatest amount of money on supplies was

    (1) 1985
    (2) 1984
    (3) 1983
    (4) 1982
    (5) 1981

39. Of the following years, the one in which there was the greatest increase over the preceding year in the amount of money spent on salaries is

    (1) 1981
    (2) 1984
    (3) 1985
    (4) 1982
    (5) 1983

40. Of the bureau's expenditures for equipment in 1985, one-third was used for the purchase of mailroom equipment and the remainder was spent on miscellaneous office equipment. How much money did the bureau spend on miscellaneous office equipment in 1985?

    (1) $400,000
    (2) $40,000
    (3) $4000
    (4) $800,000
    (5) $80,000

41. A car dealer advertises two different payment plans for a new car. If the buyer pays cash, the car costs $5700. If the buyer pays on the installment plan, he pays 20% of the cash cost as a down payment, and then $200 a month for 24 months. How much more money must a buyer pay on the installment plan than on the cash plan?

    (1) $1140
    (2) $1000
    (3) $520
    (4) $480
    (5) $240

42. Two cars leave the same location at 2:00 P.M. If one car travels north at the rate of 30 m.p.h. and the other travels east at the rate of 40 m.p.h., how many miles apart are the two cars at 4:00 P.M.?

    (1) 50
    (2) 500
    (3) 100
    (4) 120
    (5) 150

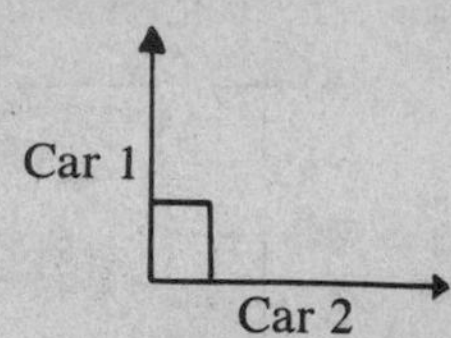

Items 43 to 46 refer to the following graph.

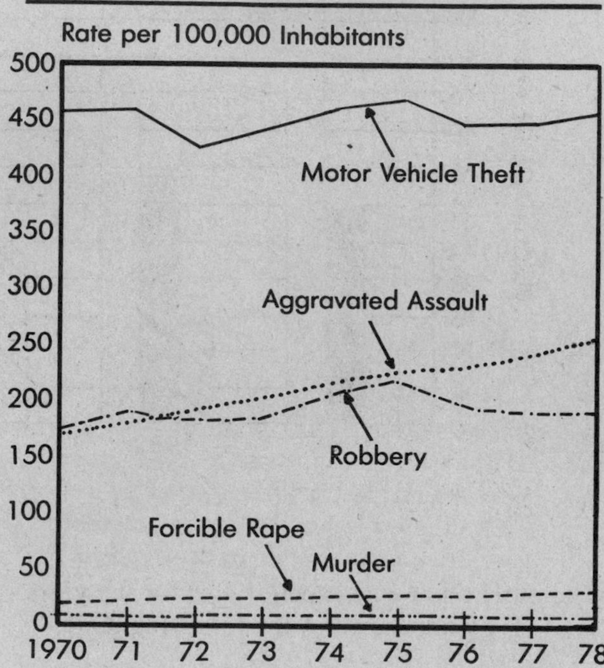

43. Next to motor vehicle thefts, which crime rate was the highest in 1971?

    (1) murder
    (2) forcible rapes
    (3) robbery
    (4) aggravated assaults
    (5) motor vehicle thefts

44. Which crime has steadily increased?

(1) murder
(2) forcible rapes
(3) robbery
(4) aggravated assaults
(5) motor vehicle thefts

45. In a city of 10,000,000, how many motor vehicle thefts would probably have occurred in 1977?

(1) 4500
(2) 40,000
(3) 45,000
(4) 50,000
(5) Not enough information is given.

46. Approximately what percent of all recorded crimes in 1978 were motor vehicle crimes?

(1) 10
(2) 20
(3) 30
(4) 40
(5) 50

47. In one year at James Madison Elementary School twice as many boys were registered for kindergarten as girls. If 90 children attended kindergarten that year, how many pupils were boys and how many were girls?

(1) 20 boys and 70 girls
(2) 30 boys and 60 girls
(3) 45 boys and 45 girls
(4) 60 boys and 30 girls
(5) 75 boys and 15 girls

48. Find x if $x^2 + 5x + 6 = 0$.

(1) 2,3
(2) −2, −3,
(3) 2, −3
(4) −1, −2
(5) 1,2

49. If the perimeter of a rectangular building is 68 yards and the width is 48 feet, what is the length of the building in feet?

(1) 30
(2) 54
(3) 55
(4) 56
(5) Not enough information is given.

50. If a distance estimated at 150 feet is really 140 feet, the percent of error in this estimate is

(1) $6\frac{2}{3}\%$
(2) $7\frac{1}{7}\%$
(3) 10%
(4) 1%
(5) 0.71%

GO ON TO THE NEXT PAGE

Items 51 to 54 are based on the diagram of building lots A and B shown below.

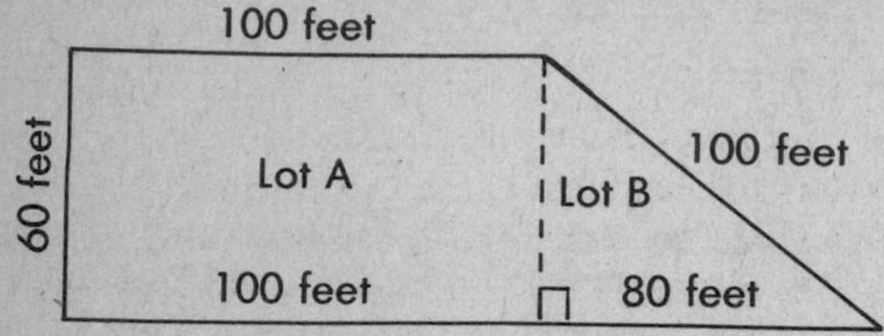

51. What is the total area of the two building lots in square feet?

(1) 2400
(2) 4800
(3) 6000
(4) 8400
(5) 14,000

52. The builder has decided to fence in the two lots to prevent curious passersby from getting too close to the construction site. How many feet of fencing are required to surround the entire property?

(1) 400
(2) 440
(3) 500
(4) 540
(5) 600

53. What is the ratio of the area of Lot A to Lot B?

(1) 5:2
(2) 3:2
(3) 2:1
(4) 4:3
(5) 2:5

54. A fence costs $20.45 per foot. Approximately how much would it cost to completely enclose lot A only?

(1) $21,000
(2) $15,000
(3) $12,000
(4) $6500
(5) $6000

55. The heights of the five starters on the Redwood High basketball team are as follows:

Joe	5 feet 11 inches
Keith	6 feet 4 inches
Neal	6 feet
Sal	6 feet 6 inches
George	6 feet 4 inches

The average height of these boys is

(1) 6 feet
(2) 6 feet 1 inch
(3) 6 feet 2 inches
(4) 6 feet 3 inches
(5) 6 feet 4 inches

56. What is the median height for the five starters?

(1) 5 feet 11 inches
(2) 6 feet 1 inch
(3) 6 feet 1 inch
(4) 6 feet 6 inches
(5) 6 feet 4 inches

END OF MATHEMATICS TEST

ANSWER KEY FOR GED SAMPLE TEST II

After completing the Practice Test Battery, check your answers against the key answers that follow. Enter the total number of correct answers for each test in the box provided on your Answer Sheet. Then turn to the Error Analysis on page 701 to see how well you did.

TEST 1. WRITING SKILLS—PART ONE

1. (5)	12. (2)	23. (2)	34. (1)	45. (3)
2. (1)	13. (5)	24. (2)	35. (3)	46. (4)
3. (4)	14. (3)	25. (5)	36. (4)	47. (1)
4. (1)	15. (5)	26. (5)	37. (2)	48. (1)
5. (3)	16. (2)	27. (2)	38. (5)	49. (5)
6. (4)	17. (2)	28. (3)	39. (2)	50. (4)
7. (1)	18. (4)	29. (3)	40. (5)	51. (5)
8. (2)	19. (5)	30. (5)	41. (4)	52. (3)
9. (3)	20. (1)	31. (4)	42. (3)	53. (4)
10. (4)	21. (5)	32. (3)	43. (5)	54. (5)
11. (4)	22. (4)	33. (4)	44. (5)	55. (1)

TEST 2. SOCIAL STUDIES

1. (4)	14. (3)	27. (3)	40. (2)	53. (5)
2. (1)	15. (3)	28. (1)	41. (5)	54. (1)
3. (3)	16. (2)	29. (4)	42. (1)	55. (4)
4. (5)	17. (5)	30. (5)	43. (3)	56. (1)
5. (4)	18. (4)	31. (5)	44. (3)	57. (2)
6. (2)	19. (3)	32. (3)	45. (2)	58. (1)
7. (4)	20. (1)	33. (5)	46. (1)	59. (4)
8. (1)	21. (2)	34. (1)	47. (3)	60. (3)
9. (1)	22. (2)	35. (1)	48. (5)	61. (1)
10. (4)	23. (4)	36. (1)	49. (5)	62. (4)
11. (3)	24. (2)	37. (4)	50. (2)	63. (2)
12. (5)	25. (1)	38. (1)	51. (2)	64. (5)
13. (2)	26. (2)	39. (5)	52. (4)	

TEST 3. SCIENCE

1. (2)
2. (5)
3. (3)
4. (4)
5. (1)
6. (5)
7. (5)
8. (2)
9. (2)
10. (1)
11. (5)
12. (4)
13. (2)
14. (1)
15. (3)
16. (1)
17. (5)
18. (3)
19. (4)
20. (1)
21. (5)
22. (4)
23. (2)
24. (1)
25. (4)
26. (1)
27. (2)
28. (1)
29. (1)
30. (4)
31. (3)
32. (1)
33. (1)
34. (5)
35. (4)
36. (4)
37. (2)
38. (1)
39. (2)
40. (2)
41. (4)
42. (4)
43. (5)
44. (1)
45. (2)
46. (3)
47. (5)
48. (1)
49. (3)
50. (5)
51. (4)
52. (2)
53. (1)
54. (2)
55. (5)
56. (2)
57. (2)
58. (4)
59. (1)
60. (5)
61. (4)
62. (2)
63. (1)
64. (5)
65. (2)
66. (4)

TEST 4. INTERPRETING LITERATURE AND THE ARTS

1. (3)
2. (2)
3. (5)
4. (4)
5. (4)
6. (4)
7. (2)
8. (3)
9. (1)
10. (3)
11. (4)
12. (1)
13. (4)
14. (4)
15. (3)
16. (4)
17. (3)
18. (1)
19. (5)
20. (2)
21. (4)
22. (3)
23. (2)
24. (4)
25. (5)
26. (3)
27. (1)
28. (1)
29. (3)
30. (5)
31. (2)
32. (4)
33. (1)
34. (2)
35. (3)
36. (1)
37. (3)
38. (5)
39. (2)
40. (5)
41. (3)
42. (3)
43. (5)
44. (3)
45. (2)

TEST 5. MATHEMATICS

1. (3)
2. (3)
3. (4)
4. (5)
5. (3)
6. (5)
7. (4)
8. (5)
9. (4)
10. (4)
11. (2)
12. (5)
13. (3)
14. (2)
15. (4)
16. (2)
17. (1)
18. (4)
19. (4)
20. (2)
21. (1)
22. (4)
23. (4)
24. (3)
25. (2)
26. (2)
27. (5)
28. (4)
29. (3)
30. (3)
31. (5)
32. (4)
33. (3)
34. (3)
35. (2)
36. (3)
37. (1)
38. (3)
39. (4)
40. (5)
41. (5)
42. (3)
43. (3)
44. (4)
45. (3)
46. (5)
47. (4)
48. (2)
49. (2)
50. (2)
51. (4)
52. (2)
53. (1)
54. (4)
55. (3)
56. (2)

ERROR ANALYSIS FOR GED SAMPLE TEST II

Circle the number of each question you answered incorrectly. Count the number of circles in each content area and write the total number missed in the column headed "Number Incorrect." A large number of incorrect responses in a particular area indicates the need for further study in that area.

Subject Area	Questions	No. Incorrect
TEST 1. WRITING SKILLS	55	
Sentence Structure	1, 3, 11, 12, 15, 18, 20, 22, 24, 25, 32, 33, 38, 49, 50, 52, 53	
Usage	4, 5, 6, 8, 9, 10, 14, 17, 26, 29, 31, 34, 35, 36, 37, 40, 44, 46, 54	
Capitalization	16, 30	
Punctuation	7, 10, 19, 21, 39, 43, 45, 55	
Spelling/Possessives/ Contractions	2, 23, 27, 28, 41, 42, 47, 48, 51	
TEST 2. SOCIAL STUDIES	64	
History	10, 21, 23, 36, 37, 38, 39, 43, 44, 46, 47, 48, 61, 63, 64	
Economics	1, 2, 4, 5, 6, 7, 8, 9, 12, 13, 14, 18, 19, 20, 21, 22, 26, 27, 28, 29, 30, 31, 35, 36, 37, 38, 40, 41, 42, 49, 50, 58, 59, 60	
Geography	15, 16, 18, 32, 33, 34, 39, 56, 57, 62	
Political Science	6, 7, 10, 11, 24, 25, 26, 27, 28, 29, 30, 51, 52, 53, 54, 55, 56, 57, 61, 63, 64	
Behaviorial Science	1, 2, 3, 4, 5, 12, 13, 15, 16, 17, 18, 23, 24, 25	
TEST 3. SCIENCE	66	
Biology	1, 2, 3, 4, 5, 6, 7, 8, 15, 16, 17, 18, 20, 21, 22, 23, 27, 28, 29, 33, 34, 35, 36, 40, 41, 61, 62, 63, 64, 65	
Chemistry	30, 31, 32, 37, 38, 39, 48, 49, 50, 51, 52, 53, 54	
Earth Science	9, 10, 11, 12, 13, 14, 24, 25, 26, 57, 58, 59, 60	
Physics	19, 42, 43, 44, 45, 46, 47, 55, 56, 66	
TEST 4. INTERPRETING LITERATURE AND THE ARTS	45	
Popular Literature	1, 2, 3, 32, 33, 34, 35	
Classical Literature	4, 5, 6, 7, 8, 9, 10, 11, 12, 13, 14, 15, 23, 24, 25, 26, 27, 36, 37, 38, 39, 40, 41	
Commentary	16, 17, 18, 19, 20, 21, 22, 28, 29, 30, 31, 42, 43	
TEST 5. MATHEMATICS	56	
Measurement	7, 11, 12, 14, 15, 21, 25, 27, 29, 30, 33, 35, 36, 41, 42	
Algebra	17, 18, 28, 32, 48	
Geometry	5, 8, 9, 19, 20, 23, 26, 31, 34, 49, 51, 52, 53, 54	
Numeration	6, 10, 13, 16, 22, 47, 50	
Statistics	1, 2, 3, 4, 24, 37, 38, 39, 40, 43, 44, 45, 46, 55, 56	

EXPLANATORY ANSWERS FOR GED SAMPLE TEST II

TEST 1. WRITING SKILLS—PART I

1. **(5)** *tissue. They can.* Adding the period here eliminates a run-on sentence, two complete sentences incorrectly joined.

2. **(1)** Change the spelling of *ocurrs to occurs.* Occurs is spelled with two "c's" and one "r."

3. **(4)** *some irritants*. The new sentence reads: In certain cells that line the bronchial tubes some irritants can directly cause a chemical reaction. No other choice creates a correct and meaningful sentence.

4. **(1)** *swell and increase.* The two verbs have a single subject, *membranes.* Therefore, both verbs must agree in tense (present) and number (plural).

5. **(3)** Change *left* to *leave.* "Narrow the airway" and "leave the sufferer" must be parallel for clarity.

6. **(4)** Change *same persons* to *same person.* You are talking about the variation in the response of *one* person.

7. **(1)** No correction is necesary.

8. **(2)** Change *were* to *are.* The paragraph is written in the present tense.

9. **(3)** *Between attacks some asthmatics*. "They" is vague. To whom does it refer?

10. **(4)** Punctuate, since the subject episodes requires a plural verb.

11. **(4)** *imported into.* We know from reading the paragraph that coffee comes from another country into the U.S.

12. **(2)** *is*. The new sentence reads: Almost half the world's coffee supply is bought by the U.S., one of the world's biggest coffee drinkers.

13. **(5)** No correction is necessary.

14. **(3)** *primarily grown.* Growth is a noun; grown is the correct form of the verb, required by this sentence.

15. **(5)** *Beans are generally imported as.* The sentence fragment requires a verb, and the paragraph is about importation of coffee.

16. **(2)** Change *south* to *South.* Capitalize points of the compass when they refer to a specific area.

17. **(2)** Change *were* to *are*. This will make sentence 7 conform to the present tense used throughout the paragraph.

18. **(4)** *blends.* These blends . . . Correct the original comma splice by making two sentences.

19. **(5)** No correction is necessary.

20. **(1)** Change the comma to a period after *businesses.* Change *they* to *They.*

21. **(5)** No correction is necessary.

22. **(4)** *individual jobseekers. Personnel officers.* This correction elminates a comma splice by creating two complete sentences. In addition, "personnel" is the correct word to use to refer to employees.

23. **(2)** Change the spelling of *carrer* to *career.* This is a frequently misspelled word, and appears on the GED Master List of Frequently Misspelled Words.

24. **(2)** Change *being* to *are.* Without this change, sentence 6 is a fragment, missing a verb.

25. **(5)** No correction is necessary.

26. **(5)** *also help clients.* Since the paragraph is written in the present tense, "help" is the correct choice.

27. **(2)** Change the spelling of *assistence* to *assistance.* This is a frequently misspelled word, and appears on the GED Master List of Frequently Misspelled Words.

28. **(3)** Change the spelling of *several* to *several.* This is a frequently misspelled word, and appears on the GED Master List of Frequently Misspelled Words.

29. **(3)** Change *required* to *require.* This makes the tense agree with the sense of the paragraph.

30. **(5)** Change *english* to *English.* Capitalize the names of languages.

31. **(4)** Change *nor* to *or.* When used as a pair of conjunctions (joining words), *either* is used with *or* and *neither* is used with *nor.*

32. **(3)** *two years. Inspectors.* Break this into two sentences to correct the comma splice.

33. **(4)** *to walk and climb about.* The parallel structure of the verbs ''to walk'' and ''to climb'' from a clean and correct sentence.

34. **(1)** *must also have.* No correction is necessary.

35. **(3)** Change *requires* to *require.* The plural subject "governments" must match the plural verb "require."

36. **(4)** *occurs.* The new sentence reads: Most training of inspectors occurs on the job.

37. **(2)** *They begin.* Watch the tense of the verbs throughout the other sentences in the paragraph to make sure they all fit together and convey your intended meaning.

38. **(5)** No correction is necessary.

39. **(2)** *with microphones, sound, and videotape.* Since ''sound'' describes the word ''recorders,'' setting it off with a comma makes the sentence confusing.

40. **(5)** Change *been* to *being.* "Being" is the correct tense of the verb.

41. **(4)** *studio to another, from film to live.* "Another" is spelled with one "n" and appears on the GED Master List of Words Frequently Misspelled. Also, "film" is singular.

42. **(3)** change the spelling of *telefone* to *telephone.* The "F" sound in telephone is spelled with the letters "ph."

43. **(5)** No correction is necessary.

44. **(5)** *they dismantle.* This paragraph is written in the present tense. Therefore, to keep the tenses the same, change "dismantled" (past) to "dismantle" (present).

45. **(3)** *networks, on the other hand,.* Set off interrupting words and expressions (such as "on the other hand," "yes," and "well") with commas. This indicates they can be removed from the sentence without changing its grammatical structure.

46. **(4)** *depends largely.* This paragraph is written in the present tense. Therefore, to keep the tenses the same, change "depended" (past) to "depends" (present). Even though "depends" ends in an "s" it is singular and matches the singular subject "success."

47. **(1)** Change the spelling of *courtous* to *courteous.* This is a frequently misspelled word and appears on the GED Master List of Frequently Misspelled Words.

48. **(1)** Change *weather* to *whether.* "Whether" is a conjunction meaning "if the case is that." "Weather" refers to atmospheric conditions such as rain or snow.

49. **(5)** *use, and showing various.* For the clearest sentences, place all elements in the same grammatical form. This is called parallel structure. Therefore, change the infinitive "to show" to "showing" to parallel "describing" and "demonstrating."

50. **(4)** Change *needing* to *needed.* Correcting the form of the verb changes 5 from a fragment to a complete sentence.

51. **(5)** Change the spelling of *reciepts* to *receipts.* This follows the "i before e" rule. This word appears on the GED Master List of Frequently Misspelled Words.

52. **(3)** *register sales, adjust.* Change "adjusting" to "adjust" to parallel register and perform. For the clearest sentence, place all elements in parallel (or the same) grammatical form.

53. **(4)** *to.* The new sentence reads: One benefit of this equipment is to increase workers' productivity—enabling them to provide better customer service.

54. **(5)** *They also handle returns.* Omit the "s" from "handles" to make the plural subject "they" match the plural verb "handle."

55. **(1)** Delete the comma after *shelves.* Overuse of commas confuses the meaning of a sentence.

TEST 1. WRITING SKILLS—PART II

SAMPLE ESSAY RESPONSE

Computers have changed the way we live in many ways. Many everyday chores can now be done more easily because of computers. Computers have also created new jobs. Life is easier today because of computers.

Many daily tasks have become easier because of computers. Thanks to computers, you can deposit and withdraw money without even going into the bank, which can save you a lot of time. Tellers can quickly figure out how much money is in an account with the use of computers. The telephone system works better because of computers. It's easier to call long distance today than it was in the past. Because of computers, you can call information and get a number in seconds. Computers have made life easier, especially in banking and telephoning.

Computers have also created a tremendous job market in the United States. Data keypunch operators and word processors are a result of the invention of computers. There is also a whole new computer service field. Because of computers, people have jobs writing and correcting programs. People build, repair, and sell computers. Some people now have jobs teaching classes that show others how to work computers. There are new jobs in the television, film, and music industry since computers have become popular. In music, for example, people have jobs creating sound effects and backup music in different ways with the help of computers.

Computers have a great effect on the way we live today. Many daily chores can be done in less time because of computers. Many new jobs have been created by the invention of the computer. The computer has made the world better.

TEST 2. SOCIAL STUDIES

1. **(4)** The pie graph shows approximately $\frac{1}{4}$ of employed women working part-time and $\frac{3}{4}$ of employed women working full-time. That means the ratio of women employed part-time to women employed full-time is 1 to 3. (1) and (5) are incorrect since the graph shows only employed women, not all women; (2) and (3) are simply inaccurate when compared with the areas on the graph.

2. **(1)** By knowing in advance what the public is willing to buy, business saves itself a lot of time and money.

3. **(3)** Each of the kinds of surveys is highlighted by an example.

4. **(5)** The selection does not refer to family relationships.

5. **(4)** The leader is left with the impression that surveys help business and are therefore necessary.

6. **(2)** All nations which need to trade with each other are tied together by economics. Whatever drastically affects one affects its trading partners in some way.

7. **(4)** When prices drop, it is generally because of the availability of too many goods. When this happens, factories stop producing and workers are laid off.

8. **(1)** As stated in the second sentence of paragraph 2, factories produced less or closed down when the Depression began.

9. **(1)** The first sentence states that the collapse began when Great Britain raised its interest rates "to bring home needed capital."

10. **(4)** The system of checks and balances is intended to prevent any one branch of government from gaining too much power.

11. **(3)** Only Congress can pass legislation. The president has the power to veto legislation of which he does not approve. Congress, in turn, can override a presidential veto by a $\frac{2}{3}$ majority. This is the only example provided which illustrates how two branches of government can be checked and balanced by each other.

12. **(5)** It is expected that there will be 111,000,000 persons at work in the United States in 1990. Adding up the individual categories will give you this number.

13. **(2)** The chart indicates 17.5 million government workers. Of the choices offered, only finance, insurance, and real estate, with 6.3 million workers, is about one-third as large.

14. **(3)** Because it is a circle and cut like a pie, it is called a "pie" graph.

15. **(3)** Genocide occurred when the Romans killed the Carthaginians and destroyed their city.

16. **(2)** As defined in paragraph 1, the aim of genocide is destruction of a racial, political, or cultural group. Proof that the Romans were successful in destroying the Carthaginians is that few traces of their civilization remain.

17. **(5)** As stated in the last paragraph, immortality is insured by art, religion, and wisdom.

18. **(4)** As stated in paragraph 2, Carthage was the center of Phoenician trade. The Romans destroyed the Carthaginians because they wished to take over this profitable trade and they feared this would never be possible if the Carthaginians were allowed to survive.

19. **(3)** Economist C expresses the socialist's point of view because this economist wants the government to assume ownership of basic industries.

20. **(1)** Economist A is concerned with government protection of the consumer. The Truth in Packaging Act, which outlaws deceptive containers, and the Truth in Lending Act, which requires retailers and lenders to provide consumers with the true cost of credit, are both intended to protect the consumer.

21. **(2)** Economist B advocates the free private enterprise system which was the policy of the U.S. government during most of the 19th century.

22. **(2)** *Laissez-faire* economics calls for the removal of government intervention in the marketplace. Without government regulation, the law of supply and demand will determine what is produced and how much people will pay.

23. **(4)** The concept of land was central to the American Indian tribes but totally different from the European concept which allowed for purchase, payment, and deeds. The confiscation of land took place throughout the U.S. until the Indians were confined to limited areas called reservations. The words quoted were spoken by an American Indian during treaty talks in South Dakota in 1866.

24. **(2)** Because of the large number of locks on the door and the fact that the door appear to be an apartment door, the cartoon is a comment on the American preoccupation with urban crime.

25. **(1)** No matter how many locks you have, you are never completely safe.

26. **(2)** Taxes added at each stage of processing are value added taxes.

27. **(3)** The table shows that the more a person earns, the more he is required to pay. For example, the person who earns $16,500 would pay 25% of his income in taxes, while the person who earns $6,500 would pay only 15% in taxes. This is an example of a progressive tax.

28. **(1)** Since the Dittmeirs earn less than the stipulated level of income ($9,000 in this case), the federal government provides payments to increase their family income. This is an example of the negative income tax.

29. **(4)** A tax which takes a higher percentage of income from the poor than from the rich is a regressive tax.

30. **(5)** A tax added to an existing tax is a surtax.

31. **(5)** While Japan may seem highest at first glance, closer examination of the graphs shows that this is not so. The scale of all graphs except the U.S. go from 0 to 8 million barrels a day. The U.S. graph goes from 0 to 40 million barrels a day. Thus, the U.S., at 15 million barrels a day, uses more petroleum than any other country shown.

32. **(3)** At 2 million barrels a day, West German oil consumption is slightly higher than United Kingdom consumption. (1) is wrong because German consumption is the same as or higher than Italian consumption. (2) is wrong because Japan uses more oil than does West Germany. (4) is wrong because there is no mention of the OPEC boycott. (5) is wrong because the U.S. consumes much more petroleum than does West Germany.

33. **(5)** Six countries show a smooth, unchanging line, indicating a steady rate of consumption throughout 1983. Japan, the exception, has a variable pattern on a month-to-month basis.

34. **(1)** According to the charts, the U.S. and Japan are the largest consumers of petroleum.

35. **(1)** The passage presents both sides of the problem, leaving the reader to decide which one is correct.

36. **(1)** Botulism is food poisoning caused by a bacterial spore.

37. **(4)** As stated in the last sentence, the heat necessary to destroy the spore would change the texture and flavor of meat products.

38. **(1)** Consumer groups believe processors are using nitrates just so that they can keep their products on store shelves for longer periods of time.

39. **(5)** According to the passage, in the northern colonies—New England—land was rocky and good soil was scarce. Therefore, fur trading and fishing were developed. The southern colonies were more suited to the development of agriculture.

40. **(2)** The bill says 900 cu. ft. of water were used from Feb. 21 to Mar. 21 and that 100 cu ft. of water equals 748 gallons. Multiply $9 \times 748 = 6732$ gallons.

41. **(5)** 900 cubic feet were used during the winter period. The cost for the water was $62.71. Divide 62.71 by 9; the answer is $6.97.

42. **(1)** The total amount of water consumed was 23,188 gallons. The total bill was $93.90. Divide $93.90 by 23,188 to get an average cost of $.004 per gallon. (Round numbers to $94 and 23,000 gallons.)

43. **(3)** The only reason mentioned in the choices that would explain England's involvement in the "Triangular Trade" is choice (3).

44. **(3)** The 1920's were a time of transition or change. (See last sentence of the passage.)

45. **(2)** In 1918 the soldiers came home from World War I. The last sentence of paragraph 1 speaks of "a nation trying to adjust to the aftermath of a world war."

46. **(1)** Jazz and flappers (people who adopted a certain style of clothing and distinctive mannerisms) were fads of the 1920's.

47. **(3)** The second sentence speaks of the era's "pervading temperament."

48. **(5)** The second sentence explains how historians classified the era, implying there are other methods of classification. There is nothing to suggest the twenties were unique (2), or that the changes that marked the period were unparalleled (3). (1) is contradicted by sentence 4. The second paragraph indicates a "Red Scare," referring to Communists, so (4) is incorrect.

49. **(5)** Skilled workers, as represented by the smoothly sailing ship, are not foundering under the "winds" of inflation. The unskilled workers, in contrast, are in danger of capsizing.

50. **(2)** According to the cartoon, skilled workers fare much better than unskilled workers during periods of inflation.

51. **(2)** The entire passage deals with nutrition programs for the elderly.

52. **(4)** The text states "nearly a quarter of a million," which is 250,000.

53. **(5)** The passage deals only with nutrition for the elderly.

54. **(1)** It is most likely that more elderly are living on their own, causing the problems described in the article.

55. **(4)** The article states that some of the nutritional problems the elderly experience are directly related to loneliness and isolation.

56. **(1)** Of the states mentioned, only Nevada has no shading at all, indicating that it has no hazardous waste sites.

57. **(2)** All three of these states have the shading that indicates "over 60" sites per state. In addition, these are three of the most densely populated states in the nation.

58. **(1)** Of the choices, only a cancelled check is proof.

59. **(4)** Consumers cannot prove anything simply by keeping a balance; however, by doing so they will know how much money they have available to spend.

60. **(3)** The final paragraph states that electronic transactions take place immediately.

61. **(1)** These words, from the Declaration of Independence, list grievances against the King of England. They were written to justify the American Revolution.

62. **(4)** Acid rain, spawned over the high smokestacks of the industrial Midwest, regularly falls in the forests, lakes, and streams of the Northeast, causing devastating ecological damage to wildlife and forests.

63. **(2)** "Off-year elections," that is, years spaced midway between presidential contests, show a consistently lower level of voter participation. (3) is incorrect because presidential candidates do not run in "off-years." No information is provided to support (1), (4), or (5).

64. **(5)** The number of votes amassed by third-party candidates was only significant enough to show up on the chart in 1968, 1972, and 1980. It appears that 1968 was the only year in which the number of "third-party" votes could have changed the outcome. No information is provided to support (1), (2), (3) or (4).

TEST 3. SCIENCE

1. **(2)** Arteries carry blood away from the heart.

2. **(5)** The left ventricle pumps blood into the aorta, which distributes blood throughout the body.

3. **(3)** Blood goes to the lungs to pick up oxygen. The oxygen-rich blood then returns to the heart for distribution throughout the body.

4. **(4)** This is the only correct sequence according to the diagram.

5. **(1)** The animal described is a shark which belongs to the class of fish. The clue words are cold-blooded, cartilaginous skeleton, and gill openings.

6. **(5)** The platypus feeds its young milk. Therefore, it is a mammal.

7. **(5)** Only birds and mammals are warm-blooded. Since all birds have feathers, this animal cannot be a bird. Therefore, it must be a mammal. The animal described is a bat.

8. **(2)** Frogs have "two lives." The young tadpoles have gills and live in the water, while the adult frogs have lungs and most species can live on land or in water. Animals that can live both on land and in water are amphibians.

9. **(2)** Find the difference between the lowest and highest temperatures expected for the cities named for each traveler. Julie will experience temperatures ranging from a low of 33° in Atlanta to a high of 75° in Miami. This is a range of 42°, which is the widest range of the five scheduled trips.

10. **(1)** Pat will experience temperatures ranging from 14° in Chicago to 43° in Denver. These are the coldest temperatures expected for the five trips shown.

11. **(5)** The announcer is referring to a hurricane, a common weather pattern in the Caribbean during late summer.

12. **(4)** Gravel and other large particles have settled out of water and eventually become cemented together. Gravel and the larger particles settle first of all the materials which form sediments. (1), (2), and (3) refer to igneous rocks; (5) refers to metamorphic rocks.

13. **(2)** 155 tornadoes occurred in May as indicated by the highest point on the dotted line representing tornadoes. (1) is wrong because the greatest number of tornado deaths occur in April, not May. (3) is wrong because there are fewer tornado deaths in fall than in spring. (4) is not covered by the information in the graph. (5) is wrong because the graph shows a total of more than 700 tornado deaths for the 27-year period from 1953 to 1980.

14. **(1)** Act promptly when you sight a tornado. Go into a designated shelter area as soon as the weather reports warn you. If there is no designated shelter, seek out a building and hide in an interior hallway, closet, or bathroom on as low a floor as possible. Do not stay in your automobile, but lie flat in a ditch or ravine with your head covered.

15. **(3)** Desirable weight for a man 5′8″ (68″) is 145. At 130, Bill is underweight.

16. **(1)** Obesity is defined at more than 20 percent over recommended weight. At 5′4″, Jan should weigh about 120 pounds. Her weight of 150 is 30 pounds over the recommended weight. This is more than 20 percent over the recommended weight and therefore classifies Jane as obese.

17. **(5)** Look at the weight columns for men and women. In almost every case, the desirable weight for men is 10 pounds more than the desirable weight for women of the same height. This is the only conclusion that is supported by the information provided by the table.

18. **(3)** It is easier to obtain all the necessary nutrients on a higher calorie diet. Therefore, women must choose their foods more carefully than men if they are to get all the necessary nutrients without gaining weight.

19. **(4)** The work done is $W=F \times D$, but the distance is not given. However, $D=R(\text{rate}) \times T(\text{time})$, or $D = 2(\text{m/sec}) \times 6\ (\text{sec}) = 12$ m. Substituting we get: $W = F \times D$, $W = 40 \times 12$, $= 480$ joules.

20. **(1)** As stated in the last sentence of paragraph 2, most back problems occur in the neck and lower back.

21. **(5)** The back contains ligaments, tendons, bones, vertebrae, discs, and nerves.

22. **(4)** As stated in the second sentence of paragraph 2, "The vertebrae are separated and cushioned by oval pads called discs."

23. **(2)** The last paragraph states that the ligaments may rupture (tear) if the back flexes suddenly.

24. **(1)** In an undisturbed cross-section of rock, the farther down you go, the older the species found there. If *A* is the bottom layer of rock, then *A* predates *B, C,* and *D* and is their ancestor.

25. **(4)** When the population of hawks increases, the population of its prey decreases and vice versa.

26. **(1)** Because of the absence of competition from antibiotic-sensitive strains, the antibiotic-resistant strains have become more prevalent. This is an example of natural selection.

27. **(2)** On the graph, the actual number of deer and the capacity of the range intersect in the year 1915.

28. **(1)** Overgrazing decreased the support capacity of the range.

29. **(1)** A decrease in animals that prey on the deer would cause the deer population to increase.

30. **(4)** The last sentence states that atoms are composed of protons, neutrons, and electrons. Molecules are groups of atoms.

31. **(3)** The fifth sentence says, "Groups of atoms make molecules."

32. **(1)** The first sentence states that matter is made up of "particles so utterly small that they have never been seen."

33. **(1)** The second paragraph advises against moving an injured person "unless absolutely necesary because of the danger of fire . . ."

34. **(5)** Paragraph 5 recommends that you control excessive bleeding by applying pressure.

35. **(4)** Everyone should know the basic rules of first aid for all of the reasons given.

36. **(4)** To dehydrate something is to deprive it of water.

37. **(2)** Isotopes have a different number of neutrons. The number of protons is the same, so the atomic number is the same. However, one isotope has more neutrons than the other, so their atomic weights will vary.

38. **(1)** Isotopes have the same atomic number (the lower number to the left of the chemical symbol) and different atomic mass (the upper number to the left of the symbol). ${}^{12}_{6}C$ and ${}^{13}_{6}C$ represent isotopes of carbon.

39. **(2)** One-half of the strontium 90 will disintegrate every 20 years.

    8 grams $\times \frac{1}{2}$ = 4 grams (after 20 years)
    4 grams $\times \frac{1}{2}$ = 2 grams (after 40 years)

40. **(2)** As stated in the passage, one of the dangers of genetic engineering is "the accidental development of a mutant bacterium which may change the whole life pattern on earth."

41. **(4)** Since the common cold is a virus infection, interferon might be helpful in curing it.

42. **(4)** According to the first sentence of the third paragraph, people cannot hear sounds below 20 vibrations per second or above 20,000 per second.

43. **(5)** Since 20 vibrations per second is the lowest sound that the human ear can detect and 20,000 is the highest, 1,000 vibrations per second is considered medium pitched.

44. **(1)** According to the final paragraph, a sound coming from the left side is heard in the left ear first.

45. **(2)** The second paragraph states that the ear is most sensitive to frequencies between 500 and 4000 vibrations per second. The singer is trying to reach 512 vibrations per second, which is in this sensitive range. Since the average person is able to detect a change in pitch of only .3%, he will be able to detect a fault of 1.5 vibrations per second ($512 \times .003 = 1.5$).

46. **(3)** The third paragraph indicates that supersonic vibrations are useful in depth sounding which is a means of measuring the depth of the sea.

47. **(5)** The third paragraph states that it is believed that bats are guided during flight by supersonic sounds which are reflected back to their ears.

48. **(1)** Two substances (sulfur + oxygen) combine to form a more complex substance (sulfur dioxide). This is an example of a combination reaction.

49. **(3)** The hydrogen of HCl is replaced by aluminum to form $AlCl_3$. This is a single replacement reaction.

50. **(5)** Splitting the nucleus of a heavy element to release enormous amounts of energy is an example of atomic fission.

51. **(4)** Two compounds exchange ions as the magnesium combines with the chlorine and the hydrogen with the oxygen in this double replacement reaction.

52. **(2)** Sulfurous acid is broken down to form water and sulfur dioxide. This is a decomposition reaction.

53. **(1)** Two substances (sodium + chlorine) combine to form a more complex substance (sodium chloride). This is a combination reaction.

54. **(2)** As indicated on the graph, when water reaches the boiling point, it changes to vapor.

55. **(5)** Since force = m × a, multiply the mass by the acceleration for each block:

Block	Mass ×	Accel. =	Force
1	2	3	6
2	4	6	24

Therefore, the second block requires 4 times as much force as the first.

56. **(2)** The acceleration due to gravity is $9.8 m/sec^2$. After 10 seconds, the object will achieve a velocity of $9.8 \times 10 = 98$m/sec.

57. **(2)** As stated in paragraph 2, the system will be able to locate the distress site within 1 to 3 miles.

58. **(4)** Paragraph 1 mentions air and maritime (sea) distress victims. Paragraph 3 mentions tracking a Japanese adventurer.

59. **(1)** Paragraph 1 states that SARSAT reduces the time needed to locate victims. Paragraph 2 mentions the accuracy with which SARSAT can locate distress sites. There is no mention of cost, ease of use, or reliability.

60. **(5)** Earthquakes are changes that occur suddenly after long periods of inactivity. All of the other changes are examples of regular or cyclic change.

61. **(4)** DNA mediates protein synthesis through m-RNA, which it makes; therefore answer choices (1) and (2) are incorrect. Transcription leads to translation, so (3) is wrong. Translation is defined as the process of assembling a protein from amino acids; therefore choice (4) is correct.

62. **(2)** As defined in the passage, transcription is the process by which DNA makes m-RNA.

63. **(1)** As stated in the passage, m-RNA is a complement of DNA.

64. **(5)** From the passage, all we can assume is that scientists can create models of DNA and RNA to study.

65. **(2)** Since the second sentence of the paragraph states that DNA replicates for the "propagation of life," we can assume it determines eye color. All the other processes listed here are a result of environmental factors, not heredity.

66. **(4)** Copper is the metal most widely used in electrical wiring because it is almost as good a conductor of electricity as silver and considerably less expensive.

TEST 4. INTERPRETING LITERATURE AND THE ARTS

1. **(3)** The author describes the other parts of the city as "American" and says that he regarded "New York as a foreign city." Therefore, we can conclude that he was the child of immigrants. We know that he was young when he remarks that he was in his final weeks of high school. (3) best describes these two attributes.

2. **(2)** We can infer that "Fatima" must be a cigarette, because it is the only choice that would be sold in a candy store.

3. **(5)** The last line tells us the author is happy, as it describes the warmth he felt upon returning to his neighborhood. His ability to remember his childhood in such detail and distinguish its various elements marks him as sensitive. We have already established he was in his last weeks of high school.

4. **(4)** Undershaft is a maker of cannon.

5. **(4)** It is hypocritical, because he degrades it while acknowledging its necessity.

6. **(4)** Undershaft tells how he danced in the streets for pennies, indicating a childhood of poverty.

7. **(2)** We can infer that "tosh" means "nonsense" by the phrase "on the other hand," which indicates that "tosh" must be a contrast to the description that comes after it. Although there may be a certain amount of *tosh* in the Salvation Army, it is still religion.

8. **(3)** As a member of the Salvation Army, Barbara is in charge of a "shelter" for homeless and hungry men and women. She is obviously interested in doing good.

9. **(1)** Poe uses words like "withering," "lonesome," "misty," and "ghoul-haunted" to establish an atmosphere of mystery and horror.

10. **(3)** "immemorial" means "beyond memory."

11. **(4)** These words establish the haunted mood of the poem.

12. **(1)** The fact that the spittle crackles before it hits the ground indicates that the temperature is colder than fifty below zero.

13. **(4)** The final sentences tell us the dog knew "it was no time for traveling." "Its instinct told it a truer tale than was told to the man by the man's judgment."

14. **(4)** See lines 28 and 29. The only choice lower than 50 below is − 65°.

15. **(3)** Both halves of choice (3) establish the frigid, forbidding Yukon, "exceedingly cold and gray."

16. **(4)** His "maiden station break" is his initial ("maiden") speech, the first break in the action of running the FCC.

17. **(3)** The audience is worried about what Minow will say. This is revealed in the phrase "a certain nervous apprehension" which Minow uses to describe his audience.

18. **(1)** He is comparing and contrasting his reasons for assuming the role of FCC chairman.

19. **(5)** He says, "Above all, I am here to uphold and protect the public interest."

20. **(2)** The phrase "good old days" tell us the shows appeared on television in the past. That Minow regards them as excellent is shown in the phrase "eminently worthwhile."

21. **(4)** cliche. It is a familiar expression.

22. **(3)** He cites the profit television has enjoyed but explains that he believes it is a "vast wasteland."

23. **(2)** The first two lines explain how nature destroys walls. The second two discuss the way hunters scatter the rocks.

24. **(4)** The neighbor likes the sentence so much he says it twice. (lines 17 and 29)

25. **(5)** The speaker questions the necessity of walls. "*Why* do they make good neighbors?" he wonders.

26. **(3)** The neighbor never questions why they need a wall between them, although their land is naturally separated by apple orchards and pine trees.

27. **(1)** Although the speaker is resigned to not changing the neighbor's mind, he still questions the validity of walls.

28. **(1)** In the first paragraph, the author says that Japanese society stresses "harmonious social relations."

29. **(3)** In the first paragraph, the author says that to prepare their children for Japanese society, Japanese parents urge them to "fit in." Thus, Japanese parents correct their children by saying, "People will laugh at you," and urge their children to fit in, not stand out.

30. **(5)** In the second paragraph, the author notes that Japanese society "places less emphasis on profit than ensuring that every worker will retain a place in the economic order."

31. **(2)** The Japanese all work together for a common goal, the author notes. In the third paragraph, he says that the Japanese believe that "discharging their duties to others" is far more than "just a job."

32. **(4)** The narrator says that the principal's speech, although simpler and clearer than his own, "did not say anything."

33. **(1)** As he hands him the new speech, the principal tells Wright: "Listen, boy, you are going to speak to both *white* and colored people that night." From this we can infer that the principal was afraid Wright would offend the whites in the audience.

34. **(2)** Richard wanted to deliver his own speech because "it said what he wanted to say."

35. **(3)** In the final paragraph, Wright announces his intention of isolating himself by saying, "I did not want to see any of them again."

36. **(1)** The first paragraph describes how poor mothers are forced to beg to support their children and how later these same children become thieves, foreign mercenaries, or slaves.

37. **(3)** To dramatize the plight of the starving, Swift proposes that children be sold as food.

38. **(5)** He is not serious in his suggestion that we cook and eat children, but he is deadly serious that something must be done to lessen the poverty of his country.

39. **(2)** He is showing that in many cases animals are treated better than children, for more money can be made from the animals.

40. **(5)** He partly blames the landlord's greed for the plight of the starving.

41. **(3)** He would support any measure that would help the starving women and children.

42. **(3)** In the second paragraph, the author explains that comics of the past appealed to the "male-adolescent outlook."

43. **(5)** In the last sentence, the author names the "uneven but fascinating new talents" in comics.

44. **(3)** Since many of the qualities of man and his universe are discussed, we can infer the legend also covered other aspects of the world.

45. **(2)** "He was handsome to look upon." (see line 25)

TEST 5. MATHEMATICS

1. **(3)** Look at the three graphs. They show that
   - Farm Population *decreased* from 30 million in 1940 to 8 million in 1978
   - Number of Farms *decreased* from 6.4 million in 1940 to 2.8 million in 1978
   - Average Farm Size *increased* from 160 acres in 1940 to 400 acres in 1978

2. **(3)** To find the population per farm in 1975, find the total farm population for 1975 on the first graph and number of farms on the second graph.

$$\text{Average population per farm} = \frac{\text{farm population}}{\text{number of farms}}$$
$$= \frac{\text{8 million}}{\text{2.8 million}} = \text{2.86 people per farm}$$

3. **(4)** Percent of increase is found by dividing amount of increase by original size and multiplying by 100.
   Average farm size in 1940 = 160 acres
   Average farm size in 1978 = 400 acres
   Amount of increase = 400 − 160 = 240 acres
   $240/160 = 1.5 \times 100 = 150\%$

4. **(5)** There is no data on the number of cattle per farm; therefore, this question cannot be answered based on the information given.

5. **(3)** The hour hand makes a complete revolution (360°) in 12 hours. Therefore, it rotates $1/12 \times 360°$ or 30° per hour. In 3 hours, the hour hand will rotate $30° \times 3 = 90°$.

6. **(5)** There is no information concerning the number of students in the class; therefore, not enough information to solve the problem.

7. **(4)** Set up a proportion:

$$\frac{\text{amount contributed}}{\text{total allowance}} = \frac{x}{100\%}$$
$$\frac{7.50}{30.00} = \frac{x}{100}$$
$$30x = 750$$
$$x = 25\%$$

8. **(5)** Use the formula page for volume of a rectangular container, $V = L \times W \times H$. Substituting, $V = 30 \times 20 \times 10 = 6000$.

9. **(4)** From the formula page, $V = \pi r^2 h$. Substituting, $V = \pi \times \left(\frac{1}{2}\right)^2 \times 10$.
(Remember that the radius is half the diameter, $\frac{1}{2}$ of 1 foot = $\frac{1}{2}$ foot.)
$V = \pi \times \frac{1}{4} \times 10$
$V = 2.5\pi$

10. **(4)** In Roman numerals:

M	1000
CM	900
L	50
X	10
IX	9
Total	1969

11. **(2)** Use the formula for interest from the formula page:
Interest = \$2000 × .06 × t (.06 is the decimal equivalent of 6%)
\$240 = 120 t
240/120 = t
2 = t

12. **(5)** \$42.50 is 15% off the regular price. Therefore, \$42.50 is 85% of the regular price (100% − 15% = 85%). If \$42.50 = .85 regular price, then regular price = \$42.50/.85.

13. **(3)** 1.28 liters ÷ 4 = .32 liters
.32 liters = .32 ÷ .001 ml
= 320 ml

14. **(2)** When the gauge reads $\frac{1}{4}$ full the tank has $250 \times \frac{1}{4} = 62.5$ gallons of oil. 250 − 62.5 = 187.5 gallons are needed to fill the tank.

15. **(4)** At 80% of maximum speed, the machine can produce
3500 × .80 = 2800 parts per hour
In 40 hours it can produce 2800 × 40 = 112,000 parts

16. **(2)** Work back from 1973:
1973 − 73 = 1900. That leaves 94 − 73 = 21 years.
1900 − 21 = 1879.
The ages at which he married and retired are not necessary to solve the problem.

17. **(1)** Multiply the first two monomials together; then multiply this product by the third:
$(x+3)(x+4) = x^2 + 7x + 12$
$(x^2+7x+12)(x+2) = x^3 + 9x^2 + 26x + 24$

18. **(4)** The graph of Dan's path underwater might look like this:

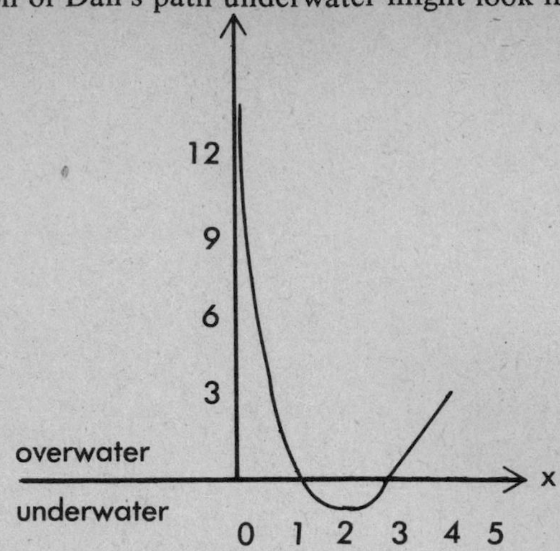

or, noting where the parabola crosses the x-axis, $(x-1)(x-3) = y$. To check, when $y = 0$, $x = +1$ or $+3$.

19. **(4)** The important factor is the thickness of the box and of the card. Dividing $\frac{1}{2}$ by $\left(\frac{1}{100}\right)$, we get the number of cards/box = 50 cards.

20. **(2)** The area of a circle, from the formula page, is
$A = \pi r^2$, or substituting,
$2.25\pi = \pi \times r^2$
Solving for r we get,
$r = \sqrt{2.25} = 1.5$ or $1\frac{1}{2}$ feet

21. **(1)** 7(15) + 4.5(8). Look at each job separately to find the total number of hours worked at each rate of pay. On the first job, Jim worked 3 + 4 + 8 = 15 hours at $7.00, hence the first part: 7(15) represents job one. Find the same information for job two: the total hours worked is 4 + 4 = 8. The rate of pay is 4.50 per hour, hence 4.5(8).

22. **(4)** The packer needs to convert the weight of each box to the same units in order to compare them and arrange them from heavier to lighter.

D	320 ounces = 320/16 =	20 pounds
E		5.7 pounds
F		35 pounds
G	77.4 ounces = 77.4/16 =	4.8 pounds
H		10.3 pounds

Rank them from heavy to light: (F(35), D(20), H(10.3), E(5.7), G(4.9)

23. **(4)** To calculate the answer we need to know the length of each shelf, the number of shelves, and the amount of edging in each package.
Length of each shelf: $3\frac{1}{2}$ feet
Number of shelves: 7
Amount of edging in each package: 9 feet
How many shelves can we cover with one package of edging?
Amount of edging in each package/length of shelf =
$9/3\frac{1}{2} = 9/7/2 = 9/1 \times 2/7 = 18/7 = 2$ and $4/7$ (There's waste)
Each package will do two shelves. Therefore, 4 packages of edging are required to trim 7 shelves.

24. **(3)** To set up a ratio, substitute X for the unknown quantity.
number of hits/number of times at bat = X / 85 = 271 / 1000.
$1000X = 271 \times 85$
$1000X = 23035$
$X = 23035/1000$
$X = 23.035$ Use 23.

25. **(2)** $°F = \left(\frac{9}{5} C\right) + 32°$
$= \left(\frac{9}{5} \times 12°\right) + 32°$
$= \frac{108}{5} + 32°$
$= 21.6° + 32°$
$= 53.6°$

26. **(2)** From the formula page you know that the area of a triangle is $\frac{1}{2}$ bh.
Therefore, Area $= \frac{1}{2}(122 \times 124)$
$= \frac{1}{2}(15{,}128)$
$= 7564$ square feet
7564 square ft × \$2.00 per square feet = \$15,128

27. **(5)** Let x = the number of copies the machine can make in 7 minutes.
Since 7 minutes = 7(60 seconds) = 420 seconds,
$$\frac{\text{copies} \rightarrow 8}{\text{seconds} \rightarrow 12} = \frac{x}{420} \text{ (cross-multiply)}$$
$12x = 3360$
$x = 280$ copies

28. **(4)** Multiply the numerator and the denominator by y to simplify the complex fraction.
$$\frac{\frac{x}{y} + 2}{\frac{x}{y} - 2} \cdot \frac{y}{y} = \frac{x + 2y}{x - 2y}$$

29. **(3)** Balance the checkbook by adding deposits and subtracting withdrawals. From the given information:

Date	Item	Deposits (+)	Withdrawals (−)
9/1	Balance	$257	
9/2	Deposit	375	
9/6	Withdraw		150
9/10	Withdraw		35
9/12	Deposit	42	
9/19	Withdraw		140
9/26	Withdraw		28
	Totals	$674	$353
10/1	Balance $674 − 353 = $321		

30. **(3)** We already know the balance on Dec 1 is $421. Subtracting a check for $193.47 would leave her with: $421 − $193. 47 = $227.53. To get the balance up to $600.00 she would need the difference, or $600.00 − $227.53 = $372.47

31. **(5)** Memorial Park is a rectangle measuring 1200 feet by 100 feet. The area of a rectangle can be found on the formula page
$A = L \times W$, or substituting,
$A = 1200 \times 100 = 120{,}000$

32. **(4)** The problem is in the form,
$(x^2 - y^2) = (x+y)(x-y)$,
where x is m^2 and y is 9.
$(m^4 - 81) = [(m^2)^2 - 9^2] = (m^2+9)(m^2-9)$,
which becomes,
$(m^2+9)(m+3)(m-3)$

33. **(3)** Bill needs a total of $750.00 for the receiver. One hundred dollars will be covered by his brother, to be repaid later. Calculate the number of weeks by setting up an equation

$$\frac{750 - 100}{35} = \frac{650}{35} = 18.5 \text{ weeks of saving.}$$

The best answer is 19, since he will not have all of the money at the end of the 18th week.

34. **(3)**

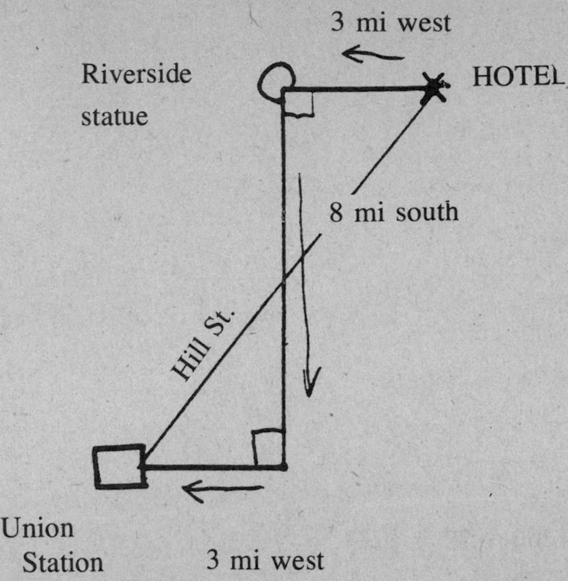

Redraw the west and south distances as the legs of a right triangle.

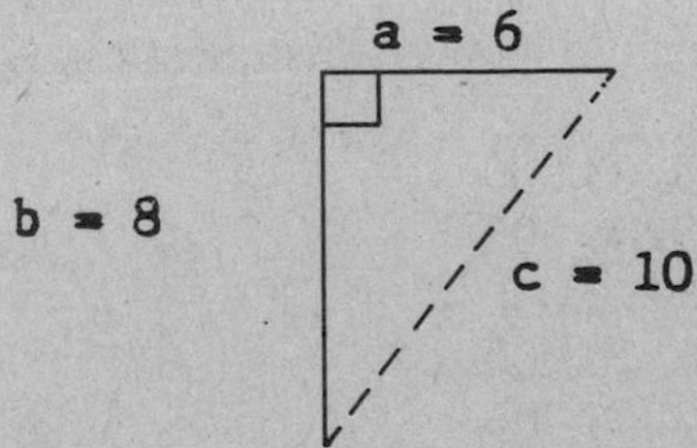

Use the Pythagorean Theorem from the formula list:

$c^2 = a^2 + b^2$

$c^2 = 6^2 + 8^2$

$c^2 = 36 + 64$

$c = \sqrt{100}$

$c = 10$

35. **(2)** 48 − 40 = 8 hours overtime
Salary for 8 hours overtime:

$$1\frac{1}{2} \times \$8.60 \times 8 = \frac{3}{2} \times \$8.60 \times \overset{4}{\cancel{8}}$$

$$= \$103.20$$

Salary for 40 hours regular time:

$$\$8.60 \times 40 = \$344.00$$
$$\text{Total salary} = \$344.00 + \$103.20$$
$$= \$447.20$$

36. **(3)** From March 31 to May 15 is 45 days $= 1\frac{1}{2}$ months $= \frac{1.5}{12}$ year.

$$\text{Interest} = \$200 \times .08 \times \frac{1.5}{12}$$

$$= \$\frac{24}{12}$$

$$= \$2$$

She must pay \$200 + \$2 = \$202.

37. **(1)** Add the percentages for salaries and equipment. The totals are the same for 1981 and 1983.

1981		1983	
Salaries =	10%	Salaries =	25%
Equipment =	60%	Equipment =	45%
Total	70%	Total	70%

38. **(3)** You must look at both charts to answer this question. Money spent on supplies:
1985—25% of \$1,200,000 = \$300,000
1984—20% of \$1,000,000 = \$200,000
1983—30% of \$1,500,000 = \$450,000
1982—35% of \$1,200,000 = \$420,000
1981—30% of \$ 800,000 = \$240,000
The greatest amount of money was spent on supplies in 1983.

39. **(4)** Money spent on salaries
1981—60% of \$ 800,000 = \$480,000
1982—50% of \$1,200,000 = \$600,000
Difference + \$120,000
1983—45% of \$1,500,000 = \$675,000
Difference + \$75,000
1984—70% of \$1,000,000 = \$700,000
Difference + \$25,000
1985—65% of \$1,200,000 = \$780,000
Difference + \$80,000
In 1982 there was an increase of \$120,000 from the amount spent the preceding year on salaries. This amount represented the greatest increase of the years given.

40. **(5)** The total expenditure for equipment in 1985 was 10% of the annual budget. The budget was $1,200,000 (see lower chart). 10% represents $.10 \times 1{,}200{,}000 = \$120{,}000$. $\frac{1}{3}$ was spent on mailroom equipment and the remaining $\frac{2}{3}$ was spent on miscellaneous, or $\frac{2}{3} \times 120{,}000 = 80{,}000$.

41. **(5)** Installment Plan
20% down payment = $5700 × .20 = $1140
$200 per month for 24 months = $200 × 24 = $4800
Total cost = $1140 + $4800 = $5940
$5940 − $5700 = $240

42. **(3)**

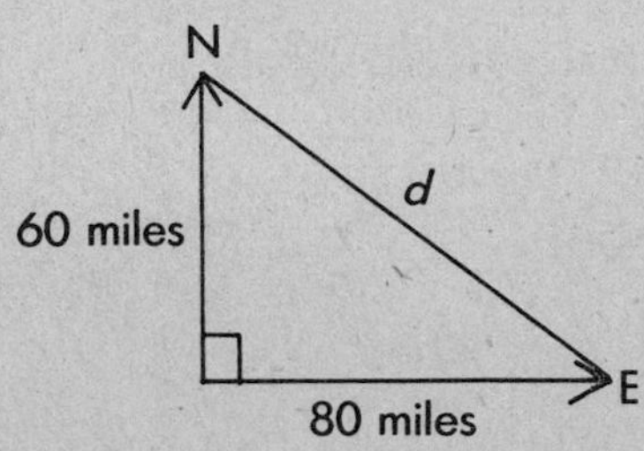

The car traveling north travels 30 m.p.h. × 2 hrs. = 60 mi.
The car traveling east travels 40 m.p.h. × 2 hrs. = 80 mi.
Using the Pythagorean Theorem,

$$60^2 + 80^2 = d^2$$
$$3600 + 6400 = d^2$$
$$10000 = d^2$$
$$\sqrt{10000} = d$$
$$100 = d$$

43. **(3)** In 1971 the rate for robbery was about 180 while the rate for aggravated assaults was about 160.

44. **(4)** Look at the slope of the graphs. Aggravated assault has an always-increasing slope.

45. **(3)** In 1977, the rate of motor vehicle thefts was 450 thefts/100,000 inhabitants. Set up a proportion and solve for x:

$$\frac{450 \text{ thefts}}{100{,}000 \text{ people}} = \frac{x \text{ thefts}}{10{,}000{,}000 \text{ people}}$$

$$100{,}000x = 4{,}500{,}000{,}000$$
$$x = 45{,}000$$

46. **(5)** Adding all the rates for total crime in 1978 we get:
$450 + 250 + 190 + 30 + 10 = 930$
Divide: $\frac{\text{Motor Vehicle Crimes}}{\text{Total Crimes}} = \frac{450}{930} = .48$
This is approximately 50%.

47. **(4)** Let the unknown number of girls be represented by X.
X girls + 2X boys = 90 pupils total.
$3X = 90$
$X = 30$ (number of girls)
$2X = 60$ (number of boys)
30 girls + 60 boys total 90 pupils

48. **(2)** Factor the expression on the left side of the equation:
$x^2 + 5x + 6 = 0$
$(x+3)(x+2) = 0$
Set each factor equal to 0 and solve for x:
$x + 3 = 0$ $\quad$ $x + 2 = 0$
$x = -3$ $\quad$ $x = -2$

49. **(2)** The formula for perimeter of a rectangle is
$P = 2L + 2W$
Notice perimeter is given in *yards,* but the length and width are in *feet.*
Change yards to feet so all units are the same.
68 yards = $68 \times 3 = 204$ feet
Substitute in the formula and solve for L.
$P = 2L + 2W$
$204 = 2L + 2(48)$
$204 = 2L + 96$
$108 = 2L$
$54 = L$

50. **(2)** There was an error of 150 ft. − 140 feet = 10 feet The percent of error is the error divided by the actual distance, 10 feet ÷ 140 feet = .0174 × 100% or about $7\frac{1}{7}$%.

51. **(4)** Lot A is a rectangle. From the formula page you know that the area of a rectangle is length × width.
Area of Lot A = 100 feet × 60 feet = 6000 square feet
Lot B is a triangle. From the formula page you know the area of a triangle is $\frac{1}{2}$ base × height.
Area of Lot B = $\frac{1}{2}(80 \times 60) = \frac{1}{2}(4800) = 2400$ square feet
Total area = 6000 square feet + 2400 square feet = 8400 square feet

52. **(2)** To find out how much fencing is required, add all the sides:
$100 + 100 + 80 + 100 + 60 = 440$ feet
Remember that the right triangle has the dimensions corresponding to 3:4:5 or 60:80:100.

53. **(1)** $\frac{\text{area Lot A}}{\text{area Lot B}} = \frac{6000}{2400} = \frac{5}{2} = 5:2$

54. **(4)** The perimeter of Lot A = 100 + 60 + 100 + 60 = 320 ft.
At \$20.45 per foot, we get
$20.45 \frac{(\$)}{(\text{ft})} \times 320\ (\text{ft}) = \$6544$
or \$6500, when rounded off.

55. **(3)** To find the average height, add the heights and divide by 5:

$$\begin{array}{l} 5'\ 11'' \\ 6'\ \ 1'' \\ 6' \\ 6'\ \ 6'' \\ \underline{6'\ \ 4''} \\ 29'\ 22'' = 30'\ 10'' \end{array}$$

$$5\overline{)30'\ 10''} = 6'\ 2''$$

56. **(2)** As defined on the formula page, median is the point in an ordered set of numbers at which half of the numbers are above and half are below this value.
Arrange the heights in order from short to tall:
5′ 11″ 6′ 6′ 1″ 6′ 4″ 6′ 6″
The median is the middle number, or 6′ 1″